THE
IRAN-CONTRA
SCANDAL

The Iran-Contra Scandal:

THE DECLASSIFIED HISTORY

EDITED BY

PETER KORNBLUH AND MALCOLM BYRNE

A NATIONAL SECURITY ARCHIVE DOCUMENTS READER

THE NEW PRESS, NEW YORK 1993

PUBLISHED IN THE UNITED STATES BY THE NEW PRESS, NEW YORK
DISTRIBUTED BY W. W. NORTON & COMPANY, INC.
500 FIFTH AVENUE, NEW YORK, NY 10110

LIBRARY OF CONGRESS CATALOGING-IN-PUBLICATION DATA
Iran-Contra Scandal : the declassified history /
edited by Peter Kornbluh and Malcolm Byrne. — 1st ed.
p.   cm. — (The National Security Archive document series)
Includes bibliographical references.
ISBN 1-56584-024-0 (cloth) — ISBN 1-56584-047-X (pbk.)
1. Iran-Contra Affair, 1985–1990—History—Sources.   I. Kornbluh, Peter.
II. Byrne, Malcolm.   III. Series.
E876.I735   1993
973.927—dc20   92-53732
                                          CIP

First Edition

ESTABLISHED IN 1990 AS A MAJOR ALTERNATIVE TO THE LARGE, COMMERCIAL PUB-
LISHING HOUSES, THE NEW PRESS IS INTENDED TO BE THE FIRST FULL-SCALE
NONPROFIT AMERICAN BOOK PUBLISHER OUTSIDE OF THE UNIVERSITY PRESSES.
THE PRESS IS OPERATED EDITORIALLY IN THE PUBLIC INTEREST, RATHER THAN
FOR PRIVATE GAIN; IT IS COMMITTED TO PUBLISHING IN INNOVATIVE WAYS WORKS OF
EDUCATIONAL, CULTURAL, AND COMMUNITY VALUE, WHICH, DESPITE THEIR INTEL-
LECTUAL MERITS, MIGHT NOT NORMALLY BE "COMMERCIALLY VIABLE." THE NEW
PRESS'S EDITORIAL OFFICES ARE LOCATED AT THE CITY UNIVERSITY OF NEW YORK.

FOR OUR SONS, GABRIEL KORNBLUH AND KIAN BYRNE

SO THAT THEY WILL BETTER UNDERSTAND THE MEANING OF IRAN-CONTRA—THAT

THE REAL DANGER TO OUR DEMOCRACY COMES FROM WITHIN.

ACKNOWLEDGMENTS

When the Iran-Contra scandal broke on November 25, 1986, the National Security Archive was already conducting major documentation projects on the Contra war, and U.S. policy toward Iran. Under the direction of the Archive's founder and first Executive Director, Scott Armstrong, whose long-standing interest in, and Freedom of Information Act (FOIA) research on, both Central America and the Middle East laid the initial groundwork for these projects, the Archive made the scandal a major focus of its work. On May 5, 1987—the day Congress opened hearings on the scandal—the Archive published its first book on the subject, *The Chronology: The Documented Day-by-Day Account of the Secret Military Assistance to Iran and the Contras*, edited by Malcolm Byrne, Scott Armstrong, and Tom Blanton. Two years later, the Archive published (with Chadwyck-Healey) *The Iran-Contra Affair: The Making of a Scandal, 1983–1988*, an indexed microfiched collection of 4,600 documents relating to the scandal.

This volume has evolved from these earlier publications and reflects the prodigious efforts of the many former colleagues, individuals, and organizations who contributed to them. We are deeply indebted to Scott Armstrong for establishing this issue as a top priority, and to the other members of the original Iran-Contra team.

To produce this book, the editors drew on the energies of a talented and dedicated Archive staff. Beyond her official job of tracking FOIA requests on Iran-Contra and other Archive projects, Lynda Davis provided a steady copyeditor's eye for error, and a thorough dedication to finalizing the manuscript. Tom Blanton, the Archive's executive director, provided his unparalleled knowledge of the Iran-Contra operations to assure that the book was factually correct and complete. Without their contributions, this book could not have been finished.

Lynne Quinto and Mary Burroughs contributed to typesetting a number of the documents in the book. Karin Edlund provided indispensable support in organizing the documents and preparing them for publication, as did Susan Breece.

A number of the documents reproduced in this book would never have seen the light of public scrutiny if not for the legal talents of several individuals and organizations. Eleanor Smith of Zuckerman, Spaeder, Goldstein, Taylor & Kolker, (formerly of Public Citizen) along with Sheryl Walter, the Archive's general counsel, waged a successful legal battle to force the declassification of Oliver North's personal notebooks in 1990 after the FOIA requests of the Archive and Public Citizen for the notebooks were denied. Kate Martin, Gary Stern, and Mark Srere of the ACLU's Center for National Security Studies obtained, through a FOIA lawsuit, the internal CIA investigative records relating to the Joseph Fernandez case. The Public Citizen Litigation Group's Kathy Meyer, Michael Tankersley, and Alan Morrison, along with Sheryl Walter and Kate Martin, have also been instrumental in winning court orders prohibiting the Reagan and Bush administrations from destroying backup computer tapes of the White House's electronic mail—or PROFS—system. The documents released pursuant to this lawsuit, and those that will be released in the future, make a major contribution to the history of the Iran-Contra operations.

Years of litigation work and research on the Iran-Contra scandal would not have been possible without the generous fiscal and moral support of the late Philip M. Stern, the J. Roderick MacArthur Foundation, the Ruth Mott Fund, the Mary Reynolds Babcock

Foundation, the Arca Foundation, C.S. Fund, Deer Creek Foundation, The Fund for Constitutional Government, Time Warner Inc., The Rockefeller Family Fund, and individual donors too numerous to list here, but who deserve our thanks.

The editors also wish to acknowledge the work of a number of reporters and authors who have continued to inspire our interest and advance our knowledge of the Iran-Contra operations and other U.S. government ventures that evolved from those covert activities. We, and many other people, be they researchers or concerned citizens, have benefited from the recent investigative journalism of Larry Bensky, John Canham-Clyne, David Corn, Brian Donovan, Seymour Hersh, James G. Hershberg, Martha Honey, David Johnston, George Lardner, Sam Meddis, Robert Parry, Walter Pincus, David Rogers, Craig Unger, and Murray Waas. We particularly want to recognize the unmatched contribution to recent scholarship on the Iran-Contra affairs of Theodore Draper, whose articles in the *New York Review of Books* and extraordinary book, *A Very Thin Line*, helped to focus attention on the deeper constitutional issues raised by the scandal, and who graciously provided the foreword to this volume.

Finally, we are indebted to the work of Independent Counsel Lawrence Walsh and his office, not for assistance on this book (none was requested or provided) but for substantially advancing the documentary record on the scandal. Against considerable political odds, Walsh's six-year investigation has fundamentally changed the way the Iran-Contra operations, and the Reagan and Bush administrations' efforts to cover them up, will be understood by future historians. For its unparalleled contribution to uncovering the truth in the face of executive branch obstruction and presidential pardons, the Office of the Independent Counsel must be commended.

This is the Archive's second collaboration with André Schiffrin and the specialists at the New Press. The expertise, guidance, and patience of our editor David Sternbach, copyeditor Ted Byfield, designer Charles Nix, production manager Kim Waymer, publicist Claudia Guerra, and other members of this important publishing house, were essential to this project and will be to many more.

CONTENTS

FOREWORD

If ever the constitutional democracy of the United States is overthrown, we now have a better idea of how this is likely to be done. During the course of the Iran-Contra affairs, from 1984 to 1986, something in the nature of a junta was at work inside the U.S. government. We usually think of a junta as plotting to overthrow a president; this junta came into being to overthrow an established constitutional rule of law with the help of a president. The main lesson from this experience is that the chief danger to our political system is from within, not from without.

The Iran-Contra affairs are not a warning for our days alone. If the story of the affairs is not fully known and understood, a similar usurpation of power by a small, strategically placed group within the government may well recur before we are prepared to recognize what is happening. For this reason, I have felt that we cannot know too much about this case history of the thin line that separates the legitimate from the illegitimate exercise of power in our government.

Fortunately, there is much that can be known. In writing my own book, *A Very Thin Line*, I discovered that well over fifty thousand pages of documentation had been released, largely as a result of the official investigations of the affairs. Beyond the final reports of the congressional Iran-Contra committees and the Tower Board, there were thirteen volumes of open hearings and associated exhibits, many of them with well over a thousand pages; twenty-seven volumes of depositions, also with exhibits, some with over fifteen hundred pages; two additional volumes of documents comprising over twenty-three hundred pages; and still more thousands of pages of testimony and documents produced at the trials of Lt. Col. Oliver L. North and Vice Admiral John M. Poindexter. In 1990, after these proceedings concluded, about twenty-five hundred pages of North's personal notebooks were released as the result of a Freedom of Information Act lawsuit filed by the National Security Archive.

Rarely, if ever, have we been given such an opportunity to learn just how our government really works. In addition to the documentary evidence, dozens of officials, including the highest, testified publicly or privately for hours and even days under oath about what they knew and did. They could not merely say what they might have chosen to say under different circumstances. They were questioned closely, often by skilled lawyers who had the benefit of thousands of documents to prepare them for what to look for and how to check answers. Nothing comparable on this scale has ever opened the national security branches of government to such scrutiny. Each administration, of course, has its own ways, but a good deal is common to all of them and reveals patterns of behavior that do not change easily.

Even with this small library of documentation, the Iran-Contra affairs were still a largely unknown story. Unavoidably, most of the public's knowledge came from the congressional hearings, especially as they unfolded on television. At best, they told only part of the story, even if someone had listened to every word. For another thing, ordinary journalism could not cope with the immense amount of material now at our disposal. Daily stories in the newspapers or sound bites on television could not conceivably cope with this vast outpouring. Matters essential to the understanding of these events were buried in thousands of pages of testimony and documents.

For those who may not be able to immerse themselves in the massive record of the Iran-Contra affairs but still wish to examine the actual documents that describe this important story, this volume is indispensable. By providing the most significant primary materials relating to the affairs, this volume allows the facts to speak for themselves. In this way, the documents also help to carry the story forward, giving the reader an intimate sense of how the president and his men manipulated the system and perverted its constitutional character.

THEODORE DRAPER

INTRODUCTION

On October 5, 1986, an antiquated U.S. cargo plane was shot down over southern Nicaragua by a surface-to-air missile. Within hours, Vice President George Bush's office received a telephone call from a resupply operative stating that the plane was missing, and the CIA station chief in neighboring Costa Rica sent a coded message to Washington warning tersely that the "situation requires we do necessary damage control." But the sole surviving crew member, Eugene Hasenfus, was beyond U.S. control—before long, his Nicaraguan captors had placed him in front of television cameras to tell the world the story of a U.S. government-sponsored covert arms resupply operation for the Contras.

Half a world away Lt. Col. Oliver North, the National Security Council staffmember in charge of the hitherto-secret effort to circumvent the law banning U.S. aid to the Contras, received word of the Hasenfus plane while he was engaged in highly sensitive negotiations with Iranian government representatives. The talks were part of another major NSC-run covert operation—an arms-for-hostages trade with Iran which made a farce of President Ronald Reagan's highly publicized maxim that "America will never make concessions to terrorists." North abruptly dropped the negotiations and returned to Washington to handle the emergency in Central America.

One month later, the arms-for-hostages deals were exposed when a Lebanese weekly magazine published an account of a secret trip to Teheran in May 1986 by former National Security Advisor Robert McFarlane. The *Al-Shiraa* story was quickly picked up by the Western media and broadcast around the world. For the second time in less than five weeks, the White House was plunged into a major political crisis.

For most Americans, the two events—trading arms for hostages in Iran and providing illicit paramilitary aid to the Contras in Central America—were unconnected incidents played out at opposite ends of the globe. But on November 25, 1986, President Reagan and Attorney General Edwin Meese shocked the nation by disclosing that the two operations were, in fact, interrelated: the president opened the press conference by stating that he had not been "fully informed" of the nature of one of the activities undertaken in connection with the Iran initiative. Then Attorney General Meese disclosed the existence of a "diversion memo," written by North in the spring of 1986, which revealed a transfer of "residual funds" from the U.S. arms sales to Iran to finance the Contra war. The six-page document, actually a status report on the hostage negotiations, contained just one reference to the Contras:

> $12 million will be used to purchase critically needed supplies for the Nicaraguan Democratic Resistance Forces. This material is essential to cover shortages in resistance inventories resulting from their current offensives and Sandinista counter-attacks and to "bridge" the period between now and when Congressionally-approved lethal assistance...can be delivered.

The attorney general announced that North had been "relieved of his duties" at the NSC because he, alone, was cognizant of this merger between Iran and Contra; his superior, National Security Advisor John Poindexter, who, Meese informed the American public, "generally" knew of and approved the plan, was permitted to resign.

THE OFFICIAL STORY

In retrospect, it is clear that the attorney general's emphasis on the diversion constituted an effort to spin the burgeoning scandal away from the Oval Office and thereby save the presidency from another Watergate impeachment scenario. In his memoirs, Lt. Col. North argued that the Reagan administration, in effect, used the diversion as a diversion:

> This particular detail [the diversion] was so dramatic, so sexy, that it might actually—well, *divert* public attention from other, even more important aspects of the story, such as what *else* the President and his top advisers had known about and approved. And if it could be insinuated that this supposedly terrible deed was the exclusive responsibility of one mid-level staff assistant at the National Security Council (and perhaps his immediate superior, the national security adviser), and that this staffer had acted on his own (however unlikely *that* might be), and that, now that you mention it, his activities might even be *criminal*—if the public and the press focused on *that*, then maybe you didn't have another Watergate on your hands after all.[1]

Indeed, the November 25 news conference, we now know, was part of an early campaign of obfuscation and deception by high U.S. officials to mislead the public about the scope of both the Iran and Contra operations as well as the connection between them. After the Hasenfus plane was shot down, President Reagan and other members of his administration vociferously denied any U.S. role in what they described as a "private" resupply initiative. After the *Al-Shiraa* story broke, the president went on national television on November 13 to portray the purpose of the U.S. approach to Iran as an effort to bolster moderate factions and to wean the Iranians away from the Soviet Union, but not to ransom hostages. "We did not—repeat—did not trade weapons or anything else for hostages nor will we," Reagan categorically told the American people.

Any wrongdoing, according to the slant of the November 25 press conference, was the responsibility of a third country involved with Iran—Israel. According to Meese, Israeli shipments of U.S. weapons to Iran in 1985 were unauthorized by, and unknown to, President Reagan—and, furthermore, they "did not involve,

at that time, the United States." The diversion, too, was Israel's doing: "No American person actually handled any of the funds that went to the forces in Central America," Meese told reporters. Monies transferred to the Contra war went straight from Israel to rebel bank accounts—a statement contradicted by the diversion memo itself, which made it clear that funds would be sent by Israel to "a private United States corporation account in Switzerland"[2] and dispensed from there—and, Meese maintained, "that was the end, so far as we know, of anyone in the United States Government knowing anything about what happened to them."[3]

If the November 25 press conference had been the last word on the Iran-Contra scandal, the American public would have been left with only the official story: The United States had sent what the president described as "small amounts of defensive weapons and spare parts" to Iran, not as ransom, but with the objective of improving relations, bolstering moderates, influencing Iran away from the USSR, and, lastly, if possible, helping to obtain the release of hostages in Lebanon. This was not "negotiating with terrorists," rather—given Iran's strategic importance in the Middle East—it was a perfectly prudent and legitimate foreign policy initiative. Nor was there any illegality involved: the arms shipments had taken place in 1986, and although Congress had not been informed "in a timely fashion," the operations were legal because the president had signed a Finding authorizing the necessary covert operations. Shipments in 1985, for which there was no requisite Finding, had been conducted by Israel without the knowledge or approval of the president. In fact, Israel was responsible for the most egregious aspect of this whole operation—the diversion of funds to the Contras. The Justice Department had investigated and concluded that, out of the whole U.S. government, only one NSC staffer knew the details of this illicit transfer of funds. But nobody in the Reagan administration had any knowledge of what the Contras had done with the Iranian money because no U.S. official, pursuant to the law, was involved in aiding them—only "private benefactors" were involved.

IRAN-CONTRA THE LARGER PICTURE

Despite a sustained effort to cover up the truth, culminating in President Bush's Christmas Eve, 1992, pardon of Caspar Weinberger—aborting his trial on charges of concealing critical evidence from investigators—and of five other former officials, the official story has given way to a far more insidious set of facts. The Iran and Contra operations, we now know, had much more than diverted funds in common; according to the congressional committees investigating the Iran-Contra scandal, they also shared the "common ingredients" of "secrecy, deception, and disdain for the law" by a U.S. president and his men.[4] Both operations incorporated a wide variety of illicit components and initiatives, involving different U.S. actors and agencies, as well as many other countries besides Israel. Far from being "out of the loop," the highest members of the Reagan administration, starting with President Reagan and Vice President Bush, knew of, and played integral roles in, a number of these schemes. The question of what they knew, and when they knew about the infamous diversion—the answer to which appears lost forever in the hundreds of documents either shredded by Oliver North or erased from the White House computer system by John Poindexter—has been rendered moot. In comparison to many of the other activities undertaken in the Middle East and Central America, the diversion appears a relatively minor transgression.

NICARAGUA: THE CONTRA RESUPPLY OPERATIONS

On the Contra side of the scandal, the resupply operations by so-called private benefactors were actually part of a protracted and wide-ranging White House program of deception, surrogate operatives, and third-country financing used illegally to sustain an unpopular war against the Sandinistas. From the beginning, the Contra war relied on official deceit and foreign intermediaries; the very first Presidential Finding presented to Congress in December 1981, for example, depicted the CIA's Contra program as an arms interdiction campaign, when in fact the CIA was already organizing Nicaraguan exiles to roll back the Nicaraguan revolution, and using security agents of the Argentine military dictatorship to train and equip a counterrevolutionary force. An official disdain for law also accompanied the Contra war early on. Despite the passage of the first Boland Amendment in 1982, which prohibited the Reagan administration from attempting to overthrow the Sandinista government, CIA covert operations continued to work toward exactly that goal. By October 1984, when the second Boland Amendment terminating all U.S. assistance to the Contras was passed, the Reagan White House had already arranged alternative financing and created a shadow CIA to sustain the war.

Between 1984 and 1986, the record shows, the Reagan administration conducted a concerted effort to circumvent Congress's constitutional power of the purse by turning to friendly countries for arms and financing. Third-country financing was discussed within the National Security Planning Group (NSPG), which included the president, vice president, and every major national security official in the administration. Officials from the CIA, the NSC, and the departments of Defense and State participated in approaches to counterparts in Israel, South Africa, Taiwan, South Korea, Brunei, and Saudi Arabia, among other nations. President Reagan personally interceded with Saudi King Fahd to obtain a larger contribution for the Contra cause.

President Reagan and Vice President Bush and other high U.S. officials also participated in an extensive program of bribery, coersion, and quid pro quos aimed at the countries of Central America whose political, military, and logistical support was pivotal to sustaining the Contra war. Quid pro quos, which Vice President Bush, at a June 1984 NSPG meeting, declared "would be wrong," were used to "entice" cooperation from Honduras, Guatemala, Costa Rica, and Panama. In the case of Honduras, which served as a territorial base for Contra operations, both the president and vice president directly participated in efforts to purchase continuing Honduran involvement in the Contra war.

It was President Reagan who directed his then–national security advisor, Robert McFarlane, to transfer the Contra program from the CIA to the NSC after congressional authorization for the CIA's Contra program expired in mid 1984. NSC staffer Oliver North became the central coordinator of the war, setting up a surrogate arms procurement and distribution resupply system through Richard Secord who, in the name of the United States, employed retired CIA and Defense Department special operations personnel, foreign saboteurs, anticommunist mercenaries, and even international terrorists. But North was by no means the "lone ranger" portrayed in the official story: hundreds of his memoranda, declassified during the Iran-Contra hearings and for subsequent judicial proceedings, show that he reported his activities and received authorization from his superiors. Moreover, North shared parts of the Contra account with CIA Central America Task Force Chief Alan Fiers, and Assistant Secretary of State Elliott Abrams.

The model of transferring a prohibited CIA operation to the National Security Council was also used in another, lesser-known facet of the Contra side of the scandal—a domestic propaganda and lobbying campaign "to alter public opinion and change the vote in Congress on Contra aid."[5] In an effort to build what Reagan administration officials called a "public diplomacy" program, William Casey authorized the transfer of a senior CIA official, whose specialty was propaganda, to the NSC. From an office down the hall from Oliver North's, this official oversaw the creation of a propaganda apparatus which drew upon the talents of U.S. military pychological warfare specialists, conducted "covert propaganda" operations to influence the media, and employed private-sector public relations specialists, fund-raisers, and lobbyists to pressure Congress to renew official Contra assistance and return the CIA to the battlefield. This operation was more successful than its paramilitary counterpart. It is perhaps the height of irony that less than two weeks after the Hasenfus plane was shot down, Ronald Reagan signed a new Contra aid bill authorizing $100 mil-

lion for the CIA to officially re-enter the fray and prosecute the war.

IRAN: ARMS FOR HOSTAGES Despite assuming office on a pledge that Washington would "never negotiate with terrorists," the Reagan administration bartered sophisticated U.S. armaments for Iran's promise to obtain the release of Americans held hostage in Lebanon. While President Reagan publicly denounced the Iranians as part of a "confederation of terrorist states," U.S. officials were secretly arranging the first arms sales to Iran. As early as August 1985, before the initial shipment, Secretary of State Shultz told both the president and the vice president that the United States was "just falling into the arms-for-hostages business and we shouldn't do it."[6]

The first arms shipment arrived in Iran on August 20, 1985; the last shipment arrived on October 28, 1986. In all, the weapons totaled 2,004 TOW antitank and eighteen HAWK antiaircraft missiles, plus 240 HAWK spare parts—not the "small amounts" of defensive weapons that, as Reagan claimed in November 1986 could easily "fit into a single cargo plane."[7] In return, Iran obtained the release of three hostages, although another three were seized by Lebanese terrorists in the interim, and four more shortly thereafter. Not until December 4, 1991, was the last hostage, Associated Press correspondent Terry Anderson, given his freedom.

All shipments of arms to Iran were authorized by the president of the United States. Although Israel did act as a conduit for U.S. arms going to Iran in 1985, it did so with the explicit consent of the Reagan White House. The Israelis, according to the Iran-Contra final report, "were unwilling to proceed without evidence of a clear, express, and binding consent by the U.S. Government."[8] Reagan's national security advisor, Robert McFarlane, obtained the president's authorization before giving Israel the go-ahead—and informed other senior members of the administration, including Vice President Bush, Secretary of State Shultz, and Defense Secretary Weinberger. "President has decided to do it thru

Israelis," Weinberger's notes record McFarlane telling him in November 1985.[9] Other U.S. agencies, notably the CIA and the Defense Department, played major roles in facilitating the 1985 Israeli shipments. The CIA arranged for the November 1985 shipment of HAWK missiles to be transported from Tel Aviv to Teheran; and the Pentagon replenished Israel's stocks of missiles to replace those weapons sent to Iran.

The shipments of U.S. missiles in the fall 1985 from Israel to Teheran appear to have been illegal: they involved the CIA and covert operations but were not accompanied, as mandated by law, by a prior Presidential Finding to Congress, and they also seem to have violated the Arms Export Control Act. Under pressure from the CIA's general counsel, President Reagan did sign a "retroactive" Finding on December 5, 1985, authorizing the earlier shipments through Israel. But this Finding was never presented to Congress; later the original copy was destroyed by Admiral Poindexter because he felt it would be "politically embarrassing" to the president. In January 1986, Reagan signed a second Finding authorizing weapons sales directly from the United States to Iran. The White House, however, withheld this Finding from Congress until after the scandal broke eleven months later.

It was the need to conceal the illegal November 1985 shipments, and protect the president from the impeachable offense of knowingly violating the law, that created a panic within the administration in November 1986. As the arms-for-hostages scheme began to unravel, U.S. officials, including Casey, Poindexter, McFarlane, and North, created a cover story—complete with false chronologies, fallacious testimony to Congress, and an effort by both the president and the attorney general to mislead the American public—that no one in the U.S. government had known that missiles were being sent to Iran in November 1985. The Israelis, according to this ficticious account, had told U.S. officials that the shipments were "oil-drilling equipment." The cover-up was complicated by Secretary of State Shultz, who had contemporaneous notes from November 1985 showing that

the White House knew exactly what was being sent to Iran.[10] It was the need to iron out this cover-up story that prompted Attorney General Meese's internal "inquiry" on November 21, 1986. The fortuitous discovery of the diversion memo in Oliver North's file cabinet the next day provided the White House with the necessary documentation to shift the focus away from Reagan's role in illicit shipments of arms to Iran.

Even the diversion, however, was wholly misrepresented in the official story. Money was disbursed to the Contras through a bank account in Switzerland controlled by Oliver North and his two main private-sector operations managers, Richard Secord and Albert Hakim. North deliberately inflated the price of arms going to Iran in order to generate a surplus that could be used for the Contras as well as other operations. Of $16.1 million in profits stemming from arms sales to Iran, only $3.8 million was actually diverted to the Contra resupply operations. Other funds were spent to acquire equipment, such as a cargo freighter, necessary for future extraofficial programs. When the operations were exposed, the bank account had a balance of over $6 million; another $10 million was expected from Brunei.[11] Had *Al-Shiraa* not exposed the arms-for-hostages missions in November 1986, it is likely that profits from Iran would have underwritten additional "off-the-shelf" covert operations elsewhere.

THE AFTERMATH: HISTORY AND ACCOUNTABILITY In the six years following the revelation of Iran-Contra operations, the official investigations have become an integral part of the story. From the short tenure of the Tower Commission, through the televised theatrics of the congressional Iran-Contra committees, to the lengthy, probing, and methodical criminal prosecutions of Independent Counsel Lawrence Walsh, the public understanding of the breadth and depth of these multifaceted covert operations has been significantly advanced. On the other hand, the ability of the legislative and executive branches to hold U.S. officials accountable for their actions has proven virtually nonexistent.

The Tower Commission, appointed by President Reagan on December 1, 1986, to conduct "a comprehensive review" of the NSC's operational role in Iran-Contra, issued its findings on February 26, 1987. The commission, made up of John Tower, Edmund Muskie, and Brent Scowcroft, interviewed a number of participants in the scandal, including President Reagan and Vice President Bush—one of only two times Bush has been officially questioned about the matter—and discovered substantial new documentation, including internal computer messages written between Admiral Poindexter, Oliver North, and Robert McFarlane. But the chief thrust of the Tower Commission report was to exonerate President Reagan and advance the "NSC rogue staff" theory that Poindexter, North, and others were operating on their own initiative, without presidential knowledge or approval. The Iran-Contra scandal, the commission concluded, was basically the result of Ronald Reagan's "hands-off management style."

The select congressional committees went one step further and held the president accountable for both the policies and the lawlessness within his administration. "[T]he ultimate responsibility for the events in the Iran-Contra Affair must rest with the President," stated the 690-page final report issued in November 1987. "It was the President's policy—not an isolated decision by North or Poindexter—to sell arms secretly to Iran and to maintain the Contras 'body and soul.'"[12] But the committees deliberately avoided investigating those areas of the scandal, such as the quid pro quos in Central America, that would have brought new charges of illegality into the Oval Office. At a January 1987 meeting of the Senate select committee, the senators concluded that "the country didn't need another Watergate."[13]

The record of the congressional investigation is a mixed one. On the one hand, the Iran-Contra committees produced an in-depth, comprehensive, and invaluable report that not only detailed the decision making process and covert operations but raised the broader issues of the Constitutional threats represented by the Reagan administration's conduct. The committees also generated more than fifty thousand pages of declassified documents, depositions and hearings, creating an unparalleled historical record of the scandal.

On the other hand, the select committees' leadership permitted politics and publicity to dictate both the process and the product of the investigation— seriously compromising the result. Lt. Col. Oliver North's appearance, for example, in the televised hearings in the summer of 1987 transformed him from the scapegoat of the scandal into its hero. To obtain North's testimony, and that of Admiral John Poindexter, Congress let them set the terms of their appearances and granted them immunity, undermining the future ability of the independent counsel to prosecute these key players for criminal misconduct. And once Admiral Poindexter had testified that he did not tell President Reagan of the diversion, the committees decided, prematurely to wrap up the hearings and close down their investigation.

The responsibility for establishing the full history of the Iran-Contra operations, and for holding U.S. officials legally accountable for crimes committed under the guise of national security, fell to Independent Counsel Lawrence Walsh. Unfortunately, the independent counsel, as Theodore Draper has observed, "was only conditionally independent." Already compromised by congressional grants of immunity, Walsh faced a hostile administration determined to protect its own by withholding documents necessary to prosecute Iran-Contra crimes. For this reason, Walsh was forced to drop charges against both North and Poindexter relating to the diversion itself; and his entire case against the former CIA station chief in Costa Rica was dismissed after the very Justice Department for whom Walsh ostensibly worked refused to declassify certain documents needed for the trial.

In the end, those officials who admitted to, or were convicted of, criminal acts—none of whom received more than a minor fine as punishment—were pardoned by President Bush on December 24, 1992. The pardons also preempted the scheduled trials of former

CIA official Duane Clarridge and former secretary of defense Caspar Weinberger, and prevented public exposure of a conspiracy at the highest levels of the Reagan White House to cover up the president's role in the illegal sale of arms to Iran. "The pardons in themselves perfect[ed] the cover-up," Walsh would later say.[14]

But although Walsh's hard-won convictions against North and Poindexter were ultimately thrown out—ironically because they had admitted to their crimes before Congress under grants of immunity—their trials, and that of CIA deputy director Clair George substantially advanced the historical record on both the Central America and Middle East sides of the scandal. Had North never been prosecuted, for example, we would likely never have learned about the Reagan administration's quid pro quo operations or the role of then Vice President Bush in implementing those operations. Had Weinberger never been indicted, his notes of policy meetings and conversations at the highest levels of the Reagan White House would not have been added to the historical record, and key evidence that President Bush was in fact "in the loop" on the arms-for-hostages initiative might have remained concealed. And without Walsh's efforts, Bush's own personal notes on the Iran-Contra scandal might also have remained concealed. Although the pardons undermined the pursuit of justice in the scandal, the independent counsel's final report to Congress, containing many important components of the Iran-Contra affair overlooked by, or deliberately withheld from, Congress, supplies perhaps the most important verdict in the scandal—the verdict of history.

USING THIS DOCUMENTS READER The labyrinthine complexity of the Iran-Contra scandal cannot be overstated. Both of these covert operations, which took place at different ends of the world, involved numerous other nations, dozens of intermediaries, mercenaries, officials, and U.S. government agencies, as well as the expenditure of millions of dollars. The connection between the two—a handful of overlapping individuals channeling funds from one operation into

the other—was, undoubtedly, the simplest aspect of the Iran and Contra operations.

This book is an effort to tell the story of these multifaceted operations through a representative selection of the many documents generated by the scandal. The paper trail is a lengthy one; and, admittedly, it is not an easy task to distill the scandal into one hundred records. Congressional and judicial investigations, as Theodore Draper points out in his Foreword, forced the Reagan and Bush administrations to declassify literally hundreds of thousands of pages of top-secret and secret documents; the National Security Archive, through the Freedom of Information Act (FOIA), has obtained the declassification of thousands of pages more.

While the record of documents, depositions, hearings, and trial testimony is fascinating in its totality, not every interested individual has the time to spend months if not years sifting through the vast quantity of material available on the scandal; for those readers, this book organizes, and provides access to some of the most important documentation now available. Individuals who want to explore the fuller record are urged to consult the Archive's microfiched collection of forty-six hundred documents, *The Iran-Contra Affair: The Making of a Scandal, 1983–1988*, and other Archive holdings on the scandal which include twenty-four hundred pages of Oliver North's personal notebooks, and numerous exhibits from the trials of former national security advisor John Poindexter and former CIA deputy director Clair George.

The records in this reader have been selected from those holdings. The book includes a number of never-before-published documents that were obtained well after the Iran-Contra committees finished their investigation and issued their final report. Notebook pages from Oliver North's daily diary, for example, were released in 1990 after a year-long FOIA lawsuit filed by the National Security Archive and Public Citizen against the Office of the Independent Counsel. Internal CIA reports on the case of Joseph Fernandez were obtained as the result of a similar lawsuit filed by the

Center for National Security Studies in May 1992. CIA documents released at the trial of Clair George in July 1992 are also among the most recently declassified documents included in this book.

Most of the documents are original photoreproductions; in a few cases, however, the documents have been transcribed for reasons of space. Almost all the selected documents were once highly classified internal U.S. government records; several unclassified briefs and papers from the Office of the Independent Counsel, which are generally inaccessible to the public at large, have been included.

This volume is divided into three distinct parts comprising eight chapters, with a contextual introduction to each chapter. Within each introduction, the documents included here are referred to by number. The records are generally, but not always, organized chronologically. Those readers who prefer to begin with a comprehensive overview of the Iran-Contra operations are urged to read the chronology at the back of the book in order to place the individual documents within the broader context of events.

With the electoral defeat of George Bush, the political salience of the Iran-Contra affair has finally run its course. As the scandal passes into history, the extraordinary quantity of declassified documents left in its wake is, perhaps, the affair's most enduring legacy. To be sure, the U.S. government has continued to censor this story, hiding the truth behind the continuing classification, in part or in full, of thousands of documents. Nevertheless, more documents have been declassified over the past six years regarding the Iran and Contra operations, and the national security policy making related to both, than on any other foreign policy issue in recent memory. Although the interpretation of the scandal remains, after all this time, politically contentious, the selection in this book will enable students of history to research the many issues that arise from this dramatic episode, and to arrive at their own conclusions.

Most important, access to these documents can facilitate and enrich the public debate over foreign and domestic issues that affect every citizen and, ultimately, the strength of the U.S. democratic system. "A popular government without popular information or the means of acquiring it, is but prologue to a farce or a tragedy or perhaps both," wrote James Madison more than 150 years before the Iran-Contra scandal. By providing the means of acquiring this information, and thereby lifting a corner of the veil of secrecy that so often shrouds the conduct—and misconduct—of the U.S. government, the editors of this volume hope that future farce and tragedy can be avoided.

PETER KORNBLUH
MALCOLM BYRNE
JANUARY 5, 1993

NOTES

1. Oliver North, *Under Fire: An American Story* (New York: HarperCollins, 1991), pp. 7–8.

2. Oliver North, "Release of American Hostages in Beirut," ca. April 4, 1986. The memorandum makes it clear that the Israelis would deposit $15 million in the corporate account (which belonged to Secord and Hakim), and that money would be dispensed from there to the CIA to repay the Pentagon for the missiles, and to the Contras.

3. *Washington Post* transcript of Meese press conference, November 26, 1986.

4. See the *Report of the Congressional Committees Investigating the Iran-Contra Affair*, 100th Congress, 1st sess., November 13, 1987, p. 11. (Hereafter referred to as the *Iran-Contra Affair*.)

5. Ibid., p. 5.

6. See Shultz's testimony during the Iran-Contra hearings, 100–7, p. 27.

7. See Reagan's November 13, 1986, speech to the nation.

8. *Iran-Contra Affair*, p. 166.

9. Weinberger's notes are quoted in the Federal indictment, *United States of America v. Caspar W. Weinberger*, October 30, 1992, p. 4.

10. Secretary of Defense Weinberger also had contemporaneous notes on the 1985 arms shipments but, unlike Shultz, he apparently did not intercede to advocate that the administration tell the truth to Congress.

11. Due to a typographical error committed by Fawn Hall, this money never arrived in the Enterprise account.

12. *The Iran-Contra Affair*, p. 21.

13. A participant of the meeting is quoted in Seymour Hersh, "The Iran-Contra Committees: Did They Protect Reagan?," *New York Times Magazine*, April 29, 1990.

14. Walsh is quoted in *Newsweek*, January 4, 1993, p. 17.

GLOSSARY

This glossary is divided into three sections: people, organizations, and legal events.

I. PEOPLE

Abrams, Elliott

Elliott Abrams served as assistant secretary of state for inter-American affairs from 1985–1989. As the senior State Department official in charge of Latin America and the chair of the Restricted Inter-Agency Group (RIG), Abrams played an important role in the Contra resupply operations and in supervising Contra policy. In August 1986, he solicited $10 million from a representative of the Sultan of Brunei to be used to purchase arms for the Contras. In October 1991, Abrams pled guilty to two misdemeanor charges of withholding information from Congress and was sentenced to community service and two year's probation. On December 24, 1992, he received a presidential pardon.

Allen, Charles E.

During the Iran-Contra Affair, Charles Allen served as the CIA's national intelligence officer for counterterrorism. In late 1987, Allen received a formal Agency reprimand for "bending CIA regulations" in providing assistance to the NSC during the Iran initiative, according to a news report.

Anderson, Terry A.

Terry Anderson, Beirut bureau chief for the Associated Press, was kidnapped in Lebanon on March 16, 1985, and was released on December 4, 1991.

Arias Sánchez, Oscar

Costa Rican President Oscar Arias Sánchez angered Reagan administration officials in September 1986 when he publicly exposed, then shut down, the secret Santa Elena airstrip in northern Costa Rica used by the Enterprise to resupply Contras on the southern front—the border between Costa Rica and Nicaragua.

Bahramani, Ali Hashemi

Ali Hashemi Bahramani was the central figure in the so-called "second channel" to government leaders in Iran, which came into play in early August 1986. In his early twenties, he was believed to be a nephew of Speaker of the Parliament Ali Akbar Hashemi-Rafsanjani, although published accounts of his background and precise relationship to Hashemi-Rafsanjani are contradictory. He is most often referred to as "the Relative" or "the Nephew" in documents and official reports.

Buckley, William

A CIA counterterrorism expert and station chief in Beirut, William Buckley was kidnapped by Islamic Jihad on March 18, 1984. His release was a major goal for the United States in the early stages of the Iran initiative. Islamic Jihad announced his death in October 1985, but reports from former American hostages suggested he died in early June of that year after prolonged torture and maltreatment.

Bush, George

George Bush served as vice president of the United States during both terms of the Reagan administration. Although his role in the Iran-Contra affair was not a major focus of the various investigations into the scandal, documentary evidence points to his knowledge of, and involvement in, both the Iran initiative and U.S. Contra policy. While Bush denied being "in the loop" on the issues, documents show that throughout 1986 he attended numerous high-level meetings on the Iran initiative, and that he supported trading arms for hostages. He also participated in administration quid pro quo arrangements with Honduras in 1985 and 1986 aimed at ensuring that the Honduran government continued its support for the Contras. On Christmas Eve, 1992, he pardoned Caspar Weinberger and Duane Clarridge, preempting scheduled trials for both. In addition, Bush pardoned Elliott Abrams, Robert McFarlane, Alan Fiers, and Clair George.

Bustillo, Juan Rafael

Juan Rafael Bustillo served as commander of El Salvador's air force during the period of covert NSC assistance to the Contras. As the senior Salvadoran official in charge of Ilopango air base outside San Salvador, Bustillo permitted Contra resupply efforts to be run from that facility. His key U.S. contact was former CIA agent Felix Rodriguez.

Calero, Adolfo

Head of Nicaragua's Coca-Cola bottling company during the Somoza dictatorship, Adolfo Calero was picked by the CIA to become the political chieftain of the largest Contra organization, the Nicaraguan Democratic Force (FDN), in June 1983. He later was named to be one of a three-member directorate of the United Nicaraguan Opposition (UNO), and worked closely with Oliver North on behalf of the Contras.

Casey, William J.

As director of central intelligence 1981–1987, William Casey was the guiding force behind U.S. covert operations and an avid proponent of the Iran initiative and the Contra war. He regularly provided guidance to Oliver North and authorized use of CIA assets in both operations. He died in May 1987.

Cave, George W.

One of the CIA's top experts on Iran before retiring in 1980, George Cave contracted with the CIA as early as January 1986 to assist in various aspects of the Iran initiative, including interpreting at negotiating sessions and communicating one-on-one with Iranian intermediaries.

Channell, Carl R. ("Spitz")

As president of the National Endowment for the Preservation of Liberty (NEPL) and several political action committees, Spitz Channell became the most prominent fund-raiser and lobbyist for Contra aid. He secretly funneled over $2 million of tax-exempt donations into an Enterprise-controlled Swiss bank account used to buy arms for the Contras. In April 1987, Channell pleaded guilty to one count of conspiracy to defraud the United States and was sentenced to two years probation.

Cicippio, Joseph James

A deputy comptroller at the American University of Beirut, Joseph Cicippio was taken hostage on September 12, 1986, reportedly by the Organization of Revolutionary Justice, and released on December 2, 1991.

Clarridge, Duane R. ("Dewey")

Between 1981 and 1988, Duane "Dewey" Clarridge held senior posts in the Operations Directorate of the CIA—first, as chief of the Latin American Division, then as chief of the European Division. From 1981 to 1984, he was the top CIA official responsible for the covert war in Nicaragua. In November 1985, he assisted Oliver North in the disastrous HAWK missile shipment to Iran. He was indicted in November 1991 on seven counts of perjury and false statements. His trial was aborted by President Bush's pardon on December 24, 1992.

Clines, Thomas G.

A former CIA operative and long-time associate of Richard Secord, Thomas Clines played an important behind-the-scenes role in the Iran-Contra affair in 1985 and 1986, including purchasing and shipping arms to the Contras for Secord's Enterprise. In 1990, Clines was found guilty of four tax-related felonies and was sentenced to sixteen months of prison, fined $40,000 and ordered to pay the costs of his prosecution.

Cruz, Arturo, Sr.

A former member of the Sandinista junta and Nicaraguan ambassador to Washington, Arturo Cruz, Sr., became a forceful opponent of the Sandinista National Liberation Front in 1983. According to NSC memoranda, in February 1985, Cruz was transferred from the CIA payroll to a payroll controlled by Oliver North; he received a stipend of approximately $7,000 a month. When the United Nicaraguan Opposition was created in June 1985 at the behest of U.S. officials, Cruz was named a director.

Dunn, Bert

Bert Dunn played a leading operational role for the CIA during the first several months of the Iran initiative in 1985 and early 1986. He served as chief of the Near East Division in the CIA's Directorate for Operations until April 1986. (See entry for Twetten, Thomas.)

Dutton, Robert C.

Working under Richard Secord, retired Air Force Lt. Col. Robert Dutton supervised the day-to-day operations of the Contra resupply program beginning in the spring of 1986.

Fernandez, Joseph

A key player in the Contra program since early 1983, CIA agent Joseph Fernandez facilitated resupply operations to the southern front, despite the Boland Amendment ban on Agency involvement in the Contra war. As CIA station chief in Costa Rica from 1984 to 1986, Fernandez (code-named Tomas Castillo) worked closely with Oliver North and Robert Owen on Contra matters. On April 24, 1989, he was indicted on four counts of lying to investigators about his activities, but the case was later dropped after the Bush administration refused to allow disclosure of classified documents deemed necessary for his defense.

Fiers, Alan D.

Alan Fiers succeeded Duane Clarridge in 1984 as the CIA official in charge of day-to-day covert operations in Central America. At the time, he was chief of the Agency's Central American Task Force (sometimes referred to in official reports as "C/CATF"), and a member of the Restricted Inter-Agency Group (RIG), and the "mini-RIG," or "RIGlet," with Oliver North and Elliott Abrams. In July 1991, Fiers pleaded guilty to two misdemeanor counts of withholding information from Congress and was sentenced to community service and one year probation. He was pardoned by President Bush on December 24, 1992.

Gadd, Richard L.

As a deputy to Richard Secord, Gadd supervised the Enterprise's day-to-day Contra resupply operations between January and April 1986, when he was replaced by Robert Dutton. One of his companies, Airmach, received a major contract from the State Department's Office of Nicaraguan Humanitarian Assistance (NAHO) to ship nonlethal equipment to Central America.

George, Clair E.

As deputy director for operations at the CIA during the 1980s, Clair George had overall responsibility for all Agency covert operations. As such, he was knew of, and was involved in, both the Iran and Contra facets of the scandal. In September 1991, he was indicted on multiple counts of perjury, false statements, and obstruction, but the jury failed to reach a unanimous verdict on any of the charges, and the judge declared a mistrial on August 26, 1992. After a retrial in November, on December 9, 1992, George was found guilty on two counts of lying to Congress. He received a presidential pardon fifteen days later.

Ghorbanifar, Manucher

Manucher Ghorbanifar, an Iranian weapons dealer, acted as middleman in the U.S. arms deals with Iran from mid 1985 through mid 1986. Although he repeatedly misled all sides, he remained the principal go-between until the "second channel" emerged in summer 1986.

Gregg, Donald P.

A career CIA officer, Donald Gregg became Vice President Bush's national security advisor in 1982 after a stint on the NSC staff. Questions about Gregg's connections with Felix Rodriguez (see that entry) and the Contra resupply operations generated controversy, mainly because of their implication that his boss, George Bush, may also have been aware of the program.

Hakim, Albert

Iranian expatriate Albert Hakim was Richard Secord's business partner beginning in 1983. He managed finances for the Enterprise, and attended most of the sessions with the Iranian intermediaries as a translator and, occasionally, as a negotiator. In November 1989, he pleaded guilty to a single count of supplementing North's salary and was sentenced to two years' probation and a $5000 fine.

Hasenfus, Eugene

Eugene Hasenfus was the sole survivor of the October 5, 1986 crash of a C-123K cargo plane shot down during a Contra resupply mission. Captured by the Sandinistas, Hasenfus stated that he believed he was working on a CIA-sanctioned operation, and identified two other members of the resupply program as Max Gomez (a code name for Felix Rodriguez) and Ramón Medina (a code name for Luis Posada Carriles).

Jacobsen, David P.

David Jacobsen was director of the American University Hospital in Beirut. He was kidnapped on May 28, 1985, by Islamic Jihad and released November 2, 1986, apparently as part of the arms-for-hostages deals.

Jenco, Lawrence Martin

Lawrence Jenco, a Roman Catholic priest and former head of the Beirut office of Catholic Relief Services, was kidnapped on January 8, 1985, by Islamic Jihad. CIA Director Casey directly attributed his release, on July 26, 1986, to the ongoing negotiations with Iran.

Kangarlou, Mohsen

Mohsen Kangarlou was an official in the Iranian prime minister's office and a principal figure in the "first channel" of the Iran initiative. He is referred to as "the Second Iranian" in the congressional Iran-Contra committees' final report and as "the Australian" by Secord and other participants. Although credited by William Casey with the release of Ameri-

can hostages Benjamin Weir and Lawrence Jenco, Kangarlou apparently also "played a role" in the abduction of American Frank Herbert Reed. Adnan Khashoggi and Manucher Ghorbanifar identified him as an "extremist."

Karrubi, Hassan

An Iranian official reportedly close to Ayatollah Khomeini, Hassan Karrubi was a figure in the so-called first channel to Iran. He is identified in the congressional Iran-Contra committees' final report as "the First Iranian." Described by Adnan Khashoggi and Manucher Ghorbanifar as a "moderate," he took part in several meetings with Americans from November 1984 to the spring of 1986.

Khashoggi, Adnan

A Saudi billionaire arms dealer and associate of Manucher Ghorbanifar, Adnan Khashoggi made several large-scale loans in 1985 and 1986, which allowed U.S.-sanctioned arms sales to Iran to go forward.

Khomeini, Ruhollah

A long-time foe of the shah of Iran and the principal figure responsible for the Iranian Revolution of 1979, Ayatollah Ruhollah Khomeini was Shiite Iran's supreme religious figure until his death in 1989.

Kilburn, Peter

A librarian at the American University of Beirut, Peter Kilburn was kidnapped December 3, 1984, and murdered, reportedly at the behest of Muammar Qaddafi in retaliation for the April 1986 U.S. bombing of Libya.

Kimche, David

While director-general of Israel's Ministry of Foreign Affairs, former Mossad official David Kimche met with Robert McFarlane on several occasions, beginning in July 1985 about a possible arms deal with Iran. He was replaced by Amiram Nir as the chief Israeli contact in late 1985.

Ledeen, Michael A.

Michael Ledeen was a consultant to the NSC on counterterrorism and certain Middle East issues from November 1984 to December 1986. A controversial figure, he played an important part in the early phases of the Iran arms deals, helping to establish contact with Prime Minister Shimon Peres and other Israelis promoting the initiative.

Levin, Jeremy
The Beirut bureau chief for Cable News Network, Jeremy Levin was kidnapped by Islamic Jihad on March 7, 1984; he later escaped.

McFarlane, Robert C.
As national security advisor from 1983 to late 1985, Robert McFarlane helped to conceive key aspects of both the Iran arms deals and U.S. Contra policy. One of the prime movers behind the Iran initiative at the outset, McFarlane later urged that it be shut down, citing the unreliability of the Iranian go-betweens.

On the Contra front, McFarlane coordinated and approved virtually every activity undertaken by Oliver North and repeatedly lied about NSC involvement with the rebels. In 1988, McFarlane pleaded guilty to four counts of withholding information from Congress and was sentenced to community service, two years' probation, and a $20,000 fine. He received a presidential pardon on December 24, 1992.

McMahon, John N.
John McMahon served as deputy director of the CIA from 1982 until March 1986. After he learned that the CIA had played a part in the November 1985 shipment of HAWK missiles to Iran without the legally required authorization, McMahon demanded that President Reagan sign an appropriate Presidential Finding before he would allow any further CIA involvement in the operation.

Meese, Edwin, III
Edwin Meese served as counselor to the president from 1981 to 1985, and attorney general from 1985 to 1988. He came under fire from Congress in connection with hostage ransom operations conducted with his approval by Drug Enforcement Administration agents and Oliver North, and for the political nature of his "informed inquiry" into the Iran arms deals in late November 1986. Court records indicate that during that period Meese also attempted to cover up high-level administration knowledge of possibly illegal arms deals with Iran.

Miller, Richard R.
As president of International Business Communications (see entry in the Organization section of this glossary), Richard Miller played a major role in the NSC's political and paramilitary operations in collaboration with Oliver North and Carl "Spitz" Channell. On May 6, 1987, Miller pleaded guilty to one count of conspiring to defraud the United States and was sentenced to community service and two years' probation.

Monge, Luis Alberto
As president of Costa Rica in the early 1980s, Luis Alberto Monge tacitly supported the Reagan administration's southern front strategy by giving the Enterprise permission to construct a secret airstrip in northern Costa Rica. Monge also allowed the Contras to conduct political and paramilitary operations from Costa Rican territory.

Najafabadi, Mohammad Ali Hadi
Referred to as "the Adviser" in the congressional Iran-Contra committees' final report, Mohammad Ali Hadi Najafabadi was a member of Iran's Parliament and chairman of its Foreign Affairs Committee. He was the highest official to meet with the McFarlane delegation to Teheran in May 1986; Robert McFarlane described him as "a considerable cut above the Bush Leaguers we had been dealing with."

Negroponte, John D.
As ambassador to Honduras, John Negroponte oversaw the expansion of CIA and Defense Department activities in that country during President Reagan's first term in office, and was referred to in press accounts as a "proconsul" and "the boss" of Contra operations there. In March 1985, he participated in the NSC's quid pro quo effort to garner continued Honduran cooperation in the Contra war after Congress banned official U.S. assistance.

Nimrodi, Yaacov

A former Israeli defense attaché and representative of Israeli arms manufacturers in Teheran, Yaacov Nimrodi became one of the key Israeli middlemen in the first phase of the Iran initiative through the end of 1985. Following several months of botched Israeli efforts, including the problem-ridden November 1985 HAWK missile shipment, U.S. officials cut Nimrodi and his colleagues out of the initiative.

Nir, Amiram

While serving as counterterrorism adviser to Israeli Prime Minister Shimon Peres, former journalist Amiram Nir was the principal Israeli contact in the second phase of the Iran initiative beginning in January 1986. In July 1986, Nir met with Vice President George Bush to discuss the Iran initiative, telling him, among other things, that the Iranian intermediaries represented "the most radical elements" in the regime. In late 1988, Nir was killed in a plane crash in Mexico.

North, Oliver L.

From his official position as deputy director for political-military affairs on the NSC staff, Lt. Col. Oliver North (known by the code names BG [Blood and Guts], William P. Goode, Mr. Green, and Steelhammer) simultaneously ran the NSC's covert Contra resupply operations and the arms-for-hostages initiative with Iran. In March 1988, he was indicted on multiple counts of conspiracy, obstruction of justice, misleading Congress and accepting an illegal gratuity. After goverment-imposed restrictions on the use of classified information led to the the major conspiracy charges being dropped, a jury eventually found North guilty on three counts, but an appeals court panel later vacated two of the verdicts and reversed the third, citing the possibility that North's immunized congressional testimony may have affected the proceedings.

Owen, Robert W.

From the spring of 1984 to 1986, former Senate aide and public relations specialist, Robert Owen served as Oliver North's "eyes and ears" with the Contras, traveling back and forth to Central America as a courier and intelligence gatherer. North arranged for Owen to be given a contract with the State Department's Nicaraguan Humanitarian Assistance Office (NHAO), which effectively paid for his work on the Contra resupply operations.

Peres, Shimon

Israeli Prime Minister Shimon Peres presided over Israel's role in the clandestine Iran initiative, which included providing aircraft for the operation, contacts inside Iran, and a bureaucratic channel through which to funnel weapons to Teheran. His friends Adolph Schwimmer and Yaacov Nimrodi and his counterterrorism adviser, Amiram Nir, also played important parts in the initiative.

Poindexter, John M.

As deputy national security advisor under Robert McFarlane, between 1983 and December 1985, and as McFarlane's successor, career navy officer and physicist John Poindexter played a major decision-making role in U.S. covert operations in Central America and Iran, authorizing the operations conducted by his aide, Oliver North, and reporting directly to the president. Allowed to resign after the scandal erupted, he was indicted in April 1988 and found guilty in April 1990 of five felonies of conspiracy, obstruction of Congress, and false statements. He was sentenced to six months in prison on each count, but an appeals panel reversed the convictions in November 1991. On December 7, 1992, all charges against him were dismissed.

Polhill, Robert B.

A business professor at Beirut University College, Robert Polhill was kidnapped, apparently by Islamic Jihad, on January 28, 1987, and freed on April 22, 1990.

Rafsanjani, Ali Akbar Hashemi

Ali Akbar Hashemi Rafsanjani, speaker of Iran's Parliament, was reported to be a major proponent of forging an opening to the United States in the mid 1980s. During the Iran initiative, U.S. officials sought to appeal to Rafsanjani through various intermediaries, particularly his nephew ("the Relative"), who they presumed to be acting with the Speaker's approval.

Raymond, Walter, Jr.

In 1982, Walter Raymond, Jr., a career CIA expert in clandestine overseas media operations, was transferred by CIA Director William Casey to the NSC staff to build a "public diplomacy" capability within the executive branch. He became the key U.S. official overseeing implementation of NSDD 77 and the Reagan administration's public diplomacy operations on behalf of the Contras. He chaired weekly meetings of the Central America Public Diplomacy Working Group, attended by Lt. Col. Oliver North, which coordinated operations designed to influence and manipulate public opinion on Central America.

Reagan, Ronald W.

President of the United States from January 20, 1981, to January 20, 1989, Ronald Reagan established the policy framework and provided specific authorization for the Contra resupply operations and the arms-for-hostages transactions with Teheran that comprised the Iran-Contra affair. While his knowledge of the actual diversion of funds to the Contras from arms sales to Iran has never been established, the congressional report on the scandal asserted that "it was the President's policy—not an isolated decision by North or Poindexter—to sell arms secretly to Iran and to maintain the Contras" despite congressional prohibitions, and concluded that Reagan bears the "ultimate responsibility."

Reed, Frank Herbert

The headmaster at the Lebanese International School, Frank Herbert Reed was taken hostage in Beirut on September 9, 1986, and freed on April 30, 1990.

Reich, Otto

Otto Reich served as the first director of the Office of Public Diplomacy for Latin America and the Caribbean (S/LPD) between 1983 and 1986. Under his direction, the office became the most visible agency producing and disseminating pro-Contra, anti-Sandinista information to influence public opinion on contra assistance. Reich reported to Walter Raymond, Jr., at the National Security Council and to Oliver North, and took his guidance from Raymond's Central America Public Diplomacy Working Group.

Rodriguez, Felix I.

An anti-Castro Cuban and career CIA operative until 1977, Felix Rodriguez's involvement in support of the Contras dates back to at least 1983. With Donald Gregg's assistance, in February 1985, Rodriguez traveled to El Salvador and, in September, became coordinator of the Contra resupply network at the Ilopango air-base outside San Salvador.

Schwimmer, Adolph ("Al")

Adolph Schwimmer was an Israeli businessman and part-time adviser to Israeli Prime Minister Shimon Peres. Along with partner Yaacov Nimrodi, Schwimmer pushed for major Israeli and U.S. arms sales to Iran in 1985, and held numerous meetings with U.S. and Iranian intermediaries until they were closed out of the initiative by U.S. officials in late 1985 following the problem-ridden HAWK missile shipment to Teheran.

Secord, Richard V.

Richard Secord was the linchpin in secret White House operations to transfer weapons to Iran and to the Contras. A retired air force major general, Secord had an extensive background in intelligence and covert operations. After resigning under the cloud of the EATSCO scandal in 1983, Secord went into business with Iranian expatriate Albert Hakim, eventually connecting with Oliver North and becoming the primary "private-sector" operative controlling both aspects of the White House's secret operations. In 1988, Secord was charged with several counts arising from his participation in the Iran-Contra affair. He pleaded guilty to a single felony count of false statements to congressional committees, for which he received two years' probation on January 24, 1990.

Shultz, George P.

A strong supporter of Contra aid, Secretary of State George Shultz participated in high-level administration meetings at which funding for the rebels outside of congressionally approved channels was discussed, and he approved several initiatives to circumvent the ban on aid, including quid pro quos with Honduras and soliciting funds from Brunei. He also attended meetings on the Iran initiative in 1985 and 1986 at which he repeatedly expressed his strong opposition to trading arms for hostages. As the scandal began to break in November 1986, Shultz made it clear to the president that he could not support a cover-up of the arms-for-hostages operations.

Singlaub, John K.

A retired army major general and former commander of U.S. forces in Korea, John Singlaub was chairman of the World Anti-Communist League (WACL) and its affiliate, the United States Council for World Freedom (USCWF). Singlaub became a "lightning rod" to divert public attention away from the NSC-sponsored Contra resupply operations. In 1984 and 1985, he publicly claimed to be raising millions of dollars for the Contra program by providing American donors with an offshore bank account. In reality, with the help of the NSC, Singlaub raised funds mainly from foreign countries such as South Korea and Taiwan while communicating frequently with Oliver North.

Steen, Alan B.

A journalism professor at Beirut University College, Alan Steen was kidnapped with two other Americans and an Indian, apparently by Islamic Jihad, on January 28, 1987. He was released on December 3, 1991.

Sutherland, Thomas M.

Thomas Sutherland was dean of the School of Agriculture at the American University of Beirut. He was kidnapped on June 9, 1985, by Islamic Jihad and freed on November 18, 1991.

Tambs, Lewis A.

Former college professor and conservative activist Lewis Tambs served as U.S. ambassador to Costa Rica, where he helped to establish a southern front in the Contra war and worked closely with CIA Station Chief Joseph Fernandez in securing Costa Rican support for Contra resupply operations.

Teicher, Howard J.

In his capacity as a senior director for political-military affairs at the NSC, Howard Teicher helped to prepare a draft National Security Decision Directive in June 1985 which would have authorized the United States to permit its allies to sell arms to Iran in order to provide Iran's leaders with an alternative to the Soviet Union. Teicher traveled to Teheran as part of the McFarlane mission in May 1986. In 1992, he asserted that he had briefed Vice President Bush on the arms deals and that Bush was well informed about the operation.

Tracy, Edward Austin

An illustrator and author of children's books, Edward Tracy was taken hostage in Beirut on October 21, 1986. The Revolutionary Justice Organization claimed responsibility for the act, declaring that Tracy was in fact a spy for Israel and the CIA. He was released on August 11, 1991.

Turner, Jesse J.

A professor of computer science and mathematics at Beirut University College, Jesse Turner was kidnapped, apparently by Islamic Jihad, on January 28, 1987, and was freed on October 22, 1991.

Twetten, Thomas

Thomas Twetten served as deputy chief of the Near East Division "DC/NE" in the CIA's Directorate for Operations until April 1986, when he succeeded Bert Dunn (see that entry) as chief of the division, "C/NE." As such, he assumed the CIA's leading operational role in the arms-for-hostages deals. He met frequently with Oliver North and others, and attended negotiating sessions with Iranian intermediaries. In April 1988, Twetten was promoted to associate deputy director for operations at the CIA.

Weinberger, Caspar W.

Caspar Weinberger served as secretary of defense throughout the Iran-Contra affair and its aftermath. Although he frequently expressed his disapproval of the arms-for-hostages deals during 1985 and early 1986, the Tower Commission criticized him for being more concerned with his own position than with protecting the president from the consequences of the policy. Weinberger also participated in key meetings on third-country aid to the Contras and oversaw the Defense Department's involvement in several major operations relating to the Contras. On June 16, 1992, he was indicted on five counts of obstruction, perjury, and false statements. On September 29, the obstruction count was dismissed; it was replaced on October 30 with a one-count indictment of lying to Congress, although this count was also dismissed. In advance of his scheduled trial, Weinberger was pardoned by President Bush on December 24, 1992.

Weir, Benjamin

A Presbyterian minister, Benjamin Weir was kidnapped by Islamic Jihad on May 8, 1984. He was released on September 14, 1985, as a result of a U.S.-authorized Israeli arms shipment to Iran.

II. ORGANIZATIONS

Dawa al-Islamiya

Al Dawa al-Islamiya is a dissident Iraqi Shiite political party headquartered in Teheran. Several members were arrested in the aftermath of the December 1983 bombing spree in Kuwait which damaged the U.S. and French embassies. Release of the so-called Dawa prisoners became an issue in negotiations between U.S. representatives led by Oliver North and Iranian intermediaries.

Enterprise

Richard Secord adopted the designation "Enterprise" to describe the various combined operations in which he and Albert Hakim were engaged. Primarily, these were the arms sales to Iran and the Contra resupply program those sales helped to fund, and included the purchase of the freighter *Erria* among other activities. The Enterprise had the characteristics of what Lt. Col. Oliver North described in congressional testimony as CIA Director Casey's vision of an "off-the-shelf,"

self-sustaining entity, outside the bounds of congressional oversight, which could be called upon on short notice to conduct covert actions around the world .

Hezbollah

The Hezbollah or "Party of God," is a loose, even unconnected, assortment of Shiite groups or cells whose broad purpose is to spread the Islamic revolution. Originally inspired and still funded primarily by Iran, Hezbollah followers have claimed credit for a number of terrorist attacks in the Middle East in recent years.

International Business Communications (IBC)

A Washington, D.C., public-relations firm founded in 1984 by former Reagan presidential campaign aide Richard Miller, International Business Communications served as the bridge between the Reagan administration's Contra arms program and its public diplomacy campaign to win congressional support for official Contra assistance. IBC received more than $440,000 in contracts from the State Department's Office of Public Diplomacy for Latin America and the Caribbean to conduct a sophisticated Contra public-relations campaign directed at Congress. Richard Miller and his partner, Francis Gomez, worked closely with Carl "Spitz" Channell and the National Endowment for the Preservation of Liberty to raise $10 million, some $2.7 million of which were funneled directly into Lt. Col. Oliver North's Contra resupply operations. (See entry for Richard Miller in the Names section of this glossary).

Islamic Jihad

A terrorist group based in Lebanon, the Islamic Jihad organization was reported to have ties to Hezbollah and to operate with the support of Iran's Revolutionary Guard Corps. In early 1984, Islamic Jihad began a string of kidnappings of Americans, including CIA Station Chief William Buckley. The group's leader, Imad Mughniyah, reportedly hoped to swap the American hostages for release of his brother-in-law and other members of the so-called Dawa prisoners being held in Kuwait.

National Endowment for the
Preservation of Liberty (NEPL)

In 1985, the Washington, D.C.-based tax-exempt National Endowment for the Preservation of Liberty emerged as the single most important fund-raising and public-relations firm working with the Reagan administration on behalf of the Contras. In collaboration with Oliver North and IBC director Richard Miller, NEPL founder Carl "Spitz" Channell raised $10 million that was used to pay for political lobbying and Contra resupply operations.

Nicaraguan Democratic Force (FDN)

Founded in August 1981 in Guatemala City, Guatemala, the Nicaraguan Democratic Force became the largest and most active of the various Contra organizations. It was also the most closely associated with CIA/NSC operations, and it received the majority of U.S. assistance to the Contras until 1988.

Nicaraguan Humanitarian Assistance Office (NHAO)

The Nicaraguan Humanitarian Assistance Office was created after Congress passed $27 million in nonlethal assistance for the Contras on August 15, 1985. To dispense this money, President Reagan mandated (in Executive Order 12530) the creation of a special agency, the NHAO, to be housed in the Department of State. Although the $27 million was supposed to be used only for food, medicine, clothing, and other nonlethal materials, unbeknownst to Congress the NHAO became part of the Contra resupply operations.

Office of Public Diplomacy for Latin
America and the Caribbean (S/LPD)

The Office of Public Diplomacy for Latin America and the Caribbean was established in July 1983 pursuant to NSDD 77, which mandated the creation of a centralized "public diplomacy" apparatus within the executive branch. Although housed in the State Department, in reality S/LPD "report[ed] directly to the NSC," according to internal NSC memoranda, and worked closely with Lt. Col. Oliver North and Walter Raymond, Jr., in secretly undertaking "political ac-

tion" programs, "white propaganda operations," and contracting with private-sector public-relations firms to lobby Congress.

United Nicaraguan Opposition (UNO)

Formed in June 1985 at the behest of U.S. officials before a critical vote in Congress on Contra aid, the United Nicaraguan Opposition was meant to portray the Contras as a coalition of civilian-led democrats. UNO's nominal leaders, Adolfo Calero, Alfonso Robelo, and Arturo Cruz, Sr. (known as the "Triple A"), were supposed to share power equally. In reality, the organization was dominated by Calero and FDN commander Enrique Bermúdez, who controlled Contra military operations. In March 1987, after months of infighting, Cruz resigned and UNO broke up.

III. LEGAL EVENTS

Arms Export Control Act of 1976

The 1976 Arms Export Control Act governs (both cash and credit) foreign military sales by the United States to foreign governments, restricting arms exports in several ways. It prohibits a recipient country (in the case of the Iran initiative, Israel) from transferring U.S. arms to a third country without prior written consent from the president of the United States, which cannot be granted unless a variety of legal and policy conditions are met.

Boland Amendment II

The second Boland Amendment, which derived from a widespread belief in Congress that the Reagan administration had systematically violated the first Boland Amendment, sought to terminate all funding for covert operations related to U.S. support for the Contras. Passed in October 1984, Boland II was written to apply specifically to the CIA, the Defense Department, and any other U.S. agency involved in intelligence operations, which appeared to include the NSC. Nevertheless, Contra supporters later argued that the NSC was exempt from this law, and therefore could continue to resupply the Contras.

Economy Act of 1915

The Economy Act authorizes, among other things, the transfer of arms from one U.S. government agency to another, provided the receiving agency reimburses the cost of the transfer. This act came into play during the Iran initiative as the preferred legal means for providing weapons to Teheran, since it did not require informing Congress of the transfer of weapons from Defense Department to the CIA.

Foreign Assistance Act of 1961, as amended

This statute provides the overall framework for U.S. foreign aid. The Hughes-Ryan Amendment to the act, passed in 1974, requires that the president authorize, through a Finding, that CIA foreign operations be "important to the national security" before any funds can be expended, and that Congress be informed of the operation.

The Contra Humanitarian Assistance Bill

Passed in June 1985 by the House of Representatives and signed into law that August, the $27 million aid bill provided monies for nonlethal assistance, defined as "food, clothing, medicine, and other humanitarian assistance" and specifically excluding weapons, ammunition, and other equipment that can be used to inflict bodily harm. To administer these funds, President Reagan signed Executive Order 12530 in late August, establishing the Nicaraguan Humanitarian Assistance Office (NHAO) within the State Department (see entry in the Organizations section of this glossary).

National Security Decision Directive 77

NSDD 77, "Management of Public Diplomacy Relative to National Security," was signed by President Reagan on January 14, 1983. The directive mandated the creation of a "public diplomacy" bureaucracy to conduct both domestic and international information campaigns. The public diplomacy program primarily focused on winning the public debate over official U.S. assistance to the Contras.

National Security Decision Directive Draft of 11 June 1985

Drawing on a CIA study by Graham Fuller, NSC staff members produced in June 1985 a draft NSDD, "U.S. Policy toward Iran," which called for a "major change" in Washington's approach to Iran, including encouraging Western allies to provide "selected military equipment" to the government in Teheran. Despite opposition from Secretary of State George Shultz and Defense Secretary Caspar Weinberger, the ideas incorporated in the document nevertheless became the intellectual justification for the arms sales to Iran in 1985–1986.

PART I

THE CONTRAS

I. THE CONTRA WAR:
ABROAD AND AT HOME

On December 1, 1981, President Ronald Reagan signed a Finding that authorized a Central Intelligence Agency covert action program to "support and conduct...paramilitary operations against...Nicaragua" (Document 1). The Finding, which CIA director William Casey presented to the congressional intelligence committees that day, was all of one paragraph in length; it stated that the main military purpose of the operation was to interdict weapons allegedly flowing from Nicaragua to leftist rebels in El Salvador.[1] The CIA, Casey informed the committees, would organize, train, and arm a force of five hundred Nicaraguan exiles to accomplish this mission. This counterrevolutionary army, known as the Contras, subsequently became the most contentious issue between the executive and legislative branches during the Reagan era.

From its inception, the CIA's Contra operation was steeped in what the committees investigating Iran-Contra described as "pervasive dishonesty." Congress was not informed that months before the Finding was signed the CIA had initiated contacts with Nicaraguan exiles in Miami and Central America as well as discussions with other Latin American governments about overthrowing the Sandinistas. In August, the head of the CIA's Latin America division, Duane Clarridge traveled to Tegucigalpa to confer with Honduran military officials who were already working with Argentine operatives to organize small groups of Nicaraguan exiles into a paramilitary force. "I speak in the name of President Ronald Reagan," Clarridge told them. "We want to support this effort to change the government of Nicaragua."[2]

Nor did the oversight committees know that in No-

vember President Reagan had signed National Security Decision Directive 17 authorizing a much broader set of covert operations than was indicated in the Finding. According to planning papers accompanying NSDD 17, the CIA would conduct "political and paramilitary operations against the Cuban presence and the Cuban-Sandinista support infrastructure in Nicaragua," as well as build "popular support...for an opposition front that would be nationalistic, anti-Cuban and anti-Somoza." Most of these operations would be conducted by foreigners, but in some instances U.S. personnel might "take unilateral paramilitary action." Initially the program was budgeted at $19.95 million, but "more funds and manpower [would] be needed."[3] Creating and supporting an interdiction force was not part of these plans.

FOSTERING THE COUNTERREVOLUTION
In the fall of 1981, the Contras consisted of scattered groupings of some 250 men who had sought refuge in Honduras and Guatemala; most were remnants of Anastasio Somoza's personal army, the Nicaraguan National Guard. Their ragtag bands roamed the Honduran-Nicaraguan border, resorting to random violence and chicken theft in order to survive.[4] Under CIA direction, these groups were united into one organization—the Nicaraguan Democratic Force (FDN)—and were transformed into a paramilitary army operating out of Honduras, equipped with trucks, planes, automatic weapons and artillery. Later in 1982, the CIA recruited former Sandinista war hero Edén Pastora and his followers in Costa Rica, and began to funnel funds and arms into what became known as the southern front.

With the influx of U.S. funds, equipment, and personnel, the frequency and destructiveness of the Contra attacks increased rapidly. "In a 100 day period from 14 March to 21 June, at least 106 insurgent incidents occurred within Nicaragua," the Defense Intelligence Agency reported in July 1982. Attacks during this period included sabotage of highway bridges, sniper fire on small military patrols, the burning of customs warehouses and crops, and "the assassination of minor government officials."[5] Such attacks, U.S. Ambassador Anthony Quainton reported in October, were resulting in "some heavy costs for the Sandinistas."[6]

The CIA's clandestine war did not stay covert for long. In March 1982, *The Nation*, the *New York Times* and the *Washington Post* published major articles exposing the operations; in November, *Newsweek* ran a cover story, "A Secret War for Nicaragua." Contrary to the limited inderdiction operation that the Contra campaign was supposed to be, reported the *New York Times*, it had "become the most ambitious paramilitary and political action operation mounted by the CIA in nearly a decade."[7]

As the visibility of the Contra program increased, U.S. legislators became increasingly uneasy about its scope and purpose. In order to hold the Reagan administration accountable to its stated goal of interdicting arms, in December 1982 the U.S. Congress passed the first Boland Amendment. It read:

> None of the funds provided in this Act may be used by the Central Intelligence Agency or the Department of Defense to furnish military equipment, military training or advice, or other support for military activities, to any group or individual, not part of a country's armed forces, for the purpose of overthrowing the government of Nicaragua or provoking a military exchange between Nicaragua and Honduras.[8]

The first congressional initiative to curtail the Contra campaign failed to have any impact whatsoever. To be sure, U.S. officials publicly declared the administration's adherence to the law. "We are complying with the law," President Reagan told reporters on April 14, 1983. "We are not doing anything to try to overthrow the Nicaraguan government."[9] Behind the scenes, however, the CIA continued its paramilitary warfare unabated. The CIA's 1983 "Pyschological Operations in Guerrilla Warfare" training manual—more commonly known as the "murder manual" because it advised the rebels on the "selective use of violence" against "carefully selected" civilian targets such as judges, village magistrates, and local Sandinista officials—exhorted the Contras to "work for the moment when the overthrow can be achieved."[10]

Following passage of the first Boland Amendment, however, the Reagan administration did begin to recast the rebels as fighters for freedom and democracy. To offset charges that the rebels were led by ex-military officials of Somoza's hated National Guard, in late 1982 the CIA rounded up eight prominent Nicaraguan civilians in exile who had opposed the Somoza regime and appointed them to the newly U.S.-created "directorate" of the FDN. At the cost of $1.8 million, the Agency hired a Miami public relations firm to publicize an image of the Contras as a nationalist democratic force. And in May 1983, President Reagan proclaimed them to be "freedom fighters" and for the first time publicly acknowledged his administration's support for them.

These public relations efforts delayed but failed to deter a growing movement in the House of Representatives to terminate Contra funding. Anyone "with any sense," concluded House Intelligence Committee Chairman Edward Boland, "would have to come to the conclusion that the operation is illegal, [and] that the purpose and mission of the operation was to overthrow the government in Nicaragua."[11] In December, congressional opponents of Contra funding failed to ban assistance outright but did manage to impose a $24 million ceiling on further aid.

With the politics of Contra funding becoming increasingly controversial, the administration moved to update its rationale for the CIA's operations. On September 19, 1983, the White House presented a broader, far more ambitious, and ambiguous, Presidential Finding to the intelligence committees (Document 2). This Finding portrayed the CIA's Contra operations as pressure against alleged Sandinista subversion in Central America, and as an inducement for democracy within Nicaragua and peace in the region. A CIA "scope paper" accompanying the Finding detailed efforts to escalate "paramilitary action" as well as to covertly provide "financial and material support" to "Nicaraguan opposition leaders and organizations" in order to foster an internal political opposition front (Document 3).

Under Director William Casey's explicit directions—"What [more] can we do to the economy to make those bastards sweat?"—the CIA initiated a series of major sabotage attacks on Nicaraguan installations in the fall of 1983.[12] On September 8, CIA assets launched a major sabotage operation on oil pipeline and dock facilities at Puerto Sandino. On October 10, covert operatives set an oil storage facility ablaze, forcing the evacuation of the city of Corinto. Between January 1 and April 24, 1984, the CIA stepped up these operations, sending teams of specially trained operatives to sow mines in the ports of Nicaragua. These operations were part of a White House plan to increase dramatically the level of aggression before Congress banned further CIA operations. "Given the distinct possibility that we may be unable to obtain additional [congressional] funding," reported a Senior Interagency Working Group to National Security Advisor Robert McFarlane in January, "our objective should be to bring the Nicaraguan situation to a head in 1984."[13]

The Contras publicly claimed credit for sowing the mines; in reality the operations were conducted by CIA contract agents—Unilaterally Controlled Latino Assets (UCLAs)—without any Contra involvement. The purpose of the mining, was to "severely disrupt the flow of shipping essential to Nicaraguan trade during the peak export period," National Security Council (NSC) staffers Oliver L. North and Constantine Menges noted in a top-secret action memo to their superior, Robert McFarlane (Document 4). And even more explosive acts of sabotage were being planned. McFarlane approved North's and Menges's recommendation

for a covert operation to destroy a Mexican oil tanker in a Nicaraguan port as part of "our overall goal of applying stringent economic pressure," and briefed President Reagan on March 5, 1984 (Document 4). The operation never took place, however, presumably because the CIA's minings were exposed in the press four weeks later, creating a furor in Congress.

In the wake of the mining scandal, the Senate refused to pass President Reagan's request for $21 million in supplementary Contra funding; instead, on October 10, Congress agreed to a second Boland Amendment, Boland II, a joint resolution banning further U.S. support for the Contra war (Document 5). The law stated that during fiscal year 1985,

> no funds available to the Central Intelligence Agency, the Department of Defense, or any other agency or entity of the United States involved in intelligence activities may be obligated or expended for the purpose of which would have the effect of supporting, directly or indirectly, military or paramilitary operations in Nicaragua by any nation, group, organization, movement, or individual.

The amendment included a clause enabling the president to obtain $14 million in new Contra aid after February 28, 1985, if both houses of Congress passed the request as a joint resolution. But the intent of the law was clear. According to its sponsor, Representative Boland,

> This prohibition applies to all funds available in fiscal year 1985 regardless of any accounting procedure at any agency. It clearly prohibits any expenditure, including those from accounts for salaries and all support costs....[I]t clearly ends U.S. support for the war in Nicaragua. Such support can only be renewed if the President can convince the Congress that this very strict prohibition should be overturned.[14]

As with the previous laws, the Reagan administration simply circumvented this one. Indeed, since the spring of 1984, the NSC and the CIA had been making financial and organizational preparations to continue the war without congressional authorization (see Chapter II, "Third-Country Quid Pro Quos"). With the CIA and the Defense Department explicitly banned from supporting the Contras, President Reagan directed his NSC staff to assume management of the rebel insurgency. Lt. Col. Oliver North, according to his own testimony, was tasked to "keep them together body and soul" using extraofficial financing, and nonofficial personnel, until Congress could be convinced to renew official aid. Meanwhile, over the next two years the Reagan administration would conduct a concentrated propaganda and public relations campaign to influence public perceptions of the Contra war, and lobby for the needed votes in Congress to allow the CIA to reengage.

PUBLIC DIPLOMACY
AND THE CONTRA IMAGE

The tasking to the NSC of a project that the CIA could not itself legitimately undertake followed a formula already in use to implement an illicit propaganda program, euphemistically known as "public diplomacy." The CIA is prohibited by the 1947 National Security Act from conducting domestic operations and by President Reagan's Executive Order 12333 from activities "intended to influence United States political processes, public opinion...or media." In 1982, however, William Casey authorized the transfer of one of the CIA's senior propaganda specialists, Walter Raymond, Jr., to the NSC, where he became the principal coordinator of a major new effort to influence and manipulate Congress, the press, and the public on the issue of the Contras. A chapter drafted by Iran-Contra investigators, but blocked from inclusion in the final report by Senate Republicans, concluded that the Reagan administration had used

> one of the CIA's most senior specialists, sent to the NSC by Bill Casey, to create and coordinate an inter-agency public diplomacy mechanism.

> [This program] did what a covert CIA operation in a foreign country might do—[it] attempted to manipulate the media, the Congress and public opinion to support the Reagan administration's policies [in Nicaragua].[15]

Once at the National Security Council, Raymond, according to his résumé, assumed "overall responsibility for NSC staff coordination concerning public diplomacy." In the spring of 1983, he oversaw the implementation of Reagan's National Security Decision Directive 77, "Management of Public Diplomacy Relative to National Security," which mandated the creation of a new bureaucracy throughout the executive branch "to strengthen the organization, planning and coordination of the various aspects of public diplomacy."[16] The public diplomacy initiative, which Raymond described in his memos as "a new art form," was eventually applied to a number of controversial foreign policy issues; from mid 1983 to mid 1986, however, the bureaucracy focused almost exclusively on salvaging the president's Contra war.

On Raymond's recommendation, in July 1983 the National Security Advisor William Clark established the most visible component of this new bureaucracy, the Office of Public Diplomacy for Latin America and the Caribbean (S/LPD), and designated an aggressive ideologue, Otto Reich, to direct it. To highlight the importance of this program, Raymond had urged that Reich and the pro-Contra public diplomacy project be given "a White House cachet."[17] Hence, a July 1, 1983, directive from Clark appointing Reich stated, "the President has underscored his concern that we must increase our efforts in the public diplomacy field to deepen the understanding of and support for our policies in Central America" (Document 6).

The Office of Public Diplomacy was housed in the State Department but, unbeknownst to the public or Congress, it reported directly to the NSC. Reich and his deputies attended the weekly meetings of the Central American Public Diplomacy Task Force, chaired by Raymond at the NSC, which included representatives from the CIA, Defense Department, Agency for International Development, and NSC. The ubiquitous Oliver North attended a number of these meetings (his calenders record some seventy public diplomacy sessions with Raymond between 1984 and 1986) maintained direct contact with Reich over a secure telephone and influenced the public diplomacy operations through his position on the Restricted Interagency Group (RIG). The task force, Raymond advised in a memo for Casey, "takes its policy guidance from the Central American RIG,"[18] the committee dominated by North, CIA Central America Task Force Chief Alan Fiers and Assistant Secretary of State Elliott Abrams—the three men responsible for all Contra operations.

Fostered by a CIA specialist in propaganda, and responsive to NSC operatives, the Office of Public Diplomacy also drew on the expertise of pyschological warfare officials from the U.S. military for its mission. Col. Daniel "Jake" Jacobowitz, an S/LPD deputy director, had an established background in "psyops." (After Jacobowitz left the S/LPD, he joined the Psychological Operations Board in the Office of the Secretary of Defense.) A confidential-sensitive "Public Diplomacy Action Plan" written by Jacobowitz in March 1985 provides an example of a psywar approach to targeting U.S., as opposed to foreign, audiences (Document 7). Under such headings as "Central Perceptions," "Situational and Perceptional Impediments," "Assets," "Themes," and "Audiences," Jacobowitz outlined an "educational campaign" to convince Congress to renew Contra aid. The "overall theme," according to the plan was: "The Nicaraguan Freedom Fighters (FF) are fighters for freedom in the American tradition; FLSN are evil."

To advance this theme systematically, other psyops officers were detailed to the Office of Public Diplomacy from the 4th Psychological Operations Group at Fort Bragg. A group of five such men, who Jacobowitz referred to as his "A-team," arrived in June 1985 to set up information and analysis systems necessary for the production of "persuasive" public diplomacy publica-

tions. Among their responsibilities, Jacobowitz informed Reich, would be "looking for exploitable themes and trends [and] inform us of possible areas for our exploitation" (Document 8). "We realize that the cadre of U.S. officers…possessing these skills is limited and in great demand," Reich wrote to Raymond in January 1986 seeking more psyops personnel for the office; "however, the overall national interest would be well served if some of these assets are placed in S/LPD to work on a problem of vital national importance—Central American public diplomacy" (Document 9).

The public diplomacy goal in the case of Nicaragua policy, Raymond declared, was to "concentrate on gluing black hats on the Sandinistas and white hats on UNO [United Nicaraguan Opposition, i.e., the Contras]."[19] The Office of Public Diplomacy advanced this goal through a number of overt and covert activities. On the surface, S/LPD functioned as a ministry of information, producing and distributing vituperative and one-sided booklets, reports, and briefings—topics ranged from "Nicaragua's Military Build-up and Support for Central American Subversion," and "The Sandinistas and Middle Eastern Radicals," to "Who Are the Contras?"—for the executive branch, Congress, reporters, editorial boards, college libraries and faculties, religious groups, and conservative advocacy organizations. S/LPD officials also served as lecturers and talk-show guests, booking 1,570 speaking engagements during its first year of operation alone.

Less visible, however, were S/LPD's multifaceted efforts to shape and manufacture press coverage on Nicaragua. Working with North and Raymond, S/LPD set up a system to declassify selected tidbits of information and leak them at propitious times to favored journalists in order to influence the debate over Nicaragua. A manipulation of the media under any circumstances, this program sometimes crossed the line between information and disinformation. In perhaps the most famous example, in November 1984 S/LPD officials helped promote the dramatic but false story that Soviet MiG fighter jets had been delivered to Nicaragua, significantly influencing the public perception of a Sandinista military threat that, in reality, never existed.

S/LPD also sought to shape coverage of Nicaragua by monitoring the media and interceding with editors to denounce stories that did not conform with the administration's view. After National Public Radio aired its first major report of Contra human rights atrocities, for example, Ambassador Reich demanded an unprecedented meeting with the editors, producers, and reporters, at which he informed them that S/LPD was "monitoring" all NPR programs on Central America and considered them biased against the Contras and U.S. policy.[20] When CBS ran a series of reports and a documentary on Central America that "upset" President Reagan and Vice President Bush, Reich spent more than three hours with CBS personnel transmitting the administration's objections. "This is one example of what the Office of Public Diplomacy has been doing. It has been repeated dozens of times over the past few months," Secretary of State Shultz informed the president (Document 10). He continued, "we are attempting to build the kinds of relationships with the news media that will enable us to dispel the disinformation and misinformation which has been so prevalent in coverage while at the same time aggressively expressing our policy objectives."

To further advance those objectives, S/LPD conducted "white propaganda" operations—covertly sponsoring reporting and articles in the media through ostensibly independent authors and sources. A March 13, 1985, confidential/eyes-only memorandum from Johnathan Miller to White House Director of Communications Patrick Buchanan reported on five examples of S/LPD's "white propaganda operation," which included two opinion pieces contracted for by the Office and published in the Wall Street Journal and the Washington Post, and NBC News coverage of the Contras arranged by S/LPD consultants (Document 11). "I will not attempt...to keep you posted on all activities since we have too many balls in the air at any one time and since the work of our oper-

ation is ensured by our office's keeping a low profile," Miller boasted. "I merely wanted to give you a flavor of some of the activities that hit our office on any one day...." Subsequently, the legal department of the General Accounting Office concluded that S/LPD's operations amounted to "prohibited covert propaganda activities designed to influence the media and the public to support the Administration's Latin American policies."[21]

THE CONTRA LOBBY

Just as Oliver North secretly recruited private-sector intermediaries to obtain guns for the Contras, the public diplomacy apparatus recruited a network of public relations specialists, fund-raisers, and lobbyists to obtain votes for them. In violation of antilobbying laws preventing congressionally appropriated monies from being used to generate propaganda "designed to influence a member of Congress," the Office of Public Diplomacy entered into secret contracts with private-sector consultants to engage in activities specifically designed to influence the Contra aid votes. Public diplomacy, as to Iran-Contra committees observed, "turned out to mean public relations–lobbying, all at taxpayers' expense."[22]

S/LPD's main contractor was International Business Communications (IBC), a public relations firm owned by two former government officials, Frank Gomez and Richard Miller. In early 1984, Reich hired Gomez for the first of seven no-bid contracts. Initially, the contracts were small and short term, calling for providing information kits, drafting briefing books, writing opinion pieces, and other public affairs activities on behalf of the Contra program. But after Congress cutoff Contra aid, IBC's contractual relationship with S/LPD dramatically expanded. In fiscal year 1985, according to an internal memo on outside contracts, IBC received $114,400 for "classified special services."[23] In September 1985, Ambassador Reich authorized a secret contract for $276,186 for IBC to upgrade its Contra media work and build a comprehensive mailing list of organizations and individuals in a position to influence the debate on Central America (Document 12). In all, IBC's U.S. government contracts totaled $441,084.

At the same time that Miller and Gomez were under contract to the Office of Public Diplomacy, IBC acted as a key adjunct to Oliver North's resupply network. Along with Carl "Spitz" Channell, whose National Endowment for the Preservation of Liberty (NEPL), American Conservative Trust (ACT), and Sentinel served respectively as the principal fundraiser, Congressional lobbyist, and Contra publicist, IBC worked closely with the White House to promote a "freedom fighter" image of the rebel forces and a "Soviet outpost" image of the Sandinista government. Miller, Gomez, and Channell, taking direction from North, designed and financed a million-dollar TV advertising campaign around the Contra aid votes. IBC also set up the Contras' Washington office down the street from the National Zoo, and conducted national speaking tours and press conferences for the rebel leaders—activities that were virtually indistinguishable from those called for in the S/LPD contract.

Much of the political lobbying and Contra publicity campaign were paid for with funds raised by Spitz Channell and his nonprofit "educational" organization, the NEPL. Channell, a disciple of legendary conservative fundraiser Terry Dolan, raised $3.9 million in 1985 and over $7 million in 1986 for the Contra cause, mostly from conservative multimillionaire widows who he publicly wined and dined and privately disparaged as "the blue-rinse brigade."[24]

The key to Channell's fund-raising success was the imprimatur of the Reagan White House. White House Chief of Staff Donald Regan, National Security Adviser Poindexter, Assistant Secretary Abrams, and communications director Patrick Buchanan all met with donors at the White House on various occasions. Oliver North delivered his public diplomacy slide-show briefing to groups brought over to the NSC by Channell, and also met with individual donors at the Hay Adams hotel in downtown Washington, D.C. There, he and Channell combined to deliver a "one-two punch." North would tell donors of the Contras' dire need for food, medicine, and arms and would then leave the table, whereupon Channell would explain to them that their donation of $100,000, $300,000, or even $1 million could mean the difference between winning or losing the fight against communism in Central America. Although North testified that he "never solicited" donations, he did write fundraising appeals on NSC stationary to thirty of NEPL's largest donors. "Because you cared, the spark of liberty still glows in the darkness of Nicaragua," North wrote to prominent, wealthy Americans such as Nelson Bunker Hunt, Robert Mosbacher, and Ellen Garwood in January 1986 (Document 13). "Once again your support will be essential."

As the ultimate inducement to contributors, the White House offered a private visit with the president. For donations of $300,000 and over, Channell essentially sold tickets to the Oval Office. Reagan met with several individual donors, and did a "drop-by" for Channell's donor groups at the White House on several other occasions. "They were very instrumental last year in helping us win the vote for aid to the Nicaraguan DRF [Democratic Resistance Forces] through their television programs and advertisements," North noted in a memo to Poindexter about a January 30, 1986, meeting between a donor group from the American Conservative Trust and Reagan. "The meeting is an opportunity to express Administration support for the efforts of ACT as we gear up for a Congressional vote during March."[25] An opinion by the counsel to the president, Fred Fielding, noted that while there was no legal problem with Reagan meeting these donors, "objections may be raised that the President is violating the spirit of the anti-lobbying provisions by enlisting these private groups to lobby Congress. Care should accordingly be taken," Fielding advised, "to avoid any suggesion of White House control of these groups" (Document 14).

Of the $10 million raised domestically, $5 million went to salaries and expenses for Channell, Miller, Gomez, and their employees, $2.7 million was funneled through IBC into a bank account in Switzerland used by North to purchase arms, and $2.3 million went into a broad political lobbying campaign that included pro-Contra and anti-Sandinista television advertisements, carefully scheduled Contra tours through swing-vote districts and paid lobbyists on Capitol Hill. This campaign, combined with the other activities of the public diplomacy apparatus, and the secret resupply operations that made the rebels appear to be a self-sustaining force, had a demonstrable impact on eroding opposition to Contra aid in the House of Representatives, and contributed, at least in part, to the passage in June 1986, of $100 million in new funds for the CIA to spend on the paramilitary war. By then, the Reagan administration had managed to glue black hats on the Sandinistas and white hats on the Contras. Public diplomacy "has played a key role in setting out the parameters and defining the terms of the public discussion on Central America policy," stated a self-congratulatory meritorious honor award for the Office of Public Diplomacy. "Despite the efforts of a formidable and well established Soviet/Cuban/ Nicaraguan propaganda apparatus, the achievements of U.S. public diplomacy are clearly visible."[26]

THE DECLASSIFIED CONTRAS

The image of the Contras fostered by the public diplomacy strategists to garner support in Congress—that of independent, nationalist freedom fighters struggling to bring democracy to Nicaragua and capable of winning this victory with U.S. support—belied the rebels' reality. In December 1984, then–CIA Deputy Director for Intelligence Robert Gates wrote a memo to Casey stating that it was "time to talk absolutely straight about Nicaragua" (Document 15). The assessment of CIA intelligence analysts, Gates reported, challenged the conventional wisdom about the Contras' viability: "the Contras, even with American support, cannot overthrow the Sandinista regime." The resistence "eventually will wither," Gates wrote; the problem of dealing with the Sandinistas required an overt policy of trying to overthrow them.

Oliver North still maintained that the Contras could win. In mid 1985, he drew up a "Political/Military Strategy for Nicaragua" (Document 16). North acknowledged that "the American people currently consider U.S. full-scale military involvement in Nicaragua as unacceptable." But he foresaw the time when Congress would renew funding for the CIA's contra operations—which "combined with the current and significant foreign and domestic support [would] allow the proposed strategy to be implemented."

North's three-phase plan called for, among other things, developing an FDN operational base inside Honduras, a southern front in Costa Rica and "an aerial resupply system for both fronts." Escalating Contra attacks would attempt to "disrupt the economic infrastructure of Nicaragua with priority to the electrical grid, water, transportation, and communications systems." In the third and "final phase," according to North's scenario, the Contras would bring about the "defeat and demobilization of [the] Sandinista armed forces" and proceed with "implementation of the UNO/FDN political program."

Ironically, the internal reporting of North's personal intermediary with the Contras, Robert Owen, who delivered the strategy paper to Contra leader Adolfo Calero, offered the most candid assessment of why such a scenario was unlikely. In Document 17, an eyes-only report that offered an "overall perspective" on Owen's two years of clandestine work with the Contra leadership, he depicted the people and organizations he had worked with considerably differently than President Reagan's description of the Contras as "the moral equivalent of our founding fathers."

The Contra organizations were simply products of the United States, unable to act independently on their own, Owen reported to North. The United Nicaraguan Opposition, which the Reagan administration fostered in June 1985 to convince Congress to appropriate $27 million in "humanitarian" assistance to the Contras, had failed to become a viable organization. "[A]lmost anything it has accomplished is because the hand of the USG[overnment] has been there directing and manipulating." The predominant Contra force, the FDN, was little better than a dictatorship run by "strong man" Adolfo Calero. Calero, was "a creation of the USG and so he is the horse we chose to ride." But, Owen warned, the Contra leaders around Calero, were "not first rate people; in fact they are liars and greed and power motivated. They are not the people to rebuild a new Nicaragua."

The reality, as Owen saw it, was that the Contra leaders were simply profiteers, content to make money off the war while waiting for the United States to militarily install them in power. There were "few of the so called leaders of the movement who really care about the boys in the field," he wrote. "THIS WAR HAS BECOME A BUSINESS TO MANY OF THEM; THERE IS STILL A BELIEF [THAT] THE MARINES ARE GOING TO HAVE TO INVADE, SO LETS GET SET SO WE WILL AUTOMATICLY [sic] BE THE ONES PUT INTO POWER." In conclusion, Owen noted, the future of the Contra movement remained in doubt, even if the Congress passed new funds for the CIA to direct the battle: "The Agency has done a shitty job in the past. There is no evidence they are going to change," he wrote. "If the $100 million is approved and things go on as they have these last five years, it will be like pouring money down a sink hole" (Document 17).[27]

NOTES

1. Roy Gutman, *Banana Diplomacy* (New York: Simon and Schuster, 1988), p. 85.

2. Ibid., p. 57.

3. See the *Washington Post*, May 8, 1983.

4. Editor's interview with original member of the September 15 Legion. For more information on the origins of the Contra forces, see Peter Kornbluh, *Nicaragua: The Price of Intervention* (Washington, D.C.: Institute for Policy Studies, 1987).

5. Defense Intelligence Agency, "Insurgent Activity Increases in Nicaragua," July 16, 1982. This document, originally classified secret, can be found in the National Security Archive's microfiche collection, *Nicaragua: The Making of U.S. Policy, 1978–1990.*

6. State Department Cable, "Assessment of Recent Counterrevolutionary Activity," October 20, 1982. This cable is reproduced in ibid.

7. *New York Times*, December 9, 1982.

8. See *Congressional Quarterly*, "The Iran-Contra Puzzle," pp. 24, 25.

9. *New York Times*, April 14, 1983.

10. For a comprehensive discussion of the Contra manual, see Kornbluh, *Nicaragua*, pp. 39–46.

11. Rep. Boland's statement is printed in *Congressional Record*, July 27, 1983, p. H5722.

12. Casey is quoted in Bob Woodward, *Veil: The Secret Wars of the CIA, 1981–1987* (New York: Simon and Schuster, 1987), p. 282.

13. *Report of the Congressional Committees Investigating the Iran-Contra Affair* (Washington, D.C.: Government Printing Office, November 17, 1987), p. 36. (Hereafter referred to as The Iran-Contra Affair.)

14. See *Congressional Record*, October 10, 1984, p. H11974.

15. The draft chapter was made available to Robert Parry and Peter Kornbluh and cited in their article, "Reagan's Pro-Contra Propaganda Machine," *Washington Post* Outlook Section, September 4, 1988. For a more comprehensive treatment of the public diplomacy program, see their "Iran-Contra's Untold Story," *Foreign Policy* 72 (Fall 1988).

16. NSDD 77 is dated January 13, 1983. It can be found in the National Security Archive's microfiche collection, *The Iran-Contra Affair: The Making of a Scandal, 1983–1988.*

17. See Walter Raymond, Memo to Clark, "Central American Public Diplomacy," May 18, 1983. This document can be found in the National Security Archive's microfiche collection, *The Iran-Contra Affair: The Making of a Scandal, 1983–1988.*

18. See Walter Raymond, memo prepared for Casey, "Central American Public Diplomacy," August 7, 1986. This document can be found in the National Security Archive's microfiche collection, *The Iran-Contra Affair: The Making of a Scandal, 1983–1988.*

19. Cited in Parry and Kornbluh, "Iran-Contra's Untold Story," pp. 5, 6.

20. Reporters at NPR believed that this meeting left a distinct impact on NPR's reporting on the Contra war. See ibid., p. 17. For a fuller discussion of the impact of Reich's intervention at NPR, see Robert Parry, *Fooling America: How Washington Insiders Twist the Truth and Manufacture the Conventional Wisdom* (New York: Morrow, 1992), pp. 214, 215.

21. GAO Letter to Representative Jack Brooks, September 20, 1987.

22. The Iran-Contra Affair, p. 34.

23. Frank Gardner to Otto Reich, "Outside Professional Service Contracts," May 17, 1985. This document is available in the National Security Archive's microfiche collection, *The Iran-Contra Affair: The Making of a Scandal, 1983–1988*.

24. For a comprehensive treatment of Channell's fund-raising activities, see Peter Kornbluh, "The Contra Lobby," *Village Voice*, October 13, 1987.

25. North to Poindexter, "Meeting with the American Conservative Trust," January 28, 1986. The document can be found in the National Security Archive's microfiche collection, *The Iran-Contra Affair: The Making of a Scandal, 1983–1988*.

26. This award was signed by Elliott Abrams in June 1986. The document can be found in the National Security Archive's microfiche collection, *The Iran-Contra Affair: The Making of a Scandal, 1983–1988*.

27. North also seems to have concluded by this time that the Contras could not win without direct U.S. intervention. Since this was still politically unpalatable, he lofted another idea to engage the U.S. militarily. In a May 6, 1986, computer note (released in full to the National Security Archive through the FOIA on November 30, 1992) he lobbied Admiral Poindexter on the issue of the rebels seizing territory and creating a "liberated zone in Nicaraguan territory." North wrote that "it is entirely likely that within the next 6 to 8 weeks, the resistance will make a major effort to capture a principal coastal population center, run up the blue and white Nicaraguan flag, salute it—and scream like hell for help. At that point the rest of the world will wait to see what we do—recognize the new territory—and UNO as the govt—or evacuate them as in a Bay of Pigs." North foresaw Guatemalan and Salvadoran air force attacks on Sandinista tanks counterattacking the rebel zone, and, of course, recommended a forceful U.S. role: "U.S. direct assistance to the Democratic Govt of Nic wd be limited to offshore support, air cover (but not bombing), and a guarantee that the introduction of Cuban troops, Migs or a seaborne assault wd be met w/ U.S. military force. My guess is tha most of the Latin Americans (not Mexico) will follow our lead w/recognition and that the whole thing wd be over in two to three months at the most. I believe that the American body politic wd respond very favorably to the image of the DRF engaged in a final desperate struggle and that we could act within 4–5 days with significant help—including prompt Congressional action on funds, authorities, etc." The Contras never seized any territory, and this plan, one of the most extraordinary put forth by North to unseat the Sandinistas, never came to fruition.

DOCUMENT 1: Ronald Reagan, Presidential Finding on Covert Operations in Nicaragua, December 1, 1981.

PAGE 1 OF 1

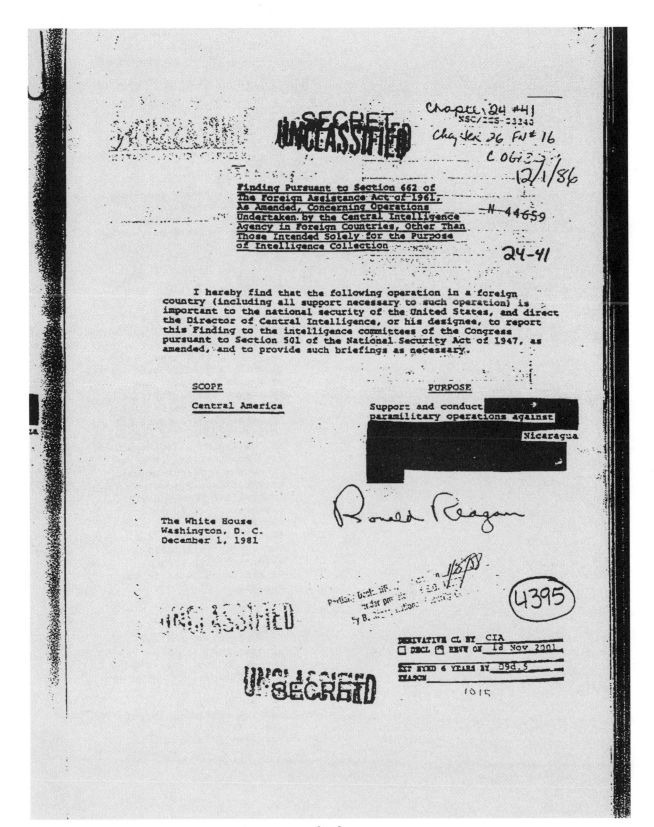

Finding Pursuant to Section 662 of
The Foreign Assistance Act of 1961,
As Amended, Concerning Operations
Undertaken by the Central Intelligence
Agency in Foreign Countries, Other Than
Those Intended Solely for the Purpose
of Intelligence Collection

I hereby find that the following operation in a foreign country (including all support necessary to such operation) is important to the national security of the United States, and direct the Director of Central Intelligence, or his designee, to report this Finding to the intelligence committees of the Congress pursuant to Section 501 of the National Security Act of 1947, as amended, and to provide such briefings as necessary.

SCOPE

Central America

PURPOSE

Support and conduct paramilitary operations against Nicaragua

The White House
Washington, D. C.
December 1, 1981

Ronald Reagan

[11]

DOCUMENT 2: Ronald Reagan, Presidential Finding on Covert Operations in Nicaragua, September 19, 1983.

PAGE 1 OF 3

<u>Finding Pursuant to Section 662 of
The Foreign Assistance Act of 1961
As Amended, Concerning Operations
Undertaken by the Central Intelligence
Agency in Foreign Countries, Other than
Those Intended Solely for the Purpose
of Intelligence Collection</u>

I hereby find that the following activities are important to the national security of the United States, and direct the Director of Central Intelligence, or his designee, to report this Finding to the Intelligence Committees of the Congress pursuant to Section 501 of the National Security Act of 1947, as amended, and to provide such briefings as necessary.

<u>SCOPE</u>

NICARAGUA

<u>PURPOSE</u>

[   ] in cooperation with other governments, provide support, equipment and training assistance to Nicaraguan paramilitary resistance groups as a means to induce the Sandinistas and Cubans and their allies to cease their support for insurgencies in the region; to hamper Cuban/Nicaraguan arms trafficking; to divert Nicaragua's resources and energies from support to Central American guerrilla movements; and to bring the Sandinistas into meaningful negotiations and constructive, verifiable agreement with their neighbors on peace in the region.

[   ] in cooperation with other governments, provide support to opposition leaders and organizations [

Provide training, support and guidance to Nicaraguan resistance forces [

ALL PORTIONS OF THIS DOCUMENT
ARE CLASSIFIED SECRET

SECRET

CL BY _____

[12]

DOCUMENT 2: Ronald Reagan, Presidential Finding on Covert Operations in Nicaragua, September 19, 1983.

PAGE 2 OF 3

SECRET

Seek support of and work with other foreign governments and organizations as appropriate to carry out this program and encourage regional cooperation and coordination in pursuit of program objectives. CIA may support [   ] in order to hamper arms trafficking through Nicaragua, support indigenous resistance efforts and pressure the Sandinistas.

U.S. support to paramilitary activities in Nicaragua will be terminated at such time as it is verified that: (a) the Soviets, Cubans, and Sandinistas have ceased providing through Nicaragua arms, training, command and control facilities and other logistical support to military or paramilitary operations in or against any other country in Central America, and (b) the Government of Nicaragua is demonstrating a commitment to provide amnesty and nondiscriminatory participation in the Nicaraguan political process by all Nicaraguans.

-2-

SECRET

DOCUMENT 2: Ronald Reagan, Presidential Finding on Covert Operations in Nicaragua, September 19, 1983.

PAGE 3 OF 3

SECRET

The Director of Central
Intelligence is directed to
ensure that this program
is continuously reviewed to
assure that its objectives
are being met and its
restrictions adhered to.

The White House
Washington, D.C.

Ronald Reagan

Date: September 19, 1983

-3-

SECRET

SCOPE OF CIA ACTIVITIES
UNDER THE NICARAGUA FINDING

The Finding replaces the 1 December 1981 Finding which
authorized certain covert action programs in Nicaragua and Central
America. This program remains a critical element of U.S. policy
in the region which recognizes that Nicaragua's Sandinista regime,
with Soviet and Cuban active support, is implementing a strategy of
full support for insurgent elements whose aim is the overthrow of
democratic governments in the region. The political and
paramilitary pressures created by this program are linked and
are essential (1) to enable friendly Central American nations
to strengthen democratic political institutions and achieve
economic and social development, free from Soviet, Cuban,
and Sandinista interference and (2) to induce a negotiated
political resolution of international tensions in Central
America.

This Finding authorizes the provision of material support
and guidance to Nicaraguan resistance groups; its goal is to induce
the Sandinista government in Nicaragua to enter into meaningful
negotiations with its neighboring nations; and to induce the
Sandinistas and the Cubans and their allies to cease their
provision of arms, training, command and control facilities and
sanctuary to regional insurgencies. This support is to be provided
[   ] in cooperation with others, as appropriate. The
provision of political support and funding to opposition leaders
and organizations [   ]—in order to
maintain their viability—is also authorized.

POLITICAL ACTION: Financial and material support will be provided
to Nicaraguan opposition leaders and organizations to enable them
to deal with the Sandinistas from a position of political strength
and to continue to exert political pressure on the Sandinistas to
return to the original promises of the revolution — free
elections political pluralism, basic human rights and a free press.

PARAMILITARY ACTION: Arms and other support will be provided to
Nicaraguan paramilitary forces operating inside Nicaragua for the
purpose of pressuring the Sandinista government and its Cuban
supporters to cease their support for regional insurgencies.
[   ] instructors will train these forces to attack targets
in Nicaragua in order to deny facilities, interrupt support
networks and to raise the price the Cubans and Nicaraguans and
their allies must pay for continued support of insurgent groups
elsewhere in Central America. [   ]

U.S. support for paramilitary forces inside Nicaragua will
be terminated when it is verified that: (a) the Soviets, Cubans,
and Sandinistas have ceased providing arms, training, command
and control facilities and logistical support for military or

SECRET

paramilitary operations in or against any country in Central
America, and (b) Nicaragua has committed itself to providing
amnesty and non-discriminatory participation in the Nicaraguan
political process by all Nicaraguans.

PROPAGANDA AND CIVIC ACTION: Guidance and media assistance will
be provided to Nicaraguan opposition elements and paramilitary
forces
Propaganda will be used to promote pluralism, human rights,
freedom of the press, free elections and democratic processes
inside Nicaragua and throughout the region. Paramilitary units
will be trained in field medicine, basic agriculture and
political/psychological action in order to assist local populations
and to gain and maintain popular support.

FUNDING REQUIRED: $19,000,000 is included in the Fiscal Year 1984
CIA budget for this program. Additional funding requirements, to
be determined by developments in the area, could be as much as
$14,000,000. Any such additional funding will have to come from
the Agency's Reserve for Contingencies or other authorized sources.

-2-

SECRET

S E C R E T

RISKS: This proposal carries with it the risks that the Cubans may increase their military presence in Nicaragua to defend their installations and to control rising internal opposition to the Sandinistas, and that the Nicaraguans may increase their covert. activities or take direct military action against Honduras. The USSR is not likely to take an active direct military role in Central America.

The Sandinista regime may heighten repression in Nicaragua, but this would only continue the course of action in which the Sandinistas have been engaged since 1979 to eliminate democratic pluralism.

S E C R E T

DOCUMENT 4: Oliver North and Constantine Menges, Memorandum for Robert McFarlane, "Special Activities in Nicaragua," March 2, 1984.

PAGE 1 OF 2

UNTOP SECRETFIED

SYSTEM IV
NSC/ICS-400215

MEMORANDUM

NATIONAL SECURITY COUNCIL

N 44842

~~TOP SECRET~~

March 2, 1984

ACTION

MEMORANDUM FOR ROBERT C. MCFARLANE

FROM: OLIVER L. NORTH
               CONSTANTINE MENGES

SUBJECT: Special Activities in Nicaragua

On the night of February 29, ▮▮▮▮▮▮▮ emplaced four magnetic mines in the harbor at Corinto, Nicaragua. No attempt was made by the Sandinistas to engage the ▮▮▮▮▮ during the mission. In accord with prior arrangements, ARDE's "Barracuda Commandos" took credit for the operation. ARDE has also declared that the entire Nicaraguan littoral is now a "war zone" and that all shipping within the Nicaraguan claimed 12nm territorial sea is subject to attack. ▮▮▮

▮▮▮▮▮▮▮▮▮▮▮▮▮▮▮ Our intention is to severely disrupt the flow of shipping essential to Nicaraguan trade during the peak export period. ▮▮▮▮▮▮▮▮▮▮▮▮▮▮▮▮▮▮▮▮▮▮▮▮▮▮▮▮

▮▮▮▮▮▮▮▮▮▮▮ In this case, our objective is to further impair the already critical fuel capacity in Nicaragua. This will substantially reduce EPS mobility and hamper their ability to support the ERP/FMLN guerrillas in El Salvador.

▮▮▮▮▮▮▮▮▮▮▮▮▮▮▮▮▮▮▮▮▮▮▮▮▮▮▮▮▮▮▮▮▮▮▮▮

▮▮▮▮▮▮▮ While we could probably find a way to overtly stop the tanker from loading/departing, it is our judgement that destroying the vessel and its cargo will be far more effective in accomplishing our overall goal of applying stringent economic pressure. It is entirely likely that once a ship has been sunk

~~TOP SECRET~~
Declassify: OADR

UTOP SECRETFIED

EXHIBIT
OLN-77

DOCUMENT 4: Oliver North and Constantine Menges, Memorandum for Robert McFarlane, "Special Activities in Nicaragua," March 2, 1984.

PAGE 2 OF 2

TOP SECRET

TOP SECRET   2

N 44843

no insurers will cover ships calling in Nicaraguan ports. This
will effectively limit their seaborne trade to that which can be
carried on Cuban, Soviet Bloc, or their own bottoms. The
following plan has been developed:

-- No legal or financial action will be taken to deter ▮▮▮

-- ▮▮

-- ▮▮

-- ▮▮

-- ▮▮

Given past performances by Sandinista military seamen under fire
(surrender or jumping overboard), there is little reason to
expect that the Nicaraguan civilian crews of a gasoline laden
vessel will attempt to "run for it." It is anticipated that the
operation can be safely executed without injury or loss of life.
No American citizens will be directly involved in the operational
event.

RECOMMENDATION

That you approve this operation and brief the President using the
points above.

Approve _PC/ ___   Disapprove _____

cc: Ken deGraffenreid

TOP SECRET   TOP SECRET

PUBLIC LAW 98-473—OCT. 12, 1984

98 STA

*Public Law 98-473
98th Congress

Joint Resolution

Making continuing appropriations for the fiscal year 1985, and for other purposes.

Oct.
[H.J.

Resolved by the Senate and House of Representatives of the United States of America in Congress assembled,

TITLE I

That the following sums are hereby appropriated, out of any money in the Treasury not otherwise appropriated, and out of applicable corporate or other revenues, receipts, and funds, for the several departments, agencies, corporations, and other organizational units of the Government for the fiscal year 1985, and for other purposes, namely:

*　　*　　*　　*　　*

SEC. 8066. (a) During fiscal year 1985, no funds available to the Central Intelligence Agency, the Department of Defense, or any other agency or entity of the United States involved in intelligence activities may be obligated or expended for the purpose or which would have the effect of supporting, directly or indirectly, military or paramilitary operations in Nicaragua by any nation, group, organization, movement, or individual.

Nic

[signature]
Speaker of the House of Representatives.

[signature] Strom Thurmond
Vice President of the United States and
President of the Senate. *pro / i*

APPROVED

OCT 12 1984

[signature] Ronald Reagan

EXHIBIT
BGS-23

file NSC 90736

THE WHITE HOUSE

WASHINGTON

July 1, 1983

MEMORANDUM FOR THE SPG PRINCIPALS

SUBJECT: Public Diplomacy (Central America)

The President has underscored his concern that we must increase
our efforts in the public diplomacy field to deepen the understanding of and support for our policies in Central America.
This effort must focus both on the foreign and domestic audiences.
To coordinate this program and to insure that the effort has the
appropriate treatment of foreign policy issues, it is essential
to designate an overall coordinator who will be responsible for
the development and implementation of a public diplomacy strategy
concerning Central America.

Secretary Shultz and I have discussed this at some length and
have agreed to ask Otto Reich to assume this responsibility for
the SPG. He will replace Senator Stone who has assumed other
duties. Mr. Reich will focus not only on the developments in
Central America but also on the impact that these activities
have in Latin America as well as elsewhere overseas and in the
United States. For this assignment he will function as the
Secretary's advisor and as SPG Coordinator for Public Diplomacy
for Central America/Caribbean. Mr. Reich will carry out his
responsibilities in the context of the International Political
Committee with substantive policy guidance to be provided by
established policy making bodies in his field. The Public Affair
and International Information Committees will also play key roles
in this overall effort.

Mr. Reich will need staff support, to include officers detailed
from appropriate agencies and departments. His office will be
established in the Department of State. The Department of State
will provide Mr. Reich with appropriate office space, logistic
support, operating budget and clerical support.

Mr. Reich's activities should commence immediately. He should
keep the SPG regularly informed and should attend all SPG meetin
concerning Central America.

William P. Clark

[21]

DOCUMENT 7: Daniel "Jake" Jacobowitz, "Public Diplomacy Action Plan: Support for the White House Educational Campaign," March 12, 1985.

PAGE 1 OF 9

O.K.

ACTION PLANS

NSC

COPY _____ OF _____

12 March 1985

C026

CONFIDENTIAL - SENSITIVE

PUBLIC DIPLOMACY ACTION PLAN
SUPPORT FOR THE WHITE HOUSE EDUCATIONAL CAMPAIGN

GOAL:

Congressional passage of aid to the Nicaraguan Freedom Fighters.

CENTRAL PERCEPTIONS

    PRIMARY PERCEPTION:
    -Vote for U.S. aid to the freedom fighters is a vital
national interest of the United States.

    SUPPORTING PERCEPTIONS:
        --U.S. history requires support to freedom fighters.
        --U.S. troops will eventually be required if aid is
        not given now.
        --Amount of aid is so miniscule that it hardly
        matters.
        --FSLN are puppets of Soviets
        --Nicaragua will become a Soviet military base if
        not resisted.
        --FSLN is racist and represses human rights.
        --FSLN is involved in U.S. drug problem.
        --FSLN are linked to worldwide terrorism.
        --FDN are freedom fighters.

    SPECIAL PERCEPTION:
        --Failure to vote for U.S. aid to the freedom
        fighters must be seen as a political liability.

IMPEDIMENTS:

    Situational:
        Deadline: Mid-April.
        Possible partisan response in House.
        Possible party-bolting in Senate
        Could be victim of budget cutting.
        Don't know what themes will cause Americans to share
        the administration's concern regarding Central
        America. (military build-up, communist threat on the
        continent drugs?)

CONFIDENTIAL - SENSITIVE

DOCUMENT 7: Daniel "Jake" Jacobowitz, "Public Diplomacy Action Plan: Support for the White House Educational Campaign," March 12, 1985.

PAGE 2 OF 9

```
            CONFIDENTIAL  -  SENSITIVE
                  12 March 1985

                      (2)


Perceptional:
            Idea that U.S. Actions violate international law.
            Idea that U.S. actions preclude peaceful solutions
            in Central America
            Idea that aid to the Contras hurts "the moderates in
            Nicaragua.
            Idea that U.S. is "immoral" in supporting a covert
            action.


ASSETS:

       --The Great Communicator.
           ---electoral mandate
       --Respected key administration figures (Shultz,
       Weinberger).
       --Supportive private sector organizations.
       --Some supportive congressmen.
       --Historical U.S. policies
       --Afghan precedent
       --Cuban threat
       --Some supportive media representatives.


THEMES:

       -Overall theme:  The Nicaraguan Freedom Fighters (FF) are
    fighters for freedom in the American tradition, FSLN are evil.

       -Major themes:

    Freedom fighters are fighting democracy's battle.

           --Sub-themes:  FSLN are outpost of the the Soviet
    empire.
                   ---Military build-up.
                   ---Communist connection.
                   ---The drug connection.
                   ---Human rights violations:
                       ----Freedom of the press.
                       ----Right of assembly.
                       ----Freedom of speech.
                       ----Forced military conscription.
                       ----Persecution of church groups.
                       ----Destruction of the economy.
```

CONFIDENTIAL - SENSITIVE

DOCUMENT 7: Daniel "Jake" Jacobowitz, "Public Diplomacy Action Plan: Support for the White House Educational Campaign," March 12, 1985.

PAGE 3 OF 9

CONFIDENTIAL - SENSITIVE
12 March 1985

(3)

--Sub-themes; FDN are the good guys:
    ---FSLN goal is participation in an ongoing,
    viable democratic process, not fighting for
    "power-sharing."
    ---U.S. support for Contadora principles has
    not diminished.
    ---Central American democracies support our
    policies, and are worried that we will change
    them.
    ---Goal is to change Sandinista behavior; not
    overthrow them.
    ---FDN are the underdogs.
        ---- Anti-Somoza credentials.
        ---- Religious.
        ---- Anti-military.
        ---- Mostly poor peasants.
        ---- Poorly armed because of lack of
             U.S. support.
        ---- U.S. image will be destroyed if we
             sell out another ally
        ---- Thousands are joining resistance,
             despite its poverty of resources
             because it represents the ideals
             of the Nicaraguan people and their
             original goals in overthrowing
             Somoza
Subthemes; Regional geopolitics require defense of
democracy in this hemisphere.

-Soviets will view failure to support contras as
license to move massively in CA.
    --Cam Ranh Bay Comparison
        ---U.S. Congress sold Vietnam out by
        failure to vote for ammo, Russkies moved
        into Cam Ranh Bay.
    --$14 million so small compared to U.S.
    budget, Soviets will believe that U.S. will
    pay no price no matter how obvious the threat.
    --West Coast surveillance
    --WWII Nazi sub-comparison
    --With control of Nu Soviets will be able to
    threaten both ends of Panama canal.
AUDIENCES:

    -U.S. Congress
    -U.S. Media
    -Interest groups

CONFIDENTIAL - SENSITIVE

DOCUMENT 7: Daniel "Jake" Jacobowitz, "Public Diplomacy Action Plan: Support for the White House Educational Campaign," March 12, 1985.

PAGE 4 OF 9

CONFIDENTIAL   -   SENSITIVE
12 March 1985

(4)

ACTIONS: (Related actions are listed under same key letter.
Subordinate actions are listed as numbered subset of a key
letter. Thus action A-1 must precede A-2. Actions in the B
series are independent of A series and can proceed
simultaneously. Completed actions are denoted by preceding $,
as $2-2. New actions are designated by +, as +ZZ-1

A. Johnathan Miller, John Blacken, John Scafe and Jake
Jacobowitz will meet daily at 1800 to report progress,
monitor progress, devise and revise themes and actions.
Johnathan Miller retains overall control. (ASAP)

B-1. Public opinion survey to see what turns Americans
against Sandinistas (JS, to contact WH, results due by
March 11).

B-2. Review and restate themes in view of results of
public opinion poll (JSM, JB, JJ, March 13).

B-3. Prepare or assign articles directed to special
interest groups at rate of one per week beginning Mar 4
[examples: article on Nicaraguan educational system for
NEA, article by retired military for Retired Officers
Association, etc.] (JB, Mar 4 until vote)

C-1. Assign knowledgeable person to prepare a complete
list of publicly and privately expressed Congressional
objections to voting for the aid. (Arturo Cruz, Jr., JSM
to contact ASAP)

C-2. Construct themes for approaches to Congressmen based
on overall listed perceptions which will directly attack
the reasons listed as above. (JSM, JB, JJ, ASAP upon
completion of survey of Congressional objections)

C-3. Presidential breakfasts, lunches, WHSR meetings and
Camp David meetings with key Congressional leaders. (WH,
Mar 24 until vote)

C-4. President call key congressmen. (WH, two days before
vote)

D-1. Insure NSC details U.S. intelligence agencies to
research, report to S/LPD, and clear for public release
all Sandinista military actions violating Geneva
Convention/civilized standards of warfare. (JJ to draft
memo from Walt Raymond to community, Feb 28)

CONFIDENTIAL   -   SENSITIVE

DOCUMENT 7: Daniel "Jake" Jacobowitz, "Public Diplomacy Action Plan: Support for the
White House Educational Campaign," March 12, 1985.

PAGE 5 OF 9

CONFIDENTIAL - SENSITIVE
12 March 1985

(5)

E. Update Green Book; send to congressmen, media outlets,
private organizations and individuals interested in
Nicaragua. (LT, DR, JB, Mar 25)

F. Release report on Soviet Military Build-up in Central
America and the Caribbean (LT, KS of DOD, Mar. 25)

G. Release paper on Nicaraguan media manipulation (JJ,
March 15).

H. Have a geopolitical paper written by Zbigniew
Brzezinski that points out geopolitical consequences of
Communist domination of Nicaragua (JJ contacted CM by Feb
28, CM will contact Zbig, plus Shlesinger, Jim Woolsey,
and Frank Cramer by Mar 4. S/LPD to prepare dummies for
edit--assignment not yet made, paper due by Mar 20)

Urbina

I-1. H and ARA prepare a list of key congressmen
interested in Nicaragua. (JSM to contact H and ARA ASAP,
Mar 1)

I-2. Briefings on Nicaragua for Congressional staffers.
North on NU aggression and external involvement, Burghardt
on diplomatic situation. (WH, Mar 3-9)

I-3. Briefings in OEOB for members/Senators: Shultz,
McFarlane, Gorman and Shlaudeman to brief (requires
General Gorman to be placed on contract (WH, Mar 10-23)

I-4. Induce a mixed friendly and unfriendly CODELS to
visit Nicaraguan refugee camps in Honduras and Costa Rica
(include visit to FF camp and hospital in Honduras)
accompanied by press (North, Fox, Holwill, JSM to contact,
April 1).

I-5. CODELS visit regional leaders of Central America.
Regional Leaders convey importance of resistance fighters
in NU (WH, during Easter Recess, Apr 4-14)

J-1. S/LPD and WH Media Relations prepare a list of key
media outlets interested in Central American issues,
including newspapers, radio and TV stations (including
SIN). Where possible identify specific editors,
commentators, talk shows, and columnists. (JanB, Mar 8)

J-2. Contact with key media outlets as identified above
(WH to contact Lew Lehrman, S/LPD, PA to support, ASAP and
continuing until vote)

CONFIDENTIAL - SENSITIVE

DOCUMENT 7: Daniel "Jake" Jacobowitz, "Public Diplomacy Action Plan: Support for the White House Educational Campaign," March 12, 1985.

PAGE 6 OF 9

CONFIDENTIAL - SENSITIVE
12 March 1985

(6)

$J-3. Send resource book on the Contadora process to congressmen, media outlets, private organizations and individuals interested in Nicaragua. (JC, JJ to check status, Feb. 26)

$K-1. Encourage FDN to select articulate freedom fighters with proven combat records and to make them available for contact with U.S. media representatives. (GC contacted by JJ Feb 26,)

K-2. Encourage U.S. media reporters to meet individual FDN fighters with proven combat records and media appeal. (GC contacted by JJ Feb 26)

L. Assign to other agencies drafting of one op-ed piece per week for signature of Administration officials. WH will specify theme and thrust for the op-ed and retain final editorial rights. (Ongoing beginning week of Mar 4)

M-1. ARA, S/LPD, NSC draft talking points on aid to Nicaraguan Freedom Fighters (JSM to contact asap, Mar 11).

M-2. ARA and PA call newspaper editorial boards and give them background on the Nicaraguan Freedom Fighters. (JSM to contact, Mar. 10)

N-1. WH, ARA, S/LPD, NSC provide H with a list of Nicaraguan emigres and masked freedom fighters to serve as potential witnesses to testify before hearings on aid to Nicaraguan Freedom Fighters. (JSM to contact NSC, Mar. 15)

N-2. Contact eyewitnesses to see if they would testify before Congress about their aborted attempts to deal with the FSLN. (JJ contacted GC Feb 26, task deadline Mar. 15)

O. -Draft and distribute a paper on why Nicaraguans flee their country. (JS to contact Macias ASAP, paper due Mar 15)

P. Themes, publications, interviews, and taped programs produced for this effort will be coordinated with USIA for overseas distribution and programming to USIS audiences overseas, particularly foreign media. (ongoing throughout life of plan)

Q-1. Production and distribution of La Prensa chronology of FSLN harassment. (TS Mar 11)

Q-2. Narcotics involvement document (NN Mar 15)

CONFIDENTIAL - SENSITIVE

DOCUMENT 7: Daniel "Jake" Jacobowitz, "Public Diplomacy Action Plan: Support for the White House Educational Campaign," March 12, 1985.

PAGE 7 OF 9

CONFIDENTIAL - SENSITIVE
12 March 1985

(7)

Q-3. PA or S/LPD reprint 10,000 copies of Secretary Shultz' speech at the Commonwealth Club of San Francisco (JC, Mar 7)

Q-4. S/LPD prepare paper detailing history of FDN's offers to negotiate with the FSLN (DR, Mar 11)

Q-3. Document outlining "72-hour Document" (JSM to decide on contractor week of Feb 25. FG to contact week of Feb 25.)

Q-4. S/LPD request declassification of Nicaragua's Development as a Marxist-Leninist State (U), by Linn Poulsen (JJ, memo on OR's desk, Feb 28) and publish as State Dept. document (MCE and TS Mar 15)

Q-5. S/LPD request Bernard Nietschmann to prepare or revise prior paper on suppression of Indian by FSLN (JJ Mar 1, paper deadline Mar 25)

R-1. Presidential report to Congress certifying reasons for releasing funds to FF (WH Apr 8)

R-2. NSDD (NSC April 8)

R-3. Major Presidential speech on Central America Note: S/LPD suggests mention of FSLN suppression of Blacks and Indians(WH Apr 8)

+S-1. NSC task appropriate agencies to prepare a report on the economic costs to the United States of a Marxist/Leninist regime on the Central American Isthmus. (S/LPD draft language for NSC memo, Feb. 26. NSC task agencies by Mar. 5; reports due Mar. 31.)

+S-2. S/LPD consolidate replies to NSC tasker on economic costs to U.S. of a Marxist/Leninist regime on the Central American Isthmus; prepare and distribute. (Apr. 5)

CONFIDENTIAL - SENSITIVE

DOCUMENT 7: Daniel "Jake" Jacobowitz, "Public Diplomacy Action Plan: Support for the White House Educational Campaign," March 12, 1985.

PAGE 8 OF 9

```
                    CONFIDENTIAL  -  SENSITIVE
                         12 March 1985

                              (8)



     Wang 0515D

     28 February 1985 version DESTROY ALL EARLIER VERSIONS!

     Drafted by J. Jacobowitz

     Copy distribution:  Copy 1--JSM
                              2--JS
                              3--OJR
                              4--JB
                              5--NSC(ON)
                              6--Jiffy
                              Original held by JJ
```

DOCUMENT 7: Daniel "Jake" Jacobowitz, "Public Diplomacy Action Plan: Support for the White House Educational Campaign," March 12, 1985.

PAGE 9 OF 9

```
                    ACTION PLAN HEADINGS

        GOAL:

        PSYCHOLOGICAL CLIMATE:

        ASSUMPTIONS:

        CENTRAL PERCEPTIONS:

        IMPEDIMENTS:

        ASSETS:

        THEMES:

        AUDIENCES:

        ACTIONS:

        Documentation:

        TIMELINE:
```

DOCUMENT 8: Daniel "Jake" Jacobowitz, Memorandum for Otto Reich, "Duties of TDY [Psychological Operations] Military Personnel," May 30, 1985.

PAGE 1 OF 2

<u>MEMORANDUM</u>   May 30, 1985

TO: S/LPD – Ambassador Reich   *FRANK*

FROM: S/LPD – Jake Jacobowitz

SUBJECT: Duties of TDY Military Personnel

   Contrary to popular belief, there is no danger that our <u>five</u> TDY troops will languish unburdened by important tasks of state. They are reporting for duty on Tuesday, due to the fact they are driving up here on Monday. In any case we have enough to keep them busy until the Contras march into Managua.

   At least one of them with analytical experience will be put to work doing a daily cable digest. That is, using his trained military analytical skills he will not only read and classify the daily cable traffic, but he will go back and rationalize our entire cable handling system, which has now totally broken down, due to the fact that I'm too busy, Tim is too busy, David is too busy, we're all too busy. The expected benefit will be that a sharp analyst will call to our attention anything the Sandys and all other bad guys have done, are about to do, or would like to do. Since he is a PSYOP type he will also be looking for exploitable themes and trends, and will inform us of possible areas for our exploitation. He will feed to Mark as well as the rest of the office. This will enable other officers to be informed and still have time to do projects, thereby raising everyone's productivity.

   Another will immediately begin reworking the Cubaganda paper. In view of Radio Marti, we now need to get that paper out--within the month.

   The ex-journalist will do the outside-the-wire-services-news-service you suggested. As you outlined, we'll feed it to people like Newt Gingrich to read on C-Span during the open orders and enter into the Congressional Record. This soldier will also feed to and from the cable analyst.

   These people are a natural to help Ledeen on exploitation of the Nidia Diaz papers. One or more of them may have worked on the Grenada documents. Whichever is a good Spanish reader will work on this.

DOCUMENT 8: Daniel "Jake" Jacobowitz, Memorandum for Otto Reich, "Duties of TDY [Psychological Operations] Military Personnel," May 30, 1985.

PAGE 2 OF 2

(2)

I expect that at least one of them will have some experience in the leaflet field, meaning he can help with layout of books. So far, our productions have mainly featured no graphics, etc. If any who show up have this ability, I expect to be able to punch up the visuals in our written productions.

One or more should be able to complete some of the production that we have never been able to get around to due to higher priorities. I have a file full of items that need to be written up and exploited, but current operations preclude taking the time to develop the themes available, etc. I'd like to put one of the officers on that. Additionally, since one of the enlisted men is only an E-4, we can use him for gopher work, especially in the Pentagon, etc.

I feel the best thing to do organizationally is just have the whole bunch report to me to keep them out of everybody's hair. Whatever you want done by your "A-Team," just pass on to me through either of the Deputies. Also, whatever hot projects develop that are appropriate for their talents will be fed to them as we become more aware of their individual strengths and weaknesses.

DOCUMENT 9: Otto Reich, Memorandum for Walter Raymond, "Denial of Detail of Personnel by DoD," January 5, 1986.

PAGE 1 OF 2

United States Department of State

*Coordinator of Public Diplomacy for
Latin America and the Caribbean*

Washington, D.C. 20520

January 5, 1986

TO: NSC - Mr. Walt Raymond

FROM: S/LPD - Otto J. Reich

SUBJECT: Denial of Detail of Personnel by DoD

With Col. David Brown's letter of December 17, 1985 (Tab 1), the Department of Defense has turned down our request for a detail of two officers and two non-commissioned officers to S/LPD on a non-reimbursable basis.

This denial of desperately needed resources appears to conflict with the President's expressed desire for an effective public diplomacy effort, as expressed in the attached NSC memoranda (Tabs 3 and 4). According to Col. Brown's letter to me, the prime basis for the denial of resources was "not uniquely military or of primary benefit to the Department of Defense." The skills requested in S/LPD's letter of September 18, 1985 (Tab 2)--intelligence analysis and production of persuasive communications--are combined only in military Psychological Operations personnel.

Prior to S/LPD's request, five TDY personnel from the 4th Psychological Operations Group served in S/LPD from June 4 to November 4, 1985. The two officers and three non-commissioned officers did the initial setup of information handling and analyzing systems to be operated by the permanent detailees. These systems, when fully operational, will provide information analysis capability fundamental to the production of effective persuasive public diplomacy documents. Analysis of Soviet, Cuban and Nicaraguan propaganda campaigns and their effect on democratic response to specific Central American issues, the synthesis of all-source intelligence, and the ability to convert abstract analyses into effective U.S. policy responses are skills normally combined in those who have worked in strategic PSYOP. We realize that the cadre of U.S. officers and NCO's possessing these skills is limited and in great demand; however, the overall national interest would be well served if some of these assets are placed in S/LPD to work on a problem of vital national importance--Central American

DOCUMENT 9: Otto Reich, Memorandum for Walter Raymond, "Denial of Detail of Personnel by DoD," January 5, 1986.

PAGE 2 OF 2

- 2 -

public diplomacy. S/LPD currently coordinates government-wide efforts to ensure that the public and Congress under-stand U.S. policy in Central America.

The five military personnel who were temporarily detailed to S/LPD were highly effective in support of our mission. They developed systems for continued analysis of Soviet, Cuban and Nicaraguan propaganda and political war-fare actions by military analysts. The product of such analysis will permit an effective U.S. reaction to these initiatives at a strategic level. S/LPD's mission will suffer unless personnel are obtained to operate the analytical systems these personnel set up. By placing personnel in these positions, DoD has an opportunity to shape U.S. public diplomacy initiatives on Central America. I urge that DoD reconsider its turndown of support to S/LPD. As outlined by the President, the mission of S/LPD requires support from outside agencies to succeed.

Attachments:

    Tab 1 - December 17, 1985, letter from Col. David Brown.
    Tab 2 - September 18, 1985, letter to Col. Brown.
    Tab 3 - NSC memorandum dated July 1, 1983.
    Tab 4 - NSC memorandum dated August 1, 1984.

DOCUMENT 10: George Shultz, Memorandum for the President, "News Coverage of Central America," April 15, 1984.

PAGE 1 OF 2

THE SECRETARY OF STATE

WASHINGTON

LIMITED OFFICIAL USE

MEMORANDUM-FOR: THE PRESIDENT

FROM: George P. Shultz

SUBJECT: News Coverage of Central America

At the entertainment following the State Dinner for President Blanco, you indicated to Otto J. Reich, Coordinator of Public Diplomacy for Latin America and the Caribbean, your concern regarding the uneven coverage of news from Central America. As an example, you mentioned a CBS News piece from Nicaragua several months ago which showed film purchased from a Cuban crew showing only farm machinery being unloaded from a Soviet freighter which we knew was also carrying weapons.

To illustrate what the Office of Public Diplomacy has been doing to help improve the quality of information the American people are receiving, Ambassador Reich has asked me to relay to you one example of a related news piece. Recently, the CBS Evening News showed a two-part documentary entitled "Behind Rebel Lines" (from El Salvador). We understand from Ambassador Thomas Pickering that both you and Vice President Bush were upset about this film, and with good reason.

Immediately upon viewing the documentary, Ambassador Reich asked for a tape because it was obvious that it was unbalanced and conveyed a deceptive image favorable to the guerrillas and distorting of U.S. and El Salvadoran Government goals and tactics in the conflict.

Ambassador Reich spent nearly one hour with CBS News' diplomatic correspondent privately reviewing the film (and four other pieces of CBS news items on Central American which had been shown over a period of several days before the March 25 El Salvadoran elections). The correspondent took copious notes of Ambassador Reich's analysis and objections about the news pieces which he subsequently passed to network executives. Shortly thereafter, Ambassador Reich was referred to the Washington Bureau Chief for CBS News who was interested in following up on this story. Ambassador Reich has since spent about two hours with him and the CBS executive is arranging for a "screening" of the "Behind Rebel Lines" documentary where Ambassador Reich will, privately and confidentially, explain to those responsible for producing it the reasons for our

LIMITED OFFICIAL USE

[35]

DOCUMENT 10: George Shultz, Memorandum for the President, "News Coverage of Central America," April 15, 1984.

PAGE 2 OF 2

LIMITED OFFICIAL USE

-2-

objections. He explained that this was not an effort to embarrass anyone but simply to try to point out flaws in the information the American people are receiving. So far, everyone at CBS has been very cordial and cooperative with Ambassador Reich.

This is one example of what the Office of Public Diplomacy has been doing. It has been repeated dozens of times over the past few months. It is a very slow and arduous effort to try to show to the networks that they are not illustrating to the American people an accurate picture of what is happening in Central America. We are attempting to build the kinds of relationships with the news media that will enable us to dispel the disinformation and misinformation which has been so prevalent in coverage while at the same time aggressively expressing our policy objectives.

With regard to the documentary in question, I will let you know of the outcome of the CBS News inquiry as soon as Mr. Reich has completed his work.

DRAFTED: S/LPD:OJReich
4/15/84   632-7023

CLEARANCES: ARA:RHolwill (Substance)
            PA:JMcCarthy (Substance)

LIMITED OFFICIAL USE

DOCUMENT 11: Johnathan Miller, Memorandum for Patrick Buchanan, "White Propaganda Operation," March 13, 1985.

PAGE 1 OF 2

FILE COPY

United States Department of State

Washington, D.C. 20520

March 13, 1985

DEPARTMENT OF STATE A/CDC/MR

REVIEWED BY ~~Tzmith~~ DATE 5-10-8

RDS☐ or XDS☐ EXT. DATE _____
TO AUTH. ____ REASON(S) _____
ENDORSE EXISTING MARKINGS ☐
DECLASSIFIED, RELEASABLE☐
RELEASE DENIED☐
PA or FOI EXEMPTIONS _____

~~CONFIDENTIAL~~/EYES ONLY

TO: Mr. Pat Buchanan
        Assistant to the President and
        Director of Communications
        The White House

FROM: S/LPD - Johnathan S. Miller

SUBJECT: "White Propaganda" Operation

Five illustrative examples of the Reich "White Propaganda" operation:

- Attached is a copy of an op-ed piece that ran two days ago in The Wall Street Journal. Professor Guilmartin has been a consultant to our office and collaborated with our staff in the writing of this piece. It is devastating in its analysis of the Nicaraguan arms build-up. Officially, this office had no role in its preparation.

- In case you missed last night's NBC News with Tom Brokaw, you might ask WHCA to call up the Fred Francis story on the "Contras." This piece was prepared by Francis after he consulted two of our contractors who recently had made a clandestine trip to the freedom fighter camp along the Nicaragua/Honduras border (the purpose of this trip was to serve as a pre-advance for many selected journalists to visit the area and get a true flavor of what the freedom fighters are doing; i.e., not baby killing). Although I wasn't wild about the tag line, it was a positive piece.

- Two op-ed pieces, one for The Washington Post and one for The New York Times, are being prepared for the signatures of opposition leaders Alphonso Rubello,

CONFIDENTIAL
DeCl: OADR

DOCUMENT 11: Johnathan Miller, Memorandum for Patrick Buchanan, "White Propaganda Operation," March 13, 1985.

PAGE 2 OF 2

CONFIDENTIAL

- 2 -

Adolpho Callero and Arturo Cruz. These two op-ed pieces are being prepared by one of our consultants and will serve as a reply to the outrageous op-ed piece by Daniel Ortega in today's New York Times.

- Through a cut-out, we are having the opposition - leader Alphonso Rubello visit the following news organizations while he is in Washington this week: Hearst Newspapers, Newsweek Magazine, Scripps Howard Newspapers, The Washington Post (Editorial Board), and USA Today. In addition, the CNN "Freeman Report," the "McNeil-Lehrer Report," the "Today Show" and CBS Morning News have been contacted about the availability of Mr. Rubello.

- Attached is a copy of a cable that we received today from Managua. The cable states that Congressman Lagomarsino took up Daniel Ortega's offer to visit any place in Nicaragua. You may remember that Ortega received a good deal of publicity on his "peace" proposal when he stated that he welcomed visits by Members of Congress, stating that they would be free to go anywhere they wished. As the cable notes, the Congreman's request to visit an airfield was denied. Do not be surprised if this cable somehow hits the evening news.

I will not attempt in the future to keep you posted on all activities since we have too many balls in the air at any one time and since the work of our operation is ensured by our office's keeping a low profile. I merely wanted to give you a flavor of some of the activites that hit our office on any one day and ask that, as you formulate ideas and plans of attack, you give us a heads-up since our office has been crafted to handle the concerns that you have in getting the President's program for the freedom fighters enacted.

Attachments:

1. Op-ed piece by Professor Guilmartin.
2. 85 Managua 1523.

CONFIDENTIAL

DOCUMENT 12: Office of Public Diplomacy, Secret Contract with International Business Communications, October 1, 1985 (not signed until September 2, 1986).

PAGE 1 OF 4

~~AWARD~~/CONTRACT

THIS CONTRACT IS A RATED ORDER UNDER DPAS (15 CFR 350)	RATING	PAGE OF
		1

CONTRACT (Proc Inst Ident) NO.
111-602066

EFFECTIVE DATE
10/1/85

REQUISITION/PURCHASE REQUEST/PROJECT NO.
1001-602066

ISSUED BY   CODE
U.S. DEPARTMENT OF STATE
CONTRACTS BRANCH
P.O. BOX 9115, ROSSLYN STATION
ARLINGTON, VIRGINIA 22209

ADMINISTERED BY (If other than Item 5)   CODE

ORIGINAL SECRET

NAME AND ADDRESS OF CONTRACTOR (No. street, city, county, State and ZIP Code)
INTERNATIONAL BUSINESS COMMUNICATIONS, INC.
1912 Sunderland Place, N.W.
Washington, D.C. 20036-1608

DUNS #991916230

8. DELIVERY
☐ FOB ORIGIN   ☒ OTHER (See below)

9. DISCOUNT FOR PROMPT PAYMENT
NET

10. SUBMIT INVOICES (4 copies unless otherwise specified) TO THE ADDRESS SHOWN IN:
ITEM SEE ITEM 11

11. SHIP TO/MARK FOR   CODE   FACILITY CODE
U.S.Department of State,
ARA/LPD, Room 6253,NS,
Washington, D.C. 20520, ATTN: Robert W. Kagan

12. PAYMENT WILL BE MADE BY   CODE
Financial Operations
Central Claims Division
P.O. Box 9487, Rosslyn Station
Arlington, Virginia 22209

13. AUTHORITY FOR USING OTHER THAN FULL AND OPEN COMPETITION:
☐ 10 USC 2304(c)( )   ☒ 41 USC 253(c)(6)

14. ACCOUNTING AND APPROPRIATION DATA
1960113 1001 602066 010122 2589
OBLIGATED 5276,186.00

15A. ITEM NO	15B. SUPPLIES/SERVICES	15C. QUANTITY	15D. UNIT	15E. UNIT PRICE	15F. AMOUNT
	THIS IS A COST-PLUS-FIXED-FEE CONTRACT FOR THE SERVICES SET FORTH IN SECTION C AND AT THE PRICES SHOWN IN SECTION B.	FUNDS AVAILABLE *Sarah E. Klugru* 8/28/86			NOT TO EXCEED

15G. TOTAL AMOUNT OF CONTRACT ▶ $ 276,186.

16. TABLE OF CONTENTS

√	SEC.	DESCRIPTION	PAGE(S)	√	SEC.	DESCRIPTION	PAGE(S)
		PART I — THE SCHEDULE				PART II — CONTRACT CLAUSES	
X	A	SOLICITATION/CONTRACT FORM	A1	X	I	CONTRACT CLAUSES	I1-
X	B	SUPPLIES OR SERVICES AND PRICES/COSTS	B1			PART III — LIST OF DOCUMENTS, EXHIBITS AND OTHER ATTACH.	
X	C	DESCRIPTION/SPECS./WORK STATEMENT	C1-2	X	J	LIST OF ATTACHMENTS	J1-
X	D	PACKAGING AND MARKING	D1			PART IV — REPRESENTATIONS AND INSTRUCTIONS	
X	E	INSPECTION AND ACCEPTANCE	E1	X	K	REPRESENTATIONS, CERTIFICATIONS AND OTHER STATEMENTS OF OFFERORS	K1A 17
X	F	DELIVERIES OR PERFORMANCE	F1-2				
X	G	CONTRACT ADMINISTRATION DATA	G1	X	L	INSTRS, CONDS, AND NOTICES TO OFFERORS	
X	H	SPECIAL CONTRACT REQUIREMENTS	H1-3		M	EVALUATION FACTORS FOR AWARD	

CONTRACTING OFFICER WILL COMPLETE ITEM 17 OR 18 AS APPLICABLE

17. ☒ CONTRACTOR'S NEGOTIATED AGREEMENT (Contractor is required to sign this document and return _3_ copies to issuing office.) Contractor agrees to furnish and deliver all items or perform all the services set forth or otherwise identified above and on any continuation sheets for the consideration stated herein. The rights and obligations of the parties to this contract shall be subject to and governed by the following documents: (a) this award/contract, (b) the solicitation, if any, and (c) such provisions, representations, certifications, and specifications, as are attached or incorporated by reference herein. (Attachments are listed herein.)

18. ☐ AWARD (Contractor is not required to sign this document.) Your offer on Solicitation Number _____ including the additions or changes made by you which additions or changes are set forth in full above, is hereby accepted as to the items listed above and on any continuation sheets. This award consummates the contract which consists of the following documents: (a) the Government's solicitation and your offer, and (b) this award/contract. No further contractual document is necessary.

19A. NAME AND TITLE OF SIGNER (Type or print)
RICHARD R. MILLER, PRESIDENT

20A. NAME OF CONTRACTING OFFICER
Barbara A. Garland
Contracting Officer

19B. NAME OF CONTRACTOR
BY *[signature]*

19C. DATE SIGNED
9/2/86

20B. UNITED STATES OF AMERICA
BY *[signature]*

20C. DATE SIGNED
SEP - 2 '86

NSN 7540-01-152-4069
PREVIOUS EDITION UNUSABLE

STANDARD FORM 26 (REV. 4-4
Prescribed by GSA
FAR (48 CFR) 53.214(a)

SECRET

Declassified by Robert U. Kagan 1/20/21

DOCUMENT 12: Office of Public Diplomacy, Secret Contract with International Business Communications, October 1, 1985 (not signed until September 2, 1986).

PAGE 2 OF 4

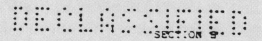

SECTION B

SUPPLIES OR SERVICES AND PRICES/COSTS

I. **CONTRACT TYPE:** This is a COST-PLUS-FIXED-FEE CONTRACT for the coordination of Latin American public diplomacy efforts, and for the design and implementation of a distribution system directly related to those efforts. The services will be performed for the Department of State's Office of the Coordinator for Public Diplomacy for Latin America and the Caribbean (ARA/LPD).

II. **SECURITY CLASSIFICATION.** This contract and all references thereto are classified SECRET.

III. **LEVEL OF EFFORT/COST CEILING BUDGET**

(A) **Ceiling Price:** The ceiling price is $276,186.00, which is comprised of $259,744.00 in estimated costs and $16,442.00 fixed fee. In no event shall the contractor exceed this estimate without prior written approval of the Contracting Officer.

(B) **Rates:** The contractor shall perform in accordance with the Statement of Work set forth in Section C within the following estimated budget:

Item	Costs
Direct Labor	$101,980.00
Other Direct Costs	$ 29,037.00
Overhead (89.48%)	$ 91,252.00
G&A (16.86%)	$ 37,475.00
TOTAL ESTIMATED COSTS	$259,744.00
Fixed Fee	$ 16,442.00
TOTAL CEILING PRICE	$276,186.00

NOTE: This contract will not result in an employer/employee relationship.

III. **PER DIEM AND TRAVEL EXPENSES:** Per diem and travel expenses shall be in accordance with the Uniform Government Travel Regulations and are reimburseable under this contract.

B-1

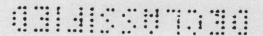

DOCUMENT 12: Office of Public Diplomacy, Secret Contract with International Business Communications, October 1, 1985 (not signed until September 2, 1986).

PAGE 3 OF 4

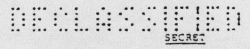

SECRET

DESCRIPTION/SPECIFICATIONS WORK STATEMENT

I.   The Contractor shall provide the following in performance of this contract:

A.   PUBLIC DIPLOMACY EFFORTS:

(1)   Provide advice and assistance for programs for Central American representatives of civic, labor, business and humanitarian groups during visits to Washington and other locations within the United States.

(2)   Provide contact with Central American refugee groups and exiles in Washington and elsewhere in the United States that will include arranging media events, interviews and public appearances.

(3)   Translate articles on Latin America and the Caribbean and make them available for distribution to U.S. news organizations and public interest groups.

(4)   Provide points of contact for public interest groups seeking to interview exiles, refugees, or other visitors.

(5)   Coordinate and, as appropriate, accompany media visits to Central America.

(6)   Provide source materials relating to the regional conflicts to persons designated by S/LPD.

(7)   Provide and present, in writing and orally, factual material on security considerations, refugee problems and political dynamics of the region to individuals designated by S/LPD.

(8)   Edit briefing and other materials for use by S/LPD.

(9)   Conduct special studies and projects for use by S/LPD.

B.   Distribution Services

(1)   Design and organize a distribution system.

SECRET
DECL/OADR

C-1

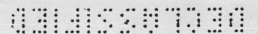

DOCUMENT 12: Office of Public Diplomacy, Secret Contract with International Business Communications, October 1, 1985 (not signed until September 2, 1986).

PAGE 4 OF 4

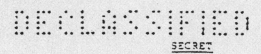

SECRET

(2) Direct the operation of this distribution system, including:

(a) Development of specialized, segmented addressee lists of persons and organizations which have solicited materials or information on Latin America and the Caribbean.

(b) Computerization, coding, maintenance and updating of lists.

(c) Retrieval, storage, mailing, and shipping of individual and bulk packets of publications

(d) Maintenance and control of inventory and reserve stocks of materials.

(e) Distribution of materials.

(f) Coordinate with FAIM/PS publication production

(g) Conduct systematic evaluations of the system.

II. CONTROL/MONITORING:

A. The Office of the Coordinator for Public Diplomacy for Latin America and the Caribbean (S/LPD) will control the number of franked envelopes provided to the Contractor and reserves the right to require, without notice, an inventory of stock usage and envelopes on hand at the Contractor's premises. All franked materials not used will be returned to S/LPD upon demand.

B. S/LPD shall perform spot checks on meetings and arrangements organized by the Contractor.

C. Media coverage, such as newspaper and periodical clippings and discussions with journalists and other members of organizations with whom the Contractor is expected to make arrangements, will be used as a means of monitoring the Contractor's performance.

D. Addressee lists will be seeded with names unknown to the Contractor and will serve as check names to ascertain performance of the distribution services.

SECRET
DECL/OADR

C-2

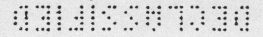

NATIONAL SECURITY COUNCIL
WASHINGTON, D.C. 20506

January 24, 1986

Dear Bunker:

During 1985, the hope freedom and democracy in Nicaragua was kept
alive with the help of the National Endowment for the Preservation
of Liberty and fine Americans such as you. Because you cared,
the spark of liberty still glows in the darkness of Nicaragua.

Without patriots like you, carrying out the President's policy of
support for a democratic outcome in Nicaragua would have been
even more difficult. Your efforts and those of the National
Endowment for the Preservation of Liberty continue to play a
crucial role in the democratic drama unfolding in Nicaragua.
Your support has been essential to those who struggle against the
tyranny and oppression of the totalitarian communist regime in
Managua. You have given hope where there would otherwise be
despair.

Last year was a challenging time for America and her President.
But, we are headed in the right direction. Today, in all of
Central America only Nicaragua is not a democracy. You can be
proud that you have made a crucial contribution in helping our
President in this vital endeavor. In the weeks ahead, we will
commence a renewed effort to make our assistance to the
Democratic Resistance Forces even more effective. Once again
your support will be essential.

All my best for the New Year and God bless you.

Sincerely,

Oliver L. North
Deputy Director
Political-Military Affairs

Mr. Nelson Bunker Hunt
2400 Thanksgiving Tower
1601 Elm Street
Dallas, TX 75201

DOCUMENT 14: Fred Fielding, Memorandum for Frederick Ryan, "Aid to Contra Meeting," January 21, 1986.

PAGE 1 OF 1

THE WHITE HOUSE
WASHINGTON

January 21, 1986

MEMORANDUM FOR FREDERICK J. RYAN, JR.
DEPUTY ASSISTANT TO THE PRESIDENT
DIRECTOR, PRESIDENTIAL SCHEDULING

FROM: FRED F. FIELDING *FFFIRO*
COUNSEL TO THE PRESIDENT

SUBJECT: Aid to Contras Meeting

N 13669

I have reviewed the proposal for a briefing for the American Conservative Trust and the National Endowment for the Preservation of Liberty on Central American issues. There is no legal prohibition that would preclude such a briefing. Objections may be raised that the President is violating the spirit of the anti-lobbying provisions by enlisting these private groups to lobby Congress. Care should accordingly be taken to avoid any suggestion of White House control of these groups, to minimize these objections.

DOCUMENT 15: Robert Gates, Memorandum for Director of Central Intelligence William Casey, "Nicaragua," December 14, 1984.

PAGE 1 OF 5

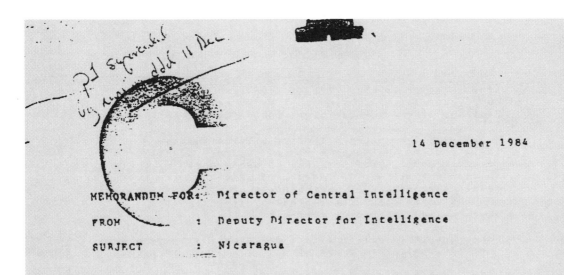

14 December 1984

MEMORANDUM FOR: Director of Central Intelligence

FROM : Deputy Director for Intelligence

SUBJECT : Nicaragua

1. It is time to talk absolutely straight about Nicaragua. To recap where we are:

-- Based on all the assessments we have done, the Contras, even with American support, cannot overthrow the Sandinista regime. Whatever small chance they had to do that has been further diminished by the new weaponry being provided by the Soviets and Cubans.

-- The Soviets and Cubans are turning Nicaragua into an armed camp with military forces far beyond its defensive needs and in a position to intimidate and coerce its neighbors.

-- The Nicaraguan regime is steadily moving toward consolidation of a Marxist-Leninist government and the establishment of a permanent and well armed ally of the Soviet Union and Cuba on the mainland of the Western Hemisphere. Its avowed aim is to spread further revolution in the Americas.

-- The FDN has been denied American assistance. Without further assistance by February, all the information we have suggests the Contras are going to begin heading into Honduras. The Hondurans will then be faced with some 12,500 armed fighters (whom the Hondurans see as closely allied with Alvarez, thereby potentially unsettling Honduras itself).

-- Flight of the Contras into Honduras will be followed not only by their families but presumably by a second wave of refugees and others who, seeing abandonment of American efforts to force the Sandinistas to alter its regime, will see the handwriting on the wall, determine that their personal futures are in peril and leave the country. It is altogether conceivable that we could be

CIIN 1951

DOCUMENT 15: Robert Gates, Memorandum for Director of Central Intelligence William Casey, "Nicaragua," December 14, 1984.

PAGE 2 OF 5

C 5074

looking at an initial refugee wave from Nicaragua over the first year of 150,000 to 200,000 people (the families of the Contras alone could account for 50,000).

Failure of the United States to provide further assistance to the resistance and collapse of the Contra movement would force Honduras to accommodate to the Nicaraguan regime. One result of this would be the complete reopening of the channels of arms support to the Salvadoran insurgency, thereby reversing the progress made in recent months.

These unsettled political and military circumstances in Central America would undoubtedly result in renewed capital flight from Honduras and Guatemala and result in both new hardship and political instability throughout the region.

2. These are strong assertions but our research as well as the reports of our people on the spot (for example our COS in Honduras) make it possible to substantiate each of the above points.

3. What is happening in Central America in many ways vividly calls to mind the old saw that those who forget the past are condemned to repeat it.

-- In 1958-60 we thought that we could reach some sort of an accommodation with Castro that would encourage him to build a pluralistic government in Cuba. We have been trying to do the same thing with the Nicaraguans, with the same success.

-- In Vietnam, our strategy consisted of a series of measures applied very gradually and over a long period of time. With each step of new US involvement the gradual approach enabled the enemy to adjust to each new turn of the screw so that by the end of the war, even in the face of the most severe bombing, the Vietnamese had developed enormous tolerance. Half measures, half-heartedly applied, will have the same result in Nicaragua

-- In 1975, the United States President announced that American assistance to UNITA in Angola was in the national interest of the United States and strongly urged the Congress to support military assistance to that group. The Congress turned it down, thereby not only proving that the United States would not involve itself in any significant way in the Third World to combat Soviet subversion and activity but, moreover, that the Congress could effectively block any moves the President did wish to make. The Boland Amendment and the cutoff of aid to the Contras is having the same

C(1N)1951

DOCUMENT 15: Robert Gates, Memorandum for Director of Central Intelligence William Casey, "Nicaragua," December 14, 1984.

PAGE 3 OF 5

C 5075

effect again, showing the Soviets and our Third World friends how little has changed in nine years, even with a President like Ronald Reagan.

In a variety of places, including Vietnam, negotiations in effect became a cover for the consolidation and further expansion of Communist control. While they might observe whatever agreements were reached for the first weeks or as long as American attention (particularly media attention) was focused on the situation, they knew they could outlast our attention span. Usually within a relatively short period of time they were openly violating whatever agreements had been achieved.

4. The truth of the matter is that our policy has been to muddle along in Nicaragua with an essentially half-hearted policy substantially because there is no agreement within the Administration or with the Congress on our real objectives. We started out justifying the program on the basis of curtailing the flow of weapons to El Salvador. Laudable though that objective might have been, it was attacking a symptom of a larger problem in Central America and not the problem itself.

5. It seems to me that the only way that we can prevent disaster in Central America is to acknowledge openly what some have argued privately: that the existence of a Marxist-Leninist regime in Nicaragua closely allied with the Soviet Union and Cuba is unacceptable to the United States and that the United States will do everything in its power short of invasion to put that regime out. Hopes of causing the regime to reform itself for a more pluralistic government are essentially silly and hopeless. Moreover, few believe that all those weapons and the more to come are only for defense purposes. Only when we acknowledge what the objective is in Central America, can we begin to have any kind of rational discussion on how to achieve it. As long as one maintains the fig leaf of curtailing the flow of arms to El Salvador, all other efforts can easily be politically dismissed.

6. Once you accept that ridding the Continent of this regime is important to our national interest and must be our primary objective, the issue then becomes a stark one. You either acknowledge that you are willing to take all necessary measures (short of military invasion) to bring down that regime or you admit that you do not have the will to do anything about the problem and you make the best deal you can. Casting aside all fictions, it is the latter course we are on. Even new funding for the Contras, particularly in light of the new Soviet weaponry, is an inadequate answer to this problem. The Contras will be able to sustain an insurgency for a time but the cost and the pain will become very high and the resistance eventually will wither. Any negotiated agreement simply will offer a cover for the consolidation of the regime and two or three years from now we will be in considerably worse shape than we are now.

Executive Register

CIIN 1951

DOCUMENT 15: Robert Gates, Memorandum for Director of Central Intelligence William Casey, "Nicaragua," December 14, 1984.

PAGE 4 OF 5

What to do?

the alternative to our present policy -- which I predict ultimately and inevitably is leading to the consolidation of the Nicaraguan regime and our facing a second Cuba in Central America -- is overtly to try to bring down the regime. This involves a mustering of political force and will, first of all within the Administration, and second with the Congress, that we have not seen on any foreign policy issue (apart from our defense rearmament) in many years. It seems to me that this effort would draw upon the following measures:

-- Withdrawal of diplomatic recognition of the regime in Managua and the recognition of a government in exile.

-- Overt provision to the government in exile of military assistance, funds, propaganda support and so forth including major efforts to gain additional support in international community, including real pressure.

-- Economic sanctions against Nicaragua, perhaps even including a quarantine. These sanctions would affect both exports and imports and would be combined with internal measures by the resistance to maximize the economic dislocation to the regime.

-- Politically most difficult of all, the use of air strikes to destroy a considerable portion of Nicaragua's military buildup (focusing particularly on the tanks and the helicopters). This would be accompanied by an announcement that the United States did not intend to invade Nicaragua but that no more arms deliveries of such weapons would be permitted.

8. These are hard measures. They probably are politically unacceptable. But it is time to stop fooling ourselves about what is going to happen in Central America. Putting our heads in the sand will not prevent the events that I outlined at the beginning of this note. Can the United States stand a second Cuba in the Western Hemisphere? One need only look at the difficulty that Cuba has caused this country over the past 25 years to answer that question.

9. The fact is that the Western Hemisphere is the sphere of influence of the United States. If we have decided totally to abandon the Monroe Doctrine, if in the 1980's taking strong actions to protect our interests despite the hail of criticism is too difficult, then we ought to save political capital in Washington, acknowledge our helplessness and stop wasting everybody's time.

10. Without a comprehensive campaign openly aimed at bringing down the regime, at best we somewhat delay the

CIIN 1951

DOCUMENT 15: Robert Gates, Memorandum for Director of Central Intelligence William Casey, "Nicaragua," December 14, 1984.

PAGE 5 OF 5

C 5077

inevitable. Without US funding for the Contras, the resistance essentially will collapse over the next year or two. While seeking funding from other countries to the Contras could help for a time, it is essential to recognize that almost as important as the money is the fact of the United States support both from an economic and political standpoint. Somehow, knowing that Taiwan, South Korea and Singapore are behind you does not carry the same weight. Economic sanctions surely would have a significant impact in the initial months, but unless accompanied by a broad range of other actions this impact will diminish over time and we will find ourselves with a Nicaragua even more closely attached to the Soviet Union and Cuba than we have now.

11. All this may be politically out of the question. Probably. But all the cards ought to be on the table and people should understand the consequences of what we do and do not do in Nicaragua. Half measures will not even produce half successes. The course we have been on (even before the funding cut-off) -- as the last two years suggest -- will result in further strengthening of the regime and a Communist Nicaragua which, allied with its Soviet and Cuban friends, will serve as the engine for the destabilization of Central America. Even a well funded Contra movement cannot prevent this; indeed, relying on and supporting the Contras as our only action may actually hasten the ultimate, unfortunate outcome.

Robert M. Gates

CIIN 1951

DOCUMENT 16: Oliver North, "U.S. Political/Military Strategy for Nicaragua" (Plan to Overthrow the Sandinista Government), ca. July 15, 1985.

PAGE 1 OF 3

Post

Partially Declassified/Released on 2/24/89
under provisions of E.O. 12356
by K. Johnson, National Security Council

AKWC865

★ U.S. POLITICAL/MILITARY STRATEGY FOR NICARAGUA

This strategy is based upon certain assumptions which are crucial to the success of United States' effort in Central America:

-- The American people currently consider U.S. full-scale military involvement in Nicaragua as unacceptable. Public acceptance of a U.S. invasion of Nicaragua could change dramatically should the Sandinista military invade either Honduras or Costa Rica.

-- Public support of current U.S. policy in Central America is rapidly growing. Support of U.S. policy among the Nicaraguans is also shifting to one of cautious but visably growing support. The U.S. Congress will vote for some level of aid which combined with the current and significant foreign and domestic support will allow the proposed strategy to be implemented.

-- The FDN and UNO are consolidating politically and support the forces led by Enrique Bermudez in Nicaragua and his forces and allied forces in the border areas of Honduras and Costa Rica.

-- The support of the FDN and the U.S. effort in Central America by the Honduran Government is very tentative; although the Honduran Government is supportive, in principle, the soon to be elctions temper overt Honduran Government action. [A Honduran military official   ] made this quite clear to tne undersigned on July 15, 1985.

-- Support for the Sandinista Government by the Nicaraguan people is eroding rapidly.

-- The Soviets/Cubans will not implement the Brezhnev Doctrine should the U.S. undertake military action in Nicaragua nor will the Soviets/Cubans intervene militarily to block the overthrow of the Sandinistas by UNO/FDN forces.

-- The global psychological warfare conducted by the Sandinistas will continue unabated.

-- Intelligence, both tactical and strategic, will continue to improve. (The FDN will receive U.S. intelligence support.)

-- A comprehensive UNO/FDN political program will be developed and widely publicized throughout the U.S., Nicaragua, and the world immediately.

FOI
3/31/87
OLN COF 4-

IRG 1

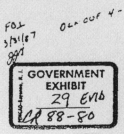

GOVERNMENT
EXHIBIT
29 EVib
CR 88-80

DOCUMENT 16: Oliver North, "U.S. Political/Military Strategy for Nicaragua" (Plan to Overthrow the Sandinista Government), ca. July 15, 1985.

PAGE 2 OF 3

2

This strategy is divided into three phases. The first phase consists primarily of a continuation of the efforts already in progress with the following objectives:

Phase I.

(1) Development of a sound FDN logistics support base in Honduras.

(2) Development of an FDN operational base in Nicaragua so that support (log) distances can be reduced and FDN troop presence in Honduras is reduced.

(3) Development of a secondary Costa Rican front with bases and operations removed as much as possible from Costa Rican territory.

(4) Establishment of an aerial resupply system for both fronts.

(5) Immediate coordination between the two fronts (northern and southern).

(6) Near term FDN urban guerrilla capability to demonstrate an active FDN presence in the urban centers.

(7) Enhanced communications and intelligence (C^{3}I) to exploit FDN capabilities.

(8) CI capability to thwart Sandinista penetration efforts of the FDN and UNO operations.

(9) Development of a robust FDN psychological warfare capability.

(10) Development of a polad/military advisory group (2-3 people) to ensure FDN maximizes political/military coordination with both the U.S. Government, private sector, Honduran/Costa Rican Governments, etc.

Phase II. This is the offensive phase of the strategy and would have the following objectives:

(1) To repeatedly but temporarily disrupt the economic infrastructure of Nicaragua with priority to the electrical grid, water, transportation, and communications systems. (A show of force action with maximum psychological benefit.)

AKW022864

[51]

DOCUMENT 16: Oliver North, "U.S. Political/Military Strategy for Nicaragua" (Plan to Overthrow the Sandinista Government), ca. July 15, 1985.

PAGE 3 OF 3

3

Phase II (continued)...

(2) To establish a strong political presence in the urban centers focusing on graffiti, leaflets, selective targetting of known FSLN population control groups, i.e., block wardens.

(3) To attack the regular Sandinista security forces to force them into a defensive posture (avoiding as possible the unproductive engagements with the BLI).

(4) To treat the Nicaraguan people much better than the Sandinista forces.

(5) To destroy the legitimacy of the Sandinista Government.

(6) To control more and more of the country by gradually and systematically replacing the Sandinista control with UNO/FDN control.

(7) To separate the foreign advisors from the Nicaraguan people and isolate these groups (both militarily and psychologically).

(8) To destroy the main armaments of the Sandinistas, priority directed to the armed helicopters, aircraft, tanks, armored personnel carriers, artillery and transportation plus C^3I.

Phase III. The third and final phase would have the following objectives:

(1) The defeat and demobilization of Sandinista armed forces.

(2) Implementation of the UNO/FDN political program.

(3) Repatriation of all foreign advisors and foreign supporters (to include the Sandinista (SIC) Americans).

(4) Identification and defranchizing (SIC) of residual Somoza supporters (people in prison a special problem).

(5) Immediate implementation of U.S. and foreign economic aid, social assistance (judicial system), and military assistance to establish professional, non-political (armed forces should be greatly and immediately reduced and armed forces placed under civilian control).

A1WO22865

DOCUMENT 17: TC (Robert Owen), Memorandum to BG (Oliver North), "Overall Perspective," March 17, 1986.

PAGE 1 OF 5

<u>EYES ONLY</u>

TO: BG   MARCH 17, 1986

FROM: TC

SUBJECT: OVERALL PERSPECTIVE

The following report is broken down into several sections. It comes from my involvement over the last few weeks, but some of the thoughts have been perculating for some time. As I have been in a somewhat unique position these last two years, I have seen and heard a number of things and people are now coming to me with bits and pieces of information which I cann't fully evaluate, I can only pass it along.

<u>FDN/UNO POLITICAL SITUATION</u>

I put it as FDN/UNO because the FDN is now driving UNO, not the other way around. UNO is a creation of the USG to garner support from Congress. When it was founded a year ago, the hope was it would become a viable organization. In fact, almost anything it has accomplished is because the hand of the USG has been there directing and manipulating.

No doubt the hope was Cruz and Robelo would turn into strong leaders to somewhat counterbalance the strength of Calero and the FDN. Both Cruz and Robelo have been disappointments. Calero, on the other hand, has used his strength and will and the FDN to further consolidate his hold on the resistance and to gain control of UNO. Perhaps UNO is the correct acronym, for there is only one leader in the Democratic Resistence, Adolfo Calero.

As long as the USG understands this to be true, then it can go forward with planning. But, if USG agencies actually believe that UNO is a strong and functioning body that truely represents all factions of the Democratic Resistence, they are fooling themselves into believing something that is not true. This is dangerous for the USG and for the effort as a whole.

To understand this, one must look at what the FDN political structure represents. Calero is the strong man and the only one who counts in the FDN; what he says is law. Under him is his strong man, or enforcer, Aristedes Sanchez. Bermudez is in the inner circle, but he is not 100% trusted, because he is seen as a potential rival for power. Also within the inner circle is Mario Calero. Off to the side, but still part of the group and acting more like temple guards are Bosco Matamoras (loyally devoted Washington rep) and Oscar Montes (the financial account). Both of these people are intensely loyal and will do whatever Adolfo says. The next ring down consists of the Tefel brothers, Hyme Morales, Statahen etc. None of these people can stand Robelo or Cruz. At every turn they will undermine them and do all in their power to see they are not given any power, thus the strength remains with Calero.

Should USG officials think any different than the above, they are not looking at the facts. If members of the USG think they control Calero, they also have another thing coming. The question should be asked, can and does Calero manipulate the USG. On several occasions, the answer is yes. Two examples are Mario Calero and Bosco. For well over a year, USG officials have wanted to remove these two, yet they remain. Why, because Calero won't budge, they are part of his security; to threaten them is to threaten him.

DOCUMENT 17: TC (Robert Owen), Memorandum to BG (Oliver North), "Overall Perspective," March 17, 1986.

PAGE 2 OF 5

BG
March 17, 1986
Page 2

I write the above only to point out the facts as I see them. Perhaps a strongman is the only thing Nicaraguans understand; perhaps Adolfo Calero is the man to lead Nicaragua back to democracy. He is a creation of the USG and so he is the horse we chose to ride. I have no problem with this, as long as we know and understand his short comings. The best way to point these out are to take a close look at who he keeps around him, only those who he intimately trusts. Unfortunately, they are not first rate people; in fact they are liars and greed and power motivated. They are not the people to rebuild a new Nicaragua. In fact, the FDN has done a good job of keeping competent people out of the organization. If it hasn't, then Nicaragua is lost forever with the type of leadership that has emerged.

Just one example of the lies which are told to keep the status quo: Honduras station reported in a cable that Dr. Tomas threatened to take the FDN medical corps on strike should Bosco be booted from Washington. This is a fact and can be verified in traffic. Tomas swore to me this was not true and no such thought ever entered his mind. He was used as one more reason to keep Bosco in place.

One other lie was spread by Mario, he told people, including an individual from the Agency, that NHAO had been responsible for putting the news crews on the DC-6. He was the one responsible, yet he blames others. This is just one example.

If the USG knows what and who it is dealing with that is all well and good, if it does not, it should learn.

NHAO FUNDING

NHAO was the worst possible vehicle which could have been devised to pay the bills. Because there is no verification it is impossible to ensure the integrity of the operation. The attached paper shows the amounts of money transferred into Miami accounts. As the black market exchange rate is about L2.75 to $1.00 while the legal rate is L2.00 to $1.00 and the suppliers are being paid at 2 to 1, there is about a 37% profit. Adolfo admitted to Duemling and Arcos he is splitting this 50-50 with Aquiles Marin, and AC's share is going to the war effort. Would you by chance know who Aquiles Marin is?

With all the money that has been deposited that adds up to about $2.3 million which is divided up between the Honduran military, the suppliers and the FDN. This does not even take into account the false receipts. For example, Francelia has received over $416,000 for medical goods. According to Tomas, up to last week he had spent maybe L250,000. There is some money going somewhere. I am not saying it is being pocketed, but there are questions unanswered.

Someone recently approached me and told me that both Adolfo and Mario have accounts in Switzerland at Lloyds Bank International. I don't even know if there is such a bank. The same person said Sanchez and his brother Cookoo (sp) have overseas accounts in the Dutch Netherland Antilles. The person said he'd provide the account numbers, then recently retracted the offer. Don't know whether it is bullshit or not. If it is true the USG is being had.

THE SEACORDS CONNECTION

What you had hoped to remain quiet is now openly being discussed on the street. For examp:

DOCUMENT 17: TC (Robert Owen), Memorandum to BG (Oliver North), "Overall Perspective," March 17, 1986.

PAGE 3 OF 5

BG
March 17, 1986
Page 3

the following names have been used in connection with Seacords operation:

- Tom Klines
- Larry Sterns
- George Stockman
- Patrice Gentry
- Peter (aka Pablo) Duncan
- Alberto Coppo (in Peru)
- Antonio Molina (Hondo Colonel)
- One Lt. Col. Oliver North
- Star Production
- General Equipment and Leasing Corp. in Geneva
- Stanford Technologies Trading Group and Transfer Ltd. in Arlington,Va.

The word is these people and companies have been involved in the procurement and trans-portation of arms and aircraft for the FDN. Some people are complaining these people are making money on sweetheart deals and that the prices they are getting are not as good as they could be.

On several occasions Adolfo even complained to me about Seacords and the deal he has got. Because Seacords is connected to Gadd, Adolfo has told people he had no choice but to use him.

Among the people talking openly about these deals are:

- Carl Jenkins
- Col. Bob K. Brown
- Ed Dearborn
- Individuals in Guatemala
- Individuals in Miami

In all probability, they are talking and bad mouthing Seacords because they want part of the action. They are also blaming Seacords for whatever problem arises.

As an added problem, Mario told me in Miami why Adolfo and company are upset with me and freezing me out. I am looked on as the responsible party for a number of the problems they are having. They look at me as the one carrying the water for you. They are also saying I am intimately tied to Seacords. Among things they connect me to are:

- The purchase of the Mahls at a higher price than necessary
- Stopping the export of the Lady Ellen helicopter
- Bringing Gadd into the picture, which they are not happy with
- Stopping NHAO from funding the movement of the Push and Pull and the heliocourier, which were donated and are in Hawaii
- The use of Project Hope
- Being the Godfather and promoter of Carlos Ulvert
- Thus being responsible for the move against Bosco

Adolfo may even have thought Seacords was the one behind his not being able to buy from the Supermarket in Honduras.

Granted, alot of this may be speculation on Mario's part and others, but the perception is there. They want me out of the way; they do not trust me; and I do not believe they trust you anymore. There is still a belief the FDN can do it alone and does not need any help.

BG
March 17, 1986
Page 4

COSTA RICA

Believe it or not, the southern effort is making progress, or at least it was before State Department in its infinite wisdom decided it would be a good thing to help Pastora. If he is brought back in and given credibility, you can throw away the Southern Front.

The first hard intelligence mission inside by boat has taken place and the people are now out. Hopefully Buck was able to debrief Risa, who was in command.

5 28-foot fiberglass boats have been ordered. They are being built in Costa Rica, the first one will be delivered in about two weeks. They will be equipped with radar, depth sounders and two 150 hp engines. A fishing company is now being formed in Limon, Costa Rica to provide cover for the boats. A safehouse has been rented on a river, which flows into the ocean.

Moises Nunez, a Cuban who has a shrimping business in Punteranous, is fronting the operation. He is willing to have an American come work for him under cover to advise the operation. I discussed this with Joe and brought up the name Bill Kenny, someone who was supposedly a member of Seal Team 1 and now works with Singlaub and Heiny Aterholt. I have met with him on a number of occasions and he seems up front and willin to keep his mouth shut. Joe has agreed to have him used. Please chek him out. If he is okay, I'll take him down next week and put him in the hands of Max (Felipe Vidal) and Nunez.

If we can get two shrimp boats, Nunez is willing to front a shrimping operation on the Atlantic coast. These boats can be used as motherships. I brought this up awhile ago and you agreed and gave me the name of a DEA person who might help with the boats. I have not followed up because I have not been in Washington long enough, but will do so now if you think it appropriate.

Nunez is about to sign an agreement with the Sandinista government which will provide him with shrimping rights off the Pacific coast of Nicaragua. Paul Atha is carrying the water for Borge, the Ortegas and the rest. Nunez is doing this so he can help us. He will cooperate and do anything we ask. He believes this will provide an opportunity to use his boats for cover operations, or to implicate the Ortegas and Borge in taking money on the side for their own pocket. He is right on both counts. As of last week he was supposed to find out if he is to go to Managua, or if Atha will go to Costa Rica.

Where to next on this one?

RWO and the FUTURE

I have been active in this cause since 1983 when I brought John Hull in to meet you. I have tried to give my all and to do my best. Hopefully I've contributed something. Perhaps the time has come for me to move on to other things. I am burned beyond belief. My name has now openly been linked to you in Congress. I am looked on as your boy by Calero and gang, and thus nolonger trusted. Don't know what Allen and Company think of me, but I don't think too much of the incompetence that has come out of the Agency.

In fact, I have probably never been more discouraged. UNO is a name only. There is more and more fluff being added, but there is no substance. Create and believe in the

DOCUMENT 17: TC (Robert Owen), Memorandum to BG (Oliver North), "Overall Perspective," March 17, 1986.

PAGE 5 OF 5

BG
March 17, 1986
Page 5

boys and girls, men and women who are fighting, bleeding and dying. But the reality as I
see it is there are few of the so called leaders of the movement who really care about
the boys in the field. THIS WAR HAS BECOME A BUSINESS TO MANY OF THEM; THERE IS STILL
A BELIEF THE MARINES ARE GOING TO HAVE TO INVADE, SO LETS GET SET SO WE WILL AUTOMATICLY
BE THE ONES PUT INTO POWER.

If the $100 million is approved and things go on as they have these last five years, it
will be like pouring money down a sink hole. The Agency has done a shitty job in the
past, there is no evidence they are going to change, especially as they are going
to have the same people running it as far as I know. State Department is no better.
No one talks to each other, there is no coordination and there is little leadership.
Without significant changes, things will not get better, they will get worse. The
heavy hand of the gringo is needed.

Unless you believe I can continue to be of use to you or the project, I would like
to move on. You once said Fires would like to bring me on contract if the money is
approved. Right now, I have no desire.

I would like your blessing and help to get actively involved in counter terrorism.
If there is something I can do with Terry Arnold, that would be great. Frankly, I'd
like to continue to work with you in some capacity. If this is not possible, I'd
like some ideas.

Possible Solution

I have talked with several people about what can possibly be done to help turn things
around in Nicaragua. One of the most glaring mistakes is we have no real intelligence
network inside, thus we have to rely on what we are told by the FDN and the other groups

A solution to this, even though it would take time, is to establish an independent
intelligence network in Nicaragua. It would be trained by us, equipped by us, and
report to us. Once established, these cells would provide the necessary information
to run a solid campaign against the Sandinistas. Without a good intelligence service
inside Nicaragua, the FDN and the U.S. is running blind. Electronic intel etc. just
does not do it. This is something the Agency never established in the beginning in
1981 or 1982. Without it, how can you fight a war, with a good one, how can you help
but have a better chance of winning.

I would like to propose you meet with Tom Hewitt, who successfully established an intel
network in Cuba and ran it uncovered for several years. He has written a short paper
and I believe the time invested would be well worth it.

END of STORY

I have valued these last few years. I've learned a great deal and had fun doing it.
I just hope I have been helpful.

I will continue in whatever position you recommend. You have been my Godfather through
this. I am here to serve my country, but I will not be involved if we are not serious
and will not do what is necessary to make it work.

II. THIRD-COUNTRY QUID PRO QUOS

In December 1983, Congress appropriated $24 million for the CIA's Contra war, but stipulated that no other funds beyond that amount could be used. According to the law, when this money ran out—it was expected to last through May 1984—the Reagan administration would have to terminate its Contra operations.

This law provided the impetus for creating what CIA Director William Casey, according to Oliver North, called a "self-sustaining, off-the-shelf" operation to continue the Contra war. In order to fulfill the president's order to keep the Contras together "body and soul," the covert war, which by this time had become quite overt, reverted to a deeply clandestine effort. During the following months, operational command was transferred from the CIA to the NSC—although key Agency officials such as Casey, Central American Task Force Director Alan Fiers, and Costa Rica Chief of Station Joseph Fernandez remained heavily involved. Former covert operatives—"private benefactors," as they were called in internal administration memoranda and cable traffic—were enlisted to manage the day-to-day operations of financing, procurement, logistics, training, and weapons drops. By October 1984, when Congress passed Boland II, explicitly prohibiting the CIA and every other agency involved in intelligence activities from using any funds that would "directly or indirectly" support Contra operations, the Reagan White House had already established "the Enterprise"—a pseudo–private-sector organization conducting covert operations in Central America on behalf of the United States. The Enterprise, noted the congressional final report on Iran-Contra, "served as the secret arm of the NSC staff, carrying out with private and nonappropriated money, and without the accountability or restrictions imposed by law on the CIA, a covert Contra aid program that Congress thought it had prohibited." [1]

THIRD-COUNTRY CONTRA SUPPORT

Securing the "private and non-appropriated money" —what William Casey refers to in Document 18 as "supplemental assistance" and "funding alternatives" —to finance this surrogate Contra aid program was the administration's first major challenge as congressional funds began to dwindle in the spring of 1984. U.S. officials quickly turned to friendly foreign governments, particularly those already supportive of the Contra war. Israel was number one on the administration's list. In a secret 1983 CIA/Pentagon operation code-named TIPPED KETTLE, the Israelis had secretly provided the Pentagon with $10 million worth of munitions, taken from the PLO in Lebanon, for use in the Contra war. As early as February 1984, National Security Advisor Robert McFarlane approached an Israeli official about taking over the Contra support operations. Although they declined to assume the financing and training of the Contras, the Israelis did transfer additional PLO armaments in Operation TIPPED KETTLE II during the summer of 1984.

"The second alternative we are exploring is the procurement of assistance from [South Africa]," Casey wrote in a March 27, 1984, memorandum to McFarlane (Document 18). A visit by CIA operative Duane Clarridge to Johannesburg was arranged in April. The South Africans, according to Document 19, an April 4 cable from the chief of station, were predisposed to offer equipment, aid, and training. Unfortunately for the CIA, Clarridge arrived just as the mining of the harbors scandal erupted in Washington; to avoid further potential embarrassment, he was immediately recalled. "Current furor here over the Nicaragua project urges that we postpone taking [the South Africans] up on their offer of assistance…at least for the time being," Clarridge cabled the CIA station after his return to Washington. [2]

On their third approach, U.S. officials turned to Saudi Arabia and hit paydirt. The Saudis, who were already providing illicit funding for the CIA's covert war in Afghanistan, emerged as the key Contra donor. In May, McFarlane paid a visit to the Mclean, Virginia, home of Saudi Arabian Ambassador Prince Bandar bin Sultan and made a pitch for Contra aid. [3] According to McFarlane's later testimony, Bandar offered to "provide a contribution of $1 million per month." Mc-Farlane then turned to North for the number of a bank account where the money could be wired—North got the account number from Casey—and subsequently provided Bandar with a Cayman Islands Contra bank account. In late June, according to North's notes, he was informed that the first million-dollar installment would be transferred "w/in 24 hrs" (Document 20). The money actually began to flow in early July.

Following a private meeting at the White House between Saudi King Fahd and President Reagan in February 1985, the Saudis enlarged their contribution. "[A]s he was leaving the Oval Office and I was escorting him to the door," Reagan later testified during the trial of John Poindexter, "the King told me of the contribution he had been making to the Contras. There had been no discussion of that in our meeting until that. He told me that, and his last words were that he was going to double it." "I think that's fine," Reagan remembered replying.[4]

By late March 1985, Saudi Arabia had contributed an additional $24 million to the Contra cause, bringing their total to $32 million, and making that government the principal financier of the Contra resupply operations.[5]

Soliciting third-country support in order to circumvent the constitutional system of congressional appropriations became one of the most covert components of Reagan's Contra policy. Thus, the Saudi aid was a closely held secret. When it began, McFarlane informed President Reagan, Vice President Bush, and, of course, Oliver North (who likely informed Casey). But other members of the administration were cut out of the loop.[6] "No one in our govt can be aware," North's notes record him telling Adolfo Calero ("Barnaby"), into whose secret bank account the Saudi money was deposited (Document 20).

The compartmentalization of this secret led to an extraordinary National Security Planning Group (NSPG) meeting on June 25, 1984. President Reagan, Vice President Bush, McFarlane, Casey, and perhaps one or two others at the meeting knew that third-country funding was already in the pipeline. But the rest of those present did not.

According to minutes of the meeting, the legality of third-country funding was forcefully debated (Document 21). Casey argued that the September 19, 1983, Finding (Document 2) authorized the CIA to approach third countries and stated that the CIA was "considering Salvador, Guatemala, Honduras and [a South American nation]" as collaborators.[7] Secretary of State George Shultz disagreed, arguing that U.S.-instigated funding from third countries was a serious transgression of the law. Relating a conversation with Chief of Staff James Baker, Shultz warned that bypassing Congress in this way could be an "impeachable offense." Keeping the Saudi aid a secret, McFarlane concluded the meeting by proposing that "there be no authority for anyone to seek third party support…until we have the information we need" and admonishing everyone present to keep quiet about these operations. President Reagan then seconded McFarlane's position, warning that this gambit was so politically and legally sensitive that if the story leaked, "we'll all be hanging by our thumbs in front of the White House until we find out who did it."

Notwithstanding the disagreement among the members of the NSPG, the NSC staff continued surreptitiously to solicit friendly governments. In mid 1985, Lt. Col. North personally negotiated a $2 million contribution from Taiwan. Besides Israel, South Africa, Saudi Arabia, and Taiwan, the Reagan administration also approached, directly or through intermediaries, China, South Korea, Singapore, Brunei, Chile, Venezuela, Guatemala, El Salvador, Honduras, Costa Rica, Panama, and Great Britain for monetary, logistical, or material support for the Contra war.

QUID PRO QUOS

One of the main sticking points on the legality of third-country solicitations was the issue of offering compensation—a quid pro quo—in return for aid to the Contras. Attorney General William French Smith's office took the position that third-country funding would be legal only if it was made "without any monetary promises or inducements from the United States."[8] At the June 25 NSPG meeting then Vice President Bush offered a similar opinion on quid pro quos and third-country support for the Contras:

> How can anyone object to the U.S. encouraging third parties to provide help to the anti-Sandinistas? The only problem that might come up is if the United States were to promise to give these third parties something in return so that some people could interpret this as some kind of an exchange. (Document 21)

But the Reagan administration did promise a number of nations something in return for their Contra support, and Bush himself participated in at least one such arrangement with Honduras.

Since the inception of the Contra policy in 1981, Washington had used Honduras as a territorial platform for the paramilitary war. In return for the use of Honduran land for rebel bases and logistics, and Honduran collaboration in CIA and Contra activities, the administration opened the floodgates of U.S. military and economic aid. By 1985, little Honduras was the eighth-largest recipient of U.S. assistance in the world, receiving for that year $215 million in economic and $74 million in military aid.[9]

When Congress terminated funding for the war in October 1984, and Contra fighters began retreating into basecamps along the Honduran-Nicaraguan border, the Honduran generals decided that their cooperation was worth more and threatened to expel the Contras from Honduran soil. On February 7, 1985, the NSC's Crisis Pre-Planning Group recommended providing "incentives for [the Hondurans] to persist in aiding the freedom fighters." These enticements included releasing economic aid, expediting the delivery of U.S. weapons, and enhancing CIA spending on several projects in Honduras, which presumably included payments to selected military officials. On February 19, 1985, President Reagan authorized this explicit quid pro quo deal (Document 22).

The quid of the deal, according to a U.S. government summary of still-classified documents known as the "Stipulation," was transmitted by Vice President George Bush to President Suazo Cordoba during an official visit in March:

> Bush told Suazo that President Reagan had directed expedited delivery of U.S. military items to Honduras…[and] that currently withheld economic assistance for Honduras should be released; that the United States would provide from its own military stocks critical security assistance items that had been ordered by Honduran armed forces; and that several security programs underway for Honduran security forces would be enhanced.[10] (Document 23, para. 58)

The more sensitive pro quo "criteria" for the aid, according to the president's authorization, was to be transmitted by a secret "emissary" (believed to be NSC staffer Raymond Burghardt, fluent in Spanish) who would "very privately explain our criteria for the expedited economic support, security assistance deliveries, and enhanced CIA support."

But even these incentives were not enough to secure lasting Honduran support. When the U.S. Congress refused to pass renewed aid for the Contras in April, the Honduran military intercepted an Enterprise shipment of Chinese surface-to-air missiles being transported to the rebel camps. To secure the release of these weapons, McFarlane felt compelled to have President Reagan place a direct call to President Suazo. "The active GOH [Government of Honduras] cooperation with FDN logistics," McFarlane wrote in Document 24, a memo to the president, also forwarded to Vice President Bush, "must continue if the resistence is to survive." According to Reagan's handwritten notes of the conversations, the Honduran president agreed to "call his mil[itary] commander and tell him to deliver the armaments," but he also took the opportunity to request an additional $15 million in U.S. economic aid (Document 24).

After a new Honduran president, José Azcona, was elected, Vice President Bush again delivered Washington's message on the Contras. According to special talking points prepared for a January 1986 meeting between Bush and Azcona, "supply of the Democratic Resistance Forces" was high on the agenda of their private discussion. "We, President Reagan and I, hope we can work very quietly and discreetly with you," Bush was to tell Azcona:

It can be done with deniability. Internal resistance in Nicaragua needs support....Armed resistance and their supply. So we hope...as soon as possible, you can take a look at supply for the DRF, talk to your military and tell the military to work out ways to assure a supplied front.[11]

Other Central American nations, on which the U.S. depended for logistics and bases, also negotiated quid pro quos. The Guatemalan military demanded, and obtained, compensation in the form of U.S. military equipment for having provided the Enterprise with false EUCs—end-user certificates[12]—for purchases of Contra weapons and ammunition in Portugal, and for facilitating transport of these munitions through Guatemala (Document 25). In mid 1985, Costa Rican President Alberto Monge agreed to allow construction of a secret airstrip to bolster the "southern front" for Contra operations in return for CIA support on a secret project (Document 23, para. 66).[13] A key CIA asset in the Costa Rican government, Public Security Minister Benjamin Piza, apparently received a private photo session with President Reagan at the White House as the reward for his assistance to the southern front.[14]

THE BRUNEI PROJECT

On June 12, 1985, Congress passed a new Contra aid bill authorizing $27 million in nonlethal assistance. This funding was cast as "humanitarian assistance" to be distributed by a newly created State Department office, the Nicaraguan Humanitarian Assistance Office (NHAO).

The NHAO appropriation, which purchased food, medical supplies, and other items not typically associated with guerrilla warfare (for example, color TVs, candy, and deodorant) covered the Contra's nonlethal needs until late spring 1986. Despite the fact that the Enterprise was flush with money from the sale of arms to Iran, the Reagan administration began to search for new sources of "bridge funding" to tide the Contras over until Congress voted more funds. At a meeting of the NSPG on May 16, 1986 the problem of the shortfall was discussed at length. Finally, according to Alan Fiers, who attended the meeting, President Reagan asked, "'Well, what about Ollie's people? Can't they help?' And someone at the end of the table...said very quickly, 'That's being worked on,' and the conversation moved on."[15]

The 1986 Intelligence Authorization Act authorized the State Department to approach other governments for nonlethal assistance. At the NSPG meeting, Secretary Shultz, who was unaware of previous solicitations to Saudi Arabia and other nations, suggested several governments, including Saudi Arabia, that the State Department might ask for help. Shultz's volunteerism created a panic for Admiral Poindexter and Lt. Col. North who were concerned that their still-secret third-country funding schemes might be uncovered. On June 10, North recommended to Poindexter that they meet with McFarlane to discuss how much Shultz knew. In a computer memo Poindexter responded, "To my knowledge Shultz knows nothing about the prior financing. I think it should stay that way."[16]

In his computer memo to North, Poindexter related a discussion with Elliott Abrams during which Abrams promoted "a good prospect" for Contra bridge funding—the oil-rich island kingdom of Brunei. "They have lots of money," as Poindexter put it.[17] This discussion set in motion the "Brunei Project"—a protracted, and in the end embarrassing, U.S. effort to obtain monies from the world's richest man, Haji Hassanal Bolkiah Mu'izzaddin Waddaulah—the sultan of Brunei.

Initially, Secretary Shultz himself was to make the

solicitation during a meeting with the sultan in June. North provided Abrams with an index card on which his secretary Fawn Hall had typed the number of the Credit Suisse bank account through which the Enterprise purchased arms, even though the law stated that the solicitation was permissible only for humanitarian aid. Then Abrams gave the card to the secretary of state. But Shultz decided that it would be impolitic for him to approach the sultan directly. Instead, Abrams cabled instructions to U.S. Ambassador to Brunei Barrington King to make a discreet inquiry with Brunei's foreign minister, Pengiran Muda Mohammed Bolkiah. On July 28, King cabled Abrams that a "meeting would be possible provided that we could assure [the foreign minister] categorically there would be no publicity and no leaks" (Document 26). On August 2, King again cabled Washington that the Sultan would soon be leaving for England and a member of his entourage could meet with a U.S. emissary in London (Document 27).

Using the codename "Mr. Kenilworth," Assistant Secretary of State Abrams himself met with the foreign minister in London three days later and requested $10 million for the Contras (Document 28). "The president will know of this, and you will have the gratitude of the secretary and the president for helping us out in a jam," Abrams assured the representative.[18] The money was transferred on August 19. On September 16, according to Document 29, Ambassador King delivered a private message from Secretary Shultz to the sultan in Brunei, thanking him for "understanding our needs." As a token of diplomatic reciprocity for the $10 million, the sultan was given a VIP tour of the aircraft carrier USS *Vinson*.

In the end, however, the Brunei initiative ended disastrously for both the sultan and the Reagan administration. Although the $10 million was transferred, the money apparently did not reach the bank account for which it was intended. Oliver North later testified that his assistant, Fawn Hall, had inadvertantly transposed two numbers on the card given to Abrams, and the money had been wired to the wrong

account.[19] Even worse for U.S. relations with the sultan, on December 6, one week after the Iran-Contra scandal broke, the *Los Angeles Times* published the story of Abrams's trip to London. Still unaware that the funds had been misdirected, Abrams frantically cabled the U.S. embassy in the capital city of Bandar Seri Begawan: "We wish to prevent deposit of any funds into designated account. We need to know if funds have been deposited in order to take other appropriate action."[20]

By that time, Abrams had already appeared before the Senate Intelligence Committee and had been asked by Senator Bill Bradley about his knowledge of Contra fund-raising activities. "I don't think I knew anything that wasn't...in the newspaper," he replied. "We're not—you know, we're not in the fund-raising business," Abrams added. "We don't engage—I mean the State Department's function in this has not been to raise money, other than to try to raise it from Congress."[21]

THE NORIEGA INITIATIVE

When Congress passed $100 million in renewed Contra aid in August 1986, the Reagan administration no longer needed to solicit funding and weapons from third countries. Yet even as CIA operatives prepared to return to Central America en masse, the NSC and the State Department were busy arranging one more quid pro quo deal, involving Panamanian General Manuel Noriega.

A long-standing U.S. intelligence asset, General Noriega had already proven helpful to Washington in the Contra war. In July 1984, he had donated $100,000 to the Contra forces operating out of Costa Rica. And in March 1985, according to the quid pro quo Stipulation, the general provided a Panamanian explosives expert to assist in blowing up a Sandinista military depot in downtown Managua, a mission carried out by British mercenaries at the behest of Oliver North (Document 23, para. 98). Even after the *New York Times* in June 1986 published two front-page stories detailing his long history of narcotics trafficking, Noriega's assistance to the Contra cause protected him from U.S. pressure. Assistant Secretary Abrams informed an interagency panel reviewing U.S. policy toward Panama that a decision had been made "not to deal with the Noriega problem until after Nicaragua was settled."[22]

In late August, Noriega sent an emissary to Washington to remind the Reagan White House how helpful he could be. The emissary met with Lt. Col. North and offered this proposal:

in exchange for a promise from the USG[overnment] to help clean up Noriega's image and a commitment to lift the USG ban on military sales to the Panamanian defense forces, Noriega would assassinate the Sandinista leadership for the U.S. government.[23] (Document 23, para. 97)

When informed of this offer, National Security Advisor Poindexter responded that the United States "could not be involved in assassination, but Panamanian assistance with sabotage would be another story."

On August 24, 1986, North met with the CIA's Duane Clarridge and, according to North's notes, discussed arrangements for a meeting abroad with Noriega: "Send word back to Noriega to meet in Europe or Israel—Tell Abrams that Noriega has asked for mtg [meeting]...re cleaning up image" (Document 30). North then brought the issue up at a meeting of the Restricted Interagency Group, arguing that there "needed to be a resistance presence in the western part of Nicaragua, particularly in Managua," and that Noriega could supply that presence. At the trial of Clair George, Alan Fiers recalled the conversation:

And he said, "I can arrange to have General Noriega execute some insurgent or some—some op-

erations there—sabotage operations in that area. It will cost us about a million. Do we want to do it?" And there was significant silence at the table. And then I recall I said, "No. We don't want to do that."[24]

With Poindexter's and Shultz's approval, however, North arranged a meeting with Noriega at a hotel in London on September 22. North's contemporaneous notes of their discussion show that the two discussed developing a commando training program in Panama, with Israeli support, for Nicaraguan and Afghani rebels (Document 31). They also discussed sabotaging a number of major economic targets in Nicaragua, including the airport, the oil refinery, and the electric and telephone systems in Managua. In his memoirs, *Under Fire*, North writes that he told Noriega that "if he were willing to help train Contra units, provide logistical support, and even use his assets to destroy Sandinista targets in Managua, we would certainly compensate him for his efforts."[25] When he returned to Washington, North reported to Poindexter that Noriega would "try to take immediate actions against the Sandinistas" (Document 31).[26]

In the end, none of these operations took place. The Iran-Contra scandal broke eight weeks later; North was fired, Poindexter resigned, and William Casey fell fatally ill, removing all of General Noriega's patrons from positions of power within the Reagan administration. Without his protectors, Noriega quickly slipped to the status of a drug trafficking enemy of U.S. interests. In late December 1989, he was seized by U.S. invasion forces in Operation JUST CAUSE and removed to the U.S. to stand trial on narcotics violations. He is now serving a sentence of forty years in prison.

NOTES

1. *Iran-Contra Affair*, p. 4.

2. Duane "Dewey" Clarridge, Cable to CIA Director, "Discussions with [South Africa]," May 1, 1984. This document is reproduced in the National Security Archive's microfiche collection, *The Iran-Contra Affair: The Making of a Scandal, 1983–1988*.

3. This meeting is described in Bob Woodward's book, *Veil: The Secret Wars of the CIA, 1981–87* (New York: Simon & Schuster, 1987), pp. 352–55.

4. Reagan's videotaped deposition is quoted in the *Washington Post*, Feb. 23, 1990.

5. *Iran-Contra Affair*, p. 120.

6. McFarlane has said that he told Secretary Shultz and Weinberger that the Contras would be provided for, though not by what source. He also said that he "likely" informed Chief of Staff James Baker and possibly Attorney General Edwin Meese. See *The Iran-Contra Affair*, p. 39.

7. Subsequently, the CIA's own general counsel, Stanley Sporkin, interpreted Congress's prohibition against direct and indirect support of the Contras as precluding any Agency approach to third countries. See Stanley Sporkin to William Casey, "Nicaragua-Legal Options," January 7, 1985. This document is reproduced in the National Security Archive's microfiche collection, *The Iran-Contra Affair: The Making of a Scandal, 1983–1988*.

8. This opinion was offered by Smith's assistant Mary Lawton during a meeting between Casey and Smith on June 26, 1984. The attorney general also opposed quid pro quos, stating that "any nation agreeing to supply [funds] could not look to the United States to repay that commitment in the future." See the *Iran-Contra Affair*, p. 40.

9. See Congressional Research Service, "Honduras: U.S. Foreign Assistance Facts," November 25, 1986.

10. The quid pro quo stipulation, or statement of facts, was submitted during the trial of Oliver North in March 1989 in lieu of the declassification of approximately 107 documents. It begins, "You are instructed that the United States has admitted for the purposes of this trial the following facts to be true."

11. This document, which shows Bush to be cognizant of the illicit Contra resupply operation, has never been declassified. Bush was questioned about it by lawyers for the Office of the Independent Counsel on January 11, 1988, and his deposition was released on January 15, 1993. "I can't deny I received the [talking points]," Bush stated. See "Deposition to the Office of the Independent Counsel: Vice President George Bush," January 11, 1988, p. 106.

12. These documents, discovered by reporters in Portugal where the weapons had been purchased, provided the first major revelation of the front organization used by Richard Secord for Enterprise procurement of arms. When reporters traced the address on each certificate filed by Energy Resources International in Vienna, Virginia, they found that it was a company registered to Secord.

13. See Document 42, "Meeting with Costa Rican Security Minister Benjamin Piza," March 17, 1986.

14. Ibid.

15. See Alan Fiers, testimony at the Clair George trial, July 28, 1992, transcript, p. 1197.

16. John Poindexter, PROFS note to Robert McFarlane, June 12, 1986. This document is reproduced in the National Security Archive's microfiche collection, *The Iran-Contra Affair: The Making of a Scandal, 1983–1988*.

17. Ibid.

18. *Iran-Contra Affair*, p. 71

19. The identity of the individual into whose account the funds went has never been clearly established.

20. Elliott Abrams, Cable to the U.S. Embassy in Brunei, December 1, 1986. This document is reproduced in the National Security Archive's microfiche collection, *The Iran-Contra Affair: The Making of a Scandal, 1983–1988*.

21. See Abrams testimony as cited in the *Iran-Contra Affair*, pp. 148–49.

22. Francis McNeil, testimony in hearings before the Subcommittee on Terrorism, Narcotics, and International Communications of the Committee on Foreign Relations of the United States Senate, April 4–7, 1988, p. 40.

23. Ibid.

24. See Alan Fiers, testimony at the Clair George Trial, July 29, 1992, transcript, pp. 1236, 1237.

25. North, *Under Fire: An American Story* (New York: HarperCollins, 1991), p. 226. North also writes in his memoirs that he "admonished Noriega to stop his involvement in drug smuggling, cut his ties to the Castro government and allow a real democracy to emerge in his country." His notes of the meeting reflect none of these statements, nor any discussion of these issues.

26. See Document 23, para. 106.

DOCUMENT 18: William Casey, Memorandum for Robert McFarlane, "Supplemental Assistance to Nicaragua Program," March 27, 1984.

PAGE 1 OF 1

The Director of Central Intelligence

Washington, D.C. 20505

27 March 1984

MEMORANDUM FOR: The Honorable Robert C. McFarlane
                   Assistant to the President for
                   National Security Affairs

SUBJECT: Supplemental Assistance to Nicaragua Program

1. In view of possible difficulties in obtaining supplemental appropriations to carry out the Nicaraguan covert action project through the
remainder of this year, I am in full agreement that you should explore
funding alternatives with the Israelis and perhaps others. I believe your
thought of putting one of your staff in touch with the appropriate Israeli
official should promptly be pursued. You will recall that the Nicaraguan
project runs out of funds in mid-May. Although additional moneys are indeed
required to continue the project in the current fiscal year, equipment and
materiel made available from other sources might in part substitute for some
funding. We are therefore currently exploring two such alternatives. Please
note, however, that we are unlikely to receive materiel assistance from these
sources by mid-May.

2. The first of these alternatives is acquiring from the Israelis
additional ordnance captured by them from the PLO. A joint CIA/DoD survey
team will make a second trip to Israel in April to inspect captured PLO
ordnance. The first trip in 1983 resulted in the acquisition of some
$10 million worth [   ] machine guns
and ammunition. The purpose of the upcoming survey is to determine current
Israeli inventories and to negotiate thereafter to receive appropriate weapons
free or at a low cost. Of course the cost of packing and delivery will have
to be factored in.

3. The second alternative we are exploring is the procurement of
assistance from [another country.] [A senior military official of that
country] has indicated that he
may be able to make some equipment and training available to the [   ] through
the Hondurans.

4. Finally, after examining legalities, you might consider an
appropriate private US citizen to establish a foundation that would be the
recipient of nongovernmental funds which could be disbursed to DOE or the
FDN.

William Casey

CL BY 000800
RVW OADR

SECRET

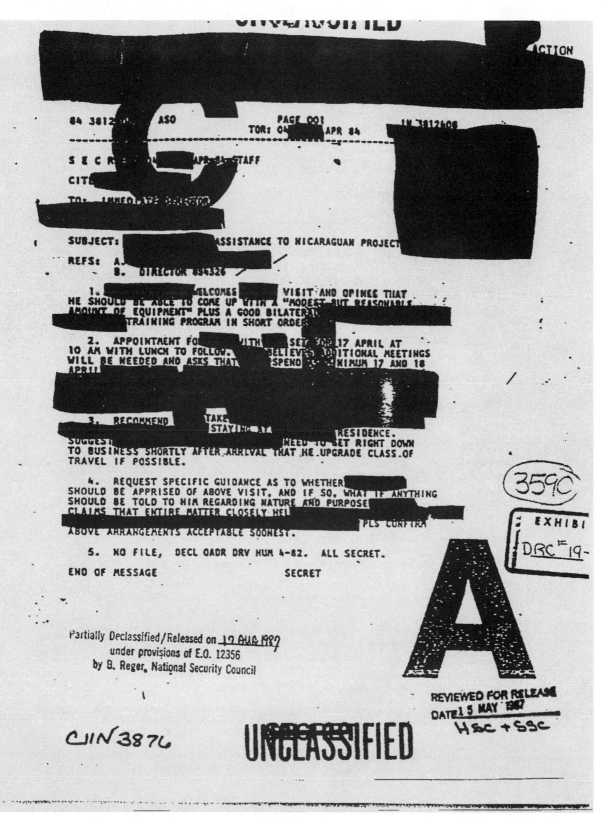

ACTION

84 3812   ASO   PAGE 001   IN 3812408
                    TOR: 04   APR 84

- -

S E C R   APR 84 STAFF
CIT

TO: IMMEDIATE DIRECTOR

SUBJECT: ASSISTANCE TO NICARAGUAN PROJECT

REFS: A.
       B. DIRECTOR 854326

1.   WELCOMES   VISIT AND OPINES THAT
HE SHOULD BE ABLE TO COME UP WITH A "MODEST BUT REASONABLE
AMOUNT OF EQUIPMENT" PLUS A GOOD BILATERAL
TRAINING PROGRAM IN SHORT ORDER

2. APPOINTMENT FO   WITH   SET FOR 17 APRIL AT
10 AM WITH LUNCH TO FOLLOW.   BELIEVES ADDITIONAL MEETINGS
WILL BE NEEDED AND ASKS THAT   SPEND MINIMUM 17 AND 18
APRIL

3. RECOMMEND   TAKE
              STAYING AT   RESIDENCE.
SUGGEST   NEED TO GET RIGHT DOWN
TO BUSINESS SHORTLY AFTER ARRIVAL THAT HE UPGRADE CLASS OF
TRAVEL IF POSSIBLE.

4. REQUEST SPECIFIC GUIDANCE AS TO WHETHER
SHOULD BE APPRISED OF ABOVE VISIT, AND IF SO, WHAT IF ANYTHING
SHOULD BE TOLD TO HIM REGARDING NATURE AND PURPOSE
CLAIMS THAT ENTIRE MATTER CLOSELY HEL
                                        PLS CONFIRM
ABOVE ARRANGEMENTS ACCEPTABLE SOONEST.

5. NO FILE, DECL OADR DRV HUM 4-82. ALL SECRET.

END OF MESSAGE   SECRET

3590

EXHIBI
DRC 19-

Partially Declassified/Released on 19 AUG 1987
     under provisions of E.O. 12356
   by B. Reger, National Security Council

REVIEWED FOR RELEASE
DATE 15 MAY 1987
HSC + SSC

CIN 3876

UNCLASSIFIED

25 Jun 84

□ Panama / Offshore Bank Accts *

□ Move w/in 24 Hrs.
   - Never let agency know of Amt, source, or even availability
   - No one in our Govt can be aware.
   - Your organization must not be fully aware.
   - Transfer w/in 24 hrs
   - Care in communications — Barnaby ⟶ Sterling
   - Accounting Arrangement
   - No more meeting here in complex.

AMX002337

□ Jonathan's Institute -
      German Representative *

□ Caribbean Conference - Columbia S.C.
      - Presidential Visit

□ New Person Magazine -

DOCUMENT 21: Minutes, National Security Planning Group Meeting on Central America, June 25, 1984.

PAGE 1 OF 14

SECRET

SYSTEM IV
NSC/ICS 400616

NATIONAL SECURITY COUNCIL
WASHINGTON, D.C. 20504

SECRET

NATIONAL SECURITY PLANNING GROUP MEETING
June 25, 1984; 2:00-3:00 P.M.; Situation Room

SUBJECT: Central America(U)

PARTICIPANTS:

The President
The Vice President

The Vice President's Office:
Admiral Daniel J. Murphy

State:
Secretary George P. Shultz
Mr. Michael Armacost
Mr. Langhorne A. Motley

Defense:
Secretary Caspar W. Weinberger
Dr. Fred Ikle

OMB:
Dr. Alton Keel

CIA:
Mr. William J. Casey
Mr. Duane Clarridge

USUN:
Ambassador Jeane J. Kirkpatrick

JCS:
General John W. Vessey, Jr.
Admiral Arthur S. Moreau

White House:
Mr. Edwin Meese, III
Mr. Robert C. McFarlane
Admiral John M. Poindexter

NSC:
Dr. Constantine C. Menges

Minutes

Mr. McFarlane: The purpose of this meeting is to focus on the political, economic, and military situation in Central America:

SECRET
DECLASSIFY ON: OADR

SECRET

A[illegible]

[69]

DOCUMENT 21: Minutes, National Security Planning Group Meeting on Central America, June 25, 1984.

PAGE 2 OF 14

SECRET

2

SECRET

to offer a status report, and to discuss next steps needed to keep our friends together while continuing to make progress toward our overall political goals. There is good news and bad new from Central America, as is always the case. The good news includes the fact that Congress will provide $62M in additional military assistance for El Salvador--$30M of which has already been spent. At the same time, we continue to need the additional $116M in aid for El Salvador which we have requested in the FY 84 supplemental, and we need to continue pressing for that.(S)

The bad news includes the fact that there seems to be no prospect that the Democratic leadership will provide for any vote on the Nicaraguan program. During the last vote in the House of Representatives, we lost by 64 votes, and that means that we need to change 32 votes in order to continue funding the anti-Sandinista program. On June 1, Secretary of State Shultz and Mr. Ortega of the Nicaraguan Directorate met in Nicaragua. The key question we need to consider now is what we believe about the prospects for further talks with Nicaragua; do we believe that Nicaragua wants to come to a reasonable agreement? Based on the answer to that question--how do we keep the friendly Central American governments together and focused on a multilateral, comprehensive, and verifiable treaty? What can we do to reinforce the confidence of the Central American and regional countries in the US in the light of questions about continuing congressional support for the anti-Sandinista program? For example, is there a need for any additional military resources for the collection of intelligence or military exercises to disrupt or deter the communist guerrilla offensive which we expect will be coming in El Salvador in late summer or autumn?(S)

What can we do to increase public understanding of the situation in Central America and of our Central American policy not only here in the United States but also in Western Europe and Latin America and among other western countries?(U)

We will begin with Secretary Shultz addressing the diplomatic situation followed by Bill Casey reporting on the freedom fighters in Nicaragua, and Cap Weinberger and General Vessey commenting on the military situation.(S)

Secretary Shultz: Mr. President, we would not have gotten the deployment of Pershing missiles in Europe if people had not seen that we had a credible, vigorous negotiation going on. Similarly, you have moved to get yourself in a position with the USSR where we have made credible proposals and they have walked out. This is useful because it shows who is at fault for the lack of progress.(S)

Similarly, in Central America, our basic thrust has to be to generate positive elements of the political and economic

SECRET

RET

DOCUMENT 21: Minutes, National Security Planning Group Meeting on Central America, June 25, 1984.

PAGE 3 OF 14

3

SECRET

situation, and to provide security help so that our efforts to disrupt the Nicaraguan export of subversion are as strong as we can get. An essential ingredient in that strategy is that we can say, if Nicaragua is halfway reasonable, there could be a regional negotiated solution--one which we support as much as we can. It is essential to have something like that going on or else our support on the Hill goes down. So it is not a question of making a prediction about the outcome of negotiations, rather it is important that we don't get sucked into something bad as it is essential to our strategy to key everything we do to support for the Contadora regional processes as I shall call it.(S)

So on our efforts to engage Nicaragua, there is one piece of very bad news. We don't have the votes in the House of Representatives to obtain additional funds for the anti-Sandinistas. The Congress will now be out for three weeks, and, therefore, anything credible going on the negotiating track can only help us. There is a sense of unease in Honduras about what is taking place for a great many reasons. The situation in El Salvador is a great big plus, assuming we get additional US military assistance; and taking what we got after the nun's case was solved, we have a good crack at the omnibus supplemental; and if not, we can use 21(d) again. Nicaragua is in trouble though not badly so, especially if the anti-Sandinista funds run out. There is some shift in attitude of the Mexicans. For example, Sepulveda went to El Salvador, and there is some Mexican impatience with Nicaragua about their posture on the negotiations. This morning I spent some time with the US Ambassador to Honduras. There are things we can do to ease the concern of the Government of Honduras. They are very concerned about the US bilateral conversations with Nicaragua, but these concerns can be assuaged. Their main problems are internal--economic, and the military change. President Suazo is upset. The most serious problem is what Honduras can do with the Nicaraguan freedom fighters who return. President Suazo is also bothered by the sharp decline in the US military presence.(S)

In the meantime, we have a negotiation going on both in the Contadora process and in this little effort with Nicaragua. Our approach is: (1) to consult closely with our friends; (2) keep our friends posted so they see we are trying to help. By and large, they see this as helpful, as contributing to the Contadora process, and us as supporting them.(S)

Today is the first US-Nicaragua meeting since June 1. We said we would not meet with the Mexicans present. Nicaragua said we have to keep the Mexicans informed. The United States said, O.K., we will inform all our friends in the Contadora countries. The first meeting was at 10:00 A.M. Mexican time or noon our time. Ambassador Shlaudeman was instructed, in the first session, only

SECRET

DOCUMENT 21: Minutes, National Security Planning Group Meeting on Central America, June 25, 1984.

PAGE 4 OF 14

SECRET

SECRET

to talk about modalities and procedure--not to table anything. But to continue these negotiations, we must have content. We think the best way for this to go on is to have a home-to-home approach (meaning alternating between the US and Nicaragua). We cannot say much about frequency. Nicaragua has lived up to its agreement about this negotiation. There was no press notification before this meeting.(S)

Our negotiating strategy is to table an Aide Memoire saying here is our approach, which we have written out and which is what we told the Core Four we would do so they would not be surprised. We have not given the Core Four the Aide Memoire, which changed recently, as a result of lengthly discussions which Fred Ikle and Admiral Moreau. We have to follow the Aide Memoire with an approach to negotiations which I discussed with almost everyone before June 1, except for Jeane Kirkpatrick, who was out of the country. Instead of a vertical approach to the negotiations taking some of the four topics on one at a time, we suggest taking some of each of the four in a horizontal approach. Ambassador Shlaudeman has a tableau of these four steps with blanks where any numbers are involved. From the standpoint of negotiations, we need to get the word to go ahead, or we need to decide on some other approach. Then, we will subvert the whole thing and it will have to abort. I have to get word to Shlaudeman.(S)

Mr. McFarlane: Now we'll receive an overview of the anti-Sandinista program from Bill Casey.(S)

Mr. Casey: The FDN in the North remains strong. ARDE in the South is on the run under pressure. In the North, we see continued support for the FDN. For example, 117 persons walked out of Nicaragua and Honduras to join up just last week, and in the central part of Nicaragua, 900 people are waiting for weapons in order to join up with the FDN. At the moment CIA has $250,000 left; about half of this is being kept in order to hold[ ]US personnel in Honduras and Costa Rica until the end of September, 1984 so that we can help immediately in the event that a continuing resolution makes more money available. Our warehouses have arms and ammunition which can hold till August. Many of the anti-Sandinistas will stay in place within the country in order to feed themselves, and they would need about $3 million to get by for the next three months. We estimate that about half will retreat into Honduras and Costa Rica in some disarray, and we have to provide humanitarian assistance to help these individuals and those they bring out with them when they come into Honduras and Costa Rica.(S)

SECRET

SECRET

DOCUMENT 21: Minutes, National Security Planning Group Meeting on Central America, June 25, 1984.

PAGE 5 OF 14

5

SECRET

The legal position is that CIA is authorized to cooperate and seek support from third countries. In fact, the finding encourages third country participation and support in this entire effort, and we are considering Salvador, Guatemala, Honduras and [a South American country] If we notify the oversight committees, we can provide direct assistance to help the FDN get the money they need from third countries. There will be some criticism, but senior members of the oversight committees recognize that we need to do this. We need a decision to authorize our permitting the FDN to obtain third country support. Meanwhile, the FDN, Misura and ARDE are acting on their own to try to get financial support from third party sources. There is a psychological gap coming up, and we should provide Honduras and Costa Rica with some type of humanitarian relief so they can assist the anti-Sandinistas. The anti-Sandinistas have something stashed away but they will be needing help.(S)

I shall offer a few words now on the Cuban-Nicaraguan military buildup. We see Cuban preparations for another military offensive in El Salvador, while at the same time the Cubans are building up their own military forces in Nicaragua. We now estimate, [

]

there are actually 7-8 thousand Cuban troops [   ] [   ] [   ] in Nicaragua. Castro is telling people such as the Nicaraguan leader Ortega that our willingness to negotiate is intended to permit the United States to buy time until we take military action against Nicaragua.(S)

Cuba and Nicaragua are moving more quickly to complete the construction of the new 3100 meter airport in Punta Huetea, [

] could support Nicaraguan and Soviet cargo jets. Two other runways at two other airports are nearing the point where they could take jet fighter planes and also Soviet cargo planes. Further, we see that 45 Nicaraguan pilots trained in the Soviet bloc have returned to Nicaragua.(S)

Secretary Weinberger: The Department of Defense objected strongly to the content of the State Department negotiating proposals with respect to the numerical restrictions which would have been placed on US forces in Central America. The content of that first step negotiating proposal and the Aide Memoire is not a negotiating position that the United States should be presenting. We don't want to appear in old paternalistic North American fashion to be taking over the negotiations. We don't think it seemly to dignify Nicaragua by having the home to home meeting approach in which US and Nicaraguan negotiating teams alternate meetings from one capital to the other. Rather, what we should be doing is helping the Central American countries

SECRET

DOCUMENT 21: Minutes, National Security Planning Group Meeting on Central America, June 25, 1984.

PAGE 6 OF 14

SECRET

6

SECRET

take the lead in the Contadora process in order to get a good Contadora treaty. This is the third choice between no negotiations and the separate bilateral negotiations proposed by State. We favor the third choice of helping the Contadora countries, who are our friends, obtain a comprehensive and verifiable Contadora treaty. (S)

On military issues we have reduced our troop levels, trying to keep to about 700. But let me emphasize, this is a self-imposed limit, and we can increase that number now. If we went along with the first step of the State negotiating proposal to Nicaragua as originally planned, we would have given up all of our flexibility. We would have given up the ability of the Defense Department to increase its physical presence in Central America above a certain low limit that was specified. On the anti-Sandinista issue, I think we need to take the offensive against the Democrats in Congress. We need to hold them accountable for not providing the resources needed to defend democracy. We need to hold the Democrats accountable. We should ask the Democrats whether they want a second Cuba. They see Ortega going after the visit of Secretary Shultz to Havana and then to Moscow. Do the American people want this? We should emphasize this to the Democrats in Congress rather than taking the bilateral negotiating tack where we would be giving Nicaragua economic aid, helping them economically. Whatever else, we need to assure that we can keep a US troop presence in Honduras of whatever size is needed to help defend our friends. (S)

General Vessey: I'm going to go over some of the material that Bill Casey covered in a general overview. In Nicaragua, we see an economy in bad shape. We see the government losing popular support, and we see the airfields being readied for jet fighters. (Admiral Moreau, would you please bring the photos to the President.) The Contras have achieved considerable success in Nicaragua in disrupting Nicaraguan military operations and preparations. In Honduras, the economy is in difficult condition, but the civilian government is functioning well, although there is a great concern in Honduras about the Contras returning into Honduras. The regional training center has been functioning well, and we have trained about 3,000 Salvadoran troops this year. (S)

Looking in overview at what we are doing to provide support, I want to mention the following things we are doing now: two spring deployment exercises are finished and no additional exercises are scheduled between now and December. The naval presence will remain continuous at about the current level. Congress approved the construction of two temporary military bases; and we are doing a number of things in the area of intelligence collection, such as the following: [   ]

SECRET

SECRET

DOCUMENT 21: Minutes, National Security Planning Group Meeting on Central America, June 25, 1984.

PAGE 7 OF 14

— 1

7

SECRET

The current policy we are following is producing results. We need to help Honduras. They have economic and military problems and they probably need an emergency package of assistance. In El Salvador we need the additional $116 million in military assistance and we need to continue reassuring our friends in Central America through firm commitments. Our policy is working now but if we don't watch it, we'll snatch defeat from the jaws of victory.(S)

President Reagan: It all hangs on support for the anti-Sandinistas. How can we get that support in the Congress? We have to be more active. With respect to your differences on negotiating, our participation is important from that standpoint, to get support from Congress.(S)

Secretary Weinberger: If the core four Central American countries agree on our negotiating proposal, that's fine; but they have not even seen the original Aide Memoire that was to be given to the Nicaraguans today, nor have they seen the new one that was just completed this past Saturday afternoon. Besides, we can't end up with a negotiation which gets us into a separate bilateral deal with Nicaragua.(S)

Secretary Shultz: I think Cap's characterization of what we are trying to do is inaccurate and unfair. As of late Saturday afternoon, the Aide Memoire was okay with the Joint Chiefs of Staff and the Office of the Secretary of Defense.(S)

Secretary Weinberger: None of our friends in Central America have seen the new Aide Memoire which, as you point out, was revised on Saturday and finished late Saturday afternoon.(S)

President Reagan: If we are just talking about negotiations with Nicaragua, that is so far-fetched to imagine that a communist government like that would make any reasonable deal with us, but if it is to get Congress to support the anti-Sandinistas, then that can be helpful.(S)

Amb. Kirkpatrick: Mr. President, at the United Nations we negotiate on everything with all the countries in the world, and I believe in diplomacy and in negotiations. But, it is very

SECRET

SECRET

AL_____

DOCUMENT 21: Minutes, National Security Planning Group Meeting on Central America, June 25, 1984.

PAGE 8 OF 14

SECRET

important to avoid getting into the situation of assuming
responsibility for something which cannot be achieved. As you
know, we often find it useful to support other countries which
are trying to achieve political settlements when we, ourselves,
remain in the background. For example, in Afghanistan, in the
Persian Gulf where we are helping those countries trying to
settle the war there without ourselves moving into the forefront.
and, in Lebanon, where we found that we were not able to bring
about a negotiated solution and where we are now working in the
background to facilitate a solution by working with our friends
and through our friends. In my judgment, the analogy of Central
America is much closer to the Persian Gulf situation than it is
to the issue of the deployment of Pershing missiles in Europe.
Let us remember that the Contadora process began in early 1983 as
an initiative of the Latin American countries, and that when you
sent me to the region in February 1983, they told me that they
wanted to try to negotiate a political settlement among
themselves. The reason the United States got out of the process
directly was because the other countries wanted us out. They
wanted to establish their own negotiating process, and they have
made some progress. Venezuela, Colombia and Panama have become
more responsible as a result of trying to achieve a negotiated
settlement. They are now much less critical of us than they
were. Now they realize how difficult Nicaragua is, and now they
have come to the hard part of the negotiation. (S)

As we now undertake separate bilateral negotiations with
Nicaragua, rather than continuing to support the 21 Contadora
objectives, these Latin American countries may well take this as
an excuse to stand aside. They will get off the hook, and they
will put us on the spot. If we give Mexico any special role,
it will further undermine the Contadora process; and in fact, the
Contadora process would then probably fall apart because any US
preference shown toward Mexico, which has been supporting the
Nicaraguans and communist guerrillas, will undermine pressure for
a genuine negotiated solution. We would then be under lots
of pressure from Congress, if the United States were negotiating
bilaterally with Nicaragua, to make additional concessions.
These bilateral negotiations with Nicaragua will scare our
friends in the region and they will neither help us in the region
nor in the US Congress. In fact, the coincidence of our
undertaking this bilateral negotiating effort at the same time as
the Congress fails to support funding for the Contras is enough
to totally unravel our entire position in the region. (S)

If we don't find the money to support the Contras, it will be
perceived in the region and the world as our having abandoned
them, and this will lead to an increase in refugees in the region
and it will permit Nicaragua to infiltrate thousands of
Nicaraguan trained forces into El Salvador. And this will be

SECRET

DOCUMENT 21: Minutes, National Security Planning Group Meeting on Central America, June 25, 1984.

PAGE 9 OF 14

9

SECRET

an infiltration we could not stop. The Democrats don't want to vote because they don't want to accept the responsibility for their votes against this program. I believe we need to make their responsibility in the Congress clear to the US public. We must require the Democrats to stand up and be counted. If you showed your commitment and the Administration's commitment with more activity, it would be a positive factor in Congress. If we can't get the money for the anti-Sandinistas, then we should make the maximum effort to find the money elsewhere; even if we couldn't find money elsewhere immediately, we should consider using the anti-Sandinistas elsewhere for the time being, for example, in El Salvador to help defend against the coming guerrilla offensive.(S)

Secretary Shultz: Several points: (1) everyone agrees with the Contra program but there is no way to get a vote this week. If we leave it attached to the bill, we will lose the money we need for El Salvador. (2) We have had a vote on the anti-Sandinista program and the Democrats voted it down. It already is on the record and the Democrats are on the record. (3) I would like to get money for the Contras also, but another lawyer, Jim Baker, said that if we go out and try to get money from third countries, it is an impeachable offense.(S)

Mr. Casey: I am entitled to complete the record. Jim Baker said that if we tried to get money from third countries without notifying the oversight committees, it could be a problem and he was informed that the finding does provide for the participation and cooperation of third countries. Once he learned that the funding does encourage cooperation from third countries, Jim Baker immediately dropped his view that this could be an "impeachable offense", and you heard him say that, George.(S)

Secretary Shultz: Jim Baker's argument is that the US Government may raise and spend funds only through an appropriation of the Congress.(S)

Secretary Weinberger: I am another lawyer who isn't practicing law, but Jim Baker should realize that the United States would not be spending the money for the anti-Sandinista program; it is merely helping the anti-Sandinistas obtain the money from other sources. Therefore, the United States is not, as a government, spending money obtained from other sources.(S)

Secretary Shultz: I think we need to get an opinion from the Attorney General on whether we can help the Contras obtain money from third sources. It would be the prudent thing to do. On the negotiations, all the other countries support this. The question is, can the US conduct the negotiations so that it is perceived as supporting the Contadora process? If people here are so

SECRET

DOCUMENT 21: Minutes, National Security Planning Group Meeting on Central America, June 25, 1984.

PAGE 10 OF 14

10

SECRET

reluctant, then we can go back and try to abort this whole thing. I am very conscious of all the negative points which have been raised. I give the chances of a positive negotiation outcome with Nicaragua as two-in-ten, but if it doesn't succeed, it needs to be clear where the responsibility is, and that we have tried to help our Contadora friends obtain a positive outcome.(S)

Mr. McFarlane: Mr. President, perhaps I might define the issues as they stand now: (1) a negotiating process in order to get a good Contadora treaty is worthwhile; (2) Marxist-Leninist regimes historically do not negotiate in order to make reasonable concessions, as we saw over many years in North Korea and Vietnam. For them negotiations are tactical exercises to split up their opponents and to obtain their goals. (3) How can there be a multilateral effort rather than one with Nicaragua in which the US is in the lead? On the military front, we had 2,200 troops and now we have about 700 there.(S)

Secretary Weinberger: We brought the numbers down to 700 on our own in order to deal with the critical perception that we were in some way militarizing the situation down there. We can always move to increase the exercises, and we can move exercises in and out so that we support our friends without creating the appearance that we are increasing the number of troops.(S)

President Reagan: Even the appearance of movement of US troops into Honduras for exercises, the movement of small units, would likely help the morale of Honduras.(S)

General Vessey: Yes, and US troop movements helped El Salvador very much during the communist offensive against the elections this year. The guerrillas in El Salvador had to turn and face the direction of US troop movements because they were afraid that our forces might have attacked or might have backed up a Honduran attack against them. So we played a positive role in blunting the Salvadoran guerrilla actions.(S)

President Reagan: I think there is merit to continuing the current negotiating session with the Nicaraguans, which has already begun because the press is eager to paint us as having failed again, and we don't want to let Nicaragua get off the hook. However, we should see these talks as only an adjunct to the Contadora. What we are doing with the Nicaraguans is that our special ambassador is there to help the Contadora process along.(S)

Secretary Shultz: Our Aide Memoire places heavy emphasis on the Contadora process. We have no intention of getting a separate bilateral agreement or treaty. If there is any glory to be obtained, then we are hoping to have the Contadora countries get

SECRET

DOCUMENT 21: Minutes, National Security Planning Group Meeting on Central America, June 25, 1984.

PAGE 11 OF 14

this if they can get a good treaty. I am of the same mind as you, Mr. President, that we must get the funds for the Contras.(S)

President Reagan: The Contra funding is like the MX spending. It is what will keep the pressure on Nicaragua, and the only way we are going to get a good Contadora treaty is if we keep the pressure on.(S)

Amb. Kirkpatrick: Mr. President I am no expert on legislative relations, but in the last week I have spoken with many congressmen, and, from what I have heard, they feel that the Administration has not attached the same priority to getting funds for the Contras as we have for the MX program and NATO issues. We have not made the impression that if the Congress cuts off the Contra funding this is of major importance to the Administration. On the question of who negotiates with whom we should remember that the Mexicans have always wanted the US and Cuba in the negotiation process. If we would go along this path of bilateral negotiations with Nicaragua as the Mexicans want, we will sooner (and I mean before November) face the issue of the Cubans being included. I can tell you Mr. President, that Venezuela, Colombia and other countries in the region do not want Cuba involved directly and they do not want the United States involved in direct talks. They have approached the United Nations Secretary General in order to invite him to help the Contadora process along. But if we start direct bilateral negotiations with Nicaragua, then Colombia, Panama, and maybe even Venezuela will blame us for their failure. The Foreign Ministers in those countries, in my judgment, lack experience, and they definitely do not want us involved right now.(S)

Secretary Shultz: Mexico, Panama, Colombia, and Venezuela say they are delighted with our initiative. Concerning our efforts in Congress to obtain the anti-Sandinista funding, Senator Kasten and others say we have really worked on this issue. In the House of Representatives General Vessey and I went up to the Congress and offered to brief the full House of Representatives on Central America--about 150 Members came. We had a good discussion. I have also spent an hour-and-a-quarter on with Tip O'Neill on this issue--this may be the first time he has listened to anyone from the Administration talk to him about this.(S)

Mr.Casey: It is essential that we tell the Congress what will happen if they fail to provide the funding for the anti-Sandinistas. At the same time, we can go ahead in trying to help obtain funding for the anti-Sandinistas from other sources; the finding does say explicitly "the United States should cooperate with other governments and seek support of other governments".

DOCUMENT 21: Minutes, National Security Planning Group Meeting on Central America, June 25, 1984.

PAGE 12 OF 14

12

SECRET

The limitation we have in the Congress is the cap on US spending; we want to get that lifted. We have met no resistance from senior members of the intelligence committees to the idea of getting help with third country funding. (S)

Mr. Meese: As another non-practicing lawyer I want to emphasize that it's important to tell the Department of Justice that we want them to find the proper and legal basis which will permit the United States to assist in obtaining third party resources for the anti-Sandinistas. You have to give lawyers guidance when asking them a question. (S)

Secretary Weinberger: I agree that we should be giving greater emphasis to obtaining funding for the anti-Sandinistas. We should make it a major issue with the Congress, Mr. President. I also agree that we should facilitate third country support for the anti-Sandinista groups. Third, I want to emphasize my concerns about the US trying to conduct separate bilateral negotiations with Nicaragua in order to get a regional settlement. We should be supporting the Contadora countries in order to help them get a good treaty; we should not be taking the lead in doing this ourselves. And, I believe we would have much better success with Congress if we are seen as helping others to obtain a good Contadora treaty and that there would be negative effects if Mexico and Cuba are seen as coming into the whole negotiating process. Honduras is not eager to have the United States undertake these separate bilateral negotiations with Nicaragua. In fact, they are very alarmed about this and that is why they are starting to pull away from security cooperation with us. (S)

Mr. McFarlane: With regard to diplomacy, Secretary Shultz should recommend specific measures so that the negotiating process will, in fact, be perceived as supportive of these friendly Central American countries in order to obtain a good Contadora treaty. The Secretary of Defense can propose such additional activities as may help our friends meet the coming guerrilla offensive in El Salvador and improve the morale of our friends in the region: Jim Baker and Ed Meese might examine the best way of getting additional money to expand our public affairs efforts and to have a greater impact in the Congress and to obtain an opinion from the Attorney General. (S)

Mr. Casey: We need the legal opinion which makes clear that the US has the authority to facilitate third country funding for the anti-Sandinistas; and at the same time, we need to find a way to provide humanitarian assistance to any anti-Sandinista and their families who might be going into Costa Rica or Honduras to escape the Nicaraguan military actions against them. We need this humanitarian assistance to be available right away. (S)

SECRET

DOCUMENT 21: Minutes, National Security Planning Group Meeting on Central America, June 25, 1984.

PAGE 13 OF 14

—

13

SECRET

President Reagan: There are persons now meeting with the Nicaraguans; and without aborting anything, we do want to keep getting a good Contadora treaty as the focus of our negotiating process. On the anti-Sandinistas, I am behind an all-out push in Congress. We must obtain the funds to help these freedom fighters. On the Contadora negotiations, there is a risk right now that our separate talks with the Nicaraguans might be misunderstood, and we need to make sure that does not happen and that our friends know they can rely on us.(S)

Secretary Weinberger: We don't need to shut off or abort any negotiations. As I have said, there is a third way between no negotiations and a separate US/Nicaragua bilateral deal. That third way, Mr. President, is that we continue actively to support our Central American friends in order to get a good Contadora treaty that provides a real solution.(S)

Secretary Shultz: Right now Shlaudeman is instructed to talk only about the US Aide Memoire, and we can keep to the Contadora process as the basis of our talks with the Nicaraguans, but then the US negotiating initiative with Nicaragua is no more.(S)

President Reagan: I don't think we should quit on it.(S)

Secretary Weinberger: We don't need to quit--just use the US talks with Nicaragua in order to support our Central American friends and get a good Contadora treaty.(S)

President Reagan: I just think, now, to back away from talks will also look like a defeat, but I can't imagine that Nicaragua would offer anything reasonable in a bilateral treaty.(S)

Mr. McFarlane: The four friendly Central American countries developed a treaty proposal in late April. Secretary Shultz and the four Contadora countries have the text of a draft Contadora treaty which needs a lot of work to become reasonable. One possible agenda item for the US-Nicaragua talks is that the US could talk about the draft Contadora treaty and use the late April document of the Central American four countries to provide criteria for how this treaty needs to be improved. Then, the US can go back to these four Central American countries with Nicaraguan comments on the draft treaty and suggestions for improving it.(S)

Mr. Meese: Is there any chance to pass the funds for the anti-Sandinistas before the Congress goes on recess?(S)

Mr. Casey: We estimate that of about 8,000 FDN fighters, 4,000 might decide to get out of Nicaragua once their ammunition

SECRET

DOCUMENT 21: Minutes, National Security Planning Group Meeting on Central America, June 25, 1984.

PAGE 14 OF 14

14

SECRET

runs out in August; and each of these may have about four family members with him. Therefore, these 16,000 possible new refugees need to have humanitarian assistance available by August.(S)

Vice President Bush: How can anyone object to the US encouraging third parties to provide help to the anti-Sandinistas under the finding? The only problem that might come up is if the United States were to promise to give these third parties something in return so that some people could interpret this as some kind of an exchange.(S)

Mr. Casey: Jim Baker changed his mind as soon as he saw the finding and saw the language.(S)

Mr. McFarlane: I propose that there be no authority for anyone to seek third party support for the anti-Sandinistas until we have the information we need, and I certainly hope none of this discussion will be made public in any way.(S)

President Reagan: If such a story gets out, we'll all be hanging by our thumbs in front of the White House until we find out who did it.(S)

The meeting adjourned at 3:50 P.M. (U)

SECRET

DOCUMENT 22: Robert McFarlane, Memorandum for the President, "Approach to the Hondurans Regarding the Nicaraguan Resistance," February 19, 1985.

PAGE 1 OF 2

SECRET

THE WHITE HOUSE

WASHINGTON

SYSTEM II
90166

February 19, 1985

SECRET   SENSITIVE

ACTION

MEMORANDUM FOR THE PRESIDENT

FROM: ROBERT C. MCFARLANE

SUBJECT: Approach to the Hondurans regarding the Nicaraguan
               Resistance

Issue

What approach would best serve our interests in convincing the
Hondurans to continue their support for the Nicaraguan resistance
forces?

Facts

In recent weeks the Hondurans have been expressing increasing
anxiety over the presence of large numbers of FDN freedom
fighters gathered on their southern border. While they have
continued their support to the FDN, there is increasing evidence
that the Sandinistas are making every effort to intimidate the
Hondurans into ceasing their assistance to the freedom fighters.
The Intelligence Community estimates that between 40-60,000
Sandinista soldiers are gathered in northern Nicaragua with the
mission of crippling the resistance in the next 60 days. We
expect that there will be increasing numbers of artillery and
rocket attacks into Honduran territory. Quick "in and out" raids
by Sandinista special troops, possibly using their new HIND
helicopters, are likely. These events could well cause the
Hondurans to reverse their recent decision to continue support
for the resistance.

Discussion

The CPPG convened on February 7, to consider the developments
described above. The group agreed that we should make an
approach to the Hondurans which emphasizes our commitment to
their sovereignty and provides incentives for them to persist in
aiding the freedom fighters. The group further agreed that the
incentives should include:

--   the release of some economic support (we are currently
       withholding disbursement of $174M until the Hondurans commit
       to certain economic reform);

SECRET   SECRET   ALU0101806 SENSITIVE
Declassify: OADR

                                              cc Vice President

DOCUMENT 22: Robert McFarlane, Memorandum for the President, "Approach to the Hondurans Regarding the Nicaraguan Resistance," February 19, 1985.

PAGE 2 OF 2

SECRET

SECRET   2   SENSITIVE

-- expedited security assistance deliveries (the Hondurans have experienced considerable delay in receiving a number of items which we could provide to them from our operating stocks); and

-- enhancements to existing CIA programs [

The group further agreed that our commitment to their sovereignty should be included in a letter from you to President Suazo and that your letter should also address the matter of the resistance in very general terms. This letter is attached at Tab A. With your approval this letter will be telegraphically transmitted to our Ambassador for delivery to President Suazo.

Following my recent trip to the region, one of my staff had very private meeting with a number of those who are very close to Suazo. This meeting apparently resulted in the Hondurans reversing their stated intention to withdraw support from the freedom fighters and force them back into Nicaragua--many of whom would have been without arms or equipment. The CPPG agreed that an emissary should again proceed to Honduras carrying the signed copy of your letter and, in a second meeting, very privately explain our criteria for the expedited economic support, security assistance deliveries, and enhanced CIA support.

Recommendations

OK   No

_RR_   _____   1. That you sign the letter at Tab A and approve its telegraphic transmission.

_RR_   _____   2. That you authorize us to proceed as outlined above.

                                              Prepared by:
                                              Oliver L. North
                                              Raymond F. Burghardt

Attachment
    Tab A - Letter to President Suazo

SECRET   SENSITIVE

SECRET

DOCUMENT 23: Court document, "U.S. Government Stipulation on Quid Pro Quos with Other Governments as Part of Contra Operations," April 6, 1989.

PAGE 1 OF 13

IN THE UNITED STATES DISTRICT COURT
FOR THE DISTRICT OF COLUMBIA

UNITED STATES OF AMERICA

v.

OLIVER L. NORTH,

Defendant.

You are instructed that the United States has admitted for purposes of this trial the following facts to be true:

1. In 1983, DCI Casey asked Secretary of Defense Weinberger if the Department of Defense ("DoD") could obtain infantry weapons that Israel had confiscated from PLO forces. Following discussions between Major General Meron of Israel and Retired Major General Richard Secord of the United States government ("USG"), Israel secretly provided several hundred tons of weapons to the DoD on a grant basis in May 1983. This was known as Operation TIPPED KETTLE. In February 1984, the CIA again asked DoD if it could obtain additional PLO weapons from Israel at little or no cost for CIA operational use. After negotiations between March 1984 and July 1984, Israel secretly provided the additional weapons to DoD in Operation TIPPED KETTLE II. The DoD then transferred the weapons to the CIA. Although CIA advised Congress that the weapons would be used for various purposes, in fact many of them were provided to the Nicaraguan Resistance as appropriated funds ran out. (The effort to funnel materiel to the Contras at a time when there were limits on the amount of funds the USG could spend to support the Resistance also found expression in 1984 in Project ELEPHANT HERD, under which the CIA was to stockpile weapons and materiel provided by DoD at the lowest possible cost under the Economy Act.) DoD assured Israel that, in exchange for the weapons, the U.S. Government would be as flexible as possible in its approach to Israeli military and economic needs, and that it would find a way to compensate Israel for its assistance within the restraints of the law and U.S. policy.

2. In late March 1984, National Security Advisor Robert C. McFarlane suggested that he pursue funding alternatives for the Resistance for use after Congressional funding ran out. McFarlane proposed putting a member of the NSC staff in touch with an Israeli official to pursue funding alternatives with the Israelis. In an "Eyes Only," Secret memo, DCI Casey agreed with McFarlane's proposal. Casey informed McFarlane that the CIA was exploring two alternative means of acquiring equipment and materiel from Israel for use by the Resistance after the funding ran out. First, the CIA was considering the acquisition from Israel of ordnance captured from the PLO. Casey advised McFarlane that in 1983 the USG had acquired some $10 million worth of weapons and ammunition in this manner from the Israelis (in Operation TIPPED KETTLE). Second, the CIA was considering procuring additional assistance from another country. Casey informed McFarlane that a foreign government official had indicated that he might be able to make some equipment and training available to the Resistance through Honduras.

3. In April 1984, McFarlane directed Howard Teicher of the NSC staff to discuss aid to the Resistance with David Kimche of the Israeli Government. McFarlane instructed Teicher to tell Kimche that the USG would not press Israel on assistance to the Resistance; that aid to the Resistance was an important matter to the USG; that the USG faced a temporary shortfall in supporting the Resistance; that the USG understood the risks involved for Israel; that Israeli aid to the Resistance should be arranged through Honduras; that the USG would furnish a point of contact; and that, although McFarlane was disappointed with Israel's reluctance to assist directly, the USG would not raise the matter further.

4. In early 1984, in a discussion with the Ambassador from Saudi Arabia, McFarlane encouraged that country to support the Resistance. A short time later, the Ambassador informed McFarlane that his government would contribute $1 million per month. The money became available during the early summer of 1984.

5. On June 25, 1984, the National Security Planning Group ("NSPG")—including President Reagan, Vice President Bush, Secretary of State Shultz, Secretary of Defense Weinberger, DCI Casey, U.N. Ambassador Kirkpatrick, CJCS Vessey, Admiral Moreau, Counselor to the President Meese, McFarlane and Admiral Poindexter (among others)—discussed third country funding for the Resistance. Director Casey noted that the CIA considered El Salvador, Guatemala, Honduras and one South American country as possible sources of

DOCUMENT 23: Court document, "U.S. Government Stipulation on Quid Pro Quos with Other Governments as Part of Contra Operations," April 6, 1989.

PAGE 2 OF 13

support for the Resistance. He suggested that the USG provide Honduras and Costa Rica with increased economic assistance as an incentive for them to assist the Resistance.

6. In Late summer and early fall 1984, CIA stations reported to CIA Headquarters concerning apparent offers by the Peoples Republic of China ("PRC") to provide assistance to the Resistance.

7. At a meeting in mid-July 1984 between DCI Casey, Deputy DCI John McMahon, and Deputy Secretary of State Dam, Casey indicated that those present ought to get moving on non-USG funding for the Resistance since Attorney General Smith had recently concluded that raising the funds in this manner would not be an impeachable offense, as had been suggested at the NSPG meeting on June 25, 1984.

8. In August 1984, the U.S. government learned of a meeting between Adolfo Calero and a senior military official of Taiwan to solicit support for the Resistance. The Taiwan official had emphasized the need for secrecy. Taiwan initially decided to reject the Resistance because of patently adverse diplomatic consequences. The Taiwan official did not inform Calero of this decision, but he recommended to his government that aid be provided to the Resistance through third parties so that it could not be traced to Taiwan. In July 1984, Calero had renewed his request to Taiwan, which again rejected his proposal for diplomatic reasons. U.S. Ambassadors in Honduras, Panama, Nicaragua, and Costa Rica, the Southern Command of the Armed Forces of the United States (SouthCom), CIA, the Defense Intelligence Agency ("DIA"), DoS, and the National Security Advisor were advised of this information.

9. In December 1984, LtCol North advised McFarlane of efforts to obtain aid for the Resistance from third countries, including Taiwan, the PRC and South Korea. Admiral Poindexter acknowledged receiving the information that LtCol North provided.

10. With McFarlane's approval, LtCol North had met with a senior military official of the PRC in a meeting arranged with the assistance of Dr. Gaston Sigur of the NSC. The meeting was precipitated by reports that the PRC had decided not to proceed with a Canadian-originated sale of anti-aircraft missiles to the Resistance using end-user certificates provided by Guatemala. LtCol North told the military official that Calero would agree to a diplomatic concession to the PRC if the Resistance pre-

vailed in Nicaragua. LtCol North advised McFarlane that the meetings with the PRC official were likely to be reported in FBI channels. The FBI had been requested to make no distribution of this information except to McFarlane. LtCol North asked McFarlane to inform FBI Director William Webster that McFarlane had endorsed the contact with the Asian official and further to apprise Webster that dissemination of intelligence regarding the meeting could jeopardize the operation.

11. General John Vessey, Chairman of the Joint Chiefs of Staff ("CJCS"), followed up on LtCol North's approach to the PRC military officer. The PRC agreed to provide anti-aircraft missiles to the Resistance, and Retired General Richard Secord consummated the transaction and arranged shipment through Guatemala. The CIA reported the details of this transaction to McFarlane.

12. LtCol North also advised McFarlane that General Singlaub had met with the South Korean Ambassador and a representative of Taiwan to urge them privately to support the Resistance.

13. In late December 1984, LtCol North advised McFarlane that a former European officer had reported that anti-aircraft missiles might be available in a South American country for use by the Resistance in dealing with the Soviet-supplied HIND attack helicopters. Calero had discovered that, while the South American country had the missiles, they would need a European country's permission for their transfer since the missiles initially had been obtained from the European country. North furnished McFarlane with a memorandum to the President recommending that the President raise the anti-aircraft missile issue with a senior European government official. The memorandum recommended that the President offer a quiet expression of USG thanks, since the European official might not be fully aware of the constraints Congress had imposed upon CIA and DoD with respect to the Resistance. In late January 1985, LtCol North recommended to McFarlane that NSC official Lyle Cox hand-carry a secure, "Eyes Only" letter to another senior European government official regarding the anti-aircraft missile matter.

14. In early January 1985, CIA Headquarters requested that U.S. officials attempt to determine why the South American country had cancelled the sale or donation of anti-aircraft missiles to the Resistance.

15. In February 1985, General Singlaub met with

DOCUMENT 23: Court document, "U.S. Government Stipulation on Quid Pro Quos with Other Governments as Part of Contra Operations," April 6, 1989.

PAGE 3 OF 13

South Korean officials and discussed the possible provision of a substantial sum of money for weapons to the Resistance from South Korea. General Singlaub also discussed this possible military aid with a senior CIA official. General Singlaub also discussed with a senior South Korean official the interdiction of a shipload of arms to the Sandinistas. In that regard, General Singlaub told the senior South Korean official that the CIA and General Stilwell of DoD knew he was meeting with the senior South Korean official.

16. In early 1985, President Reagan urged the Head of State of Saudi Arabia to continue its support for the Resistance. Saudi Arabia subsequently made a contribution of more than $25 million.

17. In early February 1985, LtCol North advised McFarlane that, as a consequence of Singlaub's recent trip, both the Taiwanese and the South Koreans had indicated to U.S. officials that they would help the Resistance. Clair George, CIA Deputy Director of Operations ("DDO"), withheld dissemination of the offers and contacted LtCol North privately to ensure that they would not become common knowledge. LtCol North sought and received McFarlane's permission to have Singlaub approach officials of the Embassies of Taiwan and South Korea to urge them to proceed with their offers. Singlaub would then put Calero in direct contact with the officials.

18. In mid-March 1985, at a meeting with DCI Casey and Deputy DCI John McMahon, Secretary of Defense Weinberger stated that he had heard that the Ambassador of Saudi Arabia had earmarked $25 million for the Contras in $5 million increments.

19. At a meeting in late March 1985 with McFarlane and Deputy DCI McMahon, DCI Casey expressed his concern that the Administration would request authorization from Congress only for non-lethal aid to the Resistance and rely on third countries to supply weapons or funds for weapons. McFarlane stated that he would take the issue to President Reagan for his decision.

20. In mid-April 1985, LtCol North advised McFarlane that the Resistance had received a total of $24.5 million since appropriated funds had run out, of which more than $17 million had gone for arms, munitions, combat operations, and combat support activities. (This money consisted primarily of the Saudi contribution of which McFarlane was aware.) Future operations included increasing the Resistance force, launching a special oper-

ations attack against Sandino Airport to destroy Soviet-supplied HIND attack helicopters, launching an operation against a Nicaraguan mines complex and opening a Southern Front along the Costa Rica-Nicaragua border. LtCol North informed McFarlane that the funds remaining were insufficient to support these operations and recommended that efforts be made to seek an additional $15 million to $20 million from current donors.

21. In early May 1985, LtCol North provided McFarlane and CJCS General Vessey with an analysis of Resistance expenditures and outlays for, among other things, weapons and other ordnance, and a summary of Resistance military operations since October 1984. LtCol North recommended that the current donors to the Resistance be approached to provide the remainder of their $25 million pledge and an additional $15 million to $20 million between May 1 and June 1, 1985. McFarlane approved LtCol North's recommendation that the current donors be approached to provide the remainder of their pledge, but McFarlane turned down the recommendation that the donors be asked to provide an additional $15 million to $20 million.

22. In early August 1985, the White House and various CIA stations learned of reports that, during the visit of David Kimche to the U.S. in May 1985, he had met with Michael Armacost, the U.S. Undersecretary for Political Affairs, and had negotiated the continuation of military aid from Israel to Central America.

23. In August 1985, Gaston Sigur approached a senior intelligence officer of South Korea to meet with LtCol North to discuss Central America and the Resistance.

24. In October 1985, the President of an Asian country was approached and advised that other concerned private and foreign sources had been supporting the Resistance with munitions and combat supplies, and that their identities had not been revealed. The Resistance had a specific need for communications equipment, and the Asian country produced some of the best in the world.

25. In November 1985, LtCol North asked Vince Cannistraro of the NSC to contact a senior South American government official to encourage the sale by that country of planes and spare parts to A.C.E., a company that was providing private support to the Resistance.

26. In early December 1985, the U.S. became aware that a South American country had offered to sell combat materiel/equipment to the Resistance. A U.S. Chief of

DOCUMENT 23: Court document, "U.S. Government Stipulation on Quid Pro Quos with Other Governments as Part of Contra Operations," April 6, 1989.

PAGE 4 OF 13

Mission requested that the developments be brought to the attention of Elliott Abrams, Assistant Secretary of State for Latin American Affairs. Abrams discussed those offers with LtCol North and other USG officials.

27. In early December 1985, a CIA officer requested that Headquarters provide the number of anti-aircraft missiles in the Resistance inventory. The CIA officer no longer had their original reporting, but recalled that the Resistance had purchased five launchers and ten missiles from the PRC.

28. In early March 1986, Retired General Secord notified LtCol North that the purchase of anti-aircraft missiles from a South American country had stalled because it wanted approval from a European country before any transfer. The arms dealer attempting to arrange the transfer had asked that a U.S. government official contact the South American government to emphasize the interest in a quick transfer of the missiles.

29. In early May 1986, LtCol North notified Admiral Poindexter that a representative of Israeli Defense Minister Rabin had offered on behalf of Israel to furnish Spanish-speaking military trainers and advisors to the Resistance. Advisors would be placed in Honduras in connection with an Israeli plan to sell the Kfir fighter to the Hondurans. Other advisors would be placed on the Southern Front. LtCol North advised Admiral Poindexter that Defense Minister Rabin wanted to meet with him privately in New York to discuss the details, and that Assistant Secretary of State Elliott Abrams liked the idea.

30. In early May 1986, McFarlane noted that the U.S. might obtain assistance for the Resistance from certain Asian countries, although he had lost confidence in the discretion of those countries. McFarlane told LtCol North that he would try to find a better alternative.

31. In May 1986, U.S. intelligence reports reflected that a South American country was aware that the Reagan administration had asked Israel, Taiwan, South Korea and an organization headed by a U.S. resident to contribute to the purchase of weapons for the Resistance. The South American country was aware that the PRC had already given anti-aircraft missiles, and that Honduras hoped that Israel would give extensive aid, including military assistance.

32. In mid-May 1986, Donald Fortier, the Director of Political-Military Affairs at the NSC, was advised that the situation for the Resistance was bleak. President Reagan needed to pursue means of obtaining additional aid promptly, including talking personally to heads of state to tell them that he was dispatching a special emissary with his personal request for their assistance to the Resistance.

33. In mid-May 1986, a senior European official notified Admiral Poindexter that the European country would not approve the transfer of anti-aircraft missiles and launchers from a South American country to El Salvador, for use by the Resistance. The European official was concerned about the risk that the intended final destination of the missiles would leak. A senior Salvadoran military official had furnished a false end-user certificate for the missiles, but the certificate was not used in light of the European response.

34. At the NSPG meeting of May 16, 1986 (attended by President Reagan, Vice President Bush, Secretary of State Shultz, Secretary of the Treasury Baker, DCI Casey, Admiral Poindexter, and LtCol North, among others), Secretary Shultz mentioned an Asian country and DCI Casey mentioned Israel, Taiwan, Saudi Arabia and South Korea as possible sources of additional support for the Resistance.

35. At the President's National Security Briefing on May 19, 1986, Admiral Poindexter discussed Israel and South Korea as possible sources of additional support for the Resistance.

36. In early June 1986, Admiral Poindexter and President Reagan discussed funding for the Resistance. Admiral Poindexter mentioned aid from third countries and the possibility of a letter from a private organization.

37. In early June 1986, LtCol North advised Admiral Poindexter to talk with Assistant Secretary of State Abrams about arranging the transfer of funds from third countries to the Resistance. North said he knew of the accounts and the means by which the funds could be transferred. North also suggested that the U.S. government renew its earlier request to a senior European official for anti-aircraft missiles. North recommended that Poindexter and McFarlane discuss how much Shultz knew about previous support for the Resistance by Taiwan and Saudi Arabia. Poindexter answered that, to his knowledge, "Shultz knows nothing about prior financing. I think it should stay that way."

38. In mid-June 1986, Admiral Poindexter advised LtCol North that he was attempting to get the State Department to seek funding for the Resistance from third countries so that North and the NSC could disengage from the effort. Assistant Secretary Abrams had

DOCUMENT 23: Court document, "U.S. Government Stipulation on Quid Pro Quos with Other Governments as Part of Contra Operations," April 6, 1989.

PAGE 5 OF 13

suggested Brunei as a potential source of funds, and Poindexter had responded that the transfer should be accomplished by having Brunei's Washington Embassy receive a person designated by Poindexter and North.

39. In the summer and fall of 1986, the DoS—particularly Abrams, Sigur, U.S. Ambassador to Brunei King, and Secretary Shultz—had discussions with a senior Brunei official in an effort to obtain a contribution from the Sultan to the Resistance. Brunei subsequently agreed to contribute $10 million to the Resistance.

40. In mid-September 1986, LtCol North reported to Admiral Poindexter after another meeting with Defense Minister Rabin of Israel. Defense Minister Rabin was pleased with the reaction of Poindexter and Secretary Shultz to Rabin's plans to introduce Kfir fighters into Honduras and in the process to provide advisors to the Resistance. Defense Minister Rabin also offered North a recently seized shipment of PLO arms for use by the Resistance. Rabin agreed that the ship Erria be sent to Haifa to pick up the weapons. Admiral Poindexter approved the plan to pick up the weapons, noting that the transaction would appear to be a private deal between Retired General Secord and the Israelis.

41. In mid-September 1986, Amiram Nir, an advisor to Israel's Prime Minister, indicated that Prime Minister Peres would raise several topics in his upcoming private discussion with President Reagan, including Israel's offer to provide captured PLO arms to the Resistance. LtCol North suggested that Admiral Poindexter tell President Reagan that the arms would be picked up by a foreign flag vessel and delivered to the Resistance. If Prime Minister Peres raised the issue, President Reagan should thank him, since the Israelis held considerable stores of weapons compatible with ordnance used by the Resistance.

CENTRAL AMERICAN COUNTRIES

42. In early July 1984, a CIA officer reported to CIA headquarters that Honduras was taking the position that it would continue to support the Resistance following the U.S. funding cut-off, but Resistance operations would have to be covert to avoid political embarrassment to Honduras.

43. In mid-August 1984, Poindexter discussed with President Reagan and others a proposal ascribed to Secretary Shultz that would permit Congress to "wink" at lethal support for the Resistance. Under Shultz's plan,

the U.S. government would supply non-lethal aid directly to the Resistance. The U.S. government would provide military aid to El Salvador, which in turn would provide lethal aid to the Resistance.

44. In mid-November 1984, a CIA officer reported to CIA Headquarters concerning support for the Resistance by Guatemala and Honduras. Guatemala had provided aircraft and had agreed to facilitate Resistance shipments of munitions and other materiel. Honduras had permitted the Resistance to operate from within its borders, had repaired Resistance aircraft at cost, had allowed government aircraft to bring in aircraft parts, had permitted the Resistance to borrow ammunition when Resistance stocks were too low, and had provided the Resistance with false end-user certificates.

45. In mid-November 1984, DCI Casey requested that LtCol North be provided with a CIA analysis of recent performance and near-term prospects for the Resistance. (Vice President Bush and McFarlane also received copies of the analysis.) According to the analysis, the Resistance had spent approximately $5 million since the funding cutoff. Calero had raised between $2 million and $2.5 million from undisclosed private donors. A Southern Front Resistance leader had received $100,000 from Panamanian Defense Forces Chief Noriega in July 1984 and $20,000 from a European official, who had previously given $40,000. In addition, the Resistance had received increased aid from some Central American governments. Honduras had facilitated the purchase of ammunition and hand grenades and had donated 10,000 pounds of equipment and two C-47 aircraft. El Salvadoran military officials continued to allow the use of a military airbase in support of ARDE air operations but had not yet supplied rifles previously promised. One European leader had reacted favorably to a request from a Southern Front Resistance leader for arms and funding but had not yet followed through, while Taiwan had refused a request for aid from FDN officials. The analysis reported several specific Resistance operations inside Nicaragua. These operations and other Resistance military activities were hindered by logistics problems, particularly difficulties in airlifting supplies into Nicaragua.

46. In December 1984, a CIA assessment concluded that the future of the FDN without U.S. government support depended on the FDN's ability to obtain continued private funding and continued support from Hon-

DOCUMENT 23: Court document, "U.S. Government Stipulation on Quid Pro Quos with Other Governments as Part of Contra Operations," April 6, 1989.

PAGE 6 OF 13

duras. The leader of that government had threatened to cease support for the FDN unless it received a signal of U.S. government support. LtCol North urged McFarlane to visit Central America and deliver a signal of U.S. resolve.

47. In mid-January 1985, in anticipation of McFarlane's trip to Central America, LtCol North furnished an analysis of U.S. government policy options in Central America. The options included seeking a negotiated solution toward Nicaragua, restoring U.S. government support to the Resistance, or using U.S. military force to overthrow the Sandinista regime. North recommended the second option—restoration of U.S. government support to the Resistance—and discussed in detail variations on the provision of that support. The possibilities included legislation authorizing only third country support; restoration of the original CIA-managed program; U.S. non-lethal and third country lethal support; seeking congressional clarification on third country support; overt assistance to a new state established by the Resistance; and funding a collective security organization that would, in turn, provide aid to the Resistance. North recommended that the Administration discuss these options with congressional and Central American leaders before selecting one. North noted that support for military operations by the Resistance should be accompanied by support for non-military activities. In addition, an effort should be made to identify leaders within the FSLN who did not support the Sandinista Revolution. The Department of State ("DoS"), the Office of the Secretary of Defense ("OSD"), CIA, Joint Chiefs of Staff ("JCS"), and NSC felt that the third option—non-lethal U.S. support with third country lethal assistance—should be pursued.

48. In mid-January 1985, LtCol North arranged a visit to Central America for McFarlane with stops in Panama, Costa Rica, El Salvador, Honduras, and Guatemala. One purpose of the trip was for McFarlane to discuss with his counterparts in those countries their continued willingness to support the Resistance. At McFarlane's request, North arranged a secret meeting between McFarlane and Calero during the visit to Honduras. North accompanied McFarlane on the trip, together with (among others) Vice Admiral Moreau and General Gorman, Commander-in-Chief of U.S. Southern Command.

49. In the course of McFarlane's trip, Alan Fiers (CIA's C/CATF) briefed him privately on political action programs in support of U.S. government objectives.

McFarlane was advised before his departure that Guatemala would continue to support the Resistance, provided that it received a quid pro quo from the United States in the form of foreign assistance funds or credits, diplomatic support or other forms of assistance. In El Salvador, McFarlane urged President Duarte to continue his support for the Resistance, including facilitating Resistance resupply operations, and McFarlane told Duarte that such regional support was essential to resumption of U.S. government support.

50. On February 2, 1985, the CIA reported to NSA, DoS, DIA, FBI, White House, NSC staff, and U.S. SOUTHCOM (among others) that Honduran military officers were assisting the Resistance in transporting materiel (including ammunition) bought on the international arms market through Guatemala to Resistance camps in Honduras. The report noted that the Resistance was having difficulty maintaining their logistical network.

51. At a February 7, 1985 meeting of the Crisis Pre-Planning Group attended by Admiral Poindexter, Don Fortier (NSC), Ray Burghardt (NSC), Michael Armacost (DoS), Fred Ikle (DoD), Nestor Sanchez (DoD), Clair George (CIA), Alan Fiers (CIA), VADM Arthur Moreau (JCS) and LtCol North, among others, the CPPG principals agreed that a Presidential letter should be sent to President Suazo of Honduras and to provide several enticements to Honduras in exchange for its continued support of the Nicaraguan Resistance. These enticements included expedited delivery of military supplies ordered by Honduras, a phased release of withheld economic assistance (ESF) funds, and other support. The CPPG was in agreement that transmission of the letter should be closely followed by the visit of an emissary who would verbally brief the "conditions" attached to the expedited military deliveries, economic assistance, and other support. The CPPG did not wish to include this detail of the *quid pro quo* arrangement in written correspondence.

52. On February 12, 1985, North proposed that McFarlane send a memo to Shultz, Weinberger, Casey and Vessey informing them of the recommendation of the CPPG that expedited military deliveries, economic funding, and other support should be offered as an incentive to Honduras for its continued support to the Nicaraguan Resistance. The memo stated that this part of the message should not be contained in a written doc-

DOCUMENT 23: Court document, "U.S. Government Stipulation on Quid Pro Quos with Other Governments as Part of Contra Operations," April 6, 1989.

PAGE 7 OF 13

ument but should be delivered verbally by a discreet emissary. The McFarlane memo sought approval to send a Presidential letter to Suazo through an emissary. If Shultz, Weinberger, Casey, and Vessey agreed, then President Reagan's letter would be signed and delivered through the U.S. Ambassador to Suazo, and a U.S. government emissary would advise Honduran officials of U.S. government expectations concerning support for the Resistance.

53. On February 19, 1985, McFarlane sent a memorandum to President Reagan informing him of the recommendation of the CPPG to provide incentives to Honduras so that it would maintain its aid to the Resistance. The memorandum described each of the agreed-upon incentives. It further recommended a Presidential letter to the leader of Honduras, to be delivered by an emissary who would very privately explain U.S. criteria for the expedited economic support, security assistance deliveries, and other support. President Reagan personally authorized the entire plan.

54. Later in February 1985, President Reagan sent the agreed-upon message to Suazo via the U.S. Ambassador. The letter urged that Honduras do all in its power to support "those who struggle for freedom and democracy." Shortly thereafter, McFarlane sent a memorandum to Shultz, Weinberger, Casey, and Vessey informing them that President Reagan's letter had been sent and proposing steps to be taken to implement the President's intent. The memorandum requested DoD to commence expedited delivery of military items, as previously planned and personally authorized by President Reagan, and it requested necessary documentation to enhance other support programs in Honduras.

55. In early March 1985, Vice Admiral Moreau was advised that military leaders of Honduras had offered assurances that the Resistance could continue to deliver supplies through Honduras, and that Honduras would continue to supply end-user certificates for arms purchases by the Resistance. Major munitions deliveries were scheduled for mid-to-late March. LtCol North recommended that Honduran military officials be told that the United States Government would soon discuss enhancing other support programs. Vice Admiral Moreau was informed that senior Salvadoran military officials had provided maintenance and storage for the Resistance at a military airfield. President Duarte was concerned that further support for the Resistance would be detected by congressional investigators and would result in a cut-off of U.S. security assistance for El Salvador.

56. In early March 1985, Vice President Bush sought McFarlane's judgment as to whether he (Vice President Bush) should encourage a private group to donate a plane load of medical supplies that would arrive in Honduras coincident with the Vice President's meetings with President Suazo. Bush strongly favored such a flight, noting that the group was supportive of the Resistance. At LtCol North's recommendation, McFarlane advised Bush that the flight was a good idea.

57. In early March 1985, Secretary Weinberger informed McFarlane that the DoD had commenced expedited procurement and delivery of military and other items to Honduras.

58. When Vice President Bush met with President Suazo, Bush told Suazo that President Reagan had directed expedited delivery of U.S. military items to Honduras. Vice President Bush also informed Suazo that President Reagan had directed that currently withheld economic assistance for Honduras should be released; that the United States would provide from its own military stocks critical security assistance items that had been ordered by Honduran armed forces; and that several security programs underway for Honduran security forces would be enhanced.

59. In March 1985, LtCol North proposed that McFarlane send a memorandum to Secretary Shultz, Secretary Weinberger, DCI Casey, and CJCS Vessey recommending that the U.S. government furnish additional assistance to Guatemala through the State Department. North advised McFarlane that the assistance was a means of compensating Guatemala for the assistance it was providing to the Resistance. Guatemala had provided end-user certificates for the purchase of nearly $8 million of munitions to be delivered to the Resistance. The ammunition and weapons identified in the certificates would be delivered in several shipments to be receipted by Guatemalan military officers and turned over to Resistance representatives at the point of arrival. North advised McFarlane that Guatemala had presented a list of military equipment that it needed. North noted that once U.S. government approval had been obtained for some of what Guatemala wanted, Guatemalan officials could be made to understand that the additional U.S. government assistance was the result of Guatemala's assistance to the Resistance.

DOCUMENT 23: Court document, "U.S. Government Stipulation on Quid Pro Quos with Other Governments as Part of Contra Operations," April 6, 1989.

PAGE 8 OF 13

60. In late March 1985, the CIA reported to NSA, DoS, DIA, White House, NSC staff, USSOUTHCOM, and U.S. Ambassadors in Honduras, Panama, Nicaragua and Costa Rica that a ship was scheduled to arrive in Honduras in mid-April 1985, carrying munitions worth almost $2 million that the Resistance had purchased on the international arms market. The CIA reported that a Honduran military official had agreed to arrange transportation of the weapons from the port of arrival to Resistance units.

61. In late March 1985, North advised McFarlane that the initial deliveries of U.S. arms from DoD to Honduras had gone well. The Honduran government had expressed its gratitude through those who were supporting the Resistance. North proposed that McFarlane ask Secretary of Defense Weinberger to convey President Reagan's and McFarlane's thanks to DoD personnel who had effected the expedited procurement for the Honduran government, including Assistant Secretary of Defense Richard Armitage and General Gast.

62. On April 25, 1985, McFarlane informed President Reagan that military support for the Resistance from Honduras was in jeopardy as a consequence of the House vote refusing to provide new funds for the Resistance. The Honduran military had stopped a shipment of ammunition from an Asian country en route to the Resistance after it had arrived in Honduras. McFarlane recommended that President Reagan call President Suazo to make clear that the Executive Branch was determined to maintain pressure on the Sandinistas. During the call between the two leaders, Suazo urged that the U.S. government continue to oppose Communism. President Reagan's personal notes of his telephone call reflect that President Suazo told President Reagan that the Honduran military commander would be ordered to deliver the ammunition to the Resistance. President Reagan pledged his continued support for the Resistance; President Suazo raised the subject of U.S. government aid for his country and the fact that he hoped Secretary Shultz and Secretary Weinberger would meet with a high-level group of Honduran officials in Washington.

63. On April 26, U.S. Ambassador Negroponte notified McFarlane that President Suazo had called Negroponte immediately after Suazo's telephone conversation with President Reagan to say that Suazo was satisfied with the U.S. government commitment to continue support for the Resistance. President Suazo told Ambassador Negroponte that he (Suazo) had assured President Reagan of his full support and had promised that he (Suazo) would check into the interdicted munitions shipment, which he did immediately after the conversation with President Reagan by calling a senior Honduran military official. Suazo told Negroponte that Honduras supported the Resistance fully, and Suazo asked that Negroponte convey his strongest assurances to President Reagan that Honduras would not let down the Resistance. Ambassador Negroponte recommended under the circumstances that the Honduran delegation be received in Washington by Vice President Bush in President Reagan's absence.

64. In May 1985, President Reagan personally approved increased U.S. special support to Honduras and Guatemala for joint programs with those countries.

65. During the period when the Boland Amendments were in effect, individuals within the State Department, DIA, National Security Agency ("NSA"), White House, and NSC, among others, were informed about the following support for the Resistance by Central American countries: that Honduras had agreed to provide the Resistance with end-user certificates for hand grenades and for rounds for grenade launchers, which the Resistance wanted to purchase from South Korea; that the relative success of the Resistance since the United States government funding cutoff depended upon its ability to raise private funds and to operate from Honduras with its approval; that a Honduran military official in charge of providing support to the Resistance had agreed to provide the Resistance end-user certificates for automatic rifles; that a senior Guatemalan military officer had said that a decision had been made at the highest levels of his government to continue its support for the Resistance: that the bulk of Guatemala's aid to the Resistance consisted of providing end-user certificates for items purchased from other countries.

66. In August 1985, Costa Rican President Monge indicated to U.S. officials that he would be willing to provide assistance to the Resistance if the United States government would help fund a certain operation in Costa Rica. The U.S. officials concluded that the operation could be funded if President Monge would take certain specified actions to assist the Resistance.

67. In the fall of 1985, Benjamin Piza, a senior Costa Rican official, agreed to permit the Resistance to construct an airstrip in Santa Elena in northern Costa Rica.

DOCUMENT 23: Court document, "U.S. Government Stipulation on Quid Pro Quos with Other Governments as Part of Contra Operations," April 6, 1989.

PAGE 9 OF 13

Payments were made to Colonel Montero, an official of the Costa Rican Civil Guard, for the official's services in guarding the Santa Elena airstrip.

68. In October 1985, Honduras seized a shipment of NHAO humanitarian goods in response to reports that Honduras was facilitating NHAO shipments. The U.S. Ambassador requested that LtCol North travel promptly to Honduras to brief its senior military leaders on NHAO procedures and plans, and to assure its leaders about U.S. government handling of aid to the Resistance.

69. In October 1985, following meetings with Honduran military officials, Colonel Comee of USSOUTHCOM informed General Galvin (CINC, USSOUTHCOM) that Honduras was wavering in its support for the Resistance because U.S. government help had not been fully implemented; Honduran officials were thinking of signing the Contadora Agreement in light of their conclusion that the Resistance could not prevail without more U.S. government assistance. The Honduran officials were particularly angry that the U.S. Embassy there had recently denied any connection with the Resistance, referring inquiries to representatives of Honduras. In Comee's view, the U.S. government had to respond to the concerns of Honduras or lose its support for the Resistance.

70. In December 1985, individuals within the DoS, CIA, DIA, White House, NSC, and USSOUTHCOM were informed about the refusal of Honduras to permit NHAO flights into the country. The refusal stemmed from the failure of the U.S. government and Honduran officials to keep a senior Honduran military official informed of Resistance activities. The senior military official was concerned, among other reasons, because there was no local point of contact for coordination between Honduran government officials, the Resistance, and the United States Government.

71. In December 1985, CIA reported to Headquarters that LtCol North would arrive for a meeting with a senior Honduran military official, and that U.S. Ambassador Ferch wanted LtCol North to know that the military official was anxious for the meeting. The most significant operational problem arising from Honduras' refusal to permit use of its airfields was not the restriction on NHAO flights into Honduras, but the restriction on resupply flights into Nicaragua, which threatened to force 5,000 Resistance troops to withdraw from Nicaraguan into Honduras.

72. In mid-December 1985, LtCol North and Admiral Poindexter visited Costa Rica, El Salvador, Guatemala, Panama, and Honduras to urge those countries to provide continued support for the armed Resistance. Admiral Poindexter assured them that the U.S. Government was committed to supporting the armed forces in those countries. Poindexter made clear to a senior Honduran military official that his country's support for the Resistance—particularly logistical support—was essential.

73. In Costa Rica, Admiral Poindexter met with and was briefed by U.S. and Costa Rican officials on the progress of the Resistance airfield at Santa Elena.

74. On December 20, 1985, Admiral Poindexter discussed with President Reagan the provision of U.S. arms to Honduras.

75. In late December 1985, Ambassador Ferch met with Honduran President Suazo and a senior U.S. official concerning the resumption of NHAO flights into Honduras. President Suazo took the request under advisement.

76. In late December 1985, Deputy Assistant Secretary of State William Walker and Chris Arcos of NHAO met in Honduras with one of its senior military officials and other officials as a follow-up to the Poindexter trip in mid-December. The follow-up team also stopped in El Salvador, where they discussed with the Ambassador the use of Ilopango military airfield as an alternate transshipment point for NHAO humanitarian assistance.

77. In January 1986, the American Embassy in Honduras furnished Secretary of State Shultz and Assistant Secretary Abrams with a statement of U.S. objectives in Honduras for 1986. The Embassy noted that Honduras had collaborated over a broad range of security issues—including support for the Resistance—during 1985. As a goal for the coming year, the Embassy listed the encouragement of Honduran support for the Resistance and pointed out that Honduran cooperation would turn upon the extent of U.S. government security assurances and military and economic support. According to the Embassy, Honduras regarded support for the Resistance primarily as a U.S. government program. The responsibility for ensuring Honduran support for the Resistance was assigned to the Ambassador, other officers from other government agencies assigned to the Embassy, and the U.S. Military Group.

78. In mid-January 1986, LtCol North prepared talk-

DOCUMENT 23: Court document, "U.S. Government Stipulation on Quid Pro Quos with Other Governments as Part of Contra Operations," April 6, 1989.

PAGE 10 OF 13

ing points for a meeting between Admiral Poindexter, Vice President Bush, and Honduran President Azcona. North recommended that Admiral Poindexter and Vice President Bush tell President Azcona of the need for Honduras to work with the U.S. government on increasing regional involvement with and support for the Resistance. Poindexter and Bush were also to raise the subject of better U.S. government support for the states bordering Nicaragua.

79. In mid-January 1986, the State Department prepared a memorandum for Donald Gregg (the Vice President's national security advisor) for Vice President Bush's meeting with President Azcona. According to DoS, one purpose of the meeting was to encourage continued Honduran support for the Resistance. The memorandum alerted Gregg that Azcona would insist on receiving clear economic and social benefits from its cooperation with the United States. Admiral Poindexter would meet privately with President Azcona to seek a commitment of support for the Resistance by Honduras. DoS suggested that Vice President Bush inform President Azcona that a strong and active armed Resistance was essential to maintain pressure on the Sandinistas, and that the United States government's intention to support the Resistance was clear and firm.

80. In late January 1986, a U.S. official inquired of DoS, CIA Headquarters, DIA, U.S. Ambassadors in Tegucigalpa, Managua, San Jose, and Panama City, and USSOUTHCOM concerning an upcoming approach to President Azcona about the resumption of NHAO flights into Honduras. The official believed that Azcona would permit a temporary resumption of flights based on an agreement by the United States government to open negotiations on increased aid to Honduras.

81. In late January 1986, the U.S. official was instructed that, in seeking President Azcona's permission to resume flights and truck transportation in support of the Resistance into and through Honduras, the categories of supplies should not be specified because Resistance flights from Ilopango airfield in El Salvador and Aguacate airfield in Honduras would have mixed (lethal and non-lethal) loads.

82. In late January 1986, LtCol North visited Costa Rican government officials and Resistance leaders on the Southern Front to discuss progress of the Resistance. These meetings and their purpose were approved by Admiral Poindexter and DCI Casey and known to others in DoD, CIA, and DoS.

83. On January 30, 1986, U.S. Ambassador Ferch met with President Azcona to request Honduras' assistance in supplying the Resistance. The Ambassador sought permission to overfly Honduras when dropping material to the Resistance; to truck material to the Resistance, and for the Resistance to position private contractor aircraft at Aguacate, a military airfield in Honduras, for resupply missions into Nicaragua.

84. On February 22, 1986, there was a meeting in the office of DoD official Fred Ikle attended by Nestor Sanchez (DoD), Fiers (CIA), General Gordon, LtCol North, a representative of the Joint Chiefs of Staff, and others with respect to strategy for the Resistance. Although much of the discussion focused on what would be done in the event funding were restored, North stated that the past external support for the Resistance from the private sector had been ruptured because there was no unity of command and people did not know who to talk to. Ikle praised the effort of Retired General Singlaub in that regard. North also indicated that DoD's FOCAL POINT system had not worked; for example, there had been problems obtaining maps for the Resistance from the Defense Mapping Agency.

85. In late February 1986, Secretary Shultz, Secretary Weinberger, Admiral Poindexter, DCI Casey and other senior officials received intelligence reports that a Salvadoran government official had acknowledged that, at the request of the United States government, Ilopango military airfield was being used to help the Resistance as a temporary alternative and supplement to airfields in Honduras.

86. In late February 1986, a CIA officer reported to CIA Headquarters concerning the conditions imposed by Honduras for the resumption of direct resupply flights to the Resistance into and out of that country. A key condition was that for the trial run there could be no leaks or publicity. The CIA officer noted that the problem with leaks arose in part from the involvement of external agencies in Washington, Miami, San Salvador and Guatemala City.

87. In March 1986, a CIA official notified CIA headquarters that Honduras had approved a private lethal shipment to the Resistance to arrive on a certain date. In addition, Honduras had approved shuttle flights to move lethal materiel for the Resistance from one military airfield in Honduras to another military airfield. It devel-

DOCUMENT 23: Court document, "U.S. Government Stipulation on Quid Pro Quos with Other Governments as Part of Contra Operations," April 6, 1989.

PAGE 11 OF 13

oped that the same aircraft scheduled to perform the shuttle flight for lethal materials was scheduled to perform a NHAO flight at the same time.

88. In mid-March 1986, LtCol North prepared a memorandum from Admiral Poindexter to President Reagan concerning a photo opportunity for Benjamin Piza, a senior Costa Rican official. The memorandum noted that Piza had been instrumental in helping the U.S. organize the Southern Front. Piza had intervened with another senior Costa Rican official on numerous occasions and had personally assisted in the development of a logistics support base for Resistance forces deployed north from Costa Rica. Admiral Poindexter noted that during his trip to Central America he had met with Piza to discuss future plans for the Resistance and support for them through Costa Rica. At the photo opportunity with President Reagan and Piza were (among others) Chief of Staff Donald Regan, Admiral Poindexter, Joseph Fernandez (CIA's San Jose Chief of Station (COS)), and LtCol North.

89. On March 20, 1986, the White House Situation Room was advised that senior Honduran military leaders planned to ask the United States for permission to control lethal aid sent through that country to the Resistance in Nicaragua, and that they wanted to receive some sophisticated weapons given the Resistance that were not already in Honduras' inventory.

90. On March 22, 1986, Admiral Poindexter advised President Reagan in a memorandum prepared by North that Elliott Abrams, Gen. Jack Galvin (CINC, USSOUTHCOM) and a team of experts had just returned from visits with three Central American leaders and that the delegation had been successful in obtaining commitments for continued support to the Nicaraguan Resistance. Vice President Bush and Chief of Staff Regan received copies of the memorandum.

91. In late March 1986, Elliott Abrams offered Honduran President Azcona immediate additional security assistance. LtCol North prepared a memorandum from Admiral Poindexter to President Reagan (with copies to Vice President Bush and Chief of Staff Regan) describing the results of Abrams' discussions with Azcona. The details of the enhanced security assistance to Honduras were worked out between Col. Royer (Chief of the Latin America Division of DoD's DSAA) and various Honduran military officials. The Honduran army and navy specifically requested a sophisticated ground-to-air mis-

sile on the ground that the U.S. had already furnished such weapons to the Resistance. The total cost for the items ultimately agreed upon was approximately $20 million. Among those aware of the additional assistance to Honduras (in addition to President Reagan, Vice President Bush, Regan, and Admiral Poindexter) were LtGen Gast (Director of DSAA), Assistant Secretary of Defense Richard Armitage, and Deputy Assistant Secretary of Defense Nestor Sanchez.

92. In early May 1986, President Reagan wrote to Presidents Duarte and Azcona, thanking them for their support for the Resistance and affirming his commitment to obtain U.S. government funding for the Resistance. In the letter to President Duarte, President Reagan announced that he would propose legislation that Duarte had sought extending U.S. participation in an international trade agreement of benefit to El Salvador. In the Azcona letter, President Reagan announced that the U.S. was disbursing ESF funds that Honduras sought. LtCol North had proposed that these letters be sent, and Donald Fortier of the NSC staff had forwarded them to President Reagan. Assistant Secretary of State Abrams, DCI Casey, and Undersecretary Fred Ikle of DoD concurred in sending the letters.

93. In May 1986, the CIA reported to NSA, DoS, DIA, the White House, the NSC staff, SouthCom, and U.S. Embassies at San Jose, Managua, Tegucigalpa, and Panama City about donations from donors in Latin America and the United States to Resistance forces fighting on the Southern Front. A Nicaraguan Resistance leader had received funds from Panamanian Defense Forces General Manuel Noriega.

94. In May 1986, Nestor Sanchez, DoD Deputy Assistant Secretary of Defense, provided the Secretary of Defense with a translation of a memorandum to President Reagan from President Azcona, calling for substantial increases in military aid for the next five years and increasing coordination between and among the U.S., Honduras' armed forces, and the leadership of the Resistance regarding UNO/FDN military operations. The letter articulated conditions for continuing to help the U.S. maintain all facets of the Resistance, including military.

95. In May 1986, President Azcona indicated to President Reagan that Honduras' continued support for the Resistance depended upon significant increases in U.S. government military aid to the Honduran armed forces and the Resistance. President Azcona noted that his

DOCUMENT 23: Court document, "U.S. Government Stipulation on Quid Pro Quos with Other Governments as Part of Contra Operations," April 6, 1989.

PAGE 12 OF 13

armed forces wanted weapons and ammunition for use by the Resistance—including grenades and launchers aboard a ship about to leave Europe—transferred to Honduran armed forces to assure the military success of the Resistance. President Azcona stated that in past months these matters had been discussed with William Taft of DoD, Abrams, Admiral Poindexter, and General Galvin.

96. On July 29, 1986, there was a discussion in the RIG about how the Resistance should best fight the war. Attending were Abrams, Sanchez, Fiers, LtCol North, General Galvin, LtGen Moellering, and Colonel Croker. Fiers indicated that UNO/South was in desperate straits, that UNO/North was not in good shape, and that all funds for resupply were exhausted on July 1.

97. In late August 1986, North reported to Admiral Poindexter that a representative of Panamanian leader Manuel Noriega had asked North to meet with him. Noriega's representative proposed that, in exchange for a promise from the USG to help clean up Noriega's image and a commitment to lift the USG ban on military sales to the Panamanian defense forces, Noriega would assassinate the Sandinista leadership for the U.S. government. North had told Noriega's representative that U.S. law forbade such actions. The representative responded that Noriega had numerous assets in place in Nicaragua and could accomplish many essential things, just as Noriega had helped the USG the previous year in blowing up a Sandinista arsenal.

98. North advised Admiral Poindexter that the British persons who had run the operation against the arsenal had used a Panamanian civilian ordnance expert. North noted that Noriega had the capabilities that he had proffered, and that the cost of any operations could be borne by Project Democracy.

99. Admiral Poindexter responded that if Noriega had assets inside Nicaragua, he could be helpful. The USG could not be involved in assassination, but Panamanian assistance with sabotage would be another story. Admiral Poindexter recommended that North speak with Noriega directly.

100. In early September 1986, General Galvin of SouthCom and an official of the U.S. Military Group met in Tegucigalpa to discuss Honduran support for the Resistance with a senior Honduran military official. General Galvin advised the senior Honduran military official that a U.S. military official would go to Honduras to work with the Resistance. The senior Honduran military official expressed concern about leaks to the media concerning arrangements between the U.S. Embassy, the Honduran military, and President Azcona in supporting the Resistance. General Galvin and the senior Honduran military official also discussed U.S. cooperation with Honduras in various military and intelligence areas.

101. In mid-September 1986, LtCol North notified Admiral Poindexter that Noriega wanted to meet with him in London within a few days. North had discussed the matter with Assistant Secretary of State Abrams, who had raised it with Secretary of State Shultz. Shultz thought that the meeting should proceed. Admiral Poindexter approved.

102. In mid-September 1986, LtCol North advised Admiral Poindexter that former U.S. Ambassador Negroponte, General Gorman of SouthCom, senior CIA official Duane Clarridge, and LtCol North had worked out arrangements for support of the Resistance with General Bueso-Rosa, a former Honduran military officer who had recently been convicted of offenses in the U.S. LtCol North suggested that efforts be made on Buego-Rosa's behalf to deter him from disclosing details of these covert activities.

103. In late September 1986, LtCol North advised Admiral Poindexter that Costa Rican Interior Minister Garron had disclosed the existence of the Santa Elena airstrip. North stated that President Arias of Costa Rica had breached his understanding with the U.S. government. Assistant Secretary of State Abrams and Secretary of State Shultz wanted to cancel Arias' scheduled visit with President Reagan and replace his appointment by scheduling a meeting with President Cerezo of Guatemala. Admiral Poindexter agreed.

104. A U.S. official met with President Cerezo of Guatemala in September 1986. Cerezo told the U.S. official that he intended to pursue U.S. government goals in Central America, including specific support for the armed Resistance, but that he would seek additional military aid from the U.S. in return.

105. President Reagan, Vice President Bush, Shultz, Weinberger, and Poindexter were informed of the U.S. official's meeting with President Cerezo. It was reported to these officials that, in return for Guatemalan support for the Resistance, Cerezo would ask Secretary of State Shultz to triple military assistance to Guatemala, to double economic assistance to Guatemala, and to undertake other forms of support for Guatemala.

DOCUMENT 23: Court document, "U.S. Government Stipulation on Quid Pro Quos with Other Governments as Part of Contra Operations," April 6, 1989.

PAGE 13 OF 13

106. In late September 1986, LtCol North reported to Admiral Poindexter on his London meeting with Noriega. Noriega would try to take immediate actions against the Sandinistas and offered a list of priorities including an oil refinery, an airport, and the Puerto Sandino offload facility.

107. At the end of September 1986, LtCol North reemphasized to Admiral Poindexter that President Arias of Costa Rica should not be invited to meet President Reagan in light of Arias' disclosure of the Santa Elena airstrip. North recommended that Presidents Duarte and Cerezo be invited to meet President Reagan instead, because El Salvador and Guatemala had supported the Resistance.

DOCUMENT 24: Robert McFarlane, "Recommended Telephone Call to His Excellency
Roberto Suazo Cordova, President of the Republic of Honduras," with Reagan's Notes, April 25, 1985.

PAGE 1 OF 2

050376   THE WHITE HOUSE   SYSTEM II
                    WASHINGTON   9044

                    April 25, 1985

SECRET

RECOMMENDED TELEPHONE CALL

TO: His Excellency Roberto Suazo Cordova,
                    President of the Republic of Honduras

DATE: Thursday, April 25, 1985

RECOMMENDED BY: Robert C. McFarlane

PURPOSE: To reassure the Honduran Government regarding
                    our intention to support the Nicaraguan
                    democratic resistance forces.

BACKGROUND: One of the most serious consequences of the
                    House's action yesterday is the deep concern
                    it has created in Honduras. [A high Honduran
                    military official] and other high officials are threatening to
                    deny sanctuary to the FDN and disarm the
                    resistance forces on the Honduran border.
                    This morning, [a senior military official] of the Honduran
                    General Staff told Alfonso Robelo that this
                    vote "finishes Honduran support." The
                    Honduran military this morning stopped a
                    shipment of ammunition to the FDN base at Las
                    Vegas. The active GOH cooperation with FDN
                    logistics, which we have seen in the past two
                    months, must continue if the resistance is to
                    survive.

                    It is imperative, therefore, that you make
                    clear the Executive Branch's political
                    commitment to maintaining pressure on the
                    Sandinistas, regardless of what action
                    Congress takes. President Suazo will need
                    some overt and concrete sign of this
                    commitment in order to forestall his military
                    in taking action against the FDN. Two
                    actions which would signal our commitment
                    are:

                    -- impose a trade embargo, using either
                        IEPA or the Trade Expansion Act (we are
                        urgently examining the alternatives and
                        will send you a recommendation); and/or

                    -- downgrade diplomatic relations.

                                                        000836

SECRET   SECRET   ALU009743
Declassify: OADR

                                            cc Vice President

000054

[98]

DOCUMENT 24: Robert McFarlane, "Recommended Telephone Call to His Excellency
Roberto Suazo Cordova, President of the Republic of Honduras," with Reagan's Notes, April 25, 1985.

PAGE 2 OF 2

SECRET

SECRET   2

BACKGROUND: (Continued...)

While we consider and prepare for these
specific measures, it is essential that you
call President Suazo to reassure him that we
intend to continue our support for the
freedom fighters and that you are examining
actions for which Congressional approval is
not required.

TOPICS OF
DISCUSSION: 1. Yesterday's House vote for aid to the
Nicaraguan democratic resistance.

2. Commitment to persist in effort to obtain
funds from the Congress for continued U.S.
support.

3. Urge GOH not to take any actions which
would jeopardize the struggle for liberty and
democracy in Nicaragua.

Date of Submission: ALU0097414

Action

[handwritten notes, largely illegible]

SECRET   SECRET

DOCUMENT 25: Oliver North, Memorandum for Robert McFarlane with Attachments, "Guatemalan Aid to the Nicaraguan Resistance," March 5, 1985.

PAGE 1 OF 11

TOP SECRET

MEMORANDUM

SYSTEM IV
NSC/ICS-400215

NATIONAL SECURITY COUNCIL

March 5, 1985

TOP SECRET

ACTION

MEMORANDUM FOR ROBERT C. MCFARLANE

FROM: OLIVER L. NORTH

SUBJECT: Guatemalan Aid to the Nicaraguan Resistance

Attached at Tab I is a memo from you to Secretaries Shultz and Weinberger, Director Casey, and General Vessey asking for their views on increased U.S. assistance to Guatemala. Your memo is cast as suggestion which derives from trip to the region.

The real purpose of your memo is to find a way by which we can compensate the Guatemalans for the extraordinary assistance they are providing to the Nicaraguan freedom fighters. At Tab II are end-user certificates which the Guatemalans have provided for the purchase of nearly $8M worth of munitions to be delivered to the FDN. These nine documents are a direct consequence of the informal liaison we have established with [a Guatemalan military officer] and your meeting with he and [a high Guatemalan official] The ammunition and weapons identified in these documents will be delivered in several shipments (2 by aircraft and 1 by sea) starting on or about March 10, 1985. All shipments will be delivered to Guatemala, be receipted for by Guatemalan military officers, and turned over to FDN representatives at La Aurora Airport and Puerto Barrios on arrival. Adolfo is convinced, and I agree, that the Guatemalans have not removed or withheld any equipment/munitions from the FDN deliveries which have occurred to date.

During one of the meetings with the Guatemalans in which the process above was arranged, one of the Guatemalan officers presented a "wish list" of items which they desperately need in order to prosecute their war against the Cuban-supported guerrillas. A copy of the list is attached at Tab III. Each of the items identified are in priority within four principal categories: Aircraft, Ground Forces Equipment, Weapons and Munitions, and Non-Tactical Military Equipment.

TOP SECRET
Declassify: OADR

TOP SECRET

AKW037446

DOCUMENT 25: Oliver North, Memorandum for Robert McFarlane with Attachments, "Guatemalan Aid to the Nicaraguan Resistance," March 5, 1985.

PAGE 2 OF 11

TOP SECRET

TOP SECRET   2

Your memo at Tab I does not refer to the arrangements which have been made for supporting the resistance through Guatemala. It does, however, urge that we take steps now to improve their situation. Once we have approval for at least some of what they have asked for, we can ensure that the right people in Guatemala understand that we are able to provide results from their cooperation on the resistance issue.

RECOMMENDATION

That you sign and transmit the memo at Tab I.

      Approve ____   Disapprove _____

Attachments
    Tab   I - McFarlane Memo to Shultz/Weinberger/Casey/Vessey
    Tab II - Guatemalan End-User Certificates
    Tab III - Guatemalan Military Equipment Requirements

AKW037447

TOP SECRET   TOP SECRET

DOCUMENT 25: Oliver North, Memorandum for Robert McFarlane with Attachments, "Guatemalan Aid to the Nicaraguan Resistance," March 5, 1985.

PAGE 3 OF 11

GUATEMALAN MILITARY EQUIPMENT REQUIREMENTS

The following military equipment and services have been identified as the highest priority for the Guatemalan Army in combatting the Communist guerrillas. They are listed in sequence of highest to lowest need within each category.

Aircraft:

-- New or refurbished helicopters and spare parts for existing inventory.

-- Spare parts for fixed wing cargo aircraft.

-- New or refurbished ground attack aircraft and spare parts for existing inventory.

-- New trainer aircraft and related spare parts.

Ground Forces Equipment:

-- Communications equipment, including secure voice systems.

-- Various vehicles for troop and logistical transport.

-- Engineering equipment, including bulldozers, road-graders, and survey instruments.

Weapons and Munitions:

-- Light and medium weapons, including M-16 rifles, M-60 machine guns, pistols (9mm and .45 caliber), 81mm and 60mm mortars, and 90mm recoilless rifles.

-- Ground force munitions, including mortar, recoilless rifle, and artillery rounds, assorted mines and explosives, and 7.62 x 51 linked ammunition, plus hand grenades.

-- Aerial munitions, including 200 and 500 pound bombs and 2.75 inch rockets with appropriate warhead mixes.

Additional Non-Tactical Supplies and Equipment:

-- Field hospital equipment, general medical supplies, and training for paramedics.

-- Tactical radars for use in detecting border infiltration.

AKW015565D

DOCUMENT 25: Oliver North, Memorandum for Robert McFarlane with Attachments, "Guatemalan Aid to the Nicaraguan Resistance," March 5, 1985.

PAGE 4 OF 11

ESTADO MAYOR DE LA DEFENSA NACIONAL

S/r.

REPUBLICA DE GUATEMALA, C. A.

CERTIFICACION DE DESTINO FINAL

No.DL-D4rr-00780-85.

Guatemala, 14 de febrero de 1,985.

Señores:
ENERGY RESOURCES INTERNATIONAL
440 Maple Ave. East
Viena, Va., 22180.

Señores:

Nos dirigimos a ustedes, para manifestarles que por es te medio estamos extendiendo CERTIFICACION DE DESTINO FINAL por DIEZ MIL (10,000) libras de explosivo (HE) - C4 o TNT y UN MIL QUINIENTOS (1,500) detonadores variados, los cuales serán destinados para uso exclusivo del Ejército de Guatema la y no serán reexportados ni vendidos a otro país, siendo Guatemala el destino final.

Sin otro particular, aprovecho la oportunidad para sus cribirme atentamente.

Stamp and signature of
high Guatemalan official

AKW015560

DOCUMENT 25: Oliver North, Memorandum for Robert McFarlane with Attachments, "Guatemalan Aid to the Nicaraguan Resistance," March 5, 1985.

PAGE 5 OF 11

...ADO MAYOR DE LA DEFENSA NACIONAL

S/r.   REPUBLICA DE GUATEMALA, C. A.

CERTIFICACION DE DESTINO FINAL

No. DL-24rr-00781-85.

Guatemala, 14 de febrero de 1,985.

S. Flores:
ENERGY RESOURCES INTERNATIONAL
440 Maple Ave. East
Viena, Va., 22180.

Señores:

       Nos dirigimos a ustedes, para manifestarles que por es-
te medio estamos extendiendo CERTIFICACION DE DESTINO FINAL
del material que a continuación se detalla, el cual será des
tinado para uso exclusivo del Ejército de Guatemala y no será reexportado ni vendido a otro país, siendo Guatemala el -
destino final:

      A. 150 ametralladoras
      B. 150 morteros de 60mm. -completos-.
      C. 100 morteros de 81mm. -completos-.
      D. 150 lanzagranadas M-79
      E. -30 fusiles sin retroceso de 57mm.

       Sin otro particular, aprovecho la oportunidad para sus-
cribirme atentamente.

Stamp and signature of
high Guatemalan official

AKW015561

DOCUMENT 25: Oliver North, Memorandum for Robert McFarlane with Attachments, "Guatemalan Aid to the Nicaraguan Resistance," March 5, 1985.

PAGE 6 OF 11

L.TADO MAYOR LE LA DEFENSA NACIONAL

S/r.

REPUBLICA DE GUATEMALA. C. A.

CERTIFICACION DE DESTINO FINAL

No. DL-D4rr-00782-85.

Guatemala, 14 de febrero de 1,985.

Señores:
ENERGY RESOURCES INTERNATIONAL
440 Maple Ave. East
Viena, Va., 22180.

Señores:

Nos dirigimos a ustedes, para manifestarles que por es
te medio estamos extendiendo CERTIFICACION DE DESTINO FINAL
del material que a continuación se detalla, el cual será --
destinado para uso exclusivo del Ejército de Guatemala y no
será reexportado ni vendido a otro país, siendo Guatemala -
el destino final:

A. 10,000 granadas M-79.
B. -3,000 granadas de 60mm.
C. -2,000 granadas de 81mm.

Sin otro particular, aprovecho la oportunidad para su:
cribirme atentamente.

Stamp and signature of
high Guatemalan official

AKW015562

[105]

DOCUMENT 25: Oliver North, Memorandum for Robert McFarlane with Attachments, "Guatemalan Aid to the Nicaraguan Resistance," March 5, 1985.

PAGE 7 OF 11

ESTADO MAYOR DE LA DEFENSA NACIONAL

S/r.

REPUBLICA DE GUATEMALA, C. A.

CERTIFICACION DE DESTINO FINAL

No. DL-D4rr-00783-85.

Guatemala, 14 de febrero de 1,985.

Señores:
ENERGY RESOURCES INTERNATINAL
440 Maple Ave. East
Viena, Va., 22180.

Señores:

Nos dirigimos a ustedes, para manifestarles que por este medio estamos extendiendo CERTIFICACION DE DESTINO FINAL
del material que a continuación se detalla, el cual será des
tinado para uso exclusivo del Ejército de Guatemala y no será reexportado ni vendido a otro país, siendo Guatemala el -
destino final:

A. 3,000 granadas RPG-7.
B. --100 lanzagranadas RPG-7.

Sin otro particular, aprovecho la oportunidad para suscribirme atentamente.

Stamp and signature of
high Guatemalan official

AKW015563

[106]

DOCUMENT 25: Oliver North, Memorandum for Robert McFarlane with Attachments, "Guatemalan Aid to the Nicaraguan Resistance," March 5, 1985.

PAGE 8 OF 11

[TADO MAYOR DE -LA DEFENSA NACIONAL

s/r.   REPUBLICA DE GUATEMALA. C. A.

CERTIFICACION DE DESTINO FINAL

No.DL-D4rr-00784-85.

Guatemala, 14 de febrero de 1,985.

Señores:
ENERGY RESOURCES INTERNATIONAL
440 Maple Ave. East
Viena, Va., 22180.

Señores:

Nos dirigimos a ustedes, para manifestarles que por es
te medio estamos extendiendo CERTIFICACION DE DESTINO FINAL
por DOS MIL (2,000) minas anti-personales y UN MIL (1,000)
minas anti-tanque, las cuales serán destinadas para uso exclusivo del Ejército de Guatemala y no serán reexportadas -
ni vendidas a otro país, siendo Guatemala el destino final.

Sin otro particular, aprovecho la oportunidad para sus
cribirme atentamente.

Stamp and signature of
high Guatemalan official

AKW015564

DOCUMENT 25: Oliver North, Memorandum for Robert McFarlane with Attachments, "Guatemalan Aid to the Nicaraguan Resistance," March 5, 1985.

PAGE 9 OF 11

L. íADO MAYOR DE JA DEFENSA NACIONAL
_____
S/r.   REPUBLICA DE GUATEMALA, C. A.

<u>CERTIFICACION DE DESTINO FINAL:</u>

No. DL-D4rr-00785-85.

Guatemala, 14 de febrero de 1,985.

Señores:
ENERGY RESOURCES INTERNATIONAL
440 Maple Ave. East
Viena, Va., 22180.

Señores:

Nos dirigimos a ustedes, para manifestarles que por es
te medio estamos extendiendo CERTIFICACION DE DESTINO FINAL
por TRES MIL (3,000) LAW ROCKETS, que vienen destinados para uso exclusivo del Ejército de Guatemala y no serán reexportados ni vendidos a otro país, siendo Guatemala el desti
no final.

Sin otro particular, aprovecho la oportunidad para su
cribirme atentamente.

Stamp and signature of high
Guatemalan official

AKWO15565

DOCUMENT 25: Oliver North, Memorandum for Robert McFarlane with Attachments, "Guatemalan Aid to the Nicaraguan Resistance," March 5, 1985.

PAGE 10 OF 11

L_íADO MAYOR DE _L_ DEFENSA NACIONAL

S/r.   REPUBLICA DE GUATEMALA. C. A.

CERTIFICACION DE DESTINO FINAL

No. DL-D4rr-00786-85.

Guatemala, 14 de febrero de 1,985.

Señores:
ENERGY RESOURCES INTERNATIONAL
440 Maple Ave. East
Viena, Va., 22180.

Señores:

Nos dirigimos a ustedes, para manifestarles que por este medio estamos extendiendo CERTIFICACION DE DESTINO FINAL por DIEZ (10) lanzacohetes tierra-aire y CINCUENTA (50) misiles tierra-aire, los cuales vienen destinados para uso exclusivo del Ejército de Guatemala y no serán reexportados ni vendidos a otro país, siendo Guatemala el destino final.

Sin otro particular, aprovecho la oportunidad para suscribirme atentamente.

Stamp and signature of
high Guatemalan official

AKW015565A

[109]

DOCUMENT 25: Oliver North, Memorandum for Robert McFarlane with Attachments, "Guatemalan Aid to the Nicaraguan Resistance," March 5, 1985.

PAGE 11 OF 11

ESTADO MAYOR DE LA DEFENSA NACIONAL

REPUBLICA DE GUATEMALA. C. A.

s/r.

CERTIFICACION DE DESTINO FINAL

No.DL-D4rr-00778-85.

Guatemala, 14 de febrero de 1985.

Señores ENERGY RESOURCES INTERNATIONAL
440 Maple Ave. East
Viena, Va., 22180.

Señores:

Nos dirigimos a ustedes, para manifestarles que por es
te medio estamos extendiendo CERTIFICACION DE DESTINO FINAL
por CINCO MILLONES (5.000,000) de cartuchos Ball Ammo, cali
bre 7.62mm., los cuales serán destinados para uso exclusivo
del Ejército de Guatemala y no serán reexportados ni vendidos a otro país, siendo Guatemala el destino final.

Sin otro particular, aprovecho la oportunidad para sus
cribirme de ustedes atentamente.

Stamp and signature of
high Guatemalan official

AKW0155658

[110]

DOCUMENT 26: American Embassy in Bandar Seri Begawan, Brunei, Telegram to Secretary of State, "Brunei Project," July 28, 1986.

PAGE 1 OF 3

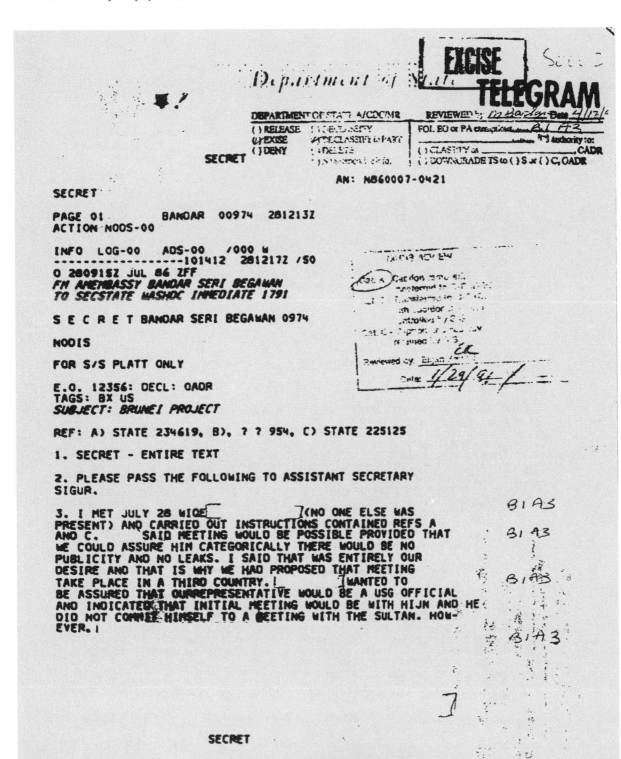

DOCUMENT 26: American Embassy in Bandar Seri Begawan, Brunei, Telegram to Secretary of State, "Brunei Project," July 28, 1986.

PAGE 2 OF 3

SECRET

_____| I ASSURED
HIM THAT VERY PRIVATE CHANNEL WOULD BE USED AND THAT
KNOWLEDGE WAS LIMITED IN BRUNEI TO THE TWO OF US.

4. AFTER FURTHER DISCUSSION WE AGREED THAT BEST LOCALE
FOR MEETING WOULD BE LONDON DURING PERIOD AUGUST 8-11
(SULTAN IS TRAVELLING TO THE UK AT INVITATION OF HIS
OLD SCHOOL SANDHURST WHERE HE WILL TAKE THE SOVEREIGN'S
PARADE)./ |TIME DURING VISIT, WHEN MEETING MIGHT
BE ARRANGED, AS FOLLOWS:

-- FRIDAY - AUGUST 8 - EVENING ONLY

-- SATURDAY - AUGUST 9 - AM ONLY

-- SUNDAY - AUGUST 10 - ENTIRE DAY

-- MONDAY - AUGUST 11 - EVENING ONLY

5. SULTAN AND HIS PARTY WILL BE STAYING AT THE
DORCHESTER WHILE|
                    |VISITORS. HOWEVER, FROM WHAT I
HAVE HEARD A STREAM OF FAVOR SEEKERS, UJERSONS WITH
INVESTMENT PROPOSALS AND BRITISH OFFICIALS ARE CONSTANTLY
IN AND OUT OF THE DORCHESTER WHENEVER THE SULTAN IS IN
RESIDENT. (HE OWNS THE HOTEL.) YOU MAY THEREFORE WISH
TO CONSIDER PROPOSING A DIFFERENT AND MORE DISCREET NEARBY
VENUE FOR INITIAL MEETING.

5. |AND I AGREED IT WOULD BE BEST FOR ARRANGEMENTS
SECRET
SECRET

PAGE 03   BANDAR 00974 2812132

TO BE SET UP BEFORE SULTAN'S DEPARTURE FOR LONDON IN
ORDER TO AVOID CONFUSION AND KEEP NUMBER OF PERSONS
INVOLVED TO AN ABSOLUTE MINIMUM. THEREFORE HOPE YOU CAN
PROVIDE NAME OF REPRESENTATIVE AND PROPOSED TIME AND PLACE
OF MEETING THIS WEEK SO THAT WE WILL HAVE TIME TO GET ANY
REACTION BEFORE THEY DEPART. I WOULD RECOMMEND AUGUST 11
BE ELIMINATED AS POSSIBLE DAY OF MEETING SINCE SULTAN OFTEN
DECIDES TO BREAK OFF VISITS EARLY.

6. IN REGARD TO YOUR REQUEST IN REF A FOR HOW BEST TO

SECRET

DOCUMENT 26: American Embassy in Bandar Seri Begawan, Brunei, Telegram to Secretary of State, "Brunei Project," July 28, 1986.

PAGE 3 OF 3

SECRET

APPROACH THIS SUBJECT WITH ☐

☐ AND WE SHOULD THINK ABOUT HOW ANY POSSIBLE COOPERATION ON HIS PART WOULD BE ACKNOWLEDGED. IN VIEW OF ☐ DESIRE TO DEAL ONLY WITH USG OFFICIAL I DOUBT THAT THERE IS A ROLE FOR A PRIVATE AMERICAN.

AND THIS IS WHY WE SHOULD TRY TO MAKE CLEAR THE FULL FORCE OF THE USG BEHIND OUR PRESENTATION. I THINK WHAT HE NEEDS TO FEEL IS THAT HE HAS AN OPPIBTUNITY TO BE A PARTNER WITH THE US IN A MATTER OF GLOBAL SECURITY SIGNIFICANCE. KING

SECRET

SECRET

DOCUMENT 27: American Embassy in Bandar Seri Begawan, Brunei, Telegram to Secretary of State, "Brunei Project," August 2, 1986.

PAGE 1 OF 2

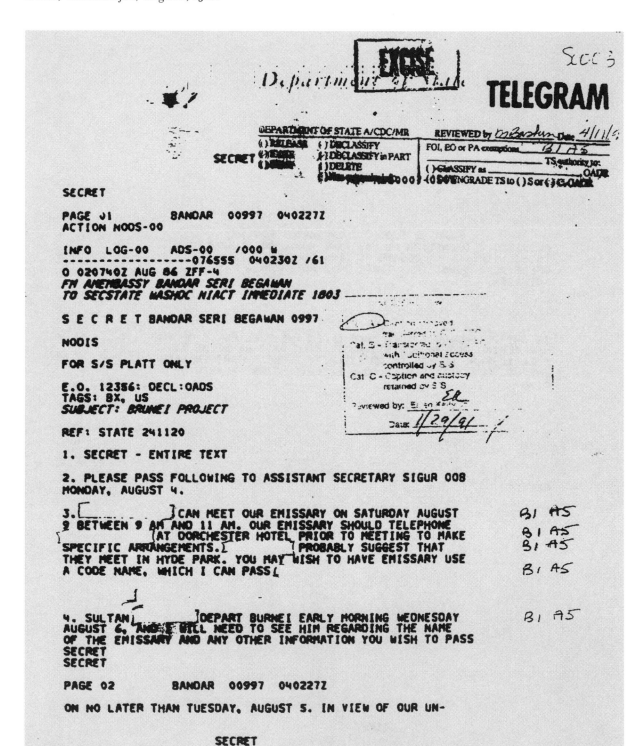

DOCUMENT 27: American Embassy in Bandar Seri Begawan, Brunei, Telegram to Secretary of State, "Brunei Project," August 2, 1986.

PAGE 2 OF 2

SECRET

RELIABLE COMMUNICATIONS (THE LINE IS DOWN RIGHT NOW), HOPE
YOU CAN GET A MESSAGE OUT TO ME ON MONDAY MORNING.
KING

SECRET

SECRET

DOCUMENT 28: George Shultz, Telegram to the American Embassy in Bandar Seri Begawan, Brunei, "Brunei Project," August 5, 1986.

PAGE 1 OF 1

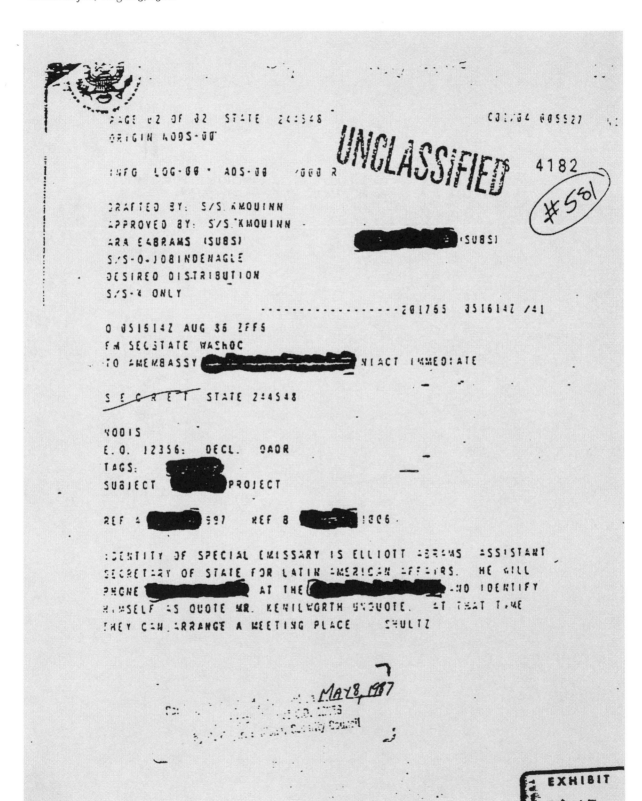

DOCUMENT 29: American Embassy in Bandar Seri Begawan, Brunei, Telegram to Secretary of State, "Brunei Project," September 16, 1986.

PAGE 1 OF 2

Department of State TELEGRAM

SECRET

AN: N860009-0170

SECRET

PAGE 01   BANDAR   01165   161105Z
ACTION NODS-00

INFO LOG-00   ADS-00   /000 W
----------------242621   161107Z /10
O 160750Z SEP 86 ZFF-4
FM AMEMBASSY BANDAR SERI BEGAWAN
TO SECSTATE WASHDC IMMEDIATE 1903

S E C R E T BANDAR SERI BEGAWAN 1165

NODIS

S/S FOR PLATT ONLY

E.O.6802356: OADS
TAGS: BX US PGOV
SUBJECT: BRUNEI PROJECT

REF: 39B) STATE 289965, (B) BSB 1158

1. SECRET ENTIRE TEXT

2. PLEASE PASS TO ASSISTANT SECRETARY SIGUR.

3. MANY THANKS FOR YITF TIMELY RESPONSE. I WAS RECEIVED BY THE SULTAN TODAY. NOTXUE ELSE WAS PRESENT. I DELIVERED MESSAGE FROM SECRETAR AND CONFIRMED THE EXACT MAGNITUDE OF PROJECT.

4. THE SULTAN WAS CORDIAL AND SEEMED PLEASE THAT THIS RELATIONSHIP HAS BEEN ESTABLISHED. I SAID THAT WE DEEPLY APPRECIATE HIS UNDERSTANDINGRF OUR NEEDS AND HIS VALUABLE ASSISTANCE. I WAS POJASED THAT HE WOULD HAVE AN OPPORTUNITY THIS WEEK TO SEE SOMETHING OF OUR COMMITMENT TO THE SECURITY OF HIS REGION EG THE WORLD, AND I THOUGHT HE WOULD ENJOY EHE PROGRAM THAT HAD BEEN ARRANGED FOR HIM ABOQRD THE AIRCRAFT CARRIER USS VINSON.
SECRET
SECRET

PAGE 02   BANDAR   01165   161105Z

THE SULTAN SAID HE WAS VERY MUCH LOOKING FORWARD TO THE

SECRET

DOCUMENT 29: American Embassy in Bandar Seri Begawan, Brunei, Telegram to Secretary of State, "Brunei Project," September 16, 1986.

PAGE 2 OF 2

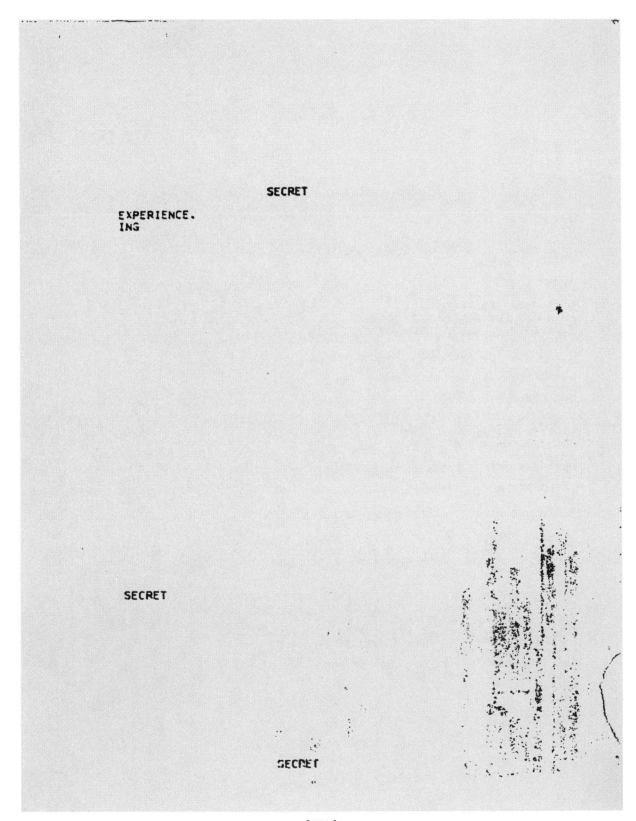

SECRET

EXPERIENCE.
ING

SECRET

SECRET

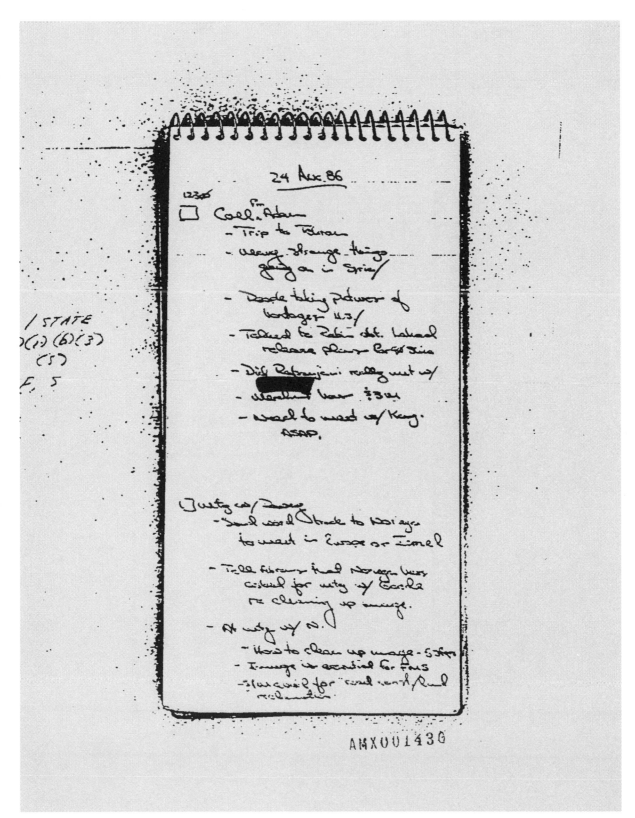

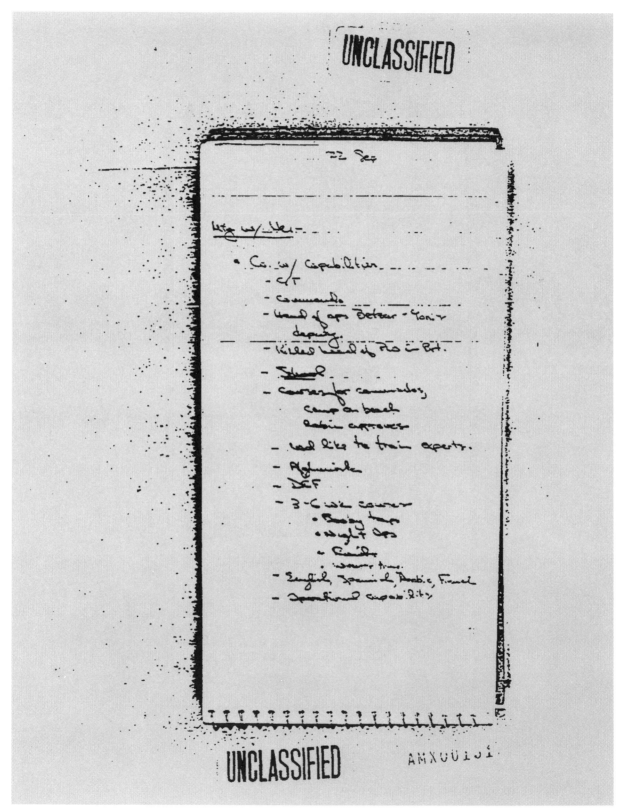

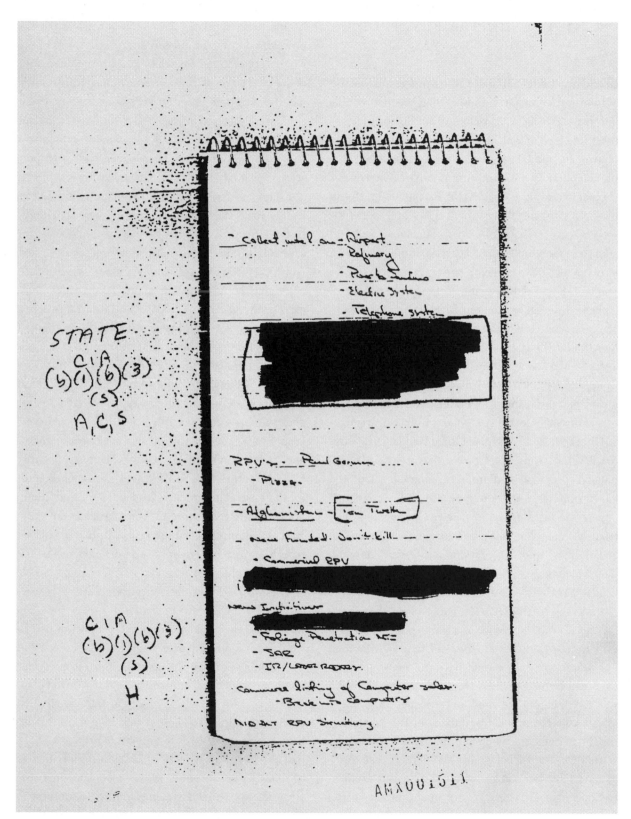

III. THE CONTRA RESUPPLY OPERATIONS

In addition to the Saudi donations of $32 million, the administration's Contra fund-raising secured $2 million from Taiwan, $2.7 million from domestic donations, and $3.8 million in diverted profits from the sale of arms to Iran.[1] These funds—approximately $40.5 million plus $27 million appropriated by Congress for "humanitarian aid"—enabled the Reagan White House to conduct what Oliver North described as a "full-service" covert Contra operation. The money financed all the components of the NSC-run paramilitary war: a network of "private-sector" personnel necessary to manage day-to-day operations, the procurement of Contra arms and equipment, logistics and infrastructure, rebel payrolls, basecamp upkeep, training, sabotage, and combat activities. Between the summer of 1984 when congressionally appropriated Contra funds expired and the fall of 1986 when Congress renewed aid, this resupply operation sustained the Contras as the vanguard of U.S. policy toward Nicaragua.

Out of the Old Executive Office Building next door to the White House, Lt. Col. North coordinated the financial, political, and military components of the Contra operations. An organizational flowchart discovered in his files by the Tower Commission illustrates the complex "resource management," "financial accounting," and "op[erations and] arms" network over which he presided (Document 32). In his memoranda, North referred to this network as "Project Democracy," or "PRODEM." He saw his task as keeping the Contras "together as a viable political opposition, to keep them alive in the field, to bridge the time between…when we would have no money and the time when the Congress would vote again."[2] North was the "kingpin" of the Contra forces, as Admiral Poindexter described his staff aide, the "switching point that made the whole system work."[3]

Iran-Contra mythology has erroneously cast North as a veritable lone ranger within the Reagan administration; he was the central figure, but he did not run the Contra program alone. Other U.S. officials, from the president down, participated in various aspects of the resupply operations. President Reagan lent the weight of the Oval Office to the domestic fund-raising efforts, met with heads of state who were providing money for the Contra war, and interceded, as did Vice President Bush, with Honduran officials to facilitate the shipment of arms to the Contras. Bush's office placed a key operative, Felix Rodriguez, in El Salvador, where he played a pivotal role in the airlift operations in addition to working on Salvadoran counterinsurgency operations. National Security Advisors McFarlane and Poindexter supervised, and were ultimately responsible for, North's activities. CIA director William Casey also provided guidance and resources, and CIA officials including Deputy Director Clair George, Central America Task Force chief Alan Fiers, and Costa Rican Station Chief Joe Fernandez contributed to various managerial and operational aspects. Fiers, along with North and Assistant Secretary for Inter-American Affairs Elliott Abrams, made up the core of the Restricted Interagency Group—the "mini-RIG" or "RIGlet"—which essentially governed all aspects of the Contras' political and military operations. Other National Security Council staffers, such as Gaston Sigur, senior director for Far Eastern and Asian affairs, were enlisted to help obtain funds and arms; U.S. ambassadors in Costa Rica, Honduras, El Salvador, and Brunei all played roles in approaching their host governments on behalf of the resupply effort.

The cover story for the resupply operations, however, was that it was to be the work of "private benefactors." Therefore, North recruited a network of private-sector intermediaries, many of them retired CIA or special operations agents, to manage the various components of the Contra effort and to provide plausible denial for the Reagan administration. His first recruit was Robert Owen, a tall, blue-eyed, blond-haired former aide to then-Senator Dan Quayle. They had met in 1983 when Owen brought John Hull, one of Quayle's constituents who owned land in Costa Rica and was working with the Contras, to confer with

North. Owen became one of the first outsiders to discuss setting up a surrogate Contra resupply program with North. Although he had no covert operations credentials, in May 1984 Owen agreed to become North's personal liaison with the Contras and undertook his first trip to Honduras and Costa Rica, carrying photographs and CIA intelligence maps to the Contras, and returning with information about their financial and military needs. Owen, who described himself as "but a private foot soldier who believed in the cause of the Nicaraguan Democratic Resistance,"[4] soon became the key bagman of the resupply operation. In numerous "intelligence reports" he assumed the codename "TC," which stood for "The Courier." Owen also used codenames for North, sometimes referring to him as "Steelhammer," or "BG"—initials for "Blood and Guts."

To handle the critical arms-procurement and resupply activities, North turned to retired Major General Richard Secord in mid 1984. Secord came highly recommended by CIA Director William Casey: "He's got the right experience for this sort of thing. He knows the right people, he gets things done, and he keeps his mouth shut."[5] As a twenty-eight-year veteran of the U.S. Air Force, Secord had a long history of experience in covert and unconventional operations, including clandestine air resupply activities in Southeast Asia. Moreover, he had already assisted in CIA/Contra supply operations. In 1983, before he retired under the shadow of scandal, Secord participated in the secret CIA/Pentagon operation, codenamed TIPPED KETTLE, to obtain PLO arms from Israel for the Contras. "Following discussions between Major General Meron of Israel and Retired Major General Richard Secord of the United States government, Israel secretly provided several hundred tons of weapons," according to Document 23. Secord was, as North later informed Poindexter, someone who could "do something in 5 min[utes] that the CIA cannot do in two days."[6]

While Secord provided the covert paramilitary expertise, his business partner, an expatriate Iranian named Albert Hakim, provided the financial arm of the operation, setting up a maze of dummy corporations and bank accounts to disguise the money trail. Shell companies such as Energy Resources International, Lake Resources, Udall Corporation, and Amalgamated Commercial Enterprises (ACE) fronted for the acquisition of arms, the purchase of boats and planes, the construction of landing strips, and payments to pilots and crews, among other Contra-related expeditures (Document 32). The Enterprise, as Secord and Hakim termed their Contra support operation, soon employed an international team of retired paramilitary and military operatives, accountants, and subcontractors whose role, according to Oliver North, was to "replicate what the CIA had been doing since 1981."[7]

THE ENTERPRISE

When Congress passed the Boland Amendment in October 1984 banning further U.S. support for the Contras, this surrogate system was already in place. "General Secord had been engaged," North later testified, "and the money had started to flow to the Nicaraguan Resistance."[8] With $1 million per month in Saudi funds being deposited into a secret Cayman Islands bank account controlled by Calero, the Enterprise had access to sufficient funds to buy the arms and build the operations. Initially, the Contras paid directly for the services of the Enterprise, as well as for those of a second broker, GeoMiliTech Consultants Corporation, represented by retired Major General John Singlaub, which purchased $5.3 million worth of arms for the FDN in Eastern Europe. In addition, Calero provided North with hundreds of thousands of dollars in unsigned Bank of America traveler's checks, which North used as a slush fund for salaries, expenses, bribes, and other "special operations," and goods ranging from groceries to tires for his family car.

Initially, the Enterprise played the role of arms procurer, purchasing $9 million worth of rifles, grenades, surface-to-air missiles, mortars, rocket-launchers, ammunition, uniforms, and other equipment from arms brokers in Canada and Portugal, and selling them to the FDN for $11,348,926—a profit of over $2.3 million. Secord's first two transactions, made in the fall of 1984, were through a shadowy Canadian company, TransWorld Arms, which initially acquired the weapons from the People's Republic of China. The first shipload suffered repeated delays—members of the Enterprise referred to it as "the slow boat from China"—and failed to arrive in Central America until April 1985. For the rest of the Contra weapons, therefore, Secord turned to a close associate, former CIA agent Thomas Clines, whose company, Defex-Portugal Ltd., procured arms in Portugul, Poland, and elsewhere in Europe.[9]

From the outset, North and other U.S. officials facilitated the procurement of these arms. To disguise their destination, North obtained from Guatemala false end-user certificates—government certifications that the arms are for the exclusive use of the country to which they are being transported. When authorities in Beijing balked at selling the arms in November, ostensibly because of a close relationship between the Taiwanese and Guatemalan militaries, North, with the help of the NSC's specialist on Asia, Gaston Sigur, arranged a lunch meeting at Washington's Cosmos Club with the Chinese military attaché. "I advised him that the purchase was not really intended for use by the Guatemalans but rather for the Nicaraguan resistance forces," North reported to McFarlane on December 4, 1984 (Document 33). North then told the attaché that when a Contra government took power in Nicaragua, it would extend diplomatic recognition to the People's Republic of China.[10] Eventually the sale went through.

The shipment from China included surface-to-air missiles, a weapons system that North and others spent considerable time and energy attempting to acquire for the Contra war effort. "The FDN is in urgent need of anti-aircraft weapons," North reported in his December 4 memo. In November the Sandinistas had acquired sophisticated Soviet-built HIND helicopters to use against the Contras, setting in motion a flurry of activity in Washington to find a way to neu-

tralize these effective counterinsurgency weapons. In early December, North contracted with David Walker, a retired British major with extensive special operations experience, dubbed "Britain's Colonel North" by the London tabloids, to carry out a sabotage attack on the HINDs as they sat on the tarmac at Sandino Airport in Managua. If that proved an impossible mission, Walker advised, the Contras should obtain the British-made shoulder-held Blowpipe missile to shoot the HINDs out of the sky.

In a top-secret memo dated December 20, 1984, regarding a visit to Washington by British Prime Minister Margaret Thatcher, North wrote that Walker had "informed [me] that BLOWPIPE surface-to-air missiles may be available in Chile for use by FDN in dealing with HIND helicopters. This information was passed through…to Adolfo Calero who proceeded immediately to Santiago."[11] The Chileans proved willing to give the Contras forty-eight missiles and training free, along with the purchase of eight launchers at $15,000 a piece,[12] but there was a hitch: the Pinochet regime "must obtain British permission for the transfer." North proposed that President Reagan "very privately" ask Thatcher for this favor.

Despite repeated efforts over the next eighteen months, the Enterprise never obtained the Blowpipes from Britain or Chile, although Secord's handwritten account ledger for May 1986 contains an entry "BP $1,000,000 Chile." Nor was David Walker able to destroy the HINDs on the ground. Instead, North authorized Walker to undertake operations "in Managua and elsewhere in an effort to improve the perception that the Nicaraguan resistance could operate anywhere that it so desired."[13] In the early morning hours of March 6, 1985, Walker conducted a spectacular act of sabotage, blowing up a central military arms depot in downtown Managua with the aid of a Panamanian ordnance technician supplied by General Manuel Noriega. This mission, for which the Contras were supposed to claim credit, was to be one of a series of "highly visible operations" designed to influence an upcoming vote in Congress to renew Contra aid.[14] But the ensuing fire spread to an adjacent hospital, and it became politically counterproductive for the FDN to take responsibility. Nevertheless, North reported to McFarlane, the Enterprise paid Walker $50,000 for the operation.[15]

As the first year of the Reagan administration's efforts to circumvent congressional prohibitions on aiding the Contras came to a close, North assessed the status of the resupply program. In his May 1, 1985, summary of "FDN Military Operations," North calculated that the Contras had received $24.5 million from Saudi Arabia and had expended $17,145,594 "for arms, munitions, combat operations, and support activities." The funds, North claimed, had enabled the FDN to grow "nearly twofold" and to "become an effective guerrilla army." The remaining $7.3 million in the Contra coffers, according to Document 34, would be used to expand further the Contra forces, to conduct "major" special operations and ground offensives, and to open "a southern front along the Costa Rican–Nicaraguan border." Even so, North concluded, in order for the Contras to "advance beyond these limited objectives" they would need "additional funds."

THE CONTRA AIRLIFT OPERATION

On June 12, 1985, Congress partially retreated on its Contra aid ban and passed $27 million in nonlethal "humanitarian" assistance. The legislation, signed by President Reagan on August 8, required him to ensure that the money was "used only for the intended purpose and...not diverted" for military purposes—both the CIA and the Pentagon were prohibited from running the program. Therefore, the task of administering the funds fell to the State Department, which created a new bureaucratic entity, the Nicaraguan Humanitarian Assistance Office (NHAO), to handle the job. To head the NHAO, Secretary Shultz appointed Robert Duemling, a career diplomat with a spotless record.

Publicly, the Reagan administration cast the NHAO as an overt program, providing food, clothing, medicine, and shelter to the Contra forces. In reality, however, the NHAO program became both a complement to, and a cover for, the covert NSC resupply operations. With $27 million available for nonlethal assistance, North's operation could now concentrate exclusively on the provision of lethal equipment. Moreover, the new program could serve as the perfect cover for transferring and air-dropping lethal, in addition to nonlethal, supplies to the Contras.

Unbeknownst to Congress, Ambassador Duemling took his marching orders from the RIG, made up of Oliver North, Alan Fiers, and Elliott Abrams—the same men responsible for overseeing the various components of the resupply operations. Without informing Duemling of the illicit resupply operations, North, with the help of Abrams, pressured the NHAO director into putting Rob Owen on the public payroll (Document 35). Owen subsequently received $50,000 for ten months' work, which included traveling to Central America at taxpayers' expense. He then would file one set of reports on the overt aid program to NHAO while providing another set of reports on the covert program to North. North also engineered the employment of Richard Gadd, a retired air force operative who was already working for Secord on Contra resupply operations, as the main NHAO contractor flying nonlethal goods from the United States to Central America. Once in Central America, Gadd would use the same planes to drop guns and ammunition to the Contras. In this manner, NHAO contractors by day became NSC-run operatives by night, and U.S. tax dollars directly contributed to the illicit resupply operations. "What was really happening," as CIA Central America Task Force Director Alan Fiers described it, was that "Ollie was highjacking the NHAO operation."[16]

The passage of the "humanitarian" aid enabled Oliver North to proceed with plans to expand and restructure the resupply operations. On June 28, Contra leaders Enrique Bermudez and Adolfo Calero, as well as key members of the Enterprise, were called to Miami for a program review that lasted until 5 A.M. Initially, the discussion focused not on arms but on corruption. "Ollie started the meeting by heavily criticizing Calero in front of Bermudez about recent reports of corruption in the Contra organization," Richard Secord recalls. "He all but pistol whipped Calero."[17] According to Secord, North's concern was "a very serious one":

> He was afraid that…since they were dependent on contributions that the image of the resistance could be badly damaged; it could ruin us, in fact, and he was very, very hard on this point…. [T]his wasn't exactly the program review I expected.

Following the meeting, North removed financial control of the Contra operations from the FDN leadership, and turned it over to Secord and Hakim. From July onward, all monies raised for Contra operations were deposited directly into their Credit Suisse bank account in Switzerland.

Out of the Miami meeting came a consensus that an arms airlift capability was necessary if the Contras were going to establish and maintain a fighting presence inside Nicaragua. The FDN possessed only a few old aircraft left behind by the CIA, and none of what Secord called "the sinews of war"—the logistical, communications, and maintenance infrastructure needed to keep Contra units in Nicaragua supplied with weapons, ammunition, and food—which the CIA had formerly provided. "You either had to develop an airdrop capability or they were going to be forced from the field," Secord asserted.[18]

Organizing a logistics network with planes, maintenance facilities, crews, and communications was the first step toward establishing the resupply airlift. Secord hired Richard Gadd, whose company EAST, Inc., specialized in clandestine transport, to acquire the planes and put together the logistical infrastructure.[19] Through intermediaries such as the former CIA proprietary, Southern Air Transport, the Enterprise eventually acquired two Fairchild C-123k planes—a small, rugged cargo aircraft used in similar covert airdrop operations in Southeast Asia—and two Canadian-built Caribou planes.[20] Several short-take-off-and-landing (STOL) planes, made by the Maule Company in Georgia, completed the small Contra air force.

The second step was to secure a mission base. Initially, North wanted to use Honduras, where the FDN camps were located, but Honduran authorities, who officially denied any Contra presence in their country, resisted. Instead, with Poindexter's authorization, North chose the Ilopango air base outside San Salvador. "I met with President Duarte and received his permission," North boasts in *Under Fire*.[21] To obtain the more important permission of the Salvadoran military, North solicited the help of the U.S. MilGroup commander in San Salvador, Colonel James Steele. North also turned to Felix Rodriguez, a Cuban-American Bay of Pigs and CIA veteran, who was already in San Salvador flying counterinsurgency helicopter missions for the Salvadoran air force.[22]

In a letter dated September 20, 1985, North laid out plans to base the resupply operations at Ilopango (Document 36).[23] "[Y]ou are the only person in the area who can set-up the servicing of these aircraft," North wrote. He requested that Rodriguez approach the military commander at Ilopango, General Rafael Bustillo, and Salvadoran Defense Minister General Vides Casanova for permission to base the airlift operations there.

Using the nom de guerre Max Gomez, Rodriguez subsequently became the Enterprise's key liaison with the Salvadoran military. He coordinated the resupply operations at Ilopango, obtaining authorization for aircraft landings and departures as well as overseeing maintenance, fueling, loading, and unloading. His deputy, another anti-Castro Cuban named Luis Posada Carriles (aka Ramón Medina), had recently escaped from prison in Venezuela, where he was being held for the 1976 bombing of a Cuban jetliner which killed seventy-three people. Posada managed three safehouses, an office, and vehicles for the nineteen Enterprise crew and maintenence men living in San Salvador.

Not surprisingly, Ilopango also became the distribution point for the NHAO shipments. Tegucigalpa was supposed to be the distribution center, but on October 10, when the first NHAO-chartered plane arrived carrying not only food and clothing but also an NBC camera crew (allowed on board by Contra leaders in New Orleans), the publicity-sensitive Honduran authorities confiscated the shipment and banned further flights. At North's urging, NHAO flights were redirected to Ilopango (Document 37). There, under the direction of Felix Rodriguez, the nonlethal aid was simply mixed in with lethal equipment when it was distributed to Contra camps in Honduras. "We didn't differentiate between one and the other," Rodriguez later testified at the Clair George trial. "To me, it was—you know, it was just one operation... I was just handling both like the same thing."[24]

THE SOUTHERN FRONT

The third step in building a successful resupply airlift was establishing a secondary base to facilitate weapons drops to Contra forces fighting in southern Nicaragua. A backup base was necessary, Secord determined, because the Enterprise aircraft could not safely fly from Ilopango to southern Nicaragua and back. "It was a very long round trip to make nonstop in a C-123, 9 hours or more," Secord later testified. "And in order to—on a sustained basis—do this operation, it was my firm belief that we had to have an emergency landing field somewhere in that area. Of course, that is Costa Rica."[25]

Building a southern front against the Sandinistas had been a CIA priority since mid 1982, when the Agency recruited one of the heroes of the revolution, Edén Pastora, and began funding his small rebel band, ARDE, based in Costa Rica. "A combination of Pastora's popular support in Nicaragua and the military strength of the FDN would increase the threat to the Sandinistas," a December 1982 CIA intelligence report noted.[26] CIA strategists entertained the hope that a simultaneous invasion from the southern and northern fronts could divide Nicaragua and create a rebel-held zone.

Pastora subsequently fell out of favor with his CIA patrons because he refused to unite his Costa Rican-based forces with FDN forces fighting out of Honduras. And on May 30, 1984, he was the target of an assassination attempt at La Penca, his jungle headquarters just inside Nicaragua's border with Costa Rica. A bomb, placed by an unidentified terrorist posing as a journalist, killed three people including American reporter Linda Frazier, and injured seventeen others. Pastora, miraculously, survived.

But the CIA continued its effort to foster a viable southern front, bribing Pastora's commanders to abandon him and unite with the north. Building a force out of these "newly allied commanders"—NACs as they were referred to in CIA cable traffic—was a primary goal of Casey, North, Fernandez, and Owen.

At the center of Contra activity in Costa Rica was John Hull, a U.S. rancher who owned a 1750-acre farm and managed thousands of acres of strategically located land in the north used by Contra forces and their mercenary supporters. Soon after Fernandez became chief of station in San Jose, both North and Casey inquired about Hull and directed Fernandez to "take good care of him." Hull was "one of my station's assets," Joe Fernandez told investigators from the CIA's Office of the Inspector General. He "had been very helpful to us on Pastora, when we had been providing assistance. We had been using him for FI [foreign intelligence]...used his airfield for drops, etc." (Document 40).

A number of anti-Castro Cubans and Civilian Military Assistance (CMA) mercenaries also conducted Contra support operations on Hull's ranch, and Robert Owen, one of Hull's close friends, frequently met with him. After five CMA members were arrested on Hull's property in April 1985 for participating in cross-border attacks, two of them told reporters that the NSC was providing Hull $10,000 per month for his Contra-related activities.

When Ambassador Lewis Tambs was transferred from Bogotá, Colombia, to San Jose in July 1985, it was Lt. Col. North, not Secretary of State Shultz, who gave him his instructions: "Before I went (to Costa Rica) Ollie said when you get down there you should open the southern front. In the subsequent meetings and conversations (of the RIG) that was confirmed by

Abrams," Tambs testified. According to a CIA chronology, the ambassador informed his embassy staff that the southern front was his "single most important objective" (Document 41).[27]

On August 10, 1985, North flew to San Jose to confer with Tambs and Fernandez directly about constructing an airstrip in northern Costa Rica and to set in motion an effort to obtain permission from President Alberto Monge for the operations. Ten days later, Owen and Fernandez scouted a site on a little peninsula in northern Costa Rica known as Santa Elena. In a "for your eyes only" report to "BG" on August 25, Owen informed North that he and Fernandez had met with Costa Rican Minister of Public Security Benjamin Piza[28] and his deputy, Johnny Campos, and agreed that a company would be formed to purchase the Santa Elena land from its American owner:

> The cover for the operation is a company, owned by a few "crazy" gringos, wanting to lease the land for agricultural experimentation and for running cattle. A company is in the process of being formed. It might be a good idea to have it be a Panamanian Company with bearer shares, this way no names appear as owners. The gringos will own two planes, registered to the company and duely [sic] registered in the country in question. Cattle will be purchased as will some farming equipment.... (Document 38)

Subsequently, a ficticious company named Udall Research Corporation was created, and North sent an emissary, Robert Haskell, to negotiate a deal with the owner, a North Carolina businessman named Joseph Hamilton. "Our goal…was simply to get his okay to use the land but as it turned out he wanted to be protected just in case anything went wrong," Haskell later testified. Udall Reasearch sent a down payment of $125,000 and Haskell, using the alias Robert Olmsted, along with William Goode (a North alias), and Richard Copp (Secord's alias) became co-owners of the property. To establish a cover story for construction on the site and presence of Costa Rican Civil

Guard troops to maintain security, Piza later dictated to Secord what a backdated letter from "Robert Olmsted" should say. The letter, on Udall Research Corporation stationery, authorized the Costa Rican government to make "improvements or repairs" on the airstrip and to use the facility for "Civil Guard training" (Document 39).

The airstrip was to be simple and rudimentary: a leveled six-thousand-foot dirt runway, with fuel storage facilities and guard quarters. But construction was delayed; actual work did not begin until January 1986 and was not completed until May. The February election of President Oscar Arias, who opposed Costa Rican involvement in the Contra war, further complicated the project. Nevertheless, Piza managed to keep the operation going. As compensation for Piza's work, North arranged to have him and his wife brought to Washington for a photo session with President Reagan. "Security Minister Piza has been highly instrumental in helping us to organize a southern front of opposition to the Sandinistas….and has personally assisted in the development of a logistics support base for [Contra] forces deployed north from Costa Rica," stated a briefing paper from Poindexter to President Reagan (Document 42).

Even before the Santa Elena airstrip was finished, North ordered weapons resupply drops to Contra rebels based along the Nicaraguan–Costa Rican border. Secord decided to use a Southern Air Transport (SAT) L-100 aircraft leased to Gadd for the NHAO program. In early April, according to the *Iran-Contra Affair*, "North coordinated virtually every aspect of the first drop of lethal supplies into Nicaragua by way of the Southern front. He was in regular communication with Secord and others to ensure that the drop was successful."[29] Fernandez requested flight path directions from CIA headquarters and intelligence on the position of Sandinista forces in the drop area, and relayed the information to the SAT crew (Document 43). Secord sent a KL-43—a computer device used for transmitting encrypted communications—message to his field manager Rafael Quintero on April 8, instructing him to coordinate the drop from Ilopango and to inform U.S. MilGroup Commander James Steele that "we intend to drop tomorrow nite or more likely Thurs nite."[30]

Despite all these preparations, the April 10 maiden resupply flight to the southern front failed. The plane, according to Document 44, another KL-43 cable from Secord, "arrived over DZ [drop zone] on time but never saw inverted L or strobe lite. They remained in area 25 minutes and then aborted." Despite some objections from Colonel Steele, the mission was attempted again on April 11, and succeeded in dropping ten tons of assault rifles and other gear. The successful mission reenergized the Contra war strategists. "Our plans during next 2–3 weeks include air drop at sea for UNO/KISAN indigenous force…maritime deliveries NHAO supplies to same, NHAO air drop to UNO South, but w/ certified air worthy air craft, lethal drop to UNO South," CIA station chief Fernandez cabled North in Washington on April 12 (Document 45). He continued:

> My objective is creation of 2,500 man force which can strike northwest and link-up…to form solid southern force…. Realize this may be overly ambitious planning but with your help, believe we can pull it off.

THE SUCCESS AND FAILURE OF THE RESUPPLY OPERATIONS

Between April and October 1986, "Project Democracy" resupply planes flew some twenty-six missions to the southern front. Not all the flights were successful; some were aborted due to mechanical and logistical problems or bad weather. But in September alone, according to the Iran-Contra committees, 180,000 pounds of weapons, ammunition, and other gear were air-dropped to Contra groups operating in southern Nicaragua. In the north, resupply flights to FDN forces were far more frequent. During the same time period, Enterprise planes undertook over sixty-five missions, airlifting at least several hundred thousand

pounds of guns, grenades, mortars, ammunition, food, uniforms, and other cargo to FDN troops.[31] "The surge is now in full force," Secord's chief manager, Robert Dutton, reported to North in mid September.[32] Dutton was so proud that he even put together a photo album of the planes, pilots, and weapons; he gave it to North who passed it to Poindexter to show to "the top boss."[33]

Nevertheless, the resupply operations were fraught with problems. Due to the age of the aircraft (even Dutton admitted they were in "very poor operating condition"), limited maintenance, and a lack of basic instrumentation such as fuel gauges, proper radar, and nightscope equipment, the flights were extremely hazardous, prompting complaints from the Contra leaders and creating dissent among the flight crews. One note, uncovered in the wreckage of the Hasenfus plane, cited a "criminal disregard" for the lives of the men working at Ilopango. "How can we be pressed into service," it read, "without the equipment…without parachutes, without minimal survival gear, without adequate communications with the DZ? Is it simply greed that drives some of you to drive the rest of us?"[34]

These problems, along with disagreements with Secord, Dutton, and other Enterprise officials, prompted Felix Rodriguez to quit Ilopango. At the end of April he traveled to Washington, and on May 1 met with Vice President George Bush to tell him he was leaving El Salvador. A scheduling paper prepared for the meeting stated that the purpose was to "brief the Vice President on the status of the war in El Salvador and resupply of the Contras" (Document 46). Before Rodriguez could tell Bush, however, Oliver North and U.S. Ambassador to El Salvador Edward Corr showed up to tell the vice president what a fabulous job Rodriguez was doing. Rodriguez later testified before the Iran-Contra committees that he became too embarrassed to say anything about his plans to resign, and left the meeting without mentioning the Contras.[35]

Eventually, North talked Rodriguez into returning to El Salvador, but his disaffection only grew. At issue was whether Secord was profiteering off his Contra support operations, and whether the aircraft at Ilopango belonged to the Enterprise or the FDN. On August 6, Rodriguez defied an order by Rafael Quintero to leave one of the C-123 planes in Miami for repairs and flew it with a load of medicine to Ilopango. Oliver North began calling other U.S. officials for help. "Ollie called me, and when he was excited he used to say, 'My hair's on fire,'" Alan Fiers testified at the Clair George trial. "And he called up...and he said, 'My hair's on fire, and Felix is going crazy. Do something about it. The man's going to blow the whole operation.'"[36] Rodriguez had "made off with an airplane," North advised Donald Gregg, Bush's national security advisor. "Will you call him and find out what the hell is going on?" By then, Rodriguez was on his way to Washington to brief Gregg in full on his belief that the Enterprise was employing corrupt individuals such as Thomas Clines, overcharging for weapons, and not operating in the best interests of the Contras.

On August 12, Gregg called together a group of U.S. officials who were, in one form or another, involved in the resupply operations, to review these allegations. In attendence were U.S. Ambassador to El Salvador Edwin Corr; Colonel James Steele, who had taken over Rodriguez's role as liaison with General Bustillo at Ilopango; North's deputies, Robert Earl and Raymond Burghardt; and CIA Central American Task Force Chief Alan Fiers. According to Fiers, "it was a highly unusual meeting to [have] with the National Security Advisor of the vice president." The meeting, he said, focused on the integrity of the private benefactors. Gregg informed the group that Rodriguez was "concerned that the private benefactors are bad characters, or characters of disrepute. They're ripping off the Contras, and [are] generally folks that are not to be trusted."[37]

Like Bush's briefing with Rodriguez in May, the August meetings raise serious questions about the knowledge and involvement of the vice president and his staff. Gregg testified that his August 8, 1986, meeting with his old CIA friend, Rodriguez, was the first time he had heard about the resupply operations—although Oliver North's notebooks record a meeting with Gregg on September 10, 1985, in which they discussed using Ilopango as a Contra resupply base. Gregg also claimed that he never passed Rodriguez's information on to Bush. "[It] was a very murky business... I wasn't sure what this amounted to," Gregg stated. "I frankly did not think it was vice presidential."[38]

On the southern front, a different set of problems developed. The airlift suffered from a frequent inability to find the drop zone and from the inability of the Contras to recover all the cargo that had been dropped from the plane. Communications were the key difficulty. The southern-based Contras had no "commo officer" at Ilopango to communicate and coordinate flight path, arrival time, and drop zone information between the Contras and the resupply crews; from San Jose, Costa Rica, Joe Fernandez assumed that function, using the KL-43 device that North had given him. According to the CIA chronology, Document 41, in May Fernandez met with his superior, Alan Fiers, to discuss his role as a communications officer for the resupply operation. The two agreed that Fernandez was skirting the Boland Amendment and should try and place a Contra officer in that role at Ilopango. Fernandez, nevertheless, continued to relay information relating to resupply flights to Contra and Enterprise officials at Ilopango.

But the Santa Elena airstrip became the biggest problem. In May, just as the strip was finally becoming operational, the new Costa Rican president, Oscar Arias, took office and informed the CIA station chief that "I'm not going to permit that airstrip to be used" (Document 40). U.S. officials simply ignored the message.[39] On June 9, the first munitions-laden plane to use the strip for an emergency landing became mired in the mud, risking discovery by Costa Rican authorities. When Fernandez was informed of the stuck plane, he described himself as being so upset, "I was shaking. [I was afraid of] being PNGed [named persona non grata and expelled] because the new Costa Rican President had cancelled the construction." Fernandez told Quintero to get the plane "the hell out of Costa Rica" (Document 40). The potential crisis was averted when the plane was able to take off again before being detected.

The airstrip issue remained a problem, and in the late summer Arias took further action to shut down the strip. In early September, the new minister of public security, Hernan Garron, decided to call a press conference to expose the airstrip. North's notebook entries for 12:05 A.M. on September 6 show a call from Fernandez: "Security minister plans to make public Udall Role w/Base West and alledge [sic] violation of C.R. law by Udall…." North immediately set up a conference call with Assistant Secretary Elliott Abrams and Ambassador Tambs to discuss how to coerce Arias into canceling the press conference: "Tell Arias:—Never set foot in WH [White House].—Never get 5 [cents] of $80M[illion in AID funds]," read North's notes from that conversation (Document 47). Tambs did call Arias and dissuaded him from holding a press conference—at least temporarily.

On the evening of September 24, Minister Garron announced the discovery and seizure of a "secret airstrip in Costa Rica that was over a mile long and which had been built and used by a company called Udall Services for supporting the Contras." Garron named Robert Olmstead as the American responsible for the base.[40] The press conference set off a flurry of activity in Washington and Panama to cover the trail of evidence leading back to the White House. "Udall Resources," North wrote in a computer message to Poindexter, "will cease to exist by noon today. There are no USG[overnment] fingerprints on any of the operation and Olmstead is not the name of the agent—Olmstead does not exist" (Document 48).

On September 30, one day after the *New York Times* ran a story headlined "Americans Reportedly Supervised Airstrip Project Near Nicaragua," North provided Poindexter with a fuller report on the situation and a press guidance document designed to conceal the U.S. role in the resupply operations (Document 49). "The damage done by this revelation is con-

siderable," North advised with little effort to hide his anger. "It has…resulted in the loss of a facility important to keeping the resistance [sic] supplied and in the field against the Sandinistas." North recommended a series of steps to punish Arias for the revelations and to pressure him "to demonstrate his goodwill toward the resistance."

The press guidance invoked a series of lies: the cover story that the property owners had been interested in developing tourism and had offered the site for Civil Guard training; that no U.S. government personnel had been involved in the airstrip's construction; and that the U.S. government respected the Arias administration's position of neutrality on the Contras. The guidance was approved by Poindexter.

THE HASENFUS PLANE SHOOTDOWN

The revelation of the airstrip also damaged another North project—his ongoing effort to have the CIA purchase the Enterprise's assets. In June 1986, Congress had approved $100 million in Contra aid funds, and the CIA was scheduled to reenter the field of battle in October. "We are rapidly approaching the point where the Project Democracy assets in Cent-Am [Central America] need to be turned over to CIA for use in the new program," North wrote in a computer message to Poindexter in late July (Document 50). "The total value of the assets (six aircraft, warehouses, supplies, maintenence facilities, ships, boats, leased houses, vehicles, ordnance, munitions, communications equipment, and a 6520' runway on property owned by a PRODEM proprietary) is over $4.5M[illion]."

In his PROFS computer note to Poindexter, North advanced several specious arguments for why the CIA should purchase the Enterprise's resupply operation for a discounted price of $2.25 million. Failure to do so, he said, would result in a month-long delay in aid—"a disaster" for the rebels. Moreover, the Contras were out of food; Secord was willing to borrow $2 million to feed them, North reported, but could only recover this money if the CIA bought the Enterprise assets. The implication was that if the CIA didn't buy the assets, the Contras would starve.

In fact, at that time the Enterprise was flush with $7 million in the bank—profits from the sale of over-priced U.S. armaments to Iran. Why North kept this money a secret, and indeed tried to augment it by selling the resupply assets to the CIA, is one of the Iran-Contra scandal's enduring mysteries. According to Albert Hakim, the money was to be used for future "off-the-shelf" covert operations that Casey wanted to conduct, possibly in Africa. A report on the Enterprise's assets prepared by Dutton and Secord stated that they preferred to sell the entire operation to the CIA at a price "negotiated at some level below the $4M" with the "proceeds from the sale going back into a fund for continued similar requirements."[41]

In any event, Poindexter responded to North's pleas by talking to CIA Deputy Director Robert Gates about the issue and authorizing North to speak directly to Casey about the matter: "I did tell Gates that I thought the private effort should be phased out," Poindexter replied in a computer message. "Please talk to Casey about this. I agree with you."[42]

Bolstering their case for selling the assets to the CIA appears to be the reason that North and company were willing to risk continuing to fly resupply missions after the Costa Rican press conference on September 24. Had they simply decided to close down the operations and wait for the CIA to reengage in mid October, the history of the Iran-Contra scandal might have been different. However, five more airdrops were conducted, the last on October 5 using a C-123 cargo plane loaded with five tons of guns and ammunition.

Project Democracy's last flight took off from Ilopango at 9:50 A.M. with a full tank of fuel. Flown by two veteran pilots, William Cooper and "Buzz"

Sawyer, it carried a cargo "kicker," Eugene Hasenfus, and a Contra to maintain radio communications with the FDN troops in the drop zone. According to a KL-43 message from Dutton to North, the mission was to resupply Contras in the north, but the plane took a southern route to avoid Sandinista mobile gunners.[43] Before the C-123 could reach the drop zone, though, it was struck by a shoulder-held surface-to-air missile fired by a teenage Sandinista soldier. Hasenfus, the one crew member with a parachute, was the only survivor of the fiery crash.

The first report that the plane was missing was a telephone call from Felix Rodriguez to the office of the vice president. A CIA cable the following day titled "Disappearance of Southern Front Supply Aircraft" stated that there was "a remote possibility" that the plane had landed at one of a number of small airfields in the area and "has been so far unable to communicate its location" (Document 51). North was in Frankfurt, negotiating with the Iranians. Dutton cabled his office on October 6 that Joe Fernandez was checking other landing sites and the Contras were organizing search parties. But by the end of the day, CNN was broadcasting footage of a captured American prisoner, Eugene Hasenfus, near the wreckage. North saw the broadcast in Germany and immediately left for Washington.

According to North's memoirs, when he got back from Frankfurt, Casey summoned him to CIA headquarters at Langley, Virginia, "for a long serious talk." As North relates the conversation, they agreed that, despite cover-up efforts, the story of the administration's role was going to come out sooner or later. "'It's over,' Casey said, referring to Project Democracy. 'Shut it down and clean it up. Bring everybody home.'"[44]

NOTES

1. The Iran arms sales generated a profit of $16.1 million for the Enterprise, $3.8 million of which was actually diverted to the Contra effort. North's famous diversion memorandum projected that $12 million was to be diverted to the Contra program.

2. *The Iran-Contra Affair*, p. 37.

3. John Poindexter, deposition in *Report of the Congressional Committees Investigating the Iran-Contra Affair*, Appendix B, vol. 20, p. 1059.

4. Robert Owen, testimony in *Joint Hearings before the Select Committees on the Iran-Contra Investigation*, May 14, 1987, vol. 100-3, p. 322.

5. Casey's chief of station in Costa Rica, Joseph Fernandez, did not share this opinion of Richard Secord. In early 1987, during an interview with investigators from the CIA's Office of the Inspector General, Fernandez stated that he had a "negative" impression of Secord. "I nicknamed him 'dickhead.' Ollie would get very upset when I called him that. He'd say, 'Don't say that.'" North records Casey's recommendation of Secord in *Under Fire: An American Story* (New York: HarperCollins, 1991), p. 251.

6. Quoted in *Newsweek*, March 9, 1987, p. 32.

7. *Under Fire*, p. 254.

8. *The Iran-Contra Affair*, p. 42.

9. Clines never reported the income from his work for the Enterprise. On September 18, 1992, he was convicted in Baltimore of income tax evasion and sentenced to sixteen months in prison. To date, he is the only player in the Iran-Contra scandal to have served a jail sentence.

10. To play Taiwan off against the PRC, North informed McFarlane that retired Maj. Gen. John Singlaub, another player in the Contra fund-raising/arms procurement business, was, at the same time, approaching Taiwanese officials for Contra support.

11. Oliver North, Memorandum to Robert McFarlane, "Follow-up with [Great Britain] re: Terrorism and Central America," December 20, 1984. This document was originally classified top-secret/sensitive and can be found in the National Security Archive's microfiche collection, *The Iran-Contra Affair: The Making of a Scandal, 1983–1988.*

12. For the story of the Contra approach to the Pinochet government, see Peter Kornbluh, "The Chilean Missile Caper," *The Nation*, May 14, 1988.

13. Quoted in *The Iran-Contra Affair*, p. 338.

14. See North's status report, "FDN Military Operation," April 11, 1985. This document can be found in the National Security Archive's microfiche collection, *The Iran-Contra Affair, The Making of a Scandal, 1983–1988.*

15. Ibid.

16. Alan Fiers, testimony at the Clair George Trial, July 28, 1992, transcript, p. 1180.

17. See Richard Secord's interview in *Playboy*, October 1987.

18. Richard Secord, testimony in *Joint Hearings before the Select Committees on the Iran-Contra Investigation*, May 5–8, 1987, vol. 100-1, p. 59.

19. In 1983 Richard Gadd, a retired air force lieutenant colonel, set up several companies, including Eagle Aviation Services and Technology (EAST), American National Management Corp. (which listed Richard Secord as an officer), and AirMach, a cargo company that later received a major contract from the NHAO to carry Contra supplies to Central America.

20. FAA records show that the first Fairchild C-123k acquired by the Enterprise originally came from storage at the Air Force Museum in July 1983, was refurbished by a Roy Stafford of Jacksonville, Florida, and then was sold three months later to a shadowy company called Doan Helicopter of Daytona Beach. Doan, in turn, leased the plane in 1984 to Barry Seal, a well-known drug-smuggler who was working with the DEA on a sting operation against the Medellín cartel and the Sandinistas. The plane was outfitted by the CIA with special cameras, which Seal used to photograph a Sandinista official allegedly loading cocaine onto the plane in Nicaragua. This plane, with tail number N4410F, is the same one that was shot down over Nicaragua on October 5, 1986. See the *Miami Herald*, October 9, 10, 1986.

21. *Under Fire*, p. 254.

22. According to a CIA résumé introduced as evidence at the trial of Clair George, Rodriguez was a CIA "independent contractor" between 1960 and 1970, and a contract employee from 1970 to 1976, serving mostly in Vietnam before retiring after a helicopter crash. In 1984, he had applied for reemployment but was turned down, according to the document. By then, however, Rodriguez had friends in high places in Washington. Donald Gregg, the national security advisor to Vice President George Bush, had been Rodriguez's CIA superior in Vietnam. In December 1984 and January 1985, Gregg ushered Rodriguez around Washington to get official support for his going to El Salvador to implement a Tactical Task Force plan for the counterinsurgency campaign against the Salvadoran rebels. Rodriguez met North during his visit to Washington, D.C., in January 1985; on January 27, he also sat down with Robert Owen to discuss Contra pyschological and counterintelligence operations.

23. According to Rodriguez's memoir, *Shadow Warrior* (New York: Simon and Schuster, 1989), the letter arrived via Federal Express to his home in Miami, and was then sent first-class by his wife to San Salvador, where it arrived nine days later.

24. See Rodriguez, testimony at the Clair George trial, August 4, 1992, transcript, p. 1912. Rodriguez's role created problems for both CIA and Contra officers at Ilopango: a CIA cable released at the George trial, dated January 25, 1986, stated that "additional confusion [was] being introduced into San Salvador scenario by Felix (Rodriguez), who has somehow become involved in the San Salvador end of the NHAO system…. He has come in conflict with both UNO/FDN air force commander Col. Juan (Gomez) and UNO/FDN San Salvador logistics chief Lopez by insisting that all matters relating to the Ilopango logistics system be channelled through him."

25. Richard Secord, testimony in *Joint Hearings before the Select Committees on the Iran-Contra Investigation*, May 5–8, 1987, vol. 100-1, p. 61.

26. Quoted in Peter Kornbluh, *Nicaragua: The Price of Intervention* (Washington, D.C.: Institute for Policy Studies, 1987), p. 29.

27. During the Iran-Contra hearings, Tambs was asked if he thought his mission might be contrary to, and in violation of, the Boland Amendment. Theodore Draper points out, in *A Very Thin Line* (New York: Hill and Wang, 1991), that Tambs's response was that "he had never read the amendment and that, anyway, 'I have difficulty reading the contract for a refrigerator'" (p. 98).

28. Owen's reference to Piza, who was a key CIA asset in Costa Rica, later became the subject of significant controversy at the trial of Oliver North. When the defense sought to introduce the document containing Piza's name, the independent counsel, at the request of the CIA, informed Judge Gerhard Gesell that the name could not be declassified, and the trial was recessed for the day. Owen had, however, turned over an unredacted copy of his memo as part of a deposition to the Christic Institute, which was investigating the La Penca bombing. The document, in turn, had been acquired by the National Security Archive as part of its Iran-Contra collection. When reporters called the Archive about the document, they were provided with the full text. The next day at the trial, North's lawyers charged the prosecution with fraud for attempting to classify a name that was already in the public domain and called for a mistrial, but the judge denied the motion.

29. *The Iran-Contra Affair*, p. 66.

30. Richard Secord, KL-43 Message to Rafael Quintero, April 8, 1986. This document can be found in the Nation Security Archive's microfiche collection, *The Iran-Contra Affair: The Making of a Scandal, 1983–1988.*

31. Data on airdrop missions and amount of cargo is drawn from table 3.1 in *The Iran-Contra Affair*. The statistics are imprecise; the flight logs compiled by pilots and crew often did not reflect the weight of the cargo. See *The Iran-Contra Affair*, pp. 79–81.

32. *The Iran-Contra Affair*, p. 75.

33. Ibid.

34. This document, believed to be written by John Piowaty, can be found in the National Security Archive's microfiche collection, *The Iran-Contra Affair: the Making of a Scandal, 1983–1988.*

35. For his account of this meeting see Rodriguez testimony in *Joint Hearings before the Select Committees on the Iran-Contra Investigation*, May 27, 1987, vol. 100-3, p. 301. Gregg later claimed that the briefing paper should have read "resupply of the copters"—a reference to the helicopters used for Salvadoran counterinsurgency operations. For a discussion of the document, see the *Washington Post*, September 9, 1987.

36. Alan Fiers, testimony at the Clair George trial, July 28, 1992, transcript, p. 1217.

37. Ibid., July 27, 1992, transcript, pp. 1219–20.

38. *The Iran-Contra Affair*, p. 74.

39. In his interview with CIA inspector general investigators, Fernandez states that Ambassador Tambs told Assistant Secretary of State for Inter-American Affairs Elliott Abrams of Arias's position. According to Fernandez, Abrams replied, "We'll have to squeeze his balls [and] get tough with him." See Document 40.

40. *Tico Times* (San Jose, Costa Rica), September 26, 1986, p. 1.

41. This untitled and undated report can be found in the National Security Archive's microfiche collection, *The Iran-Contra Affair: The Making of a Scandal, 1983–1988.*

42. John Poindexter, PROFS note to Oliver North, July 26, 1986. This document can be found in the National Security Archive's microfiche collection, *The Iran-Contra Affair: The Making of a Scandal, 1983–1988.*

43. Robert Dutton, KL-43 Message to Oliver North, October 5, 1986. This document can be found in the National Security Archive's microfiche collection, *The Iran-Contra Affair: The Making of a Scandal, 1983–1988.*

44. *Under Fire*, p. 297.

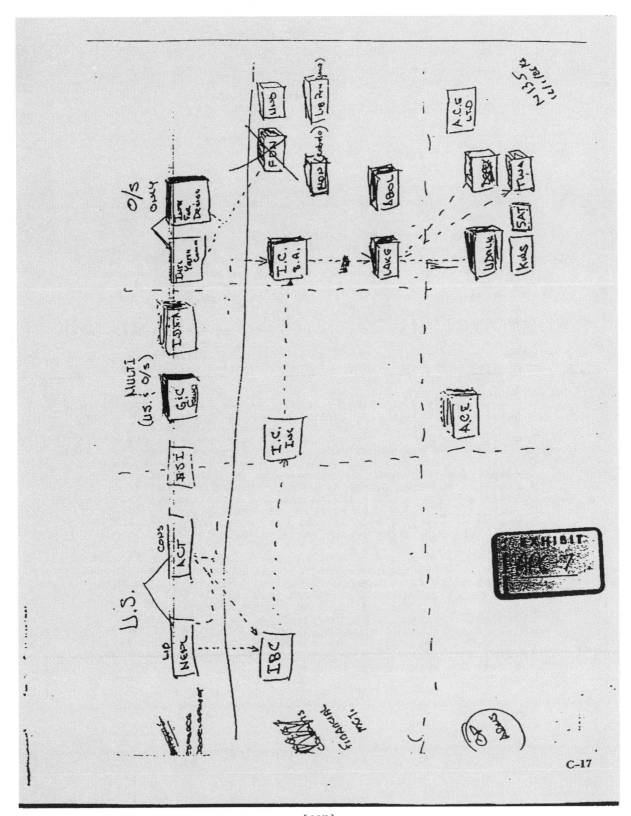

DOCUMENT 33: Oliver North, Memorandum for Robert McFarlane, "Assistance for the Nicaraguan Resistance," December 4, 1984.

PAGE 1 OF 3

TOP SECRET

MEMORANDUM

SYSTEM IV
NSC. ICS-4....

NATIONAL SECURITY COUNCIL

December 4, 1984

TOP SECRET

ACTION

MEMORANDUM FOR ROBERT C. MCFARLANE

FROM: OLIVER L. NORTH

SUBJECT: Assistance for the Nicaraguan Resistance

In accord with prior understanding, I met on Wednesday, November 28, with [a senior military official] Embassy of the Peoples Republic of China. Gaston Sigur arranged the luncheon meeting at the Cosmos Club and was present throughout.

As agreed, I explained to [a senior military official] that our purpose in the meeting was to clarify questions which had been raised in Canada regarding an arms transaction destined for Guatemala. I explained that an intermediary had advised that the PRC had apparently made a decision not to proceed with the Canadian-originated arms sale. This offer of purchase included 10 SA-7 missile launchers (referred to by the Chinese as HY-5), 30 missiles, 1 training unit, and 10 tracking units.

[the senior military official] professed to be unaware of the Canadian transaction. I advised him that the purchase was not really intended for use by the Guatemalans but rather for the Nicaraguan Resistance Forces. Further, the intermediary had indicated that the problem appeared to be the number of Guatemalan military officers who are graduates of the Taiwanese Defense Academy. As a consequence of the apparent reluctance to proceed with the sale showing a Guatemalan end user certificate, the Canadian arms dealer is preparing to re-initiate discussions for a similar delivery via Chile. [the senior military official] was advised that the FDN would prefer to have the delivery as soon as possible, since the Soviet HIND-D helicopters were being assembled as we spoke.

[the senior military official] was further advised that Adolfo Calero, the Head of the FDN, was willing to commit to a recognition of the PRC once the Resistance Forces had succeeded. [the senior military official] indicated that he understood the message and would confer with [another senior PRC official.] He observed, for the record, that the PRC steadfastly refused to become involved, in any way, in the internal affairs of another country. I indicated that we fully appreciated this position and noted that it was too bad that the Soviets, Bulgarians, and East Germans involved in Nicaragua did not feel the same way.

TOP SECRET

TOP SECRET
Declassify: OADR

AKW037366

DOCUMENT 33: Oliver North, Memorandum for Robert McFarlane, "Assistance for the
Nicaraguan Resistance," December 4, 1984.

PAGE 2 OF 3

TOP SECRET

TOP SECRET

Later that afternoon, MGEN Jack Singlaub (U.S. Army, Retired)
visited to advise of two meetings he had held early in the day
regarding support for the Resistance. Singlaub passed on the
following points:

Meeting with [a senior official] Embassy of Korea

-- The FDN is in urgent need of anti-aircraft weapons and other
crew-served weapons ammunition (particularly 60 and 81mm
mortar rounds). Units in the field are also in need of
large quantities of boots and clothing since the number of
ralliers has exceeded expectations by 2,000.

-- The Resistance Forces are also in urgent need of expertise
in maritime operations.

-- The USG is unaware of the Singlaub mission and he is making
this request based on his long friendship with the Korean
people. Because of the law restricting USG involvement, no
USG official can solicit on behalf the Resistance Forces.

-- If Korea would like to help, Singlaub can arrange a meeting
with Adolfo Calero. If it is necessary for a USG official
to verify Calero's bona fides, this can be arranged.

Meeting with [   ][a senior official
          (Taiwan)]   the senior Taiwanese
                                                        official

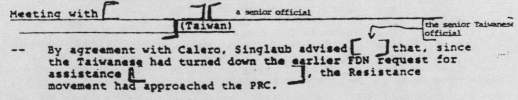

-- By agreement with Calero, Singlaub advised [   ] that, since
the Taiwanese had turned down the earlier FDN request for
assistance [   ], the Resistance
movement had approached the PRC.

-- The Resistance still is in need of financial support,
the senior Taiwanese munitions, and training assistance.
official

-- [   ] noted that this was a "considerably different
situation" than that which he had been aware of earlier.
While not committing to support, he noted to Singlaub that
senior PRC military this new information might make a difference in Taipei.
official

Prior to the North/[   ]/Sigur meeting, deGraffenreid contacted
the FBI to determine the level of surveillance we were
maintaining on [   ]. The FBI has reported that we have very
close surveillance and monitoring of [   ] activities. It is
thus very likely that the November 28 has been reported in FBI's
counter-intelligence/counter-espionage channels. Subsequent
discussions and or communications [   ] may also be monitored. The FBI has been
requested to make no distribution except to the National Security
Advisor on any intelligence we collect on [   ] regarding this
matter.

TOP SECRET   the senior PRC   the senior PRC
                          military official   military official

TOP SECRET

AKW037357

DOCUMENT 33: Oliver North, Memorandum for Robert McFarlane, "Assistance for the Nicaraguan Resistance," December 4, 1984.

PAGE 3 OF 3

TOP SECRET

TOP SECRET   3

Unless otherwise directed, our contact for FDN weapons and munitions purchases (a retired military officer) will be apprised of the FBI surveillance [   ] in order that he may be appropriately discreet. [   ]

of the senior PRC military official

This weekend, at the request of Sec. John Lehman, I met with Mr. David Walker, a former British SAS officer who now heads two companies (KMS and SALADIN) which provide professional security services to foreign governments. Walker had been approached several months ago, prior to initiating the current financial arrangement for the FDN. In addition to the security services provided by KMS, this offshore (Jersey Islands) company also has professional military "trainers" available. Walker suggested that he would be interested in establishing an arrangement with the FDN for certain special operations expertise aimed particularly at destroying HIND helicopters. Walker quite accurately points out that the helicopters are more easily destroyed on the ground than in the air. A discreet check by Clarridge [   ] gives Walker a "clean bill of health." Unless otherwise directed, Walker will be introduced to Calero and efforts will be made to defray the cost of Walker's operations from other than Calero's limited assets.

Because requests to the FBI can sometimes become lost in their bureaucracy, a call from you to Judge Webster would be appropriate. In the secure call you should advise Judge Webster that you have endorsed the contact with [   ] and that dissemination of any intelligence regarding this matter could jeopardize a very sensitive operation. (Unspoken in this call is the avoidance of an espionage case being opened against those who have been in contact with [   ].

senior PRC military official

RECOMMENDATION

That you place a secure call to Judge Webster urging him to report any intelligence [   ] regarding contacts with the NSC directly to you and no others."

on the senior PRC military official

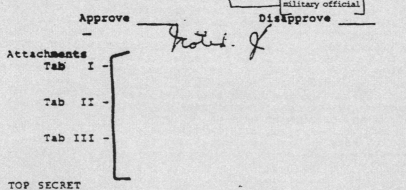

Approve _____   Disapprove _____

Attachments
    Tab   I - [
    Tab II -
    Tab III -

TOP SECRET

TOP SECRET   AKW037335

DOCUMENT 34: Oliver North, Memorandum for Robert McFarlane, "FDN Military Operations," May 1, 1985.

PAGE 1 OF 5

TOP SECRET

MEMORANDUM

SYSTEM IV
NSC/ICS-400453

NATIONAL SECURITY COUNCIL

May 1, 1985

TOP SECRET

SENSITIVE

ACTION

MEMORANDUM FOR ROBERT C. MCFARLANE

FROM: OLIVER L. NORTH

SUBJECT: FDN Military Operations

Attached at Tab A is a summary analysis of how the FDN has expended funds which have been made available since USG funding expired in May 1984. From July 1984 through February 1985, the FDN received $1M per month for a total of $8M. From February 22 to April 9, 1985, an additional $16.5M has been received for a grand total of $24.5M Of this, $17,145,594 has been expended for arms, munitions, combat operations, and support activities. No additional funds have been received by the FDN since April 9 even though there is a commitment for a total of $25M. The following information is noteworthy:

-- most expenditures have been for purchases of arms, ammunition, and other ordnance items;

-- the $2.5M indicated for upkeep of base camps on the Honduran and Costa Rican borders includes costs of approximately $350K per month (an expense which will increase as the number of recruits continues to grow) and $50K for the operation conducted in Managua against the ammunition depot at the EPS military headquarters;

-- the funding has allowed the growth of the resistance from 9,500 personnel in June 1984 to over 16,000 today--all with arms;

-- when the May 1985 sealift arrives ($5M has already been deposited for this delivery), an additional 6,000 fighters can be equipped and fielded after a 3 week training period;

-- the relocation of base camps along the Honduran border has been ordered for mid to late April 1985 in order to disperse the target for a Sandinista attack (cost for this relocation have not yet been fully quantified); and

-- the acquisition of two small transport aircraft at the cost of $186K is prudent given the increased patrolling activity by the EPS along the Honduran border, thus complicating trail-borne resupply for columns operating deep inside Nicaragua.

TOP SECRET
Declassify: OADR

TOP SECRET

SENSITIVE

AKW037369

DOCUMENT 34: Oliver North, Memorandum for Robert McFarlane, "FDN Military Operations," May 1, 1985.

PAGE 2 OF 5

2

Summary of Operations to Date

The FDN has grown nearly twofold since the cut-off of USG funding. In this period, they have reoriented from conventional to guerrilla warfare tactics. Despite the lack of any internal staff organization (G-1, G-2, G-3, G-4) when the USG withdrew, the FDN has responded well to guidance on how to build a staff. Although there was a basic lack of familiarity with how to conduct guerrilla-type operations, since July, all FDN commanders have been schooled in these techniques and all new recruits are now initiated in guerrilla warfare tactics before being committed to combat. In short, the FDN has well used the funds provided and has become an effective guerrilla army in less than a year. The listing of combat operations at Tab B (confirmed by reliable intelligence) is indicative of what the FDN has been able to accomplish with funds already made available. It is important to note that although funds started to flow in July, purchases made possible by this funding did not arrive in FDN hands until October 1984.

Future Operations

Plans call for remaining resources on hand ($7,354,000) to be used as follows:

-- increasing the force to a total of 25,000 by mid-Summer;

-- a major special operations attack against Sandino airport with the purpose of destroying the MI-24 helicopters and the Sandinista Air Force maintenance capability;

-- a major ground operation against the mines complex in the vicinity of Siuna, Bonanza, and La Rosita (Nicaragua)--the purpose of the operation is to secure the principal lines of communication in and out of Puerto Cabezas; and

-- the opening of a southern front along the Costa Rican-Nicaraguan border which will distract EPS units currently committed to the northern front.

It is apparent that the $7M remaining on hand will be insufficient to allow the resistance to advance beyond these limited objectives, unless there is a commitment for additional funds. The $14M which the USG may be able to provide will help to defray base camp, training, and support expenses but will not significantly affect combat operations until several months after Congressional approval due to lead-time requirements. Efforts

AKW037370

DOCUMENT 34: Oliver North, Memorandum for Robert McFarlane, "FDN Military Operations," May 1, 1985.

PAGE 3 OF 5

TOP SECRET

TOP SECRET   3   SENSITIVE

should, therefore, be made to have the current donors deliver the remainder of their $25M pledge ($8.5M) and to seek an additional $15-20M which will allow the force to grow to 35-40,000. If a commitment for these funds is made between now and June 1985, supplies could be ordered in July, allowing the force to reach these levels by the end of October 1985.

RECOMMENDATION

That the current donors be approached to provide the remainder of their $25M pledge and an additional $15-20M between now and June 1, 1985.

Approve ☑   Disapprove _____

Attachments
    Tab A - Summary Analysis of FDN Expenditures
    Tab B - Summary of Combat Operations: Oct 1984 - Mar 1985

TOP SECRET   TOP SECRET   SENSITIVE

AKW037371

DOCUMENT 34: Oliver North, Memorandum for Robert McFarlane, "FDN Military Operations," May 1, 1985.

PAGE 4 OF 5

As of April 9, 1985

FDN Expenditures and Outlays

July 1984 through February 1985

Quantity	Item	Cost
Independent Acquisition		
5,000	G-3 rifles	$1,500,000
25,000	Magazines	140,000
3,000,000	Rounds 7.62 x 51	420,000
1,000,000	Rounds 7.62 x 51	217,000
30,000	Hand grenades	285,000
Airlift #1 - February 1985		
1,000	81mm grenades	$ 48,000
2,000	60mm grenades	82,000
10,000	50 cal API	15,000
500,000	Rounds 7.62 x 39	87,500
498,000	Rounds 7.62 x 51	74,700
Freight, Demurrage, Ins., etc.		174,550
Airlift #2 - March 1985		
750,000	Rounds 7.62 x 39	$ 210,000
1,000	RPG-7 grenades	265,000
8,910	Hand grenades	84,645
60	60mm mortars	96,000
1,472 Kqs	C-4	47,104
Lot	Fuses and detonators	9,500
785	G-3 rifles	235,500
785	G-3 magazines	7,065
785	Cleaning kits	6,280
2,000	60mm grenades	89,500
10,000	50 cal links	3,000
Freight, Demurrage, Ins., etc.		187,000
Sealift #1 - April Arrival		
1,500	RPG-7 rockets	$ 398,475
2,400,000	Rounds 7.62 x 39	297,600
3,900,000	Rounds 7.62 x 51	322,200
1,000	Belts for 7.62 x 39	15,000
5	SA-7 launchers	25,000
10	SA-7 rockets	450,000
5,000	M-79 grenades	155,250
Freight, Ins., and other exp		216,500
5,000	M-79 grenades	150,000

AKW037416

[142]

DOCUMENT 34: Oliver North, Memorandum for Robert McFarlane, "FDN Military Operations," May 1, 1985.

PAGE 5 OF 5

2

FDN Expenditures and Outlays
July 1984 through February 1985 (Cont'd...)

Quantity	Item	Cost

Sealift #2 - May Arrival

Quantity	Item	Cost
5,100,000	Rounds 7.62 x 39	
5,600,000	Rounds 7.62 x 51	
1,700,000	Rounds linked 7.62 x 51	
100,000	Hand grenades	
15,000	M-79 grenades	
11,000	60mm grenades	
3,500	81mm grenades	
1,000	82mm grenades	
3,000	RPG-7 rockets	
1,200	Claymore mines	
50,000	50 cal API	
10,000	12.7 ammo	
30	57mm recoiless rifles	
1,500	57mm ammo	
400	Anti-tank mines	
3,000	G-3 rifles	
3,000	G-3 cleaning kits	
3,000	AK rifles	
25,000	G-3 magazines	
15,000	AK magazines	
4,000	Swedish K magazines	
80	HK-21 machine guns	
80	RPG-7 launchers	
80	M-79 launchers	
150	9mm pistols	
5,000	AK-39 links or belts	
10,000	C-4	
Lot	Fuses and detonators	
	Deposit paid	$5,000,000
	Estimated cost	$6,000,000

Miscellaneous Expenses Since July 1984

Quantity	Item	Cost
30,000	Uniforms	$ 480,000
30,000	Boots	600,000
	Radio and comm equip	150,000
	Air and ground transp	250,000
	Military gear	275,000
	Aid to southern front	650,000
	Aid to Misuras	150,000
	Food, family asst, upkeep of base camps, air force hospitals, etc.	$2,500,000
	Political activity - offices in various countries and cities, travel, p.r.	600,000
	Acquisition two transp airplanes	186,000

AKW037417

[143]

DOCUMENT 35: Robert Duemling, "Highlights of RIG Meeting of October 17, 1985," October 18, 1985.

PAGE 1 OF 2

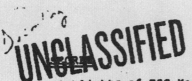

UNCLASSIFIED

#593 Ø RIG

S 4262

Highlights of RIG Meeting of Oct. 17, 1985

Participants:
ARA - Abrams, Michel, Walker, Melton
NSC - North, Burghardt
CIA -
NHAO - Duemling, Arcos

N.B. - This meeting was called on urgent basis to discuss fall-out from the episode involving NBC-TV crew riding UNO aircraft to Tegucigalpa, and renewed complaints from UNO that aid was not moving fast enough. Also, Triple-A were in town and had met with NHAO the previous afternoon (10/16) for two hours.

Status report

Duemling opened the meeting with brief status report on recent grants, L/Coms and disbursements. He noted the extreme difficulty of dealing with haphazard and incomplete UNO documents/proposals, citing requests for construction of a hospital and dispensaries without any supporting documentation. He also noted the ineffectiveness of UNO's designees ▮▮▮▮▮▮ ▮▮▮▮▮ who have no authority and apparently little understanding of the substance of UNO requests.

Buttressing UNO

With some asperity, North lamented the NBC-TV crew episode and repeated his concern that funds are not flowing fast enough. He asserted that an expediter (Rob Owen) is needed, contending that the NBC-TV episode would not have occurred if Owen had been employed and on the scene.

Abrams supported the concept of an expediter. Duemling outlined his reservations about introducing a middleman in the NHAO-UNO relationship and about Owen in particular. ▮▮▮▮▮ pointed out from long experience that UNO will never be able to provide tidy or efficient paper work.

After considerable discussion, the meeting agreed that Rob Owen would be employed under the following conditions:
1. He will work for UNO, not NHAO.
2. He will serve as an expediter. Whenever NHAO is dissatisfied with an UNO presentation, it will buck it back to UNO for upgrading by Owen.
3. If Owen fails to perform, or becomes a liability, NHAO's commitment to him will be terminated. (Abrams and North agreed that Owen will be expendable if he becomes a political or diplomatic liability. Duemling pointed out Owen's association with Singlaub and North, and fact that Amb ▮▮▮▮▮▮ had specifically rejected the idea of an American legman running around ▮▮▮▮▮ on behalf of UNO and NHAO. Abrams said that we could defend his employment to Congress by noting that UNO had specifically asked for him, as he had already demonstrated effectiveness in working on UNO's behalf. If later experience proves

UNCLASSIFIED

Partially Declassified/Released on MAY 8, 1987
under provisions of E.O. 12356
By B. Reger, National Security Council

⑭

DOCUMENT 35: Robert Duemling, "Highlights of RIG Meeting of October 17, 1985," October 18, 1985.

PAGE 2 OF 2

UNCLASSIFIED

- 2 -

S   4263

otherwise, we will simply say that our experiment did not work and we therefore terminated it.)

4. Owen will be offered a much more restricted mandate than had been requested in the UNO letter. For example, he will not be granted authority to contract for additional assistance; his personal compensation will be at a much lower rate; precise limits will be placed on allowable expenditures for travel, etc.

UNO End-runs

Duemling expressed exasperation with UNO's practice of demanding action with scant consideration for constraints imposed on NHAO, and then complaining to their friends if they are not immediately gratified. Duemling stated that he could put up with the shortcomings of UNO and its members, but he would quit if he did not have the confidence of the persons represented at this meeting. (This announcement appeared to have a sobering effect, and served notice that constant complaining and end-running by UNO would not be tolerated.)

Duemling also pointed out that, in the interest of expediting aid, he had approved several invoices that were impossible to verify. He had done this in response to repeated complaints from Calero that UNO's credit had dried up and people were starving. But his action constituted an act of faith pure and simple, and was without even the minimum documentary evidence to confirm delivery.

Discussion of this problem led to agreement that NHAO will provide CIA with a list of disbursements (on a continuing basis) and CIA will instruct its personnel in the field to attempt to verify deliveries. ████ pointed out that their efforts will not cover 100% of NHAO's disbursements but they will make a best effort. These reports from the field will be provided to NHAO for use in reporting to Congress on verification measures. Abrams emphasized the importance of verification, stating that it cannot be sacrificed.

RWDuemling 10/18/85

Cleared by Arcos

UNCLASSIFIED

September 20, 1985

Dear Felix:

AFTER READING THIS LETTER PLEASE DESTROY IT. You may keep the photographs.

Within the next 15 days, the Unified Nicaraguan Opposition (UNO)/ Nicaraguan Democratic Force (FDN) air arm will commence operations with two new types of aircraft: the C-7, CARIBOU and the M-740, MAULE STOL (see enclosures). These aircraft will be used for air drop/aerial resupply to units inside Nicaragua.

Two contract C-7s are scheduled to arrive in Honduras on or about October 10. Initially the aircraft will be flown by U.S. citizens who are employees of the firm contracted to provide delivery services for the FDN. It is intended that these aircraft will operate primarily at night, performing paradrops to units deep inside. Nicaraguan aircrews will be trained to fly these missions as soon as possible.

The resistance has also purchased a number of new MAULE aircraft shown in the enclosed photograph. These STOL a/c will be used for day and night short-haul missions to include MEDEVAC and aerial resupply. Each aircraft comes with a spare parts package and a maintenance line has been established. Two aircraft have already been delivered. More will follow. All will be flown by Nicaraguan pilots or other Latin Americans -- not U.S. citizens.

Eventually both types of aircraft will also operate in support of the southern front from fields in Costa Rica. Neither Costa Rica or Honduras have adequate sites for maintaining these aircraft. The only location which provides sufficient OPSEC, ramp space and occasional hangar time for servicing these aircraft is at Ilopongo.

Since this is a completely compartmented operation, being handled by the resistance, you are the only person in the area who can set-up the servicing of these aircraft with (two high Salvadoran military officers)   , both have a high regard for you and you may use my name privately with either of them but no others. You must not advise the [CIA]; you must also keep knowledge of this project from del Amico, who is not working with our people.

Would you, therefore, approach (two high Salvadoran military officers) with the following proposal:

--   Service space for one C-7 on a one day a week basis. A representative of the C-7 contractor will ensure that all parts and maintenance items are delivered to FDN service technicians (three) as needed. No Salvadoran parts or maintenance will be required.

iRG 1   AKW022740

2

--   <u>Service space</u> for occasional MAULE maintenance with parts
and supplies handled the same as above. Again, no
Salvadoran parts or labor will be required.

--   This plan requires <u>only</u> discrete use of the ESAF/FAS space
and no use of FMS; MAP; and/or Agency funds, equipment,
and/or personnel. The contractor will guarantee discretion.

the two high   Please advise soonest as to Salvadoran acceptance of this
Salvadoran   proposal. If (   ) agree, a representative of the
military   maintenance contractor will arrive and seek you out. He will
officers   identify himself as coming from Mr. Green.

Warm regards, hope all is well with you. We hear nothing but
good reports about your work. Keep it up. Vaya con Dios!

Mr. Felix Rodriguez
215 N.E. 114th Street
North Miami, FL 33161

AKWQ22741

[147]

DOCUMENT 37: Alan Fiers, CIA Cable to [Central American Location],
"Plans to Establish Alternative Supply Mechanism for Resistance Forces," December 24, 1985.

PAGE 1 OF 1

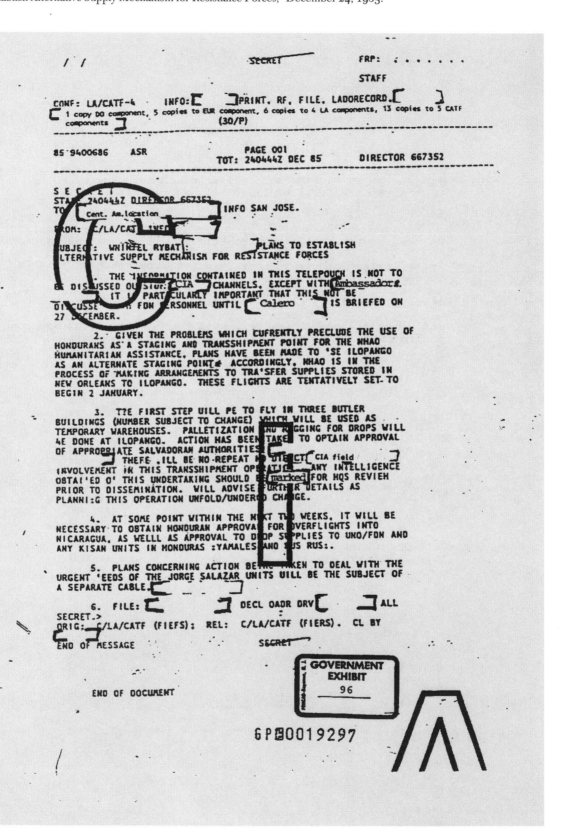

TO:　　　BG: FOR YOUR EYES ONLY　　　　　　　August 25, 1985

FROM:　　TC

SUBJECT: August   1985 Trip

Itinerary: August 19 — Washington-Miami
　　　　　　　　　 20 — Miami-San Jose
　　　　　　　　　 21 — San Jose
　　　　　　　　　 22 — San Jose-New Orleans
　　　　　　　　　 23 — New Orleans-Washington

Meeting with Ben and Johnny

This took place in Ben's office and in attendence were Joe and Johnny. Very cordial meeting with the emphasis on where the best place to locate the farm. Two sites were discussed, but the decision was made to use just one, as there would be less chance of discovery.

The area decided on is on the west coast, bordered by a National Park on the north, the ocean to the west, the Pan American Highway to the east, and mountains and hills to the south. The property is owned by an American living in New York. It is managed by a Colonel in the Civil Guard who will be glad to turn it over to Colonel Jose Ramon Montero Quesada, who has been designated by Ben to be administrator for the project. Am presently waiting for the name of the American so information on him can be found out and he can be approached by a company wishing to rent the land for a year with the option to buy. A guess is the cost will run between $10,000 and $20,000 for a year.

The cover for the operation is a company, owned by a few "crazy" gringos, wanting to lease the land for agricultural experimentation and for running cattle. A company is in the process of being formed. It might be a good idea to have it be a Panamanian Company with bearer shares, this way no names appear as owners. The gringos will own two planes, registered to the company and duely registered in the country in question. Cattle will be purchased as will some farming equipment and some land plowed.

The main house, which sits next to the Pan American highway, will be vacated and used by the Gringos. It will be possible to use third country nationals, although this was not extensively discussed. The Colonel will provide a cook, the peones to work the farm, and security.

A number of improvements will need to be made to the property. They Include:

- Building an airstrip next to the main house
- Putting in gas storage tanks by the house and a hangar and maintenance shed
- Building a road usable by 4 wheel drive to the 2nd site, about 10,000 meters
- Leveling and grading a second strip, about 800 meters
- Drilling a well by this site
- Building storage facilities
- Clearing a road to the beach

Once the new strip is completed it will be designated a military zone and will be guarded by the Colonel's people. The cover is it will be being used for mortar and rifle practice. There are no houses or farms near by and the strip is right off the water and in a draw between two ridge lines, so it is well out of sight.

DOCUMENT 38: TC (Robert Owen), Memorandum for BG (Oliver North), "August 1985 Trip," August 25, 1985.

PAGE 2 OF 4

BG
August 25, 1985
Page 2

Initial costs for the project include:

- Construction costs
- Purchase of at least two vehicles, both 4 wheel drive, a truck and pickup
- Cost of land, cattle and farming equipment
- Establishing the company, lawyers and registration costs
- Colonel's costs; should not be too high
- Salaries for gringos
  - Air ops (Spanish speaking)
  - 2 pilots
  - Mechanic
  - Loadmaster/packer/rigger
  - Civil engineer to oversee construction of the strips
- Registration of two planes in country
- Fuel

Requirements in the States for the project:

- Form company
- Off shore bank account
- Contact and negotiate with present owner
- Budget project
- Contract personnel

Next trip to the country should be with a civil engineer and air ops officer to begin the project with site survey, follow-up meeting with the Colonel, transfer of the property, establish company, begin construction.

The time table will depend on how quick the company is formed and personnel contracted.

The rest of the meeting was spent discussing the move of forces away from the border area. They want this done as soon as possible. They might be willing to help facilitate the move by providing trucks to take the people to a jumping off point. Johnny was more in front then his boss. It was left that they would be kept informed.

They were concerned with a base reported to be some 10 to 15 klics inside. If it was still there this weekend it was to be raided.

It was a very positive meeting and they want to work with us, but there are serious concerns. The biggest on both sides is █████████████████████████

BG
August 25, 1985
Page 3

Meeting with Robelo

On the evening of the 21st I met with Robelo at the request of Joe. This followed our previous meeting and Joe thought I could reinforce the need for Negro and his boys to move quickly. A number of issues were covered and as we already discussed them I will just briefly mention the significant points.

The Move: On Friday a decision was supposed to be rendered as to how best to carry out moving the approximately 280 people and some 16,000 lbs of supplies. The only two viable options are either :

- Across the lake after an air drop to include rubber boats and motors.
- By truck at night withouty equipment to a location probably above Boca San Carlo, the equipment would follow. The heavy stuff could even be cached, then picked up later and air dropped in once they are settled.

Once a plan is finalized it will take a period of time to set up the logistics. Earliest possible time for a jump off is probably at least 10 to 14 days. Even then it is pushing it the way these people operate.

There is resistance against the move, especially by Negro and his staff. They will drag their feet as long as possible. They complain they don't know the area.

If they go by boat they will have to be supplied with the following:

- Between 8 and 10 18 ft. zodiacs
- The same number of motors plus an extra 3 in case of breakdowns. They should be probably around 50 hp.
- Fuel tanks to be used for the motors.

This could be done by air out of Salvador.

They would move across the lake to between San Miguelito and Morrillo. The trip would take about 6 hours each way and would require a number of trips depending on the number of boats.

Meeting with Pastora and Negro: Pastora wants Negro to join him and work with BOS. Says the Gringos are out to screw Negro, thus he should protect himself and his people and join BOS. He reminded Negro if he goes inside he goes into his territory.

Negro believes Pastora is finished. His people in the field only talk to him on the radio in hopes he will beable to supply them with ammo or whatever.

Human Rights Violation: The internal investigation shows Chepon did order the torture and the ultimate execution. It was decided Negro should decide what punishment he deserves and was supposed to decide by Friday. He gave Robelo indications if Chepon is forced out of the movement he may choose to resign. If this is the case, the whole movement may be better off. If Negro decides on this course of action, it was suggested to Robelo he and Cruz go public immediately to get a jump on the press.

BOS: It is thought the organization may be receiving as much as $50,000 a month for expenses and travel; most probably from Perez.

BG
August 25, 1985
Page 4

Robelo's Personal Feelings: To quote Robelo, "I'm tired of the lack of equivalency in the Triple A. Cruz and I were integrated into the FDN to clean their face."

Major things he is concerned about include:

- He has not received his $30,000 for August.
- Calero gave Fred budgets for the FDN in the Miami meeting, including one for an FDN Red Cross, not an UNO Red Cross.
- Cliff took Calero's side in the meetings in Tegu.on almost every issue.
- By the next meeting of the Triple A he wants an inventory of money funneled into the FDN and where it is going.
- Wants to be consulted on what is bought
- Made it very clear he will not accept anymore money from Calero.
- Is finding it extremely difficult to work with Calero as he believes Calero looks on him and Cruz as appendages, not equals.

He made it clear he was not threatening to quit, yet. But he also wanted the message conveyed that things must change and he expects Calero to be more accommodating, or at least to make a pretense of it.

Meeting with Wycho

I flew to New Orleans and spent about 6 hours with Wycho on Thursday night. I brought him as up to date as possible and answered his questions as best as possible.

His concerns were: what was going to be the CR's stand, would his financial situation be taken care of, and deep down he was subtly asking if he had what it will take, or was he walking into a no-win situation. I think this is his biggest concern; that is why I promised he would have a gringo by his side to advise him and provide him with as much help as possible.

If he decides, he would like someone to call or visit his boss to explain the situation as he believes he owes him a great deal, including an explanation.

His decision is due on Monday, August 26.

DOCUMENT 39: Robert Olmsted, Letter from Udall Research Corporation to Benjamin Piza Carranza, Public Security Minister of Costa Rica, December 19, 1985.

PAGE 1 OF 1

UDALL RESEARCH CORPORATION

P.O. Box 7284 • Panama City 5, Republic of Panama
Telephone 692641/692652 • Telex 2752 RINO PG

December 19, 1985.

Sr. Benjamin Piza Carranza
Ministro de Seguridad Pública
San José, Costa Rica

Dear Mr. Minister:

Per your verbal request, the UDALL RESEARCH CORPORATION is pleased to make available to the Government of Costa Rica the use by the Government of the airfield at Potrero Grande area. It is our understanding that this area is needed for Civil Guard training and as an emergency alternate airfield for Murcielago.

UDALL RESEARCH CORPORATION understands that the Government of Costa Rica will be responsible for any improvements or repairs to the airstrip at Potrero Grande, as the Government may deem desirable. Any improvement or repair shall be for the sole benefit of the owner, at no cost. Furthermore, we authorize unrestricted right of access for the Civil Guard through the Hacienda Santa Elena to the Potrero Grande area.

This non-remunerated permission is unconditional, except that we request the Government observe the same stringent restrictions aimed at land conservation and preservation of the local ecology as does UDALL RESEARCH CORPORATION. The period of this authorization will extend as long as UDALL RESEARCH CORPORATION is the owner in control of Hacienda Santa Elena.

Respectfully,

Robert Olmsted

cc: files

DOCUMENT 40: CIA Office of the Inspector General, Cole Black and George Jameson, CIA Interview with Joseph Fernandez, January 24, 1987.

PAGE 1 OF 11

INTERVIEW WITH JOE FERNANDEZ
Date: 24 January 1986
Present: Cole Black and George Jameson

[The ▓▓▓ hou▓ ▓ of the interview was devoted to ensuring
that ▓andez u▓▓▓tood his right to remain silent, and that
he ▓ ▓oing to speak voluntarily without any promises or
com▓▓ents from the Agency. He raised an interesting issue in
reg▓▓ to "contempt," specifically, could he be held in
cont▓▓ of Cong▓▓▓ if it were determined that he had violated
one o▓▓▓ acts ▓▓ pposed to refusing to testify). As with
all q▓▓▓▓▓▓▓ sed relating to the possibility of
illega▓▓▓▓▓ ssociated penalties, we responded that they
were unc▓▓▓▓▓ this case, and that he had to assume that there
was some risk of self-incrimination. After carefully weighing
his decision, Fernandez said that he wanted to provide the
details of all activities he had been involved in. At that
point, he raised the issues of privileged communication in
regards to Ambassador Tambs ▓▓▓▓▓▓▓▓▓▓▓▓▓▓▓▓▓▓▓▓▓▓▓▓▓▓▓▓▓
▓▓▓▓▓▓▓▓▓▓▓▓▓▓▓▓▓▓▓▓▓▓▓ We responded that these would both
be considered before anything he told us was released outside
of the Agency. With that, he b▓▓▓ his narrative.]

I arrive in San Jose as Chief of ▓▓tion on 2 July 1984.

In early August...about the first week, a conference was held
with the ▓▓▓▓▓▓▓▓▓▓▓▓▓▓▓▓▓▓▓▓▓▓▓▓▓▓▓▓▓▓ together with
the DCI, the DDO, Dewey Clarridge and Ollie North. SouthCom
presented the usual overview briefings. ▓▓▓▓▓▓▓▓▓▓▓▓▓ gave
presentations for the DCI and DDO.

This was the first time I met North....He approached me at a
cocktail party and asked if I had had any contact with John
Hull. I responded, "No, but ▓▓▓▓▓▓▓▓▓▓▓▓▓▓ had.▓▓▓▓▓▓▓
and ▓▓▓▓▓▓▓▓▓ I also knew that ▓▓▓▓▓▓▓▓▓▓▓▓▓▓▓▓▓▓▓
had. North said, "Take good care of him because he has a close
friend in the White House." I said, "Who?" He said, "The
President...and he also has lots of other friends in
Washington." I just didn't believe him. The President knew
personally one of my station's assets! That was a new
experience. As an aside, John Hull had been very helpful to us
on Pastora, when we had been providing assistance. We had been
using him for FI...used his airfield for drops, etc.

Later in a private session with the DCI, he asked, "What is the
name of that fellow up near the border who helps Pastora?" I
responded, "John Hull," and proceeded to describe him as a
"John Wayne" type, a true patriot. The rest of the
conversation went something like this, "Well, ta▓▓▓▓▓▓▓
him because I know about him." This lent credibility to
North's comment. In my mind, then, I had the idea that Hull
was a special person.

(#6)

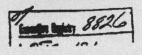 8826

DOCUMENT 40: CIA Office of the Inspector General, Cole Black and George Jameson,
CIA Interview with Joseph Fernandez, January 24, 1987.

PAGE 2 OF 11

I was always very careful about Hull. I treated him with kid
gloves. But by the summer of '86, he was getting too involved
with the press. In spite of his previous contributions, I
wanted ███████ to do with him, so I terminated him...for
opera████ █████ reasons.

Sep██ ██ct 1984 ████ President of Costa Rica was faced with
gro████ scandals relating to his administration. He named
Ben██ ██ Piza as Public Security Minister.

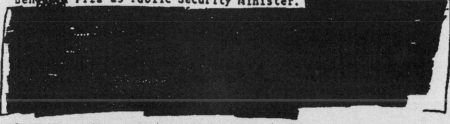

Jan '85: McFarlane visited. He met with the President, the
Vice President and various Ministers, including Piza. He was
accompanied by North and Fiers. They discussed the Nicaraguan
problem.

Spring '85: Ambassador Curtain ██████ departed. In the spring
or early summer, the Sandinistas attacked a Costa Rican Civil
Guard squad in Costa Rica. This was a "watershed." Throughout
the year there were constant problems of the Sandinistas
shelling across the border. The Resistance was constantly
getting caught transporting arms by the Civil Guard and the
Rural Guard. It was a high point of exasperation ███████
He was blaming the U.S. and, by extension, the CIA...and, by
extension, Joe Fernandez. We were trying to keep the Southern
Front viable. We had no control over Pastora. (My last
personal contact with him had been in August '84.) We tried to
keep him from politically attacking the rest of the
Resistance. It was hopeless. As he became more erratic, I
distanced myself from him. The Costa Ricans were yelling at me
for something I couldn't do anything about.

Then Pastora kidnapped 15 or 20 "Peaceniks"...some██ in ██
Summer of '85, and took the group into Nicaragua.███ ██ook
lightly...he was always doing crazy things...I kne██ ████████
never have harmed them. But HQS was frantic. The██ ████████
an urgent request for information. I called Pastora at his
home...."O.K., I'll give the order for them to be███

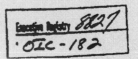

DOCUMENT 40: CIA Office of the Inspector General, Cole Black and George Jameson, CIA Interview with Joseph Fernandez, January 24, 1987.

PAGE 3 OF 11

released"....I subsequently found out from Ollie that the White House had convened...that committee that is activated every time there's a highjacking. I said, "Why didn't y'all ask us! It happen   time." I was surprised that Washington took such a   rest. We had a much larger problem that no one   tention to.

July   Ambassador Tambs arrives. About that time, 300 peop   nder Chamorro moved into Nicaragua because of my cons   appeals. This solved some of our problems. But there was   wing [Sandinista] military threat to the west and east of h   knew i   n't possible for him to remain there for long.   t him to move further north...on the other side o   re-useless....In Tamb's first meeting he said that   n given "a mission from the White House: create a Southern Front." That was "the single most important objective" he had.

Late summer or early fall: Tambs met with the President... Monge. He obtained an agreement that, if the Resistance could be forced to enter Nicaragua, Costa Rica would clandestinely support the resupply. Monge felt that this would diminish the risk to Costa Rican neutrality.   also served the U.S. objectives, first, to reduce the   ficulties with the Costa Ricans; and, second, to get peop   ack inside where they could fight. Piza was directed to wo   t the details [of resupply].

Tambs spoke to Piza.   Piza selected a place...on the weste   p of Cabo Santa Elana...Potrero-Grande. He said   his is the place that could be used for eventual resupply o   Resistance." At this point, there was no thought of t   rivate benefactors," or anyone else who would use it. Pi   dded another element: the place is also suitable for use by U.S. military aircraft if Nicaragua invades...under the Rio Treaty. "There's no other place which lends itself to large U.S. transport aircraft." Potrero Grande was inaccessible from the North and South...a series of canyons and mountains...natural protection...very defensible.

Tambs, about that same time, introduced me to Rob Owen, whom he described as "a friend of Ollie's who has contacts with various Resistance groups." He was the most knowledgeable per   about what the people in the Resistance were doing! I told   about him last time. He had contacts on the working leve   been at it since 1982. He also had contacts with John   t   told that Hull considered him his "surrogate son."   he that he was being paid by some foundation in Wash   n, never knew where he got his money from. It was c   fr Tambs that he was a close friend of North's, and   to Costa Rica it was to find out things for Nor   several times for breakfast before he was flyin   .

DOCUMENT 40: CIA Office of the Inspector General, Cole Black and George Jameson,
CIA Interview with Joseph Fernandez, January 24, 1987.

PAGE 4 OF 11

Throughout, I never tasked him. I wanted to know what he was
finding out for background. I didn't want any surprises. I
never prepared an ops or intelligence report. Subsequently, I
heard--▮▮▮▮▮▮ the paper--that he was carrying funds for
Hull'▮▮▮▮▮▮ assistance. (I've heard that Hull manages
prop▮▮▮ or se▮▮▮ senators...Durenburger, Quale...and others
in ▮▮▮gton.) ▮▮▮not sure that's true. I never asked. He
nev▮▮ ▮lunteered. I knew that he [Hull] was spending personal
fund▮▮▮.CBN, the Christian Broadcast Network, sent a boatload
of ▮▮▮ to a Pacific coast port in John Hull's name. That's
the ▮▮▮ instance ▮how of that he got outside support.

After ▮▮▮▮ted Potrero Grande, he asked me to take a
look at ▮▮▮n't want to go. I told him that I didn't
know anyth▮▮g about that kind of stuff. He insisted. I talked
to the Ambassador and he asked me to go...and to take Rob.
Pi▮▮ designated a Civil Guard colonel as his "field man"...Col.
Jose Montero...and put a helo at our disposal. Rob took
pictures, from the air and on the ground...walked it...sketched
it...paced it off. I understand that he delivered that
information to North. I don't think he told me that. I think
I heard it somewhere else.

Around the Fall of '85...I don'▮▮▮all exactly. It was after
Owen had visited the site. Ass▮▮▮cretary Elliot Abrams was
named as Ass't Secretary for La▮▮▮merica. Shortly
thereafter, he came to Costa Ri▮▮▮He told Tambs that he
wanted to meet me. I went to h▮▮tel room▮▮▮
▮▮▮▮▮▮▮▮▮▮▮▮▮▮▮▮▮▮▮▮▮▮▮▮▮▮▮▮▮▮ At one point, Abrams
says, "Tell me about 'Point West▮▮▮ I don't know where the
term came from. I think it was ▮▮ite House term. I said,
"What are you talking about?" H▮▮▮d, "That airstrip." I
flipped out and said, "Mr. Secretary, as far as I know, there
were only five people in this country that know about it...now
there are eight." He said, " We all know about it in
Washington." I said, "Who?" He said, "Fiers...North." I was
very upset. It was apparently being discussed back in
Washington and I hadn't been cut in. Anyway, I gave him a
briefing on I▮. It was clear to me at that point that the
RIG...the Regional Intelligence Group was doing the planning.
That was the point at which I learned that there was ▮▮nior.
official knowledge. [Why hadn't you notified HQS?] ▮▮▮▮▮ the
Ambassador's initiative. I felt comfortable with th▮▮▮▮
wasn't my idea. I wasn't responsible for it.

Fall '85: This is when I really started getting i▮▮▮ved ▮▮h
North on Potrero Grande. It was owned by a man n▮▮
Hamilton. He owned a textile factory in Costa R▮▮
North Carolina. This information was conveyed b▮▮
North. He was to contact Sen. Helmes, or someo▮▮ ▮his st▮
to find out if the guy was reliable. I told Tam▮▮ that I

8929
OIC-184

DOCUMENT 40: CIA Office of the Inspector General, Cole Black and George Jameson, CIA Interview with Joseph Fernandez, January 24, 1987.

PAGE 5 OF 11

wanted an agreement that there would be no Nicaraguan presence at the strip...for operational security reasons. He agreed to that...so did Piza. In fact, Piza made that one of <u>his</u> conditio   that it would become an official site of the Minist   Security, manned and guarded by the Civil Guard   cov   to be that it was a Civil Guard training site an alt   to the smaller strip an Murc o...farther north and unprotected from a Nicaraguan inv   . So, it became known as "Murcielago II" among us. Thos Washington kept referring to it as "Point West."

I ca   ecall   ely how I met Quintero. I believe it was over   the green line here, not the PRT-250. I had tal   h. He said he was sending <u>Robert Olmstead</u>, a "person idence," to negotiate a private lease with Hamilton. North asked me to contact Olmstead and brief him on the situation in Costa Rica. (Olmstead is a CPA...a former mariner Lt. who served with North. During combat he was shot in the head and lost an eye. I also understood from North that he was doing this voluntarily...without pay.) I subsequently learned that it was a protracted negotiation. Hamilton wanted a lot...a access road constructed....The cover for the negotiations was that a group o   lthy American investors wanted to lease the property fo   esort....Hamilton ultimately had some doubts about   tly whom Olmstead represented....Tambs called Ham   and gave him his personal assurances. Hamilton then worke   an agreement. Olmstead's firm, Udahl Resource Corp., purc   the property. The down payment was $50,000...it include   veral 100 acres, plus a ranch house....

The property is bordered north a   outh by national parks...actually one park, spli   this property. Part of the agreement was that the activity wouldn't upset the ecological balance...it even protected sea turtle eggs. The idea was to put in a 3,000-foot strip, with a smaller strip up in the mountains by the ranch....North advised me that Quintero was coming down and would be responsible for construction. Quintero hired Montero to be the "contractor." Quintero even agreed that Montero could farm the arable land. Montero brought down two engineers....I never met them. Quintero paid them. He once told me that Montero was ripping him of

Work started on the strip in late '85 and continued   arly '86. In discussing the airstrip with Tambs and Nor   as North's intention to use it for resupply aircraft o   Salvador. Those that couldn't make it roundtrip,   t Protero Grande and refuel...and fly back. There   lot construction delays...probably engineered by Mont   more money. The rainy season came. There was o   with aviation gas drums. "Avgas" is a controlle   stance Costa Rica because of the drug traffic....The d   were flo

5

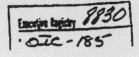

DOCUMENT 40: CIA Office of the Inspector General, Cole Black and George Jameson, CIA Interview with Joseph Fernandez, January 24, 1987.

PAGE 6 OF 11

in from Ilopango and dropped on the uncompleted strip. (They were still there when it was discovered by the press.) I have no idea where the money came from. I assumed the construction was being _____ by the RIG.

One t___ ___ ___ July, there was a flight from Ilopango with_ _ knowl__ They hit bad weather and had to land at Potr_ Grande. Quintero was in San Jose. He called me to his hote_ _ He said, "I was told not to tell you, but -e tried to run _ _ght and had to abort. We ran into trouble and had to land _ _otrero Gr__." I was so upset, I was shaking. I could_ _sion b__ NGed...because the new Costa Rican Presi__ _d j__ _ncelled the construction. He said, "Worst than th_ _ _ _aircraft is stuck in the mud." I told him to get th_ _ _aft the hell out of Costa Rica! It took him two days. That was the last time anyone was at the strip as far as I know.

Let me go back...I was here in the Fall of '85...in Allen Fier's office. He said, "Do you know that an airstrip is being built in northwest Costa Rica?" I said, "Sure," and told him about Tambs, Abrams....He said, "O.K., just so you know"....It's as though no one o__ _ed me to report on it....Let me repeat...I handled no money. I never met the engineers. I had nothing to do w__ the construction.

The idea was that the Maule [a S___ aircraft] would shuttle from the main strip up to the sm__ strip by the rang___ house....Also, in the future, it__d be used for exfiltration and infiltration. North at some point told me that he expected the Agency to take over the strip when funding became available. He never told me who__ discussed that with.

Nov '85: About six Commanders, nominally aligned with Pastora south of the Rama Road in southern Nicaragua, linked up with FDN forces north of the Rama Road. They signed an agreement to cooperate in the field, regardless of the political affiliation of their groups. That was important to us! It showed that what couldn't be accomplished by Pastora could be accomplished by the Commanders out of tactical necessity. But in the November-December period, they were running out of supplies. The Commanders had to tell many of their men to return to their homes and wait until supplies became available. They did receive some supplies from the FDN, but not much. By late December, they couldn't hold out any longer. Pastora's Commanders made it back to San Jose and asked to meet with us....There were a series of meetings. I was finally able persuade them that they should leave Pastora, unite join Chamorro, and re-enter. We were expecting funding _o __ approved by Congress in March...and then in April_ _ the advantages and signed a political agreement __ ___ '86. They name Negro Chamorro their leader. We called the__

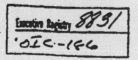

DOCUMENT 40: CIA Office of the Inspector General, Cole Black and George Jameson, CIA Interview with Joseph Fernandez, January 24, 1987.

PAGE 7 OF 11

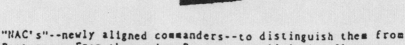

"NAC's"--newly aligned commanders--to distinguish them from Pastora....From that point Pastora's political influence declined... We also convinced Negro Chamorro to leave that marshy ████████ of the lake. His people moved north...around the la████████ed to Costa Rica.

So, ████ was no█████ng in March...or in April. I can't rec██ ██en the humanitarian flights started coming in.

Word ████ possibly Quintero--said around April that they could deli███ large a███ of supplies to the Southern Front. So the ████ ame th███ with a flight...an L-100. During that time ████████ flight support. You remember all ████ that I ██████ still had hopes.

In February '86, a new Costa Rican president was elected...not inaugurated until April. Piza though he would be supported in his activities.

Sometime in December '85, Piza ████████████████ ██████████asked for "one thing...I would like to meet the President...President Reagan." I conveyed that to Ollie. He said, "O.K." One of us told ████s. Piza and his wife, with me and my wife, saw the Preside██ ██ 19 March...at 0930. North lead us into the Oval Office. ████ were the President, Poindexter, and Regan....We had ████ oto opportunity....The wives left. Piza, North and I ████into the area outside of Poindexter's office. ████...Piza and I met with Poin███er about 20 minutes...I'm not sure if North was present. ████ of the conversation was about Costa Rican problems...vi████ of the new President...all political-military stuff. There████ no reference to resupplying the Resistance, or t████ airstrip. I don't think there had yet been a PB delivery.

As we came out of Poindexter's office, North told Piza that a man by the name of Richard Secord wanted to meet with him. I did not know the name. He said that Quintero would accompany him, and that they would meet at Piza's hotel...The Four Seasons. Piza asked me to accompany him....It seemed to me that Piza had fully expected to meet someone. I said, "It likes like something's been going on that I don't kno████ut." Piza said, "It's about the airstrip." We met in Piza█ ██m. Piza said to Secord, "I'm very concerned about how █████ing to cover this airstrip"....Then Piza dictated what a████ from Udahl Research Corp to him should say. Secord ████ down word for word. It was very precise. Secord ████ get a letter to you this afternoon." I don't kno██ ██it done, but when we got back to Costa Rica, Piza s██ the letter and it's going in my personal file." ████ that letter again until the press conference [████████ signed by Olmstead]....My impression of Secord ██ ██l

Executive Registry 8832
OIC-187

DOCUMENT 40: CIA Office of the Inspector General, Cole Black and George Jameson, CIA Interview with Joseph Fernandez, January 24, 1987.

PAGE 8 OF 11

negative. I nicknamed him "dickhead." Ollie would get very upset when I called him that. He'd say, "Don't say that."

The inaug_____ ___ on May 8th. A group came down from Washing____ ____ told Abrams that President Arias was very retice____ [sic] ____ the strip. Abrams said that we'll have to "sque__ _is bal___ __et tough with him." That day $40M was rele__ _ I turned to Abrams and said, "There's always the bala___ _ and laughed.

The ___ _n of Ari___ reticence...after he was elected, but befor_ ____ inaugu___ _n, Tambs briefed Arias and his brother about __ ____ ___ _d other things we were doing. He said, "If you__ __ ___ the Resistance out of Costa Rica, they'll have to b_ ___ __ed." Arias said, "I'll have to think about that." Subsequently, at lunch, I briefed them about our _____ _____ Tambs raised again the airstrip. The President asked me what I thought about it. I said, "Mr. President, the U.S. Government is _not_ involved in the construction of that strip...is _not_ providing the funds"....I knew it had to be coming from private funds because there _were_ no U.S. funds available for it.

The President and I hit it off w___ __ He didn't get along so well with Tambs....It was the th___ week in May...he called me for a meeting. Tambs told me to __ ahead....The Minister of Government and the Minister of P___ _ Security--no longer Piza--were there. Their names a__ __t important. It was in the President's study. He reviewed __ _ _hole situation and finally said, "Now, I'm not going to perm__ _hat airstrip to be used." I said, "I understand." I asked __m to keep a presence of Civil Guard on the property unti__ __ fuel drums could be removed. I informed Tambs of what __d been said. He asked me to inform Ollie.

After that, they had a change of heart. It was in June...all the Ministers met...Tambs attended. Several Ministers said, "We need the strip for its original purpose...to defend Costa Rica." Tambs only presented the argument for keeping it. There was no "pressure," as has been reported in the press. (I may have told Fiers about this verbally.) But it still did not carry the day.

Three months later--there were no guards--poachers got on the property and word got out that it's a Contra trainin_ ____ facility. I reported _this_ to HQS. The Ministers ___ ___ in and questioned me about it. About a week later, o_ _ agents said that the new Ministry of Public Defen__ _s _ public that the airstrip was to have been used fo_ ___ _un__ the Contras. There was a lot of Leftist pressur_ __ rationale was to expose it and let the press se_ ___ nothing there....I contacted North--Tambs was o_ __ the

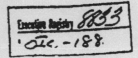

8

DOCUMENT 40: CIA Office of the Inspector General, Cole Black and George Jameson,
CIA Interview with Joseph Fernandez, January 24, 1987.

PAGE 9 OF 11

country. Allen called me back. [How soon after your call to
North?] Within an hour. He called me from his home. He
wanted me to contact the President's brother and tell him to
"put a lid ███████" He also said that Abrams had been informed
and wa███████████ntact Tambs in North Carolina. I was
conce█████bout ████ent....The next call I got...Allen called
and █████if I'd ██████cted the brother yet and I said, "No."
He █████ "You'll be hearing from the Ambassador because Abrams
told ███ to contact the President and tell him to put a lid on
it"████ambs called me and said he had. Six or seven weeks
late█████ Minist██ ██nt a force up there and explained to the
pres████ there ██ ██othing there...and showed them Piza's
lette█

About the ████ ██liveries...other than what I told you
before....It looks like the first may have been May, rather
than April. There may have been one in June, but I'm not sure
if that one was lethal or humanitarian. It may have been the
8th or 9th....For the early ones, I asked for a "hostile risk"
from HQS. On two occasions...on later flights, they actually
landed at Santa Maria Air Field...the major international
airport in Costa Rica. When they landed they were empty....I
don't know which two flights it was.

One other thing...this is a peculiar area. In late July I was
at HQS. We were faced with another "life or death" situation
in the South. I told Allen the situation. He told me to go to
█████ to see if the FDN could do something for the Southern
Forces. I did travel at Allen's direction. I talked with
████████████ I said, "Will you see if you can help?" They
never gave me an answer. We never received any supplies...and
I never heard anything more about it again.

The last flight was 23 September. We were hoping for another
and never got it. The last PB flight was Hassenfus. That one
wasn't for us. It was for the FDN north of the Rama Road. I
was never told about it. I've had no contact with Raphael
[Quintero] since that day. I spoke with North just once...one
minute before the President announced that he was being
dismissed. We were on the phone and he said, "I've got to
go." We sat there and watched it on TV.

[In response to questions re communications and the
relationship between supply drops and military activity:] The
drops were to guerrilla groups throughout the area. Their
level of operations were directly dependent on their level of
supplies. The PB's would advise me that they were ready for a
flight. I would advise the Commanders. They would looked for
a secure area and say something like, "We have control over the
area of the Parrot's Beak and can secure it for █████ days."
I'd relay that to Quintero. He would set the f████ ██ then tell
me and tell me what the cargo was and how many █████les. I█ ██

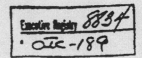

DOCUMENT 40: CIA Office of the Inspector General, Cole Black and George Jameson, CIA Interview with Joseph Fernandez, January 24, 1987.

PAGE 10 OF 11

would relay that a flight was coming in...everything but the nature of the cargo and the number of bundles. After the drop, they would radio in an inventory.

I used ▨▨▨▨▨, the open phone and the KL-43...I just found ▨▨▨ its n▨▨▨ I got it in late '85. Quintero delivered it. ▨▨▨d gotte▨ ▨▨ from North. He had ▨▨ tapes too! Mine didn▨▨ ▨ve a printout capability. [Did HQS know you had it? After ▨▨very, very long pause:] Yes. ▨▨▨ visited San Jose befo▨▨▨e became Div Chief [April '86]. I told him that I was in c▨▨▨ication ▨▨▨ North and told him about the commo gear. He s▨▨▨▨at he ▨▨▨ clear about the situation...that he didn't ▨▨▨ .that he'd look into it and let me know. It was ▨▨▨▨▨that the was unsure as to how to handle it. After tha▨▨▨▨call [re Hassenfus], I asked ▨▨▨▨ what to do with it [mid-October]. He said to give it back to North. I was going to give it to him when he came down for Thanksgiving. I didn't want to send it through the mails. So I brought it out in December and left it in Miami..in a plain box at my Mother's house. [Did ▨▨▨▨mention it at the May conference?] No. The May meeting centered on our communication problems between the South and Salvador. Nothing was said about communications with ▨▨lie.

I was always <u>reactive</u>! On a coup▨▨ of instances, I was specific about their needs becaus▨▨I had the info...straight intelligence reporting. I was not active. I got the information, then relayed it: "C▨n you resupply?" It was always, "NO." Then in September, ▨e informed me, "We're ready for frequent flights."

[Re any planning or command role:] There was one message in which he [North] asked me how I could see the eventual development of the Southern Front.... There are three main groups of non-indian, non-indigenous forces. The idea was to resupply them so they could link up....A "carrot" concept: drop ahead of them and make them go and get the supplies. But this was for our later resupply...when we were permitted to resupply them. They still haven't come to pass.

We never talked strategy with the Commanders. They are really autonomous. Planning is done in the field on a day-to-day basis.

I didn't "<u>plan</u>" resupply operations. It was, "Let ▨e know when." I was always <u>re</u>-acting...it was always a su▨▨▨▨ thing. I communicated with Quintero about specif▨▨▨igh▨▨ With North, it was more general: "Can't you <u>do</u> a▨▨▨ing?

I heard the name "Gadd" associated with resupply▨▨▨ the impression that Ollie didn't <u>control</u> Gadd--▨▨▨▨▨▨ control Secord. He could only ask....I don't ▨▨▨ Secord

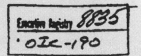

Exotion Registry 8835
OIC-190

10

DOCUMENT 40: CIA Office of the Inspector General, Cole Black and George Jameson, CIA Interview with Joseph Fernandez, January 24, 1987.

PAGE 11 OF 11

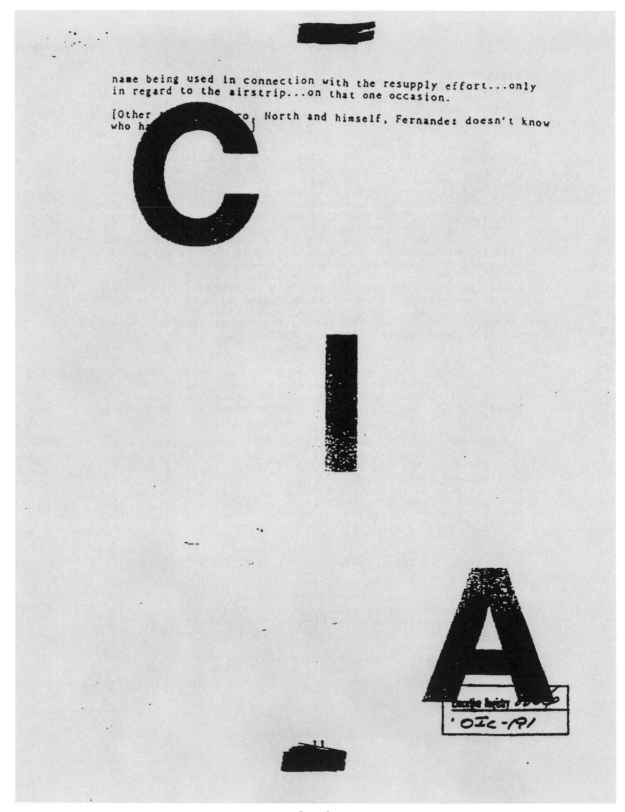

name being used in connection with the resupply effort...only in regard to the airstrip...on that one occasion.

[Other   ro North and himself, Fernandez doesn't know who ha

DOCUMENT 41: CIA, "Sequence of Events" (Chronology of CIA Station Activities in Costa Rica), ca. February 1987.

PAGE 1 OF 8

ATTACHMENT

SEQUENCE OF EVENTS*

2 July 1984: Fernandez becomes Chief of Station, San Jose.

Early August 1984: Fernandez meets Ollie North for the first time at a regional conference ▮▮▮▮▮ In attendance are the DCI, DDO, Dewey Clarridge, ▮▮▮▮▮▮▮▮▮ station chiefs. Both North and the DCI--on separate occasions--raise the name of John Hull, advising Fernandez to "take good care of him."

September or October 1984: Costa Rican President Monge names Benjamin Piza as Minister of Public Security.

January 1985: Bud McFarlane visits Costa Rica, accompanied by North and Allen Fiers. He meets with President Monge, the Vice President and various Ministers, including Piza. ▮▮

July 1985: Ambassador Tambs replaces Ambassador Winsor. In his first meeting, Tambs announces that he has been given "a mission by the White House to create a united Southern Front." He went on to say that this was his "single most important objective."

Late Summer/Early Fall 1985: Tambs meets with President Monge and obtains an agreement that Costa Rica will clandestinely support the resupply of the CONTRAS if they can be persuaded to enter Nicaragua. Piza is directed to work out the details of the resupply.

Late Summer/Early Fall 1985: Piza selects Potrero Grande on the western tip of Cabo Santa Elana in northwest Costa Rica as the site for a resupply airstrip. "About the same time," Tambs introduces Fernandez to Rob Owen, whom he describes as "a friend of Ollie's who has contacts with various Resistance groups."

---

* These events represent primarily the recollections of Joe Fernandez, with some inputs from ▮▮▮▮▮▮▮ Allen Fiers and Louis Dupart. Those which reflect direct communications between Lt. Colonel North and Fernandez or General Secord are based on material found in the files of North.

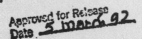

Approved for Release Date 5 March 92

15

DOC #8

DOCUMENT 41: CIA, "Sequence of Events" (Chronology of CIA Station Activities in Costa Rica), ca. February 1987.

PAGE 2 OF 8

Late Summer/Early Fall 1985:

Fernandez and Owen,

fly to Potrero Grande in a helo
[Owen "took pictures from the air and ground...walked it...sketched it...paced it off." Fernandez believes this material was then given to North.]

Fall 1985: Shortly after being named Assistant Secretary of State for Latin America, Elliot Abrams visits San Jose and asks to meet with Fernandez at his hotel. Fernandez goes, accompanied by [redacted] Abrams asks about "Point West" (Potrero Grande) and comments that North and Fiers "know all about it." [Fiers believes he first heard about the airstrip at a RIG (Restricted Inter-Agency Group) meeting in early 1986.]

Fall 1985: Tambs notifies North that Potrero Grande is owned by a man from North Carolina named Hamilton, the owner of a textile factory in Costa Rica. Tambs asks North to contact Senator Helms or someone on his staff to find out if "this guy is reliable."

Fall 1985: North calls Fernandez and tells him that he is sending Robert Olmstead, a "person of confidence," to Costa Rica to negotiate with Hamilton.

Fall 1985: During the negotiations for Potrero Grande, Hamilton becomes suspicious about whom Olmstead represents. Tambs calls Hamilton and gives him his "personal assurances." Olmstead's firm, Udahl Resource Corp., purchases the property. The down payment is $50,000.

Late Fall 1985: North calls Fernandez and tells him that Rapheal Quintero is coming to Costa Rica and would be responsible for constructing the airstrip. Quintero hires Montero as "contractor." Montero selects two engineers and work on the airstrip begins.

Late Fall 1985: On a visit to HQS, Fernandez is asked by Fiers if he knows "that an airstrip is being built in northwest Costa Rica." [Fiers does not recall raising the subject until the spring when Fiers visited San Jose, at which time he cautioned Fernandez to make certain that his activities were legal.]

November 1985: Six of Pastora's Commanders link up with FDN forces in the vicinity of the Rama Road and sign an agreement to cooperate in the field.

16

DOCUMENT 41: CIA, "Sequence of Events" (Chronology of CIA Station Activities in Costa Rica), ca. February 1987.

PAGE 3 OF 8

December 1985:

Late December 1985: Out of supplies, and with most of their forces having been sent home, Pastora's Commanders return to San Jose and ask to meet with Agency representatives. With the promise of support, they agree to combine forces with Negro Chamorro. [It was anticipated at this time that Congress would release funds for the CONTRAS in early 1986.]

Late 1985: Quintero delivers a KL-43 to Fernandez which he has obtained from North.

January 1986: Pastora's former Commanders sign a political agreement with Chamorro, naming him as their leader. [The inducements were sharing immediately in the humanitarian aid, and then sharing in addition support once Congressional restrictions were lifted.]

February 1986: A new Costa Rican President (Arias) is elected.

19 March 1986: Piza and his wife, accompanied by Fernandez and his wife, meet the President in the Oval Office. Also present are North, Poindexter and Regan.

8 April 1986: HQS receives a request from UNO/South, via Fernandez, for resupply flight routes for a C-123. HQS provides San Jose: entry points and checkpoints; true and magnetic course headings; speed and altitude data; drop zone approaches; weather data; air defense OB; and disposition of ground force units. [HQS was unaware of a commo problem between UNO/South and Ilopango at the time and assumed this info was being passed via the UNO/South Commo Center.]

9 April 1986: Fernandez is in contact with Quintero and is passing "current intelligence for drop crew."

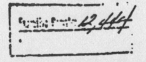

17

DOCUMENT 41: CIA, "Sequence of Events" (Chronology of CIA Station Activities in Costa Rica), ca. February 1987.

PAGE 4 OF 8

<u>10 April 1986</u>: Secord tells North he has procurred 90 55-gallon drums of av gas" and will move it to Protrero Grande between 15-17 April. [Construction of the airstrip was still in progress.]

<u>12 April 1986</u>: Fernandez reports to North that the air drop was "successfully completed in 15 minutes."

<u>15 April 1986</u>: North tells Fernandez that "a plane load of ordnance for your friends" was delivered to Ilopango the day before and asks, "When and where do you want this stuff?". North also asks if a UNO/South communicator had been placed at Ilopango and, if so, to have him coordinate with Quintero "so that we have things wired together."

<u>April 1986</u>: While visiting San Jose before becoming C/LA, ████████ is told by Fernandez about the KL-43 and his communications with the PB's. [Fernandez stated that he also told ██████ about his communications with North, but ██████ disputes this. ██████ also does not recall being told that the device had been supplied by NSA.]

<u>2 May 1986</u>: Secord tells North that "we have 20 men equipment from Aguacate," but that Fernandez has delayed the operation because of a "lack of boats for trip north by Indians."

<u>Early May 1986</u>: ████████████ Fiers attend a regional conference ████████████ In a private session with ████████████████████ Fernandez, they discuss the former's relationship with the PB's at Ilopango. The discussion then turns to the problem that UNO/South has in communicating securely with either the PB's or UNO/FDN, and Fernandez' role in relaying communications for them. Everyone understands the Agency's policy regarding contacts with the PB's. It is agreed that the UNO/South communications problem has to be solved so that Fernandez can cease his contacts with the PB's. It is also agreed that the solution is to locate a UNO/South communicator at Ilopango. Fernandez is given this task for action.

<u>8 May 1986</u>: Arias is inaugurated. After the inauguration ceremony, Tambs tells Abrams that Arias has misgivings about the airstrip. Abrams responds, "We'll have to...get tough with him."

<u>Late May 1986</u>: Arias ████████████████████ says, "I'm not going to permit the airstrip to be used." ████████████ ████████████ pass the information on to North.

18

DOCUMENT 41: CIA, "Sequence of Events" (Chronology of CIA Station Activities in Costa Rica), ca. February 1987.

PAGE 5 OF 8

<u>4 May 1986</u>: HQS receives a request simila to that of 8 April. HQS responds and COS San Jose passes the data to the PB's at Ilopango. [This resupply flight probably did not take place.]

<u>28 May 1986</u>: HQS provides the following guidelines to COS ▓▓▓▓▓▓▓▓▓▓▓▓▓ San Jose ▓▓▓▓▓▓▓▓▓▓▓ regarding interactions with UNO/FDN and UNO/South: Station may provide advice and commo equipment, and may engage in intelligence exchange; Station may <u>not</u> provide materiel or monetary support. [Some have interpreted this cable as providing Fernandez guidance on <u>his</u> contacts with the <u>PB's</u>.]

<u>2 June 1986</u>: Secord tells North that "pursuant to request" from Fernandez, we are preparing to make two drops totalling about 39,000 lbs to Southern Front troops," and that the mission "may go as soon as this next weekend." He also says that Fernandez "has provided Ralph with some current intel but we still do not have radar predictions."

<u>June 1986</u>: A PB resupply flight diverts to Potrero Grande in bad weather. The aircraft becomes stuck. Quintero, who is in San Jose at the time, asks Fernandez to come to his hotel room where he tells him about the aircraft. Fernandez tells him to remove it immediately, and then delays a visit to Washington until he is assured that the plane is being removed. [Fernandez had not been aware of this flight since it was intended to resupply the UNO/FDN forces.]

<u>6 June 1986</u>: Secord tells North that "all aircraft out of mud and back at Ilopango....Half of munitions load also back at Ilopango and remainder will be picked up by Caribou today." He also describes the conditions at Potrero Grande, saying that the strip "will have limited utility during heavy rains," but that it "can still be used as divert base since highest 3,000 ft. is useable even during worst conditions." [From early June on, Fernandez did not believe the airstrip was useable and was not aware of any other aircraft landing there.]

<u>16 June 1986</u>: North notifies Fernandez that an FDN resupply flight is scheduled for the next day, but that it can be delayed for one night "to do your drop if we can get the necessary info for the pilots." He then says, "To facilitate, have asked Ralph to proceed immediately to your location."

<u>18 June 1986</u>: [Repeat 24 May entry.]

<u>June 1986</u>: [Fernandez recalls "one or two" resupply flights taking place in June but cannot recall whether they involved "lethal" or "humanitarian" cargo.]

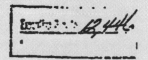

DOCUMENT 41: CIA, "Sequence of Events" (Chronology of CIA Station Activities in Costa Rica), ca. February 1987.

PAGE 6 OF 8

<u>19 June 1986</u>: Someone by the name of "Bob" notifies North that he had "talked w/SAT" [probably Southern Air Transport] but that "Bill" will not fly "the MSN" unless some insurance problems can be resolved. He goes on to say that if this problem cannot be resolved then "Bill" will only "fly goods to west [Protrero Grande]...via C-7." [Written by hand at the bottom of this message are the names "Carl Jenkins" and "Ferguson." Another notation reads, "Jenkins now in Costa Rica."]

<u>30 June 1986</u>: Fernandez tells North that "UNO south force deteriorated badly past 7 days," and requests "you come work with us." [This entry comes from the most recent dated message in OIG possession from the North files.]

<u>9 July 1986</u>: [Repeat 24 May entry.]

<u>12 July 1986</u>: Fernandez is notified that a review of Agency policy does not permit him to continue his efforts to place a UNO/South communicator at Ilopango. [Some have interpreted this cable as directing the COS San Jose to terminate his contacts with the PB's.] ████████ questions the cable after it has been transmitted and is told that UNO/South had solved the problem itself.

<u>5-6 September 1986</u>: North learns that the new Minister of Public Security intends to call a press conference regarding the airstrip. ████████████████████████ In a conference call between North, Tambs, Abrams and Fiers, it is decided to put pressure on Arias. ████████████████ ████████████ The press conference is called off. ██████████

<u>Prior to 8 September 1986</u>: Quintero notifies Fernandez about a planned resupply mission, and Fernandez relays the information to the UNO/South. [Info received: A/C type; expected date and hour of air drop; primary and alternate drop zones; and number of bundles.]

<u>8 September 1986</u>: Following the exchange of flight information, there is a resupply mission for UNO/South. [This sequence of events was repeated on 11, 14, 17, 19 and 23 Sept.]

<u>18 September 1986</u>: San Jose Station issues its weekly intel report. Among other things, the report describes the first three September air drops for UNO/South.

<u>24 September 1986</u>: San Jose Station issues its weekly intel report. Among other things, the report summarizes the six September air drops of supplies for UNO/South.

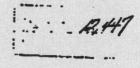

20

DOCUMENT 41: CIA, "Sequence of Events" (Chronology of CIA Station Activities in Costa Rica), ca. February 1987.

PAGE 7 OF 8

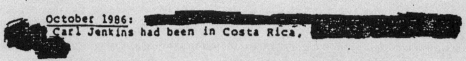

October 1986: ▮▮▮▮▮▮▮▮▮▮▮▮▮▮▮▮▮▮▮▮▮▮
Carl Jenkins had been in Costa Rica. ▮▮▮▮▮▮▮

5 October 1986: When the Hausenfus flight is overdue,
Fernandez receives "several telephone calls" from Quintero
inquiring about a possible emergency landing or crash.

October 1986: After the downing of the Hausenfus aircraft,
Fernandez asks ▮▮▮▮▮ what he should do with the KL-43 and is
told to return it to North.

14 October 1986: In the aftermath of the Hassenfus affair,
the DDO testifies before HPSCI that CIA was not involved
"directly or indirectly in arranging, directing, or
facilitating resupply missions conducted by private individuals
in support of the Nicaraguan Democratic Resistance."

Late October 1986: Fiers, during a trip to San Jose,
learns that a US reporter has information about telephone calls
between Fernandez and the PB's. Fernandez describes his
contacts with the PB's at Ilopango. [Upon his return, Fiers
reported the matter to ▮▮▮▮▮▮▮

6 November 1986: Louis Dupart, the CATF Compliance Officer
visits San Jose Station on other matters and learns for the
first time about the Fernandez' contacts with the PB's since
early April.

10 November 1986: ▮▮▮▮▮▮▮ meets with the DDO and reports on
the activities of Fernandez. The DDO asks him to followup on
the matter.

14 November 1986: A story appears in San Jose's Tico Times
about telephone calls between a "safehouse" in San Salvador and
a San Jose Embassy "private line," as well as the "unlisted"
home phone of an Embassy "political and economic analyst."

26 November 1986: In a memo to the DDO regarding the
Fernandez investigation ▮▮▮▮▮▮▮ concludes that there has been no
illegalities, but recommends an OGC review.

30 November 1986: The New York Times runs a story about
the telephone calls between San Salvador and the "unlisted"
number in San Jose.

4 December 1986: NBC broadcasts a report about the
"unlisted" telephone number in San Jose.

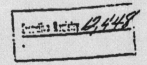

21

DOCUMENT 41: CIA, "Sequence of Events" (Chronology of CIA Station Activities in Costa Rica), ca. February 1987.

PAGE 8 OF 8

_____ _____. _____ (____) makes a t'_phonic request
_arding the facts relating to the NBC alle__ ions.

5 December 1986: Jameson and Dupart complete their
analysis of the legislation in effect at the time of the
contact with the PB's, and present it to the DDO. They
conclude that the activities, although contrary to Agency
policy, were not contrary to law. [The activities were
intended to facilitate "authorized information-sharing," and
can be distinguished from participation in "logistics
activities" which were prohibited by law. The analysis
concludes that the Intelligence Authorization Act of FY 86
permitted "advice on the effective delivery and distribution of
material to the resistance." Furthermore, since "the Agency
was authorized to pass such information directly to assist the
UNO/FDN, it logically follows that the Agency has the legal
authority to provide such information to the private
benefactors for the same purpose."]

7 December 1986: Fernandez cables details of his September
contacts with Ilopango to be included in the response to HPSCI.

9 December 1986: An interim response is sent to HPSCI.

10 December 1986: Fernandez is interviewed in Miami by
Dupart and confirms the facts as known at that time.

14 December 1986: Fernandez is recalled for temporary
service on a career panel.

29 December 1986: A final report is sent to HPSCI.

11 January 1987: OIG has its initial interview with
Fernandez. [OIG subsequently learned that Fernandez had not
been completely truthful in this interview, particularly about
his part in the construction of Potrero Grande, his single
contact with General Secord, and the extent of his
relationships with North and Quintero.]

21 January 1987: The Tower Commission interviews Fernandez
twice. After being confronted with copies of his messages to
North in the second session, he describes his activities in
much more detail. [OIG subsequently learned that, even in
Fernandez' second session with the Commission, he failed to be
completely truthful in regard to his contact with Secord.]

24 January 1987: OIG and Jameson interview Fernandez and
he admits his previous evasions and untruths.

2 February 1987: OIG interviews Fernandez for the last time.

22

DOCUMENT 42: John Poindexter, Agenda for the President, "Meeting with Costa Rican Security Minister Benjamin Piza," and Attachment "Talking Points," March 17, 1986.

PAGE 1 OF 2

THE WHITE HOUSE

WASHINGTON

<u>MEETING WITH COSTA RICAN SECURITY MINISTER BENJAMIN PIZA</u>

DATE: Wednesday, March 17, 1986
LOCATION: Oval Office
TIME: 9:40-9:45 a.m.

FROM: JOHN M. POINDEXTER

I.   <u>PURPOSE</u>: Brief photo opportunity with Costa Rican Security Minister Benjamin Piza and his wife, Teresita Pozuelo Piza.

II. <u>BACKGROUND</u>: Security Minister Piza has been highly instrumental in helping us to organize a southern front of opposition to the Sandinistas. He has intervened with President Monge on numerous occasions and has personally assisted in the development of a logistics support base for the United Nicaraguan Opposition (UNO) forces deployed north from Costa Rica. During my trip to Central America, I met with Minister Piza to discuss future plans for the Nicaraguan resistance and support for them through Costa Rica.

Although Minister Piza leaves office on May 8, 1986, when the Arias Government is inaugurated, he will continue to play an important role in Costa Rican politics and diplomacy. As such, he is a key figure in maintaining support for the our policies in the region. Your brief meeting and photo provide an opportunity for us to thank him for his assistance.

Brief talking points are attached at Tab A.

III. <u>PARTICIPANTS</u>: The President, Don Regan, John Poindexter, Minister Benjamin Piza and, his wife, Teresita Pozuelo Piza, Joseph Fernandez, and Oliver North.

IV. <u>PRESS PLAN</u>: None.

V.   <u>SEQUENCE OF EVENTS</u>: Mr. Piza and his wife are escorted into the Oval Office for a photo with you.

Prepared by:
Oliver L. North

Attachment
Tab A - Talking Points

Declassify: CADR

AKW651204

DOCUMENT 42: John Poindexter, Agenda for the President, "Meeting with Costa Rican Security Minister Benjamin Piza," and Attachment "Talking Points," March 17, 1986.

PAGE 2 OF 2

<u>TALKING POINTS</u>

-- I am very pleased to have the opportunity to meet with and your gracious wife.

-- I have fond memories of my visit to your lovely country.

-- Admiral John Poindexter has told me of your dedication to the cause of democracy in Central America.

-- I want you to know, personally, my sincere gratitude for your efforts on behalf on those who struggle for freedom in Nicaragua. I know that you have acted in principle and at considerable personal risk.

-- We all hope that this support will continue after May 8 and that the Nicaraguan democratic resistance will be provided with what they need in order to achieve a democratic outcome in their country.

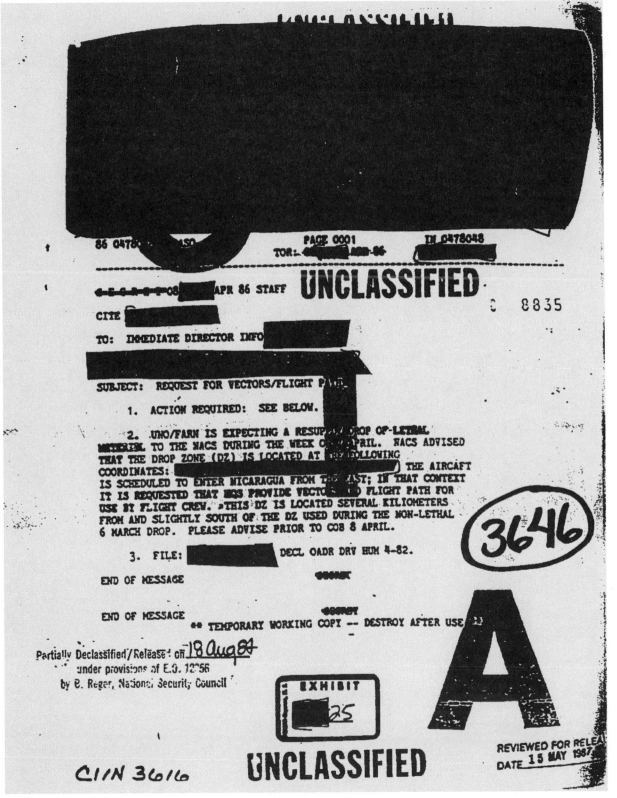

86 0478   PAGE 0001   IN 0478048

TOR: APR 86

08   APR 86 STAFF   **UNCLASSIFIED**   0   8835

CITE

TO: IMMEDIATE DIRECTOR INFO

SUBJECT: REQUEST FOR VECTORS/FLIGHT PATH

1. ACTION REQUIRED: SEE BELOW.

2. UNO/FARN IS EXPECTING A RESUPPLY DROP OF LETHAL
MATERIEL TO THE NACS DURING THE WEEK OF APRIL. NACS ADVISED
THAT THE DROP ZONE (DZ) IS LOCATED AT THE FOLLOWING
COORDINATES: THE AIRCAFT
IS SCHEDULED TO ENTER NICARAGUA FROM THE EAST; IN THAT CONTEXT
IT IS REQUESTED THAT HQS PROVIDE VECTORS AND FLIGHT PATH FOR
USE BY FLIGHT CREW. THIS DZ IS LOCATED SEVERAL KILIOMETERS
FROM AND SLIGHTLY SOUTH OF THE DZ USED DURING THE NON-LETHAL
6 MARCH DROP. PLEASE ADVISE PRIOR TO COB 8 APRIL.

3. FILE: DECL OADR DRV HUM 4-82.

END OF MESSAGE   SECRET

END OF MESSAGE   SECRET
          ** TEMPORARY WORKING COPY -- DESTROY AFTER USE **

(3646)

Partially Declassified/Released on _18 Aug 87_
   under provisions of E.O. 12356
by E. Reger, National Security Council

EXHIBIT
25

A

UNCLASSIFIED

REVIEWED FOR RELEASE
DATE 15 MAY 1987

CIIN 3616

[175]

DOCUMENT 44: Richard Secord, KL-43 Encrypted Message, Report on Failure
of April 10 Mission and Plans to Attempt Again on April 11, 1986.

PAGE 1 OF 1

''

Coop: 4/11/86 1000

10145GZ Apr 86. L-100 arrived over DZ on time but never saw
inverted L or strobe lite. They remained in area 25 minutes and
then aborted. Ralph coordinating with ___ who says troops saw
and heard L-100. I want to try again tonight an hour earlier but
Steele has informed Ralph that he will not permit another "half
ass" operation. He says we have to establish air/ground radio
contact before he will permit op to go forward. This is
assinine -- no black ops ever use this procedure. The answer is
to sort out why the troops did not have signals properly
displayed, including most importantly the strobe lite. Also Sat
wants their bird back. I will handle Sat if you take care of
Steele. This must be done right away or we must return the bird.
Rgds, Dick. BT

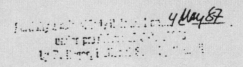

4 May 87

DOCUMENT 45: Joseph Fernandez, KL-43 Encrypted Message, Report on Sucessful Air Drop and Plans to Create 2500-man Southern Front, April 12, 1986.

PAGE 1 OF 1

UNCLASSIFIED

████ 4/12/86 1200

'1030 hours local April 12. Per UNO South Force, drop successfully completed in 15 minutes. Force requested to send full report/ inventory. When told, █████ almost cried in grateful appreciation. Our plans during next 2-3 weeks includes air drop ████████████████████████████████ maritime deliveries NHAO supplies to same, NHAO air drop to UNO South, but w/certified air worthy aircraft, lethal drop to UNO South, █████ visit to UNO South Force with photogs, UNO newspapers, caps and shirts, and transfer of 20 UNO/FARN recruits ████████████ carrying all remaining cached lethal material to join UNO South Force. My objective is creation of 2,500 man force which can strike northwest and link-up with quiche to form solid southern force. Likewise, envisage formidable opposition on Atlantic Coast resupplied at or by sea. Realize this may be overly ambitious planning but with your help, believe we can pull it off.

New subject. AFP story appeared in morning paper █████ on U.S. attorney south Florida investigation arms, drugs traffic involving insurgents and U.S. sympathisizers. Terrell, CMA named. Focus on Mar 1985 shipment ft. Lauderdale ████ via ████

New subject. Ref Cruz split. Why not offer Cruz provisional presidency in secret agreement signed by principals? Regards, DV. BT

UNCLASSIFIED

3650

EXHIBIT 29

UNCLASSIFIED
OFFICE OF THE VICE PRESIDENT
WASHINGTON

April 16, 1986

SCHEDULE PROPOSAL

TO:　　　　　　　　DEBBIE HUTTON

FROM:　　　　　　　DON GREGG

REQUEST:　　　　　VP Meeting with Felix Rodriguez, a
counterinsurgency expert visiting
from El Salvador.

PURPOSE:　　　　　To brief the Vice President on the status
of the war in El Salvador and resupply
of the Contras.

BACKGROUND:　　　The Vice President has met previously
with Mr. Rodriguez during his visits to
Washington and will be interested in
the current information he will be able
to provide.

DATE:　　　　　　　Anytime on April 28 - MAY 2 ~~22 or 23~~.

DURATION:　　　　　15 minutes

LOCATION:　　　　　OEOB

PARTICIPANTS:　　The Vice President　　　　　Felix Rodriguez
Craig Fuller
Don Gregg

REMARKS REQUIRED:　None required.

MEDIA COVERAGE:　　Staff photographer

CONTACT:　　　　　Don Gregg, 4213

RECOMMENDED BY:　　Don Gregg

3513a.

5/1 or 5/2 per Justine

5/1 - 11:30 - OEOB WW

UNCLASSIFIED

DOCUMENT 47: Oliver North, Notebook Entries for September 6, 1986.

PAGE 1 OF 1

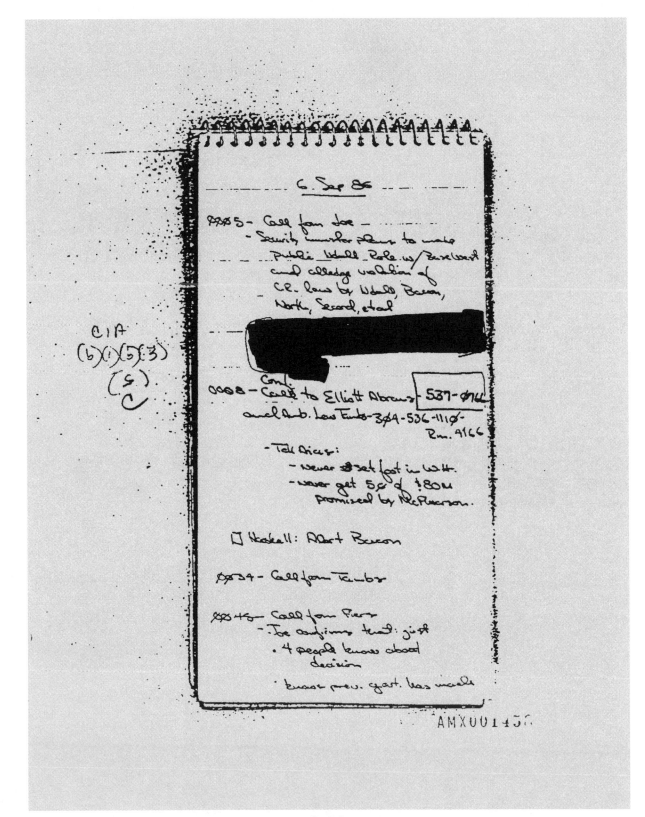

DOCUMENT 48: Oliver North, PROFS Note to John Poindexter, "Private Blank Check," September 25, 1986.

PAGE 1 OF 1

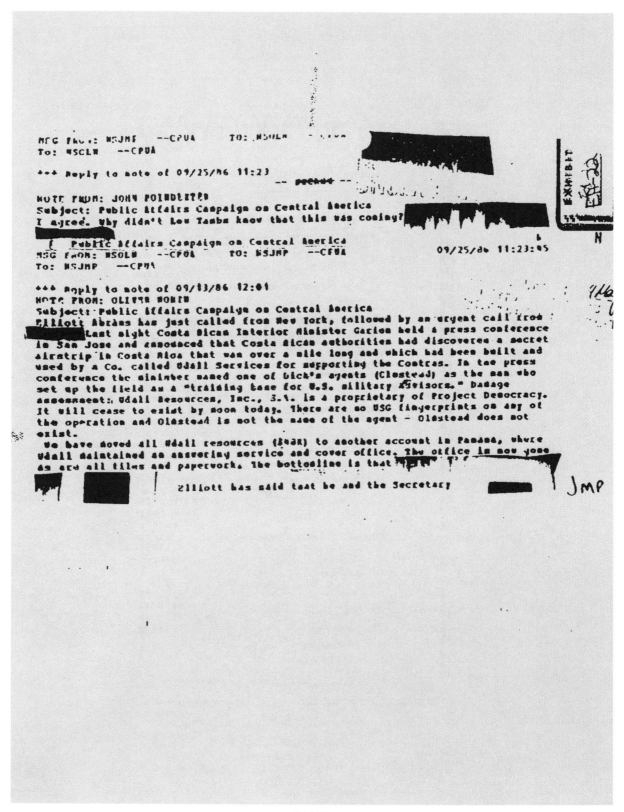

DOCUMENT 49: Oliver North, Memorandum for John Poindexter, "Press Guidance re Costa Rican Airstrip," September 30, 1986.

PAGE 1 OF 3

TOP SECRET

Non-Log

NATIONAL SECURITY COUNCIL
WASHINGTON D C 20506

September 30, 1986

JMP HAS SEEN

TOP SECRET

ACTION

MEMORANDUM FOR JOHN M. POINDEXTER

FROM: OLIVER L. NORTH

SUBJECT: Press Guidance re Costa Rican Airstrip

Attached at Tab I is draft press guidance regarding the airstrip at Santa Elena, Costa Rica, which was divulged by the Costa Rican Security Minister at a press conference on Friday, September 26. This story has now been picked up by the New York Times (Tab II) and is generating press questions at State and Defense.

The press guidance at Tab I has been coordinated with State (Abrams), Defense (Armitage), and CIA (Fiers). Due to the extreme sensitivity of the issue, your approval is requested before the guidance is used in responding to queries.

The damage done by this revelation is considerable. As indicated in the CIA report at Tab III, the logistics support provided by Project Democracy has had a profound impact on the ability of the resistance to sustain itself in the field. Operational tempo has been maintained and in those areas of Nicaragua where forces can be located and resupplied they retain the offensive.

The airfield at Santa Elena has been a vital element in supporting the resistance. Built by a Project Democracy proprietary (Udall Corporation, S.A. -- a Panamanian company), the field was initially used for direct resupply efforts (July 1985 - February 1986). Since early this year, the field has served as a primary abort base for aircraft damaged by Sandinista anti-aircraft fire. The photographs at Tab IV show the field in June 1986 and a damaged Project Democracy C-123 which made an emergency landing on the field early this month.

The Arias Administration revelations regarding this facility have caused Project Democracy to permanently close Udall Corporation and dispose of its capital assets. It has also resulted in the loss of a facility important to keeping the resistance supplied and in the field against the Sandinistas.

TOP SECRET
Declassify: OADR

TOP SECRET

OUO

IRG 1 1

DOCUMENT 49: Oliver North, Memorandum for John Poindexter, "Press Guidance re Costa Rican Airstrip," September 30, 1986.

PAGE 2 OF 3

TOP SECRET

TOP SECRET   2

There is already an effort underway in certain quarters to
"re-invite" President Arias for a meeting with President Reagan.
Those who counsel such a course of action are unaware of the
strategic importance of the air facility at Santa Elena and the
damage caused by the Arias' government revelations. While such a
visit might well be desirable in the future, we should insist
that Arias demonstrate his goodwill toward the resistance through
practical steps before he is welcomed in the Oval Office. Such a
visit now could also lead to further speculation about USG
involvement with the airstrip.

While we wait for Arias to prove his goodwill for our policy,
there are important reasons to receive both Presidents Duarte and
Cerezo in the Oval Office. Cerezo should be invited in lieu of
Arias because Guatemala is increasingly supportive of our
Nicaragua program. Duarte will be in the U.S. between October
17-21. Both he and Ambassador Rivas-Gallant have asked if it is
possible to have a "3-minute photo opportunity" with the President
in order to present him with a copy of Duarte's book. Given the
active support for the Nicaraguan democratic resistance provided
by El Salvador, such a brief meeting is highly appropriate.

RECOMMENDATIONS

1. That you approve the press guidance at Tab I and authorize us
to pass it to Dan Howard/Paul Hanley for their use if asked.

        Approve ✗   Disapprove _____

2. That you approve a brief photo op session with President
Duarte during your NSC briefing time in the October 17-21
timeframe. If you approve, an appropriate memorandum will be
prepared.

        Approve _____   Disapprove _____

                    *Prepare a schedule proposal.
                    Coordinate with Burghardt.*

Attachments
    Tab I - Press Guidance
    Tab II - NYT Article by James Lemoyne of September 29, 1986
    Tab III - CIA Special Analysis, "Nicaragua: Rebel Resupply
              Increasing," TCS 2922/86 of September 23, 1986
    Tab IV - Photographs

TOP SECRET   TOP SECRET   0001

DOCUMENT 49: Oliver North, Memorandum for John Poindexter, "Press Guidance re Costa Rican Airstrip," September 30, 1986.

PAGE 3 OF 3

September 30, 1986

PRESS GUIDANCE RE AIRSTRIP IN COSTA RICA

DID U.S. PERSONNEL SUPERVISE CONSTRUCTION OF THE AIRSTRIP IN NORTHERN COSTA RICA?

"The U.S. Embassy in San Jose, Costa Rica, has reported that during the Administration of Former President Monge the Ministry of Public Security was offered the use of a site on the Santa Elena Peninsula which could be used as an extension of the civil guard training center at Murcielago. The site included a serviceable airstrip which could have supplemented the small one which is located near the training center. The offer was reportedly made by the owners of the property who had apparently decided to abandon plans for a tourism project. The Embassy has no information on the Ministry's decision concerning the offer. No U.S. Government funds were allocated or used in connection with this site nor were any U.S. Government personnel involved in its construction. Any further inquiries should be referred to the Government of Costa Rica."

WAS THE AIRSTRIP INTENDED FOR USE BY THE CONTRAS?

The Government of Costa Rica has made clear its position that it will not permit the use of its territory for military action against neighboring states. The U.S. Government respects that position.

DOCUMENT 50: Oliver North, PROFS Note to John Poindexter, "Private Blank Check," July 24, 1986.

PAGE 1 OF 1

From: NSOLN   --CPUA
To: NSJMP   --CPUA

Date and time   07/24/86 15:33:57

*** Reply to note of 07/15/86 14:07
NOTE FROM: OLIVER NORTH
Subject: PRIVATE BLANK CHECK

We are rapidly approaching the point where the PROJECT DEMOCRACY assets in CentAm need to be turned over to CIA for use in the new program. The total value of the assets (six aircraft, warehouses, supplies, maintenance facilities, ships, boats, leased houses, vehicles, ordnance, munitions, communications equipment, and a 6520' runway on property owned by a PRODEM proprietary) is over $4.5M.

All of the assets - and the personnel- are owned/paid by overseas companies with no U.S. connection. All of the equipment is in first rate condition and is already in place. It wd be ludicrous for this to simply disappear just because CIA does not want to be "tainted" with picking up the assets and then have them spend $8-10M of the $100M to replace it - weeks or months later. Yet, that seems to be the direction they are heading, apparently based on NSC guidance.

If you have already given Casey instructions to this effect, I wd vy much like to talk to you about it in hopes that we can reclama the issue. All seriously believe that immediately after the Senate vote the DRF will be subjected to a major Sandinista effort to break them before the U.S. aid can become effective. PRODEM currently has the only assets available to support the DRF and the CIA's most ambitious estimate is 30 days after a bill is signed before their own assets will be available. This will be a disaster for the DRF if they have to wait that long. Given our lack of movement on other funding options, and Elliot/Allen's plea for PRODEM to get food to the resistance ASAP, PRODEM will have to borrow at least $2M to pay for the food. That's O.K., and Dick is willing to do so tomorrow - but only if there is reasonable assurance that the lenders can be repaid. The only way that the $2M in food money can be repaid is if CIA purchases the $4.5M+ worth of PRODEM equipment for about $2.25M when the law passes. You should be aware that CIA has already approached PRODEM's chief pilot to ask him where they (CIA) can purchase more of the C-135K A/C. The chief pilot told them where they can get them commercially from the USAF as excess - the same way PRODEM bought them under proprietary arrangements. It is just unbelievable. If you wish I can send you a copy of the PROJECT DEMOCRACY status report which includes a breakdown of assets. It is useful, nonattributable reading. Warm Regards, North

GOVERNMENT
EXHIBIT
196 ε4√

JmP44a

DOCUMENT 51: CIA Cable to Joseph Fernandez, "Disappearance of Southern Front Supply Aircraft," October 6, 1986.

PAGE 1 OF 1

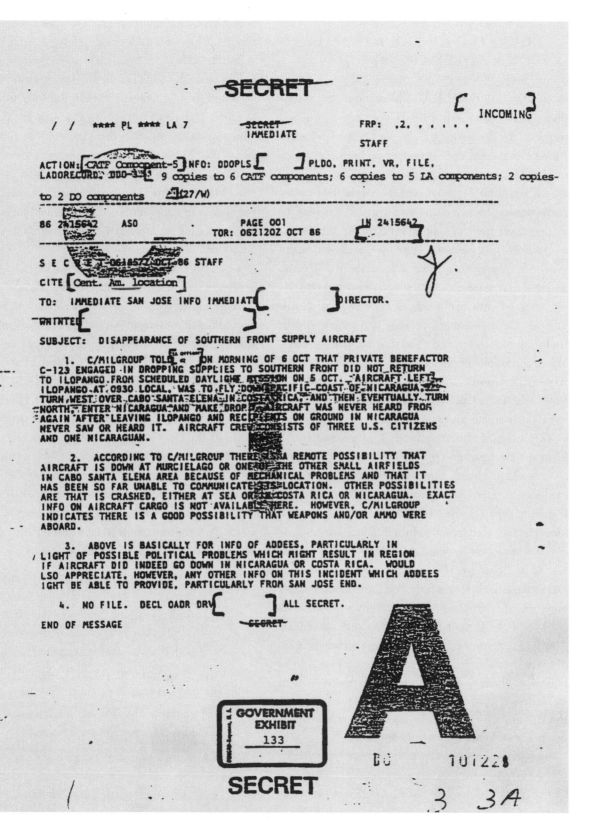

~~SECRET~~

[INCOMING]

/ / **** PL **** LA 7   ~~SECRET~~   FRP: .2. . . . . .
                        IMMEDIATE   STAFF

ACTION: [CATF Component-5] NFO: DDOPLS [   ] PLDO, PRINT, VR, FILE,
LADORECORD, DDO-   9 copies to 6 CATF components; 6 copies to 5 IA components; 2 copies-
to 2 DO components   27/W)
_____

86 2415642   ASO   .   PAGE 001   IN 2415642
                          TOR: 062120Z OCT 86
_____

S E C R E T 061857Z OCT 86 STAFF

CITE [Cent. Am. location]

TO: IMMEDIATE SAN JOSE INFO IMMEDIATE [   ] DIRECTOR.

PRINTED [

SUBJECT: DISAPPEARANCE OF SOUTHERN FRONT SUPPLY AIRCRAFT

   1. C/MILGROUP TOLD [   ] ON MORNING OF 6 OCT THAT PRIVATE BENEFACTOR
C-123 ENGAGED IN DROPPING SUPPLIES TO SOUTHERN FRONT DID NOT RETURN
TO ILOPANGO FROM SCHEDULED DAYLIGHT MISSION ON 5 OCT. AIRCRAFT LEFT
ILOPANGO AT 0930 LOCAL, WAS TO FLY DOWN PACIFIC COAST OF NICARAGUA,
TURN WEST OVER CABO SANTA ELENA IN COSTA RICA, AND THEN EVENTUALLY TURN
NORTH, ENTER NICARAGUA AND MAKE DROP. AIRCRAFT WAS NEVER HEARD FROM
AGAIN AFTER LEAVING ILOPANGO AND RECIPIENTS ON GROUND IN NICARAGUA
NEVER SAW OR HEARD IT. AIRCRAFT CREW CONSISTS OF THREE U.S. CITIZENS
AND ONE NICARAGUAN.

   2. ACCORDING TO C/MILGROUP THERE IS A REMOTE POSSIBILITY THAT
AIRCRAFT IS DOWN AT MURCIELAGO OR ONE OF THE OTHER SMALL AIRFIELDS
IN CABO SANTA ELENA AREA BECAUSE OF MECHANICAL PROBLEMS AND THAT IT
HAS BEEN SO FAR UNABLE TO COMMUNICATE ITS LOCATION. OTHER POSSIBILITIES
ARE THAT IS CRASHED, EITHER AT SEA OR IN COSTA RICA OR NICARAGUA. EXACT
INFO ON AIRCRAFT CARGO IS NOT AVAILABLE HERE. HOWEVER, C/MILGROUP
INDICATES THERE IS A GOOD POSSIBILITY THAT WEAPONS AND/OR AMMO WERE
ABOARD.

   3. ABOVE IS BASICALLY FOR INFO OF ADDEES, PARTICULARLY IN
LIGHT OF POSSIBLE POLITICAL PROBLEMS WHICH MIGHT RESULT IN REGION
IF AIRCRAFT DID INDEED GO DOWN IN NICARAGUA OR COSTA RICA. WOULD
LSO APPRECIATE, HOWEVER, ANY OTHER INFO ON THIS INCIDENT WHICH ADDEES
IGHT BE ABLE TO PROVIDE, PARTICULARLY FROM SAN JOSE END.

   4. NO FILE. DECL OADR DRV [   ] ALL SECRET.

END OF MESSAGE   ~~SECRET~~

GOVERNMENT
EXHIBIT
133

A

DO   101221

SECRET

3   3A

IV. "DAMAGE CONTROL": COVERING UP THE RESUPPLY OPERATIONS

Within hours of the Hasenfus plane crash, the resupply agents moved to cover up the operation. "Situation requires we do necessary damage control," Joseph Fernandez cabled Robert Dutton on his KL-43 transmitter.[1] Dutton quickly had the rest of the resupply air fleet flown out of Ilopango; subsequently, the CIA destroyed this evidence of the Enterprise operations. In an operation that was kept secret until the publication of Oliver North's memoirs, Agency operatives flew the remaining planes to a remote airfield where bulldozers had dug a large pit. "The planes were pushed into the pit, covered with explosives, and blown up," North writes. "The remaining wreckage was saturated with fuel and then cremated. The fire burned for days. When the smoke finally cleared, the charred remains were buried." According to North, this was "the only time an air force had been given a funeral. One might call it the ultimate cover-up."[2]

This dramatic effort to erase U.S. fingerprints failed, however, because the crew of the downed plane was not traveling "clean." The Sandinistas quickly found evidence to trace the aircraft back to El Salvador and the United States. Hasenfus, for example, carried a identification card issued to him by the Salvadoran Air Force stating that he was an "adviser" to the "Grupo U.S.A." at Ilopango. The business card of NHAO official Philip Buechler was found on the body of another crew member. William Cooper's body carried an ID card from the former CIA proprietary Southern Air Transport. Moreover, enterprising journalists soon obtained telephone records from the safehouses in El Salvador which showed multiple telephone calls to the office of Tomas Castillo (aka Joseph Fernandez) at the U.S. embassy in San Jose, and to Oliver North's office in the Old Executive Office Building.

Back in Washington, U.S. officials nevertheless concocted cover stories to explain the flight. Awaiting Oliver North's return from Germany, his colleague El-liott Abrams presided over an October 8 meeting of the RIG where it was decided that the Contra organization "UNO [would] be asked to assume responsibility for flight and to assist families of Americans involved" (Document 52). Contra officials dutifully informed the *New York Times* that the flight was theirs. U.S. officials also leaked the story that General John Singlaub, whose publically known fund-raising activities had acted as a "lightening rod" to divert press attention from the NSC's third-country solicitations, was behind the resupply operation—a charge he angrily denounced as a lie attributable to Assistant Secretary Abrams.[3]

From the president down, as Theodore Draper describes it, "a denial reflex took over in official circles."[4] The operative line was "no U.S. Government connection." President Reagan responded to reporters' questions about the Hasenfus plane by stating that "there [was] no government connection with that at all." On the basis of a briefing by his own assistant secretary for Inter-American affairs, Secretary Shultz told the TV networks that "private people" who "had no connection with the U.S. Government at all" were responsible for the downed resupply flight. Abrams, perhaps the most audacious liar within the administration, went on CNN on October 11 to deny categorically that "this was in any sense a U.S. government operation."[5] The following exchange took place between Abrams and Robert Evans of the Evans and Novak show:

EVANS: Mr. Secretary, can you give me categorical assurance that Hasenfus was not under the control, the guidance, the direction, or what have you, of anybody connected with the American government?

ABRAMS: Absolutely. That would be illegal. We are barred from doing that, and we are not doing it. This was not in any sense a U.S. government operation. None.

NOVAK: Now, when you say, gave [a] categorical assurance, we're not playing word games that are so common in Washington. You're not talking about the N[SC] or something else?

ABRAMS: I am not playing games.

NOVAK: National Security Council?

ABRAMS: No government agencies, none.

DECEIVING CONGRESS

Abrams made similar statements in testimony before the House Subcommittee on Western Hemispheric Affairs on October 15, the Senate Foreign Relations Committee on October 10, and the House Intelligence Committee on October 14, which were all investigating the Hasenfus incident. In the latter two appearances, Abrams was accompanied by CIA Deputy Director Clair George, and CIA Central America Task Force Chief Alan Fiers, both of whom were well aware of the NSC resupply role. According to minutes of a closed hearing of the House Intelligence Committee, which were classified top-secret/veil, George and Fiers carefully limited their answers to the CIA while Abrams purported to speak for the entire U.S. government. Representative Lee Hamilton "asked whether the witnesses could assure the Committee that the USG[overnment] was not involved in any way in supplying the Contras. Mr. George said this was true for the Agency, and Mr. Abrams said it was true for the Government as a whole" (Document 53). Both George and Fiers, who knew Abrams's statement to be false, kept their silence.

At the CIA, the cover-up took the form of denying any CIA involvement in the resupply operations, despite Joseph Fernandez's substantial role. In preparation for George's testimony before the Senate committee on October 10, and the House Intelligence Committee on October 14, George and Fiers decided simply to ignore the contribution of the CIA station chief in Costa Rica in setting up the Santa Elena airstrip and facilitating the air drops to the southern front, as well as their own roles in assisting Oliver North. "I would like to state categorically that the Central Intelligence Agency was not involved directly or indirectly in arranging, directing or facilitating resupply missions conducted by private individuals in support of the Nicaraguan democratic resistance," began George's opening statement before the committees. To support this falsehood, Fernandez, according to an internal CIA report obtained by the ACLU's Center for National Security Studies, misled both CIA investigators and the Tower Commission about his contribution to the resupply effort:

> Once Fernandez was confronted with copies of KL-43 messages between him[self], North and Quintero, he described a somewhat more extensive involvement in the resupply effort than he had described previously...the available KL-43 messages seemed to indicate...that Fernandez may have been serving as an adviser to both UNO/South and the PB's [private benefactors] on the resupply effort; or that he may have been planning—if not directing—certain of the operations.[6]

Later, when Louis Dupart, the CIA officer assigned to the Central America Task Force to assure that it complied with the law, threatened to inform the CIA inspector general that evidence of Fernandez's involvement contradicted George's statement to Congress, George concocted a story that he had authorized an investigation into Fernandez's activities. As Alan Fiers testified,

> We had to get something on the record... Mr. George agreed, and he said, "I want you to select a date back in early November when we were all here." And he went back, looked at his calendar, and said, "How about the 10th?" And we agreed tentatively...and he said, "...you go write me a memo that says we met on that date and I instructed you to conduct the investigation."... Chief Latin America Division 2 wrote such a memo... dated the 26th of November for the deputy director of operations...The following information is

submitted as a follow-up to our meeting on this topic on 10 November.7

In their congressional testimony, the CIA officials also suppressed information that would lead back to North's operation and misled Congress about the identity of "Max Gomez," the operative identified by Eugene Hasenfus as overseeing the Ilopango missions. According to Fiers, who wrote the first draft of the opening statement for the October 10 appearance before the Senate Foreign Relations Committee, George excised all references to "the story of the metamorphosis" of the NHAO flights from Ilopango into the "private benefactor" flights. Testifying before a grand jury in August 1991, Fiers quoted George as stating, "this puts the spotlight on the White House... the private benefactor operations and the White House connection to them; and I don't want to be the first person to do that."8 Similarly, the deputy director refused to accept Fiers's arguments that, if asked, he should acknowledge that "Max Gomez" was the alias of former CIA operative Felix Rodriguez. "I said, look, we've got to say that Max Gomez is Felix Rodriguez, because he in fact is, and I know that to be the case. And Clair said, 'no, we're just going to say that we're checking.'"9 Although the deputy director had a document in his hearing briefing book clearly identifying Rodriguez as Max Gomez, as a former CIA operative, and as an actor in the resupply operations, when George was questioned during an October 10 hearing before the Senate Foreign Relations Committee he dissembled. "We are in the process of tracing all of those named, seeing if we have any record of any relationship at any time with them," he told Senator Claiborne Pell. "We have an indication of a former CIA official using that name as an alias," George told Senator John Kerry when he asked about Max Gomez. "Before I sort of say...he is involved...I would like to make sure that I know what I am talking about."10 Following the testimony, according to Fiers, Donald Gregg sent buttons to Langley headquarters for CIA officials to wear which read "Who is Max Gomez?"

and "Where is Max Gomez?" Fiers remembered that "two or three of us were in Mr. George's office and we were laughing about these buttons and sort of passing them around...[Clair] was the one [that] had one that said, 'I am Maximo Gomez.'"11

THE PATTERN OF DECEIT

The orchestrated deception that accompanied the Reagan administration's efforts to cover up its illicit Contra operations followed a pattern of lying that began in the summer of 1985 following initial press reports on the NSC activities. The first article to name North was an AP wire story written by Robert Parry that appeared on June 10, 1985; the *Miami Herald's* Alfonso Chardy followed on June 24 with a story entitled "U.S. Found to Skirt Ban on Aid to Contras," in which former FDN directorate member Edgar Chamorro recounted a meeting with North in May 1984 during which the colonel promised that the White House would "find a way" to sustain the Contras.12

As is so often the case in Washington, D.C., these reports drew no political response until they were picked up in August by the *New York Times* and the *Washington Post*. On August 16, the chairman of the House Subcommittee on Western Hemispheric Affairs, Michael Barnes, wrote to Robert McFarlane asking for answers to "serious questions regarding the violation of the letter and spirit of U.S. law prohibiting support for the Nicaraguan rebels" (Document 54). A similar letter arrived several days later from Lee Hamilton, the chairman of the House Intelligence Committee.

"Barnes is really a trouble maker. We have good answers to all of this," McFarlane's then-deputy, John Poindexter, scrawled on a cover memo when the congressman's letter arrived at the NSC (Document 54). He directed North to draft a response that, Poindexter later admitted, would "withhold information" about the resupply operations.13 McFarlane, however, did most of the drafting (Document 55). After reviewing a number of documents relating to the resupply operations—documents that showed explicit NSC involvement—he wrote to Barnes on September 12 that, "based on this review, I want to assure you that my actions, and those of my staff, have been in compliance with both the spirit and the letter of the law…. There have not been, nor will there be, any expenditures of NSC funds which would have the effect of supporting directly or indirectly military or paramilitary operations in Nicaragua…." The letter continued, "none of us has solicited funds, facilitated contacts for prospective potential donors, or otherwise organized, or coordinated the military or paramilitary efforts of the resistance [sic]." [14]

Similar letters were sent to Representative Hamilton, and to Senators Patrick Leahy and David Durenberger. North later admitted to the Iran-Contra committees that they were "false, erroneous, misleading, evasive, and wrong." [15] On March 11, 1988, McFarlane pled guilty to four counts of "withholding information" from Congress.

During his review of the documents, McFarlane selected a half-dozen memoranda that clearly contradicted his categorical denials and ordered North to alter them—a process that North later described as "cleaning up the historical record." [16] The memos, all from North to McFarlane, included North's December 4, 1984, report on securing arms from China (Document 23), a proposal to interdict a North Korean ship transporting arms for the Nicaraguan government, a status report on FDN military operations, and a set of proposals for providing assistance to the Contras if Congress refused to do so. In the latter document, "Fallback Plan for the Nicaraguan Resistance," dated March 16, 1985, North proposed that the Saudis be asked for another donation of $25–30 million. As a cover for the continuing flow of funds, he advised, "the name of one of several existing non-profit foundations we have established…will be changed to Nicaraguan Freedom Fund"—a plan okayed by McFarlane. North also recommended that President Reagan make a speech telling the American public to "send your check or money order to the Nicaraguan Freedom Fighters, Box 1776, Gettysburg, PA," a proposal that McFarlane tabled as premature (Document 56).

This document, a three-page memorandum classified as top-secret, was eventually altered to become an unclassified half-page memo regarding a discussion between McFarlane and Senators Durenberger and Lugar about options on the Contra war (Document 57). But North did not get around to changing the documents until the scandal began to unravel in November 1986. [17] Only then did he direct his secretary, Fawn Hall, to redo these documents, even as both of them were shredding hundreds of others. The alterations prompted one of the more comical scenes of the cover-up. As FBI investigators moved to seal North's office on November 25, Hall realized that several of the original and altered versions were in plain view on her desk. Speaking in a whisper, she called her boss who was meeting with Secord and his lawyer, Thomas Green, for instructions on what to do. North advised her simply to pick up the incriminating documents and smuggle them out of the building. Hall took papers out of the room, stuffed them beneath her undergarments and walked passed the guards. [18]

A GULLIBLE CONGRESS

After the first round of congressional inquiries in 1985, the NSC staff changed its method of recordkeeping. No longer did North write "logged" memoranda to his superiors—memos that would be stored in the NSC filing system. Instead, North communicated directly with McFarlane and Poindexter through computer messages known as PROFS notes under the heading "Private Blank Check." [19] This system, he believed, was irretrievable and would prevent Congress from ever obtaining documentation on the resupply operations.

In the face of McFarlane's categorical denials of illegal activities, Congress lost interest in the evidence of the NSC resupply operations. Only after another spate of AP and *Miami Herald* reports in the late spring of 1986, which named North, Robert Owen, John Singlaub, and John Hull as collaborating on a major resupply program, did congressional officials once again focus on the NSC. On June 4, Texas Representative Ron Coleman introduced House Resolution 485, which directed President Reagan to turn over all documents involving contacts between NSC staffmembers and the Contras relating to funding and supply of weapons, military activities, and contacts with Owen, Singlaub, and Hull. In late July, the resolution was referred to three committees for evaluation.

At first, Poindexter tried to stonewall Congress by sending a letter on July 21 to the Chairmen of the House Intelligence, Foreign Affairs, an Armed Services committees in which he simply reiterated McFarlane's false statements from the year before. But on the advice of Republican supporters on the House Intelligence Committee, Poindexter agreed to allow North to testify in closed session, fully expecting that he would lie. "I did think he would withhold information and be evasive, frankly, in answering questions," Poindexter later told the Iran-Contra committees. "My objective all along was to withhold from the Congress exactly what the NSC staff was doing."[20]

Oliver North did not let his superior down. When he appeared before the intelligence committee on August 6, North denied giving the Contras any military advice or knowing of specific military operations. He claimed not to have seen General Singlaub for twenty months and to have only "casual contact" with Robert Owen. "Session was success," NSC aide Bob Pearson reported in a PROFS note to Poindexter. "Hamilton will entertain motion soonest to report unfavorably on Resolution of Inquiry.... North's remarks were thorough and convincing" (Document 58). Poindexter added a two-word note when forwarding this message to North: "Well done."

Indeed, without asking any hard questions, the House Intelligence Committee took North at his word, and Chairman Hamilton even thanked Admiral Poindexter for his cooperation. According to notes of the session taken by a committee staffer, at the end of the hearing Hamilton "expressed his appreciation for the good faith effort that Admiral Poindexter had shown in arranging a meeting and indicated his satisfaction in the responses received" (Document 59). On August 12, Hamilton informed Representative Cole-

man that the committee would rule unfavorably on his resolution. "Based on our discussions and review of the evidence provided, it is my belief that the published press allegations cannot be proven."[21]

FINAL DENIAL

Had the Coleman resolution passed and Congress aggressively pursued evidence of the NSC Contra operations, the Iran-Contra scandal might have evolved very differently. Even after the Hasenfus plane went down, however, and irrefutable evidence had emerged linking the White House to the resupply flights, Congress failed to take action. Only in the aftermath of Attorney General Edwin Meese's press conference on November 25, 1986, prompted by the unraveling of the Iran arms-for-hostages initiative, did Congress actively scrutinize the testimony of U.S. officials regarding the Contras.

Elliott Abrams provided the first opportunity. As Meese was revealing the diversion to the American public, Assistant Secretary of State Abrams was testifying before the Senate Select Committee on Intelligence about the State Department's knowledge of Contra funding sources. He was asked by Senator Bill Bradley of New Jersey whether he had ever discussed Contra fund-raising problems with members of the NSC staff. "We're not—you know, we're not in the fundraising business," Abrams replied, even though he personally had solicited funds from Brunei. "We don't engage—I mean the State Department's function in this has not been to raise money, other than to try to raise it from Congress."[22]

After the *Los Angeles Times* story revealed his Brunei contacts, Abrams returned to the Senate intelligence committee on December 8, still insisting, under oath, that "I have never lied to this committee." An irate Senator Thomas Eagleton reminded Abrams of his earlier testimony:

EAGLETON: "We're not, you know, we're not in the fundraising business." No one intimidated that out of you. That was your answer....You're not in the fundraising business. Today I asked were you at any time in the fundraising business.

ABRAMS: We made one solicitation to a foreign government.

EAGLETON: Were you then in the fundraising business?

ABRAMS: I would say we were in the fundraising business. I take your point.

EAGLETON: Take my point? Under oath, my friend, that's perjury. Had you been under oath, that's perjury.

ABRAMS: Well, I don't agree with that, Senator.

EAGLETON: That's slammer time.

Abrams objected. "You've heard my testimony," he told Senator Eagleton. "I've heard it," Eagleton replied, "and I want to puke."[23]

On October 7, 1991, Abrams pleaded guilty to two misdemeanor counts of withholding information from Congress; he was sentenced to two years' probation and one hundred hours of community service. Robert McFarlane also pleaded guilty to withholding information from Congress for the false letters to Representative Barnes and others. From the CIA, Alan Fiers pleaded guilty to deceiving Congress about his knowledge of Contra resupply operations, and his superior, Clair George, was found guilty on two counts of perjury relating to his testimony before congressional committees investigating the Hasenfus plane shootdown. All received presidential pardons on December 24, 1992. Oliver North and John Poindexter were both found guilty on charges that included destroying evidence and obstruction of justice in an effort to cover up the NSC's Contra program; their convictions were later overturned on appeal and dismissed (see Part Three).

NOTES

1. Fernandez also inquired, "Did this A/C [aircraft] have tail number? If so, we will have to try to cover quickly as record of this tail number could lead to very serious implication." Indeed, the tail number of the C-123 was visible in photographs of the wreckage, and journalists were able to trace the plane back to a previous owner, a known drug-smuggler named Barry Seal. The plane turned out to be the same aircraft used by the CIA and Seal in a drug sting operations against the Sandinistas in 1984. For the Fernandez cable, see the *Iran-Contra Affair*, p. 144.

2. Oliver North, *Under Fire: An American Story* (New York: HarperCollins, 1991), p. 272.

3. See Singlaub's testimony in *Joint Hearings before the Select Committees on the Iran-Contra Investigation*, May 20–21, 1987, vol. 100-3.

4. Theodore Draper, *A Very Thin Line* (New York: Hill and Wang, 1991), p. 355.

5. The Abrams exchange with Evans and Novak is exerpted in Draper, *A Very Thin Line*, p. 356.

6. CIA Office of the Inspector General, "Special Investigation into Certain Activities of the COS [Chief of Station] San Jose," April 24, 1987.

7. Alan Fiers, testimony at Clair George trial, July 29, 1992, transcript, pp. 1362-63.

8. Office of the Independent Counsel, Grand Jury Testimony of Alan Fiers, August 16, 1991, transcript, pp. 11, 12.

9. Ibid., p.21.

10. Transcript of the hearing before the Senate Foreign Relations Committee, October 10, 1986, pp. 55, 56.

11. Alan Fiers, testimony at the Clair George trial, July 29, 1992, transcript, p. 1327.

12. Robert Parry, along with AP colleague Brian Barger, and Alfonso Chardy broke almost every substantive story regarding the resupply operations. For Edgar Chamorro's account of the meeting with North see Peter Kornbluh, *Nicaragua: The Price of Intervention* (Washington, D.C.: Institute for Policy Studies, 1987), p. 62.

13. *Iran-Contra Affair*, p. 123.

14. The issue with Barnes did not end there. The congressman wrote to McFarlane again on September 30 to request access to NSC documents on Oliver North's contacts with the Contras. On October 17, Barnes met with McFarlane in his NSC office. Pointing to a stack of documents on his desk, Reagan's national security advisor offered to allow Barnes to read the materials then and there, knowing that Barnes would likely decline. For Barnes, the offer wasn't serious; there were no assurances that the documents were anything but the ones McFarlane wanted Barnes to see, and they could not be properly evaluated unless his staff was allowed to read them also. On October 29, Barnes requested that McFarlane turn the documents over to the House Intelligence Committee—which McFarlane declined to do. The congressman then dropped the issue. Ibid., p. 129.

15. Ibid.

16. Ibid., p. 126.

17. North failed to consider that the letterhead of the National Security Council had changed during the year that had passed since the originals were written. When the documents were altered they were put on stationery that was not available at the time they were dated.

18. See Fawn Hall's testimony in *Joint Hearings before the Select Committees on the Iran-Contra Investigation*, June 8, 1987, vol. 100-5, p. 505.

19. Ibid., p. 138.

20. Ibid., p. 142.

21. Ibid., p. 141.

22. See Elliott Abrams, Exhibit EA-30, "Testimony in Hearings before the Senate Select Committee on Intelligence, November 25, 1986," in *Joint Hearings before the Select Committees on the Iran-Contra Investigation*, June 2–3, 1987, vol. 100-5, p. 650.

23. See Elliott Abrams, Exhibit EA-30A, "Testimony in Hearings Before the Senate Select Committee on Intelligence, December 8, 1986," in *Joint Hearings before the Select Committees on the Iran-Contra Investigation*, June 2–3, 1987, vol. 100-5, p. 663.

DOCUMENT 52: Vincent Cannistraro, PROFS Note to John Poindexter and Robert McFarlane, "Downed Plane," October 8, 1986.

PAGE 1 OF 1

UNCLASSIFIED

From: NSVMC   --CPUA **UNCLASSIFIED** and time   10/08/86 16 08.12
To: NSRAM   --CPUA   JOHN M. POINDEXTER NSLRP   --CPUA   JOHN M. POINDEXTER
NOTE FROM: Vincent Cannistraro
SUBJECT: Downed Plane
At RIG meeting with Elliott Abrams today the question of the captur [American
held by the Nicaraguans was discussed. Following decisions were made:

--Demands for consular access would continue. Elliott thought Nics would
accede to our request today. (He later called me to say the Nics had still not
responded and we should be prepared to escalate tomorrow if there is no
movement. Believes we may have to make this a "hostage crisis" to exert
leverage on Sandinistas.

███

--Press Guidance was prepared which states no U.S.G. involvement or
connection, but that we are generally aware of such support contracted by the
Contras.

--UNO to be asked to assume responsibility for flight and to assist
families of Americans involved. Elliott will follow up with Ollie to
facilitate this.

--ARA will attempt to identify appropriate legal counsel and ask UNO to
engage him. Lawyer will be asked to donate services pro bono. Alternatively,
private money can be found, according to Elliott.

--HPSCI and SSCI have been briefed and there were no problems.

--Elliott said he would continue to tell the press these were brave men
and brave deeds. We recommended he not do this because it contributes to
perception U.S.G. inspired and encouraged private lethal aid effort.

cc: NSWP   --CPUA   NSRLE   --CPUA

Partially Declassified/Released on 6 July 1987
under provisions of E.O. 12356
by B. Reger, National Security Council

1667

EXHIBIT
OLN-133

E-50
12/17/86

UNCLASSIFIED

DOCUMENT 53: "Memorandum for the Record: Testimony before the House Permanent Select Committee on Intelligence Regarding the Crash of a C-123 in Nicaragua," October 14, 1986.

PAGE 1 OF 4

14 October 1986

MEMORANDUM FOR THE RECORD

SUBJECT: Testimony before the House Permanent Select Committee on Intelligence Regarding the Crash of a C-123 in Nicaragua

1. On 14 October at 1500 in Room H-405 The Capitol, the HPSCI heard testimony on the above topic. A transcript was taken; testimony was at the Top Secret Veil level. (S)

2. Present from the Committee were:

Lee Hamilton (D., IN), Chairman
Bob Stump (R., AZ), Ranking Minority Member

Louis Stokes (D., OH)	Andy Ireland (R., FL)
Dave McCurdy (D., OK)	Henry Hyde (R., IL)
Dan Daniel (D., VA)	Dick Cheney (R., WY)
George Brown (D., CA)	Bob McEwen (R., OH)
Matt McHugh (D., NY)	
Bernard Dwyer (D., NJ)	

Present for the opening statement, but not returning after a 30 minute voting recess were Representatives Tony Beilenson (D., CA), Bob Kastenmeier (D., WI), and Robert Roe (D., NJ).

Present from the Committee staff were:

Tom Latimer, Staff Director

Mike O'Neil	Steve Berry
Duane Andrews	Dave Addington
Martin Faga	Diane Dornan
Dick Giza	Bernie Raimo
Jeanne McNally (U)	

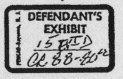

DEFENDANT'S
EXHIBIT
15
CC 88-80

3. Present from the Central Intelligence Agency were:

Clair E. George, Deputy Director for Operations
Alan Fiers, Chief, Central American Task Force, DO
Norman Gardner, Special Assistant to the DDO
Dave Gries, Director of Congressional Affairs
Patricia Taylor, Deputy Director for House Affairs, OCA (C)

OCA TS4289-86
Copy # 1

CL BY 0188893
DECL OADR
DRV FM NSDD-159

000210   DO   172454

TOP SECRET VEIL

DOCUMENT 53: "Memorandum for the Record: Testimony before the House Permanent Select Committee on Intelligence Regarding the Crash of a C-123 in Nicaragua," October 14, 1986.

PAGE 2 OF 4

4. Present from the Department of State were:

Assistant Secretary Elliot Abrams
William Walker, Robert Kagen, Michael Kozak, and John McAteer.
(U)

5. Mr. George read his prepared opening statement
(attached) categorically denying that the CIA was involved
either directly or indirectly in arranging, directing, or
facilitating resupply missions conducted by private individuals
in support of the Nicaraguan Democratic Resistance. The
hearing then recessed for 30 minutes for voting. Mr. Abrams
reaffirmed Mr. George's statement, said that the Department of
State and the US Government do not follow Americans overseas,
and noted the sensitivity of the use by the CIA as well as the
private benefactors of Ilopango Air base in El Salvador--a fact
which has been denied by the Salvadoran government. (S)

6. Mr. Hamilton asked whether the witnesses could assure
the Committee that the USG was not involved in any way in
supplying the contras. Mr. George said this was true for the
Agency, and Mr. Abrams said it was true for the Government as a
whole. Did we ask El Salvador to permit the private
benefactors to use Ilopango? No. Could the flights use
Ilopango without Salvadoran Air Force permission? No. Mr.
Fiers noted that we became aware of the private flights in
April or May of 1986. What do we know about these private
groups? Mr. George said we know what the contras have told us
about what has been dropped to them and we knew of the
existence of private Americans at Ilopango. Whose plane was
it? We do not know. Mr. Fiers said that we sometimes knew the
destination of the flights, but that we did not know who flew
the aircraft. Are any foreign governments providing support to
the contras? Not to our knowledge, and certainly not at our
behest. (TSV)

7. Mr. Stokes asked whether the denial of US involvement
included the Vice President. Mr. Abrams said Mr. Gregg of the
Vice President's staff had introduced Mr. Rodriguez to
Salvadoran Air Force officials in 1984 to serve as an adviser
on air/ground operations. Mr. Rodriguez'actions since that
time were on his own. Mr. George clarified the former
relations between the Agency and Southern Air Transport for Mr.
Stokes and denied that there was any relationship between the
Agency and Four Aces air service, Dick Secord, or retired
General Singlaub. Mr. Stokes asked about Doane Helicopter, and
Mr. George said he thought it had been associated with Barry
Seal in a narcotics operation several years ago. (S)

172-

14

DOCUMENT 53: "Memorandum for the Record: Testimony before the House Permanent Select Committee on Intelligence Regarding the Crash of a C-123 in Nicaragua," October 14, 1986.

PAGE 3 OF 4

Mr. McCurdy wanted to know whether President Duarte's denial of knowledge of contra support activities could jeopardize his position. Mr. Abrams responded. Mr. McCurdy stressed the importance of maintaining a dialogue with the Agency and the administration; he emphasized that not only our credibility but also the Committee's was on the line--and we certainly had better be right in our categorical denials. (S)

9. Mr. Daniel asked whether any money authorized for El Salvador had found its way into contra support. Mr. George said not from the CIA, and Mr. Abrams said that State keeps a close check on such funds and would investigate any allegations of impropriety. Mr. Daniel said that Congress should learn from this incident to understand the consequences of its actions. The unprofessional private benefactor system and the embarrassment it had caused was a direct result of the Congressional decision to deny US support to the contras. (S)

10. Mr. Cheney said he hoped the administration understood the public skepticism and confusion caused by revelations of a disinformation campaign directed at Libya and then stout denials of any involvement in the plane crash in Nicaragua. Our credibility is at a low point. (C)

11. Mr. Brown asked to see the guidance provided to CIA stations regarding contact with the private benefactors and the legal opinion given the DDO on the relevance of EO 12333 to DO contacts with the benefactors. He also asked for information on the number of benefactor flights and the amount of goods supplied to the contras. (See attached follow-up memo.) (TSV)

12. Mr. McHugh asked about Ramon Medina. Mr. George said we had no traces on that name. Was Felix Rodriguez supplying the contras? Mr. George said we did not know, and Mr. Fiers said his name had surfaced in that regard but that we had no specific evidence. Mr. McHugh said it was hard to believe that the Agency did not know who was flying the planes and aiding the contras. Mr. George explained that he believed it absolutely necessary to keep the Agency away from even the appearance of improperly aiding the contras. Mr. Abrams said that it was unreasonable to expect the US Government to know what conservative backers of the contras were doing while criticizing any efforts of the USG to find out about left wing groups raising money for the Sandinistas. A spirited exchange between Mr. Hyde and Mr. McHugh and Mr. Abrams followed--the upshot being that Mr. McHugh still thought it did not ring true that we did not know who the Americans were at Ilopango. (S)

DO 172452

TOP SECRET VEIL

DOCUMENT 53: "Memorandum for the Record: Testimony before the House Permanent Select Committee on Intelligence Regarding the Crash of a C-123 in Nicaragua," October 14, 1986.

PAGE 4 OF 4

Mr. McCurdy wanted to know whether President Duarte's denial of knowledge of contra support activities could jeopardize his position. Mr. Abrams responded. Mr. McCurdy stressed the importance of maintaining a dialogue with the Agency and the administration; he emphasized that not only our credibility but also the Committee's was on the line--and we certainly had better be right in our categorical denials. (S)

9. Mr. Daniel asked whether any money authorized for El Salvador had found its way into contra support. Mr. George said not from the CIA, and Mr. Abrams said that State keeps a close check on such funds and would investigate any allegations of impropriety. Mr. Daniel said that Congress should learn from this incident to understand the consequences of its actions. The unprofessional private benefactor system and the embarrassment it had caused was a direct result of the Congressional decision to deny US support to the contras. (S)

10. Mr. Cheney said he hoped the administration understood the public skepticism and confusion caused by revelations of a disinformation campaign directed at Libya and then stout denials of any involvement in the plane crash in Nicaragua. Our credibility is at a low point. (C)

11. Mr. Brown asked to see the guidance provided to CIA stations regarding contact with the private benefactors and the legal opinion given the DDO on the relevance of EO 12333 to DO contacts with the benefactors. He also asked for information on the number of benefactor flights and the amount of goods supplied to the contras. (See attached follow-up memo.) (TSV)

12. Mr. McHugh asked about Ramon Medina. Mr. George said we had no traces on that name. Was Felix Rodriguez supplying the contras? Mr. George said we did not know, and Mr. Fiers said his name had surfaced in that regard but that we had no specific evidence. Mr. McHugh said it was hard to believe that the Agency did not know who was flying the planes and aiding the contras. Mr. George explained that he believed it absolutely necessary to keep the Agency away from even the appearance of improperly aiding the contras. Mr. Abrams said that it was unreasonable to expect the US Government to know what conservative backers of the contras were doing while criticizing any efforts of the USG to find out about left wing groups raising money for the Sandinistas. A spirited exchange between Mr. Hyde and Mr. McHugh and Mr. Abrams followed--the upshot being that Mr. McHugh still thought it did not ring true that we did not know who the Americans were at Ilopango. (S)

DO   172452

DOCUMENT 54: Michael Barnes, Letter to Robert McFarlane, August 16, 1985, with Cover Note, and Comments by John Poindexter, August 17, 1985.

PAGE 1 OF 3

August 17, 1985

JMP

UNCLASSIFIED

N 29810

This was brought up to me first thing this morning from the Situation Room. Do you want to send RCM a copy before it is staffed?

YES____   NO _✗

Bob   Kay

Send Bud an info copy with staffing indicated. Barnes is really a trouble maker. We have good answers to all of this. Staff to:

North - action
Sible
Regan   ⎫
Thompson   ⎬ coord.
Burghardt   ⎭

UNCLASSIFIED

DOCUMENT 54: Michael Barnes, Letter to Robert McFarlane, August 16, 1985, with Cover
Note, and Comments by John Poindexter, August 17, 1985.

PAGE 2 OF 3

#565

Congress of the United States N 9646

Committee on Foreign Affairs

House of Representatives

Washington, DC 20515

August 16, 1985

The Honorable Robert C. McFarlane
Assistant to the President
for National Security Affairs
Executive Office of the President
The White House
Washington, D.C. 20500

EXHIBIT
OLN-107

Dear Mr. McFarlane:

I am writing in response to recent press reports detailing the
activities of certain National Security Council staff members in
providing advice and fundraising support to Nicaraguan rebel
leaders.

These reports raise serious questions regarding the violation
of the letter and the spirit of U.S. law prohibiting support
for the Nicaraguan rebels. The Congress, in passing the Boland
Amendment (Section 8046 of P.L. 98-473), prohibited "the Central
Intelligence Agency, the Department of Defense, or any other
agency or entity of the U.S. involved in intelligence activities"
from supporting the rebels. It would be stretching the integrity
of the law to suggest that this prohibition was not intended to
cover the NSC. President Reagan, himself, in his executive order
on the nation's intelligence agencies, describes the National
Security Council as the highest government entity with
responsibility for intelligence activities.

In addition, the Boland Amendment strictly prohibits assistance
"for the purpose of which would have the effect of supporting,
directly or indirectly, military or paramilitary operations" of
the Nicaraguan insurgents. Reports quote Administration
officials describing Marine Lt. Col. Oliver North as providing
"tactical influence" on rebel military operations, facilitating
contacts for prospective financial donors, and otherwise
organizing and coordinating rebel-efforts. These activities
clearly have "the effect of supporting" the Nicaraguan rebels.

Congressional intent in passing the Boland Amendment was to
distance the United States from the Nicaraguan rebel movement,
while the Congress and the nation debated the appropriateness of
our involvement in Nicaragua. The press reports suggest that,
despite congressional intent, during this period the U.S.
provided direct support to the Nicaraguan rebels.

DOCUMENT 54: Michael Barnes, Letter to Robert McFarlane, August 16, 1985, with Cover Note, and Comments by John Poindexter, August 17, 1985.

PAGE 3 OF 3

N 9647

The Honorable Robert C. McFarlane
Page Two
August 16, 1985

In order to clarify the circumstances surrounding Lt. Col. North's activities, as chairman of the subcommittee with jurisdiction over United States policy toward Nicaragua, I request that you provide Congress with all information, including memoranda and any other documents, pertaining to any contact between Lt. Col. North and Nicaraguan rebels leaders as of enactment of the Boland Amendment in October, 1984.

Thank you for your attention to this request.

Sincerely,

Michael D. Barnes
Chairman
Subcommittee on Western
Hemisphere Affairs

MDB:na

DOCUMENT 55: Robert McFarlane, Draft of Letter to Congressman Michael Barnes, September 12, 1985.

PAGE 1 OF 4

CONFIDENTIAL
UNCLASSIFIED

Dear Congressman Barnes:

C52105

This is in reply

~~I am pleased to have the opportunity to respond~~ to your letter of
August 16, regarding the activities of members of the NSC staff
in connection with the Nicaraguan democratic resistance. Like
you, I take these charges very seriously and consequently have
thoroughly examined the facts and circumstances which could bear
upon these charges in any fashion.

Based on this review, I *want to* ~~can~~ assure you that my actions, *and* ~~as~~ those
of my staff, have been *in compliance* ~~fully consistent~~ with both the spirit and
the letter of the law. In your letter, you referred specifically
to the *prescriptive* ~~prohibitionary~~ language of Section 8066 of P.L. 98-473—the
Boland Amendment. There have not been, nor will there be, any
expenditures of NSC funds which would have the effect of
supporting directly or indirectly military or paramilitary
operations in Nicaragua by any nation, group, organization,
movement, or individual. Indeed, our actions *have been must* ~~are~~ and ~~will~~ be in
conformity, not only *with* ~~to~~ this proscription, but *with* ~~to~~ _all_ laws.

Your letter affords, *a useful* ~~an~~ opportunity to *comment upon allegations* ~~respond to charges made by~~
~~unnamed Administration officials~~ in the media regarding the
activities of Lieutenant Colonel North and other members of my
staff. Various NSC staff officers have been in contact with
members of the Nicaraguan resistance since the opposition began
to organize in 1982. These staff contacts, as well as my own,

CONFIDENTIAL

UNCLASSIFIED
CONFIDENTIAL

GOVERNMENT
EXHIBIT
103 _EVID_

DRAF

A-00127782

IRG 1

DOCUMENT 55: Robert McFarlane, Draft of Letter to Congressman Michael Barnes, September 12, 1985.

PAGE 2 OF 4

and of *these* ~~our~~ President, have been *important* ~~critical~~ in determining the course of our policy. Discussions with the resistance leaders have helped us to assess the *integrity* ~~sincerity~~ of their commitment to the cause of democracy and justice in Nicaragua. We have also discussed the *evolving character of U.S. support* ~~changing political situation in Washington~~, as we moved from covert support for their cause in 1982-84 to the *more restrictive,* ~~essen~~ *exclusively political support allowed* ~~by~~ ~~constraints imposed by the Boland restrictions in 1984-85 to the~~ *October of last year to the* current situation in which we are able to provide *only* ~~overt~~ humanitarian assistance.

Contrary to reports that we used ~~Rather than using~~ these contacts ~~for~~ "tactical influence" or *to* *to provide* ~~planning~~ military operations, we urged the resistance leaders to forge a representative political front, involving credible non-military figures, aimed at achieving a democratic outcome in Nicaragua. We have also emphasized that the resistance must investigate charges of human rights violations ~~and~~ punish any *put in place measures to prevent such acts* ~~from taking place.~~ guilty parties. Throughout, we have scrupulously abided by the spirit and the letter of the law. None of us has solicited funds, facilitated contacts for prospective potential donors, or otherwise organized or coordinated the military or paramilitary efforts of the resistance.

Since October 1984 when the Boland restrictions were enacted, Lieutenant Colonel North has travelled to Central America eight times for the purpose of meeting with foreign government officials regarding our Central America policy. During these

ALU0127763

DOCUMENT 55: Robert McFarlane, Draft of Letter to Congressman Michael Barnes, September 12, 1985.

PAGE 3 OF 4

CONFIDENTIAL

trips, as well as in other meetings in the U.S., he has conferred with leaders of the Nicaraguan resistance. He acknowledged to both the foreign government officials and the opposition leaders that, while we could no longer contribute directly or indirectly to the military/paramilitary prosecution of their resistance, we would continue to seek Congressional support for their cause. He further urged, as I did during my January 1985 trip to the region, that every effort be made to broaden their political base ~establish a political program providing for a negotiations toward reconciliat as a means of obtaining increased international support for their cause. We also urged that they make clear their commitment to a political, not a military solution int in their international contacts,

These efforts led to the March 1 San Jose Declaration in which the freedom fighters offered to lay down their arms and enter into a church-mediated dialogue with the Sandinistas. As this process matured this past Spring, the President met with the three principal resistance leaders and encouraged them to desist from military activites when it appeared that their proposal might be accepted by the Sandinistas. These actions resulted in the June 12 statement of democratic objectives announced by the Unified Nicaraguan Opposition (UNO) in San Salvador, El Salvador. Our emphasis throughout has been on a political rather than a military solution.

Recent contacts with the resistance have focused on ensuring that the $27 million in humanitarian assistance is properly administered and fully compliant with the legal requirements

A_U0127704

CONFIDENTIAL
UNCLASSIFIED

DOCUMENT 55: Robert McFarlane, Draft of Letter to Congressman Michael Barnes, September 12, 1985.

PAGE 4 OF 4

contained in the legislation. In short, we want to do it right. I well recognize that the Administration and the Congress may differ as to how we can best achieve our shared goal of a democratic outcome in the Central American region. Nonetheless, we agree on the desirability of this outcome and that it must be achieved within the limits of our law.

Mr Chairman, like you, I am most concerned that ~~I am also sure that you share my grave concern about the~~ at a time when humanitarian is being extended to the ~~wide-ranging consequences of making available internal~~ UNO there be no misgivings as to the existence of any ~~Presidential documents, particularly those concerning sensitive~~ parallel efforts to provide directly or indirectly, support for ~~relations with other governments. At the same time, I want to~~ ~~assure you that~~ I remain fully prepared to discuss these matters with you and other members of your committee.

Thank you again for this opportunity to clarify a most unfortunate misrepresentation of the facts.

Sincerely,

military or paramilitary activities in Nicaragua. There has not ~~this~~ been nor will there be any such activities by the NSC staff. In the interest i providing such assurances as may be helpful in forging mutual trust and confidence

The Honorable Michael D. Barnes
House of Representatives
Washington, D.C. 20515

DOCUMENT 56: Oliver North, Memorandum for Robert McFarlane, "Fallback Plan for the Nicaraguan Resistance," March 16, 1985.

PAGE 1 OF 4

ROUTING			
To	Name and Address	Date	Initials
1	Robert McFarlane	3/17	W
2			
4			
5			
6			

XX ACTION		FILE	
APPROVAL		INFORMATION	
COMMENT		PREPARE REPLY	
CONCURRENCE		RECOMMENDATION	
DIRECT REPLY		RETURN	
DISPATCH		SIGNATURE	

REMARKS:

cc: Oliver North (#2 and 3)
     Jim Radzimski (#4)

TOP SECRET   SENSITIVE

E Y E S   O N L Y

TOP SECRET

NSC/ICS CONTROL NO.   400246

COPY NO.   1   OF   4

HANDLE VIA SYSTEM IV CHANNEL ONLY

NSC INTELLIGENCE
DOCUMENT

Warning Notice
Intelligence Sources and Methods Involved
NATIONAL SECURITY INFORMATION
Unauthorized Disclosure Subject to Criminal Sanctions

E Y E S   O N L Y   AKW03740

TOP SECRET   SENSITIVE

TOP SECRET

DOCUMENT 56: Oliver North, Memorandum for Robert McFarlane, "Fallback Plan for the Nicaraguan Resistance," March 16, 1985.

PAGE 2 OF 4

TOP SECRET

MEMORANDUM

NATIONAL SECURITY COUNCIL

SYSTEM IV
NSC/ICS-400246

March 16, 1985

TOP SECRET

SENSITIVE

ACTION

MEMORANDUM FOR ROBERT C. MCFARLANE

FROM: OLIVER L. NORTH

SUBJECT: Fallback Plan for the Nicaraguan Resistance

The plan attached at Tab I has been developed, pursuant to our discussion on Friday regarding fallback options. It is premised on the assumption of a major Congressional budget battle and an assessment that the Congress will not rescind the restrictions in Section 8066 of the FY-85 C.R. (Tab A). Should you determine in your meeting with Senators Durenburger and Lugar (Tuesday, March 19, 0730) that the Congress will not endorse a resumption of USG support to the resistance, the plan at Tab I provides a workable alternative.

Secrecy for the plan is paramount. We could not implement such an option if it became known in advance and it also mandates that present donors continue their relationship with the resistance beyond the current funding figure. The plan would require the President to make a major public pronouncement which, in turn, must be supported by other Administration officials, resistance leaders, and regional Heads of State once it has been announced.

RECOMMENDATION

That, if Durenburger and Lugar indicate an unwillingess to support resumption of USG aid to the resistance, you discuss the attached plan with Secretary Shultz following your meeting.

Approve _____   Disapprove _____

Attachments
      Tab I - Fallback Option Plan
            Tab A - Section 8066 of the FY-85 C.R.

TOP SECRET
Declassify: OADR

TOP SECRET

SENSITIVE

AKW037402

DOCUMENT 56: Oliver North, Memorandum for Robert McFarlane, "Fallback Plan for the Nicaraguan Resistance," March 16, 1985.

PAGE 3 OF 4

FALLBACK OPTION PLAN FOR THE NICARAGUAN RESISTANCE

Assumptions. The Congress is unwilling to support release of $14M in USG funds for the purpose of supporting, directly or indirectly, military or paramilitary operations in Nicaraguan. The FY-86 budget is seriously jeopardized by Congressional action and will require a major effort on the part of the President immediately after the MX vote through mid-July. There will be insufficient time or assets available to organize the kind of Administration-wide effort required to achieve an affirmative vote in both Houses on the Nicaraguan resistance program.

Section 8066 of the law (Tab A) expires on October 1, 1985. There are currently $28M requested in the FY-86 intelligence budget for the purpose of supporting paramilitary operations by the Nicaraguan resistance. The current funding relationship which exists between the resistance and its donors is sufficient to purchase arms and munitions between now and October--if additional monies are provided for non-military supplies (e.g., food, clothing, medical items, etc.). The current donors will have to be convinced of the need to continue their funding for munitions after October 1, 1985. A commitment for another $25-30M from the donors will be necessary for munitions in 1986 in anticipation that the $28M requested in the intelligence budget is not approved.

Concept. In lieu of forwarding the report to the Congress required by Section 8066 of PL 98-473, the President would announce on or about April 2 that the American people should contribute funds ("...send your check or money order to the Nicaraguan Freedom Fighters, Box 1776, Gettysburg, PA...") to support liberty and democracy in the Americas. He would note that the monies raised would be used to support the humanitarian needs of those struggling for freedom against Communist tyranny in Central America. By necessity, the speech must be dramatic and a surprise. It cannot be leaked in advance.

Prior to the speech, the following steps must be taken:

-- Calero, Cruz, and Robelo (the principle leadership of the Nicaraguan armed and unarmed resistance) must be covertly advised of this plan and must assure of their support.

-- The Nicaraguan Freedom Fund, Inc., a 501(c)3 tax exempt corporation, must be established and obtain a Post Office Box 1776 in Gettysburg, Philadelphia, Valley Forge, or Yorktown. (This process is already underway.)

TOP SECRET

TOP SECRET   2   SENSITIVE

-- Presidents Suazo, Monge, and Duarte (and the appropriate
   leadership of each of those countries) must be apprised of
   this plan 1-2 days in advance of the announcement. They
   must be prepared to fully support the President's
   proclamation.

-- The current donors must be apprised of the plan and agree to
   provide additional $25-30M to the resistance for the
   purchase of arms and munitions.

-- Public groups and political action committees already
   mobilized for the Congressional campaign to relieve the 8066
   constraints will have to be mobilized for the new approach
   (advertising, posters, mailings, phonecalls, etc.) several
   hours before the President speaks.

-- Assuming a Presidential speech on or about April 2 at 8:00
   p.m., a briefing for senior Administration officials should
   be held at 7:00 p.m. that day in Room 450 OEOB to ensure
   that public commentary after the speech by these official is
   supportive of this proclamation

Additional Requirements.

-- Informal contact several months ago with a lawyer
   sympathetic to our cause indicated that such a procedure
   would be within the limits of the law. Fred Fielding should
   be asked to do conduct a very private evaluation of the
   President's role in making such a request.

-- The name of one of several existing non-profit foundations,
   we have established in the course of the last year, will be
   changed to Nicaraguan Freedom Fund, Inc. Several reliable
   American citizens must be contacted to serve as its
   corporate leadership on its board of directors along with
   Cruz, Calero, and Robelo

-- Calero, Cruz, and Robelo will support support such an option
   if properly approached. They should then be photographed
   with the President on the day of his announcement and
   prepared to appear on U.S. and other media supporting the
   President's program.

-- You will have to make a quick (one day) trip to the region,
   preferably the day before announcement in order to brief
   Heads of State and regional leaders. For obvious reasons,
   this must be a very secret trip.

-- The President's speech must be prepared in total secrecy
   much the same as Ben Elliott worked on the Grenada
   announcements.

TOP SECRET   SENSITIVE

TOP SECRET

AKW037405

DOCUMENT 57: Oliver North, Action Memorandum for Robert McFarlane, "Fallback Plan for the Nicaraguan Resistance," Altered Version, March 16, 1985.

PAGE 1 OF 1

NATIONAL SECURITY COUNCIL
WASHINGTON D.C. 20506

March 16, 1985

ACTION

MEMORANDUM FOR ROBERT C. MCFARLANE

FROM: OLIVER L. NORTH

SUBJECT: Fallback Plan for the Nicaraguan Resistance

Congress is apparently reluctant to rescind the restrictions in
Section 8066 of the FY-85 C.R. (Tab A). Should you determine in
your meeting with Senators Durenburger and Lugar (Tuesday,
March 19, 0730) that the Congress will not endorse a resumption
of USG support to the resistance, we will need to develop a
fallback plan for getting on with support for the resistance.
The best fallback we have is to stress that, while President
Reagan is unwilling to use U.S. troops in Nicaragua, all
available intelligence supports the realization that we will have
to in the 1990's, if there is not a democratic outcome now.

RECOMMENDATION

That, if Durenburger and Lugar indicate an unwillingness to
support voting on USG aid to the resistance again this spring,
you ask them for fallback options.

           Approve ✓   Disapprove _____

Attachment
      Tab A - Section 8066 of the FY-85 C.R.

AXW020480

DOCUMENT 58: John Poindexter, PROFS Note to Oliver North, August 11, 1986, with Forwarded PROFS Message from Bob Pearson, "HPSCI Interview of North," August 8, 1986.

PAGE 1 OF 1

UNCLASSIFIED

From: NSJMP   --CPUA
To: NSOLN   --CPUA   OLLIE NORTH   Date and time   05.11.86 15.44.09

-- SECRET --

NOTE FROM: JOHN POINDEXTER
Subject: HPSCI interview of North
Well done.
*** Forwarding note from NSWRP   --CPUA   08/03/86 09:29 ***
To: NSRBH   --CPUA

NOTE FROM: BOB PEARSON
SUBJECT: HPSCI interview of North

Session was success - Hamilton will entertain motion soonest to report unfavorably on Resolution of Inquiry and made clear believes HPSCI can turn aside future offers of similar resolutions. North's remarks were thorough and convincing. Hamilton underlined his appreciation to Admiral and to Bud for full cooperation offered by NSC. He restated there were no facts uncovered by or known to HPSCI to substantiate the allegations in the resolution of inquiry or media reports on North's activities.

In response to specific questions. Ollie covered following points:

o contact with FDN and UNO aimed to foster viable, democratic political strategy for Nicaraguan opposition. gave no military advice. knew of no specific military operations.

o Singlaub - gave no advice. has had no contact in 20 months: Owen - never worked from OLN office. OLN had casual contact. never provided Owen guidance.

o threats/harassment - in response to question. OLN recounted incidents of harassment/threats prior to '85 vote and again prior to '86 vote. speculated that possibly due in part to active measures effort.

cc: NSPBT   --CPUA   NSOLN   --CPUA
    NSRKS   --CPUA   NSPWR   --CPUA
    NSPWH   --CPUA   NSJMP   --CPUA   JOHN M. POINDEXTER
    NSRCM   --CPUA   ROBERT MCFARLANE

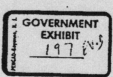
GOVERNMENT
EXHIBIT
197 N-5

JmP 25a

UNCLASSIFIED

DOCUMENT 59: Steven Berry, "Memo to the Files: August 6, 1986, 8:35 a.m. White House Situation Room. Discussion with Mr. Ollie North Regarding House Resolution 485...," September 3, 1986.

PAGE 1 OF 2

UNCLASSIFIED

September 3, 1986

MEMO TO THE FILES

FROM: Steven K. Berry, Associate Counsel

RE: August 6, 1986, 8:35 a.m., White House Situation Room.
        Discussion with Mr. Ollie North regarding House Resolution 485,
        directing the President to provide to the House of Representatives
        certain information concerning the activities of Lieutenant Colonel
        Oliver North or any other member of the staff of the National
        Security Council in support of the Nicaraguan Resistance, submitted
        by Congressman Tom Coleman.

In attendance: Bob Pearson, Counsel, NSC; Ollie North, Special Assistant,
NSC; Ron Sable, Director of Legislative Affairs, NSC; Tom Latimer, HPSCI;
Steve Berry, HPSCI.
Members present: Chairman Hamilton, Mssrs. McCurdy, Kastenmeier, Daniel,
Roe, Stump, Ireland, Hyde, Cheney, Livingston and McEwen.

Mr. Ollie North indicated that his principle mission was to coordinate
contacts with the FDN (the Nicaraguan Resistance) and U.S. government
officials. One of the main purposes of his job was to assess the long-term
viability of the FDN as a democratic institution and to explain the U.S.
government's relationship to that organization including the explanation of
the Boland Amendment. North indicated he gave the FDN and their officials
advice on human rights and political advice concerning the need for an
improved civic image. North also explained the United States' legal position
with regard to the guidelines and limitations of U.S. support as outlined
under the Boland Amendment. Prior to the ban on assistance to the Nicaraguan
Resistance of October 1, 1983, North indicated he had given books to the
leadership of the FDN which focused on creating guerrilla movements and
popular support for their goals, ideas and objectives. In support of that
concept, North asked the FDN leaders to focus on the principles and the
tactics espoused by such individuals as Maosetung and Sungsu and Cheginerria
and also asked that they focus on the internal and external support necessary
to continue the movement. North indicated that he stressed these points with
Calero, Bermudez, Cruz, Robello, and Pastora when he was an active
participant.

When queried regarding his relationship with General Singluab, Colonel
North indicated that although he knew him he had no association as indicated
in press reports and it was unfortunate that General Singlaub made those
statements.

Mr. Roe asked Mr. North to comment on his relationship with Robert W.
Owen, a former Hill staffer who was employed by the Nicaraguan Humanitarian
Assistance Office ($50,000 contract), to facilitate delivery of supplies to
the FDN and UNO. Colonel North indicated that he had talked to Robert Owen,
had only a casual and formal contract with him, was familiar with Owen but
that his contacts were greatly exaggerated and were not nearly as extensive as
the press had reported.

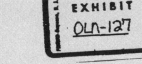

EXHIBIT
OLN-127

UNCLASSIFIED

DOCUMENT 59: Steven Berry, "Memo to the Files: August 6, 1986, 8:35 a.m. White House Situation Room. Discussion with Mr. Ollie North Regarding House Resolution 485...," September 3, 1986.

PAGE 2 OF 2

UNCLASSIFIED

-2-

Similarly, Mr. North indicted he did not know Mr. Terrill, an individual who had appeared on numerous news shows and who had been quoted in newspapers supporting allegations of improper activities of Colone North. Furthermore, it seemed as though Mr. Terrill was not who he said he was and had never been an Army officer.

Mr. North in a direct response to a question regarding the proprieties of his activities after October 1, 1984, responded that be did not in any way, nor at any time violate the spirit, principles or legal requirements of the Boland Amendment.

Congressman Ireland indicated that he had heard of several personal difficulties Colonel North and his family had experienced since the newpaper articles diclosed his joo, duties and responsibilities in the NSC.

To summarize, Colonel North, his wife and children, have been targets of organized protests and pickets in front of his home, his personal property was damaged, fences torn down, his car damaged, his house had been broken into, his dog had been poisoned, his family received continuous threatening phone calls during all hours of the day and night and his children had been threatened. At the suggestion of the FBI and Secret Service his family was moved for several weeks to Camp Perry while improved security procedures were installed in his home at North's expense.

Near the conclusion of the meeting. Congressman McCurdy supported by several other Members of the Committee indicated that although it was no longer necessary for the Intelligence Committee to meet to report on H. Res. 485 to stay its privileged status, he hoped the Intelligence Committee would meet to adversely report H. Res. 485 in the near future. The Chairman responded that action would be more appropriately done at a Full Committee Meeting after all Members had been notified of the Committee meeting.

The Chairman expressed his appreciation for the good faith — effort that Admiral Poindexter had shown in arranging a meeting and indicated his satisfaction in the responses received. Ron Sable from the NSC staff expressed the Administration's concern and his hope that this meeting had satisfied the Committee's concern with regard to the allegations of improper conduct by Lt Col North and further expressed his hope that this meeting would be the final chapter in the Committee's inquiries. The Chairman indicated that, barring any new or additional information, he too thought the Committee would be satisfied with the information that it had received.

UNCLASSIFIED

PART TWO

IRAN: ARMS FOR HOSTAGES

V. THE IRAN INITIATIVE: PRESIDENTIAL AUTHORIZATION

When the Shah of Iran went into permanent exile in January 1979, the United States hoped it could establish positive ties with his eventual successor. Even after Ayatollah Ruhollah Khomeini emerged as the uncontested ruler, President Jimmy Carter tried to reach a *modus vivendi* with the new regime. But the November 1979 takeover of the U.S. embassy in Teheran changed Washington's official attitude to barely restrained hostility as Carter immediately imposed a wide-ranging embargo on Iran, which included deliveries of military equipment.

After Ronald Reagan's inauguration in January 1981, which coincided with the release of the remaining fifty-two American hostages from Teheran, the new president assigned the Khomeini regime a prominent place on his foreign policy agenda and hardened Washington's approach toward Teheran further. The United States not only objected to what it saw as Iran's support for terrorist acts overseas but it feared that an Iranian victory in its bloody war against Iraq, underway since September 1980, might prompt Khomeini to spread his revolutionary brand of Islamic fundamentalism throughout the volatile Persian Gulf region. That would not only threaten Western access to oil but might leave the Soviet Union in a position to exploit the ensuing instability politically or militarily.

Accordingly, Reagan administration officials took a number of steps to prevent their worst fears from coming to pass. Notably, in the spring of 1983, the United States initiated Operation STAUNCH, a voluntary, worldwide arms embargo against Teheran, which Washington pursued vigorously with its allies. And in January 1984 the State Department formally declared Iran a sponsor of international terrorism.

But from the early days of the administration, dissenting voices in the government had called for a different tack toward Teheran, based in part on the concern that such an inflexible stance might backfire. For example, at a Senior Interdepartmental Group (SIG) meeting held on July 21, 1981, participants agreed that current U.S. efforts to prevent other countries from selling arms to Iran "would have only a marginal effect on...the war" with Iraq and might actually "increase opportunities for the Soviets to take advantage of Iran's security concerns."[1]

ARMS TO IRAN?

Echoes of that early judgment clearly resonated in a draft National Security Decision Directive (NSDD), which came to the attention of top administration officials in mid 1985 (Document 60). Drawn up at the behest of National Security Advisor Robert McFarlane, the draft NSDD proposed to change U.S. policy toward Iran from efforts to isolate it from the world community to encouraging limited contacts by U.S. allies in hopes of creating an opening to the Khomeini regime.

"Dynamic political evolution is taking place inside Iran," the paper began:

> Instability caused by the pressures of the Iraq-Iran war, economic deterioration and regime infighting create the potential for major changes in Iran. The Soviet Union is better positioned than the U.S. to exploit and benefit from any power struggle that results in changes in the Iranian regime....

The specifics of this suggested "program" included one phrase that caught everyone's eye, a plan to

> [e]ncourage Western allies and friends to help Iran meet its import requirements so as to re-

duce the attractiveness of Soviet assistance.... This includes provision of selected military equipment....

In short, the authors proposed authorizing Western arms sales to Iran, and effectively bringing an end to Operation STAUNCH.

The secretaries of state and defense, George Shultz and Caspar Weinberger, reacted instantly. In a cover note, Weinberger wrote to an aide, "this is almost too absurd to comment on....like asking Qadhafi to Washington for a cozy chat" (Document 61). Shultz responded almost as bluntly; after all, as secretary of state in January 1984 he had taken the lead in designating Iran a sponsor of international terrorism. Only CIA Director William Casey, whose analysts had helped formulate the assumptions and ideas contained in the document, supported the proposal. At the time, it appeared that the combined opposition of Shultz and Weinberger would close the book on revising Washington's posture toward Iran.

However, in early July McFarlane saw another opportunity to press the issue. In separate meetings with Israeli Foreign Ministry official David Kimche and NSC consultant Michael Ledeen, who with McFarlane's permission had recently visited Israeli Prime Minister Shimon Peres, McFarlane learned about an approach to Israel that certain Iranians had made involving an exchange of U.S.-made weapons for the release of American hostages in Lebanon. According to McFarlane, Kimche suggested that the United States consider authorizing a token transfer of TOW (Tube-launched, Optically-tracked, Wire-guided) missiles to the Iranian faction, as a sign of goodwill.

McFarlane leaped at the idea. Over the next several days, he contacted both Shultz and Weinberger to tell them about the proposal. In a cable to the secretary of state, McFarlane wrote:

The short term dimension concerns the seven hostages; the long term dimension involves the establishment of a private dialogue with Iranian officials on the broader relations.... [They]

sought specifically the delivery from Israel of 100 TOW missiles....[2]

Weinberger's military assistant, Lt. Gen. Colin Powell, recalled that McFarlane "described to the Secretary [Weinberger] the so-called Iran Initiative...and what the purposes of such an initiative would be," and that the national security advisor referred to both arms and hostages in the conversation.[3]

McFarlane also briefed President Reagan on the proposal, initially at a July 18 meeting with White House Chief of Staff Donald Regan present. Recollections vary as to what exactly was discussed at this session. On August 6, the idea received a more formal review at the White House in a meeting attended by Reagan, Vice President George Bush, Shultz, Weinberger, and Regan.[4] Specifically, the debate focused on whether Israel should provide one hundred TOW missiles to Iran in exchange for four hostages as part of a renewed dialogue between Iran and the United States. Shultz and Weinberger again rejected the idea, Shultz going so far as to warn, prophetically, that "we were just falling into the arms-for-hostages business and we shouldn't do it."[5]

Despite their objections, President Reagan gave the go-ahead a few days later,[6] and on August 20, 1985, Israel delivered a palett of TOW missiles to Iran. The shipment was supposed to result in the release of American hostages, but none followed—Iran had failed to deliver as promised. Nevertheless, with the president's approval, the Israelis dispatched another consignment of missiles, which arrived in Iran on September 15. This time, Benjamin Weir, a Presbyterian minister held since May 8, 1984, was released.

In their public pronouncements after the arms deals were exposed, Reagan and his aides insisted that the long-term goal of the operation was to reopen relations with "moderate" officials in Iran who would pursue a more pro-Western policy after Khomeini. They also claimed that bringing the Iran-Iraq War to an end and stemming the tide of terrorism were important factors in the decision. In contrast, they deliberately downplayed resolution of the hostage issue as either a pre-condition for attaining other goals or a subsidiary benefit of the Iran initiative.[7]

But at other times, these same officials, including the president himself, revealed that in fact the hostage predicament occupied the central place in Reagan's thinking. McFarlane told the Tower Commission that the plight of the hostages "was terribly important" to Reagan, that he would meet with their families "almost every time he took a trip…. [A]nd it would be a very anguishing kind of a thing."[8] CIA Director Casey wrote after one meeting, "I suspect he would be willing to run the risk and take the heat in the future if this will lead to springing the hostages." Reagan himself acknowledged this in his memoirs: "I felt a heavy weight on my shoulders to get the hostages home."[9]

This strong personal desire meshed with a more practical, political motivation. As Thomas Twetten of the CIA's Near East Division told the Tower Commission:

The political reality of this thing was it would be very nice if you could get a strategic thing done…. But the real thing that was driving this was that there was in early '86, late '85, a lot of pressure from the hostage families…and there were articles in the magazines about the forgotten hostages, and there were a lot of things being said about the U.S. Government isn't doing anything…. And there [was] a lot of fear about the yellow ribbons going back up and that this President would have the same problems that the last President had had with the Iranian hostages.[10]

This powerful combination of personal and political incentives helps to explain why the president kept the initiative going despite disappointments at virtually every stage. After the August-September TOW transactions, "the lesson to Iran was unmistakable," according to the Iran-Contra final report. "All U.S. positions and principles were negotiable, and breaches by Iran went unpunished. Whatever Iran did, the U.S. could be brought back to the arms bargaining table by the promise of another hostage."[11]

A QUESTION OF LEGALITY

The next phase of the Iran initiative got underway in October 1985 after another in the series of meetings of American, Israeli, and Iranian intermediaries. This time, rather than TOWs, Iran sought HAWK (Homing-All-the-Way-Killer) antiaircraft missiles in exchange for hostages. McFarlane briefed President Reagan about the proposal on November 17 as Reagan was about to leave for a Geneva summit with Soviet leader Mikhail Gorbachev. According to McFarlane, the president's reaction to the HAWKs-for-hostages idea was "cross your fingers or hope for the best, and keep me informed."[12]

As with the earlier TOW proposal, McFarlane made sure to tell other top-level officials, including Shultz and Weinberger, about the plan. The secretary of state got a secure telephone call "out of the blue" from McFarlane indicating that Iran was about to release a number of American hostages, for which Israel would provide one hundred missiles. Shultz once again objected to the overall idea, which he called a "straight-out arms-for-hostages deal."[13]

Secretary of Defense Weinberger also received calls about the HAWK missiles. Although he later told Iran-Contra investigators that he did "not have any recollection" of being informed of the November shipments, Weinberger's own handwritten notes record a call from McFarlane from Geneva on November 19: "McFarlane…wants us to try to get 500 Hawks for sale to Israel to pass on to Iran for release of 5 hostages." When Weinberger objected during a second phone conversation the next day that "we shouldn't pay Iranian[s] anything," McFarlane told him that the "President has decided to do it thru Israelis."[14]

Weinberger learned more about the operation through highly classified electronic intercepts—transcripts of intercepted telephone conversations—which he began to receive in the fall of 1985.[15]

This was a series of intelligence reports and they were garbled and sometimes tried to use other language to refer to hostages or to refer to weapons, things of that kind. I think there could well have been references to hostages but the whole gist of it was that American officials were negotiating and discussing matters involving arms with the Iranian representatives.[16]

According to information released during the trial of Lt. Col. Oliver North, the intercepts were more explicit than that. A stipulation of facts that was entered into the record as a substitute for the intercepts themselves indicates that "the reports of very late November and early December 1985 revealed that HAWK missiles were shipped to Iran from Israel in connection with hostage recovery efforts" (Document 62). The Stipulation notes that several high-level officials received the intercepts over the course of late 1985 through late 1986. Besides North, McFarlane and Poindexter, they were distributed to Weinberger, CIA Director Casey, CIA Deputy Director John McMahon, and National Security Agency chief William Odom, as well as several other intelligence officials.

On December 7, top-level administration officials gathered in the White House residential quarters to discuss the Iran initiative. President Reagan presided. Others attending included Weinberger, Shultz, Regan, Poindexter, and McMahon. "President wants to free hostages," Weinberger recorded in his notes of the meeting. In clear terms, the secretary of defense explained to President Reagan that sending missiles to Iran was against the law:

> I argued strongly that we have an embargo that makes arms sales to Iran illegal [and] President couldn't violate it [and] that "washing" transaction thru Israel wouldn't make it legal. Shultz, Don Regan agreed.[17]

According to Weinberger's notes, the president responded that "he could answer charges of illegality but he couldn't answer charge that 'big strong President Reagan passed up a chance to free hostages.' "[18] Implying that the consequences of proceeding with the arms-for-hostages transfers might include a prison

term, Weinberger retorted, "visiting hours are Thursday."[19]

Although Reagan gave verbal approval to the HAWK deal before it took place, his formal authorization—in the form of a written Presidential Finding—did not come until Deputy CIA Director John McMahon demanded that one be drafted "retroactive[ly]" to cover his agency's involvement.[20] A copy of the unsigned draft has survived (Poindexter tore up the original), showing explicitly that the scope of the operation was "hostage rescue"—specifically, to provide "assistance by the Central Intelligence Agency to private parties in their attempt to obtain the release of Americans held hostage in the Middle East" (Document 63). Significantly, the Finding made no mention of a larger strategic opening.

A NEW FINDING

The disarray brought about by the HAWK shipment (described in the following chapter) prompted administration officials to take direct control of future deliveries of weapons to Iran. North provided the immediate impetus. In a December 9, 1985, memorandum to Poindexter, he wrote, "We could, with an appropriate covert action Finding, commence deliveries ourselves, using [Richard] Secord as our conduit to control [Manucher] Gorbanifar [sic] and delivery operations."[21] Over the next few weeks, CIA and NSC officials formulated a new Presidential Finding that incorporated these elements, as spelled out in a detailed new proposal offered by an Israeli intermediary early in January 1986. Another meeting of NSC principals, including Vice President George Bush and Attorney General Edwin Meese, took place on January 7 to review the latest effort, and Shultz and Weinberger once again rose to object. Weinberger memorialized the meeting in his daily notes:

> Met with President, Shultz, Poindexter, Bill Casey, Ed Meese, in Oval Office. President decided to go with Israeli-Iranian offer to release our 5 hostages in return for sale of 4000 TOWs to Iran by Israel—

George Shultz + I opposed—Bill Casey, Ed Meese + VP favored—as did Poindexter.[22]

Reflecting the will of the majority, Poindexter presented the final version of the Finding to the president on January 17. A cover memorandum attached to the Finding explained the details (Document 64). By signing it, the president moved the United States to the forefront of the arms-for-hostages deals: from now on, North and his colleagues would deal directly with representatives of the government of Iran—the same regime the State Department continued to classify a sponsor of international terrorism. The president also ordered that the operation be kept secret from Congress, a decision that would cause serious problems with the legislature after the deals were exposed. Witnessing the authorization were the vice president, the chief of staff, the national security advisor, and one other NSC staff member. In his diary for that day, President Reagan wrote, "I agreed to sell TOWs to Iran."[23]

With the Finding signed, the pattern for the rest of the operation was set. Poindexter, the new national security advisor, knew the rules of the game, having previously served as McFarlane's deputy. He continued to grant a great deal of leeway to North, who made the most of the situation, often deciding important matters on his own, striking outlandish deals with the Iranians, and acting in the name of the president on issues that were far beyond his competence. Yet all of these activities continued to take place within the framework of the president's broad authorization. Until the press reported the existence of the operation, nobody in the administration questioned the authority of Poindexter's and North's team to implement the president's decisions.

KEEPING THE WHEELS TURNING

The next major event in the initiative came in late May 1986 when McFarlane, North, and others traveled secretly to Teheran to meet, so they thought, with some of Iran's leaders. None appeared, however, and talks with lower-level officials broke down. On his return, McFarlane briefed the president, urging that no arms

be delivered until all the hostages were set free (Document 65). Vice President Bush, Regan, and Poindexter, among others, also attended the briefings. McFarlane's forceful arguments for an "all or nothing" approach carried the day.

This presented major problems for North and the other arms dealers. In Teheran, McFarlane had refused to go along with an Iranian demand to provide more military equipment before all the remaining hostages were released. Two of the American participants, Secord and Albert Hakim, blamed the mission's failure on this decision. However, before the trip, Poindexter specifically told North that "[t]here are not to be any parts delivered until all the hostages are free.... It is either all or nothing."[24] Looking for more room to maneuver, North now set out to convince Poindexter and the president of the need to be more flexible.

But North and his colleagues well understood that the Iranians would never give up all the hostages at once, for the simple reason that to do so would remove their leverage over the Americans. From North's perspective, the only way to make progress was to agree to a series of separate weapons shipments in exchange for the release of perhaps one or two hostages at a time—through the process they termed "sequentialism." However, to reverse the "all or nothing" policy decreed by Poindexter and the president, North needed a dramatic new development.

That turning point came on July 26, when hostage Lawrence Jenco gained his freedom. His release followed weeks of effort by Israeli intermediary Amiram Nir and Iranian middleman Manucher Ghorbanifar to get Iran to produce a sign of progress for the Americans. North jumped at the opportunity to drive his message home to his superiors. In a memorandum for Poindexter and the president, North combined the "carrot" of future possible hostage releases with a "stick"—a catalog of disasters that were likely to take place, in his view, if the United States did not honor Iran's latest demands (Document 66). North warned of the consequences if Iran did not get the remaining HAWK spare parts that McFarlane had denied them in May:

It is entirely possible that if nothing is received, [deleted: Iranian intermediary Mohsen Kangarlou] will be killed by his opponents in Tehran, Ghorbanifar will be killed by his creditors (they are the beneficiaries of a $22M[illion] life insurance policy), and one American hostage will probably be killed in order to demonstrate displeasure.

On the last page of the memorandum, under North's recommendation that Poindexter obtain the president's consent to ship the remaining HAWK parts, the national security advisor wrote: "7/30/86 President approved."

North appears to have recruited one other supporter of his position—Vice President Bush. He arranged a meeting in Tel Aviv between Bush and the chief Israeli intermediary at the time, Amiram Nir, on July 29, for a briefing on the status of the Iran initiative. Nir himself described the conversation in a classified memorandum to Israeli Prime Minister Shimon Peres:

it was said with regard to the hostages, there is no choice but to deal with the most extreme [factions in Iran], because they are controlling the [captives'] fate. They are capable of delivering, where the moderates are not. Now that Jenco has been released, it is absolutely clear.[25]

Bush's aide, Craig Fuller, also prepared a memorandum of conversation after the session (Document 67). After briefing the vice president on the history of the arms-for-hostage deals, according to Fuller's notes, Nir stated that the Iranians had recently proposed an exchange in "four sequences." Nir asked Bush, "Should we accept sequencing?" then answered his own question by echoing North's view that the Iranians would not agree to turn over all the captives at once because "[t]hey fear if they give all hostages they won't get anything from us." The Israeli concluded the meeting with the observation, "We have no real choice [other] than to proceed." The next day, President Reagan approved the sequential approach.

So top-level authorization for the operation continued: North and Secord kept the wheels turning, including developing the "second channel," through which they arranged a final missile shipment in late October 1986 for a single hostage.

The denouement came with Reagan's and Meese's press conference on November 25, which "exposed" the diversion and blamed Israel. On that day, Poindexter called North to discuss how to deal with Israel; North wrote in his notes, "VP call Peres" (Document 68). Evidence suggests that they planned to have Bush tell the Israeli leader that the Iran-Contra connection had been exposed and to recommend that it would "be best if Israel w[oul]d accept that they were aware that some funds were diverted."[26] North hoped that Israel would take the fall for at least the diversion scheme.

Later, on November 25, North recorded a conversation with Nir in which the Israeli balked saying, "I cannot back this story." This was, Nir lamented, the "worst possible end to an intimate and successful joint venture."[27]

NOTES

1. L. Paul Bremer, III, memorandum to Richard Allen, "Iran SIG Meeting of July 21, 1981," September 23, 1981, as quoted in the *Iran-Contra Affair*, p. 159.

2. McFarlane to Shultz, "Israeli-Iranian Contact," July 13, 1985 (see Document 70).

3. Colin Powell, deposition in *Report of the Congressional Committees Investigating the Iran-Contra Affair*, Appendix B, vol. 21, pp. 228–31.

4. White House logs place each of these officials at the session. However, interviews and an examination of other records convinced *Washington Post* reporters Bob Woodward and Walter Pincus that Bush was not there.

5. Shultz is quoted in the *Iran-Contra Affair*, p. 167.

6. Although no record of the president's authorization exists, both the Tower Commission and the congressional Iran-Contra committees concluded that he "most likely" did approve the

proposal in advance: see *Report of the President's Special Review Board* (Washington, D.C.: Government Printing Office, February 26, 1987), p. 111-8 (hereafter referred to as Tower Commission report); the *Iran-Contra Affair*, p. 168.

7. Iran scholar James A. Bill has noted that concerns about falling oil prices also constituted "a confluence of interest…between Iran and America" during the period of the initiative. He points to remarks by North and Ghorbanifar on the subject—including a reference to George Bush's interest in the matter—and recalls that the June 1985 draft NSDD lists "Iranian moderation of OPEC pricing policy" as one of the "longer term goals" to be pursued. See James A. Bill, "The U.S. Overture to Iran, 1985–1986: An Analysis," in Nikki R. Keddie and Mark J. Gasiorowski, eds., *Neither East Nor West: Iran, the Soviet Union, and the United States* (New Haven: Yale University Press, 1990), p. 171.

8. Tower Commission report, p. B-96, fn. 69.

9. Ronald Reagan, *An American Life* (New York; Simon & Schuster, 1990), p. 510.

10. Tower Commission report, p. B-83.

11. *Iran-Contra Affair*, p. 171.

12. McFarlane interview with the Tower Commission, quoted in ibid., p. 176.

13. George Shultz, testimony in *Joint Hearings before the Select Committees on the Iran-Contra Investigation*, July 23, 1987, vol. 100-9, p. 29.

14. (Second) Weinberger Indictment, October 30, 1992, p. 4.

15. The agency that originated the intercepts, the National Security Agency (NSA), a component of the Defense Department, considered them so sensitive that even their existence was secret. Instead, they were referred to with euphemisms such as "sensitive intelligence." However, North's attorney, Brendan Sullivan, repeatedly spoke of "intercepts" during North's trial (see, for example, Sullivan's closing argument, April 19, 1989, pp. 8194–98).

16. Caspar Weinberger, testimony in *Joint Hearings before the Select Committees on the Iran-Contra Investigation*, July 31, 1987, vol. 100-10, p. 136.

17. (Second) Weinberger indictment, October 30, 1992, p. 5.

18. Ibid., pp. 5–6.

19. George Shultz, testimony in *Joint Hearings before the Select Committees on the Iran-Contra Investigation*, July 23, 1987, vol. 100-9, p. 32.

20. John McMahon, deposition in *Report of the Congressional Committees Investigating the Iran-Contra Affair*, Appendix B, vol. 17, pp. 97–98.

21. North to McFarlane and Poindexter, "Next Steps," December 9, 1985 (Document 77).

22. (Second) Weinberger Indictment, October 30, 1992, p. 7. A chronology prepared on behalf of Shultz for congressional investigators offered a similar account: "GPS[hultz] and Weinberger argue strongly against the Iran proposal, but everyone else favors going forward." See "Testimony of Secretary of State: Iran Chronology I, (5/85–10/31/86)."

23. Quoted in Tower Commission report, p. 111-12.

24. Poindexter to North, "Private Blank Check," April 16, 1986 (Document 81).

25. As quoted by ABC's *Nightline*, October 2, 1992.

26. It is not clear whether they approached Bush or the vice president actually made the call to Peres.

27. Oliver North, Notebook Entries for November 25, 1986.

DOCUMENT 60: Draft National Security Decision Directive, "U.S. Policy toward Iran," ca. June 11, 1985, with Cover Note by Robert McFarlane, June 17, 1985.

PAGE 1 OF 7

UNCLASSIFIED

THE WHITE HOUSE

WASHINGTON

June 17, 1985

SEC DEF
HAS SEEN
JUN 18 1985

SECRET/WITH
TOP SECRET ATTACHMENT

MEMORANDUM FOR THE HONORABLE GEORGE P. SHULTZ
          The Secretary of State

          THE HONORABLE CASPAR W. WEINBERGER
          The Secretary of Defense

SUBJECT: U.S. Policy Toward Iran (S)

The Director of Central Intelligence has just distributed an SNIE on "Iran: Prospects for Near-Term Instability", which I hope you have received. This SNIE makes clear that instability in Iran is accelerating, with potentially momentous consequences for U.S. strategic interests. It seems sensible to ask whether our current policy toward Iran is adequate to achieve our interests. My staff has prepared a draft NSDD (Tab A) which can serve to stimulate our thinking on U.S. policy toward Iran. I would appreciate your reviewing the draft on an eyes only basis and providing me with your comments and suggestions. I am concerned about the possibility of leakage should we decide not to pursue this change in policy with the President. If you feel that we should consider this change, then I would refer the paper to the SIG(FP) in preparation for an NSPG meeting with the President. (S)

Robert C. McFarlane

22 Jun '87

UNCLASSIFIED

(12238a)

SECRET/WITH
TOP SECRET ATTACHMENT

DOCUMENT 60: Draft National Security Decision Directive, "U.S. Policy toward Iran," ca. June 11, 1985, with Cover Note by Robert McFarlane, June 17, 1985.

PAGE 2 OF 7

UNCLASSIFIED

NSC/ICS 402

THE WHITE HOUSE
WASHINGTON

DRAFT

TOP SECRET

Partially Declassified/Released on 22 June 1987
under provisions of E.O. 12356
by B. Rogers, National Security Council

D 92

NATIONAL SECURITY DECISION
DIRECTIVE

U.S. Policy Toward Iran

Dynamic political evolution is taking place inside Iran. Instability caused by the pressures of the Iraq-Iran war, economic deterioration and regime infighting create the potential for major changes in Iran. The Soviet Union is better positioned than the U.S. to exploit and benefit from any power struggle that results in changes in the Iranian regime, as well as increasing socio-political pressures. In this environment, the emergence of a regime more compatible with American and Western interests is unlikely. Soviet success in taking advantage of the emerging power struggle to insinuate itself in Iran would change the strategic balance in the area. ▮▮▮ While we pursue a number of broad, long-term goals, our primary short-term challenge must be to block Moscow's efforts to increase Soviet influence (now and after the death of Khomeini). This will require an active and sustained program to build both our leverage and our understanding of the internal situation so as to enable us to exert a greater and more constructive influence over Iranian politics. We must improve our ability to protect our interests during the struggle for succession.

U.S. Interests and Goals

The most immediate U.S. interests include:

(1) Preventing the disintegration of Iran and preserving it as an independent strategic buffer which separates the Soviet Union from the Persian Gulf;

(2) Limiting the scope and opportunity for Soviet actions in Iran, while positioning ourselves to cope with the changing Iranian internal situation;

(3) Maintaining access to Persian Gulf oil and ensuring unimpeded transit of the Strait of Hormuz; and

(4) An end to the Iranian government's sponsorship of terrorism and its attempts to destabilize the governments of other regional states.

TOP SECRET

(1238b)

DOCUMENT 60: Draft National Security Decision Directive, "U.S. Policy toward Iran," ca. June 11, 1985, with Cover Note by Robert McFarlane, June 17, 1985.

PAGE 3 OF 7

UNCLASSIFIED

DRAFT

D 93

TOP SECRET   2

We also seek other broad and important, if less immediately
urgent, goals.

(1)   Iran's resumption of a moderate and constructive role as a
      member respectively of the non-communist political
      community, of its region, and of the world petroleum
      economy;

(2)   continued Iranian resistance to the expansion of Soviet
      power in general, and to the Soviet occupation of
      Afghanistan in particular;

(3)   an early end to the Iran-Iraq war which is not mediated by
      the Soviet Union and which does not fundamentally alter the
      balance of power in the region;

(4)   elimination of Iran's flagrant abuses of human rights;

(5)   movement toward eventual normalization of U.S.-Iranian
      diplomatic consular and cultural relations, and bilateral
      trade/commercial activities;

(6)   resolution of American legal and financial claims through
      the Hague Tribunal; and

(7)   Iranian moderation on OPEC pricing policy.

Many of our interests will be difficult to achieve. But given
the rapidity with which events are moving, and the magnitude of
the stakes, it is clear that urgent new efforts are required.
Moving forward, we must be especially careful to balance our
evolving relationship with Iraq in a manner that does not damage
the longer term prospects for Iran.

Present Iranian Political Environment

The Iranian leadership faces its most difficult challenges since
1981. The regime's popularity has declined significantly in the
past six months, primarily because of intensified disillusionment
with a seemingly unending war, the continued imposition of
Islamic social policies on a population increasingly reluctant
accept such harsh measures, and a faltering economy brought on
primarily by declining oil revenues. The impact of these
problems is intensified by the realization that Ayatollah
Khomeini's mental and physical health is fragile, which in turn
casts a pall of uncertainty over the daily decision-making
process.

TOP SECRET

DOCUMENT 60: Draft National Security Decision Directive, "U.S. Policy toward Iran," ca. June 11, 1985, with Cover Note by Robert McFarlane, June 17, 1985.

PAGE 4 OF 7

UNCLASSIFIED

DRAF

TOP SECRET   3   D   94

Unless the acceleration of adverse military, political and economic developments is reversed, the Khomeini regime will face serious instability (i.e. repeated anti-regime demonstrations, strikes, assassination attempts, sabotage and other destabilizin activities throughout, increasingly involving the lower classes) This condition will sap officials' energies and government resources, intensifying differences among Iranian leaders as the government tries to avoid mistakes that would provoke popular upheaval and threaten continued control.

While it is impossible to predict the course of the emerging power struggle, it is possible to discern several trends which must be accounted for by U.S. policy. As domestic pressures mount, decision-making is likely to be monopolized by individual representing the same unstable mix of radical, conservative and ultra-conservative factions that now control the Iranian government. The longer Khomeini lingers in power, the more likely the power struggle will intensify, and the greater the number of potential leaders who might affect the outcome of the struggle.

The ultimate strength of various clerical groups and the power coalitions they may form are not known. However, the weaknesses of various opposition groups -- inside Iran and abroad -- are evident, especially the lack of a leader with sufficient stature to rival Khomeini and his ideas. The most likely faction in a power struggle to shift Iranian policy in directions more acceptable to the West -- should their influence increase -- are conservatives working from within the government against the radicals. Radicals within the regime, and the leftist opposition, are the groups most likely to influence the course o events in ways inimical to Western interests.

The Iranian regular armed forces represent a potential source of both power and inclination to move Iran back into a more pro-Western position. Representatives of every faction inside and outside the regime recognize the potential importance of the military and are cultivating contacts with these forces. However, as long as the Army remains committed in the war with Iraq it will not be in a position to intervene in Tehran.

The other instrument of state power, the Revolutionary Guard, is becoming increasingly fractured. It will probably come apart following Khomeini's death, and might even engage in a major power struggle before then. In any scenario, the Guard will be at the center of the power struggle.

TOP SECRET   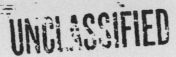 UNCLASSIFIED

DOCUMENT 60: Draft National Security Decision Directive, "U.S. Policy toward Iran," ca. June 11, 1985, with Cover Note by Robert McFarlane, June 17, 1985.

PAGE 5 OF 7

UNCLASSIFIED

DRAFT

TOP SECRET

D 95

The Soviets are well aware of the evolving developments in Iran They will continue to apply carrot-and-stick incentives to Iran in the hope of bringing Tehran to Moscow's terms for an improve bilateral relationship that could serve as a basis for major growth in Soviet influence in Iran. Moscow will clearly resist any trend toward the restoration of a pro-Western Iranian government.

Despite strong clerical antipathy to Moscow and communism, Tehran's leadership seems to have concluded that improvement of relations with the Soviet Union is now essential to Iranian interest. They do not seem interested in improving ties with u: This Iranian assessment is probably based on Tehran's view of what Moscow can do for -- and against - Iran rather than on an ideological preference to conduct relations with Moscow. The USSR already has much leverage over Tehran -- in stark contrast to the U.S.

Moscow views Iran as a key area of opportunity. ████████

██████████████████████████ In return, Moscow is certain to offer economic and technical assis· nce, and possibly even military equipment. While they have heretofore balked at providing major weapon systems, the Soviets might relax their embargo if the right political opportunities presented themselves. While Moscow woul probably not act in a manner that severely disrupts its relatior with Baghdad, given Iraq's dependency on the USSR for ground forces equipment, Moscow possesses considerable room for maneuve if it senses major openings in Tehran for the establishment of a position of significant influence.

Moscow may also pursue a strategy based on support of separatist movements. The Soviet Union has had ample opportunity to cultivate the ethnic groups that cut across the Soviet-Iranian border. Most ethnic groups are unlikely to challenge the centra government in Tehran as long as they fear severe reprisals. But in the areas of Iran adjacent to the Soviet border, the Soviets can provide a security umbrella to protect rebellious ethnic groups from reprisals.

The U.S. position in Tehran is unlikely to improve without a major change in U.S. policy. The challenge to the U.S. in the post-Khomeini period will be severe. Any successor regime will probably seize power in the name of Islam and the revolution and

TOP SECRET

UNCLASSIFIED

DOCUMENT 60: Draft National Security Decision Directive, "U.S. Policy toward Iran," ca. June 11, 1985, with Cover Note by Robert McFarlane, June 17, 1985.

PAGE 6 OF 7

UNCLASSIFIED   DRAF

TOP SECRET   D   96

can be expected to have a built-in anti-American bias. ~~A more conservative regime, still Islamic, might lessen the emphasis on revolution and terrorism and could move cautiously toward a more correct relationship with the U.S.~~ On the other hand, radical ~~forces will try to exacerbate anti-American feelings to strengthen their own positions at the expense of the conservatives.~~

Our leverage with Iran is sharply reduced by the current degree of hostility that springs from the ideology of the radical clergy, especially as it serves their foreign policy goals. Moreover, the moderate and conservative elements of the clergy may also share the radicals' belief that we are inveterately hostile to the Islamic government, making accommodation with the U.S. impossible. The clerical regime continues to believe that the U.S. has not accepted the revolution and intends to reverse the course of events and install a puppet government. This perception has been reinforced by our restoration of diplomatic relations with Iraq, efforts to cut the flow of arms to Iran, and direct threats of military action in retaliation for Iranian-inspired anti-U.S. terrorism.

U.S. Policy

The dynamic political situation in Iran and the consequences for U.S. interests of growing Soviet and radical influence, compel the U.S. undertake a range of short- and long-term initiatives that will enhance our leverage in Tehran, and, if possible minimize that of the Soviets. Particular attention must be paid to avoiding situations which compel the Iranians to turn to the Soviets. Short-term measures should be undertaken in a manner that forestalls Soviet prospects and enhances our ability, directly and indirectly, to build U.S. and Western influence in Iran to the maximum extent possible in the future. Planning for the following initiatives should therefore proceed on a fast and longer-term track. The components of U.S. policy will be to:

(1)   Encourage Western allies and friends to help Iran meet its import requirements so as to reduce the attractiveness of Soviet assistance and trade offers, while demonstrating the value of correct relations with the West. This includes provision of selected military equipment as determined on a case-by-case basis.

TOP SECRET   UNCLASSIFIED

DOCUMENT 60: Draft National Security Decision Directive, "U.S. Policy toward Iran," ca. June 11, 1985, with Cover Note by Robert McFarlane, June 17, 1985.

PAGE 7 OF 7

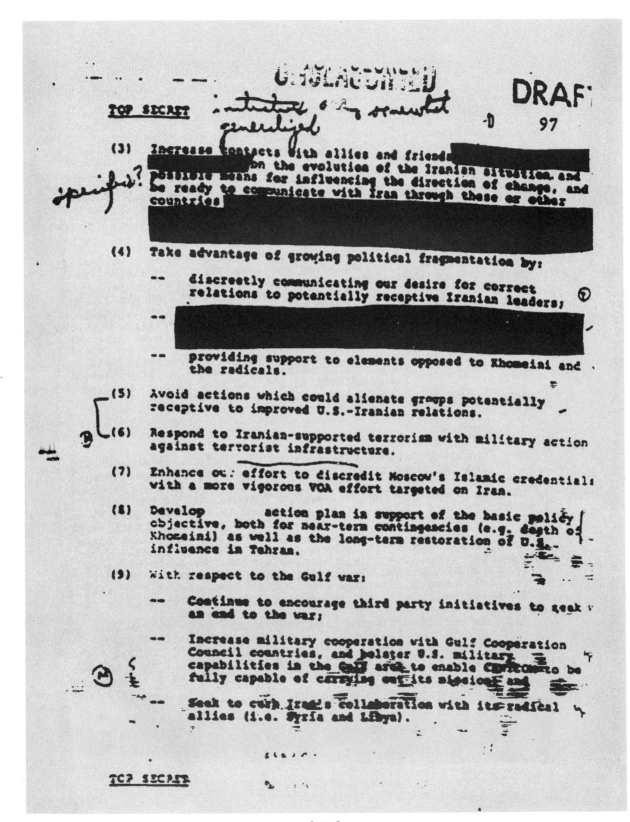

UNCLASSIFIED

DRAFT

TOP SECRET

-D 97

(3) Increase contacts with allies and friends ▮▮▮▮ on the evolution of the Iranian situation and possible means for influencing the direction of change, and be ready to communicate with Iran through these or other countries ▮▮▮▮

(4) Take advantage of growing political fragmentation by:

-- discreetly communicating our desire for correct relations to potentially receptive Iranian leaders;

-- ▮▮▮▮

-- providing support to elements opposed to Khomeini and the radicals.

(5) Avoid actions which could alienate groups potentially receptive to improved U.S.-Iranian relations.

(6) Respond to Iranian-supported terrorism with military action against terrorist infrastructure.

(7) Enhance our effort to discredit Moscow's Islamic credentials with a more vigorous VOA effort targeted on Iran.

(8) Develop an action plan in support of the basic policy objective, both for near-term contingencies (e.g. death of Khomeini) as well as the long-term restoration of U.S. influence in Tehran.

(9) With respect to the Gulf war:

-- Continue to encourage third party initiatives to seek an end to the war;

-- Increase military cooperation with Gulf Cooperation Council countries, and bolster U.S. military capabilities in the Gulf area to enable Centcom to be fully capable of carrying out its missions; and

-- Seek to curb Iran's collaboration with its radical allies (i.e. Syria and Libya).

TOP SECRET

DOCUMENT 61: Colin Powell, Handwritten Note to Caspar Weinberger, with Weinberger's Response, June 18, 1985 (Powell Note to Richard Armitage Attached).

PAGE 1 OF 2

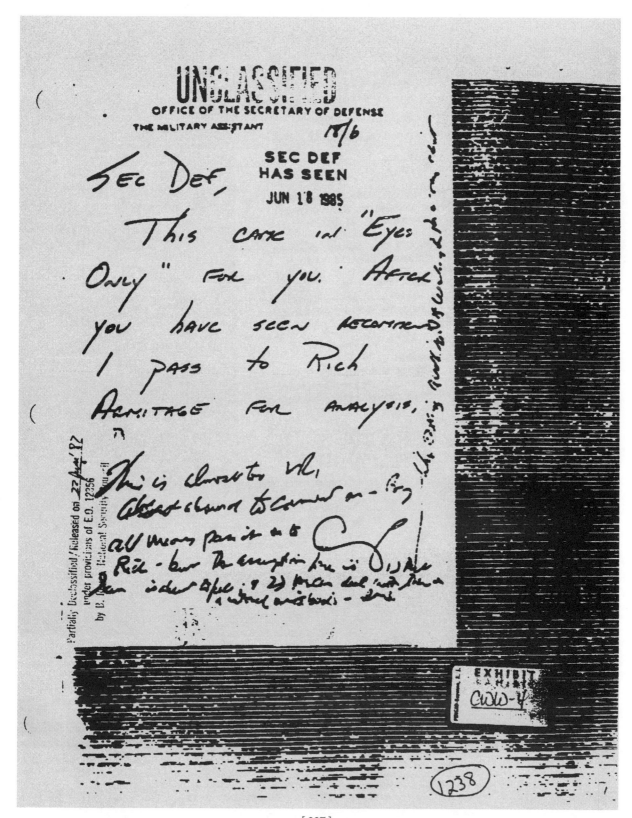

UNCLASSIFIED
OFFICE OF THE SECRETARY OF DEFENSE
THE MILITARY ASSISTANT

SEC DEF
HAS SEEN
JUN 18 1985

Sec Def,

This came in "Eyes Only" for you. After you have seen recommend I pass to Rich Armitage for analysis.

EXHIBIT
CWs-4

1238

DOCUMENT 61: Colin Powell, Handwritten Note to Caspar Weinberger, with Weinberger's Response, June 18, 1985 (Powell Note to Richard Armitage Attached).

PAGE 2 OF 2

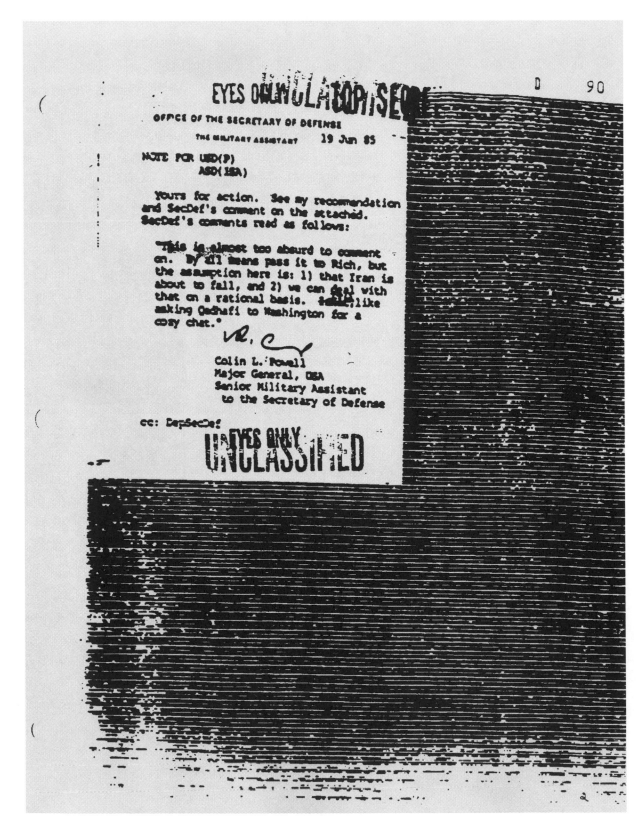

DOCUMENT 62: *United States of America v. Oliver L. North*, "Unclassified Substitute Stipulation," May 5, 1989.

PAGE 1 OF 2

UNITED STATES DISTRICT COURT
FOR THE DISTRICT OF COLUMBIA

UNITED STATES OF AMERICA)
)
        V.   )   Criminal No. 88-0080 --
)   02 - GAG
OLIVER L. NORTH,   )
)
      Defendant.   )
)

FILED

MAY 5 1989

Clerk, U.S. District Court
District of Columbia

<u>UNCLASSIFIED SUBSTITUTE STIPULATION</u>

For purposes of this trial the parties stipulated and agreed as follows:

Defense Exhibit 82 for Identification, which is not in evidence, consists of a group of highly accurate and reliable intelligence reports obtained by lawful and authorized intelligence collection methods at the request of LtCol North and at the direction of his supervisors. The reports are the result of an extensive use of intelligence assets devoted to following and reporting the Iranian initiative.

The reports generally range from two to several pages and are in chronological order commencing on September 1985 and ending in December 1986. There is no particular pattern of frequency of the reports, but the reports are frequent. These reports provide an accurate record of information obtained by various methods of surveillance.

These reports remain classified to the TOP SECRET CODEWORD level. Codeword is defined by the intelligence community as

DOCUMENT 62: *United States of America* v. *Oliver L. North,* "Unclassified Substitute Stipulation," May 5, 1989.

PAGE 2 OF 2

highly sensitive and compartmented information that is distributed only to individuals who have a specific need to know this information. Individuals must have special clearances for this particular information. These reports also contain other restrictions to limit the dissemination of the information to a very small group of very senior government officials and their designated assistants.

The intelligence was able to be collected based in large part on information provided by LtCol North and provides information regarding the pricing and delivery of missiles and military material sold to Iran and the release of American hostages held in Lebanon. The reports show individuals involved, including General Secord. The reports contained information about pricing of this material and those recipients of the reports at the Central Intelligence Agency, National Security Council, and Department of Defense who knew the actual cost of this material to the DoD could have known the Iranians were being significantly overcharged. The reports of very late November and early December 1985 revealed that HAWK missiles were shipped to Iran from Israel in connection with hostage recovery efforts.

The documents are addressed exclusively for National Security Advisor Mr. McFarlane, Admiral John Poindexter, LtCol Oliver North, Director of Central Intelligence Mr. Casey, Deputy Director of Central Intelligence Mr. McMahon (later, Mr. Gates), Secretary of Defense Mr. Weinberger, Assistant to the Chairman of the Joint Chiefs of Staff Vice Admiral Moreau, Director of NSA General Odom, Messrs. Rich, Lord and six other senior intelligence officials. The reports were delivered by special courier to ensure that the information would be seen promptly by the addressees and only by those authorized to receive it.

DOCUMENT 63: Unsigned Draft Presidential Finding on "Hostage Rescue—Middle East," ca. November 26, 1985.

PAGE 1 OF 1

UNCLASSIFIED

Finding Pursuant to Section 662 of the Foreign
Assistance Act of 1961, As Amended, Concerning
Operations Undertaken by the Central Intelligence
Agency in Foreign Countries, Other Than Those
Intended Solely for the Purpose of Intelligence
Collection

C401

    I have been briefed on the efforts being made by private
parties to obtain the release of Americans held hostage in
the Middle East, and hereby find that the following operations
in foreign countries (including all support necessary to
such operations) are important to the national security of
the United States. Because of the extreme sensitivity of
these operations, in the exercise of the President's constitutional authorities, I direct the Director of Central
Intelligence not to brief the Congress of the United States,
as provided for in Section 501 of the National Security Act
of 1947, as amended, until such time as I may direct otherwise.

SCOPE	DESCRIPTION
Hostage Rescue – Middle East	The provision of assistance by the Central Intelligence Agency to private parties in their attempt to obtain the release of Americans held hostage in the Middle East. Such assistance is to include the provision of transportation, communications, and other necessary support. As part of these efforts certain foreign materiel and munitions may be provided to the Government of Iran which is taking steps to facilitate the release of the American hostages. All prior actions taken by U.S. Government officials in furtherance of this effort are hereby ratified.

The White House
Washington, D.C.

Date:

7 May 1987

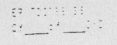

DOCUMENT 64: John Poindexter, Memorandum for the President, "Covert Action Finding Regarding Iran," with Signed Finding Attached, January 17, 1986.

PAGE 1 OF 4

THE WHITE HOUSE

WASHINGTON

January 17, 1986

ACTION

MEMORANDUM FOR THE PRESIDENT

FROM: JOHN M. POINDEXTER

SUBJECT: Covert Action Finding Regarding Iran

Prime Minister Peres of Israel secretly dispatched his special advisor on terrorism with instructions to propose a plan by which Israel, with limited assistance from the U.S., can create conditions to help bring about a more moderate government in Iran. The Israelis are very concerned that Iran's deteriorating position in the war with Iraq, the potential for further radicalization in Iran, and the possibility of enhanced Soviet influence in the Gulf all pose significant threats to the security of Israel. They believe it is essential that they act to at least preserve a balance of power in the region.

The Israeli plan is premised on the assumption that moderate elements in Iran can come to power if these factions demonstrate their credibility in defending Iran against Iraq and in deterring Soviet intervention. To achieve the strategic goal of a more moderate Iranian government, the Israelis are prepared to unilaterally commence selling military materiel to Western-oriented Iranian factions. It is their belief that by so doing they can achieve a heretofore unobtainable penetration of the Iranian governing hierarchy. The Israelis are convinced that the Iranians are so desperate for military materiel, expertise and intelligence that the provision of these resources will result in favorable long-term changes in personnel and attitudes within the Iranian government. Further, once the exchange relationship has commenced, a dependency would be established on those who are providing the requisite resources, thus allowing the provider(s) to coercively influence near-term events. Such an outcome is consistent with our policy objectives and would present significant advantages for U.S. national interests. As described by the Prime Minister's emissary, the only requirement the Israelis have is an assurance that they will be allowed to purchase U.S. replenishments for the stocks that they sell to Iran. We have researched the legal problems of Israel's selling U.S. manufactured arms to Iran. Because of the requirement in U.S. law for recipients of U.S. arms to notify the U.S. government of transfers to third countries, I do not recommend that you agree with the specific details of the Israeli plan. However, there is another possibility. Some time ago Attorney

DOCUMENT 64: John Poindexter, Memorandum for the President, "Covert Action Finding Regarding Iran," with Signed Finding Attached, January 17, 1986.

PAGE 2 OF 4

2

General William French Smith determined that under an appropriate finding you could authorize the CIA to sell arms to countries outside of the provisions of the laws and reporting requirements for foreign military sales. The objectives of the Israeli plan could be met if the CIA, using an authorized agent as necessary, purchased arms from the Department of Defense under the Economy Act and then transferred them to Iran directly after receiving appropriate payment from Iran.

The Covert Action Finding attached at Tab A provides the latitude for the transactions indicated above to proceed. The Iranians have indicated an immediate requirement for 4,000 basic TOW weapons for use in the launchers they already hold.

The Israeli's are also sensitive to a strong U.S. desire to free our Beirut hostages and have insisted that the Iranians demonstrate both influence and good intent by an early release of the five Americans. Both sides have agreed that the hostages will be immediately released upon commencement of this action. Prime Minister Peres had his emissary pointedly note that they well understand our position on not making concessions to terrorists. They also point out, however, that terrorist groups, movements, and organizations are significantly easier to influence through governments than they are by direct approach. In that we have been unable to exercise any suasion over Hizballah during the course of nearly two years of kidnappings, this approach through the government of Iran may well be our only way to achieve the release of the Americans held in Beirut. It must again be noted that since this dialogue with the Iranians began in September, Reverend Weir has been released and there have been no Shia terrorist attacks against American or Israeli persons, property, or interests.

Therefore it is proposed that Israel make the necessary arrangements for the sale of 4000 TOW weapons to Iran. Sufficient funds to cover the sale would be transferred to an agent of the CIA. The CIA would then purchase the weapons from the Department of Defense and deliver the weapons to Iran through the agent. If all of the hostages are not released after the first shipment of 1000 weapons, further transfers would cease.

On the other hand, since hostage release is in some respects a byproduct of a larger effort to develop ties to potentially moderate forces in Iran, you may wish to redirect such transfers to other groups within the government at a later time.

DOCUMENT 64: John Poindexter, Memorandum for the President, "Covert Action Finding Regarding Iran," with Signed Finding Attached, January 17, 1986.

PAGE 3 OF 4

3

The Israelis have asked for our urgent response to this proposal so that they can plan accordingly. They note that conditions inside both Iran and Lebanon are highly volatile. The Israelis are cognizant that this entire operation will be terminated if the Iranians abandon their goal of moderating their government or allow further acts of terrorism. You have discussed the general outlines of the Israeli plan with Secretaries Shultz and Weinberger, Attorney General Meese and Director Casey. The Secretaries do not recommend you proceed with this plan. Attorney General Meese and Director Casey believe the short-term and long-term objectives of the plan warrant the policy risks involved and recommend you approve the attached Finding. Because of the extreme sensitivity of this project, it is recommended that you exercise your statutory prerogative to withhold notification of the Finding to the Congressional oversight committees until such time that you deem it to be appropriate.

Recommendation

OK   NO

_RB_   __   That you sign the attached Finding.

Prepared by:
Oliver L. North

Attachment
    Tab A - Covert Action Finding   _1100 17 Jan 3._

President was briefed verbally from this paper VP, Don Regan and Don Fortier were present

DOCUMENT 64: John Poindexter, Memorandum for the President, "Covert Action Finding Regarding Iran," with Signed Finding Attached, January 17, 1986.

PAGE 4 OF 4

Finding Pursuant to Section 662 of
The Foreign Assistance Act of 1961
As Amended, Concerning Operations
Undertaken by the Central Intelligence
Agency in Foreign Countries, Other Than
Those Intended Solely for the Purpose
of Intelligence Collection

I hereby find that the following operation in a foreign country (including all support necessary to such operation) is important to the national security of the United States, and due to its extreme sensitivity and security risks, I determine it is essential to limit prior notice, and direct the Director of Central Intelligence to refrain from reporting this Finding to the Congress as provided in Section 501 of the National Security Act of 1947, as amended, until I otherwise direct.

SCOPE	DESCRIPTION
Iran	Assist selected friendly foreign liaison services, third countries and third parties which have established relationships with Iranian elements, groups, and individuals sympathetic to U.S. Government interests and which do not conduct or support terrorist actions directed against U.S. persons, property or interests, for the purpose of: (1) establishing a more moderate government in Iran, (2) obtaining from them significant intelligence not otherwise obtainable, to determine the current Iranian Government's intentions with respect to its neighbors and with respect to terrorist acts, and (3) furthering the release of the American hostages held in Beirut and preventing additional terrorist acts by these groups. Provide funds, intelligence, counter-intelligence, training, guidance and communications and other necessary assistance to these elements, groups, individuals, liaison services and third countries in support of these activities.

The USG will act to facilitate efforts by third parties and third countries to establish contact with moderate elements within and outside the Government of Iran by providing these elements with arms, equipment and related materiel in order to enhance the credibility of these elements in their effort to achieve a more pro-U.S. government in Iran by demonstrating their ability to obtain requisite resources to defend their country against Iraq and intervention by the Soviet Union. This support will be discontinued if the U.S. Government learns that these elements have abandoned their goals of moderating their government and appropriated the materiel for purposes other than that provided by this Finding.

The White House
Washington, D.C.
Date January 17, 1986

UNCLASSIFIED ~~SECRET~~

~~SECRET/SENSITIVE~~

NATIONAL SECURITY COUNCIL
WASHINGTON. D.C. 20506

MEMORANDUM OF CONVERSATION

SUBJECT: U.S.-Iran Dialogue

PARTICIPANTS:

N 15397

U.S.
The President
The Vice President
Donald Regan
John Poindexter
Robert McFarlane
Oliver North
Howard Teicher
Rod McDaniel

DATE: May 29, 1986
PLACE: Oval Office
TIME: 9:30 a.m.

<u>McFarlane</u> briefed the President on the visit to Tehran. "We did not succeed in gaining the hostages' release. The current state of government in Iran lacks competence. The competents were decapitated. One hundred thousand or more are gone. The tentative overtures to U.S. result from a recognition of their declining circumstances."

<u>McFarlane</u> described their bazaar-style negotiating tactics and apparent fear of failure. On the terms of reference, there was disagreement, but some areas of agreement as well, e.g., the Soviet threat, Afghanistan. The Iranians have never stepped up to the reality of hostage release process. Misunderstandings were caused by Ghorbanifar's letter.

On possibilities for future, the Iranians are moved by the opportunity to restore ties to serve their strategic and economic interests. "They will be back in touch with us. They have now met with North and Teicher. I recommend no more meetings until the hostages are released. A lot may be possible. You have begun to open the door to these people." (S)
The meeting ended at 9:40.

Prepared by:
Howard Teicher

~~SECRET/SENSITIVE~~
Declassify on: OADR

UNCLASSIFIED
~~SECRET~~

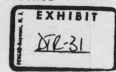
EXHIBIT
DR-31

DOCUMENT 66: Oliver North, Memorandum for John Poindexter, "Next Steps on the American Hostages," July 29, 1986.

PAGE 1 OF 3

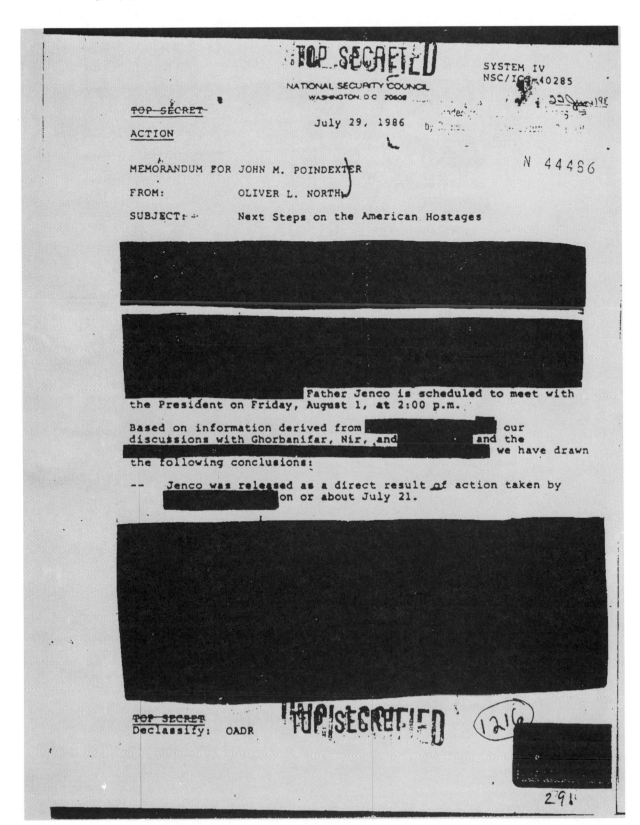

TOP SECRET

NATIONAL SECURITY COUNCIL
WASHINGTON, D.C. 20506

SYSTEM IV
NSC/ICS 40285

TOP SECRET

July 29, 1986

ACTION

N 44486

MEMORANDUM FOR JOHN M. POINDEXTER

FROM: OLIVER L. NORTH

SUBJECT: Next Steps on the American Hostages

Father Jenco is scheduled to meet with the President on Friday, August 1, at 2:00 p.m.

Based on information derived from ▮▮▮▮▮▮▮▮ our discussions with Ghorbanifar, Nir, and ▮▮▮▮▮▮▮ and the ▮▮▮▮▮▮ we have drawn the following conclusions:

--   Jenco was released as a direct result of action taken by ▮▮▮▮▮▮ on or about July 21.

TOP SECRET
Declassify: OADR

TOP SECRET

1216

DOCUMENT 66: Oliver North, Memorandum for John Poindexter, "Next Steps on the American Hostages," July 29, 1986.

PAGE 2 OF 3

TOP SECRET · ·   2   N 44487

-- _____ believed that he had consumated an arrangement with the Americans through Ghorbanifar on the terms for release of the hostages.

-- _____ expectations regarding the immediate delivery of the 240 HAWK missile parts were apparently transmitted to higher authority in Iran. Discussions with _____ in Europe (Sunday, July 27) and calls <u>from</u> him today indicate that _____ is in considerable personal jeopardy as a consequence of not having received what he believed we promised.

-- It is entirely possible that if nothing is received _____ will be killed by his opponents in Tehran, Ghorbanifar will be killed by his creditors (they are the beneficiaries of a $22M life insurance policy), and one American hostage will probably be killed in order to demonstrate displeasure.

-- Although the Dawa 17 in Kuwait continue to be mentioned as the ultimate demand on the part of the hostage holders, _____ we have not seen reference to this issue since our meeting in Tehran (Tab B).

It is obvious that the conditions for the release of the hostages arranged between Ghorbanifar and _____ are unacceptable. Nonetheless, we believe that Ghorbanifar acted on what he considered to be the following arrangement:

<u>Step 1</u>:   One hostage released and $4M to Ghorbanifar for items removed from the aircraft in Tehran during the May visit (Ghorbanifar received the $4M on July 28).

<u>Step 2</u>:   Remainder of 240 parts plus full quota of electron tubes (Item 24 on Iranian parts list) and 500 TOWs delivered to Iran.

<u>Step 3</u>:   Second hostage released and Ghorbanifar paid for remainder of 240 parts.

<u>Step 4</u>:   500 TOWs and 1 HIPAR radar delivered.

<u>Step 5</u>:   Third hostage released and Ghorbanifar paid for one radar.

<u>Step 6</u>:   Meeting in Tehran to discuss future followed by release of the last hostage and delivery of second HIPAR radar.

TOP SECRET

DOCUMENT 66: Oliver North, Memorandum for John Poindexter, "Next Steps on the American Hostages," July 29, 1986.

PAGE 3 OF 3

TOP SECRET

TOP SECRET

3

N 44488

We believe that the mixture of HAWK parts and TOWs is designed to satisfy both the military and the revolutionary guards in Iran. At this point, ███████ will probably be able to retain his credibility if just the 240 parts are delivered from Israel. We believe that he can be convinced to follow-up this delivery with a meeting in Europe to discuss next steps.

At such a meeting, we should endeavor to produce a concrete schedule that is agreeable to both parties and which allows all remaining hostages to be released simultaneously. The Jenco release ████████████ indicate that this is clearly within the power of the Iranians, if they are so inclined. While they will continue to haggle over prices, timing, and sequence, the delivery of the 240 should help to assure the Iranians that we will keep <u>our</u> word. It is important that a face-to-face meeting occur so that we can establish the terms rather than having Ghorbanifar negotiate for us. Finally, even after the parts are delivered, we still retain some leverage over █████████

--

--

RECOMMENDATION

That you brief the President regarding our conclusions on the Jenco release as indicated above and obtain his approval for having the 240 HAWK missile parts shipped from Israel to Iran as soon as possible, followed by a meeting with the Iranians in Europe.

Approve ___ 7/30/8 Disapprove ___

President approved.

Attachments

   Tab B - ████████████████████

TOP SECRET

DOCUMENT 67: Craig Fuller, Memorandum, "The Vice President's Meeting with Mr. Nir," July 29, 1986.

PAGE 1 OF 2

THE VICE PRESIDENT'S MEETING WITH MR. NIR—7/29/86 0735-0805

PARTICIPANTS: The Vice President, Mr. Nir, Craig Fuller

DATE/TIME: 7/29/86 0735-0805

LOCATION: Vice President's suite/King David Hotel, Jerusalem

1. SUMMARY. Mr. Nir indicated that he had briefed Prime Minister Peres and had been asked to brief the VP by his White House contacts. He described the details of the efforts from last year through the current period to gain the release of the U.S. hostages. He reviewed what had been learned which was essentially that the radical group was the group that could deliver. He reviewed the issues to be considered—namely that there needed to be ad [sic] decision as to whether the items requested would be delivered in separate shipments or whether we would continue to press for the release of the hostages prior to delivering the items in an amount agreed to previously.

2. The VP's 25 minute meeting was arranged after Mr. Nir called Craig Fuller and requested the meeting and after it was discussed with the VP by Fuller and North. Only Fuller was aware of the meeting and no other member of the VP's staff or traveling party has been advised about the meeting. No cables were generated nor was there other reporting except a brief phone call between Fuller and North to advise that "no requests were made."

3. Nir began by indicating that Peres had asked him to brief the VP. In addition, Nir's White House contacts with whom he had recent discussions asked him to brief the VP.

4. Nir began by providing an historical perspective from his vantage point. He stated that the effort began last summer. This early phase he said "didn't work well." There were more discussions in November and in January "we thought we had a better approach with the Iranian side," said Nir. He said, "Poindexter accepted the decision."

5. He characterized the decision as "having two layers—tactical and strategic." The tactical layer was described as an effort "to get the hostages out." The strategic layer was designed "to build better contact with Iran and to insure we are better prepared when a change (in leadership) occurs." "Working through our Iranian contact, we used the hostage problem and efforts there as a test," suggested Nir. He seemed to suggest the test was to determine how best to establish relationships that worked with various Iranian factions.

6. Nir described Israel's role in the effort by saying, "we activated the channel; we gave a front to the operation; provided a physical base; provided aircraft." All this to "make sure the U.S. will not be involved in logistical aspects." Nir indicated that in the early phase they "began moving things over there."

7. Before a second phase a meeting was desired. Nir indicated a February meeting took place with "the Prime Minister on the other side." Nir did not make it clear who else attended the meeting. He said the meeting was "dramatic and interesting." He said "an agreement was made on 4,000 units—1,000 first and then 3,000." The agreement was made on the basis that we would get the group," Nir said. "The whole package for a fixed price," he said.

8. Although there was agreement the other side changed their minds and "then they asked for the other items," according to Nir. "We were pleased because these were defensive items and we got to work with the military," said Nir. He continued, "there were 240 items on the list we were provided and we agreed to it."

9. A meeting was organized for mid May in Tehran to finalized the operation. The VP asked Nir if he attended the meeting and Nir indicated he did attend. Nir said, "two mistakes were made during this phase." "Two people were to be sent to prepare for the meeting but the U.S. had concerns about McFarlane," according to Nir. He described the meetings as "more difficult—total frustration because we didn't prepare." And he said, "their top level was not prepared adequately." During the meeting in Tehran the other side kept reminding the group that "in 1982 there was a meeting which leaked and the Prime Minister was thrown out of office." Nir said that at the end of the May meeting, "they began to see the light." "McFarlane was making it clear that we wanted all hostages released," Nir reported and, "at the last moment

DOCUMENT 67: Craig Fuller, Memorandum, "The Vice President's Meeting with Mr. Nir," July 29, 1986.

PAGE 2 OF 2

the other side suggested two would be released if those at the meeting stayed six more hours." According to Nir, "the Deputy Prime Minister delivered the request (to delay departure) and when the group said 'no,' they all departed without anything."

10. According to Nir, "the reason for delay is to squeeze as much as possible as long as they have assets. They don't believe that we want overall strategic cooperation to be better in the future. If they believed us they would have not bothered so much with the price right now." Further, according to Nir, "there are serious struggles now within the Iran power groups. Three leaders share the view that we should go ahead but each wants to prove his own toughness."

11. Turning to what Nir said was the final or most recent phase, he reported, "we felt things would just die if we didn't push forward to see what could be delivered. They asked for four sequences, but we said no to talks until they showed something."

12. According to Nir, he told them about 10 days ago he would cancel the deal. Then nine days ago their Prime Minister called saying that they were taking steps to release one—the Priest. The second one to be released would be Jacobson. The Prime Minister also said that one would be released and then "we should give some equipment." Nir indicated to the VP that the bottom line on the items to be delivered was understood to be the same or even less but it was not the way the deal was originally made. The items involved spares for Hawks and TOWs. No denial or approval was given according to Nir. Nir said he made it clear that no deal would be discussed unless evidence is seen of a release.

13. On Tuesday or Wednesday a message was intercepted between Tehran and the guards according to Nir. On Friday, three hostages were taken out and on Saturday Janco [sic] was taken out, put into a trunk and driven to a village in the Bakka [sic] Valley. Nir then described what Janco reported with regard to the conditions under which he was held and what he knew of the other hostages including Buckley. (I assume we have detailed briefing already.) The VP asked Nir if he had briefed Peres on all of this and he indicated that he had.

14. Nir described some of the lessons learned: "we are dealing with the most radical elements. The Deputy Prime Minister is an emissary. They can deliver...that's for sure. They were called yesterday and thanked and today more phone calls. This is good because we've learned they can deliver and the moderates can't. We should think about diversity and establish other contacts with other factions. We have started to establish contact with some success and now more success is expected since if these groups feel if the extremes are in contact with us then it is less risky for the other groups—nothing operational is being done...this is contact only."

15. Nir described some of the problems and choices: "Should we accept sequencing? What are alternatives to sequencing? They fear if they give all hostages they won't get anything from us. If we do want to move along these lines we'd have to move quickly. It would be a matter still of several weeks not several days, in part because they have to move the hostages every time one is released."

16. Nir concluded with the following points: "The bottom line is that we won't give them more than previously agreed to. It is important that we have assets there 2 to 3 years out when change occurs. We have no real choice than to proceed."

17. The VP made no commitments nor did he give any direction to Nir. The VP expressed his appreciation for the briefing and thanked Nir for having pursued this effort despite doubts and reservations throughout the process.

BY: CRAIG L. FULLER [initialed:] "CF 8/6/86"

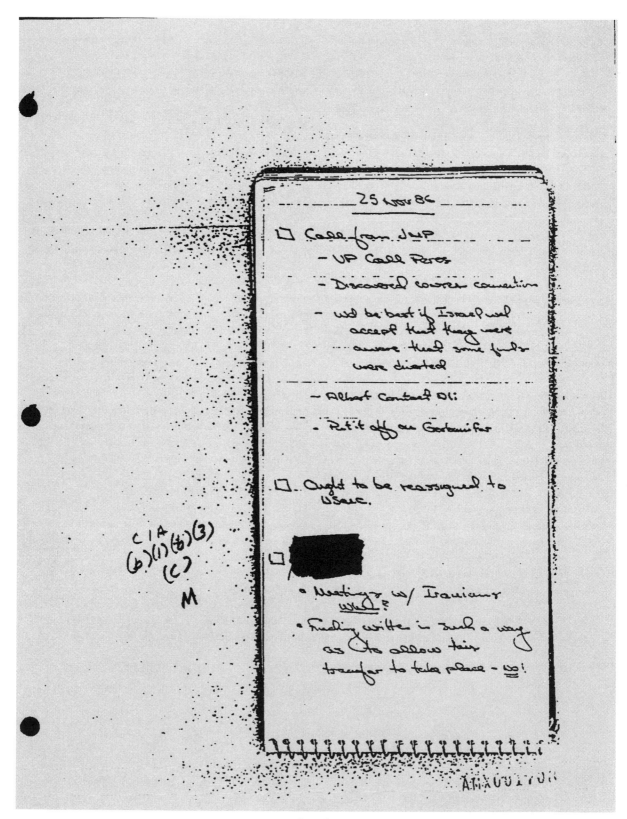

VI. DEALING IN
ARMS AND HOSTAGES

In the spring of 1985, an Iranian businessman named Manucher Ghorbanifar, using the good offices of Saudi Arabian billionaire Adnan Khashoggi, made contact with two well-connected Israelis and offered a proposition:[1] if they helped him buy U.S.-made TOW missiles, Ghorbanifar claimed he would arrange the release of William Buckley, the CIA station chief in Beirut who had been held hostage in Lebanon since March 16, 1984. Ghorbanifar was betting that Washington would leap at the chance to get any American hostage back—let alone Buckley, whose kidnapping had been a blow to vital American security interests in the Middle East.

From the outbreak of war between Iran and Iraq in the fall of 1980, Iranian agents had scoured the global arms bazaar for weapons to counter what most observers agreed was a superior Iraqi military machine. An estimated forty-one countries supplied Iran with weapons in the 1980s,[2] including Israel, which the Khomeini regime abhorred in its public pronouncements but, given its desperate circumstances, privately saw as an ally of convenience. By early 1985, the covert Israel-Iran arms pipeline was well established.

Moreover, for some time the U.S. government had been receiving a steady flow of Iranians seeking arms for various causes. Thomas Twetten, the CIA's Near East operations chief, told the Tower Commission:

> We have in the DDO [Operations Directorate] probably 30 to 40 requests per year from Iranians and Iranian exiles to provide us with very fancy intelligence, very important internal political insights, if we in return can arrange for the sale of a dozen Bell helicopter gunships or 1,000 TOW missiles or something else that is on the contraband list.[3]

THE PIECES FALL INTO PLACE
Thanks to a combination of good timing and the right connections, Ghorbanifar's overture reached the right ears. His partners in Israel were Adolph Schwimmer, founder of Israel Aircraft Industries, and Yaacov Nimrodi, an arms dealer. Both Israelis had long experience in Iran before the overthrow of the shah and were friends of Israeli Prime Minister Shimon Peres. Private citizens both, they would become Peres's unofficial liaisons to the Iran initiative.

At about the time these meetings were taking place, Michael Ledeen, a part-time counterterrorism consultant to the National Security Council, extracted permission from Robert McFarlane to travel to Israel to find out if Jerusalem was willing to undertake a joint effort to learn more about Iran's internal situation. Among others, Ledeen met with Peres, whom he knew personally. Peres took the opportunity of Ledeen's visit to pass along a request to McFarlane for U.S. approval of an arms deal between Ghorbanifar and the Israelis.[4]

Two months later, on July 3, a third Israeli intermediary, David Kimche, director general of Israel's Foreign Ministry, traveled to Washington and spoke directly to McFarlane about an Iranian opening to the United States. Ten days later, Ledeen, breathless with excitement, briefed McFarlane on the details of a new proposal by Ghorbanifar calling for one hundred TOWs in return for not just Buckley but for *all* the American hostages. In passing word to McFarlane prior to their meeting, Ledeen termed the new development "just wonderful news" (Document 69). On July 13, the same day of his talk with Ledeen, McFarlane reported on the Israeli-backed proposition to Secretary of State George Shultz (Document 70).[5]

Several factors influenced McFarlane to act on the Israeli recommendations. For some time he had pressed for a more active U.S. policy toward Iran, the latest attempt coming in the form of the draft NSDD of June 11 (Document 60), and he saw this as a ready-made opportunity to put the idea into practice. He had also long admired Israel's pragmatic geopolitical ideals and tough line on terrorism; moreover, he had previously known and worked with Kimche, a former top Mossad official who enjoyed a glowing reputation. If the Israelis, and particularly Kimche, endorsed the plan, it carried a great deal of weight with McFarlane.

Shultz, in his reply to McFarlane the following day, touched on a key "imponderable" inherent in any joint operation with Israel on Iran (Document 71). Urging "great caution," he noted that "complications" could arise from "'blessing' an Israel-Iran relationship where Israel's interests and ours are not necessarily the same." Still, he suggested that McFarlane answer the emissary, Schwimmer, by saying Washington was "receptive to the idea of a private dialogue involving a sustained discussion of U.S.-Iranian relations."

Shultz's warning anticipated only one of the problems that would surface as the initiative unfolded. Inept interlocutors, an excessively secretive process, and competing personal agendas combined with often incompatible national priorities to produce, at best, mixed results by the time the arms deals were exposed.

The negotiations and logistics behind the arms deals were highly intricate. At every stage, a series of financial transactions took place involving multiparty pricing decisions, large-scale loans, and deposits of earnest money into various accounts (Document 72).[6] Each delivery was supposed to result in the release of one or more American hostages being held in Lebanon. Ultimately, only three hostages gained their freedom while three more were taken captive during the same period, and still others in subsequent months.

PHASE ONE BEGINS

In early August 1985, McFarlane received the green light from President Reagan to pursue the first arms deal through Israel. At this point, the players who would conduct the first phase of the initiative were already in place, having held lengthy discussions during the summer to flesh out the details of a plan. The U.S. intermediary, Ledeen, and two of the Israeli go-betweens, Schwimmer and Nimrodi, were private citizens whose importance lay not only in their personal connections to Peres but in the deniability they provided should word of the arms deal leak. (Foreign Ministry official Kimche provided the only direct tie

to either government.) A CIA report from December 1985, although reflecting the viewpoint of two of the actors, helps to shed more light on some of these individuals, as well as background on the operations they carried out (Document 73).

For his part, Ghorbanifar had a murky background and his standing with his sponsors in Iran has never been entirely clear. Unconfirmed rumors linked him with both SAVAK, the Shah's intelligence service (Document 74), and Israeli intelligence.[7] Somehow, after the revolution he managed to establish ties to various officials in the Khomeini regime. Their need for weapons presumably played a part in their willingness to take a chance on him.

The CIA, on the other hand, knew Ghorbanifar as a would-be informant who had tried repeatedly to strike up a relationship with the Agency since at least 1980. To them, Ghorbanifar was little more than a "wheeler dealer" who had "deliberately provided false info" in the past to the U.S. government (see Document 74). In mid 1984, the Agency took the unusual step of issuing a "burn notice" on him, warning the entire U.S. intelligence community that he could not be trusted. In spite of his poor track record, he succeeded in convincing McFarlane and his subordinates to include him in their game plan.

A major factor in the Israeli and American calculations was the fact that Ghorbanifar's contacts in Iran were bona fide government officials who could be expected either to wield influence themselves or at least to have direct ties to the uppermost circles of power in Iran. In fact, Ghorbanifar's two main connections during the initiative were Hassan Karrubi, the head of an Iranian revolutionary organization who reportedly had close connections to Iran's spiritual leader, Ayatollah Ruhollah Khomeini, and Mohsen Kangarlou, an aide to Prime Minister Mir-Hosain Musavi.[8] Although Khashoggi and Ghorbanifar described Karrubi as a "moderate," his purported patron, Khomeini, hardly fit that category. The two also characterized Kangarlou as an "extremist." Furthermore, U.S. intelligence had concluded that Kangarlou was involved in the

1983 attacks on the U.S. and French embassies in Kuwait, which had prompted the arrests of the Dawa prisoners. In the context of bargaining with Kangarlou and Karrubi, the Reagan administration claim that it sought to establish closer relations with "moderates" seems more like an ex post facto cover story than an actual strategic motivation. (See Chronology of Events, entry for December 1983.)

Ghorbanifar's first attempt at acquiring TOWs in August 1985 brought positive results for Iran but not for the other parties. On August 20, after a series of negotiations over pricing and financing, a chartered DC-8 aircraft carrying ninety-six TOWs[9]—and Ghorbanifar—arrived in Iran without incident, but problems developed when members of Iran's Revolutionary Guard allegedly commandeered the shipment at the airport. Things went from bad to worse when none of the hostages were released as agreed. At a meeting in Paris afterward, Ledeen and the Israelis read Ghorbanifar the riot act, but the Iranian explained away the problem saying that since the faction he claimed to represent had gotten nothing, they owed nothing in return. He promised better results next time and proposed a new agreement: four hundred TOWs in return for only one hostage. It was a measure of the American and Israeli eagerness to believe in their new contact (and to achieve a demonstrable success) that they agreed to these far less advantageous terms.

The second arms-for-hostages transaction worked out as planned. On September 15, within hours after a shipment of 408 TOWs landed in the northern city of Tabriz (Ghorbanifar's suggestion, to ensure the Revolutionary Guard would not take control of the missiles again), the Rev. Benjamin Weir was released. With this success, all sides felt they had crossed an important threshold and began making new plans for the next transfer.

Despite the participants' enthusiasm, the TOW shipments of 1985 set a pattern that would recur in future deals with Iran. Iranian assurances that missile sales would result in the release of hostages regularly turned out to be empty promises. Still, the Americans and Israelis barely hesitated before committing themselves to further weapons deliveries, displaying an earnestness the Iranians exploited at every turn. Despite later claims that other motives lay behind the Iran initiative, the driving forces from the start were Iran's urgent need for arms and the United States' determination to gain freedom for the hostages.

THE HAWK FIASCO

Even though only one hostage was released after the September TOW shipments, the Americans and Israelis came away convinced that their decision to stick with Ghorbanifar had paid off, opening a new avenue to the circles of power in Iran. With optimism riding high, they began another round of talks with Ghorbanifar, centering around the provision of HAWK antiaircraft missiles in exchange for more hostages.

In the HAWK deal, the stakes were raised as high-level Israeli and U.S. officials directly participated in the transaction. Israeli Defense Minister Yitzhak Rabin leaned on McFarlane to tighten the two governments' cooperation in the covert transactions, and McFarlane assigned Oliver North to take over the U.S. side of the planning. As the operation proceeded, North brought in other Americans, including officials from the CIA and State Department, to help untangle problems as they developed.

North's notes show that he was in frequent touch with the Israeli middlemen, Schwimmer and Nimrodi, concerning logistics. On November 20, he described the latest, ever-changing arrangements to his superior, John Poindexter:

The Israelis will deliver 80 Mod[ified] HAWKS [to Lisbon] at noon on Friday 22 Nov. These 80 will be loaded aboard three chartered aircraft, owned by a proprietary which will take off at two hour intervals for Tabriz....There is a requirement for 40 additional weap[on]s of the same nomenclature for a total requirement of 120. (Document 75)

Despite North's later testimony that he felt uncomfortable treating the hostages as commodities, his discussions with the Israelis soon took on a cold, mathematical quality. His handwritten notes reflected stark calculations of how many missiles were to be swapped for each hostage:

—Deliver boxes
—One 27–2
—27–3
—26–1
—5+1 French
    * * *
—120 HAWKS =
(1) 5 AMCITS [American citizens]
(2) Guarantee that no more [10]

In other words, each shipment of twenty-six or twenty-seven missiles would yield one, two, or three hostages—"boxes"—with the breakdown being five Americans and one French hostage. The notes also imply that 120 HAWK missiles would result in freedom for five American citizens and a guarantee that no more would be kidnapped.

Even as the planners continued to nail down the logistics, problems began to materialize. On November 18, the government of Portugal, which the planners had chosen as an intermediate point on the journey in order to disguise the true origin of the flights, refused to grant landing clearances for the mission. North brought in his colleague from the ongoing Contra operation, Richard Secord, who had contacts in Portugal's armaments industry, to try to fix the problem. Secord's heavy-handed efforts reportedly included an attempt by a business associate to bribe a Portuguese official.[11] Portuguese suspicions of Secord's band of private middlemen grew when authorities checked with the U.S. embassy in Lisbon and were told by embassy officials, who had not been briefed about the mission, that it was not authorized by the U.S. government.

In his message to Poindexter on November 20, North glossed over the problems with Portugal, saying only that "[a]ll arrangements have been made by Dick Secord, who deserves a medal for his extraordinary

short notice efforts." At the same time, North searched frantically for more help. He contacted Duane Clarridge, the CIA's head of European covert operations, who until a few months earlier had worked closely with North in the Contra war. Now the two joined forces on another highly sensitive operation.

Over the next few days, Clarridge sent a series of "flash" cables to Agency operatives in Portugal ordering them to "report to office and standby to assist [deleted] on special assignment." That assignment involved "pull[ing] out all the stops"[12] to intervene directly with local authorities in order to obtain the necessary clearances. At about the same time, North got in touch with Robert Oakley, a State Department counterterrorism official, and asked him to advise embassy officials in Lisbon to use their contacts to do the same. This multipronged attempt at diplomatic arm-twisting, which at its peak included a call from McFarlane to the Portuguese foreign minister, ultimately failed, forcing an increasingly desperate North to come up with another plan.

To make matters worse, early on November 22, Schwimmer's chartered El Al flight carrying the missiles had taken off for Portugal, even though no clearances had been given, and had to be ordered back to Israel. Before it could be brought into action again, Schwimmer's lease for the aircraft ran out, sending North into a tirade. Clarridge once again stepped in, calling an official in the CIA's air branch and asking for immediate use of a 747 jet. Not having one available, the official suggested using a proprietary airline— a CIA-owned company operating under a commercial cover. That same day, Clarridge and North learned that the company in question, St. Lucia Airways, had a Boeing 707 aircraft on hand. It was good news for the operation's planners, but it did not entirely solve the problem: the smaller size of the 707 meant that fewer missiles could be carried at a time. And there was still the matter of getting clearance from Portugal. Clarridge began to look to other countries for help (Document 76).

By November 24, North, Clarridge, and others involved had worked out an alternate route. The St. Lucia 707 picked up eighteen of the original eighty missiles (the most that could fit in its cargo hold) in Tel Aviv and flew to Cyprus instead of Portugal. From there, the pilots took off for Teheran, flying over Turkish airspace en route. Once again, they ran into difficulties: not only had the Israelis neglected to provide a manifest for inspection by Cypriot airport officials but Turkish officials explicitly forbade overflights by aircraft coming from Cyprus. In both cases, the pilots apparently managed to talk their way out of the predicament,[13] and the flight finally arrived safely in Tabriz early on the morning of November 25. For the mission's architects, however, the problems had just begun.[14]

Shortly after the HAWKs reached Tabriz, Ghorbanifar called Ledeen, "on the very edge of hysteria," to say that "the most horrible thing had happened," that the "missiles had arrived and they were the wrong missiles."[15] Iranian officials tested one of the HAWKs and discovered that it was incapable of shooting down high-flying aircraft, which was their reason for purchasing them.[16] To make matters worse, some of the missiles also bore Israeli markings, which offended the Iranians. They demanded that the weapons be returned. Ghorbanifar passed a message to Ledeen, which he said came from Iran's prime minister and was to be delivered to President Reagan: "We have done everything we said we were going to do, and you are now cheating us, and you must act quickly to remedy this situation."[17] For their part, the U.S. and Israeli players blamed each other for bungling the operation, which once again failed to win the release of any hostages. The experience would lead U.S. officials to abandon Ledeen and the Israeli go-betweens, and to begin shipping arms directly to Iran instead of through Israel.

PHASE TWO BEGINS

By the end of 1985, the foundation had been laid for a major structural change in the Iran initiative. The HAWK disaster had provided the main impetus, prompting U.S. officials not only to replace the middle-

men handling the negotiations but to stop working through Israel and start dealing directly with Iran. Oliver North first broached the idea to his superiors on December 9. In a lengthy eyes-only memorandum to McFarlane and John Poindexter, who had replaced McFarlane just five days earlier as the president's national security advisor, North described the problems the initiative faced and suggested several options (Document 77). The last alternative was, "with an appropriate covert action Finding, [to] commence deliveries ourselves, using Secord as our conduit to control Gorbanifahr [sic] and delivery operations."

As noted earlier, North was now the operations manager of the arms-for-hostages initiative and firmly committed to seeing it continue. By this time, the Marine officer had introduced a new purpose to the initiative—diverting profits from the arms sales to other covert projects. After the first TOW transactions, Israel had transferred $1 million to an account controlled by the Enterprise run by Secord. A part of that amount went to finance the HAWK shipment, leaving $800,000 that would have covered additional HAWK deliveries if problems had not brought the deal to an abrupt halt. According to North, the Israelis authorized him to use the remainder for "whatever purpose we wanted." North chose to use it to help finance the Reagan administration's other main preoccupation—the Contras.[18] The diversion idea came up again on December 6, when North told Israeli officials at a meeting that he planned to skim money from the Iran initiative for the Nicaraguan rebels.[19] With the United States taking direct control over the arms deals, including pricing and financing, North was in a position to begin overcharging Iran systematically.

The United States took another step toward direct dealings with Iran on January 2, 1986, when Amiram Nir, Prime Minister Peres's adviser on counterterrorism, met with North and Poindexter to present another approach toward Iran (Document 78). Nir had worked with North on earlier operations, including the resolution of the *Achille Lauro* hijacking in 1985, and they admired each other as "can-do" operatives.

Although Nir's plan still posited the lead role for Israel, it contained some attractive aspects, including inserting Nir himself as the main point of contact with Israel—at the expense of Kimche, Schwimmer, and Nimrodi, who were phased out of the operation.[20]

Over the next two weeks, President Reagan and his top aides hashed out the proposal and, notwithstanding the objections of Shultz and Weinberger, approved an altogether new structure to the approach that placed the United States in the forefront. A key hurdle was the legal requirement to notify Congress of significant arms transactions. The most common vehicle for weapons sales to foreign governments, the Arms Export Control Act, carried restrictive reporting requirements precisely because Congress wanted public debate on major arms transactions—which were often controversial. To avoid this, the planners turned to the Economy Act as the instrument for transferring the missiles from the Defense Department to the CIA, and to a Presidential Finding (Document 64) to authorize transshipping the weapons to Iran.

The new framework also added another important feature, inserting Secord as a "commercial cutout" for the CIA, someone who would do the actual buying and shipping to Iran to provide deniability to the U.S. government. The participation of North's colleague from the Contra resupply program became the key that gave North greater leverage over pricing and profits from future arms deals.

Once the president signed the Finding authorizing the new U.S. plan on January 17, North immediately got to work. Within days, he arranged to meet in London with Ghorbanifar, who continued to be the primary intermediary on the Iran side, in order to review the next steps. During a break in the talks, North and Ghorbanifar had an extraordinary conversation which North later described: "Mr. Ghorbanifar took me into the bathroom and suggested several incentives to make [this] transaction work."[21] According to notes of their private talk, Ghorbanifar offered on behalf of the Iranians to "do," or take care of, troublesome issues for the United States, including financing the Contras:

"We do everything. We do hostages free of charge; we do all terrorist[s] free of charge; Central America for you free of charge."[22]

After the London meeting, North prepared a "notional timeline" for Poindexter describing events he expected to happen over the next month (Document 79). A notable entry revealed North's optimism in the operation as well as the continued poor quality of intelligence available on Iran (which was one of the original reasons for undertaking a cooperative arrangement with Israel). Under February 11, the schedule reads, "Khomeini steps down."[23]

North's schedule also reflected a new element that had recently been added to the deal—the provision of intelligence to Iran on Iraq's military situation in the ongoing war. The entry for January 25 reads, "Dispatch intel[ligence] sample to G[h]orba[nifar] via [CIA analyst] Charlie Allen." Word of this development provoked a strong reaction from high in the CIA. Deputy Director John McMahon, who had gone "through the overhead" in anger about the HAWK shipment in November 1985, now complained bitterly to Director William Casey: "providing defensive missiles was one thing but when we provide intelligence [on] the order of battle, we are giving the Iranians the wherewithal for offensive action." A successful Iranian offensive, he warned, could have "cataclysmic results."[24]

McMahon received no response to his protest and the first intelligence items were forwarded to Iran. It was another example of the American side yielding to ever-increasing demands from Iran without ensuring that the other side would hold up its end. Even with the intelligence package, the first direct U.S. shipment of TOWs in February resulted in no hostages being released. Still the negotiations continued.

MISSION TO TEHERAN

Over the next three months, the hectic pace of the initiative barely relaxed, even though the next shipment of matériel did not occur until late May, when McFarlane led a covert mission to the Iranian capital. During this time, certain CIA officials continued to raise objections to various aspects of the initiative; their main problem was with Ghorbanifar, whose misleading translations proved him to be untrustworthy, as the CIA had previously warned.

On March 5, George Cave, a retired CIA operative with lengthy experience in Iran, joined the operation and began dealing directly with Ghorbanifar in a series of meetings. His notes of one such get-together in early April give the flavor of a typical session at this stage of the initiative (Document 80). Within two days of coming on board, Cave, North, and the CIA's Thomas Twetten met with Ghorbanifar in Paris. At this session, Ghorbanifar abruptly changed the nature of the Iranian demand for weapons from TOWs to HAWK spare parts. He also informed the group that the site for a planned high-level gathering between U.S. and Iranian officials (to which North had referred in his note to Poindexter after the February TOW shipment) would have to be shifted from Kish Island in the Persian Gulf to Teheran. Both new pieces of information caused some reconsideration on the part of the Americans, and thus delays in moving the operation forward.

Toward the end of April, Ghorbanifar relayed yet another new condition for the release of American hostages. Rather than have them all delivered as the U.S. delegation arrived in Teheran, the Iranians wanted to receive the HAWK spare parts first and then release the captives sequentially. Poindexter was incensed: he ordered North to tell the Iranians at their next session that

> [t]here are not to be any parts delivered until all the hostages are free.... None of this half shipment before any are released crap. It is either all or nothing.... If they really want to save their asses from the Soviets, they should get on board. (Document 81)

On May 8, after a meeting with the Iranians in London, North could report to Poindexter:

> I believe we have succeeded.... Release of hostages set for 19 May in sequence you have specified. Specific date to be determined by how quickly we can assemble requisite parts. Thank God—He answers prayers.[25]

After several weeks of uphill effort, events began to gain momentum. Financial transactions to cover the multiphased delivery process took place with few complications. In keeping with the new procedures instituted following the U.S. takeover of the initiative, the Iranians deposited funds, including a sizable cost markup, into a Secord-controlled account. Secord then paid the actual cost of the weapons into a CIA Swiss bank account.

On May 25, an Israeli aircraft disguised as a foreign air carrier ferried the American delegation to Teheran. Bearing Irish passports and codenames, McFarlane, North, Cave, NSC aide Howard Teicher, Nir, and a CIA communications operator arrived at 8:30 A.M. They brought with them one of thirteen pallets of HAWK parts requested by the Iranians. The rest remained in Tel Aviv under Secord's supervision, pending a sign from Teheran that the hostages had been released. In case the group became hostages themselves, McFarlane, at least, took along a poison pill to avoid revealing secrets under torture.[26]

From the outset, the group met with disappointment (see Document 82 for one version of the events). McFarlane anticipated that a high-level Iranian delegation would greet them at the airport, but none materialized—in fact, he never met with a single senior member of the government during his stay. The presence of only "third and fourth level officials" led to largely rhetorical exchanges for the first two days. At one point, McFarlane insisted: "As I am a Minister, I expect to meet with decision-makers. Otherwise, you can work with my staff."[27] Other problems arose, including the realization that each side had different understandings of what to expect from the sessions. The Iranians thought that all of the HAWK parts would come before any hostages would be freed. McFarlane refused to budge from his instructions not to ship any more parts until all the hostages were released. Tensions grew, particularly among the Iranians when they began to see that McFarlane intended to stick to his position. Finally, McFarlane decided to leave, ignoring an offer to release two of the hostages immediately and two more after the HAWK parts arrived.

The McFarlane team considered the mission a failure, but different players had different explanations. North and Cave saw Ghorbanifar as the culprit for his role in misleading both sides. Secord and Hakim blamed McFarlane, although his firm stance amounts to the only known instance of an American willing to walk out of a meeting when Iran failed to come through as agreed.

Back in Washington, McFarlane expressed his deep frustration with the entire operation at a White House briefing on May 29. He recommended to the president that he shut down the initiative. But Reagan did not.

THE SECOND CHANNEL

On July 26, the initiative received an important boost when American hostage Lawrence Jenco was set free following frantic maneuvering by Amiram Nir and Manucher Ghorbanifar. The move helped North convince Poindexter and President Reagan a few days later to switch to sequential releases of hostages from the "all or nothing" approach that had been repeatedly urged during the Teheran mission.

One of the first orders of business at this stage was to replace Ghorbanifar, a move Poindexter had specifically authorized shortly after the trip to Teheran. The Iranian broker had not only proved his unreliability but he now faced financial ruin as a result of McFarlane's decision not to send a planeload of HAWK spare parts to Teheran as the Iranians had expected.[28] Secord and his business partner, Albert Hakim, sent out feelers to try to establish a new contact with Iran's leadership. The effort took several weeks, but by late August a breakthrough seemed to occur (Document 83). A new contact, Ali Hashemi Bahramani, a nephew of Iran's Speaker of the Parliament, appeared on the scene.[29]

Bahramani immediately impressed Secord: in his early twenties, he was described as highly intelligent and well informed on a range of topics of interest to the Americans, including the history of the initiative to date. He acknowledged that he was a member of the hard-line Revolutionary Guard. Nevertheless, Secord reported triumphantly to North, "my judgement is that we have opened up new and probably much better channel into Iran." He added, "this connection has been effectively recruited and he wants to start dealing." As in the case of Kangarlou, Bahramani's allegiance to an avowedly "extremist" group seems to have had no impact on the Americans' willingness to deal with him.

So pleased were the Americans with their new find that they paid Bahramani the extraordinary compliment of hosting a series of meetings with him in Washington. Deciding to do so required pulling more than a few strings to arrange covert transportation for him into the country. During his stay, North even led a late-night tour of the White House—including the Oval Office—for the Iranian's benefit.

The talks with Bahramani, in Washington and at other locations in Europe, were always wide-ranging, touching not only on arms and hostages but on the likelihood of gaining the release of the Dawa prisoners in Kuwait and the two sides' mutual desire (as expressed by North) to see "a non-hostile regime in Baghdad." At one point during a session in Frankfurt, West Germany, in early October, North commented that "Saddam Hussein must go." It was one of many remarks he made purporting to reflect the views of the U.S. government. (At the time, of course, official U.S. policy was tilting in favor of the Iraqi leader against Iran.) In the course of these talks, North also increasingly invoked President Reagan, claiming that the president had personally authorized certain negotiating positions, and even attributing statements to him, such as North's remark in Frankfurt that "Saddam Hussein is a [expletive]."[30]

Another topic of discussion with Bahramani was a plan to set up a joint commission of Americans and Iranians to explore future relations. However, as the Iranians started to list which officials would belong to the commission, several things became clear. First, the Americans discovered to their dismay that they had not gotten rid of the "first channel" at all: the list included Kangarlou, who was Ghorbanifar's contact, and a member of the Parliament with whom McFarlane had negotiated in Teheran. According to George Cave, this revelation "really blew our minds"—though it should not have come as a complete shock since another Revolutionary Guard official, Ali Samii, who accompanied Bahramani to the Frankfurt and Mainz meetings, had also taken part in sessions with Ghorbanifar and Kangarlou in February (also in Frankfurt) and during the May Teheran trip.[31]

Second, the Americans realized that the second channel they had developed actually answered to the same leadership circle that Ghorbanifar's first channel had. Bahramani reported at Mainz that Speaker of the Parliament Ali Akbar Hashemi Rafsanjani, "for his own politics…decided to get all the groups involved and give them a role to play." That way, all of the factions would share responsibility for any failures and "there would not be an internal war."[32] In other words, if, as U.S. officials claimed, they had wanted to deal only with "moderates" and to bolster their standing in the regime by providing arms, they now learned that they were dealing with every faction that made up the Iranian leadership.

Perhaps the most controversial aspect of the negotiations was the extent to which North and his fellow go-betweens on the American side exceeded their authority to negotiate on behalf of the U.S. government. At various times, North—the only American holding a government post—Secord, Hakim, and retired CIA Iran expert George Cave all took an active part in the talks.

The nadir came in Frankfurt in early October when the Hasenfus plane went down and North had to leave a negotiating session to return to Washington. When the rest of the Americans departed, responsibility for this highly sensitive matter of U.S. foreign policy was left in the hands of a private businessman. Hakim dutifully carried on the negotiations, producing a nine-point agreement (known as the "Hakim Accords"), which featured additional TOW and HAWK deals and a promise to "provide the plan for the release of the

Kuwaitis (17 persons)," the Dawa prisoners (Document 84). Hakim assured the Iranians the U.S. would approve the document, and he later testified that North told him President Reagan had done so.

A RECIPE FOR FAILURE

The Frankfurt episode exemplified the worst aspects of the negotiating process in the Iran initiative. Interlocutors who were not prepared for the delicate and complex task of negotiating with foreign governments regularly caved in to escalating demands from Iran based on no more than a promise of things to come. In addition, the goals of the operation quickly became confused. Although officials claimed that long-term U.S.-Iran relations ranked as the top priority, the return of the hostages quickly dominated the American agenda. This showed through not only in the Americans' passivity in the face of shifting Iranian ultimatums but in the deception and manipulation North repeatedly engaged in during the talks.[33]

Moreover, the profit motive, which most of the middlemen shared in one form or another, undermined the U.S. position. To the extent that Secord's and Hakim's ambitions included setting themselves up as brokers for future lucrative arms deals with Iran, there was a built-in incentive to keep the initiative alive no matter how badly the U.S. side fared. Likewise, North's desire to draw continually on this source of funds for his other covert projects, including the Contras, provided a similar incentive for him.

Only McFarlane, who had no conflicting priorities to reconcile, seemed to understand the costs to the United States of continuing down the same path—a path that he, as national security advisor, had initially recommended. During and after the failed May 1986 mission, he repeatedly urged that the initiative be shut down and was the only participant to quit negotiations rather than acquiesce to Iranian demands.

In the end, the Americans and Israelis provided Iran 2,004 TOW and eighteen HAWK missiles (all but one of the HAWKs was returned as unsatisfactory), 240 HAWK spare parts, and a variety of sensitive intelligence on Iraq. They were willing to provide much more, including many more HAWKs, radar equipment, and other matériel. In return, only Benjamin Weir, Lawrence Jenco, and, on November 2, 1986, David Jacobsen were freed—a partial accomplishment that was offset by later kidnappings. Ironically this sequence of events supported President Reagan's

public stance—ignored in practice—that dealing with terrorists only contributes to more terrorism. Testifying before Congress in 1987, Secretary of State Shultz summed up the general view of how the U.S. fared in the Iran negotiations: "Our guys…got taken to the cleaners."[34]

NOTES

1. Roy Furmark, an American businessman and associate of CIA Director William Casey, introduced Ghorbanifar and Khashoggi in early 1985: see the *Iran-Contra Affair*, p. 164.

2. *New York Times*, April 11, 1987, p. 2, quoted in the *Iran-Contra Affair*, p. 159.

3. Tower Commission report, p. B-3.

4. Although this request actually covered an earlier deal proposed by Ghorbanifar, the TOW-for-hostages proposition soon superseded it. In either event, Peres's intervention served to introduce Ghorbanifar to the Americans.

5. McFarlane may have betrayed his eagerness to win over Secretary Shultz by dramatizing the matter. In his cable, he claimed that he had met personally with an unidentified Israeli who had carried a message from the Israeli prime minister. In fact, the Israeli was Schwimmer, and the message had come via Ledeen.

6. The Tower Commission's charts are based on information available at the time the panel's report was published. The chart depicting Transaction One incorrectly gives the date of delivery of the missiles as August 30, 1985, instead of August 20, the date the *Iran-Contra Affair*'s authors have determined to be accurate (see page 172 fn. 94).

7. *Iran-Contra Affair*, p. 163.

8. Karrubi is referred to as the "First Iranian" and Kangarlou as the "Second Iranian" (or "the Australian") in official accounts of the affair.

9. TOW missiles are customarily packed in pallets of twelve.

10. Oliver North, Notebook Entry for November 20, 1985.

11. DCM, Country 15 (U.S. Deputy Chief of Mission, Portugal), deposition in *Report of the Congressional Committees Investigating the Iran-Contra Affair*, Appendix B, vol. 8, p. 290.

12. Duane Clarridge, cable #625908, "NSC Mission," November 22, 1985. This document is available in the National Security Archive's microfiche collection, *The Iran-Contra Affair: The Making of a Scandal, 1983-1988*.

13. *Iran-Contra Affair*, p. 184.

14. A series of financial steps, similar to the arrangements for the TOW deals, took place prior to the HAWK deliveries, without which even the fragmentary success of the mission would have been impossible. Several transactions, all based on the anticipated sale of eighty missiles, occurred on November 22, just two days before the weapons left for Tabriz. Again, sizable markups accompanied each phase of the transaction. Schwimmer and Nimrodi transferred $11.2 million to Israel's Defense Ministry, paying a rate of $140,000 per missile. Ghorbanifar entered two deposits of $18 million and $6 million, respectively, into Israeli accounts (the latter to be held in trust by Israel), making Ghorbanifar's cost per missile roughly $225,000. Iran deposited $24.72 million into Ghorbanifar's Swiss bank account, putting Teheran's cost per missile at about $300,000. (Two other Iranian deposits of $20 million each apparently went toward other missile purchases by Ghorbanifar.) Built on the modicum of trust generated by the successful TOW financing, the banking aspect of the mission took place without complications.

15. Michael Ledeen, deposition in *Report of the Congressional Committees Investigating the Iran-Contra Affair*, Appendix B, vol. 15, p. 1217.

16. There appears to have been a misunderstanding about the capabilities of the HAWK missile. Secord maintained that they were never intended for high-flying targets, as the Iranians apparently thought they were.

17. Ledeen testified that he delivered the message to Poindexter (deposition in *Report of the Congressional Committees Investigating the Iran-Contra Affair*, Appendix B, vol. 15, p. 1028).

18. *Iran-Contra Affair*, pp. 269–70.

19. Ibid.

20. Ledeen, too, found himself pushed out of the initiative shortly after the HAWK deal, courtesy of Poindexter, who told him he needed "somebody with more technical expertise" (Ledeen, deposition in *Report of the Congressional Committees Investigating the Iran-Contra Affair*, Appendix B, vol. 15, p. 1229).

21. Oliver North, testimony in *Joint Hearings before the Select Committees on the Iran-Contra Investigation*, July 8, 1987, vol. 100-7, Part I, p. 109.

22. Oliver North tape recording, January 22, 1986. North later claimed that he got the idea for the diversion from Ghorbanifar during this conversation.

23. North's information on this came from Ghorbanifar. (See Charles Allen, deposition exhibit 32 in *Report of the Congressional Committees Investigating the Iran-Contra Affair*, Appendix B, vol. 1, p. 1029.)

24. John McMahon, Cable for William Casey, "Present Status in Saga Regarding the Movement of TOW Missiles," January 25, 1986. This document is available in the National Security Archive's microfiche collection, *The Iran-Contra Affair: The Making of a Scandal, 1983–1988*.

25. North to Poindexter, "Iran," May 8, 1986, 08:07 (incorrectly dated in *The Iran-Contra Affair* as May 6: see p. 235 fn. 163). This document can be found in the National Security Archive's microfiche collection, *The Iran-Contra Affair: The Making of a Scandal, 1983–1988*.

26. *Iran-Contra Affair* euphemistically described the pill as "prescription medicine" (see Chapter 13, p. 243 fn. 11).

27. Memorandum of Conversation, "U.S.-Iran Dialogue," May 26, 1986, 3:30 p.m., p. 3. This document is available in the National Security Archive's microfiche collection, *The Iran-Contra Affair: The Making of a Scandal, 1983–1988*.

28. See Document 66.

29. Bahramani is referred to as "the Nephew" or "the Relative" in official accounts of the initiative.

30. See "Status of Frankfurt Meeting Tapes," November 13, 1986, with attached transcript, p. 10 (Bates stamp C-382). This document is included in the National Security Archive's microfiche collection, *The Iran-Contra Affair: The Making of a Scandal, 1983–1988*.

31. Samii is referred to as "the Engine" in official accounts of the affair.

32. Quoted from George Cave interview, *Iran-Contra Affair*, p. 261.

33. Acknowledging one particular "bald-faced lie" he had told to the Iranians, North admitted in his congressional testimony that he was prepared to say anything to get what he wanted: "I'd have offered the Iranians a free trip to Disneyland if we could have gotten Americans home for it" (North, testimony in *Joint Hearings before the Select Committees on the Iran-Contra Investigation*, July 7, 1987, vol. 100-7, Part I, p. 8).

34. George Shultz, testimony in *Joint Hearings before the Select Committees on the Iran-Contra Investigation*, July 23, 1987, vol. 100-9, p. 72.

UNCLASSIFIED

Chapter 9 FN#
N 10579

July 11, 1985

9-58

RCM:

JMP talked with Michael Ledeen this morning about an urgent
message from Peres for McFarlane which Al Schwimmer, a
Jewish-American who provides lots of money to Peres, wants to
deliver to RCM.

In the meantime, Schwimmer has flown down here and had lunch
today with Michael Ledeen and Ledeen has called back with the
following:

     "It is indeed a message from Prime Minister of Israel; it is
a follow-on to the private conversation he had last week when
David Kimche was here. It is extremely urgent and extremely
sensitive and it regards the matter he told David he was going to
raise with the President. The situation has fundamentally
changed for the better and that I must explain to him because it
will affect his decision. It is very important. It won't keep
more than a day or two but could keep until Saturday morning.
This is the real thing and it is just wonderful news."

Should I try to schedule Ledeen to see you?

                    _____ Yes, Friday afternoon

                    ✓   Yes, on Saturday

                    _____ No, I don't want to see Ledeen

          Other: _____

Wilma

R... 654-0524

*RCM-a
12/30/86*

UNCLASSIFIED

DOCUMENT 70: Robert McFarlane, Memorandum for George Shultz, "Israeli-Iranian Contact," July 13, 1985.

PAGE 1 OF 6

UNCLASSIFIED

P-7

N 13906

EXHIBIT
GP5-9

225C

FROM: The White House

TO: The Secretary of State's Aircraft

Please deliver the following message from Bud McFarlane to Secretary Shultz personally and to no other for him. It must repeat must be opened by the Secretary only. If it is not posible to do so, then so advise this station.

SUBJECT: Israeli-Iranian Contact

1. Top Secret Entire Text.

2. This message is for you only and until we can exchange thoughts on it, I would request that it not be shared with anyone. It concerns a proposal by an Iranian official endorse by the Government of Israel. It has a short term and a long te dimension to it. The short term dimension concerns the seven hostages; the long term dimension involves the establishment of private dialogue with Iranian officials on the broader relation

3. It may perhaps first be useful to provide some background c how this matter came to my attention. Today, I received a private emissary who asked to convey a message from Prime Minis Peres. Reduced to its essentials, the oral message expressed t Israeli position that their access to Iranian officials (which became clear has involved extensive dialogue for some time) had surfaced serious interest among authoritative persons in the Iranian hierarchy in opening a dialogue with the west. A month or so ago, the Israelis surfaced this interest in a Peres sessi with Michael Ledeen who reported it to me. Separately, Rabin

UNCLASSIFIED

ly Declassified/Released on 21 July 1987
under provisions of E.O. 12356
by S. Reger, National Security Council

DOCUMENT 70: Robert McFarlane, Memorandum for George Shultz, "Israeli-Iranian Contact," July 13, 1985.

PAGE 2 OF 6

reported the contact to Sam Lewis and he to you. Ledeen had been in Israel on his own and without any sponsorship from me but he did report the contact. I was awaiting a chance to report it to you when Sam's report reached you and following your stated disinclination, I told Ledeen to state tersely to whomever he dealt with that we did not favor such a process. He did so.

4. Last week, during David Kimche's visit, he asked for 10 minutes with me following a larger meeting. Kimche ███████ ████████████████████████████████████ that they were puzzled by our disinclination and that he was instructed to determine its accuracy. I stated flatly that we could not undertake such a dialogue (or trialogue) at this time. David did not amplify in any degree as to what they intended but clearly understood my flat turndown. He asked again ████████████ that I raise it with appropriate authorities and reconfirm it. I committed to do so but frankly thought it could wait until your trip and some of our more pressing business was behind us. My lone thought at the time was that it was interesting that Kimche ████████████

██
██
██

5. Then came today's emissary who again, ████████████ ████████████ He stated that Israel has for some time been conducting meetings with high level persons in Iran. At a recent meeting in Germany attended by Kimche, a man named Al Schwimmer (Father of the Israeli aircraft industry), and on the

DOCUMENT 70: Robert McFarlane, Memorandum for George Shultz, "Israeli-Iranian Contact," July 13, 1985.

PAGE 3 OF 6

Iranian side ▓▓▓▓▓▓▓▓▓▓▓▓▓▓▓▓▓▓▓▓▓▓▓ and an advisor to the Prime Minister named Gorbanifar, the Iranians presented a picture of contemporary Iran that was extremely pessimistic; continued economic decline, stalemate on the war front; no improvement even assuming Khomeini's passing without having "an option." Their hope and that of what they portrayed as a significant cadre of the hierarchy was to develop a dialogue with the west. At this point and often throughout the conversation Kimche reminded them that they were talking to Israelis who aren't the "west" per se and what did they have in mind? The interlocutors stated emphatically that they sought a dialogue with the United States. The Israelis pressed (in the interest of vetting the bona fides of the Iranians with the real power in Iran) for some tangible show of their ability "to deliver" in such a dialogue. The Iranians stated that they were very confident that they could in the short term, achieve the release of the seven Americans held hostage in Lebanon. But in exchange they would need to show some gain. They sought specifically the delivery from Israel of 100 TOW missiles. But they stated that the larger purpose would be the opening of a private dialogue with a high level American official and a sustained discussion of US-Iranian relations.

6. The concept raises a number of imponderable questions. First, there is your very reasonable concern raised a month ago when the issue was just intelligence sharing, ▓▓▓▓▓▓▓▓▓▓ ▓▓▓▓▓▓▓▓▓▓▓▓ That is very real and one has to consider how such a "trialogue" would be affected over time by sustained

DOCUMENT 70: Robert McFarlane, Memorandum for George Shultz, "Israeli-Iranian Contact," July 13, 1985.

PAGE 4 OF 6

UNCLASSIFIED

Israeli involvement. Surely we ought to expect that Israel's fears over any Arab (as opposed to Iranian) fallout would not always necessarily coincide with our own.

7. On the short term aspect, there is a family of questions related to our terrorism policy against negotiating with terroris (notwithstanding the thin veil provided by Israel as the cutout on this specific matter). As a footnote I have checked and determined that Iran had TOW missiles before the Shah's fall and, consequently, their using TOWs now would not necessarily raise too many eyebrows.

8. Then one has to consider where this might lead in terms of our being asked to up the ante on more and more arms and where that could conceivably lead, not just in the compromise of our position, but to the possible eventuality of the Iranians "winni: and where that would put the security of the neighboring Gulf States. Clearly that is a loser. But I would think that, given the vulnerability of the Iranian interlocutor to our discrete blowing of his cover with Khomeini, ought to enable us to control that.

9. At the end of the day, our long term interest remains in maintaining an ability to renew ties with Iran under some more sensible successor regime. Whether or not this contact is

UNCLASSIFIED

DOCUMENT 70: Robert McFarlane, Memorandum for George Shultz, "Israeli-Iranian Contact," July 13, 1985.

PAGE 5 OF 6

UNCLASSIFIED

connected to viable, stable parties in Iran remains to be seen. It could be that these people are no more than self-serving, self-promoters who seek to curry favor with an element of the military -- those who happen to want TOWs right now. But I would think their risk of exposure again, provides some insurance against that. And Israel is not noted for dealing with fools and charlatans.

10. George, I cannot judge the equities on this. We need to think about it. But I don't think we should tarry.

On balance my instincts are to see our larger interest in establishing an entree to someone in Iran and the check provided by the Iranian interlocutor's vulnerability to being "blown" as giving us some insurance against perfidy. We could make a tentative show of interest without commitment and see what happens. Or we could walk away. On balance I tend to favor going ahead.

10. As a final note, and please understand that I intend no comment on the NEA bureau for which I have profound respect, I don't believe this should go beyond you and Charlie Hill. It isn't at all that others lack judgment. It is simply a matter of the potential for compromise as the circle widens which is axiomatic.

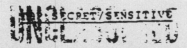

SECRET/SENSITIVE

UNCLASSIFIED

DOCUMENT 70: Robert McFarlane, Memorandum for George Shultz, "Israeli-Iranian Contact," July 13, 1985.

PAGE 6 OF 6

UNCLASSIFIED

11. The emissary will return to Israel on Tuesday. We should give him some signal by then, preferably on Monday Washington time. I will await and abide fully by your decision.

12. Finally, the President has been in the operating room for 3 hours. I will keep you advised.

Warm Regards, Bud

P.S. - I have just received word from Don Regan that the operation has been completed and was entirely successful.

RCM

DOCUMENT 71: George Shultz, Cable to Robert McFarlane, "Reply to Backchannel No. 3 from Bud" (response to Document 70), July 14, 1985.

PAGE 1 OF 3

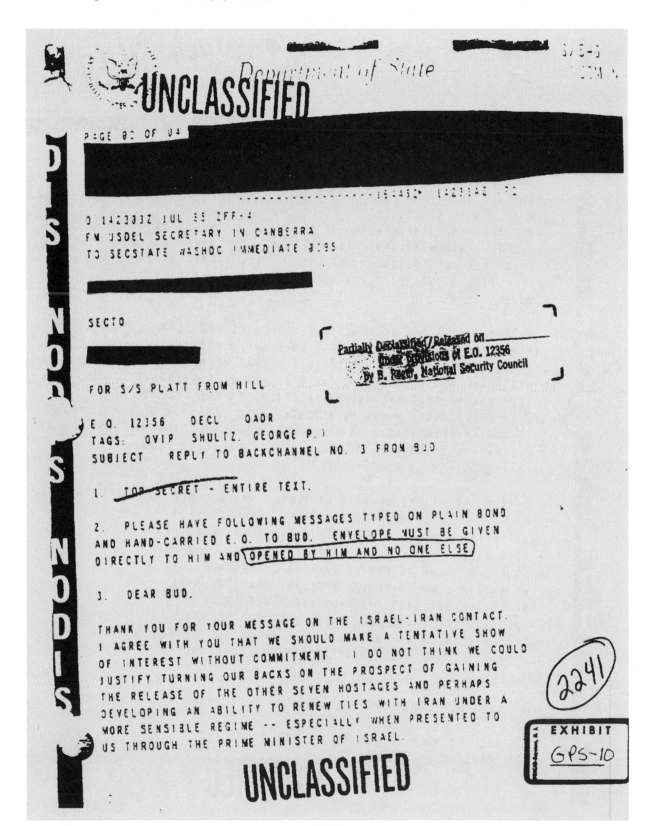

UNCLASSIFIED

P:GE 0: OF 0:

O 142333Z JUL 35 ZFF-4
FM USDEL SECRETARY IN CANBERRA
TO SECSTATE WASHDC IMMEDIATE 3:95

SECTO

Partially Declassified/Released on
Under provisions of E.O. 12356
By B. Reger, National Security Council

FOR S/S PLATT FROM HILL

E.O. 12356   DECL   OADR
TAGS: OVIP SHULTZ, GEORGE P.
SUBJECT   REPLY TO BACKCHANNEL NO. 3 FROM BUD

1. TOP SECRET - ENTIRE TEXT.

2. PLEASE HAVE FOLLOWING MESSAGES TYPED ON PLAIN BOND
AND HAND-CARRIED E.O. TO BUD. ENVELOPE MUST BE GIVEN
DIRECTLY TO HIM AND OPENED BY HIM AND NO ONE ELSE.

3. DEAR BUD.

THANK YOU FOR YOUR MESSAGE ON THE ISRAEL-IRAN CONTACT.
I AGREE WITH YOU THAT WE SHOULD MAKE A TENTATIVE SHOW
OF INTEREST WITHOUT COMMITMENT. I DO NOT THINK WE COULD
JUSTIFY TURNING OUR BACKS ON THE PROSPECT OF GAINING
THE RELEASE OF THE OTHER SEVEN HOSTAGES AND PERHAPS
DEVELOPING AN ABILITY TO RENEW TIES WITH IRAN UNDER A
MORE SENSIBLE REGIME -- ESPECIALLY WHEN PRESENTED TO
US THROUGH THE PRIME MINISTER OF ISRAEL.

2241

EXHIBIT
GPS-10

UNCLASSIFIED

DOCUMENT 71: George Shultz, Cable to Robert McFarlane, "Reply to Backchannel No. 3 from Bud" (response to Document 70), July 14, 1985.

PAGE 2 OF 3

Department of State UNCLASSIFIED S/S-O INCOMING

PAGE 02 OF 04

4. THAT BEING SAID, I FURTHER AGREE WITH YOU THAT THIS SITUATION IS LOADED WITH "IMPONDERABLES" THAT CALL FOR GREAT CAUTION ON OUR PART. I THINK YOU HAVE COVERED THEM ALL IN YOUR MESSAGE. I WOULD ONLY UNDERSCORE A COUPLE OF THEM: THE FRAUD THAT SEEMS TO ACCOMPANY SO MANY DEALS INVOLVING ARMS AND IRAN; AND THE COMPLICATIONS ARISING FROM OUR "BLESSING" AN ISRAEL-IRAN RELATIONSHIP WHERE ISRAEL'S INTERESTS AND OURS ARE NOT NECESSARILY THE SAME.

5. I SUGGEST -- AND YOUR MESSAGE INDICATES YOU LEAN THIS WAY TOO -- THAT WE GIVE THE EMISSARY A POSITIVE BUT PASSIVE REPLY. THAT IS, TELL HIM THAT HE MAY CONVEY TO HIS IRANIAN CONTACTS THAT THE U.S. HAS BEEN INFORMED OF THE IRANIAN PROPOSAL AND IS RECEPTIVE TO THE IDEA OF A PRIVATE DIALOGUE INVOLVING A SUSTAINED DISCUSSION OF U.S.-IRANIAN RELATIONS. IN OTHER WORDS, WE ARE WILLING TO LISTEN AND SERIOUSLY CONSIDER ANY STATEMENT ON THIS TOPIC THEY MAY WISH TO INITIATE.

6. GIVEN THE NATURE OF THIS MATTER, I AM INCLINED TO THINK IT SHOULD BE MANAGED BY YOU PERSONALLY; ITS SENSITIVITY REQUIRES HIGH-LEVEL MANAGEMENT; BUT THAT IN TURN RAISES THE LIKELIHOOD OF DISCLOSURE. BUT THIS IS SOMETHING THAT WE CAN GO OVER MORE CAREFULLY AFTER I GET BACK. I DO THINK IT IMPORTANT THAT YOU MAKE CLEAR TO THE EMISSARY THAT YOU AND I ARE IN CLOSE CONTACT AND FULL AGREEMENT EVERY STEP OF THE WAY; THIS IS ALL THE MORE IMPORTANT IN VIEW OF THE PRESENT LACK OF UNITY AND FULL COORDINATION ON THE ISRAELI SIDE.

7. THANK YOU AGAIN FOR YOUR MESSAGE; I CAN ONLY REITERATE HOW MUCH I VALUE OUR CLOSE CONSULTATION AND FRIENDSHIP.

UNCLASSIFIED

DOCUMENT 71: George Shultz, Cable to Robert McFarlane, "Reply to Backchannel No. 3 from Bud" (response to Document 70), July 14, 1985.

PAGE 3 OF 3

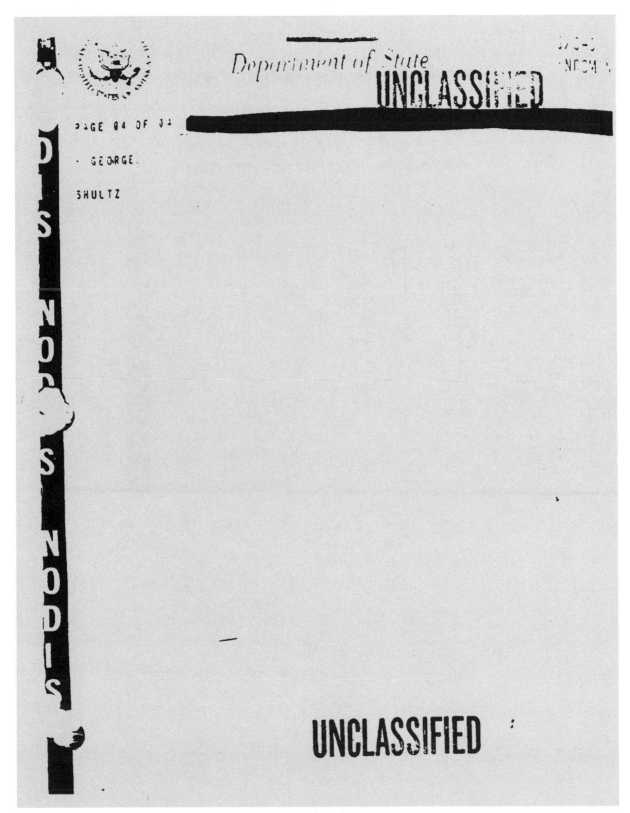

Department of State

UNCLASSIFIED

PAGE 04 OF 04

GEORGE

SHULTZ

DIS NODIS NODIS

UNCLASSIFIED

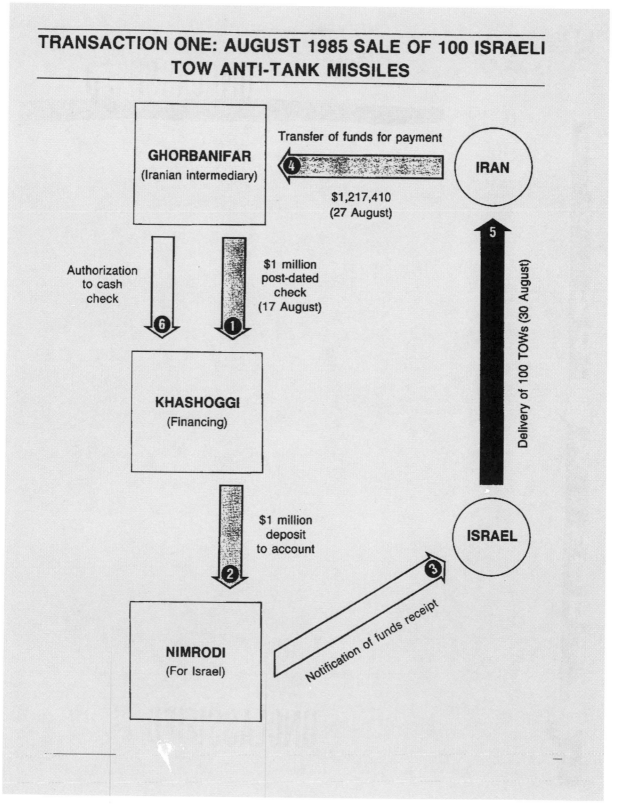

TRANSACTION ONE: AUGUST 1985 SALE OF 100 ISRAELI TOW ANTI-TANK MISSILES

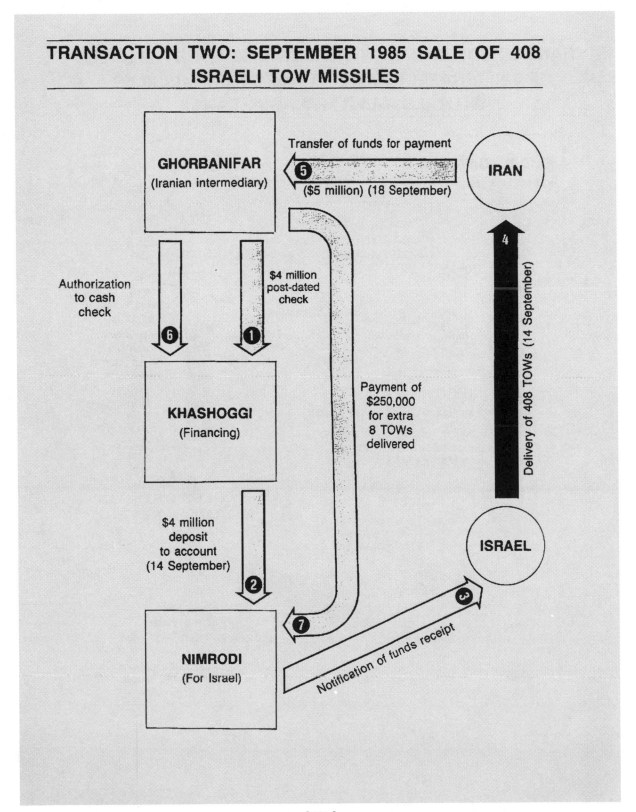

TRANSACTION TWO: SEPTEMBER 1985 SALE OF 408 ISRAELI TOW MISSILES

GHORBANIFAR
(Iranian intermediary)

Transfer of funds for payment
⑤
($5 million) (18 September)

IRAN

Authorization
to cash
check

$4 million
post-dated
check

⑥

①

KHASHOGGI
(Financing)

Payment of
$250,000
for extra
8 TOWs
delivered

Delivery of 408 TOWs (14 September)

④

$4 million
deposit
to account
(14 September)

②

ISRAEL

⑦

③

NIMRODI
(For Israel)

Notification of funds receipt

TRANSACTION THREE: NOVEMBER 1985 ABORTED SALE OF 120 ISRAELI HAWK ANTI-AIRCRAFT MISSILES WITH U.S. DELIVERY ASSISTANCE

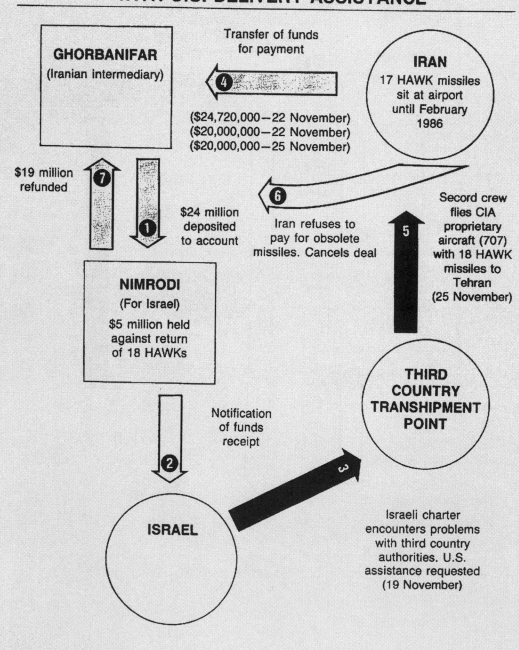

GHORBANIFAR
(Iranian intermediary)

Transfer of funds
for payment

IRAN
17 HAWK missiles
sit at airport
until February
1986

($24,720,000—22 November)
($20,000,000—22 November)
($20,000,000—25 November)

$19 million
refunded

$24 million
deposited
to account

Iran refuses to
pay for obsolete
missiles. Cancels deal

Second crew
flies CIA
proprietary
aircraft (707)
with 18 HAWK
missiles to
Tehran
(25 November)

NIMRODI
(For Israel)

$5 million held
against return
of 18 HAWKs

**THIRD
COUNTRY
TRANSHIPMENT
POINT**

Notification
of funds
receipt

ISRAEL

Israeli charter
encounters problems
with third country
authorities. U.S.
assistance requested
(19 November)

DOCUMENT 72: Tower Commission Charts Illustrating Arms Transactions with Iran (1986; misdated 1985).

PAGE 4 OF 6

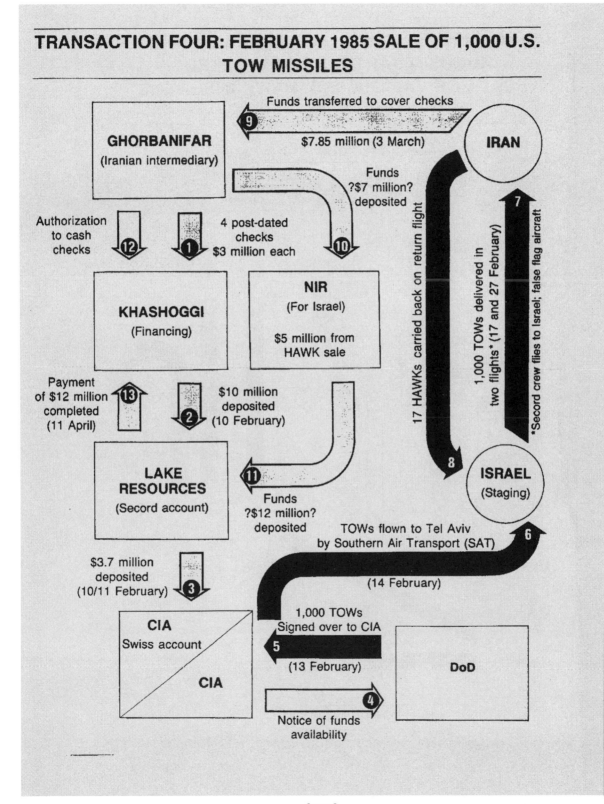

TRANSACTION FOUR: FEBRUARY 1985 SALE OF 1,000 U.S. TOW MISSILES

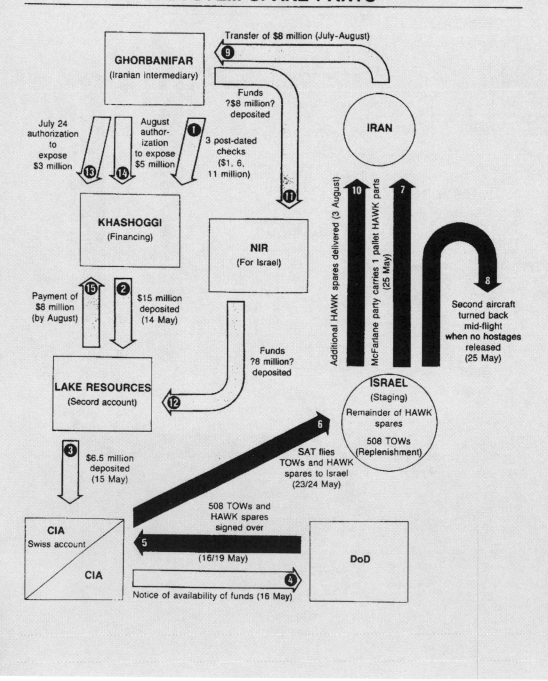

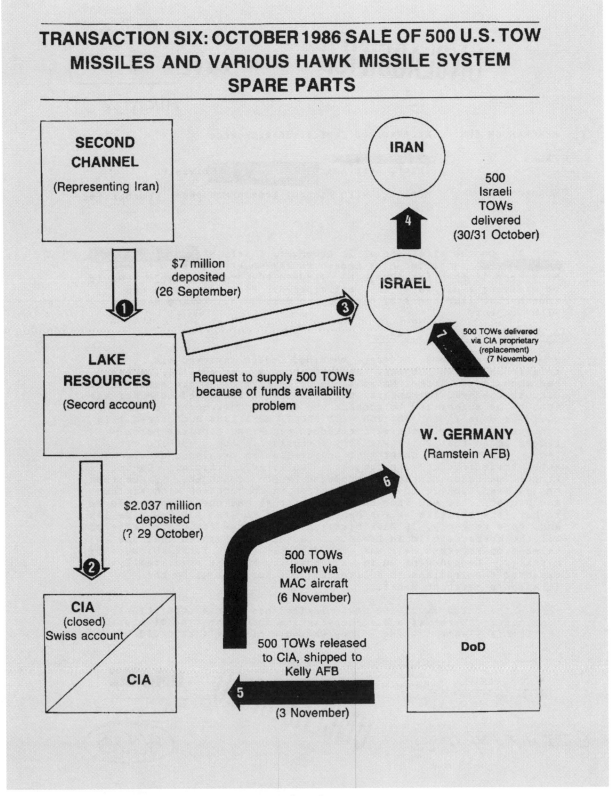

TRANSACTION SIX: OCTOBER 1986 SALE OF 500 U.S. TOW MISSILES AND VARIOUS HAWK MISSILE SYSTEM SPARE PARTS

SECOND CHANNEL

(Representing Iran)

IRAN

500 Israeli TOWs delivered (30/31 October)

$7 million deposited (26 September)

❶

ISRAEL

❸

LAKE RESOURCES

(Secord account)

Request to supply 500 TOWs because of funds availability problem

500 TOWs delivered via CIA proprietary (replacement) (7 November)

❼

W. GERMANY

(Ramstein AFB)

❹

$2.037 million deposited (? 29 October)

❻

❷

500 TOWs flown via MAC aircraft (6 November)

CIA
(closed)
Swiss account

CIA

500 TOWs released to CIA, shipped to Kelly AFB

❺

DoD

(3 November)

DOCUMENT 73: Chief, CIA Near East Division, Memorandum for Director of Central Intelligence William Casey, "Meetings with Michael Ledeen/Manuchehr [*sic*] Ghorbanifar," ca. December 23, 1985.

PAGE 1 OF 6

UNCLASSIFIED

86-4068E

Dec 85
Executive Reg stry
85- 5048

Allen Ex.#20

MEMORANDUM FOR: Director of Central Intelligence

FROM: Chief, Near East ▒▒▒▒▒ Division

SUBJECT: Meetings with Michael Ledeen/Manuchehr Ghorbanifar

1. On the afternoon of 21 December, Chief, NE ▒▒▒▒▒ contacted Mike Ledeen to lay-on arrangements to meet Manuchehr Ghorbanifar (Subject). Ledeen advised that Subject would be arriving a day later than anticipated. He suggested we get together at 1100 hours 22 December to discuss our coming meeting with Subject.

1 0282

Meeting with Michael Ledeen

- During the 22 December meeting, Ledeen reviewed his relationship with Subject. He said about a year ago, he (Ledeen) had gone to the former National Security Advisor Robert McFarlane to discuss the need for an Iran policy. Ledeen suggested to McFarlane that he be authorized to contact the Israeli Government to see what could be done in conjunction with them. McFarlane authorized this contact and shortly thereafter Ledeen met Prime Minister Peres. Ledeen added that Peres was very enthusiastic about working with Ledeen and the U.S. Government on the Iranian problem and told him about their contact with Subject. Two Israeli officials, David Kimche and Jacob Nimradi, introduced Ledeen to Subject. Since then, he has seen Subject 20-30 times, often in conjunction with Kimche and Nimradi. It was from this contact that the operation developed to have the Israelis at our behest deliver to Iran 500 Tow missiles and, more recently, 18 Hawk missiles in exchange for the release of all the hostages held in Lebanon. Ledeen is convinced that the release of Reverend Weir was tied directly to the first shipment of missiles. Ledeen went on to say, however, that he never really expected the Iranians to deliver all the hostages given the "Iranian's merchant mentality."

- The delivery of the Hawk missiles has been an operational nightmare. There was a misunderstanding about the type of missiles the Iranians were seeking. They wanted a missile that could hit a

Partially Declassified/Released on 26 JAN 88
under provisions of E O 12356
by K Johnson, National Security Council

WARNING NOTICE
INTELLIGENCE SOURCES
AND METHODS INVOLVED

UNCLASSIFIED

CL BY ▒▒▒▒
DECL OADR
DERIVED FROM
HUM 4-8

CIIN #174/E 02

(5003)

DOCUMENT 73: Chief, CIA Near East Division, Memorandum for Director of Central Intelligence
William Casey, "Meetings with Michael Ledeen/Manuchehr [sic] Ghorbanifar," ca. December 23, 1985.

PAGE 2 OF 6

UNCLASSIFIED

target at seventy-thousand feet and already had Hawk missiles in
their arsenal. What they thought they were going to get was a
modified and advanced version of the Hawk. They are quite angry
about the delivery of the missiles and have asked that they be
removed from Iran as soon as possible. Their presence in Iran is
politically troublesome to the Iranian hierarchy. They are now
asking for Hercules or Phoenix missiles.

- Ledeen stated that at a recent high-level meeting which
included the President, Secretary of State Schultz and Defense
Secretary Weinberger a decision was made not to proceed with
Ghorbanifar in an effort to release the hostages. Schultz and
Weinberger reportedly were quite unhappy about this operation.

- As an aside, Ledeen noted they had purposely overcharged the
Iranians and had used around $200,000 of these funds to support
Subject's political contacts inside Iran. Later that same evening,
Subject stated he was holding $40 million which the Iranians want
returned.   I   0283,

- Ledeen is a fan of Subject and describes him as a "wonderful
man .... almost too good to be true." He had asked Subject to come
to the U.S. to meet with us in order to straighten out his
credibility and to find a way to keep the relationship going with
him. The number one item in this latter area is his proposed Libyan
operation. Ledeen said that when he learned of our Burn Notice on
Subject, he contacted him in an effort to have him explain the
situation (see Attachment A). He commented that Subject admitted
lying to us, saying he could not reveal his source nor explain his
relationship with senior Iranian officials. He felt we would not
understand his relationship with the Iranian government. We
suggested that perhaps a new polygraph would be useful given these
latest revelations. He agreed to a polygraph to be conducted in the
Hqs area on 6 January.

- In closing out this session, Ledeen made the point that any
serious covert action operations directed against Iran using
Ghorbanifar should be run out of the White House not CIA because "it
will leak from Congress."

Meeting with Ledeen and Ghorbanifar

- At 2100 hours, we met with Ledeen and Subject at Ledeen's
home. After a few pleasantries, we began to discuss Subject's
reporting concerning the "Iranian hit team" which allegedly is

UNCLASSIFIED

SECRET

UNCLASSIFIED

I 0284

presently

Subject also said he thinks they have been given authority to assassinate He mentioned as a secondary target. When we went over this a second time, he stated he is certain that is the target.

Subject was fairly reluctant at this meeting to identify this source. However, at the meeting on the afternoon of 23 December, he identified his source as This is the same source who provided the false information last March concerning an alleged Iranian plan to assassinate Presidential candidates which did not hold up during Subject's polygraph (see Attachment E).

(Comment: Subject's reporting on this team is very reminiscent of his previous terrorist reporting which, after investigation and polygraph, turned out to be fabricated. It is our feeling there are bits of valid information in Subject's reporting but he has embellished and projected his own feelings in presenting this information as hard fact. This has been a presistant problem throughout the four years we have known him. His reporting has sometimes been useful but it is extremely difficult to separate the good from the bad information. It is hard to find in the file any instance where his reporting in fact resulted in a solid development.)

UNCLASSIFIED

DOCUMENT 73: Chief, CIA Near East Division, Memorandum for Director of Central Intelligence
William Casey, "Meetings with Michael Ledeen/Manuchehr [*sic*] Ghorbanifar," ca. December 23, 1985.

PAGE 4 OF 6

UNCLASSIFIED

I   0285

    - Subject had no additional information to add at this time
other than the fact that this operation is not directed by ▮▮▮▮

▮▮▮▮▮▮▮▮▮▮▮▮▮▮▮▮▮▮▮▮▮▮▮▮▮▮▮▮▮▮▮▮▮▮

    - At this point in the discussion, we shifted to his views on
the current divisions within the Iranian Government. He described
them as:

              line one - rightist;
              line two - hardline;
              line three - balancers.

He said that he would like to modify his earlier reporting
(Attachment B). He believes "line two" and "line three" are now
working more closely than in the past. His reporting on this is not
very substantive and did not bring forward any really new
information. He said he is working closely with the "rightist line"
▮▮▮▮▮▮▮▮▮▮▮▮▮▮▮▮▮▮▮▮▮▮▮▮▮▮▮▮▮▮▮▮▮▮▮

He said that the "rightist group" is not easily discernable because
of the physical danger associated with openly opposing the
government. Because they are not "visible", it is difficult to
measure their strength within the Armed Forces, Revolutionary Guard,
Bazar, etc. ▮▮▮▮▮▮▮▮▮▮▮▮▮▮▮▮▮▮▮▮▮▮▮

    - At this point, he provided us with a 13-page Farsi document
▮▮▮▮▮▮▮▮▮▮▮▮▮▮▮▮▮ analysis of the Islamic Jihad. He said there
is new information and details in this document which our analyst
will find very useful. (Comment: While we are having the document
fully translated, the translator's early impression is that the
document ▮▮▮▮▮ does not reveal any new information). Subject went on to say
that he could put us in touch with ▮▮▮▮▮▮ whom he describes as ▮▮▮
▮▮▮▮▮▮▮▮ supposedly would
be willing to answer all of our questions provided we give Subject
three guarantees:

      - There would be no harm done to ▮▮▮▮ or his associates;

      - That we would coordinate all our efforts with Ghorbanifar
        and;

      - That we would support ▮▮▮▮ to become ▮▮▮▮▮▮

UNCLASSIFIED

DOCUMENT 73: Chief, CIA Near East Division, Memorandum for Director of Central Intelligence William Casey, "Meetings with Michael Ledeen/Manuchehr [*sic*] Ghorbanifar," ca. December 23, 1985.

PAGE 5 OF 6

UNCLASSIFIED

I 0286

He added that this guarantee would have to come from the Director of CIA. He described ▮▮▮▮▮▮ as being in charge of purchasing weapons for Iran. When asked what support ▮▮▮▮▮ is looking for, Subject replied that we should help him be effective in his job. (Comment: What we are talking about here is facilitating ▮▮▮▮▮▮ arms purchasing efforts. We told him we would review his report carefully and get back to him with additional requirements. It is noteworthy that Ghorbanifar's contact with ▮▮▮▮▮ is very recent and he only raised the idea of cooperation with ▮▮▮▮▮ one week ago.)

- At that point, we reviewed his relations with ▮▮▮▮▮. Subject said he has known ▮▮▮▮▮ for 2-1/2 years and has developed a good personal relationship with him. He described ▮▮▮▮▮ as a "hard-line fundamentalist" who is loyal to the Regime. He said ▮▮▮▮▮ holds ▮▮▮▮▮ position within the ▮▮▮▮▮ office ▮▮▮▮▮ ▮▮▮▮▮ Subject said that he provides ▮▮▮▮▮ with information which ▮▮▮▮▮ has used effectively in enhancing his position. Ledeen interjected the observation that subject has actually "made" ▮▮▮▮▮ by his efforts in delivering missiles to the Iranians, ▮▮▮▮▮ is disliked by his competition ▮▮▮▮▮

- Subject said that because of the negotiations concerning the exchange of the hostages for missiles, there has not been a terrorist act directed against the USG since July. He implied that this might change now that the negotiations have broken off.

- Finally, we discussed his proposed Libyan operation (Attachment D). He reiterated that Qadhafi is very much interested in assassinating Muhammad ((al-Mugarieff)), Libyan opposition leader ▮▮▮▮▮ ▮▮▮▮▮ In essence, Subject is proposing a sting operation in which the Libyans would provide $10 million in exchange for al-Mugarieff's demise. Subject believes he would be able to extract these funds from Qadhafi ▮▮▮▮▮ stage his disappearance. He

UNCLASSIFIED

DOCUMENT 73: Chief, CIA Near East Division, Memorandum for Director of Central Intelligence William Casey, "Meetings with Michael Ledeen/Manuchehr [*sic*] Ghorbanifar," ca. December 23, 1985.

PAGE 6 OF 6

UNCLASSIFIED

I 0287

believes that when al-Mugarieff reappears, it would have a devastating impact on Qadhafi's image. He proposed using the funds ($10 million) obtained from Qadhafi for joint operations against the Iranians or any other target we are interested in. ▮▮▮▮▮▮▮ Both Subject and Ledeen made a strong pitch for a decision on the operation as quickly as possible. We told him that we would review the operational proposal and get back to him quickly.

▮▮▮

- Subject plans to travel to London on 24 December to be with his family for 2-3 days. He has agreed to return on 5 January to undergo a polygraph scheduled for 6 January.

- Around 2330 hours NSC staffer, Ollie North, dropped by to,say hello to Subject and to talk with him about the problem of retrieving the missiles from Iran. We departed at 2400 hours and it was arranged to get together on the afternoon of 23 December to discuss further some of his ideas. (Comments: This latter meeting took place as scheduled and the new information obtained during this session is folded into this report -- specifically arranging the date for a polygraph and the identification ▮▮▮▮▮▮▮ as his source of terrorist activities in Europe.).

- Subject is registered at the Madison Hotel in alias, Nicholas Kralis.

UNCLASSIFIED

UNCLASSIFIED   9-1

Manuchear Ghorbanifar - aka Djafar Souzani, Ja'far Suzani,
Manouch██████ Hanuel Pereira, Manoucheer Korbanifar,
Nikol██████ DPOB: 9 May 1945, Tehran, Iran; also 1942,
Isf██████ and 1938. He is an Iranian citizen. His
occ██████on is export/import businessman. Formerly a Managing
Dir██████ of Israeli-connected Star Line Shipping. He is a
fo██████ Iranian Army Officer. He claims to have worked for
SA██████ He is believed to be in periodic contact with U.S.
int██████agence service███████████████ He is a self-proclaimed
whee██████████████ his early 20's. Speaks excellent
Amer████████ ██glish. He has had a Portuguese Passport in
name of ██████ Pereira issued on 3 October 1980 and valid until
3 October 1985, number 10596/80. Greek Passport number X-10723
in the name of Nikolaos Kralis issued 27 October 1981 in
Stockholm and vaild until 26 October 1986. Iranian Passport
Number 11652209 in name of Ja'far Suzani. As of 1982 was said
to have an Iraqi passport in an Arab name. He claims to be in
a position to produce genuine passports of various
nationalities.

Prior to the Iranian Revolution, Ghorbanifar had been an
informant for Iranian Intel and claimed to have access to many
senior ranking officers in the military as well as access to
iranian underworld characters of various illicit hues. As of
late 1979 he was a member of Tehran Komite and was able to
travel freely between Europe and Iran in connection with his
import/export business. He and his brothers Ali and Reza
became implicated in abortive coup of 9 July 1980 which
resulted in curtailment of this trips to Iran. Since that time
he has been located primarily in Paris with his brother Ali but
travels to Athens, Turkey and Iran for purpose of meeting with
other exile leaders in support of his "group" in Iran. He
claimed at one time to be closely affiliated with Shahpour
Bakhtiar but later said he and his "group" were monitoring
Bakhtiar, Hadani and other exile groups.

On 17 March 1984 Ghorbanifar met with a CIA officer ██████
██████ and volunteered information on the Beirut kidnapping
of COS, Beirut and on a plot to assassinate presidential
candidates. He said he had stopped dealing with CIA in 1981
because the U.S. Government was not going to act on intel he
was giving to bring down the Khomeini regime ██████████████ On 18
March 1984 he was polygraphed ██████████████ to determine the
veracity of his information. He failed the exam on significant
issues of fabrication and he deliberately provided false info
on the Beirut kidnapping and assassination plots. At the
request of U.S. Secret Service he was re-polygraphed on 12 June
1984 and again failed the exam. His reactions indicated he was
practicing deception on all relevant questions concerning plot
to assassinate presidential candidates.

In 1985 Ghorbanifar was cited by Cyrus Hashemi as one the
latter's influential contacts and as an official of Iranian
intelligence who was interested in negotiating a settlement of
the hostage issue.

REVIEWED FOR RELEASE
Date 27 March 87

UNCLASSIFIED

C11N1022

DOCUMENT 75: Oliver North, PROFS Note to John Poindexter, "Private Blank Check: Wrap Up as of 2030 EDT," November 20, 1985.

PAGE 1 OF 1

From: NSOLN --CPUA
To: NSJMP --CPUA

Date and time   11/20/85 21:27:39

*** Reply to note of 08/31/85 13:26

UNCLASSIFIED   1100
~~SECRET~~   N 28724

NOTE FROM: OLIVER NORTH
Subject: PRIVATE BLANK CHECK
Wrap Up as of 2030 EDT.
The Israelis will deliver 80 Mod HAWKS ▮▮▮▮▮ at noon on Friday 22 Nov.
These 80 will be loaded aboard three chartered aircraft, owned by a proprietary
which will take off at two hour intervals for Tabriz. The aircraft will
file for overflight through the ▮▮▮▮FIR enroute to Tabriz from ▮▮▮▮
Appropriate arrangements have been made with the proper ▮▮▮▮ air control
personnel. Once the aircraft have been launched, their departure will be confirmed by Ashghari who will call ▮▮▮▮ who will call ▮▮▮▮
▮▮▮▮ who will direct ▮▮▮▮ in Beirut to collect the five
1st five Amcits from Hizballah and deliver them to the U.S. Embassy.
There is also the possibility that they will hand over the French hostage
who is very ill.

There is a requirement for 40 additional weaps of the same nomenclature
for a total requirement of 120. $18M in payment for the first 80 has
been deposited in the appropriate account. No acft will land in Tabriz until
the AMCITS have been delivered to the embassy. The Iranians have also asked
to order additional items in the future and have been told that they will
be considered after this activity has succeeded. All transfer arrangements
have been made by Dick Secord, who deserves a medal for his extraordinary
short notice efforts.

Replenishment arrangements are being made through the MOD purchasing office
in NYC. There is, to say the least, considerable anxiety that we will
somehow delay on their plan to purchase 120 of these weapons in the next
few days. IAW your instructions I have told their agent that we will sell
them 120 items at a price that they can meet. I have further told them that
we will make no effort to move on their purchase LOA request until we have
all five AMCITS safely delivered. In short, the pressure is on them.

Tomorrow we will dispatch a covert hostage debrief team to Wiesbaden,
under cover of an exercise. ▮▮▮▮▮▮▮▮▮▮ EUCOM will be told to prepare a
C-141 for four-hour alert to pick up any hostages who may be released
over the weekend. All of the parties above will be told that we have
info (from the same source which advised us of Wier's release) that
some, if not all, AMCIT hostages will be turned over ▮▮▮▮▮▮
between now and Sunday.

As soon as we have the release confirmed, we need to move quickly with
Defense to provide the 120 missiles the Israelis want to buy. They are very
concerned that they are degrading their defense capability, and in view of the
Syrian shoot-down yesterday the PM has placed considerable pressure on both
Rabin and Kimche for very prompt replacement. Both called several times
today.

There is the distinct possibility that at the end of the week we will
have five Americans home and the promise of no future hostage takings in
exchange for selling the Israelis 120 Mod HAWKs. Despite the difficulty
of making all this fit inside a 96-hour window, it isn't that bad a deal --
▮▮▮▮▮▮▮▮▮▮▮▮▮▮▮▮▮▮ Warm regards.
Recommend pass to RCM after review. North.

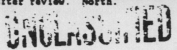

UNCLASSIFIED

EXHIBIT
CAW-6

DOCUMENT 76: Duane Clarridge, Cable for European CIA Station, "NSC Request," November 23, 1985.

PAGE 1 OF 1

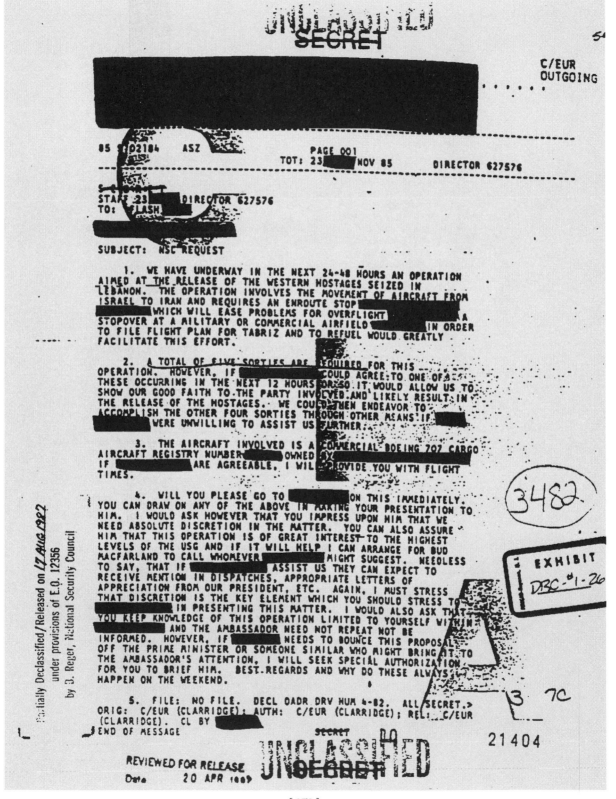

UNCLASSIFIED
SECRET

C/EUR
OUTGOING

85 [ ]2184   ASZ   PAGE 001
                        TOT: 23[ ] NOV 85   DIRECTOR 627576

STAFF 23[ ] DIRECTOR 627576
TO: FLASH

SUBJECT: NSC REQUEST

1. WE HAVE UNDERWAY IN THE NEXT 24-48 HOURS AN OPERATION AIMED AT THE RELEASE OF THE WESTERN HOSTAGES SEIZED IN LEBANON. THE OPERATION INVOLVES THE MOVEMENT OF AIRCRAFT FROM ISRAEL TO IRAN AND REQUIRES AN ENROUTE STOP [ ] WHICH WILL EASE PROBLEMS FOR OVERFLIGHT [ ] A STOPOVER AT A MILITARY OR COMMERCIAL AIRFIELD [ ] IN ORDER TO FILE FLIGHT PLAN FOR TABRIZ AND TO REFUEL WOULD GREATLY FACILITATE THIS EFFORT.

2. A TOTAL OF FIVE SORTIES ARE REQUIRED FOR THIS OPERATION. HOWEVER, IF [ ] COULD AGREE TO ONE OF [ ] THESE OCCURRING IN THE NEXT 12 HOURS OR SO IT WOULD ALLOW US TO SHOW OUR GOOD FAITH TO THE PARTY INVOLVED AND LIKELY RESULT IN THE RELEASE OF THE HOSTAGES. WE COULD THEN ENDEAVOR TO ACCOMPLISH THE OTHER FOUR SORTIES THROUGH OTHER MEANS IF [ ] WERE UNWILLING TO ASSIST US FURTHER.

3. THE AIRCRAFT INVOLVED IS A COMMERCIAL BOEING 707 CARGO AIRCRAFT REGISTRY NUMBER [ ] OWNED BY [ ] IF [ ] ARE AGREEABLE, I WILL PROVIDE YOU WITH FLIGHT TIMES.

4. WILL YOU PLEASE GO TO [ ] ON THIS IMMEDIATELY. YOU CAN DRAW ON ANY OF THE ABOVE IN MAKING YOUR PRESENTATION TO HIM. I WOULD ASK HOWEVER THAT YOU IMPRESS UPON HIM THAT WE NEED ABSOLUTE DISCRETION IN THE MATTER. YOU CAN ALSO ASSURE HIM THAT THIS OPERATION IS OF GREAT INTEREST TO THE HIGHEST LEVELS OF THE USG AND IF IT WILL HELP I CAN ARRANGE FOR BUD MACFARLAND TO CALL WHOMEVER [ ] MIGHT SUGGEST. NEEDLESS TO SAY, THAT IF [ ] ASSIST US THEY CAN EXPECT TO RECEIVE MENTION IN DISPATCHES, APPROPRIATE LETTERS OF APPRECIATION FROM OUR PRESIDENT, ETC. AGAIN, I MUST STRESS THAT DISCRETION IS THE KEY ELEMENT WHICH YOU SHOULD STRESS TO [ ] IN PRESENTING THIS MATTER. I WOULD ALSO ASK THAT YOU KEEP KNOWLEDGE OF THIS OPERATION LIMITED TO YOURSELF WITHIN [ ] AND THE AMBASSADOR NEED NOT REPEAT NOT BE INFORMED. HOWEVER, IF [ ] NEEDS TO BOUNCE THIS PROPOSAL OFF THE PRIME MINISTER OR SOMEONE SIMILAR WHO MIGHT BRING IT TO THE AMBASSADOR'S ATTENTION, I WILL SEEK SPECIAL AUTHORIZATION FOR YOU TO BRIEF HIM. BEST REGARDS AND WHY DO THESE ALWAYS HAPPEN ON THE WEEKEND.

5. FILE: NO FILE. DECL OADR DRV HUM 4-82. ALL SECRET.>
ORIG: C/EUR (CLARRIDGE); AUTH: C/EUR (CLARRIDGE); REL: C/EUR
(CLARRIDGE). CL BY [ ]
END OF MESSAGE

3482

EXHIBIT
DBC-[ ]1-26

3 7C

21404

SECRET
UNCLASSIFIED

REVIEWED FOR RELEASE
Date   20 APR 1989

DOCUMENT 77: Oliver North, Memorandum for Robert McFarlane and John Poindexter, "Next Steps," December 9, 1985.

PAGE 1 OF 4

~~UN~~ TOP SECRET
UNCLASSIFIED

N 29746

NATIONAL SECURITY COUNCIL

December 9, 1985

MEMO FOR ROBERT C. MCFARLANE
JOHN M. POINDEXTER

FROM: OLIVER L. NORTH

Attached are our plans to
date.

EYES ONLY

598

~~TOP SECRET~~
UNCLASSIFIED

DOCUMENT 77: Oliver North, Memorandum for Robert McFarlane and John Poindexter, "Next Steps," December 9, 1985.

PAGE 2 OF 4

SECRET

~~TOP SECRET~~   December 9, 1985

N 28747

NEXT STEPS

The meetings this weekend with the Israelis and Gorbanifahr were inconclusive. Gorbanifahr refused to return to Geneva with our message that no further deliveries would be undertaken until all the hostages were released. Gorbanifahr and the Israelis both believe that if he were to pass such a message to the Iranian Prime Minister or ████████████ (who provides funds for items delivered) -- one or more of the hostages would be executed. Gorbanifahr noted that nine Hizballah leaders had been summoned to Tehran on Friday and that, given the pressures inside Lebanon, all it would take for the hostages to be killed would be for Tehran to "stop saying no."

Much of what we decide to do in the days ahead depends upon whether or not we can trust Gorbanifahr. The Israelis believe him to be genuine. Gorbanifahr's earlier game plan delivered Reverend Weir. He has proposed that we "deliver something" so that he can retain credibility with the regime in Tehran. He even suggested that the weapons delivered be useful only to the Army or Air Force (not the Revolutionary Guards) and that they b "technically disabled." He urged that, if improved HAWKs were not feasible, to at least keep the door open by some kind of delivery between now and the end of the week. He said we must recognize that if TOWs are provided that they will probably go t the Revolutionary Guards.

The Israelis have willingly consented to "kick-back" arrangement which allows Israeli control over Gorbanifahr and ████████ Israel believes strongly in using any means to bridge into Iran. Their last three governments over a four year period have been consistent in this theme.

Whether we trust Gorbanifahr or not, he is irrefutably the deepest penetration we have yet achieved into the current Irani Government. There is nothing in any ████████████ which contradicts what he has told us or the Israelis over the past several months. Much of our ability to influence the course of events in achieving a more moderate Iranian Government depends the validity of what Gorbanifahr has told us -- and his credibility as one who can "deliver" on what the Iranians need. While it is possible that Gorbanifahr is doubling us or simply lining his own pockets, we have relatively little to lose in meeting his proposal; i.e., the Israelis start delivering TOWs and no hostages are recovered. On the other hand, a supply operation now could very well trigger results he claims.

~~TOP SECRET~~
Declassify: OADR

TOP SECRET

DOCUMENT 77: Oliver North, Memorandum for Robert McFarlane and John Poindexter, "Next Steps," December 9, 1985.

PAGE 3 OF 4

2

N 29748

The current situation is one in which information is incomplete, the motivation of the various participants uncertain, and our operational control tenuous in that we have had to deal exclusively through the Israelis. The near term risk to the hostages has undoubtedly been increased by Iranian "expectations" arising from earlier decisions to proceed with deliveries and by the increasing pressure against Hizballah in Lebanon.

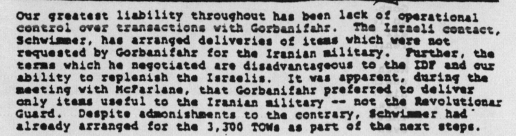

Our greatest liability throughout has been lack of operational control over transactions with Gorbanifahr. The Israeli contact, Schwimmer, has arranged deliveries of items which were not requested by Gorbanifahr for the Iranian military. Further, the terms which he negotiated are disadvantageous to the IDF and our ability to replenish the Israelis. It was apparent, during the meeting with McFarlane, that Gorbanifahr preferred to deliver only items useful to the Iranian military -- not the Revolutionar Guard. Despite admonishments to the contrary, Schwimmer had already arranged for the 3,300 TOWs as part of the next steps.

Schwimmer's arrangements would have exchanged the 3,300 TOWs for three hostages at a price which would not allow the IDF to recoup expenses, thus complicating our ability to replenish IDF stores. In short, most of the problems with this endeavor have arisen because we have been unable to exercise operational control over arrangements or their expected outcome. For example, at the meeting with McFarlane we learned for the first time that the Iranians want desperately to return the 18 basic HAWK missiles which are still in Tehran. All agree that we should only do so if the in-bound aircraft has something aboard which the Iranians want. At the end of the meeting it was agreed that we would "get back" to Gorbanifahr quickly as to our next steps. He departed for Geneva to brief ▓▓▓▓▓▓▓▓▓▓▓▓ to the effect that "technical difficulties remain to be overcome before further deliveries can be scheduled."

The question which now must be asked is should we take a relatively small risk by allowing (encouraging) a small Israeli-originated delivery of TOWs and hope for the best or should we do nothing? If such a delivery were to take place, we would have to plan to replenish the Israeli stocks on a "routine" basis to avoid drawing attention.

C

DOCUMENT 77: Oliver North, Memorandum for Robert McFarlane and John Poindexter, "Next Steps," December 9, 1985.

PAGE 4 OF 4

~~TOP SECRET~~

N 28749

If we are to prevent the death or more of the hostages in the near future, we appear to have four options available:

● Accept Gorbanifahr/Schwimmer's game plan:

  -- Stretch and replenishment to Israel over several month making it routine.

  -- 1,100 TOWs are maximum risk materielly. Cost and cove can be maintained by selling from stock to Israel over time.

  -- If hostages are recovered disclosure doesn't hurt much

● Allow the Israelis to deliver 400-500 TOWs while picking up 18 HAWKs in effort to show good faith to both factions in Iran:

  -- This could cause Iran to deliver a hostage as sign of cooperation. It will also serve to boost Gorbanifahr' reputation.

  -- Israel could do this unilaterally and seek routine replacements.

  -- This gives U.S. more breathing time (maybe!).

● Do nothing:

  -- Very dangerous since U.S. has, in fact, pursued earli Presidential decision to play along with Gorbanifahr' plan. U.S. reversal now in mid-stream could ignite Iranian fire -- hostages would be our minimum losses.

There is a fifth option which has not yet been discussed. We could, with an appropriate covert action Finding, commence deliveries ourselves, using Secord as our conduit to control Gorbanifahr and delivery operations. This proposal has considerable merit in that we will reduce our vulnerabilities i the replenishment of Israeli stocks and can provide items like the Improved HAWK (PIP II) which the Iranian Air Force wants an the Israelis do not have. Finally, Secord can arrange for thir country nationals to conduct a survey of ground and air militar requirements which is what Gorbanifahr has been attempting to obtain from the Israelis for nearly three months.

~~TOP SECRET~~

TOP SECRET

DOCUMENT 78: John Poindexter, Notes Prepared for Briefing of the President on Meeting with Amiram Nir, January 2, 1986.

PAGE 1 OF 3

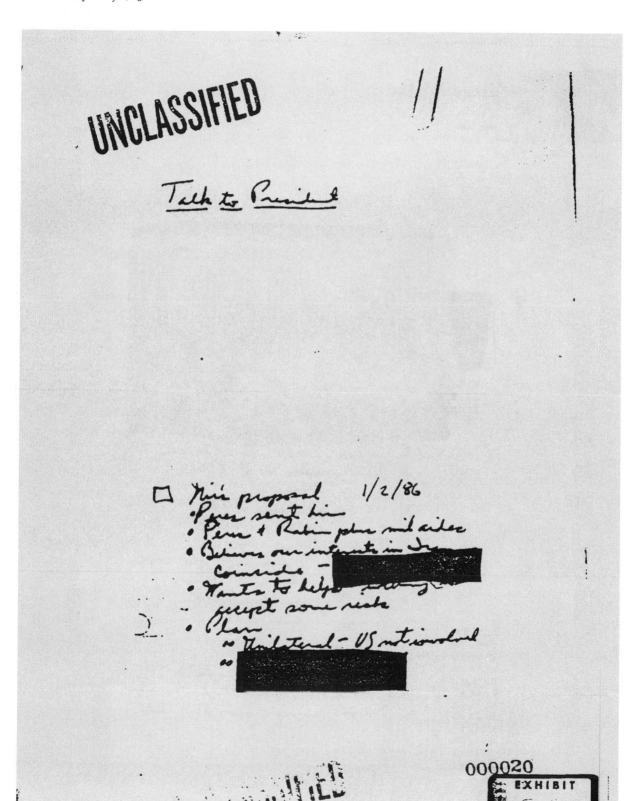

DOCUMENT 78: John Poindexter, Notes Prepared for Briefing of the President on Meeting with
Amiram Nir, January 2, 1986.

PAGE 2 OF 3

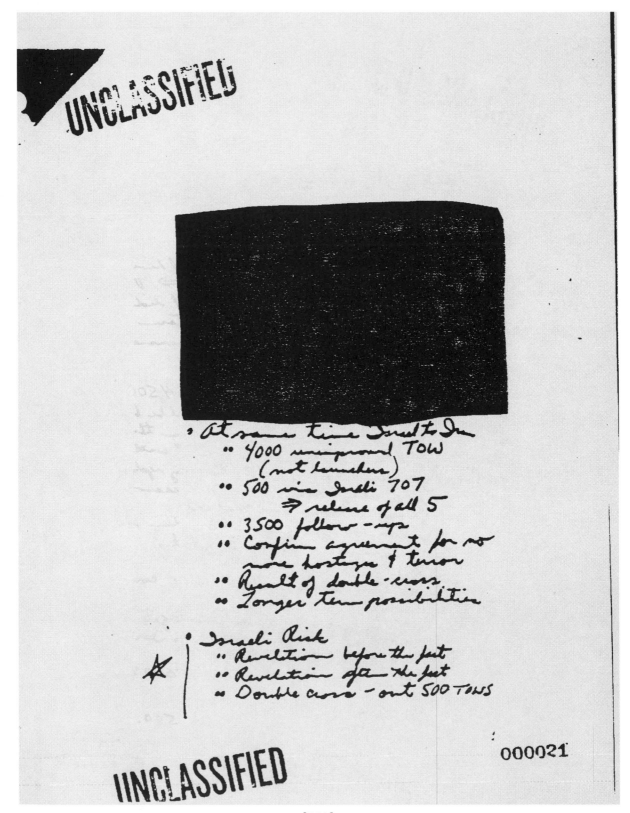

UNCLASSIFIED

• At same time Israel to Iran
  •• 4000 unimproved TOW
     (not launchers)
  •• 500 via Israeli 707
        ⇒ release of all 5
  •• 3500 follow-ups
  •• Confirm agreement for no
     more hostages & terror
  •• Result of double-cross
  •• Longer term possibilities

• Israeli Risk
  •• Revelation before the fact
  •• Revelation after the fact
  •• Double cross - out 500 TOWS

UNCLASSIFIED

000021

DOCUMENT 78: John Poindexter, Notes Prepared for Briefing of the President on Meeting with Amiram Nir, January 2, 1986.

PAGE 3 OF 3

UNCLASSIFIED

- Want from US
  - •• If discovered and have to acknowledge ⇒ US was aware and didn't object for long term reasons (or expansion of other reasons

  - •• Sell replacements 4500
    - ASAP - Could be before due to Syrian threat
    - PREPOS ASAP with regular steady replacement
    - 1/3 of war reserve
    - If not get 5, then no commitment.

DIFFERENCES
  - Better & more effective cover plan
  - No risks to US if don't get 5
  - Only 500 at risk for Israel
  - PREPOS possibility

VIEW AS TEST OF INTENTIONS.

COVERT FINDING
  - Already present for 500.

: 000022

DOCUMENT 79: Oliver North, Action Memorandum for John Poindexter, "Operation Recovery," January 24, 1986.

PAGE 1 OF 6

UNCLASSIFIED

~~TOP SECRET~~

Non-Log

NATIONAL SECURITY COUNCIL
WASHINGTON, D.C. 10506

N   9688

January 24, 1986

~~TOP SECRET~~

SENSITIVE

PLEASE DESTROY AFTER READING

EXHIBIT
DRC-15

ACTION

MEMORANDUM FOR JOHN M. POINDEXTER

FROM: OLIVER L. NORTH

SUBJECT: Operation Recovery

Please find attached at Tab A a <u>notional</u> timeline for major events in Operation Recovery. To my knowledge the only persons completely cognizant of this schedule are:

    John Poindexter
    Don Fortier
    Oliver North

    John McMahon
    Clair George
    ████████████

    Dewey Clarridge

    Richard Secord
    Amiram Nir
    Prime Minister Shimon Peres

RECEIVED
FBI
NOV 29 1986
Copy is Receipt

Partially Declassified/Released on 17 AUG 1987 under provisions of E.O. 12356 by B. Reger, National Security Council

RECOMMENDATION

That you privately discuss the attachment with the President.

       Approve _____   Disapprove _____

TC @ 7

Attachment
    Tab A - <u>Notional</u> Timeline for Operation Recovery

RECEIVED

PLEASE DESTROY AFTER READING

NC . . .

(3579)

Copy is Receipt

~~TOP SECRET~~
Declassify: OADR

~~TOP SECRET~~

SENSITIVE

UNCLASSIFIED

DOCUMENT 79: Oliver North, Action Memorandum for John Poindexter, "Operation Recovery," January 24, 1986.

PAGE 2 OF 6

~~TOP SECRET~~ UNCLASSIFIED

~~TOP SECRET~~

SENSITIVE

PLEASE DESTROY AFTER READING

N 9690

Notional Timeline for Operation Recovery

Friday, January 24

-- CIA provide cube and weight data to Copp for a/c loading.

-- CIA prepare intel sample for pass to Gorba.

-- Copp provide a/c tail # to CIA for pickup at ███████

-- ██

Saturday, January 25

-- Dispatch intel sample to Gorba via Charlie Allen.

Sunday, January 26

-- C. Allen deliver intel sample to Gorba at Churchill Hotel, London.

-- Copp finalize a/c requirements w/air carrier in Oklahoma.

██

Monday, January 27

-- Gorba place intel sample on 1300 GMT flight to Tehran fm Frankfurt, Germany.

Wednesday, January 29

-- Gorba transfer funds for purchase/transport of 1000 basic TOWs to Israeli account at Credit Suisse Bank, Geneva.

-- Israeli account manager automatically transfers deposit fm Israeli account to Copp account in same bank (bank record keeping transaction).

-- Copp's account manager automatically transfers $6M to CIA account in same bank (bank record keeping transaction).

PLEASE DESTROY AFTER READING

~~TOP SECRET~~ UNCLASSIFIED

SENSITIVE

Declassify: OADR

DOCUMENT 79: Oliver North, Action Memorandum for John Poindexter, "Operation Recovery," January 24, 1986.

PAGE 3 OF 6

UNCLASSIFIED
~~TOP SECRET~~

N

~~TOP SECRET~~   2   SENSITIVE

**RECEIVED
FBI
NOV 29 1986**

PLEASE DESTROY AFTER READING

Copy 's Receipt

Thursday, January 30

-- CIA transfers $6M to DOD account by wire service transaction.

-- CIA orders movement of 1000 TOW missiles fm DOD storage facility Anniston, Alabama, to ▮▮▮▮▮▮▮▮

-- CIA bills Copp account $26K for cost of moving 1000 TOW missiles fm Anniston, Alabama, to ▮▮▮▮▮▮▮▮

Friday, January 31

-- ▮▮▮▮▮▮▮▮▮▮▮▮▮▮▮▮▮▮▮▮▮▮▮▮▮▮▮▮▮▮▮▮

-- ▮▮▮▮▮▮▮▮▮▮▮▮▮▮▮▮▮▮▮▮▮▮▮▮▮▮▮▮▮▮▮▮

Sunday, February 2

-- ▮▮▮▮▮▮▮▮▮▮▮▮▮▮▮▮▮▮▮▮▮▮▮▮▮▮

-- Copp travels to Israel for site survey of transfer point (Eliat, Israel).

-- Copp proceeds to rendezvous in Rome w/Clarridge to establish command post.

Monday, February 3

-- ▮▮▮▮▮▮▮▮▮▮▮▮▮▮▮▮▮▮▮▮▮▮▮▮▮▮▮▮▮▮▮▮

-- ▮▮▮▮▮▮▮▮▮▮▮▮▮▮▮▮▮▮▮▮▮▮▮▮▮▮▮▮▮▮▮▮

-- ▮▮▮▮▮▮▮▮▮▮▮▮▮▮▮▮▮▮▮▮▮▮▮▮▮▮▮▮▮▮▮▮

PLEASE DESTROY AFTER READING
UNCLASSIFIED

~~TOP SECRET~~   SENSITIVE

DOCUMENT 79: Oliver North, Action Memorandum for John Poindexter, "Operation Recovery," January 24, 1986.

PAGE 4 OF 6

UNCLASSIFIED

~~TOP SECRET~~   N   9692

~~TOP SECRET~~   3   SENSITIVE

RECEIVED

NOV 29 1986

PLEASE DESTROY AFTER READING

Copy : R

Tuesday, February 4

-- 1000 TOWs sanitized and prepared for shipping ███████

-- Copp a/c packers arrive ███████ and arrange for Copp a/c to lift TOWs fm Kelly AF Base, San Antonio, TX, on CIA contract.

Wednesday, February 5

-- Copp a/c arrives Kelly AF Base for loading.

-- CIA provides remainder of first intel sample to Gorba at Iranian Embassy in Bonn, Germany.

Thursday, February 6

-- Copp a/c commence lifting TOWs fm Kelly AF Base to transfer point at Eliat, Israel.

-- Israeli AF "sterilized" 707 a/c arrives at transfer point for loading.

-- Copp aircrew arrives Eliat, Israel, to pilot Israeli a/c.

-- ████████████████████████

-- Remainder of first intel sample flown fm Germany to Tehran in diplomatic pouch on scheduled Iran Airways flight.

Friday, February 7

-- Israeli "sterile" a/c piloted by Copp crew commences movement of TOWs fm Eliat to Bandar Abbas, Iran, via Red Sea route.

-- ████████████████████████

PLEASE DESTROY AFTER READING

UNCLASSIFIED

~~TOP SECRET~~   SENSITIVE

[289]

DOCUMENT 79: Oliver North, Action Memorandum for John Poindexter, "Operation Recovery," January 24, 1986.

PAGE 5 OF 6

UNCLASSIFIED

~~TOP SECRET~~ N 9693

~~TOP SECRET~~   4   SENSITIVE

<u>PLEASE DESTROY AFTER READING</u>

RECEIVED
FRI
NOV 29 1986
Copy is Rec'd at

<u>Saturday, February 8</u>

--   Delivery of 1000 TOWs completed.

--   25 Hizballah released by Lahad.

--   Returning Israeli a/c pickup 18 HAWKs at Tehran airport for return to Israel.

<u>Sunday, February 9</u>

--   All U.S. hostages released to U.S./British or Swiss Embassy.

--   Second group of 25 Hizballah released by Lahad.

--   Israelis return $5.4M to Gorba when HAWKs land in Israel.

<u>Monday, February 10</u>

--   Gorba transfers funds to Israel account for purchase/transportation of 3000 TOWs (amount transferred is sufficient to cover purchase of 508 additional TOWs owed to Israel for Weir release and all transportation costs).

--   Israelis transfer funds to Copp account at Credit Suisse Bank, Geneva.

--   Copp transfers funds to CIA account for purchase/transportation of 3508 TOWs ($21.048M).

--   Four (4) remaining Lebanese-Jews released by Hizballah.

<u>Tuesday, February 11</u>   (Anniversary of Iranian-Islamic Revolution)

--   Khomheini steps down.

--   CIA transfers $21.048M to DOD account for purchase of 3508 TOWs at $6K each.

--   CIA starts moving TOWs to ████████████████ fm Anniston, Alabama, in lots of 1000.

PLEASE DESTROY AFTER READING   UNCLASSIFIE

DOCUMENT 79: Oliver North, Action Memorandum for John Poindexter, "Operation Recovery," January 24, 1986.

PAGE 6 OF 6

UNCLASSIFIED

~~TOP SECRET~~   N   9694

~~TOP SECRET~~   5   SENSITIVE

PLEASE DESTROY AFTER READING

RECEIVED FBI NOV 29 1986 Copy is Rare of

Thursday, February 13

-- Copp packers return to ████████████

Tuesday, February 18

-- Copp a/c pickup 1000 TOWs at Kelly AF Base, Texas; deliver to transfer point (Eliat).

-- Israeli "sterilized" 707 a/c w/Copp crew commences delivery of 1000 TOWs to Iran.

Thursday, February 20

-- Copp a/c pickup 1000 TOWs at Kelly AF Base, Texas; deliver to transfer point (Eliat).

-- Israeli "sterilized" 707 a/c w/Copp crew commences delivery of 1000 TOWs to Iran.

Saturday, February 22

-- Copp a/c pickup 1000 TOWs at Kelly AF Base, Texas; deliver, to transfer point (Eliat).

-- Israeli "sterilized" 707 a/c w/Copp crew commences delivery of 1000 TOWs to Iran.

Monday, February 24

-- Copp a/c returns to ████████████ pickup 508 TOWs for delivery to Israel.

-- Collett (British hostage) and Italian hostages released and Buckley remains returned.

Tuesday, February 25

-- Second sample of intel provided to Gorba at Iranian Embassy in Bonn, Germany.

-- ██

PLEASE DESTROY AFTER READING

UNCLASSIFIED

~~TOP SECRET~~   SENSITIVE

DOCUMENT 80: George Cave, Memorandum for Chief of CIA Near East Division,
"Meeting with G[h]orba[nifar]," April 3, 1986.

PAGE 1 OF 2

Partially Declassified/Released on e N

Meeting with Ghorbanifar of E.O. 12356

by B. Reger, National Security Coun — UNCLASSIFIED

REVIEWED FOR RELEA:

Date 14 JAN 1987   12-95

Ch 12 #9

b]. One of key issues that came up which Gorba alleges made an
lerstanding difficult was his missing reports to us. He said that he
—d turned over to adam a two page farsi report which listed all the
the iranian demands and what they were prepared to do. he wrote the
farsi report because he wanted to be sure that he got everything right.
he said that he also wrote a five page report in english which was
more detailed. thise were supposeded to have been sent via dhl along
wh with the parts list. Goode z told gorba that all he got was the
parts list. gorba said that he wrote the reports on the plane from
Tehran. he gave the reports to adam in london who said that he would
send them to us. there seems to be only two conclusions either the
xx reports don't exist. in whihc case maybe adam and gorba are playing
games with u.s, or the reports exist and after reading them, adam
decided that the demands were too great and we would not agree to them,
therefore he shortstopped the reports.

2. One of Gorba's most interesting offers was to offer us ▮▮▮▮▮
passports for the trip. each one would cos ▮▮▮▮▮▮▮▮ the passports
would be genuine and the price includes a genuine drivers license and
a bank account.

3. there was the problem of the venue. Gorba said that they can
not xxxxxxxx recieve us in kish. the hrs problem is that the desalinization
plant has borken down, the buildings have not been used since the
revolution. Also, no planes have landed on the strip in two years.
he said that a meeting on kish would place great logistical problems on
them in tehran. MAte; in the last phone conversation betweenxxxxxxx
d ibrahim spoke of the meeting still being held in kish. we
reed to consider possiblity of tehran, but wanted them to re-examine
kish and bandar -abbas. we said that plane must be with us for commo.
gorba said that would be no problem. we also said that we would

probablly want to arrive in bandar abbas. for some reason, gorba
insists that adam told him that we would be using ▮▮▮▮▮ passports.
we told him that this gave us some heartburn, but not to worry, we
would take care of the documentation if even if it meant being ▮▮▮▮▮
▮▮▮▮▮ gorba said that he will need some details on the plan,
tail number registration etc. we told him it would be 707 and not trace
ble to thexxx to us. we will devise way of getting him the tail
number.

4. we discussed the schedule in some detail. we proposed arriving
about 7-8 days after the money is deposited. this would give us time
to have the planed load of spares positioned in europe. we then haggled
for hours about what was included and what would be negotiated in tehran.
we stuck to our position that once the release takes place we would
order plane to launch and it should arrive in bandar abbas with 8
hours. it would then turn around and bring in the rest of the spares.
we are tentavilye committed to dleiver the 3,000 volswagons about
10 days later. gorba pressed for new additions. the new batteries
we said were no longer in inventoory. the radars we would discuss
in theran as they would have to be shipped by ship anyway. gorba kept
insisting that we bring some of spares with us and wt kept insisting
that we wouldn't although a small sample is an option.   B

5. they agenda for the discussion with the other side in tehran will
include syria, ▮▮▮▮▮▮ and the soviet union. we will give him
a short brief on the ussr on 4 april which he will convey to ● and company

UNCLASSIFIED

DOCUMENT 80: George Cave, Memorandum for Chief of CIA Near East Division,
"Meeting with G[h]orba[nifar]," April 3, 1986.

PAGE 2 OF 2

in discussing the whole transaction we insisted that he had to play the
key role in making it all work. after long haggling, he agreed to pre
the schedule to ▊ as outlined by us. we have got take a present, in
addition to korans, it might be a good idea to tack all the
spare parts for one unit with us. and present this as a present. we
told gorba to check with them about the availability of functioning
test and calibration equipment and the technical skill toluse the
equipment. our observation is that they have not successfully fired
a hawk for some time and in fact have had numerous missfires.

6. possibly the best indication that we might be getting
somewhere is that towards the end, gorba began discussing his cut.
goode told him that he could add on whatever he thinks irght for his
cut to the final price. he said that he had spent 300,000 dollars
already to grease the skids etc. ▊▊▊▊▊▊ it would appear that
he now feels that the deal is entering its final stages.

7. gorba stated that there is considerable pressure on the iranians
to do something because the time frame within which they can deliver ou
friends. they feel that fighting is going to break out between the
hizbullah and the syrian army at any time. gorba insists that Iranian
syrian relations are very bad at the moment and will definitely get wor
he claims that iran has stopped delivering oil to syria. believe he
aid that deliveries stopped about 34 days ago.

8. gorba claims that the iranian side is devoting considerable
time to this. the whole thing is being masterminded by rafsenjani behi
the scenes. if the transaction goes, the plan is to have khomieni
issue a fatwa against the taking of hostages. they also have a large nu
of people they wish us to brief. we must get him to discuss more of his
military contacts during his last trip. he warned us about the
primeminister who may be our primary senior contact. he said that he ▊
line ▊ he represents do not like or trust us and we must be aware of tl
at all times. he thought there was a chance that rafsenjani would at
some point put in an appearance, as he will be following everything cl
he on his own part will want us to meet with reps from the conservative
line, particularly farisi.

9. it is still apprsent that they have not given much thought to
how a continuing relationship will be maintained. gorba tried to answer
him but he was not able to cover up the basic truth that they hadn't
gone that far yet.

UNCLASSIFIED

C11N 0513 (page 2)

DOCUMENT 81: John Poindexter, PROFS Note to Oliver North, "Private Blank Check," April 16, 1986.

PAGE 1 OF 1

UNCLASSIFIED

From: NSJMP   --CPUA
To: NSOLN   --CPUA

Date and time   04/16/86 19:02:42

N 9212

*** Reply to note of 04/16/86 16:40

-- SECRET --

NOTE FROM: JOHN POINDEXTER
Subject: PRIVATE BLANK CHECK
You may go ahead and go, but I want several points made clear to them. There are not to be any parts delivered until all the hostages are free in accordance with the plan that you layed out for me before. None of this half shipment before any are released crap. It is either all or nothing. Also you may tell them that the President is getting very annoyed at their continual stalling. He will not agree to any more changes in the plan. Either they agree finally on the arrangements that have been discussed or we are going to permanently cut off all contact. If they really want to save their asses from the Soviets, they should get on board. I am beginning to suspect that
        doesn't have much authority.

cc: NSPBT   --CPUA   PAUL THOMPSON

_5/6/87_

UNCLASSIFI

EXHIBIT
ON-276

426

UNCLASSIFIE 13-24 *[handwritten: 1, Foothics, 24 7, 48, 67 N 1483]*

T... SECRET SENSITIVE

This is an account of the U.S. mission to Tehran from May 25 through May 28, together with some comments and observations. The U.S. team was headed by Mcfarland with Goode, Mcgrath, Miller and O'neil making up the rest of the team. A communicator also accompanied the team on the trip into Tehran.

The team arrived in Tehran at 0830 hours on 25 May and was left to cool its collective heels for about two hours. During this period the Iranian Air force put on a show in which one by one a squadron of F-4's took off from Mehrabad airport. The planes carried no ordanance and according to the Mehrabad base commander they were flying training missions. According to Gorba, the Iranians recently recieved a shipment of F-4 spare parts and the flights were training flights to bring some of their pilots up to snuff. The first Iranian official to show up who was connected with this operation was ████████ who was already known to the air crew. The base Commander ████████ also put in an appearance and made pleasant conversation. He was also their at our departure. It is unclear how much he was cut in on he operation. Gorba showed up about half an hour after our arrival. He said that we had arrived an hour early and this was the reason there was no one at the airport to recieve us. We were later told that the recieving party had gone to the miliary side of the base expecting us to park our plane there. Gorba told us that for security reasons we were being given the entire top floor of the Hiton Hotel, now renamed the Istiqlal(independence). ████████ finally arrived and after some small talk we departed for the hotel. While still at the airport, Gorba informed us that everything was going well and the Iranians had already dispatched a representative to secure the release of the hostages.

While on the plane Mcfarland, Goode and O'neil rehearsed a discussion of the briefs which we would run through in the hotel for the benefit of Iranian coverage of the American delegation. In short the play acting was designed to give the brief good sourcing. We expressed our concern out loud that the Iranians would not believe the Soviet invasion plan. We worried hat we could not indicate the real source of the information due to said source's sensitivity. The sensitive source, dubbed "Vladimir" by Goode was described as a Major General who had taken part in two of the war games on the invasion of Iran. O'neil subsequently gave ████ a brief glance at the briefing book to whet his appetite and give them something to which they could tie their audio coverage. None of the three briefs were given.

The first substantive meeting took place late in the afternoon of 24 May. The Iranian side consisted of ████████ a named ████████ who was introduced ████████ and a man named ████████ whom Gorba described as being in their intelligence service. This initial meeting was hostile with the Iranians listing past sins of the United States etc. The meeting ended with what appeared to be little chance of any progress. Basically the American side insisted on adherence to the agreement as we understood it, and the Iranians inisisting that America must do more to atone for its sins. At the end on the Meeting, ████████ set the tone by saying that even if no progress is made during the discussions, we were their guests and Iranians honored guests.

The first crisis occurred later in the evening when the Iranians

UNCLASSIFIED   N 1484

insisted on removing the one crew member who was staying on the plane.
They insisted that we had agreed to this at the earlier meeting.
McFarland's response to this was that we pack up and leave. O'neil
consulted with a young man named ████ who stayed in the hotel with us
during the visit. He had been intrduced to us as the one person to
contact to solve any problems which might come up. ████ was very
upset that we consulted with ████ about the plane and referred to it as
a breach of secuity on our part. He insisted that their primary concern
was our security and this was adduced as the reason we were to stay
couped up on the 15th floor of the hotel. We succeeded in getting a
crew member back on the plane the following day. It was clear that the
Iranians only wanted to search the plane. The search seemed to satisfy
them and we had no subsequent problems on this issue. ████ was also
very upset that we had our own communications(this was reason we gave
for having a man on the plane at all times). He argued that Iranian
intelligence would pick up the signals and this could jeopardize the
security of whole opeation. He said that they would put what ever we
wished at our disposal including a dedicated telex. We insisted on our
own commo and he gradually backed off. The hostile attitude of the
Iranians on the first day left us a little uneasy.
   On Monday we were left to our own devices throughout most of the day.
We finally had another meeting late in the afternoon. At this meeting,
another Iranian was introduced a█ ████. He is several cuts above
the other members of the Iranian side. He is obviously well educated
and very cultured. At this meeting, McFarland outlined the reasons we
were in Tehran. We wished to lay the groundwork for a new political and
strategic relationship between our two countries. We considered the
arms supplies as an example of our good faith and we insisted on the
release of the hostages as an example of their good faith. ████ made
the appropriate noises and said that Iran was prepared to have normal
relations with every country,except two, Israel ans South Africa.
McFarland outlined our conceraans about soviet designs on Iran and told
the Iranians that we woud provide them with a briefing which would
detail our reasons for concern. He also spoke of Sadam Hussayn's
December visit to Moscow in which the Soviets promised Sadam that they
would do everything to prevent Iraq from Losing the war.████ tried
some of the usual Iranian bravado by claiming that if the soviets
attacked, the Iranian soldiers would do well against them because of
their devotion to shoheda. This was followed by a load of shit on
shoheda. On the Iranian side ████ concentrated on the Hostage issue
and ████ on the arms transactions. ████ said that they had
already heard from their man in Lebanon who said that the group holding
the hostages had insisted on several conditions as follows: (1) Israeli
withdrawal from the Golan heights (2) Israeli withdrawal fom Southern
lebanon (3) Removal of Lahad to East Beirut (4) freeing of the
imprisoned Shi'ites in Kuwait, and (5) re-imbursement for the expenses
of holding the hostages. ████ graciously volunteered that Iran would
pay these expenses. ████ argued that we were not upholding our part
of the deal because we had promised to bring half the parts with us(no
such promise wa made). He did not repeat his sunday claim that the
parts we brought were used. He insisted tht we bring the rest of the
parts before the release of the hostages. We stuck to the terms of the
agreement. When things seemed to come unstuck, McFarland got up and
said that we would leave if they couldn't uphold their end of the

UNCLASSIFIED   N   1485

bargin. This upset ⬭⬭⬭ who said that McFarland was very f.rm and
stern cond-rol and they as Iranians liked to negotiate in a more
gentle narml atmosphere. What was encouraging about monday's meetings
was that the Iranians were far more friendly than on Sunday.
    By this time it was clear that McFarland was not going to meet any of
the principles that had been mentioned by Gorba. McFarland then told
the Iranians that they could continue negotiations with the American
staff and get back to him when some kind of agreement was reached. ⬭⬭
⬭⬭ made a big issue of the problems our presence in Tehran caused
them. He stated that a senior official could not afford the political
risk of a meeting with McFarland. He pointed out that it was Bazergan's
meeting with Brezhinsky that brought down the Bazergan government.
Based on ⬭⬭⬭s comments we can take it as a certainty that Khomieni
was not breifed on our presence or our mission. He would have to give
his blessing before any senior official would dare to meet wih a senior
American official. We ran into the same problem in our discussions with
the Bazergan governent. Gorba also let drop that ⬭⬭⬭⬭ one
of the senior personages that he had supposedly arranged for us to meet
was also not aware of our presence.
    Tuesday was a day of marathon negotiations with the Iranians stalling
for time and trying to get the most out of the American delegation. The
American delegation stuck by the terms of the original agreement and
insisted that after the terms of the Frankfurt agreement were met, we
would meet and discuss in detail their needs and the outline of our two
countries' future relations. The American delegation proposed a
specific timing for a subsequent meeting. During the late afternoon it
was agreed that the American team would draw up an agreement which would
be discussed later in the evening. To save time O'neil began working on
a translation which was later completed by he and Gorba.
    During tuesday's negotiations, all the demands of the hostages
holders evaporated except for the demand for the release of the Shi'ite
prisoners in Kuwait. Goode handled this part of the negotiations by
firmly stating that the United States would not interfere in the
internal affairs of Kuwait, particularly in an instance where Kuwaiti
due legal pocess had been carried out. We would however seek to better
the condition of Shia prisoners through the good offices of
international organizations such as the Red Cross and the Red Crescent.
Goode warned that as far as the well being of the Shi'ite prisoners in
Kuwait is concerned, there had better not be any more terrorist activity
directed at the Royal family in Kuwait.
    The draft agreement was the subject of intense negotiations with the
Iranians making some counter proposals which were designed to gain them
more time. Talks broke off around midnight with the Iranian delegation
saying it wanted to caucus. For the next two hours, heated discussions
were held within the Iranian delegation. ⬛⬛⬛⬛⬛⬛ both said
that the other would be responsible if nothing comes of the
negotiations. Finally, shortly before two on Wednesday morning, ⬭⬭
asked to see McFarland. He wanted assurances that we would deliver the
remaining spare parts two hours after the hostages were released,and
would stay after the arrival of the spare parts to discuss additional
Iranian needs. He also asked for more time to get control of the
hostages. McFarland gave ⬛⬛⬛ until 0630 wednesday morning to arrange
for the release of the hostages. The American delegation retired to
grab a couple of hours sleep knowing that we had at least out-frazzled

UNCLASSIFIED   N 1486

them.
     The first Iranian to put in an appearance Wednesday morning was
████████ who looked totally dejected and refused to make any comment
other than salam. The fact that Gorba did not show up also was a clear
indication that things had not gone too well. ████████put in an
appearance to say that they were working hard on the release, but would
need more time. He also asked if we would accept two being released
immediately and two more afer the delivery. He was told that we would
leave for the airport after finishing breakfast. We also heard from the
aircrew that the plane was beng refueled. This had been worrisome for
the Iranians had stalled on refueling the plane. ████████
██
████████████████ The American delegation departed the hotel at about
0730. ████ and ████████ accompanied the delegation to the Airport.
████did not put in an appearance after his final talk with Mcfarland.
At planeside, ████████asked to speak with McFarland. He asked for more
time saying that arranging for the release was a very delicate and time
consuming effort. McFarland told him that the plane with the spare parts
was in the air, but if no word on the release of the hostages was heard
by 0930, the plane would turn around and return to its base. O'neil was
the last of the delegation to board the plane before take-off and he and
████████had one last exchange. ████████admitted that the hostages
were not under their control. O'neil told him to get them under Iranian
control. ████████said that they would seek to do this and that he
would send Gorba to Europe to maintain contact with us. Our aircraft
departed at 0900.
     The above account is O'neil's outline recollection of what transpired
and may differ somewhat from what others recall, but it is needed for·
O'neil's comments and recomendation to make sense.

COMMENTS:

     1. If Gorba does appear, we must press him for positive
identification of the people with whom we talked. Since████████
actually forget his alias during the course of one evening's
discussions, we can assume that the others were using aliases,
particularly since we have no traces on ████████ ████████ may not be a
true name. ████████is an ████ name, but ████does not have an
████accent. He is definitely from South Tehran. If ████████ is an
alias it may explain why ████████have not been able to identify
such a person ████████
     2. It is quite possible that the Iranian side was negotiating
under the impression that we were only interested in a deal for the
hostages. This would explain why they tried so hard to get us to do
more in exchange for the hostages, i.e., the 20 hawk batteries and the
18 additional hipar radars. It was therefore a good idea to leave a
translation of the draft agreeement with them as it will give them
something to chew on. McFarland issued a stern warning that we are
getting fed up with overatures from them that don't pan out. We are
interested in a long term political and strategic relationship, and if
Iran does not pick up on this opportunity, it may be years before there
is another one.
     3.Ramadan was certainly a factor in how the negotiations went.

UNCLASSIFIED   N 1487

also the problem caused by not being able to let anyone in a postion of power. The people we were negotiating with were a couple of rungs down the ladder. The fact that ███████ breath could curl rhino hide was no help either. On the positive side was the change in the attitude of the Iranian delegation. By tuesday they were begging us to stay.

4. We also have the problem of a dishonest interlocutor. The Iranian side made it clear that they were upset with Gorba. On tuesday, ██████old O'neil that one of the problems in our negotiations was the fact that prior to our meeting, Gorba gave each side a different picture of the structure of the deal. O'neil made the point to ██████ that the letters they recieved were from Gorba, not the U.S. government. We will have to lean heavily on Gorba in the future.

5. Since both Gorba and ███████ stand to make a lot of money out of this deal, they presumably will work hard to bring it off. Gorba has very special reasons for seeing that the deal goes through. The serious problem we must address is whether the Iranians can gain control of the hostages. ██████████████████ This could be our real problem. The Iranians side may be most willing, but unable to gain control.

RECOMENDATION

Through hindsight it would have been better for Goode and O'neil to have gone in first to handle the initial negotiations. We should not have subjected a senior U.S. official to the indignities he was forced to endure. We have made the point to the Iranians that the draft agreement must be finally negotiated by senior responsible officials from both sides. If we have a subsequent response from the Iranian side it is strongly recomended that Goode and O'neil meet with the Iranian side somewhere in Europe to continue the negotiations.

TOP SECRET SENSITIVE

DOCUMENT 83: Richard Secord, KL-43 Encrypted Message to Oliver North on Meeting in Brussels with Iranian Representatives, August 26, 1986.

PAGE 1 OF 2

UNCLASSIFIED

~~TOP SECRET~~

Chapt.
Footnic 14-77

Copp: 8/26/86 1320

N 2801

261800Z Aug 86.

Partially Declassified / Released on ___ May 87
under provisions of E.O. 12356
by B. Razu, National Security Council

1. Following is summary report of three long meetings -- total circa eight hours -- with Iranian gp visiting Brussels. Meetings took place August 25 in three segments. Iranian side was ███████████ of Rafsanjani █████████████████████████

Our side included me ███ true name -- Abe in true name, and ███████ our agent. Meetings constituted comprehensive tour de force regarding Iran/Iraq War, Iranian views of U.S. and other western policies, Soviet activities, activities of nearly all important Iran government figures, hostage matters, activities in the Hague, and Iranian forces equipment and materiel shortages.

2. Special interest items included claim that ██████████ have recently tried to meet with ████ -- he has declined -- he wants to deal with the Presidents representatives. ████ is very sharp, ████████████ speaks no English. ████████████████████ claims Rafsanjani now heads supreme war council and aims to terminate war but in little more favorable military situation for Iran than current. They badly need air defense items, armor spares, TOWs, gun barrels, helo spares, and ████████████. I told them all things negotiable if we can clear the hostage matter quickly. ████ knew great deal about McFarlane msn to Thn. He also knows all about ████████ Gorba, Isareli connection, and this gps financial

~~TOP SECRET~~

UNCLASSIFIED

(939)

N 1158
12/8/86
KL

DOCUMENT 83: Richard Secord, KL-43 Encrypted Message to Oliver North on Meeting in Brussels with Iranian Representatives, August 26, 1986.

PAGE 2 OF 2

TOP SECRET   2   N 2802

~~TOP SECRET~~

greed. Gorba was nastly classified as a crook. ▮▮▮wealth of
current of information but also volunteers to discuss hostage
matter and USG connection with ▮▮▮ in next 10 days. He will
then return to Brussels for meeting with us. ▮▮▮ said
categorically he would not screw up ▮▮▮ efforts but would
carefully examine them for feasibility. ▮▮▮ will recommend two
courses to ▮▮▮

a.   Assist in current ▮▮▮ effort to release hostages or
     start new effort.

b.   ▮▮▮▮▮▮▮▮▮▮▮▮▮▮▮▮▮▮▮▮▮▮▮
     ▮▮▮▮▮▮▮▮▮▮▮▮▮ says there are many specific
     things USG can do in the Hague and on Voice of America
     programming to help start USG/GOI talks -- he will give us
     documents on these subjects at next meeting.

3. Numerous military supply problems were discussed and I will
detail these for you later this week in Washington. FYI: They
need oil barter deals.

4. My judgement is that we have opened up new and probably much
better channel into Iran. This connection has been effectively
recruited and he wants to start dealing. Recommend you plan on
bringing George to next meeting in two weeks or less.

Rgds, Dick. BT

~~TOP SECRET~~

DOCUMENT 84: Albert Hakim, Memorandum of Understanding, "Translation by Albert Hakim of the Farse [*sic*] Original of the '9 Points,'" October 8, 1986.

PAGE 1 OF 2

Translation by Albert Hakim of

the Farse Original of the "9 Points"

Note: The date is the 16th day of the 7th month of the Iranian
        year which I believe corresponds to 8 October 1986, but
        needs to be checked. It also indicates the discussions
        started in the afternoon and lasted until late at night.

Summation of Us and Hakim

1.   Iran provides funds to Mr. Hakim for 500 TOWs and, if
     willing, Iranians will provide for the Hawk spare
     parts which remain from the previous agreement.

2.   Nine working days from now the 500 TOWs and the Hawk
     spare parts (if accepted by Iran) and the gifted
     medicines will be delivered to Iran.

3.   Before executing Item 4 below, Albert will provide the
     plan for the release of the Kuwaitis (17 persons).

4.   1 1/2 (1 definitely and the 2nd with all effective
     possible effort) American hostages in Lebanon, through
     the effort of Iran, will be released by the Lebanese.

*5. Using the Letter of Credit method, (three to four days
     after delivery of shipment stipulated in Item 2)
     additional 500 TOWs (together with a maximum of 100
     launchers), within four days after the execution of
     Item 4 above, will be delivered to Iran. The method
     of Letter of Credit will be reviewed between Albert
     and *Oliver (ali)* by tomorrow night. Iran will pay
     the funds for 1500 TOWs (the 500 TOWs mentioned above
     plus an additional 1000 TOWs) and the 1000 TOWs will
     be delivered to Iran within nine days.

6.   The United States will start with the technical
     support of the Hawks (material and know-how), update
     of the military intelligence and maps, establishment
     and commissioning of the special communication link.

DOCUMENT 84: Albert Hakim, Memorandum of Understanding, "Translation by Albert Hakim of the Farse [*sic*] Original of the '9 Points,'" October 8, 1986.

PAGE 2 OF 2

and will prepare the chart related to the items
(provided by Mr. _____) indicating price and
delivery to Iran.

Israel and its cover organization, La Had, and
the text written in the Seven Step Document of
Mr. North (illegible)

**7. Before the return of Mr. *No Name* to Tehran, the
subject of the Moslem prisoners (Shia) in Lebanon and
the manner of their release by the involved parties
will be reviewed by Mr. Secord.

8. Iran will continue its effort for creating the grounds
for the release of the rest of the hostages.

9. The steps for delivery of items referred to in the
second part of Item 6 above will start.

*. The Letter of Credit will be opened in favor of
Mr. *Hosein* and he will make the money for the 500
TOWs available by using 80% of the Letter of Credit.

**. After discussion between Mr. Secord and Mr. *Samii* (
it was agreed regarding regarding the Moslem prisoners
that the sentence (text) will be written in the
following manner:

Israel and its . . . . .

*Shakastah = broken
so ordeny person would
for bottle to read —
Bazaari people —*

[303]

VII. "DAMAGE CONTROL": COVERING UP ARMS FOR HOSTAGES

On November 3, 1986, the Lebanese magazine *Al-Shiraa* broke the first public account of Robert McFarlane's secret trip to Teheran. The same day, the Hezbollah faction Islamic Jihad announced that its release the previous day of American hostage David Jacobsen had followed "overtures" from Washington. On November 4, election day for Congress in the United States, Iran's Speaker of the Parliament, Ali Akbar Hashemi Rafsanjani, gave a speech in which he confirmed McFarlane's visit and later added colorful details about the chocolate-covered cake and boxed set of pistols he had brought.

Initially, Reagan administration officials either refused to comment or claimed to know nothing about the revelations. "On the news at this time is the question of the hostages," Vice President Bush noted on November 5 in a personal diary that remained concealed for more than six years. "I'm one of the few people that know fully the details, and there is a lot of flack and misinformation out there. It is not a subject we can talk about.... This is one operation that has been held very, very tight, and I hope it will not leak."[1]

But as more and more information flowed out of the Middle East, leaks began to spring from inside the Reagan administration as well, from officials who had opposed the initiative. Several days later, the dam burst when the *Washington Post* and *Los Angeles Times* published lengthy articles on the arms deals; these went far beyond the original sketchy accounts to implicate the president and his men in a series of weapons transfers to Iran aimed at gaining the release of the American hostages held in Lebanon.[2]

CIRCLING THE WAGONS

The wave of publicity shocked the White House, which had taken every precaution to keep the initiative secret. The president now had to deal with a barrage of daily headlines and lead stories on network news broadcasts, which reflected and added to the public furor that stemmed from the revelation that the administration had been shipping arms to Iran's Ayatollah Khomeini. As a result, Reagan's carefully crafted image as the implacable enemy of terrorism, built largely at the expense of his predecessor Jimmy Carter, threatened to wash away, along with his overall credibility. Public opinion polls soon bore out the administration's fears: within the single month of November, a *New York Times*/CBS News poll found that Reagan's approval ratings had plummeted from 67 percent to 46 percent, the largest single drop for a president ever.[3]

When the story first broke, the inclination of administration decision makers was to respond by dissembling and withholding the facts. Only Secretary of State Shultz officially dissented from this approach. In a cable to John Poindexter on November 4, Shultz opted for making "clear that this was a special, one-time operation based on humanitarian grounds and decided by the President within his Constitutional responsibility."[4] Shultz apparently thought that the McFarlane mission comprised the only direct U.S. arms delivery to Iran.

In his response to the secretary, Poindexter took the opposite stance (Document 85). "I do not believe that now is the time to give the facts to the public," he wrote, citing a variety of reasons, including potential harm to the hostages and a continued opportunity to influence events inside Iran, which he said was in the midst of a "power struggle." At the end of his cable, Poindexter appended press guidance that finessed the question of whether Washington had violated its own weapons ban: "As long as Iran advocates the use of terrorism, the U.S. arms embargo will continue." To Shultz, it was "the kind of tricky and misleading statement that looks great on the surface, but then you start looking at it more carefully and you see it is going in a different direction entirely."[5]

Over the next several days, the majority view within the administration was to keep the issue moving in that "different direction"—away from the facts. In his cable to Shultz, Poindexter had noted that "VP [Vice

President Bush], Cap [Weinberger] and Bill Casey… agree with my approach." So did President Reagan.[6] During a public appearance on November 6, Reagan denied the accuracy of the *Al-Shiraa* report, describing it as nothing more than "a story that came out of the Middle East and that, to us, has no foundation."[7] The president's spokesman, Larry Speakes, later acknowledged that Reagan "knew [this remark] was wrong at the time."[8]

On November 10, the first full, top-level meeting took place at the White House to decide how to protect the initiative and the administration. Participants included the president, the vice president, Secretary of State Shultz and Secretary of Defense Weinberger, Attorney General Edwin Meese, CIA Director Casey, Chief of Staff Donald Regan, Poindexter, and his deputy, Alton Keel. Several of those present took notes. Weinberger later prepared a memorandum for the record, which contains the essential points that were discussed (Document 86).

According to Regan's notes, the president began by saying that "as [a] result of media, etc., [we] must have [a] statement," immediately adding, "we have not dealt directly with terrorists, no bargaining."[9] Weinberger's memo reflects much the same thing: "[W]e did not do any trading with the enemy for our hostages," he quotes Reagan as saying. Poindexter spoke next, presenting the rationale behind the administration's decision to make contact with Iran. According to Keel's notes,

> Main condition [was] long term strategic
> relationship
> (1) support moderates
> (2) stop terrorism
> (3) release hostages

The president and Poindexter were clearly laying out the framework for the administration's public response to revelations of the initiative. Reagan's remark would become a constant refrain in his future statements about the initiative, even though most crit-

ics, including the secretary of state, saw no distinction between dealing with the hostage-takers directly as opposed to their sponsor, Iran, which the State Department just two years earlier had declared a supporter of international terrorism. Poindexter's listing of objectives hearkened back to the January 17, 1986, Finding, although as put into practice, the operation's participants had always given the hostages' release top priority as the precondition for a new relationship between the United States and Iran.

What is striking about the records of the November 10 meeting is the number of omissions and false statements concerning the initiative. For example, there is no mention of the HAWK missile shipment whatsoever, nor of the retroactive Finding the president signed on December 5, 1985, even though the HAWKs constituted the most controversial element of the initiative. This and other misrepresentations indicate that those who knew the true story deliberately set out to cover up the facts from their colleagues and, ultimately, from Congress and the American public as well.

After the meeting, Poindexter and Meese reviewed a statement Casey had drafted to explain the administration's position. Reflecting the importance attached to projecting an image of unity, the document included the assertion that the president's aides had shown "unanimous support for the President's decisions" on Iran. Having cleared the statement with some participants, Poindexter cabled a copy to Shultz, who had left for an overseas mission. Shultz accepted most of the points raised, but balked at a single word—"decisions." He insisted that the word be deleted so that the final copy read that there had been "unanimous support for the President." It was a seemingly minor objection, but in it Poindexter saw the signs of a split developing in the administration's ranks.[10]

THE PRESIDENT GOES PUBLIC

With the cover story in hand, the president and his aides began to spread the word to Congress and to the public. On November 12, Reagan and Poindexter briefed congressional leaders, conveying the basic misinformation discussed two days earlier and stressing that no one in the administration had been left out of the loop. The next day, Poindexter gave a background briefing to the press in which he let slip that an unnamed "third country" had delivered one shipment of arms prior to the January 1986 Finding. This remark caused problems for the administration later when the president denied that any other countries had played a part in the initiative.

The same day, November 13, President Reagan gave a televised address to the nation—prepared by McFarlane, Poindexter, and North—in order to stem the growing pressure for an accounting of his administration's actions. Once again, he repeated most of the main points agreed to on November 10, including the questionable assertion that the arms deals had complied with the law, and the untrue statement that "taken together, [the missiles] could easily fit into a single cargo plane." As he had with the members of Congress, the president underscored the legality of the operation and contended that no arms had been traded for hostages.

The speech left the public cold. A poll conducted immediately afterward showed 56 percent thought that the deals amounted to an arms-for-hostages trade and 72 percent disapproved of arms sales to Iran under any circumstances.[11] According to another poll taken in this period, an astonishing 79 percent of the population considered the president's defense of the initiative "misleading."[12] Even conservative Senator Barry Goldwater concluded that Reagan had "gotten his butt in a crack."[13]

Less than a week later, on November 19, the president tried again—this time at a televised news conference. His performance was even more disastrous. Not only did he perpetuate the earlier inaccuracies but he denied any U.S. role whatsoever in the November 1985 HAWK transaction. He also insisted that the United States "had nothing to do with other countries or their shipment of arms" to Iran, including Israel.[14] But the press already knew from Poindexter's remarks the previous week that this was not the case. Reagan's refusal to own up to the truth forced his aides to issue an unusually swift correction—just twenty minutes after the conference ended. The president's credibility sank to a new low.

Behind the scenes, the unity that Reagan's aides hoped to preserve was beginning to crumble. Secretary Shultz in particular became profoundly uncomfortable after watching the news conference and asked to meet immediately with the president. The next day, with Chief of Staff Regan present, he had what he described as a "long, tough discussion, not the kind of discussion I ever thought I would have with the President of the United States."[15] Shultz conveyed to Reagan a number of the inaccuracies from his televised remarks. Based on that recounting, he told the president that he was being used by certain members of his staff to cover up the truth, and needed to take steps to review the facts.

FALSE CHRONOLOGIES

Shortly after the Iran initiative was exposed, Congress began holding hearings on the matter. Poindexter and Casey were scheduled to appear before the intelligence committees of the House and Senate on November 21. Prior to their testimony, the two witnesses gathered in Poindexter's White House office with Meese, North, Deputy CIA Director Robert Gates, and others to prepare. For assistance, they turned to a chronology of events that North and other NSC officials had taken the lead in compiling shortly after the Al-Shiraa story broke.

Several versions of the chronology, which ended up totaling seventeen single-spaced pages, have been preserved and provide a road map to the evolution of the official account of the affair.[16] In keeping with the earlier discussions and the president's public pronouncements, the drafts of the chronology focused on distancing the administration from the arms shipments of 1985, which took place before Reagan had signed any Findings, arguably making them illegal.

Poindexter and Casey had to contend with the problematic fact that the CIA had helped deliver eighteen HAWK missiles to Iran the previous November—something Reagan had denied just the day before. To manage this problem, the chronology was amended to include a contrived account: the Israelis were responsible for the shipment and had told U.S. officials that the cargo consisted of "oil-drilling equipment."

Information bolstering this cover story was contained in a CIA-prepared insert for the NSC chronology (Document 87). At the meeting in Poindexter's office, North suggested, and no one objected, that the insert be adopted with one major change—that the existing statement about the CIA's ignorance of the true nature of the shipment be expanded to read that "no one in the USG" knew at the time of the delivery that missiles were on board. North wrote this and other changes in by hand.

Secretary of State Shultz, however, became an obstacle to disseminating this obvious lie. Although North's revisions passed muster at the meeting, Shultz had contemporaneous notes of a conversation with McFarlane that proved both they and others *had* known about the HAWK shipment at the time it went forward. State Department Legal Advisor Abraham Sofaer took the matter up with an official at the Justice Department.

For Sofaer, the oil-drilling story "smelled like the kind of thing you see in a trial…in a narcotics case, for example, where they refer to the drugs as 'shirts' or something like that."[17] Acknowledging later that he was "very afraid" that a cover-up was in progress,[18] Sofaer insisted that the testimony be corrected, and he vowed to the head of the Office of Legal Counsel at the Justice Department, Charles Cooper, that if it were not he would have to resign from the State Department. At eight o'clock the next morning, Cooper personally went to the CIA to make sure the offending passages were deleted.[19]

At the same time, Vice President Bush was actively engaged in an effort to keep Secretary Shultz from resigning and the scandal from unraveling further. On November 20, the vice president met with the president. "A tough day in the White House," Bush recorded in his diary:

All kinds of odds and ends. The President tells me that at lunch, "I really had a shocker. Don Regan has just told me that George Shultz has told him Poindexter has to go or he goes."…We talked at length and I suggested to the President that the only thing he could do was call a Monday meeting which he decided to do to get the key NSC players together and to get them all to lay it on the table and to just simply say, "we're going to hammer this thing out.…"[20]

THE ATTORNEY GENERAL STEPS IN

After Sofaer raised the red flag, Cooper called Meese to fill him in. For the previous two weeks, Cooper had been looking into the legal aspects of the Iran initiative at Meese's direction. His call apparently convinced the attorney general that he should take the lead in "getting his arms around this" issue.[21] Meese met with the president on the morning of November 21 and got his permission to undertake a "fact-finding inquiry" to be completed in time for a top-level National Security Planning Group (NSPG) meeting on Iran set for November 24.

When Congress held its own investigation of the Iran-contra affair, Meese's probe became a major issue.[22] The attorney general came under strong criticism on several counts: selecting a small number of personal staff and political appointees for his team rather than seasoned criminal investigators or experts in the legal aspects of covert action; failing to promptly seal important NSC files; and disregarding standard investigative procedures such as taking notes in key interviews. Meese later insisted there were no grounds for assuming a criminal investigation was needed at the time, but officials in his own Criminal Division disagreed.[23]

The attorney general originally stated that his goal was to clarify the "confusion" within the administration surrounding the Iran initiative, which showed through in the differing accounts he had heard from various officials. There were other issues at stake, however. One was the continued viability of the initiative. The negotiations had stayed alive even after the Lebanese story broke, and the president wanted to keep them going as long as there was a chance to get more hostages out. (Indeed, the Iran intitiative continued into December.)

Meese also recognized the political problem. Public disapproval both of the arms deals and of Reagan's attempts to explain them further had intensified. Moreover, several of Reagan's aides had already voiced concerns that the November 1985 HAWK deals had been illegal,[24] which would add an explosive, new dimension to the situation if those misgivings became known—an increasing possibility as administration unity continued to dissolve.

Meese justified his focus on political considerations by claiming that he was acting as "legal adviser" to the president rather than as attorney general. As the nation's chief law enforcement officer, his duty was to root out possible wrongdoing, but by depicting himself as the president's personal counselor, he asserted that his responsibility lay primarily in protecting his "client."

At this stage, Meese's focus was Iran. His first two interviews, with McFarlane and Shultz, dealt largely with the HAWK episode and yielded diametrically opposed versions. McFarlane clung to the cover story in the false chronologies that the November 1985 shipment had been a strictly Israeli operation to deliver oil-drilling equipment to Iran, and that the United States had assisted with it at the request of Israeli Defense Minister Yitzhak Rabin. Shultz, however, recounted a detailed conversation with McFarlane before the shipment took place in which McFarlane described its true contents and its connection to a plan to get the hostages released. Shultz added that McFarlane spoke to him again later and told him the operation had not worked out as planned. The blatant contradiction disturbed the Justice Department officials—until a new discovery distracted their attention.

A SMOKING GUN?

On the same morning that Meese spoke with Shultz, two of his aides arrived at the Old Executive Office Building to review documents from North's files. Sifting through materials presented to them by an aide to North, it did not take long before they came across an unsigned, undated memorandum entitled "Release of American Hostages in Beirut" (Document 88). Written on or about April 4, 1986, the document described plans for an upcoming delivery of HAWK missile spare parts that would accompany an American delegation to Teheran. On the last page, one of the officials, Assistant Attorney General for Civil Rights William Bradford Reynolds, noticed a section that read, "The residual funds from this transaction are allocated as follows....$12 million will be used to purchase critically needed supplies for the Nicaraguan Democratic Resistance Forces." Reynolds's reaction was "holy cow or something to that effect"[25]—he had stumbled on a new dimension to the Iran deals, one that connected them to the Contras in Nicaragua. Not wanting to attract the attention of North's aide to the discovery, the two officials replaced the memo and shortly afterward met Meese for lunch at the Old Ebbitt Grill in downtown Washington.

For Meese, the document, which came to be known as the "diversion memo," had the look of a smoking gun. He saw in it a "merging" of the two operations that were currently causing the president unprecedented political complications. As he later acknowledged, "as soon as we learned about the diversion, that changed entirely the focus of what we were discovering and what would be presented to the American people."[26] From that point on, he homed in on the facts surrounding the "diversion," including the question of who had authorized it. In Meese's interview with North the next day, North maintained that only he, McFarlane and Poindexter knew about the scheme.

North's confirmation of some of the details of the plan presented Meese with both a problem and a solution. Questions of legality aside, the political explosiveness of the Iran-Contra connection was frightening. It was entirely possible, he testified at North's trial, that if word of the linkage became public, the fallout could bring about the "toppling of the president himself"[27]—the outcome he most wanted to avoid. But North also provided a convenient way to do just that—by saying that the president had been kept in the dark. Meese came to the conclusion that the administration had to disclose the diversion. The revelation would prevent charges of a cover-up and it could be handled in a way that would limit the damage to administration interests: the questionable activities would be seen as the responsibility of subordinate officials, and the larger policies of negotiating with Iran and supporting the Contras could remain unscrutinized.

Although Meese decided on this approach by the morning of November 24, he apparently did not raise it at the NSPG meeting that was supposed to be the forum to present his findings. Instead, the high-level session, which included the president, the vice president, secretaries Shultz and Weinberger, Casey, Poindexter, Regan and others, focused on Iran. Records concerning the meeting that were available as of this writing reveal that the HAWK shipment was raised in the context of a significant exchange:

> Mr. Meese told the group that the November 1985 Israeli HAWK missile shipment may have been illegal, but that the President did not know about the shipment at the time. At the end of the meeting, Mr. Meese asked whether anyone knew of anything else that had not been revealed. No one contradicted Mr. Meese's incorrect statement concerning President Reagan's lack of knowledge, although several of those present…had contrary information.[28]

Although not stated directly, the implication is unmistakable—top officials in the government acquiesced in perpetrating a cover story that Reagan did not know about this controversial operation. The record shows that the president, Shultz, Meese, and Regan knew the truth of the matter: on November 20, during Shultz's meeting with the president and Regan, the president told Shultz he had known about the operation at the time it took place; two days later, Shultz

passed on this information to Meese. Weinberger also knew that Meese's statement was false, having been briefed by McFarlane on the shipments four times in November 1985.[29] And clearly, McFarlane and Poindexter understood Reagan's role in the shipment.

THE DIVERSION AS A DIVERSION

Shortly after the NSPG meeting, Meese met briefly with the president and Regan. They discussed the diversion, which Reagan was reportedly surprised to hear about, and broached the subject of disclosure. The president decided to hold a news conference the next day.

Meese also informed Vice President Bush. "Ed Meese came to see me," Bush recorded in his diary on the afternoon of November 24.

> Then, he laid a real bomb shell on me that Ollie North had taken the money and put it in a Swiss bank account…from Iran…to be used for the Contras. They are going to blow into a major thing…. I told him that in my view, the President should ask me if I knew anything about it. I told [Meese] absolutely not.

"I'ts going to be a major flap," Bush said in his taped diary. "We got some 12 press calls today…all on a new theme: The Vice President—what's his advice? What does he think? Thank God, I've consistently said that I don't discuss what I tell the President or if I support the President."[30]

President Reagan's appearance before the packed White House press room on November 25 was brief. His role was merely to announce the broad outlines of the Iran-Contra affair then yield the podium to the attorney general, who would handle the questions. Avoiding any details, Reagan declared, "I was not fully informed about one of the activities undertaken in connection with this initiative" on Iran. He announced that North had been "relieved of his duties" for the unnamed offense, and that "although not directly involved," Poindexter had "asked to be relieved of his assignment" (Document 89). The president then retreated from the press room, followed by reporters' questions shouted after him.

True to the plan, Meese's extended remarks and answers to questions focused on North's diversion scheme and shied away from the larger issues of administration policy toward Iran and the Contras. During the course of his presentation, he made several incorrect, misleading, and false statements, including claims that the United States had played no role in the first arms shipments to Iran via Israel in August–September 1985 and that the president had not known about the November 1985 HAWK shipment until early 1986. In effect, the press conference to disclose the diversion amounted to a diversion of a different sort—

and the public, press, and Congress took the bait.

For the next several months and throughout the 1987 congressional investigation of the scandal, the diversion took center stage, finding expression in a question resurrected from the Watergate era: "What did the president know and when did he know it?" Even on this relatively narrow issue, evidence surfaced that undercut assertions about Reagan's ignorance.[31] Nevertheless, as of the time Congress wrapped up its inquiry, the cover-up had basically succeeded: the larger questions of top-level administration complicity had received short shrift and the deeper policy and constitutional issues raised by the scandal failed to generate serious national debate.

NOTES

1. See "Extracts from Vice President Bush Diary Transcripts, November 4, 1986–January 2, 1987," pp. 1, 2. The Office of the Independent Counsel requested Bush's calendars and diaries, among other documents, in late February 1987, but the diaries, which Bush dictated into a tape recorder and later had transcribed, remained concealed from investigators until December 11, 1992, when Walsh's office was advised by the White House that such documents existed. On January 15, 1993, the Bush White House released forty-five transcribed pages of his diary, along with a "privileged and confidential" fourteen-page report from his lawyer, former attorney general Griffin Bell, explaining why these documents had not been turned over earlier. Bush, according to the report, was never informed by his lawyers of the request for diaries, and Walsh's office failed to ask him directly for such documents when he was interviewed in January 1988. Although the diaries clearly catalogue the inner workings of the Reagan White House during the critical months of November and December 1986 as the scandal unraveled, the report states that "even had [Bush] been aware of the request, his present view is that he would not have believed that his dictation constituted a diary responsive to an Iran-Contra document request." See King and Spalding, "Report to President Bush," January 15, 1993, pp. 6,7.

2. See Jane Mayer and Doyle McManus, *Landslide: The Unmaking of the President, 1984–1988* (Boston: Houghton-Mifflin, 1988), p. 292ff., for one account of this period.

3. Ibid., p. 358.

4. Shultz, Cable to Poindexter, November 4, 1986. This document is available in the National Security Archive's microfiche collection, *The Iran-Contra Affair: The Making of a Scandal, 1983–1988*.

5. Shultz is quoted in the *Iran-Contra Affair*, pp. 293–94.

6. See Rodney McDaniel notes, November 6–7, 1986. They can be found in the National Security Archive's microfiche collection, *The Iran-Contra Affair: The Making of a Scandal, 1983–1988*.

7. Reagan is quoted in the *Iran-Contra Affair*, p. 294.

8. Speakes is quoted in *Landslide*, p. 295.

9. Donald Regan, notes of November 10, 1986, meeting, in the National Security Archive's microfiche collection, *The Iran-Contra Affair: The Making of a Scandal, 1983–1988*.

10. Theodore Draper has pointed out the significance of this growing "gap" between Shultz and Reagan in *A Very Thin Line* (New York: Hill and Wang, 1991), pp. 469–70.

11. Mayer and McManus, *Landslide*, p. 303.

12. Ibid, p. 316.

13. Ibid., p. 303.

14. A transcript of the president's news conference can be found in *Weekly Compilation of Presidential Documents*, vol. 22, no. 47, p. 1586.

15. George Shultz, testimony in *Joint Hearings before the Select Committees on the Iran-Contra Investigation*, July 23, 1987, vol. 100-9, p. 45.

16. For a brief description of the misrepresentations included at various stages of the chronology's construction, see the *Iran-Contra Affair*, pp. 298–300.

17. Abraham Sofaer, deposition in *Report of the Congressional Committees Investigating the Iran-Contra Affair*, Appendix B, vol. 26, p. 270.

18. Ibid., p. 268.

19. As it happened, Casey still managed to put across the "cover story," as Donald Regan later termed it, in his answers to questions from the committee.

20. "Extracts From Vice President Bush Diary Transcripts, November 4, 1986–January 2, 1987," p. 13.

21. Charles Cooper, testimony in *Joint Hearings before the Select Committees on the Iran-Contra Investigation*, June 25, 1987, vol. 100-6, p. 250.

22. See, for example, "Additional Views of Honorable Peter W. Rodino…," in the *Iran-Contra Affair*, pp. 644–47.

23. See, for example, Ralph Martin to William Weld, "Independent Counsel Request," ca. November 28, 1986, in the National Security Archive's microfiche collection *The Iran-Contra Affair: The Making of a Scandal, 1983–1988*.

24. According to the independent counsel, "During the period leading up to November 24, 1986, officials within the White House and other executive branch agencies expressed repeated concern that the 1985 arms shipments to Iran, and in particular the November 1985 HAWK missile shipment, had been illegal" ([First] Weinberger Indictment, June 16, 1992, p. 8). The document is available from the National Security Archive.

25. William Bradford Reynolds, deposition in *Report of the Congressional Committees Investigating the Iran-Contra Affair*, Appendix B, vol. 22, p. 1129.

26. Edwin Meese, testimony in *Joint Hearings before the Select Committees on the Iran-Contra Investigation*, July 29, 1987, vol. 100-9, p. 403.

27. Edwin Meese, testimony at the Oliver North trial, p. 5750.

28. (First) Weinberger Indictment, June 16, 1992, pp. 9–10.

29. (First) Weinberger Indictment, June 16, 1992, pp. 3, 23.

30. "Extracts From Vice President Bush Diary Transcripts, November 4, 1986–January 2, 1987," p. 18.

31. North testified that he wrote several memoranda to Poindexter about the matter, and that he assumed the president knew about it. Also, Poindexter, who proclaimed in July 1987 that "the buck stops here with me" on the diversion, raised doubts about his own truthfulness when he acknowledged that his intent all along had been to protect the president from political embarrassment in the scandal.

DOCUMENT 85: John Poindexter, Cable to George Shultz, "U.S. Policy on Iran (TS),"
November 5, 1986.

PAGE 1 OF 3

TA#256 R ···········C O N F I D E N T I A L···

WHITE HOUSE SITUATION ROOM

PAGE 01

N 12439

Z 05   NOV 86
FM THE WHITE HOUSE

TO
TE

T O P   S E C R E T VIA PRIVACY CHANNELS EYES ONLY #WOC652

EYES ONLY FOR SECRETARY GEORGE SHULTZ FROM ASSISTANT TO THE
PRESIDENT FOR NATIONAL SECURITY AFFAIRS JOHN POINDEXTER

SUBJ: U.S. POLICY ON IRAN (TS)

REF: SECTO 23003

1. T O P   S E C R E T -ENTIRE TEXT

2. BEGIN TEXT.

DEAR GEORGE:

1. THANK YOU FOR PROVIDING ME WITH YOUR PERSPECTIVE ON OUR PROBLEMS
WITH IRAN. I SHARE YOUR DESIRE TO FIND A WAY TO PREVENT FURTHER
SPECULATION AND LEAKS ABOUT U.S. POLICY ON IRAN. NOT ONLY WILL
SUCH COMPLICATE OUR EFFORTS TO SECURE THE RELEASE OF OTHER
HOSTAGES, BUT MAY ALSO UNDERMINE OPPORTUNITIES FOR EVENTUALLY
ESTABLISHING A CORRECT RELATIONSHIP WITH IRAN AND POSSIBILITIES
FOR AN ACTIVE U.S. ROLE IN ENDING THE IRAN-IRAQ WAR.

THE WHITE HOUSE C652   DTG:05   NOV 86 PSN: 076029
                             TOR: 309/2219Z

EXHIBIT

GPS-36

Partially Declassified/Released on Jul 20, 1987 T O P   S E C R E T
under provisions of E.O. 12356
by B. Reger, National Security Council

(2213)

DOCUMENT 85: John Poindexter, Cable to George Shultz, "U.S. Policy on Iran (TS),"
November 5, 1986.

PAGE 2 OF 3

TOP SECRET

DATE 12/06/85   WHITE HOUSE SITUATION ROOM   PAGE 02

MESSAGE (CONTINUED):

2. AT SOME POINT WE WILL HAVE TO LAY OUT ALL OF THE FACTS. I AM CONVINCED WHEN WE DO LAY OUT THE FACTS THAT IT WILL BE WELL RECEIVED SINCE IT IS A GOOD STORY. HAVING SAID THAT, I DO NOT BELIEVE THAT NOW IS THE TIME TO GIVE THE FACTS TO THE PUBLIC. THERE ARE SEVERAL FACTORS TO CONSIDER IN ADDITION TO THE NEED TO GET THE OTHER HOSTAGES OUT AND THEN BRIEF THE INTELLIGENCE COMMITTEES BEFORE THE ADMINISTRATION SPEAKS PUBLICLY ON THIS MATTER: FIRST, WHILE WE ARE NOT COMPLETELY SURE WHAT PROVOKED RAFSANJANI TO MAKE THESE RELEVATIONS (WHICH ARE NOT TOTALLY ACCURATE), IT IS APPARENT THAT A POWER STRUGGLE OF SOME SORT IS UNDERWAY IN IRAN. THIS STRUGGLE COULD PROMPT OTHER IRANIAN OFFICIALS TO MAKE ADDITIONAL RELEVATIONS. DISCLOSURES BY THE U.S. COULD LEAD TO CONTRADICTORY IRANIAN STATEMENTS AND MISINTERPRETATION OVER OUR ATTITUDES AND INTENTIONS. SECOND, WE MAY HAVE AN OPPORTUNITY TO AFFECT THE INTERNAL POLITICAL SITUATION IN TEHRAN AND TAKE ADVANTAGE OF IT TO ADVANCE OUR REGIONAL AND ANTI-TERRORIST INTERESTS. HOWEVER, OFFICIAL STATEMENTS BY THE U.S. WILL ONLY PLAY INTO THE HANDS OF RADICAL IRANIANS WHO CONTINUE TO WANT TO DISTANCE IRAN FROM THE U.S. AND THE WEST TO THE MAXIMUM EXTENT POSSIBLE.

3. I THEREFORE REMAIN CONVINCED THAT WE MUST REMAIN ABSOLUTELY CLOSE-MOUTHED WHILE STRESSING THAT OUR "BASIC POLICY TOWARD IRAN, THE GULF WAR, AND DEALING WITH TERRORISTS HAS NOT CHANGED. MOREOVER, SPECULATION ABOUT OUR EFFORTS TO SECURE THE HOSTAGES RELEASE ONLY INCREASES THE DANGER TO THE HOSTAGES."

4. TODAY I HAVE TALKED WITH VP, CAP AND BILL CASEY. THEY AGREE WITH MY APPROACH.

5. I HAVE ASKED MY STAFF TO PREPARE A CABLE TO RELEVANT POSTS EXPLAINING OUR POLICY IN THE IRAN-IRAQ WAR HAS NOT CHANGED AND WE ARE NOT GOING TO COMMENT ON NEWS REPORTS AND SPECULATION BECAUSE OF THE DANGER TO HOSTAGES. WE WILL SEND THE DRAFT OVER TO STATE.

6. TODAY I AM ESTABLISHING TWO COMPARTMENTS. ONE IS OPERATIONAL AND I AM WILLING TO BRIEF JERRY BREMER INTO IT PROVIDING HE REPORTS ONLY TO YOU. THE SECOND IS ON POLICY AND LONG TERM STRATEGY TOWARD IRAN. I WOULD LIKE TO INCLUDE ONLY

THE WHITE HOUSE 0652   DTG:05▮▮▮ NOV 86 PSN: 076029
                           TOR: 309/2219Z

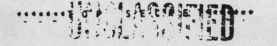

DOCUMENT 85: John Poindexter, Cable to George Shultz, "U.S. Policy on Iran (TS)," November 5, 1986.

PAGE 3 OF 3

UNCLASSIFIED   N 12441

DATE 12/16/66   WHITE HOUSE SITUATION ROOM   PAGE

MESSAGE (CONTINUED):

MIKE ARMACOST AND ARNIE RAPHEL IN THIS ONE. IT IS ESSENTIAL
THAT KNOWLEDGE OF EITHER COMPARTMENT BE EXTREMELY LIMITED.

7. TOMORROW I MEET WITH ▮▮▮▮▮▮▮▮ AND WILL BE INTERESTED IN
HIS ASSESSMENT AS TO WHAT IS HAPPENING IN TEHRAN. BY THE WAY,
WE DISAGREE WITH THE INR ARTICLE IN THIS MORNING'S SUMMARY,
QUOTE IRAN: THE POLITICAL POT BOILS UNQUOTE. WHEN YOU GET BACK
I WILL GIVE YOU MY VIEW AS TO WHAT IS HAPPENING. I THINK IT IS
VERY SIGNIFICANT THAT RAFSANJANI'S STATEMENT YESTERDAY THAT BUD
WENT TO TEHRAN IN SEPTEMBER AND OTHER FACTS ARE WRONG. SINCE
HE OBVIOUSLY KNOWS THE FACTS, I BELIEVE HE IS TRYING TO SEND US
A MESSAGE.

8. PRESS GUIDANCE ATTACHED.

                    IRAN PRESS GUIDANCE

Q: ABOUT MCFARLANE OR SPARE PARTS OR ARMS TO IRAN?

A: WE HAVE NO COMMENT ON THESE REPORTS. AS LONG AS THERE ARE
AMERICAN HOSTAGES BEING HELD IN THE MIDDLE EAST WE WILL NOT BE
RESPONDING TO QUESTIONS LIKE THIS. A SIMPLE NO COMMENT WILL BE
MADE TO ALL QUESTIONS ABOUT TALKS OR ACTIONS THAT MIGHT OR MIGHT
NOT BE TAKING PLACE. YOU SHOULD INFER NOTHING TO THESE RESPONSES.

Q: DOES THE U.S. STILL HAVE AN ARMS EMBARGO AGAINST IRAN IN THE
IRAN-IRAQ WAR?

A: AS LONG AS IRAN ADVOCATES THE USE OF TERRORISM, THE U.S.
ARMS EMBARGO WILL CONTINUE. MOREOVER, THE U.S. POSITION ON THE
IRAN-IRAQ WAR REMAINS THAT THE FIGHTING SHOULD STOP AND THE TWO
SIDES SHOULD REACH A NEGOTIATED SETTLEMENT OF THEIR DISPUTE. WE
FAVOR AN OUTCOME WHEREIN THERE ARE NO WINNERS OR LOSERS.

9. HOPE THE TALKS WITH ▮▮▮▮▮▮▮▮ GO WELL.

WARM REGARDS, JOHN

        THE WHITE HOUSE 0652   DTG:05▮▮▮▮ NOV 86 PSN: 076029
                                    TOR: 309/22192

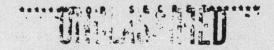

TOP SECRET

UNCLASSIFIED

DOCUMENT 86: Caspar Weinberger, Memorandum for the Record, "Meeting on November 10, 1986, with the President, Vice President, Secretary Shultz, DCI Casey, Attorney General Meese, Don Regan, Admiral Poindexter, and Al Keel, in the Oval Office," Undated.

PAGE 1 OF 3

UNCLASSIFIED

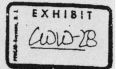

EXHIBIT
CWD-28

MEMORANDUM FOR RECORD

SUBJECT: Meeting on November 10, 1986, with the President, Vice President, Secretary Shultz, DCI Casey, Attorney General Meese, Don Regan, Admiral Poindexter, and Al Keel, in the Oval Office

The President said we did not do any trading with the enemy for our hostages. We do need to note that ▮▮▮▮▮ (Khomeni) will be gone someday, and we want better leverage with the new government and with their military. That is why we felt it necessary to give them some small defensive weapons.

We can discuss that publicly, but no way could we ever disclose it all without getting our hostages executed. (We must make it plain that we are not doing business with terrorists. We aren't paying them or dealing with them.) We are trying to get better relations with Iran, and we can't discuss the details of this publicly without endangering the people we are working through and with in Iran. I pointed out we must bear in mind we have given the Israelies and the Iranians the opportunity to blackmail us by reporting selectively bits and pieces of the total story. I also pointed out that Congress could -and probably would -- hold legislative hearings. Admiral Poindexter pointed out that we do want a better relationship with Iran.

In ~~June~~ Jan 1986, the President apparently made a formal finding under Section 501 of the Arms Export Control Act which directes the DCI not to notify Congress until further notice, and authorizes discussion with friendly groups which are trying to get a better government in Iran. I had not known of this finding before Nov ~ 1986 -- Shultz said he had not known of it either. We needed to help those elements to get a more pro-U.S. government in Iran. Poindexter continued that we assisted Israel initially because we found Israel was sending arms to Iran ▮▮▮▮▮ and also wanted the Iran-Iraq war to end as soon as possible. Admiral Poindexter said that McFarlane went to Iran in May 1986, and that was the only trip he made, and then we started working through ▮▮▮▮▮ of Rasfanjani. Previously we had used an Israeli agent called Gorbanfar. We also used many channels to try to get the hostages back. ▮▮▮▮▮ others proved no good because the Iranians always insisted that the Da▮a▮ prisoners held by Kuwait be released. We finally did authorize the release of 500 TOWS sold by Israel to Iran, and another 500 were sent last week. This was all arranged as a result of a meeting with Rasfanjani's ▮▮▮▮▮ came here to show that he was a legitimate representative of the government. Poindexter reported there were several meetings

UNCLASSIFIED
SECRET/SENSITIVE

2895

DOCUMENT 86: Caspar Weinberger, Memorandum for the Record, "Meeting on November 10, 1986, with the President, Vice President, Secretary Shultz, DCI Casey, Attorney General Meese, Don Regan, Admiral Poindexter, and Al Keel, in the Oval Office," Undated.

PAGE 2 OF 3

SECRET/SENSITIVE
-2-

in Europe and elsewhere.

I reminded John that he had always told me that there would be no more weapons sent to Iran, after the first 500 TOWS, until <u>after all</u> of the hostages were returned, but unfortunat we did send a second 500 because it "seemed the only way to get the hostages out", according to Poindexter.

Poindexter pointed out the hostage taking had stopped for a year. I pointed out that they took three more quite recently. Poindexter pointed out that this was not done by the same people or Iranians.

publicized Rasfanjani's contacts with the U.S. Rasfanjani then felt he had to speak out against the U.S. and the McFarlane trip. Because of the obvious errors in Rasfanjani's speech, Poindexter thinks he is sending a message that he "wants to work with us." Colonel North thinks we can get two more hostages out by the weekend. I don't. (We didn't.) We have told all our friends in the Mid-East, and according to Poindexter they agree, they would like a negotiated settlement and the war to end.

The President said this is what you had to do to reward Iran for the efforts of those who could help. Actually the captors do not benefit at all. We buy the support and the oportunity to persuade the Iranians.

I again pointed out we will have to answer many questions and have Congressional hearings. The President said we need to point out any discussion endangers our source in Iran and our plan, because we do want to get additional hostages released. Mr. Shultz spoke up for the first time, saying that it is the responsibility of the government to look after its citizens, but once you do deal for hostages, you expose everyone to future capture. He said we don't know, but we have to assume the captors will get someone. He said he felt the Isralies sucked us up into their operation so we could not object to their sales to Iran. He pointed out there will be a lot of questions after any statement, even after a statement such as Mr. Casey

DOCUMENT 86: Caspar Weinberger, Memorandum for the Record, "Meeting on November 10, 1986, with the President, Vice President, Secretary Shultz, DCI Casey, Attorney General Meese, Don Regan, Admiral Poindexter, and Al Keel, in the Oval Office," Undated.

PAGE 3 OF 3

SECRET/SENSITIVE

-3-

proposed to read. The President said we should release the statement, but not take any questions. Mr. Regan said we are being hung out to dry, our credibility is at stake, and we have to say enough. Shortly thereafter the meeting adjourned on the note that revised drafts of the Casey proposed statement will be sent to us.

SECRET/SENSITIVE

S E C R E T

SUBJECT: CIA Airline Involvement

In late November 1985, a CIA proprietary airline was chartered to carry cargo to Iran. ~~at the NSC's request~~ The cargo was described to us as oil drilling spare parts. Although we did not know it at the time, the cargo was actually 18 Hawk missles. The chronolgy of the incident is as follows:

On 22 November ~~1985~~, *6th* the NSC contacted the Agency with an urgent request ~~for the name of~~ a discreet, reliable airline that could transport bulky oil-drilling parts to an unspecified destination in the Middle East.

We offered the name of the CIA's proprietary airline as a company which could handle the NSC request. The NSC passed the name of ~~our airline~~ to the ~~intermediary with the Iranians.~~ *(Israelis)* *Israelis*

In ~~the~~ interim, we contacted our airline and told them that they would be receiving an urgent, legitimate charter request. The ~~NSC intermediary~~ contacted the airline that evening (22 November) and made arrangements for the airline to pick-up the parts in Lisbon.

operated by the proprietor
The destination was changed to Tel Aviv and two ~~of our airline's~~ Boeing 707's arrived in Tel Aviv 23 November. The cargo was ultimately loaded onto only one of the aircraft. Loading was completed by 24 November and the aircraft proceeded to Iran via a stop at Larnaca and then overflying Turkey. At the NSC's request, and for the protection of our aircraft, we helped arrange for the overflight clearances.

nor the Iranians knew
~~To~~ the best of our knowledge, the *rather* ~~intermediary~~ ~~did not know~~ *Israeli* that ~~they was~~ dealing with a CIA proprietary, nor did airline personnel know what they were carrying. ~~We in CIA~~ did not find out that our airline had hauled Hawk missles into Iran until mid-January ~~when~~ we were told by the Iranians. *No one in the USG*

The airline was paid the normal commercial rate which amounted to approximately $127,700. I should stress that the airline does a considerable amount of normal business in addition to its support to CIA. It had, in fact, made a ~~legitimate~~ flight into Tehran carrying commercial items prior to the 22-25 November incident. *another unrelated*

Senior CIA management found out about the flight on 25 ~~February~~ *November.* Although we did not know the nature of the cargo, we thought that any future support of this type to the NSC would require a Finding.

S E C R E T   AKW002179   110

DOCUMENT 88: Oliver North, "Release of American Hostages in Beirut," ca. April 4, 1986
(the "Diversion Memo")

PAGE 1 OF 5

~~TOP SECRET~~   ~~TOP SECRET~~   SENSITIVE

RELEASE OF AMERICAN HOSTAGES IN BEIRUT   N   590

Background. In June 1985, private American and Israeli citizens
commenced an operation to effect the release of the American
hostages in Beirut in exchange for providing certain factions in
Iran with U.S.-origin Israeli military materiel. By September,
U.S. and Israeli Government officials became involved in this
endeavor in order to ensure that the USG would:

-- not object to the Israeli transfer of embargoed materiel to
   Iran;

-- sell replacement items to Israel as replenishment for like
   items sold to Iran by Israel.

On September 13, the Israeli Government, with the endorsement of
the USG, transferred 508 basic TOW missiles to Iran. Forty-eight
hours later, Reverend Benjamin Weir was released in Beirut.

Subsequent efforts by both governments to continue this process
have met with frustration due to the need to communicate our
intentions through an Iranian expatriate arms dealer in Europe.
In January 1986, under the provisions of a new Covert Action
Finding, the USG demanded a meeting with responsible Iranian
government officials.

On February 20, a U.S. Government official met with ███████████
the first direct U.S.-Iranian contact in over five years. At
this meeting, the U.S. side made an effort to refocus Iranian
attention on the threat posed by the Soviet Union and the need to
establish a longer term relationship between our two countries
based on more than arms transactions. It was emphasized that the
hostage issue was a "hurdle" which must be crossed before this
improved relationship could prosper. During the meeting, it also
became apparent that our conditions/demands had not been accurately
transmitted to the Iranian Government by the intermediary and it
was agreed that:

-- The USG would establish its good faith and bona fides by
   immediately providing 1,000 TOW missiles for sale to Iran.
   This transaction was covertly completed on February 21,
   using a private U.S. firm and the Israelis as intermediaries.

-- A subsequent meeting would be held in Iran with senior U.S
   and Iranian officials during which the U.S. hostages would
   be released.

-- Immediately after the hostages were safely in our hands, the
   U.S. would sell an additional 3,000 TOW missiles to Iran
   using the same procedures employed during the September 1985
   transfer.

~~TOP SECRET~~
Declassify: OADR

~~TOP SECRET~~   EXHIBIT   OLN-1   SENSITIVE

UNCLASSIFIED

DOCUMENT 88: Oliver North, "Release of American Hostages in Beirut," ca. April 4, 1986
(the "Diversion Memo")

PAGE 2 OF 5

~~TOP SECRET~~ ~~UNCLASSIFIED~~ N 591

~~TOP SECRET~~ UNCLASSIFIED SENSITIVE

In early March, the Iranian expatriate intermediary demanded that
Iranian conditions for release of the hostages now included the
prior sale of 200 PHOENIX missiles and an unspecified number of
HARPOON missiles, in addition to the 3,000 TOWs which would be
delivered after the hostages were released. A subsequent meeting
was held with the intermediary in Paris on March 8, wherein it
was explained that the requirement for prior deliveries violated
the understandings reached in Frankfurt on February 20, and were
therefore unacceptable. It was further noted that the Iranian
aircraft and ship launchers for these missiles were in such
disrepair that the missiles could not be launched even if provided.

From March 9 until March 30, there was no further effort
undertaken on our behalf to contact the Iranian Government or the
intermediary. On March 26, ▮▮▮▮▮▮▮▮▮▮▮▮ made an unsolicited
call to the phone-drop in Maryland which we had established for
this purpose. ▮▮▮▮▮▮▮▮▮ asked why we had not been in contact and
urged that we proceed expeditiously since the situation in Beirut
was deteriorating rapidly. He was informed by our Farsi-speaking
interpreter that the conditions requiring additional materiel
beyond the 3,000 TOWs were unacceptable and that we could in no
case provide anything else prior to the release of our hostages.
▮▮▮▮▮▮▮▮ observed that we were correct in our assessment of their
inability to use PHOENIX and HARPOON missiles and that the most
urgent requirement that Iran had was to place their current HAWK
missile inventory in working condition. In a subsequent phone
call, we agreed to discuss this matter with him and he indicated
that he would prepare an inventory of parts required to make
their HAWK systems operational. This parts list was received on
March 28, and verified by CIA.

<u>Current Situation</u>. On April 3, Ari Gorbanifahr, the Iranian
intermediary, arrived in Washington, D.C. with instructions from
▮▮▮▮▮▮▮▮▮ to consummate final arrangements for the return of the
hostages. Gorbanifahr was reportedly enfranchised to negotiate
the types, quantities, and delivery procedures for materiel the
U.S. would sell to Iran through Israel. The meeting lasted
nearly all night on April 3-4, and involved numerous calls to
Tehran. ▮▮
▮▮▮▮▮▮▮▮▮▮▮▮▮▮▮▮▮▮▮▮▮▮▮▮ A Farsi-speaking CIA officer in
attendance was able to verify the substance of his calls to
Tehran during the meeting. Subject to Presidential approval, it
was agreed to proceed as follows:

-- By Monday, April 7, the Iranian Government will transfer
   $17 million to an Israeli account in Switzerland. The
   Israelis will, in turn, transfer to a private U.S.
   corporation account in Switzerland the sum of $15 million.

~~TOP SECRET~~ ~~TOP SECRET~~ SENSITIVE

UNCLASSIFIED

DOCUMENT 88: Oliver North, "Release of American Hostages in Beirut," ca. April 4, 1986 (the "Diversion Memo")

PAGE 3 OF 5

TOP SECRET   N   592

TOP SECRET   3   SENSITIVE

-- On Tuesday, April 8 (or as soon as the transactions are verified), the private U.S. corporation will transfer $3.651 million to a CIA account in Switzerland. CIA will then transfer this sum to a covert Department of the Army account in the U.S.

-- On Wednesday, April 9, the CIA will commence procuring $3.651 million worth of HAWK missile parts (240 separate line items) and transferring these parts to ███████ ██████████████████████████████. This process is estimated to take seven working days.

-- On Friday, April 18, a private U.S. aircraft (707B) will pick-up the HAWK missile parts at ██████ and fly them to a covert Israeli airfield for prepositioning (this field was used for the earlier delivery of the 1000 TOWs). At this field, the parts will be transferred to an Israeli Defense Forces' (IDF) aircraft with false markings. A SATCOM capability will be positioned at this location.

-- On Saturday, April 19, McFarlane, North, Teicher, Cave, ███████████ and a SATCOM communicator will board a CIA aircraft in Frankfurt, Germany, enroute to Tehran. ████████████████████

-- On Sunday, April 20, the following series of events will occur:

   - U.S. party arrives Tehran (A-hour) -- met by Rafsanjani, as head of the Iranian delegation.

   - At A+7 hours, the U.S. hostages will be released in Beirut.

   - At A+15 hours, the IDF aircraft with the HAWK missile parts aboard will land at Bandar Abbas, Iran.

Discussion. The following points are relevant to this transaction, the discussions in Iran, and the establishment of a broader relationship between the United States and Iran:

-- The Iranians have been told that our presence in Iran is a "holy commitment" on the part of the USG that we are sincere and can be trusted. There is great distrust of the U.S. among the various Iranian parties involved. Without our presence on the ground in Iran, they will not believe that we will fulfill our end of the bargain after the hostages are released.

TOP SECRET   SENSITIVE

UNCLASSIFIED

~~TOP SECRET~~   N   593

~~TOP SECRET~~   SENSITIVE

▬▬ [REDACTED]

Gorbanifahr specifically mentioned that
Qhadhafi's efforts to "buy" the hostages could succeed in
the near future. Further, the Iranians are well aware that
the situation in Beirut is deteriorating rapidly and that
the ability of the IRGC to effect the release of the
hostages will become increasingly more difficult over time.

-- We have convinced the Iranians of a significant near term
and long range threat from the Soviet Union. We have real
and deceptive intelligence to demonstrate this threat during
the visit. They have expressed considerable interest in
this matter as part of the longer term relationship.

-- [REDACTED]

-- The Iranians have been told that their provision of
assistance to Nicaragua is unacceptable to us and they have
agreed to discuss this matter in Tehran.

-- We have further indicated to the Iranians that we wish to
discuss steps leading to a cessation of hostilities between
Iran and Iraq. [REDACTED]

-- The Iranians are well aware that their most immediate needs
are for technical assistance in maintaining their air force
and navy. We should expect that they will raise this issue
during the discussions in Tehran. Further conversation with
Gorbanifahr on April 4, indicates that they will want to
raise the matter of the original 3,000 TOWs as a significant
deterrent to a potential Soviet move against Iran. They
have also suggested that, if agreement is reached to provide
the TOWs [REDACTED]

-- The Iranians have been told and agreed that they will
receive neither blame nor credit for the seizure/release of
the hostages. [REDACTED]

~~TOP SECRET~~   ~~TOP SECRET~~   SENSITIVE

UNCLASSIFIED

TOP SECRET   5   SENSITIVE

-- The residual funds from this transaction are allocated as follows:

- $2 million will be used to purchase replacement TOWs for the original 508 sold by Israel to Iran for the release of Benjamin Weir. This is the only way that we have found to meet our commitment to replenish these stocks.

- $12 million will be used to purchase critically needed supplies for the Nicaraguan Democratic Resistance Forces. This materiel is essential to cover shortages in resistance inventories resulting from their current offensives and Sandinista counter-attacks and to "bridge" the period between now and when Congressionally-approved lethal assistance (beyond the $25 million in "defensive" arms) can be delivered.

The ultimate objective in the trip to Tehran is to commence the process of improving U.S.-Iranian relations. Both sides are aware that the Iran-Iraq War is a major factor that must be discussed. We should not, however, view this meeting as a session which will result in immediate Iranian agreement to proceed with a settlement with Iraq. Rather, this meeting, the first high-level U.S.-Iranian contact in five years, should be seen as a chance to move in this direction. These discussions, as well as follow-on talks, should be governed by the Terms of Reference (TOR) (Tab A) with the recognition that this is, hopefully, the first of many meetings and that the hostage issue, once behind us, improves the opportunities for this relationship.

Finally, we should recognize that the Iranians will undoubtedly want to discuss additional arms and commercial transactions as "quids" for accommodating ███████████████████ Nicaragua, and Iraq. Our emphasis on the Soviet military and subversive threat, a useful mechanism in bringing them to agreement on the hostage issue, has also served to increase their desire for means to protect themselves against/deter the Soviets.

RECOMMENDATION

That the President approve the structure depicted above under "Current Situation" and the Terms of Reference at Tab A.

Approve _____   Disapprove _____

Attachment
    Tab A - U.S.-Iranian Terms of Reference

TOP SECRET   TOP SECRET   SENSITIVE

UNCLASSIFIED

Administration of Ronald Reagan, 1986 / Nov. 25

Remarks Announcing the Review of the National Security Council's Role in the Iran Arms and *Contra* Aid Controversy
November 25, 1986

The President. Last Friday, after becoming concerned whether my national security apparatus had provided me with a security—or a complete factual record with respect to the implementation of my policy toward Iran, I directed the Attorney General [Edwin Meese III] to undertake a review of this matter over the weekend and report to me on Monday. And yesterday Secretary Meese provided me and the White House Chief of Staff [Donald T. Regan] with a report on his preliminary findings. And this report led me to conclude that I was not fully informed on the nature of one of the activities undertaken in connection with this initiative. This action raises serious questions of propriety.

I've just met with my national security advisers and congressional leaders to inform them of the actions that I'm taking today. Determination of the full details of this action will require further review and investigation by the Department of Justice. Looking to the future, I will appoint a Special Review Board to conduct a comprehensive review of the role and procedures of the National Security Council staff in the conduct of foreign and national security policy. I anticipate receiving the reports from the Attorney General and the Special Review Board at the earliest possible date. Upon the completion of these reports, I will share their findings and conclusions with the Congress and the American people.

Although not directly involved, Vice Admiral John Poindexter has asked to be relieved of his assignment as Assistant to the President for National Security Affairs and to return to another assignment in the Navy. Lieutenant Colonel Oliver North [Deputy Director for Political-Military Affairs] has been relieved of his duties on the National Security Council staff.

I am deeply troubled that the implementation of a policy aimed at resolving a truly tragic situation in the Middle East has resulted in such controversy. As I've stated previously, I believe our policy goals toward Iran were well founded. However, the information brought to my attention yesterday convinced me that in one aspect implementation of that policy was seriously flawed. While I cannot reverse what has happened, I'm initiating steps, including those I've announced today, to assure that the implementation of all future foreign and national security policy initiatives will proceed only in accordance with my authorization. Over the past 6 years we've realized many foreign policy goals. I believe we can yet achieve—and I intend to pursue—the objectives on which we all agree: a safer, more secure, and stable world.

And now, I'm going to ask Attorney General Meese to brief you.

Reporter. What was the flaw?

Q. Do you still maintain you didn't make a mistake, Mr. President?

The President. Hold it.

Q. Did you make a mistake in sending arms to Tehran, sir?

The President. No, and I'm not taking any more questions. And in just a second, I'm going to ask Attorney General Meese to brief you on what we presently know of what he has found out.

Q. Is anyone else going to be let go, sir?

Q. Can you tell us—did Secretary Shultz——

Q. Is anyone else going to be let go? There have been calls for——

The President. No one was let go. They chose to go.

Q. What about Secretary Shultz, Mr. President?

Q. Is Shultz going to stay, sir?

Q. How about Secretary Shultz and Mr. Regan, sir?

Q. What about Secretary Shultz, sir?

Q. Can you tell us if Secretary Shultz is going to stay?

Q. Can you give Secretary Shultz a vote of confidence if you feel that way?

The President. May I give you Attorney General Meese?

Nov. 25 / Administration of Ronald Reagan, 1986

Q. And who is going to run national security?

Q. What about Shultz, sir?

Q. Why won't you say what the flaw is?

Note: The President spoke at 12:05 p.m. to reporters in the Briefing Room at the White House.

PART THREE

THE AFTERMATH:
HISTORY AND ACCOUNTABILITY

In the years following revelation of the Iran-Contra operations, the scandal continued to generate widespread public interest and to play a significant role in U.S. politics. Sustained by the televised congressional hearings in 1987, the unprecedented criminal trials of former national security officials Oliver North, John Poindexter, and Clair George, and President Bush's Christmas Eve pardons, the scandal defied every effort (most were partisan in nature) to relegate it to the dustbin of history. The media focus on Bush's lack of candor and credibility regarding his own knowledge and role, and the cover-up implied by the president's pretrial pardon of Caspar Weinberger, assured that Iran-Contra would reverberate as a national issue even beyond his departure from the Oval Office.

Indeed, unlike Watergate, for which Richard Nixon's resignation provided a national sense of closure, this scandal remains unresolved. The ongoing, if sporadic, release of documentation, such as the daily diaries of Oliver North and Caspar Weinberger, and the belated discovery that Bush himself had withheld notes pertaining to Iran-Contra, continued to provide new information, and to raise new questions, about U.S. government operations in the Middle East and Central America—further demonstrating the incomplete nature of the congressional inquiry into the scandal. More important, the Iran-Contra committees declined to use the historic opportunity of their investigation to recommend any substantive legal reforms that would strengthen congressional oversight of covert operations and impede future abuses of power by the executive branch.[1]

Nor did the complicated and lengthy judicial proceedings provide a clear signal that crimes committed in the name of national security would be punished, and perhaps thereby deter a repetition to such conduct in the future. Before Bush's December 24, 1992, pardon, the work of Independent Counsel Lawrence Walsh had yielded plea bargains to felony and misdemeanor charges—ranging from perjury to defrauding the United States Treasury—from seven Iran-Contra actors. Of these, the toughest penalty fell to Robert McFarlane, who pleaded guilty to four counts of "withholding information" from Congress and was sentenced to two years' probation, a $20,000 fine, and two hundred hours of community service. Walsh successfully prosecuted former CIA operative Thomas Clines, who became the only Iran-Contra figure to serve a prison sentence—for falsifying his tax records. And after an initial mistrial, on December 9, 1992, a jury found former CIA deputy director of Operations Clair George, guilty on two felony counts of lying to Congress. Fifteen days later, this conviction, and the plea bargains of McFarlane, Abrams, and Fiers, were annulled by presidential pardons. Walsh's two other achievements, the convictions of Oliver North in May 1989, and John Poindexter in April 1990, were later reversed by the Court of Appeals on the grounds that their trials had been tainted by their immunized testimony before Congress, and their cases were subsequently dismissed (Document 90). The independent counsel's two final prosecutions, of Caspar Weinberger and Duane Clarridge, were aborted by Bush's preemptive pardons.

"Tragedies like the Iran-Contra affair," stated Senators Daniel Inouye and Warren Rudman, chairman and vice-chairman of the congressional panel that investigated the scandal, "unite our government and our people in their resolve to find answers, draw lessons, and avoid a repetition."[2] As the Reagan-Bush era came to an end, however, many questions about the Iran-Contra affair remained unanswered and key lessons remained unlearned. And as the American public became aware in 1992 that "Irangate" had evolved into "Iraqgate"—a similarly deceitful program implemented by the Reagan and Bush administrations of aiding and arming Saddam Hussein in Iraq up to the day he invaded Kuwait—the costs of failing to implement stringent safeguards on the executive branch to ensure accountability on national security policy became increasingly evident.[3]

INITIAL INVESTIGATIONS

The Reagan administration's November 25, 1987, disclosure of the diversion set off a number of investigations. To avoid the appearance of a Watergate-style cover-up, the president quickly called for "a full and complete airing of all the facts." On November 26, Reagan announced the appointment of a blue-ribbon "Special Review Board," made up of Senator John Tower, Edmund Muskie, and Brent Scowcroft, to conduct "a comprehensive study of the future role and procedures of the National Security Council staff."[4] On that day Attorney General Meese also ordered the Justice Department's criminal division to initiate an investigation of the diversion. And on December 2, the president directed Meese to appoint an independent counsel to investigate the Iran arms transfers, the Contra resupply operations, and the connection between them.

Congress also moved to investigate the scandal. On November 29, the Senate Intelligence Committee announced that it would conduct its own inquiry. On December 4, the House and Senate agreed to establish a special joint panel to investigate and hold hearings. The Senate Select Committee on Secret Military Assistance to Iran and the Nicaraguan Opposition, and the House Select Committee to Investigate Covert Arms Transactions with Iran were formerly created by congressional resolutions on January 6, and 7, 1987, with a mandate to complete their work and produce a final report by October.

The Senate Intelligence Committee became the first investigative body to issue findings on January 29,

1987. Overshadowed by leaks of an earlier draft, the "Preliminary Inquiry into the Sale of Arms to Iran and Possible Diversion of Funds to the Nicaraguan Resistance" presented the first "general chronological framework of events" surrounding the arms-for-hostages transactions and the Contra operations.[5] Based on interviews with thirty-three witnesses—North and Poindexter refused to testify, citing their Fifth Amendment right not to incriminate themselves—and the examination of a number of documents, the intelligence committee reviewed and summarized the available evidence, and identified the major areas of inquiry for the Iran-Contra committees to investigate. The report contained no evaluation of how the oversight committee had managed to overlook these operations while they were taking place. To the delight of the White House, the report produced no evidence to contradict President Reagan's claim of ignorance regarding the diversion.

With an additional month to work, and access to many more witnesses and documents, the President's Special Review Board (known as the Tower Commission) provided a far more detailed, though still preliminary picture of the actors, decisions, and operations involved in the Iran and Contra policies. The basic thrust and the chief political purpose of the report, however, was to exonerate the president and lay the blame for the scandal on his aides and "flaws in the process" of decision making. The commissioners concluded that Reagan's hands-off management style, and inadequate policy review procedures, were responsible for what they characterized as "an unprofessional and, in substantial part, unsatisfactory operation."[6]

The Tower Commission did make two major contributions to Iran-Contra history. In early February, investigators discovered and retrieved from the National Security Council's computer backup system a major file of secret internal computer messages between North, Poindexter, McFarlane and staffmembers, including thousands of notes that the authors had deleted from the main system during the last few days before the scandal was exposed. Since much of the communications between NSC officials had been conducted electronically instead of on paper—particularly after late August 1985 when the press had first identified Oliver North and the Contra resupply operations—these PROFS notes yielded extensive new details about the Iran-Contra policies and operations.[7]

The Tower Commission also interviewed President Reagan and Vice President Bush. Although the interviews were cursory at best, they established an official record against which Reagan and Bush's honesty and credibility on their roles in the scandal could be judged.

President Reagan was interviewed for the first time on January 26, 1987, and he adopted what Theodore Draper calls an "innocence-by-ignorance" defense.[8] Although later evidence demonstrated that Reagan had directed the NSC to sustain the Contras, received almost daily briefings on the resupply efforts, interceded with foreign leaders to raise money and secure arms, and met with domestic donors for the same purpose, "the President told the Board," according to the Tower Commission report, "that he did not know that the NSC staff was engaged in helping the Contras."[9]

On the Iran arms-for-hostages-transfers, Reagan at first told the Tower investigators that he had indeed approved the first shipment by Israel of arms to Iran in August 1985. During the commission's second interview with the president on February 11, however, Reagan retracted this position. "The President said that he and Mr. Regan had gone over the matter a number of times and that Mr. Regan had a firm recollection that the President had not authorized the August shipment in advance," the commission reported. "The President said he did not recall authorizing the August shipment."[10] Then, in a February 20 letter to the commission, Reagan retracted this story also. "My answer," Reagan wrote, "and the simple truth is 'I don't remember—period.'"[11]

Tower Commission investigators interviewed Vice President Bush on December 12, 1986. They focused on a meeting he had held the previous July in Tel Aviv with Israeli official Amiram Nir. "President Bush related that his discussion with Mr. Nir was generally about counterterrorism. There was no discussion of specifics relating to arms going to the Iranians," the report stated. Below Bush's response, however, the report reproduced a detailed memorandum of conversation on the meeting with Nir, written by Bush's chief of staff, Craig Fuller, which flatly contradicted the vice president's account.[12] Fuller's notes recorded no discussion whatsoever of counterterrorism, but rather an extensive, specific discussion about "the details of the efforts from last year through the current period to gain the release of the U.S. hostages" in return for "4000 [missile] units" and "spares for Hawks and TOWS."[13] The memorandum represented the first of many documents that contradicted Bush's repeated claims to have been "out of the loop" on the Iran initiative.

THE IRAN-CONTRA COMMITTEES

The joint House and Senate Iran-Contra panel opened hearings on May 5 and ended them on August 6 after listening to over two hundred fifty hours of testimony from thirty-two witnesses. For twelve weeks, network television cameras enabled the public to visually follow the complicated proceedings.[14] The television coverage assured that the hearings would become the single most important vehicle for transmitting the story of the scandal to the American people.

To be sure, the testimony of such figures as Richard Secord, Fawn Hall, Elliott Abrams, Donald Regan, Edwin Meese, and other government officials and nongovernment players provided important, often extraordinary, insights into the internal workings of the Reagan White House, the role of the "private-sector" intermediaries, and the mechanics of running covert operations in Central America and the Middle East. But overall, the hearings presented an extremely distorted picture of the policies and events, as well as of their implications for the nation. When, for example, Oliver North testified between July 7 and 14, the hearings played more like a televison advertisement for his brand of zealotry than a major congressional inquiry into the crimes of state.

North's testimony provided the dramatic high point

of the hearings—so dramatic that the television networks preempted their soap opera programming to broadcast it live—as well as the low point in Congress's handling of their own investigation. Over strenuous objections by Independent Counsel Walsh, the committees conferred on North "use immunity"—a legal guarantee that nothing he said could be used against him in future criminal proceedings—to compel his testimony. The committees then capitulated to a series of extraordinary demands made by North's lawyer, Brendan Sullivan, among them that North not be deposed prior to his testimony; that the duration of his testimony be limited to a few days with no recourse by the committee to recall him later in the hearings; and that he be allowed to delay turning over relevant documents until three days in advance of his testimony. Sullivan's intentions were clear: to undermine the ability of the panel's investigators to prepare for questioning North on the witness stand. Nevertheless, the committees "caved in," as Senators George Mitchell and William Cohen wrote in their book, *Men of Zeal: A Candid Inside Story of the Iran-Contra Hearings*. Although some leaders of the panel believed that Sullivan was bluffing, calling that bluff meant risking contempt of Congress proceedings that might drag on beyond the committees' self-imposed October deadline. "To get North to testify, we had let him set the time and terms of his testimony," Mitchell and Cohen admitted. "This was the single most important decision made by the Committee."[15]

North's uncanny ability to cow the Congress extended through his appearance before the committees. He began his testimony as the obscure NSC staffer at the center of the scandal; he finished as a certified celebrity, to some the "national hero" that North claimed President Reagan had called him.[16] In the interim, North proudly admitted to systematically lying to Congress, shredding documents, and falsifying evidence, among many other illicit activities intended to aid the Contras and to cover up the arms-for-hostages operations. But his telegenic personality, in contrast to an abysmal performance by his congressional questioners, wholly overshadowed the substance of the story North told.

The committees' lack of will and determination in confronting Oliver North manifested itself in other areas of their investigation. To avoid extending their work into the 1988 election year, congressional leaders imposed a short (ten-month) deadline on completing the hearings and issuing a report, forcing investigators to abandon many important avenues of inquiry because of time pressures. The committees agreed to permit White House screening of classified documents before their release to investigators, thereby entrusting responsibility for access to information to the very agencies that had participated in the scandal. In the end, Congress was denied access to hundreds of records needed to complete its investigation.[17]

Most important, the committees decided not to investigate potentially illegal offenses involving President Reagan—except the diversion—to avoid creating an impeachment crisis à la Watergate. Critical evidence, such as recordings of Reagan's phone calls with foreign leaders which might have exposed additional participation by the president in illegal activities, went unrequested. The consensus of an early meeting of members of the Senate select committee, the dominant power on the joint panel, was that "we don't want to go after the President."[18]

These decisions and compromises contributed to the less-than-definitive outcome of Iran-Contra committees' investigation—their final report, issued on November 17, 1987. Drawn from the hearings, interviews with over five hundred witnesses, and a review of a million pages of documents, the 690-page *Report of the Congressional Committees Investigating the Iran-Contra Affair* provided a comprehensive treatment of the complex and interconnected covert operations run out of the Reagan White House.[19] Subsequently, the committees released two massive volumes of documents used as sources for the report, and twenty-seven volumes of formerly closed depositions with hundreds of governmental and nongovernmental actors who participated in many different components of the Iran-Contra operations.

The Iran Contra Affair presented a compendium of

the administration's skulduggery, enhancing public understanding of what it took—in terms of money, manpower, and manipulation—to conduct "off-the-shelf, self-sustaining, stand-alone" operations behind the back of Congress and the American public. At the same time, the report contained numerous informational and conceptual omissions. Although Senate committee chief counsel Arthur Liman later wrote in the *New York Times* that since the fall of 1987 "we have known all that is knowable about the affair," the committees' investigation missed significant components of the scandal—later uncovered by the office of the independent counsel—involving President Reagan and Vice President Bush.[20] In addition, drafted chapters on contentious aspects of the scandal were excluded from the final publication for political reasons.[21] And the historical, ideological, and institutional foundations of the Iran-Contra operations went largely unexplored. Nor, in the end, did the congressional authors include an examination of the role of their own legislative branch in allowing these illicit operations to evolve as they did.

To their credit, the committees did identify the important constitutional issues at the heart of the Iran-Contra scandal. In Chapter 25 on the "Power of Congress and the President in the Field of Foreign Policy," the report addressed the threat to the constitutional system of checks and balances posed by the Reagan administration's illicit efforts to raise funds—funds explicitly denied by Congress—from other sources. "This clandestine financing operation undermined the powers of Congress as a coequal branch and subverted the Constitution," the authors argued.[22] "To permit the President and his aides to carry out covert actions by using funds obtained from outside Congress undermines the Framer's belief that 'the purse and the sword must never be in the same hands.'"[23] The position adopted by Reagan's national security managers, that these funds could be used to field an army and fight a war without congressional appropriations, represented the most serious threat of all, concluded the report. "That is the path to dictatorship."[24]

Having identified the true gravity of the Iran-Contra scandal, however, the committees failed to proscribe changes in the law that would prevent future administrations from going down that path again. Instead, the congressional authors concluded that the scandal had "resulted from the failure of individuals to observe the law, not from deficiencies in existing law or in our system of governance."[25] *The Iran-Contra Affair* recommended only minor adjustments to the official system of conducting and reporting covert operations; and only a few of these recommendations were actually incorporated into the 1988 Intelligence Oversight Act.[26]

THE INVESTIGATION OF INDEPENDENT COUNSEL LAWRENCE WALSH

When the Iran-Contra committees concluded their work in November 1987, responsibility for completing the factual record, and enforcing the laws that had been violated, fell to Judge Lawrence Walsh. Pursuant to a December 4, 1986, petition filed by Attorney General Meese, a three-judge panel named Walsh—a former federal judge, deputy attorney general, diplomat, and long-standing member of the Republican party—as Iran-Contra's independent counsel. Whereas Meese had wanted Walsh's criminal inquiry to be limited to the sale of arms to Iran and the diversion of funds, the panel broadened Judge Walsh's mandate to include investigating and prosecuting violations of law derived from the "provision or coordination of support" for the Nicaraguan Contras.[27]

In many respects, Walsh's work was unprecedented. None of the nine independent counsels that had proceeded him under the 1978 special prosecutor statute had investigated national security crimes. Nor had the Classified Information Procedures Act (CIPA)—a 1980 law passed to prevent "graymail," the threat by defendants to disclose classified information if brought to trial—been used in cases involving contemporary covert operations. Walsh and his Office of the Independent Counsel (OIC) faced the daunting task of investigating and prosecuting the highest national security officials in the U.S. government—while the administration they had served was still in office.

Walsh convened a grand jury on January 28, 1987, and thereafter moved to secure indictments and plea bargains with individuals who might testify against the major figures in the Iran-Contra operations. Three months later, Carl R. "Spitz" Channell became the first to plead guilty to criminal conduct in the scandal's aftermath. Channell admitted to conspiring with Oliver North to

> defraud the IRS and deprive the Treasury of the United States of revenue to which it was entitled by subverting and corrupting the lawful purposes and operations of NEPL by using NEPL for an improper purpose, namely, to solicit contributions to purchase military and other types of non-humanitarian aid for the Contras. (Document 91)

A week later Richard Miller plead guilty to an identical charge. Under the terms of their plea bargain, both received slap-on-the-wrist penalties—two years' probation and a fifty-dollar fine—and agreed to cooperate in future legal proceedings against their coconspirator.[28]

In March 1988, Walsh also secured the cooperation of former national security advisor Robert McFarlane, allowing him to plead guilty to four misdemeanor counts of "unlawfully, willfully and knowingly" withholding information from Congress (Document 92). Although McFarlane was a key player in the scandal, on February 8, 1987, he had attempted suicide with an overdose of Valium. This self-destructive act of contrition rendered him a difficult defendant to put on trial, let alone to convict; by allowing him to plead to misdemeanors the OIC hoped McFarlane would provide critical testimony against his NSC colleagues at their forthcoming trials.[29]

North, Poindexter, Secord, and Hakim were indicted together on March 16, 1988. Their indictment contained twenty-three criminal counts including: conspiracy, wire fraud, obstruction of Congress, and destruction of government documents. The central charge relating to the diversion stated that all four had conspired to defraud the United States "by deceitfully and without legal authorization organizing, directing and concealing a program to continue funding of and logistical and other support for military and paramilitary operations in Nicaragua." They were also charged with theft of government property because they "unlawfully, willfully and knowingly did embezzle, and convert to their own use and the use of others," funds from the sale of U.S. arms to Iran.[30]

The OIC faced two overwhelming obstacles to prosecuting North et al.: the "use immunity" granted by Congress to North, Poindexter, Hakim, and others; and the need to use top-secret information—the declassification of which would be determined by the very agencies involved in the Contra and Iranian operations—during the trials of operatives and officials. These two problems resulted in hundreds of hours of additional legal work, countless pretrial hearings, and months of delay. In the end, they combined to undermine the ability of the independent counsel to prosecute, independently, the criminality of the Iran-Contra scandal.

As early as January 13, 1987, Walsh asked the Iran-Contra committees not to confer immunity on certain witnesses during their forthcoming hearings. Doing so, he argued, would create "serious—and perhaps insurmountable—barriers" to future prosecutions.[31] The Supreme Court ruling governing use immunity, known as *Kastigar* v. *United States*, held that any such grant would result in "a sweeping proscription of any use, direct or indirect, of the compelled testimony and any information derived therefrom," and placed on the prosecution "the heavy burden of proving that all of the evidence it proposes to use was derived from legitimate independent sources."[32] In practice, the burden of what the OIC called "our Kastigar problems" became far broader: not only did all evidence against North and others have to be gathered and sealed prior to their immunization—a process known in Walsh's office as "canning"—but the prosecutors themselves had to be insulated from media coverage of immunized testimony.[33] Walsh, moreover, subsequently would have to prove that all witnesses used at the trials, and perhaps even before the grand jury, had not been influenced by immunized testimony given during the nationally televised hearings. Nor could any individual who had watched the hearings, or had read about them in the newspapers, serve on a jury in the forthcoming trials. "Immunity cannot be granted without a full recognition that it will have a serious and possible destructive impact upon a subsequent prosecution," Walsh reported to Congress in April 1987.[34]

The Iran-Contra committees rejected Walsh's requests to forgo immunizing North and Poindexter, agreeing only to delay their public testimony until midsummer 1987 to allow the OIC more time to build a case and put evidence "in the can." This decision haunted Walsh's prosecutions at every stage. Originally, Walsh had planned to try North, Poindexter, Secord, and Hakim together—demonstrating their conspiratorial partnership to the jury. But Judge Gerhardt Gesell ruled in June 1988 that they must be tried separately, to avoid one defendant seeking to use immunized testimony of another during the trial. Instead of one trial for the major actors, the OIC now faced preparing for four.

Oliver North, the self-described "fall guy" of the scandal, went on trial first in February 1989. After more than two months of testimony and twelve days of deliberation, a jury pronounced him guilty on three counts: "aiding and abetting" the obstruction of Congress by falsifying chronologies about the Iran arms-for-hostages initiatives; destroying evidence by shredding documents; and accepting an illegal gratuity in the form of a $13,800 security fence paid for with funds from the diversion. On nine other charges, however, he was acquitted. "Basically, on the counts of 'not guilty' he was following orders," jury foreperson Denise Anderson told the press afterward. "And there were lots of people's orders."[35]

In Walsh's posttrial submissions to Judge Gesell, the OIC pressed for a prison sentence that would "be carefully considered by those officials who may now be weighing the advantages of deception, obstruction and personal greed against the risks of punishment," as well as "scrutinized by a citizenry whose confidence in government and the political system has been seriously undermined by the activities of this defendant" (Document 93). But on July 5, Gesell sentenced North, who he called "a low-ranking subordinate working to carry out initiatives of a few cynical superiors," to a three-year suspended sentence, two years' probation, $150,000 in fines and twelve hundred hours of community service.

North's conviction, however, did not stand. A year later, a three-judge appeals court (which included Lawrence Silberman, a minor figure in the Reagan administration's Iran initiative) overturned one count and vacated the other two on the basis that North's immunized testimony before Congress might have tainted his trial. The appeals court placed an impossible burden on the OIC: to prove that not a single sentence of testimony presented at North's trial had been influenced by his congressional testimony. When Robert McFarlane told Judge Gesell during a hearing in September 1991 that his court testimony had been "overwhelmingly" influenced by North's appearance before Congress, the judge had no recourse but to dismiss all charges.

Iran-Contra's most famous defendant then declared himself "totally exonerated." But, ironically, North was freed of any criminal culpability precisely because he had admitted to these crimes under immunity. On the issue of falsifying chronologies he had told the Iran-Contra committees that "I decided I would continue to participate in preparing a version of the chronology...that was not accurate. I did participate in that activity, wittingly and knowingly." Similarly, North told the committees that after the shootdown of the Hasenfus plane in October, he had instigated a "shredding party" in his office to eliminate incriminating evidence. "I do not deny that I engaged in shredding on November 21," North admitted, referring to the day he learned of Attorney General Meese's inquiry. And he confessed to falsifying invoices to conceal his acceptance of a $13,800 security fence paid for by money from the diversion. "The security system...was installed by Mr. [Glenn] Robinette with General Secord's money, or the Enterprise's money," North admitted to the committees. "I then tried to paper over the whole thing by sending two phony documents back to Mr. Robinette.... I have admitted to that. I am here to tell the truth, even when it hurts. Okay? They [were] phony."[36]

The dismissal of charges against North paved the way for "exoneration" of his superior at the NSC, Admiral Poindexter. In a major legal victory for the OIC, Poindexter had been convicted on all five felony charges of obstruction of Congress and perjury on April 7, 1990; he subsequently became the first Reagan administration official to be sentenced to a prison term, all of six months. But on November 15, 1991, the same appeals court that had overturned the charges against North threw out Poindexter's conviction on the same grounds. When the Supreme Court refused to hear Walsh's appeal of that ruling, all charges against Poindexter were dropped on December 7, 1992. As Walsh had predicted to Congress, the immunization of key players in the Iran-Contra scandal had created insurmountable roadblocks to bringing them to justice.

The necessity of using secret documents in court also constrained Walsh's ability to prosecute the crimes of Iran-Contra. Beginning in the spring of 1988, the OIC found itself engaged in what staffmember Jeffrey Toobin characterized as "a war over classified information."[37] The Iran-Contra defendants demanded thousands of NSC, CIA, NSA, and Defense Department documents—many of them unrelated to the Contra or Iran operations—that they claimed were critical for their defense. Some of these requests were, in fact, legitimate; most, however, constituted "graymail"—a threat to reveal such highly classified information during the judicial proceedings that the administration would terminate prosecution on national security grounds.

In 1980, Congress had passed the Classified Information Procedures Act (CIPA) in order to prevent gray-

mail.[38] CIPA enacted procedures for court review, substitutions, and negotiations over the use of such information during trial proceedings. Most important, however, CIPA provided for U.S. government control over the ultimate disclosure in court of secret documents. In practice, the law empowered first the Reagan administration and then Bush's—both of which had a clear conflict of interest in Walsh's prosecutions—to control the independent counsel's independence, and hamstring his ability to prosecute, simply by denying public disclosure of certain documentation.

Using this power, the White House blocked the pursuit of justice and history in the aftermath of the scandal. The core charges regarding the diversion conspiracy in Walsh's indictment against North et al., for example, had to be abandoned because an interagency review group—a committee made up of representatives of the very agencies that had been heavily involved in the Iran-Contra operations—made it clear that documentation on U.S. covert operations in the Middle East would not be declassified. This decision exempted the activities at the very center of the Iran-Contra scandal from public scrutiny and criminal prosecution. The OIC was forced to drop the charges relating to the diversion against North and Poindexter, and decided to forgo trying Secord and Hakim altogether.[39] In the end, no one involved would stand trial for the diversion of funds from one operation to the other.

The Bush administration also used its control over classified documentation to abort Walsh's prosecution of the former CIA chief of station in Costa Rica, Joseph Fernandez. Fernandez had played an integral part in the Contra resupply operation in the southern front and then lied about his role to the Tower Commission. After more than a year of legal preparations and extensive hearings on what classified information could be used in court, Walsh's office prepared to bring Fernandez to trial on four counts of perjury in July 1989.

Fernandez's defense strategy was to argue that he had no reason to lie because he had reported his Contra activities to his superiors as part of his other covert duties in Costa Rica. To bolster this defense, Judge Claude Hilton ruled that Fernandez could disclose the locations of three CIA stations and one facility in Central America, and identify three CIA programs in Costa Rica that had been part of the U.S. efforts to undermine the Sandinistas. As jury selection began, however, Attorney General Richard Thornburgh, acting at the behest of the CIA, intervened to block the disclosure of that information and to delay the advent of the trial.

In a letter to President Bush dated October 19, 1989, Walsh requested a meeting to discuss the CIA's efforts to abort the trial of one of its own (Document 94). If the CIA was allowed to withhold this information, Walsh argued, the United States would "lose a much more important national value—the rule of law." The president refused to meet with him.[40] On November 24, Judge Hilton dismissed all charges against Fernandez.

The Fernandez episode amounted to a flagrant abuse of the classification system aimed at hiding the truth of the CIA's role in the Contra resupply operations. The CIA's "fictional secrets," as Walsh described them, were, in fact, publicly known. The presence of CIA stations in El Salvador, Guatemala, and Honduras, and the existence in the latter country of an additional major facility at the El Aguacate air base were well established; for example, the government itself had allowed the release of Iran-Contra documents which referred to station chiefs in El Salvador and Honduras. The three CIA programs in Costa Rica were also known; in an oral history, former U.S. Ambassador to Costa Rica Curtin Winsor, Jr., had identified two of them—the development of "an intelligence net for the Costa Ricans" and a training program for an elite eight-hundred-man border patrol.[41] The third, a sophisticated radio communications program, had been identified in the press.

In his second report to Congress, the independent counsel forcefully argued that by provoking the dismissal of the Fernandez case, the Bush administration had exempted the intelligence community from legal, and thus democratic, accountability. The Justice Department's claim that national security would be damaged by admission in court of already publicly known information was a specious one:

> Revelations concerning the Iran/Contra activities of the national security agencies have already exposed such grave questions of national credibility that they dwarf the breach of deniability that is now said to require the dismissal of Fernandez. Deceiving allies, deceiving Congress, diverting United States funds to unauthorized activities...have all been extensively disclosed and acknowledged by documents and evidence previously released....[A]gainst the three-year widespread disclosure of truly sensitive information regarding these countries, the acknowledgement of these publicly known facts would barely add a drop to an already full bucket.[42]

"We suggest," Walsh's report concluded, "that the injury to national security flows from support of illegal activities undertaken by former CIA officials and not from their investigation and prosecution."[43]

THE VERDICT OF HISTORY

These and other setbacks provided ammunition for critics of the independent counsel who grew increasingly vocal about the costs of the OIC's legal work—estimated in August 1992 at $32 million—and Walsh's continued pursuit of major figures involved in the scandal. Indeed, bashing the independent counsel became a cottage industry among right-wing editorial page writers and conservative Republicans. After charges against North were dismissed, the *Wall Street Journal* editorialized that Walsh's prosecutions were "a Kafkaesque ritual" comparable "to what used to happen to people in the Soviet Union."[44] When the case against Poindexter was dropped in December 1992, Senate minority leader Robert Dole declared that Walsh had "struck out again in his costly and partisan inquisition of Republicans."[45]

The value of Walsh's work, however, derived less from his conviction rate than from the historical contribution of his prosecutions. As much as an Elliott Abrams or a Duane Clarridge, history became a "subject" of the OIC's investigation. The perpetrators of the Iran-Contra operations had falsified the historical record as part of an effort to cover up the scandal and to obfuscate their personal roles. Congress had proven unable, or unwilling to establish a complete and accurate body of evidence that historians could later judge. The OIC's investigation helped to fill the gaps in the record, and, to the extent possible, set that record straight for the judgment of history.

The prosecutions, for example, revised the way history books would treat President Reagan's role in the scandal. Both North and Poindexter sought to defend themselves by pointing the finger at their commander-in-chief, and in effect, putting the absent Reagan on trial with them. New documents introduced at North's trial, such as transcripts of the National Security Planning Group meetings (Document 23) revealed Reagan to be extensively engaged in plotting and participating in the circumvention of the law, contradicting the popular image of him as disengaged from the crimes of state. At the same time, however, the former president's testimony, via videotape, at the Poindexter trial forever changed Reagan's image as "the great communicator" and a capable leader. "To this day, I don't have any information or knowledge that ...there was a diversion," Reagan stated. "I, to this day, do not recall ever hearing that there was a diversion."[46]

The trials also provided new and important evidence about components of the Iran-Contra affair far more scandalous than the renowned diversion. In particular, the North trial produced documents that revealed, and catalogued, the Reagan administration's quid pro quos on behalf of the Contras. These schemes of bribery, blackmail, and coercion—Draper describes them as "an anthology of practices so shady that they could not be revealed without shame"—were authorized by president and implemented, in part, by the vice president and numerous other members of the administra-

tion.[47] The quid pro quos represented an extraordinary facet of Iran-Contra history that might have remained concealed had North never been prosecuted.

Walsh's investigation also uncovered the Reagan administration's extensive efforts to conceal the Iran-Contra operations. Unable to prosecute the operational side of the affair because of obstacles raised by the White House, the last three years of the OIC's work focused on exposing the cover-up and the criminality that accompanied it. Reagan administration officials from almost every agency involved in the Iran-Contra operations, the OIC determined, had sought to obstruct congressional inquiries by lying and withholding evidence. Elliott Abrams, the administration's most famous dissembler who pleaded guilty to two counts of perjury in October 1991, was not alone (Document 95).

The cover-up of a broader knowledge of the diversion itself prevailed until July 1991, when the former chief of the CIA's Central American Task Force, Alan Fiers, pleaded guilty to two counts of unlawfully withholding information from Congress about his knowledge of the Contra resupply operations. As part of his plea bargain, Fiers admitted that North had told him of the diversion, not once but twice in 1986, and that he had reported this information to his immediate superior in the Latin American division, and to Clair George, CIA deputy director for operations. "Mr. Fiers informed Mr. George that Lt. Col. North had told him that the United States was selling arms to Iran and using proceeds from the sales to assist the Contras," court papers submitted by Walsh stated. "Mr. George informed Mr. Fiers that, 'Now you are one of a handful of people who know this'" (Document 96).

Fiers's decision to go public broke the official mythology surrounding the diversion: that only North and Poindexter had known about it. More importantly, Fiers's agreement to cooperate with the OIC marked a major rupture in the code of silence that had insulated the CIA from any public scrutiny of its little-understood role in the Iran-Contra scandal. The information he shared had immediate repercussions for the agency and its highest officials.

This new evidence forced a two-month delay in the confirmation hearings of Robert Gates, Casey's deputy in 1986, and Bush's nominee to be CIA director in mid 1991.[48] Although Gates was later confirmed, the hearings became another national forum on the CIA's role in both the Iran and Contra operations.

The Fiers plea bargain also led directly to the indictment on nine counts of perjury and obstruction of Congress of Clair George, the former CIA deputy director for operations. In July 1992, the CIA's spymaster became the first Agency official ever to go on trial for crimes committed during the commission of covert operations. This historic trial offered a rare public glimpse into the inner workings of the CIA's most secret sanctum, the covert operations directorate. During the proceedings, a vast body of CIA reports and memoranda relating to the Contra war in Nicaragua were placed in the public domain as evidence. The trial also produced a number of important revelations about the Nicaragua side of the scandal, among them that in addition to evading the congressional cutoff of funding for the Contras, the CIA and the NSC had circumvented another congressional ban on funding for the Nicaraguan Catholic Church, by using monies obtained from a third country and an American corporation.[49]

The first trial of Clair George ended in a hung jury on August 26, 1992. Over the objections of his critics, Walsh announced that he would try George again. The second trial ended on December 9, with guilty verdicts on two counts of lying to Congress. The OIC hailed the convictions as "an important deterrent to protect the Congress and the public from cover-ups by high-level national security officials."[50]

By then, Walsh was preparing for what was supposed to have been his last major trial—*United States v. Caspar W. Weinberger*. The former secretary of defense was indicted on June 16, 1992, on five felony counts relating to his concealment of extensive personal notes on meetings and conversations on the Iran initiative and the Contra resupply operations and knowledge of those operations. When he was asked by

congressional investigators in April 1987 to turn over all "notes...diaries...or other such records" relating to Iran-Contra, Weinberger had quietly withheld his personal papers. "Occasionally [I] take a few notes, but not really very often," Weinberger told the House select committee that June, when, in fact, he was a compulsive notemaker and had over seventeen hundred pages relating to Iran-Contra issues.[51]

Although Weinberger would later claim not to have understood what exactly investigators were requesting of him, his own internal office documents and handwritten notes explicitly contradicted this defense. On April 17, 1987, after both the House and Senate committees had requested his personal papers, Weinberger received an "action memorandum" from former Defense Department general counsel H. Lawrence Garrett on turning over his notes and diaries:

> I know you understand the nature of the obligations placed upon us by this request. I understand that these materials...are highly personal and sensitive. Accordingly, I would of course insist that any provision of these materials to the Committees be conducted in as discreet and limited a manner as you wish.

During a meeting with Garrett four days later, Weinberger scribbled the following: "Larry Garrett in office—re demands by Sen-House Committees for briefings on black programs—Their demand for my diary" (Document 97).[52]

The Weinberger notes provided a contemporaneous record of the policymaking discussions in the Oval Office—an unparalleled source of historical evidence on the Iran-Contra affair. For the OIC, Weinberger's records of meetings with President Reagan and his top aides in November 1986 revealed a cover-up conspiracy, at the highest levels of the administration, of the president's knowledge of the 1985 arms shipments to Iran. "[T]he continuing investigation has developed new and disturbing evidence that...has provided a significant shift in our understanding of Iran/Contra [and] who participated in its cover-up,"

Walsh reported to Congress nine days after indicting Weinberger. "We are attempting to determine whether officials at the highest levels of government, acting individually or in concert, sought to obstruct official inquiries into the Iran initiative" (Document 98).

THE DENOUEMENT OF THE SCANDAL

The political context in which Walsh's investigation took place raised its profile. As the 1992 election year progressed, the issue of Iran-Contra cast a shadow over President Bush's reelection bid. In 1988, Michael Dukakis chose not use Bush's unexplained role in the scandal as a political weapon; the Clinton campaign, however, decided to parry Bush's charges on draft dodging with the Iran-Contra sword, challenging the president to come clean on what he knew and when he knew it. The Weinberger proceedings helped to focus the media on Bush's claims to have been "out of the loop" on both the trading of arms-for-hostages, and Weinberger and Shultz's strong objections to it. One pretrial motion in the Weinberger case contained the following note, dictated on August 7, 1987, by Secretary of State Shultz following a phone conversation with the secretary of defense: "VP in papers yest[erday] s[ai]d he not exposed to Cap or my arguments on Iran arms. Cap called me + sd that's terrible. He [Bush] was on other side. Its on the Record. Why did he say that."[53]

It is, perhaps, poetic justice that the Iran-Contra scandal returned to haunt the very office in which it began. On October 30, three days before the election, Walsh's OIC filed a new indictment on the first count against Weinberger, replacing the original charge of obstructing Congress—dismissed by Judge Hogan as improperly constructed—with a charge of withholding evidence from Congress. Unlike the first indictment, this one quoted numerous passages from Weinberger's notes, including notes of a January 7, 1986, meeting attended by Bush, Reagan, Weinberger, Shultz and others at which trading four thousand missiles for five hostages was explicitly discussed (Document 99). The story led the evening news, and dogged

Bush throughout the final weekend of the campaign. When the president was defeated by Clinton, Walsh provided a convenient scapegoat for those Republicans who refused to admit that the systematic problems engendered by Bush's policies might have finally come home to roost.

In the immediate aftermath of the election, the second Weinberger indictment (which was also dismissed by the judge) generated a hail of partisan acrimony. Senator Dole demanded that a special prosecutor be named to investigate allegations that Walsh had leaked the indictment to the Clinton/Gore campaign. Vice President Quayle called the timing of the second indictment "a travesty of justice" that "smell[ed] of politics." Although election analysts discounted the impact on Clinton's victory, President Bush was reported to be convinced that the Iran-Contra story had broken his surge in the polls during the final hours of the campaign and cost him any chance for a comeback.[54]

On Christmas Eve, Bush took his revenge, surprising the nation by pardoning Weinberger, Clarridge, McFarlane, Abrams, Fiers, and George. With one presidential signature, Bush effectively terminated the legal work of the OIC—the Weinberger trial had been scheduled for January 5, 1993—and erased the modicum of justice that, after six long years of effort, that office had achieved against these U.S. officials for perjury, obstruction, and other criminal acts. "The common denominator of their motivation…was patriotism," Bush asserted in his pardon statement; the prosecution of Weinberger and the others represented nothing more than "the criminalization of policy differences." He described their actions as part of a "larger Cold War struggle" at home; now that the Cold War was over, "it was time for the country to move on" (Document 100).

In response, Independent Counsel Walsh excoriated the president for using the pardons to conceal the truth. "The Iran-Contra cover-up, which has continued for more than six years, has now been completed," he submitted. By aborting the trial, Bush had assured that important details of the cover-up woud not be publicly aired. "Weinberger's notes contain evidence of a conspiracy among the highest-ranking Reagan administration officials to lie to Congress and the American public," wrote Walsh. And by concealing these notes, Weinberger had "radically altered the official investigations and possibly forestalled timely impeachment proceedings against President Reagan and other officials." Therefore, a crime that had obstructed the investiagation of the scandal, and possibly altered the direction of American history, would now go unanswered. The presidential pardons demonstrated "that powerful people with powerful allies can commit serious crimes in high office—deliberately abusing the public trust—without consequence," Walsh asserted (Document 101). Later he would tell *Newsweek* that it was "hard to find an adjective strong enough to characterize a president who has such contempt for honesty."[55]

With his presidential pardons, Bush clearly intended to shut the door, once and for all, on the scandal and "put the bitterness behind us and look to the future." Instead, the pardons only served to put the spotlight on his own role in the cover-up. The president himself, Judge Walsh informed the press, may have "illegally withheld documents" from investigators.[56] In November 1986, Bush had begun keeping his own notes on the scandal, and, despite repeated requests to turn over such documents, had failed to provide them to Congress or the OIC. The concealment of these documents fit "a disturbing pattern of deception and obstruction that permeated the highest levels of the Reagan and Bush administrations," according to the OIC's statement on the pardons. "In light of President Bush's own misconduct, we are gravely concerned about his decision to pardon others who lied to Congress and obstructed official investigations" (Document 101).

To counter these charges, President Bush promised to make public "everything" in his files—a promise he

had uttered more than once over the last six years. At the same time, he hired a lawyer (former attorney general Griffin Bell) to represent him in discussions with the OIC over the release of his notes and any legal proceedings that the independent counsel's office might initiate against him after he left office. In reality, however, the pardons left Walsh with only one recourse: to record for posterity the truth of the criminal abuses of power during the Reagan and Bush administrations in his final report to Congress. When asked on ABC's *Nightline* how history would judge Bush, Walsh was direct: the president, along with those he had pardoned, had "shown an arrogant disdain for the law." Moreover, Walsh stated, "President Bush's sugar coating [of these actions] is going to become increasingly transparent. The American public is, in the end, a very perceptive body of people."[57]

As the political uproar over the pardons subsided, and the Reagan-Bush era became a part of the past, the Iran-Contra scandal completed its transformation from tragedy to history. However, its legacy—the dangers of national security secrecy, the lack of congressional will to safeguard the checks and balances of the Constitution, inadequate public support for the principles of openness and accountability and the threat of an imperial presidency—carried a warning for, and a pressing challenge to, the American people and their system of governance. The Cold War had ended but the U.S. national security institutions and operations generated by that war remained intact. Of the many unanswered questions about Iran-Contra, the most important is how to reconstruct a national security system to complement, rather than threaten, a constitutional system premised on public access to information, democratic debate, and active consent of the governed. Until that question is addressed, the Iran-Contra scandal remains to be resolved.

NOTES

1. For an examination of the congressional recommendations on legislation in the aftermath of the scandal, see Peter Kornbluh, "Iran Contra: A Post Mortem," *The World Policy Journal,* Winter 1987–1988.

2. See their "additional views" in the *Report of the Congressional Committees Investigating the Iran-Contra Affair* (Washington, D.C.: G.P.O. November 17, 1987), p. 637.

3. For a detailed account of how the Iran operation evolved into U.S. economic and military support for Saddam Hussein, see Murray Waas and Craig Ungar, "In the Loop: Bush's Secret Mission," *The New Yorker*, November 2, 1992.

4. On December 1, 1986, Reagan issued Executive Order 12575 formerly establishing the Tower Commission and giving it a mandate. See *The Tower Commission Report* (New York: Times Books, 1987), p. 100.

5. For an overview and the text of the Intelligence Committee report see Congressional Quarterly, Inc., *The Iran-Contra Puzzle* (Washington, D.C.: CQ, 1987), pp. 63–69.

6. Tower Commission report, p. 63.

7. When the Reagan administration attempted to erase its computer data banks in mid January 1989, the National Security Archive and Public Citizen sought a court injunction to keep trillions of bytes of electronic mail, including Iran-Contra PROFS notes from being lost permanently. Through our follow-up lawsuit under the Freedom of Information Act, additional computer messages relating to the Iran-Contra operations are still being declassified.

8. Theodore Draper, "Revelations of the North Trial," *New York Review of Books*, August 17, 1989, p. 56.

9. Tower Commission report, p. 61. Several months later, President Reagan flatly contradicted his own testimony, telling a gathering of newspaper editors that "I was very definitely involved in the decisions about support to the freedom fighters. It was my idea to begin with."

10. Ibid., p. 28.

11. Ibid., p. 29.

12. See Document 67. The commission investigators obtained the Fuller memorandum of conversation after interviewing Bush. Why they did not reinterview him on the clear discrepancies between his story and the document has never been explained.

13. Tower Commission report, pp. 385-89.

14. Four days of hearings were conducted in executive session, off-limits to the public and the press.

15. William S. Cohen and George J. Mitchell, *Men of Zeal: A Candid Inside Story of the Iran-Contra Hearings* (New York: Penguin, 1989), p. 149. Mitchell, for one, understood that North and Sullivan were bluffing. On page 151 he writes: "It seemed to me that North's best hope of avoiding criminal conviction was to testify and then to get the criminal charges dismissed on the ground that the prosecution of those charges had been compromised by his testimony before Congress."

16. In the aftermath of the hearings, North became the leading conservative speaker around the nation, commanding up to $25,000 per speech, and often giving five speeches per weekend.

17. The White House denied a large computer "dump" of PROFS notes sought by the committee; it also withheld word processing diskettes that had been gathered from NSC staff offices.

18. For a description of this meeting and an overview of these decisions by the Iran-Contra committees see, Seymour M. Hersh, "The Iran-Contra Committees: Did They Protect Reagan?" *New York Times Magazine*, April 29, 1990.

19. The report was, in fact, two reports: a majority report and a minority report. The minority report (signed by Senators James McClure, and Orrin Hatch, and by Congressmen Dick Cheney, William Broomfield, Henry Hyde, Jim Courter, Bill McCollum, Michael DeWine) attempted to exonerate the Reagan administration of any wrongdoing by providing an inaccurate, distorted, and biased depiction of the events investigated by the committees. The Republican vice chairman of the committees, Senator Warren Rudman, characterized it as "a pathetic report," and suggested that the minority had separated the wheat from the chaff "and printed the chaff."

20. See Liman's opinion piece on the *New York Times* op-ed page, March 2, 1990.

21. For example, a chapter drafted on the public diplomacy operations was dropped in order to obtain Republican support for the majority report. See Robert Parry and Peter Kornbluh, "Iran-Contra's Untold Story," *Foreign Policy Magazine*, Fall 1988.

22. *Iran-Contra Affair*, p. 391.

23. Ibid., p. 390.

24. Ibid.

25. Ibid., p. 433.

26. The committees' recommendations included proposals for "timely notice"—within forty-eight hours of presidential approval—of covert operations, a requirement that all Findings be written, and an exclusion of active military officers as national security advisors. See Chapter 28 of the *Iran-Contra Affair*.

27. *Congressional Quarterly*, p. 164.

28. Miller was also sentenced to 120 hours of community service.

29. In retrospect, Jeffrey Toobin, an attorney in Walsh's office, later wrote, "the McFarlane plea bargain turned out to be one of the worst mistakes the OIC made." Indeed, rather than help the prosecution during the North trial, his confusing testimony exasperated the judge and severely undermined Walsh's case. The

jury foreperson, Denise Anderson, later told the *Washington Post* that "McFarlane was nicky-dicky. I don't trust a thing he said.... I got a headache just listening to him." See Toobin's, *Opening Arguments* (New York: Viking, 1990), p. 140.

30. *United States* v. *John Poindexter*, Oliver North, Richard Secord and Albert Hakim, March 16, 1988.

31. Quoted in *Congressional Quarterly*, p. 168.

32. Lawrence Walsh, "Immunity and Prosecution: A First Interim Report," April 28, 1987, p. 11. This document is on file at the National Security Archive.

33. Toobin cites Walsh's reaction to being told that he would have to actively avoid reading or hearing anything about the congressional testimony of immunized witnesses: "You are talking about doing something that will make me look ridiculous. How can I be the only person in America not reading the newspaper?" See Toobin, *Opening Arguments*, p. 61.

34. Walsh, "Immunity and Prosecution: A First Interim Report," April 28, 1987, p. 13.

35. For the jurors' justifications and an overview of the North trial see Peter Kornbluh, "Another Fine Mess: Oliver North's Conviction Explodes the Official Story," *LA Weekly*, May 12–18, 1989.

36. For quotes and a treatment of North's culpability on these charges, see Peter Kornbluh, Malcolm Byrne, and Tom Blanton, "Ollie Oops," *The Washington Monthly*, November 1991.

37. Toobin, *Opening Arguments*, p. 172.

38. The CIPA was passed after the Justice Department's difficulties, between 1976 and 1977, in prosecuting the former head of the CIA, Richard Helms, and two employees of the International Telegraph and Telephone corporation on charges of lying to Congress about CIA/ITT efforts to thwart the election of Salvador Allende in Chile.

39. Both plea bargained on charges unrelated to the diversion— Secord to perjury, Hakim to supplementing North's salary.

40. In a letter to Walsh dated October 25, the president's counsel, C. Boyden Gray wrote that a meeting "would not be appropriate." Walsh responded to Gray on October 31 that "you have belittled the gravity of the problem." The administration's positions, he wrote, "show an adherence to over-protective classification concepts that will be difficult to reconcile with a realistic commitment to prosecute high-ranking national security officials for crimes committed in office."

41. See Winsor's oral history interview, p. 38. The interview transcript is dated February 29, 1988, and is on file at Georgetown University as part of the Association for Diplomatic Studies Foreign Affairs Oral History Program.

42. Lawrence Walsh, "Second Interim Report to Congress by Independent Counsel for Iran/Contra Matters," December 11, 1989, pp. 39–40. This document is on file at the National Security Archive.

43. Ibid., p. 2.

44. Quoted in Kornbluh, Byrne and Blanton, "Ollie Oops," p. 33.

45. See the *Washington Times*, December 8, 1992.

46. Quoted in Draper, *A Very Thin Line*, p. 573.

47. See Draper's article, "Revelations of the North Trial," p. 59.

48. Gates had been nominated previously by Reagan to be director after Casey died in the spring of 1987. But widespread distrust in Congress regarding Gates role in the scandal led to his decision to withdraw his nomination at that time.

49. See Fiers's testimony at the George trial, July 31, 1991, p. 1442. "Oliver North and I had a discussion about that project," Fiers told the court, "yes, and whether or not outside sources could continue to fund it.... He said it could be arranged."

50. Quoted in the *Washington Times*, December 10, 1992.

51. *United States* v. *Caspar W. Weinberger*, Indictment, June 16, 1992.

52. The Garrett memo and Weinberger's notes were revealed in a pretrial court submission filed by the Office of the Independent Counsel. See "Government's Proffer of Evidence Regarding Congressional Documents Requests," December 20, 1992. p. 6.

53. The note on this conversation was reported in the *Washington Post*, August 26, 1992.

54. See Fred Barnes's column in the *New Republic*, "Pardon Me," December 21, 1992, pp. 11-12.

55. *Newsweek*, January 4, 1993. p. 16.

56. Walsh made this statement on "MacNeil/Lehrer News Hour," December 24, 1992.

57. See ABC *Nightline*, December 24, 1992.

OFFICE OF INDEPENDENT COUNSEL
FACT SHEET - DECEMBER 1992
PUBLIC INFORMATION OFFICE: 202-383-5443

Expenditures by the Office of Independent Counsel were $33.5 million as of Oct. 31, 1992, which are the latest figures available. The staff includes 11 full-time attorneys and 33 support staff. Since Independent Counsel Lawrence E. Walsh's appointment in December 1986 there have been 11 convictions; two have been dismissed on appeal.

PENDING CASES

Caspar W. Weinberger- Indicted June 16, 1992, on five counts of obstruction, perjury and false statements in connection with congressional and independent counsel investigations of Iran-contra. On Sept. 29, the obstruction count was dismissed. On Oct. 30, a second indictment was issued, charging one false statement count; the second indictment was dismissed on Dec. 11, leaving four counts remaining. The maximum penalty for each count is five years in prison and $250,000 in fines. U.S. District Judge Thomas Hogan has set a Jan. 5, 1993, trial date.

Duane R. Clarridge - Indicted Nov. 26, 1991, on seven counts of perjury and false statements about a secret shipment of U.S. HAWK missiles to Iran. The maximum penalty for each count is five years in prison and $250,000 in fines. U.S. District Judge Harold Greene has set a March 15, 1992 trial date.

COMPLETED TRIALS AND PLEAS

Clair E. George - Found guilty Dec. 9, 1992, of two felony charges of false statements and perjury before Congress. The maximum penalty for each count is five years in prison and $250,000 in fines. U.S. District Judge Royce Lamberth has set sentencing for Feb. 18, 1993. A first trial that began July 13, 1992, ended in a mistrial Aug. 26, 1992, due to the jury's inability to reach a verdict. The retrial of George on seven counts began Oct. 19, 1992.

Elliott Abrams - Pleaded guilty Oct. 7, 1991, to two misdemeanor charges of withholding information from Congress about secret government efforts to support the Nicaraguan Contra rebels during a ban on military aid. U.S. District Judge Aubrey Robinson sentenced Abrams Nov. 15, 1991, to two years probation and 100 hours community service.

Alan D. Fiers, Jr. - Pleaded guilty July 9, 1991, to two misdemeanor counts of withholding information from Congress about the diversion of Iranian arms sales proceeds to the Nicaraguan Contras and about other contra aid. U.S. District Judge Aubrey Robinson sentenced Fiers Jan. 31, 1992, to one year probation and 100 hours community service.

Thomas G. Clines - Found guilty Sept. 18, 1990, of four tax-related felonies. U.S. District Judge Norman Ramsey in Baltimore, Md., on Dec. 13, 1990, sentenced Clines to 16 months in prison and $40,000 in fines. He was ordered to pay the cost of the prosecution. The Fourth U.S. Circuit Court of Appeals in Richmond, Va., on Feb. 27, 1992 upheld the convictions. Clines began serving his jail sentence May 25, 1992.

Richard V. Secord - Pleaded guilty Nov. 8, 1989, to one felony count of false statements Congress. Sentenced by U.S. District Judge Aubrey Robinson on Jan. 24, 1990, to two years probation.

Albert Hakim - Pleaded guilty Nov. 21, 1989, to a misdemeanor of
supplementing the salary of Oliver North. Lake Resources Inc., in which
Hakim was the principal shareholder, pleaded guilty to a corporate felony
of theft of government property in diverting Iranian arms sales proceeds to
the Nicaraguan Contras. Hakim was sentenced by U.S. District Judge Gerhard
Gesell on Feb. 1, 1990, to two years probation and a $5,000 fine; Lake
Resources was ordered dissolved.

Robert C. McFarlane - Pleaded guilty March 11, 1988, to a four-count
information charging him with withholding information from Congress.
Sentenced by U.S. District Judge Aubrey Robinson on March 3, 1989, to two
years probation, $20,000 fine and 200 hours community service.

Carl "Spitz" Channell - Pleaded guilty April 29, 1987, to a one-count
information of conspiracy to defraud the United States. Sentenced by U.S.
District Judge Stanley Harris July 7, 1989, to two years probation.

Richard R. Miller - Pleaded guilty May 6, 1987, to a one-count information
of conspiracy to defraud the United States. Sentenced by U.S. District
Judge Stanley Harris on July 6, 1989, to two years probation and 120 hours
of community service.

REVERSED ON APPEAL

John M. Poindexter - Found guilty April 7, 1990, of five felonies:
conspiracy (obstruction of inquiries and proceedings, false statements,
falsification, destruction and removal of documents); two counts of
obstruction of Congress and two counts of false statements. U.S. District
Judge Harold Greene sentenced Poindexter June 11, 1990, to 6 months in
prison on each count, to be served concurrently. A three-judge appeals
panel Nov. 15, 1991, reversed the convictions. The Supreme Court on Dec.
7, 1992, declined to review the case.

DISMISSALS

Oliver L. North - U.S. District Judge Gerhard Gesell dismissed the case
Sept. 16, 1991, at the request of Independent Counsel following hearings on
whether North's immunized congressional testimony tainted the testimony of
trial witnesses. A three-judge appeals panel on July 20, 1990, vacated for
further proceedings by the trial court North's three-count conviction for
altering and destroying documents, accepting an illegal gratuity, and
aiding and abetting in the obstruction of Congress. The appeals panel
reversed outright the destruction-of-documents conviction. The Supreme
Court declined review of the case May 28, 1991. North, who was convicted
May 4, 1989, had been sentenced July 5, 1989, to a three-year suspended
prison term, two years probation, $150,000 in fines and 1,200 hours
community service.

Joseph F. Fernandez - U.S. District Judge Claude Hilton dismissed the four-
count case Nov. 24, 1989, after Attorney General Dick Thornburgh blocked
the disclosure of classified information ruled relevant to the defense.
The Fourth U.S. Circuit Court of Appeals in Richmond, Va., on Sept. 6,
1990, upheld Judge Hilton's rulings under the Classified Information
Procedures Act (CIPA). On Oct. 12, 1990, the Attorney General filed a
final declaration that he would not disclose the classified information.

UNITED STATES DISTRICT COURT FOR
THE DISTRICT OF COLUMBIA

UNITED STATES OF AMERICA :
         v. :
                        :
CARL R. CHANNELL, :
              Defendant. :
                        :

Criminal No.:
Violation: 18 U.S.C.
Section 371 (Conspiracy)

INFORMATION

The Independent Counsel informs the Court that:

INTRODUCTION

1. At all times relevant to this Information, the National Endowment for the Preservation of Liberty ("NEPL") was a non-profit corporation. From NEPL's inception in or about May 1984 to in or about August 1986, NEPL had offices located at 305 4th Street, N.E., Suite 210, Washington, D.C. From in or about August 1986 to the filing of this Information, NEPL had offices located at 1331 Pennsylvania Avenue, N.W., Suite 350 South, Washington, D.C.

2. At all times relevant to this Information, in its promotional literature and in filings with the United States Internal Revenue Service ("IRS"), NEPL purported to be an educational and charitable organization devoted to the study, analysis, and evaluation of the American socio-economic and political systems.

3. At all times relevant to this Information, NEPL made representations to the IRS as to the organization's purposes and activities and, on the basis of those representations, NEPL was duly qualified by the IRS as an organization exempt from federal income taxation under Section 501(c)(3) of the Internal Revenue Code and applicable regulations. Section 501(c)(3) of the Internal Revenue Code, among other things, exempts from federal income taxation corporations "organized and operated exclusively for religious, charitable, scientific, testing for public safety, literary or educational purposes...." A contribution to an organization properly recognized and operating as exempt under Section 501(c)(3) is deductible on the contributor's federal income tax return only if it is a "charitable contribution" within the meaning of Section 170(c)(2) of the Internal Revenue Code.

4. At all times relevant to this Information, the defendant CARL R. CHANNELL was the President of NEPL.

5. At all times relevant to this Information, the Contras were insurgents engaged in armed conflict against the Sandinista government in Nicaragua.

THE CONSPIRACY

6. From in or about April 1985 to the filing of this Information, in the District of Columbia and elsewhere, the defendant CARL R. CHANNELL, and others known and unknown to the Independent Counsel, unlawfully, wilfully [sic] and knowingly did combine, conspire, confederate and agree together and with each other to defraud the United States of America and the IRS by impeding, impairing, defeating and obstructing the lawful governmental functions of the IRS in the ascertainment, evaluation, assessment and collection of income taxes.

OBJECTS OF THE CONSPIRACY

7. It was an object of the conspiracy to defraud the IRS and deprive the Treasury of the United States of revenue to which it was entitled by subverting and corrupting the lawful purposes and operations of NEPL by using NEPL for an improper purpose, namely, to solicit contributions to purchase military and other types of non-humanitarian aid for the Contras.

8. It was an object of the conspiracy to defraud the IRS and deprive the Treasury of the United States of revenue to which it was entitled by falsely representing that contributions made to NEPL were tax-deductible when, in truth and in fact, certain of such contributions were not deductible since they were made for a non-deductible purpose, namely, to purchase military and other types of non-humanitarian aid for the Contras.

OVERT ACTS

9. The following overt acts, among others, were committed and caused to be committed, in the District of Columbia and elsewhere, by the defendant CARL R. CHANNELL and his co-conspirators in furtherance of the conspiracy and to effect the objects thereof:

(a) In or about April 1985, in Washington, D.C., the defendant CARL R. CHANNELL met with a consultant to NEPL, the principals of a public relations firm, and "Contributor A," a potential contributor to NEPL.

(b) On or about July 9, 1985, in a dining room of the Hay-Adams Hotel, Washington, D.C., the defendant CARL R. CHANNELL met with a consultant to NEPL, the principals of a public relations firm, and a United States government official ("the Official").

(c) On or about September 11, 1985, in Dallas, Texas, the defendant CARL R. CHANNELL and the Official met with at least three potential contributors to NEPL.

(d) On or about November 22, 1985, in Washington, D.C., at his government office, the Official met "Contributor B," a potential contributor to NEPL.

(e) On or about January 16, 1986, in Washington, D.C., "Contributor B" caused a check in the amount of $20,000 to be issued to NEPL.

(f) On or about March 28, 1986, in a dining room of the Hay-Adams Hotel, Washington, D.C., the defendant CARL R. CHANNELL and the Official met with "Contributor C," a potential contributor to NEPL.

(g) On or about March 31, 1986, in a dining room of the Hay-Adams Hotel, Washington, D.C., the defendant CARL R. CHANNELL and the Official met with "Contributor C," at which time "Contributor C" delivered to the defendant CHANNELL a check in the amount of $130,000 payable to NEPL.

(h) On or about April 11, 1986, in the cocktail lounge of the Hay-Adams Hotel, Washington, D.C., the defendant CARL R. CHANNELL and the Official met with "Contributor D," a potential contributor to NEPL.

(i) On or about April 15, 1986, "Contributor D" caused a wire transfer in the amount of $470,000 to be made to a NEPL bank account in Washington, D.C.

(j) On or about April 15, 1986, "Contributor D" caused the wire transfer of stocks valued at approximately $1.15 million to a NEPL brokerage account in Washington, D.C.

(k) On or about May 19, 1986, "Contributor D" caused a wire transfer in the amount of $350,000 to be made to a NEPL bank account in Washington, D.C.

(l) On or about November 18, 1986, in Washington, D.C., the defendant CARL R. CHANNELL caused to be filed with the IRS a 1985 Return of Organization Exempt from Income Tax for NEPL.

(Violation of Title 18, United States Code, Section 371.)

LAWRENCE E. WALSH
Independent Counsel

IN THE UNITED STATES DISTRICT COURT
FOR THE DISTRICT OF COLUMBIA

UNITED STATES OF AMERICA

v.

ROBERT C. McFARLANE,

    Defendant.

Criminal No.

Violation: 2 U.S.C. 192

INFORMATION

The Independent Counsel charges:

COUNT ONE

(September 5, 1985 Letter
to the House Permanent Select
Committee on Intelligence)

1. From October 17, 1983 to December 4, 1985, the defendant ROBERT C. McFARLANE was the Assistant to the President for National Security Affairs (the "National Security Advisor"), in which capacity he was responsible for developing, coordinating and implementing national security policy as approved by the President, as well as staffing and administering the National Security Council (the "NSC"). As the National Security Advisor, the defendant ROBERT C. McFARLANE had offices in the West Wing of the White House, Washington, D.C.

2. At all times relevant to this Information, the NSC was a government entity established by the National Security Act of 1947. The function of the NSC was, among other things, to review, guide and direct foreign intelligence and covert action activities. The staff of the NSC was appointed to perform such duties as might be prescribed by the NSC in the performance of its functions. The staff of the NSC had offices located in the Old Executive Office Building (the "OEOB"), Washington, D.C.

3. At all times relevant to this Information, the Contras were military insurgents engaged in military and paramilitary operations in Nicaragua.

4. From in or about December 1981 to on or about October 12, 1984, the United States Government, acting principally through the CIA, pursuant to written presidential findings, provided the Contras with financial support, arms and military equipment, as well as supervision, instruction, tactical and other advice, coordination, intelligence and direction. During fiscal year 1984, Public Law 98-212 prohibited the CIA, the Department of Defense and any other agency or entity of the United States involved in intelligence activities from obligating or expending more than $24 million for direct or indirect support of military or paramilitary operations in Nicaragua. These funds were almost entirely obligated by June 1984.

5. On October 12, 1984, Public Law 98-473 was enacted and expressly prohibited the use of funds available to certain agencies and entities of the United States from being obligated or expended in support of military or paramilitary operations in Nicaragua, stating in relevant part:

> During fiscal year 1985, no funds available to the Central Intelligence Agency, the Department of Defense, or any other agency or entity of the United States involved in intelligence activities may be obligated or expended for the purpose or which would have the effect of supporting, directly or indirectly, military or paramilitary operations in Nicaragua by any nation, group, organization, movement, or individual.

This provision of the law was commonly known as the Boland Amendment.

6. Although the Boland Amendment was modified twice, agencies and entities of the United States involved in intelligence activities were at all times between October 12, 1984 and October 17, 1986 prohibited from spending funds available to them (including, without limitation, funds for salaries and transportation) to provide lethal military or paramilitary supplies to the Contras or to participate in the planning or execution of military or paramilitary operations in Nicaragua. At no time during this period was any member of the NSC staff authorized by a presidential finding to undertake any covert or special activities with respect to Nicaragua, including any of the covert or special activities previously undertaken by the CIA. As of October 18, 1986, the provision by the CIA of military aid to the Contras was resumed pursuant to statutory authorization and appropriation.

7. On August 20, 1985, the Chairman of the House of

Representatives Permanent Select Committee on Intelligence ("HPSCI") wrote a letter on behalf of the Committee to the defendant ROBERT C. McFARLANE in the defendant McFARLANE's capacity as National Security Advisor. The letter referred to press accounts of alleged activities by the NSC with respect to the Contras and requested, among other things, a full report on the activities of the NSC to support the Contras after the enactment of the Boland Amendment.

8. On September 5, 1985, in the District of Columbia, the defendant ROBERT C. McFARLANE, having been summoned to give testimony and to produce papers upon a matter under inquiry before the United States House of Representatives, unlawfully, willfully and knowingly did make default by refusing and failing to answer fully and completely, to wit, defendant McFARLANE signed and caused to be transmitted to HPSCI, a committee of the United States Congress, a letter that stated as follows:

> This is in reply to your letter of August 20, 1985 in which you called attention to press reports of "...alleged activities by the National Security Council (staff) regarding the contras in Nicaragua..." and asked for a full report and legal justification for any such activities. Like you, I take such charges very seriously and consequently have thoroughly examined the facts and all matters which in any remote fashion could bear upon these charges. *From that review I can state with deep personal conviction that at no time did I or any member of the National Security Council staff violate the letter or spirit of the law....*

> o   o   o

> It is equally important to stress what we did not do. *We did not solicit funds or other support for military or paramilitary activities either from Americans or third parties....*

9. The underscored statements and representations unlawfully withheld material information from HPSCI because as the defendant ROBERT C. McFARLANE then and there knew and believed, a member of the NSC staff had violated the letter or spirit of the Boland Amendment by, among other things, soliciting support for military and paramilitary activities of the Contras and offering certain advice for the conduct of the Contras' military activities and organization.

(Violation of Title 2, United States Code, Section 192.)

COUNT TWO

(September 12, 1985 Letter to the House of Representatives Subcommittee on Western Hemisphere Affairs of the Committee on Foreign Affairs)

The Independent Counsel further charges:

10. Paragraphs 1 through 6 of Count One of this Information are repeated, realleged and incorporated by reference herein as if fully set forth in this count.

11. On August 16, 1985, the Chairman of the House of Representatives Subcommittee on Western Hemisphere Affairs of the Committee on Foreign Affairs wrote a letter on behalf of the Subcommittee to the defendant ROBERT C. McFARLANE in the defendant McFARLANE's capacity as National Security Advisor. The letter referred to "press reports detailing the activities of certain National Security Council staff members in providing advice and fundraising support to Nicaraguan rebel leaders" and requested "all information, including memoranda and any other documents, pertaining to any contact between Lt. Col. North and Nicaraguan rebel leaders as of enactment of the Boland Amendment in October, 1984."

12. On September 12, 1985, in the District of Columbia, the defendant ROBERT C. McFARLANE, having been summoned to give testimony and to produce papers upon a matter under inquiry before the United States House of Representatives, unlawfully, willfully and knowingly did make default by refusing and failing to answer fully and completely, to wit, defendant McFARLANE signed and caused to be transmitted to the House of Representatives Subcommittee on Western Hemisphere Affairs of the Committee on Foreign Affairs, a subcommittee of the United States Congress, a letter that stated as follows:

> This is in reply to your letter of August 16, regarding the activities of members of the NSC staff in connection with the Nicaraguan democratic resistance. Like you, I take these charges very seriously and consequently have thoroughly examined the facts and circumstances which could bear upon these charges in any fashion.

Based on this review, *I want to assure you that my actions, and those of my staff, have been in compliance with both the spirit and the letter of the law....*

∘   ∘   ∘

Throughout, we have scrupulously abided by the spirit and the letter of the law. None of us has solicited funds, facilitated contacts for prospective potential donors, or otherwise organized or coordinated the military or paramilitary efforts of the resistance.

∘   ∘   ∘

Mr. Chairman, like you, I am most concerned that at a time when humanitarian assistance is being extended to the UNO there be no misgivings as to the existence of any parallel efforts to provide, directly or indirectly, support for military or paramilitary activities in Nicaragua. *There has not been, nor will there be, any such activities by the NSC staff....*

13. The underscored statements and representations unlawfully withheld material information from the House of Representatives Subcommittee on Western Hemisphere Affairs of the Committee on Foreign Affairs because as the defendant McFARLANE then and there knew or had reason to believe, a member of the NSC staff had violated the spirit and letter of the Boland Amendment by, among other things, providing, directly or indirectly, support for military and paramilitary activities in Nicaragua.

(Violation of Title 2, United States Code, Section 192.)

COUNT THREE

(October 7, 1985 Letter
to the House Permanent Select
Committee on Intelligence)

The Independent Counsel further charges:

14. Paragraphs 1 through 8 of Count One of this Information are repeated, realleged and incorporated by reference herein as if fully set forth in this Count.

15. On September 12, 1985, having received the letter referred to in Count One of this Information and having

met with the defendant ROBERT C. McFARLANE, the Chairman of HPSCI wrote a letter, on behalf of the Committee, to the defendant McFARLANE, enclosing a series of questions "concerning allegations about the activities of Lieutenant Colonel Oliver North."

16. On October 7, 1985, in the District of Columbia, the defendant ROBERT C. McFARLANE, having been summoned to give testimony and to produce papers upon a matter under inquiry before the United States House of Representatives, unlawfully, willfully and knowingly did make default by refusing and failing to answer fully and completely, to wit, defendant McFARLANE signed and caused to be transmitted to the House Permanent Select Committee on Intelligence, a committee of the United States Congress, a letter that stated as follows:

Q–When the CIA had to withdraw from their day-to-day contact with the rebels, it has been alleged in the *New York Times* (8 Aug 85) that Colonel North tried to fill the void, partly through helping facilitate the supplying of logistics help. Did Colonel North, in his capacity as a staff member of the National Security Council, use his influence to facilitate the movement of supplies, either raised privately in this country or otherwise, to the contras?

A–*Lieutenant Colonel North did not use his influence to facilitate the movement of supplies to the resistance.*

∘   ∘   ∘

Q–General Singlaub has stated (*Washington Post,* 9 Aug 85) that he would often talk to Colonel North and inform him what he was doing and then state that if it was a dumb idea, for North to send him a signal. Is that your impression of the relationship between General Singlaub and Colonel North?

A–*There is no official or unofficial relationship with any member of the NSC staff regarding fund raising for the Nicaraguan democratic opposition. This includes the alleged relationship with General Singlaub.*

∘   ∘   ∘

Q–The Nicaraguan freedom fighters, in the last two months, are reported by the U.S. Embassy, Tegucigalpa, to have received a large influx of funds and equipment with some estimates of their value reaching as high as $10 million or more. Do you know where they have obtained this assistance?

A–*No*.

17.   The underscored answers unlawfully withheld information from HPSCI because, among other things, the defendant McFARLANE then and there, (a) knew and believed that Lieutenant Colonel North had used his influence to facilitate the movement of certain supplies to the Contras; (b) knew or had reason to believe that a member of the NSC staff had had contact with retired Major General John K. Singlaub regarding fund raising for the Contras; and (c) knew and believed that the Contras had received millions of dollars from a third country.

(Violation of Title 2, United States Code, Section 192.)

COUNT FOUR

(December 8, 1986 Testimony before the House of Representatives Committee on Foreign Affairs)

The Independent Counsel further charges:

18.   Paragraphs 1 through 6 of Count One of this Information are repeated, realleged and incorporated by reference herein as if fully set forth in this Count.

19.   On December 8, 1986, in the District of Columbia, the defendant ROBERT C. McFARLANE, having been summoned to give testimony before the United States House of Representatives Committee on Foreign Affairs, unlawfully, willfully and knowingly did make

default by refusing and failing to answer fully and completely, to wit, defendant McFARLANE withheld material information from the House of Representatives Committee on Foreign Affairs, a committee of Congress, as follows:

Q–There have also been press reports that the [nationals of a third country] have been indirectly involved in financing the contras. Are you aware of any such activities?

A–I have seen the reports and I have heard that the [nationals of such third country] have contributed. *The concrete character of that is beyond my ken*.

20.   The underscored answer unlawfully withheld material information from the United States House of Representatives Committee on Foreign Affairs because as the defendant McFARLANE then and there knew and believed, the defendant McFARLANE had been aware since 1984 that nationals of the third country referred to had expressed willingness to contribute millions of dollars to the Contras, the defendant McFARLANE had provided a representative of that third country with the number of a Contra-controlled bank account into which the funds could be deposited, and the defendant Mc-FARLANE was aware that nationals of that third country had in fact made contributions to the Contras totalling millions of dollars.

(Violation of Title 2, United States Code, Section 192.)

LAWRENCE E. WALSH
Independent Counsel

IN THE UNITED STATES DISTRICT COURT
FOR THE DISTRICT OF COLUMBIA

UNITED STATES OF AMERICA

v.

OLIVER L. NORTH,

Defendant.

Criminal No. 88-0080-02-GAG

GOVERNMENT'S SENTENCING MEMORANDUM

Preliminary Statement

The Government respectfully submits this memorandum in connection with the sentencing of Oliver L. North, scheduled for June 23, 1989. Because the Court is fully familiar with the facts of the case, we will not review those facts in detail, but will instead focus on those matters we believe are appropriate for the Court to consider in imposing sentence.

The most striking thing about North's posture on the eve of sentencing is his insistence that he had done nothing wrong. Instead, on the day of the verdict, he declared that his "vindication was not "complete," and promised to "continue the fight" until it is.[1] At the same time, he continues to profit from his notoriety, even while he decries the wastefulness and injustice of his prosecution.

The Government recognizes that sentencing North presents difficult issues. The defendant was a public official who worked tirelessly on programs he and his superiors believed should be pursued. But the crimes of which he was convicted, involving a cover-up even after those programs became known to the public, were crimes designed to protect himself and his associates, not the national security. The fact that North and at least some of his superiors were willing to conceal their work from the American people and Congress and thereby to insulate their actions from the democratic process is for this defendant, a matter of considerable pride. North has not indicated one iota of remorse for having committed crimes which, because of his position of public trust, jeopardized the constitutional processes of government. He apparently sees nothing wrong with alteration and destruction of official national security records. His participation in the preparation of a false and misleading chronology has not led to any acknowledgement of wrongdoing.[2] Certainly, he sees nothing wrong with lying to Congress, when in the view of himself and his superiors lying is necessary.

His contempt for Congress and the public is accompanied by venality in financial matters. The jury found him guilty of accepting a $13,800 security system from Richard Secord, a man with whom he had been doing business in his official capacity for two years. North does not appear to question the propriety of his other financial relationships with Secord and Hakim, including the use of large amounts of cash without accountability and his wife's trip to Philadelphia to discuss with Secord and Hakim's representative the education of North's children.

In fashioning a just sentence in this case, we urge the Court to consider the seriousness of North's abuse of the public trust, the need for deterrence, North's failure to accept personal responsibility for his actions, his lack of remorse and his perjury on the witness stand. Taking all these factors into account, as set forth more fully below, the Government submits that a term of incarceration is appropriate and necessary.

Public Officials Be Deterred From Such A *Serious Breach Of The Public Trust*

The Conduct of North in this case constituted a serious breach of the public trust. He prepared false documents for the purpose of obstructing congressional investigations; he destroyed, altered and removed official documents; and he repeatedly participated in lying to congress. North seems to believe that such activities are business as usual in government or necessary tactics in a "political firestorm." But after a non-political trial and a non-political verdict, the Court, in its sentence, should alert all government officials that such activities are indeed unlawful, and that if officials engaging in such conduct are caught and convicted, the punishment will be severe. Further, the private citizens of this country, who continue to follow this case closely, are entitled to the reassurance only this Court can give that these are serious crimes and that powerful government officials are not accorded special treatment.

Deterrence is particularly important in a case involving not only obstruction, lying and cover-up, but also personal venality. While it is understandable that a person under threat of danger might seek to protect his family, this concern arises frequently for some officials engaged in the areas of intelligence, covert action or, for that matter, law enforcement. They cannot accept private gifts from those doing business with the government. Where, as here, a public official receives a substantial gratuity from an individual with whom he has conducted official business, and proceeds to create fraudulent, back dated letters to cover it up, the Court must respond.[3]

A sentence in this case that included no period of incarceration would send exactly the wrong message to government officials and to the public. It would be a statement that fifteen years after Watergate, government officials can participate in a brazen cover-up, lie to Congress and collect a substantial gratuity and still receive only a slap on the wrist. North's view that anything goes in a political controversy would be sustained. Instead, since his acts are a serious breach of the public trust, they warrant serious punishment.

North's Refusal to Accept Personal Responsibility For His Actions Is An Appropriate Consideration in Sentencing

The evidence at trial, as confirmed by North in his own testimony, demonstrated that, acting in his position at the National Security Council, North wielded enormous power in the government. By his own description, he met with presidents and kings. He was the primary official responsible for the coordination of counterterrorism, the release of American hostages and relations with the Contras. In connection with these responsibilities, North reported directly to the President's National Security Advisor and, speaking for the White House, exercised substantial authority over numerous other officials throughout the government. Thus, North held a position of substantial public trust that far exceeded his military rank.

With his power and public trust came critical individual responsibilities. The verdict in this case constitutes a finding by the jury that Oliver North violated that public trust in substantial and serious ways. In exercising its discretion in imposing sentence, the Court should not permit the defendant to rely on his trial tactic of shifting onto others the responsibility for actions that he took. Few criminal defendants have attempted to blame so many

others for so many lawless acts. North must accept his fair share of the responsibility.

North's disregard for this basic precept of a democratic society was graphically demonstrated during his trial testimony. At one point, the Court asked the defendant whether at any time he considered in his own mind not drafting false answers to Congress but, instead, simply saying "no." In a revealing moment, the defendant stated that he never considered the possibility of not doing it. Tr. at 7447. This society cannot tolerate government officials unwilling and unable to exercise independent judgement and responsibility in refusing to perform illegal acts. The sentence in this case should carry with it a message to all citizens, including all government officials, that one cannot simply rely on real or imagined authorization of illegal conduct and expect to escape responsibility. Oliver North is not a scapegoat. He is a government official who must be held to account for the legality and honesty of his own personal actions regardless of whether others may also have transgressed the law and regardless of the ends sought to be achieved.

"Scapegoat"

Several times during the trial and pretrial proceedings this Court expressed concern that North might be a scapegoat. In this context, it commented upon the charges brought against McFarlane and the sentence imposed upon him. Now, and before sentence is imposed in this case, the Court should know that at no time was North singled out by this office as a scapegoat. His testimony free of immunity would have been welcomed if he had promptly attempted to clear the mystery surrounding these transactions. The response of this office would have been similar to that accorded McFarlane as a person who related the facts extensively, if not perfectly, without attempting to foreclose all prosecution.

A plea bargain with a grant of immunity would also have been considered if North had been willing first to give a proffer of his testimony so that it could have been checked against documents and the testimony of others for its truthfulness and completeness.

It is the opinion of this office that North deliberately and with full awareness of the consequences accepted the role of operations officer in the criminal activities charged in the indictment. Although he calls himself a "scapegoat," he invited this role. He joked about the danger that he would be jailed and bragged that he would be protected because "the old man love[s] my ass."⁴ Similarly, his decision to stand trial and gamble on acquittal, a right granted by the Constitution, was also undertaken as a challenge to the capability of our system of justice to respond to crimes with political overtones, given the expressed sympathy and support of this country's then President and Vice President.

The investigation of this office is not yet concluded. Despite his diminished credibility, North would still have usefulness as a witness if he were prepared to take the steps appropriate to such a course.

North's Lack of Remorse and Perjury
Should Be Taken Into Account

The arrogance that characterized North's exercise of power before the investigation has been the hallmark of his reaction to his indictment and conviction. Simply put, Oliver North viewed and continues to view himself as being above the law and beyond reproach. Thus, form the beginning, North has aggressively painted himself for the public as an innocent victim of an improperly motivated prosecution.

It is no wonder, then, that North was not content merely to exercise his constitutional right to put the Government to its proof at trial. Instead, he sought to pervert the processes of justice much as he had corrupted the processes of government. With supreme faith in his ability to deceive, North took the stand and perjured himself. For example, his unsupported claim that he had a $15,000 fund in a steel box in his closet echoed the flimsy lies offered by corrupt municipal officials in the days of Tammany Hall. North's attempt to use the steel box to explain his cash purchase of a car in two installments graphically demonstrated North's penchant for weaving a tale that by its conclusion is preposterous. Car salesman William Howell demolished North's account of the transaction.

Furthermore, North's testimony with respect to the documents he received from Fawn Hall on November 25, 1986, was incredible. He insisted that he returned to the Government all of the documents he received from Hall. But Hall testified that the documents removed included versions of the altered memos and none of the altered memos was in the package returned. North's perjury represents another indication of his continuing callous attitude toward the judicial process and our democratic institutions.

North's lack of remorse is particularly troubling in view of the fact that he continues to travel throughout the country, like a politician on the stump, giving speeches and discoursing on his defiance of Congress. Apparently, North has become a wealthy man in the process. The fact that this defendant is cultivating a popular following, which reinforces his lack of remorse, makes it all the more important for the Court to underscore the gravity of North's offenses by imposing a term of incarceration.

Conclusion

Oliver North's sentence will be known to, and closely evaluated by, all who view the perversion of government as a permissible means to the attainment of their goals. The sentence will also be carefully considered by those officials who may now be weighing the advantages of deception, obstruction and personal greed against the risks of punishment. It will also be noted by those serving substantial prison sentences for more personal crimes far less damaging to the nation. Most importantly, the sentence will be closely scrutinized by a citizenry whose confidence in government and the political system has been seriously undermined by the activities of this defendant.

In determining Oliver North's sentence, the Court should consider his breach of public trust and misuse of public power, the destructive effect of his criminal behavior on the functioning of government and the public's faith in government, his perjury and his total lack of remorse.

Under all these circumstances, we respectfully submit that a term of incarceration is appropriate and necessary.

Respectfully submitted
LAWRENCE E. WALSH
Independent Counsel

John W. Keker
David M. Zornow
Michael R. Bromwich
Associate Counsel

Office of Independent Counsel
555 Thirteenth Street, N.W.
Suite 701 West
Washington, D.C. 20004
(202) 383-8940

June 19, 1989

CERTIFICATE OF SERVICE

I hereby certify that I have caused a true copy of the attached Government's Sentencing Memorandum to be delivered by hand to the office of Brendan V. Sullivan, Jr., Williams & Connolly, Hill Building, 839 Seventeenth Street, N.W., Washington, D.C. 20006, this 19th day of June, 1989.

Michael R. Bromwich
Associate Counsel

NOTES

2. During North's trial testimony, for example, the following colloquy took place:

Q. At any time on November 21, 1986 did you think that what you were doing, what you were being asked to do or what you had done might be wrong?

A. Not for one fleeting moment.

Tr. at 7648

3. Information in the Government's possession shows that North's receipt of the security system gratuity was not an isolated lapse. Mrs. North's meeting in Philadelphia with Willard Zucker and the subsequent funding of a $200,00 "Button" account for the educational needs of

mony at trial of former NSC official Mary Dix concerning the abrupt change in North's attitude toward obtaining reimbursement strongly suggested that North began to use the so-called "operational account" for his own personal use in 1985 and 1986. Of course, the precise manner in which North spent funds from the operational account will never be known because according to North, he destroyed a ledger reflecting the use of the monies.

4. Testimony of Felix I. Rodriguez, Joint Hearings Before The Senate Select Committee on Secret Military Assistance to Iran and the Nicaraguan Opposition and the House Select Committee to Investigate Covert Arms transactions with Iran, May 27, 1987, Volume 3 at 306.

DOCUMENT 94: Lawrence Walsh, Letter to President Bush Regarding Administration Obstruction of
Joseph Fernandez Prosecution, October 19, 1989.

PAGE 1 OF 3

EXHIBIT A

OFFICE OF INDEPENDENT COUNSEL
SUITE 701 WEST
555 THIRTEENTH STREET, N.W.
WASHINGTON, D.C. 20004
(202) 383-8940

October 19, 1989

BY HAND

The Honorable George H. W. Bush
President of the United States
The White House
1600 Pennsylvania Avenue, N.W.
Washington, DC 20500

Dear Mr. President:

Unless different standards for the release of
information to the courts are adopted by the intelligence
agencies, we face the likelihood that former high officials
cannot be tried for crimes related to their conduct in public
office. The intelligence agencies, the Attorney General, and
my office have been trying to deal with this problem without
exposing intelligence secrets, and protecting government
deniability of publicly known facts. It seems clear that if
we continue in this effort to withhold this information we
lose a much more important national value - the rule of law.

On December 19, 1986, I was appointed Independent
Counsel with responsibility for the investigation and
prosecution of crimes growing out of the Iran/Contra matter,
as well as illegal obstructions of my work. For over two
years my office received the assistance of the Reagan
Administration, through presidential representatives,
Ambassador Abshire and A. B. Culvahouse. Now the work of
this office is being seriously hampered by the lack of any
similar point of contact in your Administration.
Accordingly, I am writing to request an appointment to
discuss this very serious problem, and to present to you in
abbreviated form the essence of the problem.

The immediate problem is the interference of the
Administration with my efforts to prosecute Joseph Fernandez,
the former CIA Chief of Station in Costa Rica. The District
Court has ruled admissible the details of certain programs
that the CIA claims to be still secret. The Court has ruled
also that the defendant may prove the existence of CIA
stations in certain Latin American countries as well as the
location of a CIA installation in one of those countries.

DOCUMENT 94: Lawrence Walsh, Letter to President Bush Regarding Administration Obstruction of
Joseph Fernandez Prosecution, October 19, 1989.

PAGE 2 OF 3

The CIA claims that although the existence of these stations
is publicly known, this evidence may not be made public even
though this refusal may force dismissal of the Fernandez
case.

This incident follows the trial of Oliver L. North
which was completed after important concessions by both the
intelligence agencies and me. They released some secrets and
I, in deference to secrecy claims by the National Security
Agency, eliminated major charges against North. This more
recent incident, as well as other information we have
received, convince me that without your help the rule of law
will be subordinated to the intelligence effort. The tail
has begun to wag the dog.

The broad question that confronts the
Administration as well as Independent Counsel is whether a
group of high public officials shall be excluded from the
reach of the law. The Constitution provides that the
President "shall take Care that the Laws be faithfully
executed" (Article 2, Section 3). These few words
incorporate the essence of Anglo-American jurisprudence, the
thirteenth century concept that no person, great or small, is
beyond the law. The question is whether this Administration
will tolerate the creation of an enclave of high public
officers free from the rule of law simply because those
public officers deal extensively with classified information.

The Classified Information Procedures Act (CIPA)
does not solve this problem. It merely provides a procedure
by which to expose it. One branch of government, the
judiciary, is left to decide the materiality of evidence,
while another, the executive, is left to decide what secrets
may be revealed. My office will do its best to utilize the
procedures of the courts, and, if appropriate, husband its
opportunities for appeal. Only the President, however, can
deal with agencies of the executive branch if they, on a
highly subjective basis, refuse to make information available
to the courts because of their concern for the difficulties
and niceties of intelligence work.

The problems of CIPA in a case prosecuted by
Independent Counsel must be reviewed from a viewpoint broader
than that of the agencies directly concerned with
intelligence issues. There is a very serious danger that a
ritualistic application of classification procedures will
insulate most if not all officers responsible for national
security from prosecution for crimes committed in office.
This danger is particularly acute in the case of former high
officials such as Poindexter, but it has also become apparent
in cases of those who held less elevated positions, such as
Fernandez. To leave these decisions solely to the unrevie-

-2-

DOCUMENT 94: Lawrence Walsh, Letter to President Bush Regarding Administration Obstruction of Joseph Fernandez Prosecution, October 19, 1989.

PAGE 3 OF 3

judgment of agencies concerned with intelligence issues runs a very real risk of emasculation of the rule of law which the Independent Counsel was appointed to further. To prevent this from happening, I am appealing to you to provide a higher level of review for these crucial decisions. We respectfully suggest that particularly in cases where the Attorney General has been superseded by Independent Counsel because of possible conflict of interest, this review should be conducted in the White House itself, either by a member of the Presidential staff or by a specially appointed Presidential body assigned that responsibility.

In summary, I believe that concern for the preservation of secrets relating to national security is being used in exaggerated form and will defeat necessary prosecutions of high government officers. I should like to meet with you to urge that: (1) the intelligence agencies be directed to use a more liberal standard for the trial of former government officials; (2) that my office be given an avenue of communication with you through someone on your staff free of agency limitations; and (3) that you consider the possible use of a Presidential commission to review any agency action which conflicts with the rulings of the trial court in the connection of prosecution of high government officials.

Respectfully yours,

Lawrence E. Walsh
Independent Counsel

-3-

DOCUMENT 95: *United States of America* v. *Elliott Abrams*, "Government's Statement of the Factual Basis for the Guilty Plea," October 7, 1991

PAGE 1 OF 3

THE UNITED STATES DISTRICT COURT
FOR THE DISTRICT OF COLUMBIA

UNITED STATES OF AMERICA

v.

ELLIOTT ABRAMS,

Defendant.

Criminal No. 91-0575

Violations: 2 U.S.C. 192.

GOVERNMENT'S STATEMENT OF THE
FACTUAL BASIS FOR THE GUILTY PLEA

COUNT ONE

From July 1985 through 1988, Elliott Abrams was Assistant Secretary of State and headed the United States Department of State's Bureau of Inter-American Affairs. As Assistant Secretary of State for Inter-American Affairs, MR. ABRAMS chaired a Restricted Interagency Group ("RIG") comprised of, among others, representatives of the United States Department of Defense, the Joint Chiefs of Staff, the Central Intelligence Agency ("CIA"), the National Security Council ("NSC"), and the Department of State. During 1985 and 1986, the RIG met regularly to coordinate the activities of these agencies in Central America.

During 1985 and 1986, Alan D. Fiers, Jr., was the Chief of the CIA's Central American Task Force, the headquarters element that managed CIA operations in Central America. During that period until November 25, 1986, Oliver L. North was a Lieutenant Colonel in the United States Marine Corps detailed to the NSC staff, where he held the position of Deputy Director, Political-Military Affairs. MR. ABRAMS dealt with Mr. Fiers and Lt. Col. North on Central American issues and discussed sensitive matters relating to Central America with them, rather than with the entire RIG.

Throughout 1985 and 1986, the Nicaraguan democratic resistance, also known as the Contras, were insurgents engaged in military and paramilitary operations in Nicaragua. Throughout 1985 and until October 18, 1986, the United States Government was prohibited by the Boland Amendment from providing lethal assistance to the Contras.

After enactment of the Boland Amendment in October 1984 and continuing into 1986, certain private individuals, including American citizens, provided financial support and supplied arms, military equipment and logistical support to the Contras. These individuals became known to ELLIOTT ABRAMS and other United States Government officials as the "private benefactors."

In 1985 MR. ABRAMS became generally aware that Lt. Col. North was working with the Contras and the private benefactors with the goal of keeping the democratic resistance alive while the Boland Amendment prohibited the United States Government from providing the Contras with lethal assistance. From at least December 1985 through October 1986, Lt. Col. North acted as the principal channel of communication between the private benefactors and United States Government officials, including the RIG.

In August 1985, Congress modified the Boland Amendment by appropriating $27 million for humanitarian, but not lethal, assistance to the Contras. President Reagan created the Nicaraguan Humanitarian Assistance Office ("NHAO") in the Department of State to administer these funds.

ON September 4, 1985, as the NHAO program was being organized, Secretary of State George P. Shultz instructed ELLIOTT ABRAMS that he had to know how the Contras were obtaining support, including lethal supplies (arms), from sources outside the United States Government. MR. ABRAMS recorded Secretary Shultz's instruction in his notebook as follows: "monitor Ollie."

In early 1986, before the NHAO funds were depleted, President Reagan requested that Congress authorize the United States Government to provide both humanitarian and lethal assistance to the Contras and to appropriate $100 million for this purpose. In March 1986, the United States House of Representatives rejected the request.

On May 16, 1986, MR. ABRAMS attended a National Security Planning Group meeting where President Reagan, among others, addressed alternative funding sources for the Contras. Following that meeting, MR. ABRAMS informed Secretary Shultz that the Sultan of Brunei was a good prospect for a substantial contribution to the Contras.

After receiving approval from Secretary Shultz to solicit a contribution from the Sultan of Brunei, MR. ABRAMS asked Lt. Col. North for advice on how to pro-

DOCUMENT 95: *United States of America v. Elliott Abrams*, "Government's Statement of the Factual Basis for the Guilty Plea," October 7, 1991

PAGE 2 OF 3

vide to the Contras any funds contributed by the Sultan of Brunei. Lt. Col. North provided ELLIOTT ABRAMS with the number of a Swiss bank account into which funds for the Contras could be deposited.

In July 1986, after the $27 million available to the NHAO program had been depleted, MR. ABRAMS and Mr. Fiers asked Lt. Col. North whether the private benefactors could provided food for the Contras. Lt. Col. North replied that he would ask the private benefactors to do so.

Congress eventually reconsidered President Reagan's request for $100 million to assist the contras, but as of October 17, 1986, the appropriation was being held in conference awaiting final enactment, and the funds were not available. It was the opinion of MR. ABRAMS that disclosure of Lt. Col. North's activities in the resupply of the Contras would jeopardize enactment of the appropriation.

On October 5, 1986, a C123K aircraft carrying arms and other supplies to the Contras was shot down over Nicaragua. Three crewmen were killed; Eugene Hasenfus, the sole survivor, was captured by the Nicaraguans.

Following press reports regarding the shootdown, the United States Senate Committee on Foreign Relations requested briefings from United States Government officials, including ELLIOTT ABRAMS, on the circumstances surrounding the downed plane and the resupply operation. MR. ABRAMS appeared before the Committee on Foreign Relations to provide the briefing on October 10, 1986.

In response to a request that he comment on an article in *The Los Angeles Times* reporting that an elaborate system supplied the Contras, ELLIOTT ABRAMS explained the United States Government's purported "distance" from that lethal supply system as follows:

> [MR. ABRAMS]:…In the last two years, since Congress cut off support to the resistance, this supply system has kept them alive. It is not our supply system. It is one that grew up after we were forbidden from supplying the resistance, and *we have been kind of careful not to get closely involved with it and to stay away from it* ….

I think that people who are supplying the Contras believe that we generally approve of what they are doing—and they are right. We do generally approve of what they are doing, because they are keeping the Contras alive while Congress makes its decision, which each House has separately, though obviously final legislation is not yet ready.

So, the notion that we are generally in favor of people helping the Contras is correct.

We do not encourage people to do this. We don't round up people, we don't write letters, *we don't have conversations, we don't tell them to do this, we don't ask them to do it*. But I think it is quite clear, from the attitude of the administration, the attitude of the administration is that these people are doing a very good thing, and if they think they are doing something that we like, then, in a general sense, they are right. But *that is without any encouragement and coordination from us, other than a public speech by the President, that kind of thing, on the public record*.

At the time MR. ABRAMS made this statement he was aware that Lt. Col. North had been in contact with people supplying the Contras, had conversations with people supplying the Contras and had asked and encouraged them to supply the Contras.

COUNT TWO

In August 1986, after receiving authorization from Secretary of State George P. Shultz, ELLIOTT ABRAMS requested from a representative of the Sultan of Brunei a contribution of $10 million to the Contras. MR. ABRAMS provided to the Sultan's representative a Swiss bank account number obtained from Lt. Col. North.

On or about September 16, 1986, MR. ABRAMS learned of a Department of State cable reporting that the Sultan of Brunei had agreed to contribute $10 million to the Contras. On or about September 26, 1986, MR. ABRAMS learned of a Department of State cable reporting that the $10 million had been sent from the Sultan to the Swiss bank account and MR. ABRAMS had that expectation on October 14, 1986.

Following the press reports regarding the shootdown described in the statement of the factual basis for Count One, the United States House of Representatives Permanent Select Committee on Intelligence requested a briefing from United States Government officials, including

DOCUMENT 95: *United States of America v. Elliott Abrams*, "Government's Statement
of the Factual Basis for the Guilty Plea," October 7, 1991

PAGE 3 OF 3

ELLIOTT ABRAMS, regarding the circumstances surrounding the shootdown and the lethal resupply operation. MR. ABRAMS appeared before the Committee to provide the briefing on October 14, 1986.

During the briefing, ELLIOTT ABRAMS responded to a series of questions regarding foreign government help for the Contras as follows:

[THE CHAIRMAN]: Do you know if any foreign government is helping to supply the contras? There is a report in the LA paper, for example, that the Saudis are.

[MR. GEORGE]: No sir, we have no intelligence of that.

[MR. ABRAMS]: I can only speak on that question for the last fifteen months when I have been in this job, and that story about the Saudis to my knowledge is false. I personally cannot tell you about pre-1985, but in 1985-1986, when I have been around, no.

[THE CHAIRMAN]: Is it also false with respect to other governments as well?

[MR. ABRAMS]: *Yes, it is also false.*

Respectfully submitted,

LAWERENCE E. WALSH
Independent Counsel

By:

Craig A. Gillen
John Q. Barrett
Thomas E. Baker
Associate Counsel
Office of Independent Counsel
555 Thirteeth Street, N.W.
Suite 701 West
Washington, D.C. 20004

DOCUMENT 96: *United States of America v. Alan D. Fiers, Jr.*, "Government's Statement of the Factual Basis for the Factual Basis for the Guilty Plea ," July 9, 1991

PAGE 1 OF 4

UNITED STATES DISTRICT COURT
FOR THE DISTRICT OF COLUMBIA

UNITED STATES OF AMERICA)
v.)
ALAN D. FIERS, JR.,)
Defendant.)

Criminal No.

Violations: 2 U.S.C. 192.

GOVERMENT'S STATEMENT OF
THE FACTUAL BASIS FOR THE
GUILTY PLEA

COUNT ONE

From October 1984 through November 25, 1986, ALAN D. FIERS, JR., was the Chief of the Central Intelligence Agency's ("CIA") Central American Task Force, which managed CIA operations in Central America. MR. FIERS worked closely with Lt. Col. Oliver L. North on Central American issues and, in particular, on matters relating to the activity of the Nicaraguan resistance fighters, known as the Contras.

During the period from October 1984 until November 25, 1986, Lt. Col. North was detailed by the United States Marine Corps to the National Security Council ("NSC") staff, where, among other things, Lt. Col. North engaged in certain activities with respect to the Contras, counter-terrorism, and a United States initiative involving the sale of arms to elements in Iran.

Beginning with the overthrow of the Shah of Iran on or about January 16, 1979, and the seizure of the United States Embassy in Iran and its staff on November 4, 1979, relations between the United States Government and the Government of Iran were characterized by mutual hostility and tension. At all times relevant to this Information, the United States Government imposed an embargo on shipments of arms to Iran. In January 1984 the Secretary of State designated Iran a sponsor of international terrorism and, thereafter, the United States Government ac-

tively urged its allies not to permit the shipment of arms to Iran, in part because of its sponsorship of international terrorism and the continuation of the Iran-Iraq war.

Despite the embargo on arms shipments to Iran and the effort to urge United States allies not to permit Iranian arms shipments, a United States Government initiative involving sales of arms to elements in Iran and efforts to obtain the release of American citizens held hostage in Lebanon was undertaken in the latter part of 1985 and continued in 1986. Millions of dollars from the proceeds of arms sales to Iran were generated and secretly used for various purposes, including the purchase and delivery of military weapons and supplies for the Contras. The use of proceeds from these arms sales to assist the Contras became known as "the diversion."

During the early Spring of 1986, Lt. Col. North told ALAN D. FIERS, JR., that Israel was selling weapons to Iran and "kicking dollars into the Contras' pot."

Shortly after receiving this information from Lt. Col. North, ALAN D. FIERS, JR., told his superior, the Chief of the CIA's Latin American Division, of North's revelation. Shortly after this conversation, the Chief of the Latin American Division was routinely reassigned and the new Chief of the Latin American Division (hereinafter referred to as C/LAD #2) began his duties in the Spring of 1986.

By late Summer of 1986, Lt. Col. North told ALAN D. FIERS, JR., that the United States was selling arms to Iran and using proceeds from the sales to aid the Contras. MR. FIERS reported this information to his superior, C/LAD #2. C/LAD #2 instructed MR. FIERS to report this information immediately to Clair E. George, the CIA's Deputy Director for Operations.

Shortly thereafter, MR. Fiers informed Mr. George that Lt. Col. North had told him that the United States was selling arms to Iran and using proceeds from the sales to assist the Contras. Mr. George informed MR. FIERS that, "Now you [FIERS] are one of a handful of people who know this."

On November 25, 1986, President Reagan held a press conference and announced that on November 21, 1986, he had become concerned about whether his national security apparatus had provided him with a complete factual record with respect to the implementation of his policy toward Iran. President Reagan stated that he had directed Attorney General Edwin Meese III to review the matter. President Reagan introduced Attorney

DOCUMENT 96: *United States of America* v. *Alan D. Fiers, Jr.*, "Government's Statement of the Factual Basis for the Factual Basis for the Guilty Plea ," July 9, 1991

PAGE 2 OF 4

General Meese and asked him to brief the media on his preliminary findings. Attorney General Meese described arms transactions to Iran involving the United States and stated that the preliminary inquiry revealed that proceeds from those arms transactions had been deposited in bank accounts under the control of the Contras.

Later that day, ALAN D. FIERS, JR., and Assistant Secretary of State for Inter-American Affairs Elliott Abrams appeared before the United States Senate Select Committee on Intelligence to give it a briefing on Nicaragua.

During the briefing, but prior to addressing specific questions on Nicaragua, Committee members asked about the revelation by Attorney General Meese regarding the diversion. Assistant Secretary of State Abrams and the defendant, ALAN D. FIERS, JR., were asked to comment on events of the day.

After Assistant Secretary of State Abrams explained his lack of knowledge of the diversion prior to the November 25, 1986 press conference, MR. FIERS expressed his purported lack of knowledge by stating:

[MR. FIERS]: No, I don't have anything to add to it except to add the footnote that the Agency was in the same boat, and *the first I knew of it was on CNN today and that that is the first that I know that the Agency knew of it at that point in time.*

. . .

[SENATOR EAGLETON]: Back to you, Mr. Abrams. Are you speaking for the sum totality of the State Department or are you speaking just of your own personal knowledge? As to who knew what and when they knew it.

[MR. ABRAMS]: Well, I am speaking for the State Department. That is, that I think that I can say with some degree of confidence that the Secretary and others who would be expected to know if I knew, or maybe even if I didn't know, were not aware that money was going into this. I think it is—you know, I haven't asked everybody individually, but I am pretty certain in saying that there was nobody in the Department of State who knew about this Iranian business.

[SENATOR EAGLETON]: All right. How about, Mr. Fiers, you said the Agency—could you give the same all encompassing answer with respect to the Agency?

[MR. FIERS]: Yeah. *Everyone that I have talked to in the Agency, and that goes—over time, I am fairly confident didn't know that this was going on. I certainly know that people below me and immediately above me didn't.*

COUNT TWO

ALAN D. FIERS, JR., was aware generally from November 1984 through November 25, 1986, that Lt. Col. North was actively involved in coordinating lethal assistance for the Contras. During this period, the United States Government, and specifically the CIA, was prohibited by the Boland Amendment from providing lethal assistance to the Contras. MR. FIERS coordinated the Central American Task Force's activities with Lt. Col. North's to facilitate North's efforts to provide Contra assistance. MR. FIERS endeavored, however, to keep the Task Force's activities within his understanding of the scope of the Boland Amendment.

MR. FIERS became aware by February 1986 that Lt. Col. North was involved specifically in coordinating flights carrying lethal supplies to the Contras from Ilopango air base in El Salvador. He learned this from Lt. Col. North and from his interactions with two individuals involved in the resupply operation: Richard Gadd and Felix Rodriguez.

MR. FIERS met Mr. Gadd in February 1986 at Charley's, a restaurant in McLean, Virginia. The meeting had been arranged by Richard Secord, at the suggestion of Lt. Col. North. At this meeting, Mr. Gadd described the C-7 airplanes that would be used by the operation to deliver supplies to the Contras. Mr. Gadd also told MR. FIERS that, in addition to his operation as a contractor of the Department of State's Nicaraguan Humanitarian Assistance Office ("NHAO"), he had also arranged for aerial deliveries of lethal supplies for the Contras to Central America.

MR. FIERS had a confrontation with Mr. Rodriguez at Ilopango air base in February 1986. MR. FIERS had become aware of Mr. Rodriguez' involvement in NHAO operations from Lt. Col. North and from intelligence reports. The confrontation occurred because Mr. Rodriguez had authorized a resupply flight that would have compromised United States Government objectives in the region. Mr. Rodriguez informed MR. FIERS that Lt. Col. North had authorized the flight. MR. FIERS spoke

DOCUMENT 96: *United States of America v. Alan D. Fiers, Jr.*, "Government's Statement of the Factual Basis for the Factual Basis for the Guilty Plea ," July 9, 1991

PAGE 3 OF 4

to Lt. Col. North by telephone in Mr. Rodriguez' presence and told Lt. Col. North that the flight would have to be cancelled. Later in the call, Lt. Col. North spoke to Mr. Rodriguez in MR. FIERS' presence and told Mr. Rodriguez to cancel the flight.

MR. FIERS became aware during March and April 1986 that the planes managed by Mr. Gadd were carrying lethal supplies to the Contras. Mr. Fiers also was aware that in April 1986 a Southern Air Transport L-100 airplane used for NHAO deliveries had been used to drop lethal supplies to Contra forces operating in southern Nicaragua. Lt. Col. North had informed MR. FIERS of the potential for such a delivery before the L-100 drop took place.

On August 12, 1986, MR. FIERS attended a meeting in the office of Donald P. Gregg, national security advisor to Vice President Bush, in which Mr. Rodriguez' complaints about the lethal resupply operation were discussed. Several other United States Government officials attended the meeting, including Lt. Col. Robert L. Earl, a Marine officer detailed to the NSC staff under Lt. Col. North, and the United States Ambassador to El Salvador, Edwin G. Corr.

At this meeting, the resupply activity at Ilopango was discussed. Ambassador Corr said that Mr. Rodriguez had been instrumental in this activity because of his personal friendship with the commander of Ilopango air base. MR. FIERS stated that the CIA was not interested in using the resupply assets at Ilopango once the CIA was authorized to provide lethal assistance to the Contras. MR. FIERS told Lt. Col. Earl that Lt. Col. North should be informed promptly about this meeting.

On October 5, 1986, one of the resupply operation's planes was shot down over Nicaragua. The plane carried arms and ammunition. The only survivor of the crash was Eugene Hasenfus, an American citizen. MR. FIERS learned of the crash on October 6, 1986. After the downing, but before October 10, 1986, MR. FIERS had a secure telephone conversation with Lt. Col. North regarding the downed plane. MR. FIERS asked Lt. Col. North whether the downed aircraft was Lt. Col. North's. Lt. Col. North told MR. FIRS that the plane was part of his operation, and that the operation was being dismantled.

During a press conference in Managua, Nicaragua, on October 9, 1986, Mr. Hasenfus, then in Nicaraguan custody, stated that he had made ten trips to supply the Contras and had worked with Max Gomez and Ramon Medi-

na, who he alleged were CIA employees. Mr. Hasenfus stated that Mr. Gomez and Mr. Medina oversaw housing for the crews, transportation, refueling and flight plans. That same day the United States Senate Committee on Foreign Relations and the United States House of Representatives Permanent Select Committee on Intelligence requested briefings from CIA officials on the circumstances surrounding the downed plane.

On October 9, 1986, MR. FIERS and Mr. George met to discuss briefing the committees. MR. FIERS and Mr. George agreed that Mr. George would read an opening statement prepared by the Central American Task Force, and that MR. FIERS would answer more specific questions, if necessary. MR. FIERS told Mr. George that the CIA would have to acknowledge that Felix Rodriguez was the "Max Gomez" named by Mr. Hasenfus because MR. FIERS knew that to be a fact. MR. FIERS also told Mr. George that they should describe how the NHAO operation at Ilopango metamorphosed into the lethal resupply operation.

Mr. George informed MR. FIERS that neither topic would be discussed. Mr. George stated that the CIA was still gathering information about Mr. Rodriguez and that, therefore, the Agency did not know conclusively who Mr. Rodriguez was. Mr. George also stated that he wanted to avoid giving the level of detail suggested by MR. FIERS about the genesis of the lethal resupply program. Mr. George told MR. FIERS that the information should not be disclosed because it would "put the spotlight" on the Administration and thus reveal Lt. Col. North's involvement in the operation. MR. FIERS acquiesced to Mr. George's plan and had a draft of Mr. George's opening statement revised to delete the information identified by Mr. George as troublesome.

On October 14, 1986, Mr. George and MR. FIERS, accompanied by Assistant Secretary of State Abrams, testified before the House Permanent Select Committee on Intelligence, during which the following exchange occurred on the matter of the downed plane:

[MR. CHAIRMAN]: You don't know whose airplane that was?

[MR. GEORGE]: I have no idea. I read–except what I read in the paper.

[MR. CHAIRMAN]: I understand, but you don't know?

DOCUMENT 96: *United States of America v. Alan D. Fiers, Jr.*, "Government's Statement of the Factual Basis for the Factual Basis for the Guilty Plea ," July 9, 1991

PAGE 4 OF 4

[MR. FIERS]: *No, we do not know.*

[MR. CHAIRMAN]: There are a number of planes that take off there to supply the Contras regularly. You don't know who they are?

[MR. FIERS]: We know what the planes are by type, we knew, for example, there were two C-123s and two C-7 cargoes. . . . We knew in some cases much less frequently that they were flying down the Pacific air corridors into southern Nicaragua for the purposes of resupply, but as to who was flying the flights and *who was behind them we do not know.*

[MR. CHAIRMAN]: And you still don't?

[MR. FIERS]: *No.*

Respectfully submitted,

LAWRENCE E. WALSH
Independent Counsel

Craig A. Gillen
Vernon L. Francis
Michael D. Vhay
Associate Counsel

July 9, 1991

DOCUMENT 97: Caspar Weinberger, Handwritten Notes on Congressional Request for Diary, April 21, 1987 ("Larry Garrett in office—re demands by Sen-House Committee for briefings on black programs— Their demand for my diary").

PAGE 1 OF 1

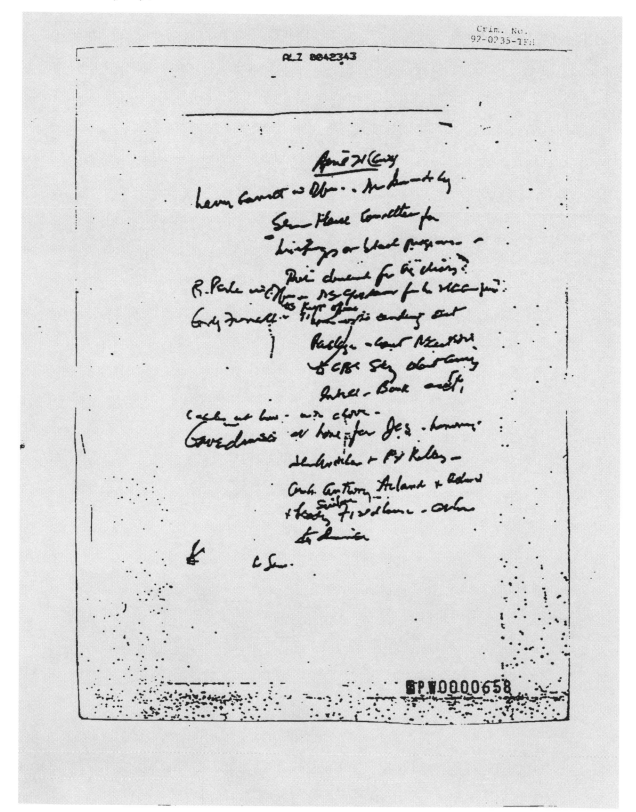

THIRD INTERIM REPORT TO CONGRESS BY INDEPENDENT COUNSEL FOR IRAN/CONTRA MATTERS

June 25, 1992

The Independent Counsel statute provides that an "independent counsel appointed under this chapter may make public from time to time, and shall send to the Congress statements or reports on the activities of such independent counsel."

Under the governing statute, Independent Counsel's responsibilities are threefold. First, he has an investigative role, 28 U. S. C. Section 594. Second, he has a prosecutorial role, 28 U. S. C. Section 594. Third, he has a reporting role, 28 U. S. C. Section 595.

The purpose of this report is to inform the Congress of the status of Independent Counsel's investigation and prosecutions in the Iran/Contra matters.

Status of the Investigation

The criminal investigation of Iran/Contra is in its final phase. We are attempting to determine whether officials at the highest level of government, acting individually or in concert, sought to obstruct official inquiries into the Iran Initiative by the Tower Commission, the Congress and Independent Counsel by withholding notes, documents and other information, by lying, and by supplying a false account of the 1985 arms sales from Israeli stocks and their replenishment by the United States.

The indictment of former Defense Secretary Weinberger by the grand jury on June 16, 1992, stemmed from that investigation. A copy of the Weinberger indictment is attached. Independent Counsel has yet to determine whether additional proposed indictments will be presented to a Grand Jury. That investigation should be completed this summer.

While pursuing the final phase of the investigation, the Office of Independent Counsel will proceed with the trial of three pending cases, *United States v. Clair E. George*, *United States v. Duane R. Clarridge*, and *United States v. Caspar W. Weinberger*. The *George* case is set for trial on July 13, 1992, before U.S. District Judge Royce Lamberth. No trial date has been set for the *Clarridge* case, but U.S. District Judge Harold Greene has stated that he hopes the trial can be held in October 1992. U.S. District Judge Thomas Hogan has set a No-

vember 2, 1992, trial date for the *Weinberger* case. In addition, Independent Counsel has been prepared to seek leave to appeal to the Supreme Court the reversal of the conviction of John M. Poindexter, but is awaiting an appeals court ruling on Poindexter's petition for rehearing in that Court.

Independent Counsel is sensitive to concerns expressed by Members of Congress and others as to the length and the resulting cost of the investigation. The investigation has continued for five and one-half years and has cost $31.4 million. This highly complex investigation posed unique problems and circumstances that stretched out our work, which I will explain in more detail later.

To speed up the completion of our investigation, I announced last December the appointment of Craig A. Gillen as Deputy Independent Counsel to direct the continuing investigation and the remaining trial work of the office, while I undertook to complete the final report of our long period of activity. I have nevertheless maintained overall responsibility for the supervision and direction of prosecutorial matters, spending one third of my time in Washington and returning to Washington full time in April for the final consideration of the Weinberger indictment. Much of the report has been drafted, but in order to complete the final phase of our investigation, and particularly while Mr. Gillen is trying cases in court, I shall continue full time in Washington where we hope to complete our investigative work by the end of this summer.

Length of Investigation

In evaluating the cost and time involved in the effort of Independent Counsel to carry out his assignment by the Appointing Panel, it is important to understand that the Iran/Contra matters posed a number of highly complicated circumstances for a prosecutor. The Iran/Contra operations were intended by the Reagan Administration to remain hidden. Because they were conducted in tandem with or in the course of covert activities, once exposed, they could not be readily explored in open court because of the national security claims.

The operations were executed by high Reagan Administration officials in support of presidential foreign policy objectives. They occurred in a broad geographic setting over a period of years. Their investigation required a thorough sifting of hundreds of thousands of documents from some of the most sophisticated and secretive agencies of government. And, although there were many witnesses to various aspects of these operations, the most central figures were not cooperative. There were few government officers who volunteered information willingly.

It was imperative for Independent Counsel to focus first on the facts that might be the subject of immunized testimony, including the diversion of funds from the proceeds of the Iranian arms sales to assist the Contras. It was necessary to gather as much material as possible before Congress granted immunity to the most central figures in the affair. After immunity was granted, it was necessary to shield our potential prosecutions from contamination by the highly publicized congressional testimony of Oliver L. North, Poindexter and others who testified under immunity grants.

Once the first major indictment was brought in March 1988, Independent Counsel turned to trial work. In the *North* case alone, 108 pre-trial motions were filed, thirty-two of which challenged the validity of charges in the 23-count indictment brought against North, Poindexter, Richard Secord, and Albert Hakim.

The decision by U.S. District Judge Gerhard Gesell to sever the four defendants in the case to preserve the right of each of the defendants to use the immunized testimony of others to exculpate himself necessitated separate trials and added more than a year to the anticipated schedule. The immunity issues ultimately brought about the reversal of North and Poindexter's convictions on appeal.

Classified information problems have also complicated Independent Counsel's prosecutions and consumed enormous time and energy. Every line of every page of the thousands of pages of classified documents that might be used in trial by either the prosecution of the defense has had to undergo review by a group of declassification experts from several agencies. Claims of national security led to the dismissal of the central conspiracy charge against North, Poindexter, Secord and Hakim. Attorney General Thornburgh's refusal to declassify publicly known but officially secret information forced the dismissal of the government's entire case against former CIA Costa Rican station chief Joseph Fernandez—and more than a year's litigation was wasted. I have previously reported to Congress at greater length on these problems.

Crimes Charges and Tried

Independent Counsel has *not* been able to prosecute the basic operational crimes committed in the course of the Iran/Contra affair due to national security claims. For instance, Count One in the North-Poindexter-Secord-Hakim indictment was dismissed due to claims that material information could not be declassified. It charged a conspiracy to defraud the United States by obstructing congressional oversight; by illegally supporting the Nicaraguan Contras; by depriving the government of the honest and faithful services of employees free from conflicts of interest, corruption and self-dealing; and by exploiting and corrupting for their own purposes a government initiative involving the sale of arms to Iran rather than pursuing solely the government objectives of the initiative, including the release of hostages in Lebanon.

Independent Counsel *has* been able to prosecute the crimes committed in the course of the Iran/Contra cover-up. These have including [*sic*] lying to and withholding information from Congress, lying to other official investigations, and withholding and destroying documents.

Criminal charges have been brought against 14 persons in three venues, including three cases that have not yet come to trial. Ten convictions have been obtained. The North and Poindexter convictions were reversed on appeal. The Fernandez case never came to trial due to classified information problems.

The Office of Independent Counsel could not complete its work without questioning all significant witnesses and pursing all important leads related to the mandate issued by the Appointing Panel, a copy of which is attached. Because of the need to try North and Poindexter separately, those two principals did not become available for questioning until mid-1990.

Since then, the continuing investigation was fueled by newly discovered documents, including the personal notes of key officials, CIA cables and tapes, and other records previously withheld from Independent Counsel and other investigating bodies. These were obtained by renewed emphasis on the fulfillment of longstanding document requests, originally made in 1987 to the National Security Agency, the National Security Council, the CIA, the White House, the Office of the Vice President, and the State and Defense Departments. Also of critical importance were changes in witness testimony.

Conclusion

In the past two years, the continuing investigation has developed new and disturbing evidence that made it necessary to re-interview many of the witnesses first questioned in 1987. This was not merely a clean-up chore—it has provided a significant shift in our understanding of which Administration officials had knowledge of Iran/Contra, who participated in its cover-up, and which areas required far more scrutiny than we previously believed.

It is not a crime to deceive the American public, as high officials in the Reagan Administration did for two years while conducting the Iran and Contra operations. But it is a crime to mislead, deceive and lie to Congress when, in fulfilling its legitimate oversight role, the Congress seeks to learn whether Administration officials are conducting the nation's business in accordance with the law.

Attachments: Appointing Mandate
                            Weinberger Indictment
                            Office Fact Sheet

UNITED STATES DISTRICT COURT
FOR THE DISTRICT OF COLUMBIA

Holding a Criminal Term

Grand Jury 91-1 Sworn in on January 16, 1991

UNITED STATES OF AMERICA :
        v. :
CASPAR W. WEINBERGER, :
Defendant. :
        :

Criminal No.

Violation:
  Title 18 U.S.C. 1001.
  (False Statements)

INDICTMENT

COUNT I
(False Statements)

The Defendant

1. From 1981 to November 1987, the defendant, CASPAR W. WEINBERGER, was the Secretary of Defense and a statutory member of the National Security Council ("NSC").

2. At all times relevant to this Indictment, the Secretary of Defense was the head of the Department of Defense ("DoD").

3. At all times relevant to this Indictment, the NSC was a government entity established by the National Security Act of 1947, whose statutory members were the President of States, the Vice President, the Secretary of State and the Secretary of Defense.

4. At all times relevant to this Indictment, the defendant, CASPAR W. WEINBERGER, as a statutory member of the NSC, advised President Ronald Reagan on the integration of domestic, foreign, and military policies relating to the national security; facilitated cooperation among the military services and other departments and agencies of the government in matters involving the national security; and reviewed, guided and directed foreign intelligence and covert action activities.

The Defendant's Handwritten Notes

5. For many years, the defendant, CASPAR W. WEINBERGER, took daily notes of his activities. These handwritten daily notes contain an extensive record of what the defendant, CASPAR W. WEINBERGER, did on a daily basis, and include summaries of telephone conversations and meetings. During 1985 and 1986, the defendant, CASPAR W. WEINBERGER, took nearly 1,700 pages of daily notes.

6. During 1985 and 1986 the defendant, CASPAR W. WEINBERGER, also took hundreds of pages of meeting notes during high-level meetings, in addition to the daily notes described in the preceding paragraph.

7. After he left the DoD, the defendant, CASPAR W. WEINBERGER, deposited these notes in the Library of Congress in the District of Columbia, where public access to the notes was subject to his exclusive personal control.

The Iran Initiative

8. Beginning with the overthrow of the Shah of Iran on or about January 16, 1979, and the seizure of the United States Embassy in Iran and its staff on November 4, 1979, relations between the United States Government and the Government of Iran were characterized by mutual hostility and tension. At all times relevant to this Indictment, the United States Government embargoed arms sales to Iran. In January 1984, Secretary of State George P. Shultz designated Iran as a sponsor of international terrorism and, thereafter, the United States Government actively urged its allies not to permit the shipment of arms to Iran.

9. In August 1985, Robert C. McFarlane, the Assistant to the President for National Security Affairs, briefed President Ronald Reagan, Secretary Shultz, and the defendant, CASPAR W. WEINBERGER, about an Israeli proposal to sell arms to Iran to obtain the release of Americans held hostage in Lebanon. This plan and subsequent efforts to obtain the release of the hostages through the sale of arms to Iran became known as the Iran initiative.

10. In August and September of 1985, Israel shipped 508 United States-supplied TOW anti-tank missiles to Iran. Following these Israeli TOW shipments to Iran, the Reverend Benjamin Weir, an American held hostage in Lebanon, was released from captivity.

11. On Saturday, November 9, 1985, the defendant, CASPAR W. WEINBERGER, spoke with Mr. McFarlane. The defendant, CASPAR W. WEINBERGER, made the following handwritten entry in his daily notes:

Bud McFarlane...wants to start "negot." exploration with Iranians (+ Israelis) to give Iranians weapons for our hostages-I objected-we'll talk later on secure.

12. On Sunday, November 10, 1985, the defendant, CASPAR W. WEINBERGER, again spoke with Mr. Mc-Farlane. The defendant, CASPAR W. WEINBERGER, made the following handwritten entry in his daily notes:

Bud McFarlane...negotiations are with 3 Iranian dissidents who say they want to overthrow government. We'll demand release of all hostages. Then we might give them-thru Israelis-Hawks but no Phoenix.

13. On Tuesday, November 19, 1985, the defendant, CASPAR W. WEINBERGER, again spoke with Mr. Mc-Farlane. The defendant, CASPAR W. WEINBERGER, made the following handwritten entry in his daily notes:

Bud McFarlane fm Geneva-update on meetings-all OK so far-Also wants us to try to get 500 Hawks for sale to Israel to pass on to Iran for release of 5 hostages Thurs.

14. Later that day, Major General Colin L. Powell, the Senior Military Assistant to the defendant, CASPAR W. WEINBERGER, spoke with him. The defendant, CAS-PAR W. WEINBERGER, made the following handwritten entry in his daily notes:

Colin Powell in office re data on Hawks-can't be given to Israel or Iran w/o Cong. notification,-breaking them up into several packages of 28 Hawks to keep each package under $14 million is a clear violation

15. The defendant, CASPAR W. WEINBERGER, then spoke with Mr. McFarlane. The defendant, CAS-PAR W. WEINBERGER, made the following handwritten entry in his daily notes:

called McFarlane in Geneva-re above-he "thanks me for call"-

16. On Wednesday, November 20, 1985, the defendant, CASPAR W. WEINBERGER, spoke with Mr. Mc-Farlane. The defendant, CASPAR W. WEINBERGER, made the following handwritten entry in his daily notes:

Bud McFarlane rmc. fm Geneva (2)-he hasn't heard of request for logistical support for hostages-return-Told him we shouldn't pay Iranian anything-he sd President has decided to do it thru Israelis.

17. Later that day, the defendant, CASPAR W. WEIN-BERGER, again spoke with Mr. McFarlane. The defendant, CASPAR W. WEINBERGER, made the following handwritten entry in his daily notes:

Bud McFarlane fm Geneva-working on broad agreement language-Israelis will sell 120 Hawks, older models to Iranians-Friday release

18. On or about Sunday, November 24, 1985, a cargo of 18 HAWK missiles was sent from Israel to Iran.

19. On Saturday, December 7, 1985, the defendant, CASPAR W. WEINBERGER, attended a meeting at the White House with President Reagan, Chief of Staff to the President Donald T. Regan, Secretary Shultz, Deputy Director of Central Intelligence John N. McMahon, newly-appointed Assistant to the President for National Security Affairs Vice Admiral John M. Poindexter, and Mr. McFarlane, who recently had resigned his position as Assistant to the President for National Security Affairs. The defendant, CASPAR W. WEINBERGER, made the following handwritten entry in his daily notes:

met with President, Shultz, Don Regan, John McMahon, McFarlane, John Poindexter-in Upstairs residence of WH (end of corridor sitting room)-re NSC Iran proposal. President wants to free hostages. Thinks Hawks + TOWs would only go to "moderate elements in Army" + would help overthrow Iranian gov't. I argued strongly that we have an embargo that makes arms sales to Iran illegal + President couldn't violate it-+ that "washing" transaction thru Israel wouldn't make it legal. Shultz, Don Regan agreed. President sd. he could answer charges of illegality but he couldn't answer charge that "big strong President Reagan passed up a chance to free hostages". President left to do his noon radio.

20. On December 10, 1985, the defendant, CASPAR W. WEINBERGER, attended a meeting at the White House with President Reagan, Chief of Staff Regan, Director of Central Intelligence William J. Casey, Admiral Poindexter, and Mr. McFarlane. The defendant,

CASPAR W. WEINBERGER, made two pages of hand-written meeting notes, including the following:

Bud

. . .

We still must replace 500 TOWs to Israel

The defendant, CASPAR W. WEINBERGER, also made the following handwritten entry in his daily notes:

Met with President [,] John Poindexter, McFarlane, Bill Casey-in Oval Office-McFarlane recommends that we not continue to deal with Iranians for hostage release-but try to get more reliable Iranians who will help overthrow government-but not link any of it to hostage release-President still wants to try to get hostage released. But forcible storming would mean many deaths-...

21. On January 6, 1986, the defendant, CASPAR W. WEINBERGER, met with Admiral Poindexter. The defendant, CASPAR W. WEINBERGER, made handwritten meeting notes, He also made the following handwritten entry in his daily notes:

John Poindexter in office. Another Israeli-Iranian scheme offering freedom to hostages in return for TOW missiles. Told him I opposed it.

22. On January 7, 1986, the defendant, CASPAR W. WEINBERGER, attended a meeting at the White House with President Reagan, Vice President George Bush, Attorney General Edwin Meese, III, Director Casey and Secretary Shultz. The defendant, CASPAR W. WEINBERGER, made the following handwritten entry in his daily notes:

Met with President, Shultz, Poindexter, Bill Casey, Ed Meese, in Oval Office. President decided to go with Israeli-Iranian offer to release our 5 hostages in return for sale of 4000 TOWs to Iran by Israel-George Shultz + I Opposed-Bill Casey, Ed Meese + VP favored-as did Poindexter.

23. On January 17, 1986, President Reagan formally approved, by Presidential Finding, a covert plan in which the United States would sell weapons to Iran through an American intermediary, rather than through Israel.

24. In furtherance of this plan, during February 1986, 1,000 TOW missiles were sold to Iran.

25. Between May and November 1986, additional weapons and replacement parts for weapons were sold to Iran, and two Americans held hostage in Lebanon were released.

26. In early November 1986, there were public reports that United States Government officials had engaged in arms-for-hostages deals with Iran.

27. On November 10, 1986, the defendant, CASPAR W. WEINBERGER, attended a White House meeting with President Reagan, Vice President Bush, Secretary Shultz, Attorney General Meese, Director Casey, Chief of Staff Regan, Admiral Poindexter, and Acting Deputy Assistant to the President for National Security Affairs Alton G. Keel, Jr. Admiral Poindexter briefed the meeting about operational details of the Iran initiative, but he omitted mention of the November 1985 HAWK missile shipment and did not acknowledge any United States role in or approval of any shipment prior to the Presidential Finding of January 17, 1986. The defendant, CASPAR W. WEINBERGER, took five pages of handwritten meeting notes. He also made the following handwritten entry in his daily notes:

Met with President in Oval Office. Shultz, V.P., Don Regan, John Poindexter, Bill Casey, Al Kheel [sic–Keel]. (see separate memo)

28. On November 12, 1986, the defendant, CASPAR W. WEINBERGER, attended a briefing for Congressional leaders at the White House with the same officials who attended the November 10, 1986 meeting. Admiral Poindexter briefed the Congressional leaders about the Iran initiative but, once again, did not acknowledge any United States role in or approval of any 1985 shipments, including the November 1985 HAWK missile shipment. In response to a question by Senate Minority Leader Robert C. Byrd, Admiral Poindexter stated that the initial contacts with the Iranians had been in 1985 but there had been no transfer of material to Iran then because it took time to asses the contacts and issue a Finding. The defendant, CASPAR W. WEINBERGER, took sixteen pages of handwritten meeting notes. He also made the following handwritten entry in his daily notes:

Attended WH Sit Rm meeting-with President, VP, Shultz, Ed Meese, Poindexter-Sen Byrd, Jim

Wright, Bob Dole, Dick Cheyney [sic–Cheney]-(see separate memo)

29. On November 13, 1986, President Reagan addressed the nation about the Iran initiative.

30. On November 19, 1986, President Reagan held a news conference about the Iran initiative.

31. On Sunday, November 23, 1986, the defendant, CASPAR W. WEINBERGER, met with Prince Bandar bin Sultan, the Saudi Arabian Ambassador to the United States. The defendant, CASPAR W. WEINBERGER, made the following handwritten note:

Prince Bandar in office-Nancy Reagan-in a 1 1/2 hr. talk Friday with him-he invited President to dinner at his Embassy-sd she thinks Shultz should go-that he has been disloyal to the President-he sd he recommended to her that I be named Secretary of State; that I could negotiate an agreement with Soviets because no one could say I was soft on them-She feels that very few are being loyal to the President + that Shultz should not have gone to Canada Friday + should support President-She would like Baker to go in as Secretary of Defense!

32. On November 24, 1986, the defendant, CASPAR W. WEINBERGER, met at the White House with President Reagan, Vice President Bush, Secretary Shultz, Director Casey, Chief of Staff Regan, Admiral Poindexter and Attorney General Meese. Mr. Meese told the group that the November 1985 Israeli HAWK missile shipment may have been illegal, but that the President did not know about the shipment at the time. The defendant, CASPAR W. WEINBERGER, took twenty pages of handwritten meeting notes. He also made a handwritten entry regarding the meeting in his daily notes.

33. On November 25, 1986, Attorney General Meese announced at a press conference that proceeds generated from mark-ups in the sales of arms to Iran had been diverted to the Nicaraguan democratic resistance, also known as the Contras.

Congressional Investigations

34. Following the November 25, 1986 press conference, several Congressional Committees conducted investigations and held hearings on these topics.

35. On December 17, 1986, the defendant, CASPAR

W. WEINBERGER, testified about the Iran initiative in closed session before the United States Senate Select Committee on Intelligence. With regard to the November 1985 Israeli HAWK missile shipment to Iran, the defendant, CASPAR W. WEINBERGER, testified as follows:

Q. In the period of time from approximately November 16th to November 21st of 1985, the President was in Geneva for the summit meeting with Mr. Gorbachev. And at or about that same time, one of the arms transfers to the Iranians was under way and there is some evidence that there was discussions [sic] at various highest levels relative to that. Do you have any reason to recollect being aware at that particular point in time of discussions?

A. No. I was not in Geneva at those meetings and I did not have any recollection of that. I know that may have been about the time I saw one of these first [intelligence reports] that I mentioned to you earlier. But that was all–my impression was that the plan was not being put forward actively, was no longer being considered. And this was confirmed in my view in the President's reaction at the December 6th [sic–December 7] meeting that I have mentioned.

36. On January 6, 1987, the United States Senate, by Senate Resolution 23, established the Select Committee on Secret Military Assistance to Iran and the Nicaraguan Opposition ("Senate Select Committee"). On January 7, 1987, the United States House of Representatives, by House Resolution 12, established the Select Committee to Investigate Covert Arms Transactions with Iran ("House Select Committee"). The two Chambers instructed their respective Committees (collectively, "Select Committees") to work together and charged them with investigating, among other things, any activity of any officer or entity of the United States Government relating to the Iran initiative.

37. On March 11, 1987, the defendant, CASPAR W. WEINBERGER, met with counsel to the Senate Select Committee. A Senate Select Committee staff memorandum prepared following the meeting states, in relevant part:

Weinberger offered that some of his recollections of these matters were a bit fuzzy, and added "I have the deepest sympathy for the President's memory problem." He then added that he "should have done what Henry Kissinger did after every meeting, he would dictate a memo of what transpired, which was used in writing his memoirs. For me, after I finish a meeting, I go off to another meeting." While Weinberger did not expressly deny that he kept diaries or dictated his thoughts about a day's events, with these comments he clearly left the impression that he did not make such notes or recordings.

38. On or about April 4, 1987, the Senate Select Committee requested that the DoD produce to it all documents relating to the Iran initiative, including "notes,...diaries,...or other such records, of attendance at, recollection of, or participation in,...any meetings, discussions, conferences, or events pertaining to the Committee's inquiry, prepared by and/or in the possession of" certain individuals, including the defendant, CASPAR W. WEINBERGER.

39. On or about April 13, 1987, the House Select Committee requested that the DoD produce to it all documents relating to the Iran initiative, including "calendars, logs, diaries, appointment books, records of meetings and handwritten notes kept by or on behalf of" certain individuals, including the defendant, CASPAR W. WEINBERGER.

40. The defendant, CASPAR W. WEINBERGER, never produced to the Select Committees his daily notes or many of his relevant meeting notes.

41. On June 17, 1987, members of the Select Committees' staffs took deposition testimony under oath from the defendant, CASPAR W. WEINBERGER, in his office at the Pentagon.

42. Pursuant to House Resolution 12, which established the House Select Committee, the June 17, 1987 deposition is deemed to have been taken in the District of Columbia.

THE GRAND JURY CHARGES:

43. On June 17, 1987, in a deposition, the defendant, CASPAR W. WEINBERGER, unlawfully, knowingly and willfully made material false, fictitious and fraudulent statements to a department or agency of the United States, to wit, the House Select Committee, in a matter within its jurisdiction, to wit, its investigation of the Iran initiative and certain aspects of assistance for the Contras.

44. It was material to the House Select Committee's investigation to determine whether the defendant, CASPAR W. WEINBERGER, had any written materials, including contemporaneous notes, that contained information relating to what the President and other senior government officials had known or done in connection with proposals to ship arms to Iran in 1985, contributions to the Contras, and other topics within the scope of the investigation of the Select Committees.

45. On June 17, 1987, the defendant, CASPAR W. WEINBERGER, appearing as a witness before duly authorized staff of the House Select Committee, made the following statements, knowing them to be false, fictitious and fraudulent:

Q. We have gone over a number of meetings?
A. Yes.
Q. Of course, your recollection is better on some and fainter on others.
A. Yes.
Q. Is there any way that you have of making a record of the highlights of meetings of this nature?
A. Now?
Q No, then.
A. *No. There wasn't.* I did dictate a memorandum on this particular one [referring to a November 10, 1986 meeting], but I've often said that I understand that Henry Kissinger made a memo of every meeting he ever attended and that enabled him to write his book rapidly. I wish I had done that with day one of the administration. I am usually getting ready for the next meeting and don't have time to write these memorandums. I took notes about this one and dictated this memorandum because it seemed to be important.
Q. Do you ever take notes that are not dictated or make jottings when you get back?
A. Yes, *occasionally, but comparatively rarely.* I don't know we kept those in any formal way. I don't think they have been filed or labeled. My handwriting is notoriously bad. I have trouble even reading it myself. *Occasionally take a few notes, but not really very often.*
Q. If there is any chance there are—
A. I think we made this examination and *whatever there is is in our so-called C&D, Correspondence and Directives.* They have been asked to paw through everything.

Q. Are you aware of any other potential source of–that might be–have made a record that might supplement your memory of some of these meetings?

A. *Well, I don't really think of anything.* We could paw through everything again. *We have done that, I think, pretty well.*

46. The above underscored material statements made to the duly authorized staff of the House Select Committee by the defendant, CASPAR W. WEINBERGER, were false, fictitious and fraudulent, as the defendant, CASPAR W. WEINBERGER, then and there well knew, in that:

a. he had, for years, including nearly seven years as Secretary of Defense, regularly taken daily notes of his meetings and telephone conversations;

b. he had, as Secretary of Defense, taken notes during meetings with the President and other high officials, including meetings related to the Iranian arms sales matter, that contained a record of what occurred at those meetings;

c. he had extensive notes that had never been provided to the Select Committees;

d. his daily notes were not stored or deposited in the DoD's Correspondence & Directives (C&D) section; and

e. these notes contained information relevant to the Select Committees' investigation.

(In Violation of Title 18, United States Code, Section 1001.)

DOCUMENT 100: George Bush, Presidential Pardon of Caspar Weinberger, Elliott Abrams, Duane Clarridge, Alan Fiers, Clair George, and Robert McFarlane, December 24, 1992.

PAGE 1 OF 3

THE WHITE HOUSE

Office of the Press Secretary

For Immediate Release   December 24, 1992

GRANT OF EXECUTIVE CLEMENCY

- - - - - - -

BY THE PRESIDENT OF THE UNITED STATES OF AMERICA

A PROCLAMATION

Today I am exercising my power under the Constitution to pardon former Secretary of Defense Caspar Weinberger and others for their conduct related to the Iran-Contra affair.

For more than 6 years now, the American people have invested enormous resources into what has become the most thoroughly investigated matter of its kind in our history. During that time, the last American hostage has come home to freedom, worldwide terrorism has declined, the people of Nicaragua have elected a democratic government, and the Cold War has ended in victory for the American people and the cause of freedom we championed.

In the mid 1980's, however, the outcome of these struggles was far from clear. Some of the best and most dedicated of our countrymen were called upon to step forward. Secretary Weinberger was among the foremost.

Caspar Weinberger is a true American patriot. He has rendered long and extraordinary service to our country. He served for 4 years in the Army during World War II where his bravery earned him a Bronze Star. He gave up a lucrative career in private life to accept a series of public positions in the late 1960's and 1970's, including Chairman of the Federal Trade Commission, Director of the Office of Management and Budget, and Secretary of Health, Education, and Welfare. Caspar Weinberger served in all these positions with distinction and was admired as a public servant above reproach.

He saved his best for last. As Secretary of Defense throughout most of the Reagan Presidency, Caspar Weinberger was one of the principal architects of the downfall of the Berlin Wall and the Soviet Union. He directed the military renaissance in this country that led to the breakup of the communist bloc and a new birth of freedom and democracy. Upon his resignation in 1987, Caspar Weinberger was awarded the highest civilian medal our Nation can bestow on one of its citizens, the Presidential Medal of Freedom.

Secretary Weinberger's legacy will endure beyond the ending of the Cold War. The military readiness of this Nation that he in large measure created could not have been better displayed than it was 2 years ago in the Persian Gulf and today in Somalia.

As Secretary Weinberger's pardon request noted, it is a bitter irony that on the day the first charges against Secretary Weinberger were filed, Russian President Boris Yeltsin arrived in the United States to celebrate the end of the Cold War. I am

more

DOCUMENT 100: George Bush, Presidential Pardon of Caspar Weinberger, Elliott Abrams, Duane Clarridge, Alan Fiers, Clair George, and Robert McFarlane, December 24, 1992.

PAGE 2 OF 3

2

pardoning him not just out of compassion or to spare a 75-year-old patriot the torment of lengthy and costly legal proceedings, but to make it possible for him to receive the honor he deserves for his extraordinary service to our country.

Moreover, on a somewhat more personal note, I cannot ignore the debilitating illnesses faced by Caspar Weinberger and his wife. When he resigned as Secretary of Defense, it was because of his wife's cancer. In the years since he left public service, her condition has not improved. In addition, since that time, he also has become ill. Nevertheless, Caspar Weinberger has been a pillar of strength for his wife; this pardon will enable him to be by her side undistracted by the ordeal of a costly and arduous trial.

I have also decided to pardon five other individuals for their conduct related to the Iran-Contra affair: Elliott Abrams, Duane Clarridge, Alan Fiers, Clair George, and Robert McFarlane. First, the common denominator of their motivation -- whether their actions were right or wrong -- was patriotism. Second, they did not profit or seek to profit from their conduct. Third, each has a record of long and distinguished service to this country. And finally, all five have already paid a price -- in depleted savings, lost careers, anguished families -- grossly disproportionate to any misdeeds or errors of judgment they may have committed.

The prosecutions of the individuals I am pardoning represent what I believe is a profoundly troubling development in the political and legal climate of our country: the criminalization of policy differences. These differences should be addressed in the political arena, without the Damocles sword of criminality hanging over the heads of some of the combatants. The proper target is the President, not his subordinates; the proper forum is the voting booth, not the courtroom.

In recent years, the use of criminal processes in policy disputes has become all too common. It is my hope that the action I am taking today will begin to restore these disputes to the battleground where they properly belong.

In addition, the actions of the men I am pardoning took place within the larger Cold War struggle. At home, we had a long, sometimes heated debate about how that struggle should be waged. Now the Cold War is over. When earlier wars have ended, Presidents have historically used their power to pardon to put bitterness behind us and look to the future. This healing tradition reaches at least from James Madison's pardon of Lafitte's pirates after the War of 1812, to Andrew Johnson's pardon of soldiers who had fought for the Confederacy, to Harry Truman's and Jimmy Carter's pardons of those who violated the Selective Service laws in World War II and Vietnam.

In many cases, the offenses pardoned by these Presidents were at least as serious as those I am pardoning today. The actions of those pardoned and the decisions to pardon them raised important issues of conscience, the rule of law, and the relationship under our Constitution between the government and the governed. Notwithstanding the seriousness of these issues and the passions they aroused, my predecessors acted because it was time for the country to move on. Today I do the same.

Some may argue that this decision will prevent full disclosure of some new key fact to the American people. That is not true. This matter has been investigated exhaustively. The Tower Board, the Joint Congressional Committee charged with investigating the Iran-Contra affair, and the Independent

DOCUMENT 100: George Bush, Presidential Pardon of Caspar Weinberger, Elliott Abrams, Duane Clarridge, Alan Fiers, Clair George, and Robert McFarlane, December 24, 1992.

PAGE 3 OF 3

3

Counsel have looked into every aspect of this matter. The Tower Board interviewed more than 80 people and reviewed thousands of documents. The Joint Congressional Committee interviewed more than 500 people and reviewed more than 300,000 pages of material. Lengthy committee hearings were held and broadcast on national television to millions of Americans. And as I have noted, the Independent Counsel investigation has gone on for more than 6 years, and it has cost more than $31 million.

Moreover, the Independent Counsel stated last September that he had completed the active phase of his investigation. He will have the opportunity to place his full assessment of the facts in the public record when he submits his final report. While no impartial person has seriously suggested that my own role in this matter is legally questionable, I have further requested that the Independent Counsel provide me with a copy of my sworn testimony to his office, which I am prepared to release immediately. And I understand Secretary Weinberger has requested the release of all of his notes pertaining to the Iran-Contra matter.

For more than 30 years in public service, I have tried to follow three precepts: honor, decency, and fairness. I know, from all those years of service, that the American people believe in fairness and fair play. In granting these pardons today, I am doing what I believe honor, decency, and fairness require.

NOW, THEREFORE, I, GEORGE BUSH, President of the United States of America, pursuant to my powers under Article II, Section 2, of the Constitution, do hereby grant a full, complete, and unconditional pardon to Elliott Abrams, Duane R. Clarridge, Alan Fiers, Clair George, Robert C. McFarlane, and Caspar W. Weinberger for all offenses charged or prosecuted by Independent Counsel Lawrence E. Walsh or other members of his office, or committed by these individuals and within the jurisdiction of that office.

IN WITNESS WHEREOF, I have hereunto set my hand this twenty-fourth day of December, in the year of our Lord nineteen hundred and ninety-two, and of the Independence of the United States of America the two hundred and seventeenth.

GEORGE BUSH

# # #

OFFICE OF INDEPENDENT COUNSEL
555 THIRTEENTH STREET N.W.
SUITE 701 WEST
WASHINGTON, D. C. 20004

FOR RELEASE AT 2 P.M. EST   CONTACT: MARY BELCHER
DECEMBER 24, 1992   (202) 383-5443

STATEMENT OF INDEPENDENT COUNSEL LAWRENCE E. WALSH

President Bush's pardon of Caspar Weinberger and other Iran-contra defendants undermines the principle that no man is above the law. It demonstrates that powerful people with powerful allies can commit serious crimes in high office -- deliberately abusing the public trust -- without consequence.

Weinberger, who faced four felony charges, deserved to be tried by a jury of citizens. Although it is the President's prerogative to grant pardons, it is every American's right that the criminal justice system be administered fairly, regardless of a person's rank and connections.

The Iran-contra cover-up, which has continued for more than six years, has now been completed with the pardon of Caspar Weinberger. We will make a full report on our findings to Congress and the public describing the details and extent of this cover-up.

Weinberger's early and deliberate decision to conceal and withhold extensive contemporaneous notes of the Iran-contra matter radically altered the official investigations and possibly forestalled timely impeachment proceedings against President Reagan and other officials. Weinberger's notes contain evidence of a conspiracy among the highest-ranking Reagan administration officials to lie to Congress and the American public. Because the notes were withheld from investigators for years, many of the leads were impossible to follow, key witnesses had purportedly forgotten what was said and done, and statutes of limitation had expired.

Weinberger's concealment of notes is part of a disturbing pattern of deception and obstruction that permeated the highest levels of the Reagan and Bush administrations. This office was informed only within the past two weeks, on December 11, 1992, that President Bush had failed to produce to investigators his own highly relevant contemporaneous notes, despite repeated requests for such documents. The production of these notes is still ongoing and will lead to appropriate action. In light of President Bush's own misconduct, we are gravely concerned about his decision to pardon others who lied to Congress and obstructed official investigations.

# # #

THE IRAN-CONTRA SCANDAL
A CHRONOLOGY OF EVENTS

SOURCE NOTES

This Chronology covers events relating to the Reagan administration's illicit Contra resupply operations and the U.S. arms-for-hostages initiative with Iran. Beginning in 1981 and extending into 1992, it includes background on U.S. activities and policies in those areas and key events relating to official investigations of the scandal. The Chronology is designed as a complement to the reader, drawing from the documents themselves (as well as from many published in the National Security Archive's document collection on microfiche, The Iran-Contra Affair: The Making of a Scandal, 1983–1988), contemporary press accounts, books and congressional publications.

Each chronology entry is followed by a citation for its sources. Documents that are included in this reader are cited by title and number, as listed in the table of contents. Documents not included in the book are cited by title or constructed title and date. (Occasionally, the date appears as part of the title or constructed title.) Ellipses indicate omission of words when a title has been shortened. Additional information, such as time and cable origin and number, is provided to distinguish documents with the same title or constructed title and date.

Books and periodicals are generally cited by an abbreviated form of the author or title of the publication. Occasionally, periodicals are cited by full title. References to parts or specific pages of publications are provided where helpful. For a listing of the abbreviated titles used in this chronology, see the "Abbreviations" section on pages 411–12.

April 25, 1980: A secret U.S. government attempt to rescue American hostages held in Teheran ends with the fiery collision of a U.S. helicopter and refueling aircraft at "Desert One," an isolated rendezvous point in the middle of Iran. Planning for a second mission begins immediately. Air Force Brig. Gen. Richard Secord, from 1975 to 1978 the official in charge of all U.S. arms sales to Iran, serves as deputy commander of the planning team. He later plays a central role in the Iran-Contra Affair. Working in air force special operations in the Pentagon at the time are Lt. Col. Richard Gadd and Col. Robert Dutton. Dutton had worked with Secord on Iran in the 1970s. Both later assist Secord in the Contra resupply program. Secord later testifies to Congress that the single greatest problem in planning for another rescue was acquiring accurate intelligence on the location of the hostages. In the aftermath of the rescue mission failures, the Defense Department puts together a new special operations apparatus in the Pentagon, preparing the way for expanded covert activities during the next decade. (*United States Air Force, Major General Richard V. Secord*, ca. 2/82; WP 11/8/86, 3/22/87; LAT 2/6/87; Maas, p. 287; *Department of Defense Telephone Directory*, 8/80, 12/81; Secord, Testimony, vol. 100-1, pp. 148–49)

Early 1981: Secretary of State Alexander Haig reportedly gives permission to Israel to ship U.S.-made spare parts for fighter planes to Iran, nearly four years before similar shipments set in motion the Iran-Contra affair. Haig's decision follows discussions between his counselor at the State Department, Robert McFarlane, and David Kimche, director general of the Israeli Foreign Ministry. In July 1985, Kimche convinces McFarlane, who by then has become President Reagan's national security advisor, of the desirability of selling U.S. missiles to Iran in the hopes of gaining freedom for American hostages in Lebanon. (WP 11/29/86)

January 21, 1981: President Reagan chairs the first National Security Council (NSC) meeting of his administration. Iran and Libya are the focus. Throughout the Reagan presidency, the Khomeini and Qaddafi governments are reportedly subjects of urgent concern in the White House. (WP 2/20/87)

December 1, 1981: President Reagan signs a covert operations Finding authorizing the CIA to "[s]upport and conduct [deleted] paramilitary operations against Nicaragua." The authorization provides $19.95 million for the CIA to organize, train, and arm

Nicaraguan exiles, who come to be known as the Contras (from the Spanish term, *contrarevolucionario*). When CIA Director William Casey presents the Finding to the congressional intelligence committees, he depicts the operation as an interdiction program, designed to stop the flow of weapons allegedly going from Nicaragua to rebels in El Salvador. (Document 1, *Signed Presidential Finding on Central America*, 12/1/81; WP 5/8/83)

December 4, 1981: President Reagan signs Executive Order 12333, the primary executive branch document establishing operating rules for intelligence agencies. According to the order, the CIA is in charge of covert operations unless the president directs otherwise. During the Iran initiative, President Reagan fails to assign formal responsibility for the secret program to the NSC; according to Senate investigators, this places him in violation of the order. The Executive Order also defines the National Security Council as "the highest Executive Branch entity" involved in intelligence, a definition that becomes important later when Reagan administration officials claim that the NSC was not covered under the second Boland Amendment, which prohibited all U.S. intelligence agencies from assisting the Contras. (*Executive Order 12333, December 4, 1981: United States Intelligence Activities*; WP 1/12/87)

June 1982: Walter Raymond, Jr., a career CIA official with expertise in clandestine overseas media operations, is transferred to the National Security Council. Donald Gregg, chief of the NSC's Intelligence Directorate, recommends Raymond as his replacement when he leaves in the next several weeks to become national security advisor to Vice President George Bush. Raymond confers with CIA Director William Casey before accepting the transfer. According to his deposition, Raymond tells Casey that in addition to his intelligence responsibilities, he would like to be involved in setting up a "public diplomacy" capability for the U.S. government to "wage the war of ideas"; Casey concurs. Eventually, Raymond is given the titles of special assistant to the president with responsibility for public diplomacy affairs and director of international communications at the NSC. (Walter Raymond, Jr., Depositions, vol. 22, pp. 8, 164–65; *State Department and Intelligence Community Involvement in Domestic Activities Related to the Iran-Contra Affair: Staff Report*, 9/7/88)

June 15, 1982: CSF Investments, which later acts as a conduit for funds acquired by the Enterprise, is incorporated in Bermuda. The Enterprise is the web of dummy corporations put together by Richard Secord and Albert Hakim to facilitate the NSC-directed Iran and Contra operations. Later, the firm pays for a Maule short-take-off-and-landing (STOL) aircraft that is later used in NSC-directed Contra resupply operations in Central America. (NSA, pp. 15–16)

July 12, 1982: Donald Gregg, head of the NSC's Intelligence Directorate, drafts a new Presidential Finding to cover CIA support for Edén Pastora's Contra forces based in Costa Rica. The draft Finding asserts that the purpose of the Contra program is to "effect changes in Nicaragua's government policies." John Poindexter, military assistant to the national security advisor, rejects the need for a new Finding. (*Proposed Covert Finding on Nicaragua*, 7/12/82)

August 18, 1982: U.S. intelligence reports indicate that Israel continues to ship arms to Iran. A recent deal between the two countries reportedly involved up to $50 million worth of matériel, possibly including arms Israel captured from the Palestine Liberation Organization in Lebanon. The Israeli government acknowledges it has been selling spare aircraft parts, including replacement tires to Iran. (*Aerospace Daily*, 8/18/82; WP 8/20/82)

November 1982: Israel reportedly sells U.S.-made TOW antitank missiles to an Iranian arms dealer, Faroukh Azzizi, in Athens. The shipment, according to documents, goes to Amsterdam before reaching Iran, its final destination. A news report later identifies Azzizi as Israel's primary middleman with Iran. The Israeli government denies violating any agreements it has with the United States concerning the sale of American-made weapons to Iran. (*Time*, 7/25/83)

December 21, 1982: Congress passes the first Boland Amendment. The legislation, named for the chairman of the House intelligence committee, Edward P. Boland, prohibits the CIA from supplying money, arms, training, or support to individuals or organizations seeking the overthrow of the Nicaraguan government or to provoke a military exchange between Nicaragua and Honduras. (WP 5/8/83)

January 14, 1983: President Reagan signs NSDD 77, "Management of Public Diplomacy Relative to National Security," a classified directive mandating the creation of an interagency bureaucracy to facilitate domestic and international "public diplomacy" operations. Under the jurisdiction of the NSC, the order establishes the Special Policy Group (SPG) to oversee four committees, including an international political committee authorized to "direct the concerned departments and agencies to implement political action strategies in support of key policy objectives." (*NSDD 77, Management of Public Diplomacy Relative to National Security*, 1/14/83)

January 25, 1983: In the first planning memorandum, Public Diplomacy Coordinator Walter Raymond lays out a strategy for implementing NSDD 77. Public diplomacy will become a "new art form," according to Raymond, and will attempt to garner international and domestic support on issues such as yellow rain, intermediate nuclear forces in Europe, and Central America. (*Public Diplomacy NSDD Implementation: First Special Planning Group Meeting*, 1/25/83)

March 1983: The State Department launches Operation STAUNCH, a program aimed at discouraging countries from selling arms to Iran. Over the next three years, U.S. officials file as many as "two or three" protests a month to foreign governments, including South Korea, Italy, Portugal, Spain, Argentina, China, Israel, Britain, West Germany, and Switzerland, urging that they halt potential sales. In November 1986, despite disclosures that the United States has sanctioned such sales itself, the State Department insists that "Operation Staunch continues to be pursued vigorously." (WP 12/10/86; Events, p.3)

March 17, 1983: Donald Gregg, national security advisor to Vice President George Bush, transmits a copy of a "Tactical Task Force Plan," written by former CIA colleague Felix Rodriguez, to National Security Advisor Robert McFarlane. Based on helicopter operations conducted when Gregg and Rodriguez served together in Vietnam, the plan is meant to enhance aerial counterinsurgency operations against the guerrillas in El Salvador. Two years later, Gregg and other U.S. officials help Rodriguez travel to Central America to implement the plan. (*Anti-Guerrilla Operations in Central America*, 3/17/83)

April 1983: Walter Raymond formally retires from the CIA so, he later testifies, there "would be no question whatsoever of any contamination" of his role overseeing public diplomacy operations. However, Raymond continues to meet weekly with CIA Director William Casey and to keep him abreast of developments in the White House public diplomacy operations. (Walter Raymond, Jr., Depositions, vol. 22, pp. 15–17)

April 18, 1983: The U.S. embassy in Beirut is bombed. Initial reports indicate that there are at least thirty-three casualties, including U.S. citizens. The CIA station chief is reported to have been killed along with members of his staff. (He is subsequently replaced by CIA Middle East specialist William Buckley, who is later taken hostage.) In a statement, President Reagan denounces "the vicious terrorist bombing" as a "cowardly act," and vows that the United States will not be deterred in its efforts to secure peace in the region. (DOS Bulletin 6/83; Woodward, p. 245)

April 27, 1983: President Reagan gives a nationally televised speech on Central America before a joint session of Congress. He categorically denies that U.S. support for the Contras is intended to oust the Sandinistas: "But let us be clear as to the American attitude toward the Government of Nicaragua. We do not seek its overthrow." Instead, Reagan claims, the United

States is trying to stop the alleged flow of arms to rebels in El Salvador. (NYT 4/28/83)

May 1983: The CIA and Defense Department conduct Operation TIPPED KETTLE—a secret negotiation with Israel to transfer armaments captured from PLO forces in Lebanon to the CIA. Maj. Gen. Richard Secord, only recently retired from the military, handles the talks. In May, Israel provides several hundred tons of weapons, valued at $10 million (see entry for July 1984). (Document 23, *U.S. Government Stipulation on Quid Pro Quos with Other Governments as Part of Contra Operations*, p. 1)

May 1, 1983: Richard Secord retires from the U.S. Air Force and from his position as deputy assistant secretary of defense for Near East and South Asian affairs. His record is clouded by allegations surrounding his involvement with Egyptian-American Transport and Services Corporation (EATSCO) and former CIA operative Edwin Wilson (see entry for January 16, 1984). (WP 12/9/86; Maas, pp. 279, 287–88; *Questions and Answers for the Record from Secretary of Defense Testimony before the House Permanent Select Committee on Intelligence, 18 December 1986*, pp. 1–2)

July 1, 1983: National Security Advisor William Clark circulates a directive among national security agencies entitled "Public Diplomacy (Central America)." The document states that "the president has underscored his concern that we must increase our efforts in the public diplomacy field to deepen the understanding of and support of our policies in Central America. This effort must focus on the foreign and domestic audiences." The directive announces the creation of the State Department's Office of Public Diplomacy for Latin America and the Caribbean (S/LPD) as a key agency to facilitate this new emphasis on affecting public opinion on Central America. (Document 6, *Public Diplomacy (Central America)*, 7/1/83)

July 25, 1983: "Hundreds of millions of dollars worth of U.S.-made military equipment" is sold to Iran each year, despite a State Department ban on such sales, according to arms dealers quoted in a news report published on this date. The sales are made by American companies, by arms dealers operating in the United States, and by third-party countries such as South Korea and Israel which are transferring often U.S.-made arms to Teheran in violation of agreements with the United States. (*Time*, 7/25/83)

Early August 1983: Around August 7, William Casey meets with a group of public relations specialists to discuss how to "sell a new product—Central America—by generating interest across-the-spectrum." The meeting is part of a push by the CIA and the White House to advance a public diplomacy program in support of the Contras and U.S. military assistance to El Salvador. Out of this meeting comes a "consensus," according to a Walter Raymond memorandum, "that we should strive for the creation of a genuinely bipartisan, centrist structure to generate public support around the issue of Central America." (*Private Sector Support for Central American Program*, 9/9/83)

September 19, 1983: President Reagan signs a second Finding changing the rationale for Contra support from interdicting arms to, among other objectives, "bring[ing] the Sandinistas into meaningful negotiations and constructive, verifiable agreement with their neighbors on peace in the region." A CIA "scope paper" accompanying the Finding states that covert operations will include "paramilitary support" for the Contras, "Propaganda and Civic Action" as well as "Political Action"— covert support of opposition parties and organizations inside Nicaragua. (Document 2, *Finding*, 9/19/83; Document 3, *Scope of CIA Activities under the Nicaraguan Finding*, 9/19/83)

October 1983: Using the pseudonym "Tayacan," CIA contract agent "John Kirkpatrick" drafts a "Psychological Operations in Guerrilla Warfare" manual for the Contras. Drawn in part from the 1968 Vietnam-era army manual, the training guide recommends the "selective use of violence" and advocates "neutralizing" minor government officials. The manual is cleared by officials at CIA headquarters. When the existence of the document becomes public knowledge a year later, Lt. Col. Oliver North writes a memo to CIA Director William Casey arguing that "neutralize" did not mean "assassinate" and urging that the Reagan administration orchestrate a defense of the manual. North also tells Casey that "scores" of copies were "inserted into Nicaragua by balloon and airdrop." (*Psychological Operations in Guerrilla Warfare*, 10/83; *FDN Manual on Psychological Warfare*, 10/22/84)

October 17, 1983: Robert McFarlane assumes the post of assistant to the president for national security affairs, replacing William Clark. (Events, p. 4)

October 23, 1983: The U.S. Marine compound at Beirut International Airport is bombed by terrorists, killing 241 servicemen. A caller to the Beirut office of Agence France Presse says that a group calling itself the Free Islamic Revolution Movement takes responsibility for the bombing. The National Security Agency reportedly intercepts diplomatic messages in 1983 showing that Iran ordered and financed the bombing. (DOS Bulletin 12/83; MH 12/7/86)

December 1983: A series of bombings of the American and French embassies in Kuwait leads to the arrest of seventeen men, some of whom are members of the Al-Dawa al-Islamiya, a terrorist organization based in Teheran. In response to their arrest, members of Hezbollah begin to kidnap Americans in Lebanon to use as bargaining chips to gain their release. Iranian intermediaries repeatedly demand freedom for the so-called Dawa prisoners in negotiations with U.S. representatives in 1985 and 1986. (Iran-Contra Affair, p. 160)

December 8, 1983: Congress passes legislation ordering a $24 million cap on CIA spending on the Contra war. The funds are expected to last until late spring; when they run out, according to language of the bill, the CIA must withdraw from Contra operations. It is this legislation that prompts Reagan administration officials to begin to approach other countries for Contra support, and to establish an alternative system through the National Security Council to sustain the Contra war against Nicaragua. (Kornbluh 1, p. 57)

1984: By early 1984, some U.S. officials have begun to harden their view toward Iran. Geoffrey Kemp, a senior member of the NSC staff with responsibility for the Near East, writes a memorandum to National Security Advisor Robert McFarlane outlining his view that Ayatollah Khomeini poses a threat to Western interests and recommending a renewal of covert operations that might include overthrowing the government of Iran. At the same time, McFarlane and others worry about post-Khomeini prospects, specifically the prospect that a weakened Iran might fall prey to Soviet influence. These fears percolate throughout the year but, in the words of one senior NSC official, produce "no ideas which any of us involved considered to be of great value in terms of significantly affecting our posture in the region." (Tower, pp. B-2–3)

According to a report by the Senate intelligence committee, during this period, "Israel had a strong interest in promoting contacts with Iran and reportedly had permitted arms transfers to Iran as a means of furthering their interests. A series of intelligence studies written in 1984 and 1985 described Israeli interests in Iran. These studies also reported Israeli shipments of non-U.S. arms to Iran as well as the use of Israeli middlemen as early as 1982 to arrange private deals involving U.S. arms." (SSCI, p. 3)

January 16, 1984: Thomas Clines pleads guilty to charges of overbilling the Pentagon for millions of dollars while he served as a partner in the Egyptian-American Transport and Services Corporation, a company involved in shipping U.S. arms to Egypt following the Camp David accords (see entry for May 1, 1983). Accused of taking at least $2.5 million dollars from EATSCO before leaving the firm, Clines engineers a plea bargain and pays a $10,000 fine on behalf of Systems Services International, which owned 49 percent of EATSCO, and another $100,000 to settle civil claims. Clines later plays a key role assisting Richard Secord, alleged to be a silent partner of EATSCO, in activities relating to the Iran-Contra Affair. (AP 1/16/84; Maas, p. 280)

January 18, 1984: In Beirut, Malcolm Kerr, president of the American University of Beirut, is assassinated by an unidentified gunman; President Reagan condemns the act. State Department officials say that the event must "strengthen our resolve not to give in to the acts of terrorists. Terrorism is repugnant and contrary to the principles for which Dr. Kerr stood." (DOS Bulletin 3/84)

January 20, 1984: Secretary of State George Shultz declares Iran a sponsor of international terrorism. According to the Tower Commission final report, "Thereafter, the United States actively pressured its allies not to ship arms to Iran, both because of its sponsorship of international terrorism and its continuation of the war with Iraq." (Tower, p. III-3)

March 2, 1984: Lt. Col. Oliver North and Constantine Menges write a top-secret action memorandum to Robert McFarlane reporting on the progress of CIA economic sabotage and mine warfare in Nicaragua. "Our intention is to severely disrupt the flow of shipping essential to Nicaraguan trade during the peak export period," they write. Not content with the slow pace of the mining, North and Menges propose to have a special operations team blow up an oil tanker in Nicaragua's ports. Such a dramatic event, they advise, would drastically reduce shipments of oil to Nicaragua and cripple the economy. McFarlane checks the "approve" box and notes on the front of the memo: "RR Briefed 3/5," indicating he has briefed President Reagan. (Document 4, *Special Activities in Nicaragua,* 3/2/84)

March 7, 1984: Jeremy Levin, the Beirut bureau chief for Cable News Network, is kidnapped. (Events, p. 7)

March 16, 1984: CIA Station Chief William Buckley is kidnapped in Beirut. Efforts to bring about his release, along with that of the other American hostages in Lebanon, becomes a high priority for Washington in the Iran initiative. At one point, Lt. Col. Oliver North asks Texas millionaire H. Ross Perot to provide up to $2 million as ransom for Buckley. All efforts fail, however, and Buckley dies in captivity in June 1985. (MH 12/7/86; LAT 1/21/87; NYT 12/25/86; Tower, pp. III-2, B-29)

March 17, 1984: Manucher Ghorbanifar, who later becomes one of the principal Iranian intermediaries of the "first channel" to Iran's government, meets with CIA agents to offer information on the kidnapping of Beirut Station Chief William Buckley

and on alleged plots to assassinate U.S. presidential candidates. The CIA, familiar with Ghorbanifar as a purveyor of dubious information since 1980, views his latest overture as another attempt to establish himself as a "broker" for contacts with Iran. (Iran-Contra Affair, pp. 164–65; *[Excised] Info on Alleged Plan to Assassinate Presidential Candidates,* 3/17/84; *Meeting with [Excised] re: Beirut Kidnapping,* 3/17/84)

March 27, 1984: Concerned that funds for the Contras are running out, CIA Director William Casey writes a memorandum to Robert McFarlane urging the White House to explore alternative sources of money and equipment to sustain the covert war. "I am in full agreement that you should explore funding alternatives with the Israelis and perhaps others," Casey writes. He advises McFarlane that the CIA is already "exploring…the procurement of assistance from [South Africa]," which, he says, has been approached earlier and showed interest. Casey also recommends establishing a "foundation" which could receive nongovernmental funds to be dispersed to the Contras. (Document 18, *Supplemental Assistance to Nicaragua Program,* 3/27/84)

March 31, 1984: Robert McFarlane meets with Prince Bandar, Saudi Arabia's ambassador to the United States, to appeal for aid to the Contras. Several days later, Bandar calls McFarlane and says that Saudi Arabia will contribute $1 million per month "as a humanitarian gesture." (Woodward, pp. 352–53)

April 4, 1984: Robert Owen, an official with Gray and Company, a Washington, D.C., public relations firm, contacts Lt. Col. Oliver North at the NSC to discuss a request by the FDN for public relations representation. Owen and another Gray and Company official, Neil Livingstone, draft a PR plan for the Contras, but Gray and Company decides not to handle the account. Two months later, Owen leaves the company to become Lt. Col. Oliver North's personal "eyes and ears" with the Contras. (Robert Owen, Testimony, vol. 100-2, pp. 326–28)

April 9, 1984: This week, the *Wall Street Journal* reveals that the CIA has mined the harbors of Nicaragua. The political uproar is immediate. Senator Barry Goldwater, chairman of the Senate intelligence committee, writes a bitter letter to CIA Director William Casey which states: "I've been trying to figure out how I can most easily tell you my feelings about the discovery of the President having approved mining some of the harbors of Central America. It gets down to one, little, simple, phrase: I am pissed off!" (*[Expression of Outrage…on CIA Mining of the Nicaraguan Harbors],* 4/9/84)

April 10–13, 1984: Duane "Dewey" Clarridge, the CIA's chief of the Latin American Division of the Directorate of Operations, travels to South Africa to negotiate assistance to the Contras.

While there, the mining of Nicaragua's harbors becomes a major scandal and Clarridge receives a cable from CIA Deputy Director John McMahon telling him to postpone further discussions. "Current furor here over the Nicaraguan project urges that we postpone taking [South Africa] up on their offer of assistance," Clarridge writes in a secret communiqué to an intermediary. "Please express to [a South African official] my deep regret that we must do this, at least for the time being...." Despite the documentary evidence, Clarridge later denies to the congressional Iran-Contra committees that the CIA had requested South African support for the Contra war. (Iran-Contra Affair, p. 38)

April 20, 1984: Robert McFarlane instructs his deputy, Howard Teicher, to approach Israeli official David Kimche about further assistance to the Contras. The message to transmit to the Israelis is that Contra support constitutes "an important matter to us and we face a temporary shortfall in goods." After hearing Teicher's appeal, however, Israeli officials decide that they do not want to risk antagonizing the U.S. Congress on this issue. (*Memorandum for Howard Teicher*, 4/20/84)

May 8, 1984: The Reverend Benjamin Weir is kidnapped in Beirut. (CSM 1/2/87)

May 30, 1984: Contra leader Edén Pastora holds a press conference at his jungle camp of La Penca, along the Costa Rican–Nicaraguan border, to denounce CIA pressure to align his southern front Contra group with the Nicaraguan Democratic Force, operating out of Honduras. During the press conference, a bomb explodes. Eight people are killed, including three journalists, one of them a U.S. citizen; seventeen more are injured. Pastora survives. The assassin, who posed as a Danish journalist, escapes and remains unidentified or captured. (See entry for May 30, 1986). (WP 7/3/86; NYT 2/6/89)

Summer 1984: By this time, according to the Tower Commission final report, "Iranian purchasing agents were approaching international arms merchants with requests for TOW missiles." The chief of the Near East Division of the CIA's Directorate for Operations told the Tower Commission, "We have in the DDO [Operations Directorate] probably 30 to 40 requests per year from Iranians and Iranian exiles to provide us with very fancy intelligence, very important internal political insights, if we in return can arrange for the sale of a dozen Bell helicopter gunships or 1,000 TOW missiles or something else that is on the contraband list." (Tower, p. B-3)

June 25, 1984: The National Security Planning Group meets to discuss bilateral negotiations with Nicaragua and the legality of U.S. efforts to sustain the Contras through third-country support. According to minutes of the meeting, Secretary of State

George Shultz tells President Reagan, Vice President Bush, CIA Director Casey, and others in attendance that Chief of Staff James Baker believes "that if we go out and try to get money from third countries, it is an impeachable offense." At the end of the meeting, Vice President Bush raises the problem of a quid pro quo with other countries. "How can anyone object to the U.S. encouraging third parties to provide help to the anti-Sandinistas? The only problem that might come up is if the United States were to promise to give these parties something in return so that some people could interpret this as some kind of an exchange." (Document 21, *Minutes, National Security Planning Group Meeting on Central America*, 6/25/84)

July 1984: Advertisements appealing to the "generosity of the American people" for funds for the Contras begin to appear in major newspapers around the United States. Sponsored by a shell organization called the Human Development Foundation, the advertisements are actually a CIA effort to camouflage new funds coming from Saudi Arabia. The advertisements are meant to create a plausible cover story for the way in which the Contras are able to sustain their operations after congressionally approved funding runs out. (Kornbluh 1, p. 67; NSA, p. 62)

The CIA and the Defense Department conduct Operation TIPPED KETTLE II, repeating a deal worked out with Israel in 1983 to purchase captured PLO arms (see entry for May 1983). (Document 23, *U.S. Government Stipulation on Quid Pro Quos with other Governments as Part of Contra Operations*, p. 2)

July 25, 1984: The CIA puts out a highly unusual "burn" or "fabricator" notice on Iranian businessman Manucher Ghorbanifar, informing the U.S. intelligence community that "[s]ubject should be regarded as an intelligence fabricator and a nuisance." Nevertheless, within a year, Ghorbanifar has secured the support of Israeli and American officials anxious to develop ties to Iran's government. (*Fabricator Notice—Manucher Ghorbanifar*, 7/25/84)

September 1984: Former journalist Amiram Nir assumes the post of counterterrorism adviser to Israeli Prime Minister Shimon Peres. In late December 1985, he takes over the lead role on the Israeli side of the arms-for-hostages deals with Iran. (Tower, p. III-5)

September 1, 1984: Two members of Civilian Military Assistance, Dana Parker and James Powell, are killed when a CIA-supplied helicopter they are piloting during an aerial attack in Nicaragua is shot down. The crash establishes CMA as the most prominent of the mercenary organizations aiding Contra operations. U.S. officials deny any connection to the attack, although CMA's Contra connections have been facilitated by officials at the U.S. embassy in Honduras. In a report to Robert McFarlane, Lt. Col. Oliver North complains that the operation was "not sponsored/directed by or briefed to any of our CIA personnel." He recommends that McFarlane authorize a request to a private individual to "donate a helicopter to the FDN for use in any upcoming operation" in order to replace the aircraft shot down. (*FDN Air Attack of 1 September*, 9/2/84)

October 10, 1984: House and Senate conferees agree on final language for the second Boland Amendment—commonly known as Boland Amendment II—terminating U.S. assistance to the Contras. The carefully worded legislation reads: "During fiscal year 1985, no funds available to the Central Intelligence Agency, the Department of Defense, or any other agency or entity of the United States involved in intelligence activities may be obligated or expended for the purpose or which would have the effect of supporting, directly or indirectly, military or paramilitary operations in Nicaragua by any nation, group, organization, movement, or individual." (Document 5, *Public Law 98-473, [Boland Amendment II], Section 8066[A]*, 10/12/84)

October 19, 1984: The State Department forwards to National Security Advisor Robert McFarlane an interagency study he requested on the situation in Iran. Its pessimistic conclusion that the United States has little prospect for developing contacts inside Iran's government is a disappointment to some officials at the NSC. They resolve to find ways to increase American influence in that country. (Tower, p. III-3)

November 1984: Michael Ledeen is hired as a consultant to the NSC on terrorism and Middle East issues. He retains this position until December 1986. (Tower, p. B-4; *Mike Ledeen*, 1/24/86, 10:40; *How Are Things*, 2/27/86, 20:22)

November 5, 1984: Lt. Col. Oliver North speaks by telephone to Alan Fiers, the CIA's new Central American Task Force (CATF) chief, about the Contras. "At the conclusion of our discussion, we briefly reviewed the prospects for a liberation government in which [Arturo] Cruz, [Sr.,] and [Adolfo] Calero would share authority," North writes in a memorandum to Robert McFarlane. (*Clarifying Who Said What to Whom*, 11/7/84)

November 19–21, 1984: Former CIA official Theodore G. Shackley meets in Hamburg, West Germany, with Gen. Manucher Hashemi, formerly chief of counterespionage for SAVAK, the Shah's secret police. Shackley is introduced to a number of Iranians, including Manucher Ghorbanifar and Hassan Karrubi. (Karrubi, referred to as the "First Iranian" in the congressional committees' final report, later plays an important role in the Iran initiative.) During one of the meetings,

Ghorbanifar raises the issue of Iran's desire for TOW missiles and, at a later point, the possibility of obtaining the release of some American hostages in Lebanon in return for cash payment. Shackley writes up his account of the sessions, including Ghorbanifar's remarks, and sends it to Vernon Walters, ambassador-at-large at the State Department. Walters forwards the memorandum to other officials at the State Department, who tell Shackley they do not intend to pursue Ghorbanifar's offer. (Iran-Contra Affair, p. 164; *American Hostages in Lebanon*, 11/22/84, pp. 1–4)

December 3, 1984: Peter Kilburn, a librarian at the American University of Beirut, is kidnapped. (NYT 12/25/86)

December 4, 1984: Lt. Col. Oliver North meets with retired British special operations major David Walker at the recommendation of Secretary of the Navy John Lehman. They discuss how to destroy Soviet-built HIND helicopters recently obtained by the Sandinista government to fight the Contras. Walker agrees to conduct for pay sabotage operations inside Nicaragua, including the possible destruction of the HINDs. He also tells North that the Contras should obtain British-built Blowpipe surface-to-air missiles from the Pinochet government in Chile to use against the helicopters. (*Assistance to the Nicaraguan Resistance*, 12/4/84)

December 7, 1984: Lt. Col. Oliver North dispatches Contra leader Adolfo Calero to Santiago, Chile, to arrange the acquisition of Blowpipe surface-to-air missiles and other weapons as suggested by British mercenary David Walker. When Calero returns, he calls North and reports that the Chileans are willing to provide forty-eight missiles free of charge but want the Contras to purchase the missile launchers for $25,000 each. North records in his notebook that the Contras will also "have to buy some items from Chileans which are somewhat more expensive." (*[North Notebook Entries for December 17, 1984]*, 12/17/84; Kornbluh 2)

December 14, 1984: The State Department produces a draft National Security Decision Directive which concludes that the United States has only limited influence in Iran and recommends no substantive change in U.S. policy under current conditions. (Tower, pp. B-2–3)

December 20, 1984: Lt. Col. Oliver North reports to Robert McFarlane on the status of efforts to obtain the British-made Blowpipe surface-to-air missiles. The Chileans say that "they would need to obtain British permission for the transfer." Attaching a memorandum for the president, North recommends that McFarlane ask Reagan to intervene personally with British Prime Minister Margaret Thatcher to request that she authorize the Chileans to give the missiles to the Contras. (McFarlane later testifies that he never gave the memo to Reagan.) For the next eighteen months, North continues to pursue options and negotiations for acquiring the missiles from Chile without success. (*Follow-up with [Deleted] re: Terrorism and Central America*, 12/20/84; Kornbluh 2)

December 21, 1984: Defex-Portugal Ltd., an arms brokerage used by Richard Secord in Europe, submits three false Guatemalan end-user certificates to Portuguese authorities. The documents list a Montreal firm, Transworld Arms, as the purchasing agent for three thousand mortar grenades, and over one million rounds of ammunition, ostensibly to be exported to the Guatemalan military. In reality, the arms are destined for the Contras. The purchase marks the first of many shipments arranged by the Secord group from Europe. (WSJ 1/16/87)

1985: The Reagan administration is "occupied on a regular basis with matters relating to terrorism and the state of U.S. hostages," according to a Senate intelligence committee report. "In particular, documents and testimony reflect a deep personal concern on the part of the President for the welfare of U.S. hostages both in the early stages of the [Iran arms-for-hostages] initiative and throughout the program." (SSCI, p. 3)

January 1985: Israeli middlemen Yaacov Nimrodi and Adolph Schwimmer begin a series of meetings that runs through late 1985 with various interested parties concerning Iran and American hostages. Both Israelis have ties to Prime Minister Shimon Peres. Key participants include Iranian arms dealer Manucher Ghorbanifar and Saudi billionaire Adnan Khashoggi. (Tower, p. B-11)

January 8, 1985: The Rev. Lawrence Martin Jenco, head of the Beirut office of Catholic Relief Services, is kidnapped. (NYT 12/25/86)

January 22, 1985: Donald Gregg, national security advisor to Vice President Bush, arranges a meeting between Bush and former CIA counterinsurgency specialist, Felix Rodriguez. The meeting is one of several in Washington, D.C., that Gregg sets up, ostensibly to arrange for Rodriguez to go to El Salvador and participate in the U.S. counterinsurgency program there. (*Statement by the Press Secretary*, 12/15/86)

January 29, 1985: Lt. Col. Oliver North meets in Miami with Adolfo Calero and Arturo Cruz, Sr., to draft a Contra statement of political principles and unity, later known as the San José Declaration. "The document was written by Calero, Cruz and North in my hotel room in Miami," North reports to Robert McFarlane. "They were convinced that this document was necessary in order to bring unity to the movement.... The only rea-

son Calero agreed to sign was because the criteria established for the Sandinistas were, he knew, impossible for them to meet." (*Using the March 1 San José Declaration to Support the Vote on the Funding for the Nicaraguan Resistance*, 4/1/85)

February 7, 1985: John Singlaub, a retired major general and head of the United States Council for World Freedom (USCWF), meets with Lt. Col. Oliver North at the NSC to discuss potential multimillion dollar Contra donations from the governments of South Korea and Taiwan. In preparation for the meeting, North requests authorization from Robert McFarlane to enable Singlaub to contact these governments again and "put [Adolfo] Calero in direct contact with each of these officers." (Tower, p. C-4)

The Crisis Pre-Planning Group, made up of the deputies to the NSPG members, meets to discuss strategies to secure continued support from Honduras for the Contras. A memorandum drafted four days later by Lt. Col. Oliver North and NSC aide Raymond Burghardt states that the CPPG agreed on several "enticements to the Hondurans": expedited delivery of military items already ordered by Honduras; enhanced CIA covert support for Honduras; and release of up to $75 million of $174 million in embargoed economic aid. (*Approach to the Hondurans Regarding the Nicaraguan Resistance*, 2/11/85)

Assistant Secretary of State for Inter-American Affairs Langhorne Motley reports in a memorandum to Secretary of State George Shultz on a meeting of the Crisis Pre-Planning Group: "It was agreed that some combination of efforts was needed to encourage the Hondurans to remain firm in their support for the FDN during the coming weeks." Motley writes that U.S. encouragement will include expedited military and economic assistance and asks that Shultz approve a memorandum written by Robert McFarlane summarizing the situation. Shultz initials the "approve" box. (*Honduran Actions with Respect to Nicaraguan Resistance Forces*, 2/7/89)

February 12, 1985: The Office of Public Diplomacy for Latin America and the Caribbean contracts with Professor John Guilmartin, Jr., to write an article on the Soviet HIND helicopters and other Soviet-bloc equipment shipped to Nicaragua. The contract states that the article must be produced in a "minimum time, in accordance with S/LPD's expectations." Later, when Guilmartin's article is published in the *Wall Street Journal*, no mention is made of the fact that it was contracted for by the public diplomacy office and financed by the American taxpayer. Internal S/LPD memoranda refer to the article as a "white propaganda operation" (see entry for March 13, 1985). (*Contract for Dr. John Guilmartin, Jr.*, 2/12/85)

February 13, 1985: Jeremy Levin, the Beirut bureau chief for Cable News Network, who was kidnapped on March 7, 1984, is freed. It is not clear whether he escaped or was released by his captors. (Events, pp. 7, 17)

The Drug Enforcement Agency wins a seat on the interagency Hostage Locating Task Force. Soon afterward, two DEA agents, William Dwyer and Frank Tarallo, are assigned to explore potential sources in Lebanon who might help locate captive Americans. The project, which eventually comes under the direction of Lt. Col. Oliver North, develops into a twenty-month on-again, off-again ransom operation, using both government and private funds (donated by Texas businessman H. Ross Perot), that ultimately fails to produce a single hostage. Congressional investigators later conclude that the use of private funds for such an operation, which they imply had the approval of Attorney General Edwin Meese, violated a number of government rules and policies governing unappropriated funds and payment of ransom to hostage-takers. (Iran-Contra Affair, pp. 361–66)

February 14, 1985: Defex-Portugal Ltd. submits nine more false Guatemalan end-user certificates to Portuguese authorities. This time the documents list Energy Resources International in Vienna, Virginia, as the purchasing agent for massive quantities of guns, bullets, mortars, grenades, artillery, and surface-to-air missiles. Later, the Energy Resources International address in Virginia is shown to be the same as that of other companies controlled by Richard Secord. (*End User Certificates*, 2/14/85)

Gen. Paul Gorman, chief of the U.S. Southern Command, sends an eyes-only cable to Ambassador Thomas Pickering and U.S. MilGroup Commander Col. James Steele in El Salvador shortly after meeting with Felix Rodriguez. Gorman writes that Rodriguez's "primary commitment" is to help the Contras but that he wants to come to El Salvador to be an adviser to the Salvadoran Air Force on long-range reconnaissance patrols. Gorman offers to fly Rodriguez to San Salvador the next day. (*Felix Rodriguez*, 2/14/85)

February 19, 1985: Robert Owen drafts a comprehensive plan for a "Public Relations Campaign for the Freedom Fighters," which calls for a "major lobbying, educational and public relations effort" to win congressional restoration of official Contra aid. Owen recommends a new Contra coalition front to offset the FDN's image as a Somocista army that violates human rights. He also suggests that the Contras be referred to as "the new revolutionaries" and that the Contra war be called "Revolutionary Counter-Communism." (*Public Relations Campaign for the Freedom Fighters*, 2/19/85)

President Reagan authorizes a plan to provide a quid pro quo to Honduras. "We should make an approach to the Hondurans which emphasizes our commitment to their sovereignty and provides incentives for them to persist in aiding the freedom fighters," states the authorization. The plan calls for a presidential letter to be sent through U.S. ambassador to Honduras John Negroponte, who would deliver it to President Roberto Suazo Córdova. The letter will not contain any language about a quid pro quo. A "special emissary" will subsequently carry the "signed copy" of the letter and "very privately explain our criteria for the expedited economic support, security assistance deliveries, and enhanced CIA support." The initialed authorization plan is marked "cc Vice President." (Document 22, *Memorandum for the President, Approach to the Hondurans Regarding the Nicaraguan Resistance*, 2/19/85)

February 20, 1985: Lt. Col. Oliver North and NSC aide Raymond Burghardt write a memorandum to McFarlane on the need to keep the quid pro quo with Honduras secret from Congress. "Notwithstanding our own interpretation" of the Boland Amendment, the memo states, "it is very clear from the colloquy during the [congressional] debate…that the legislative intent was to deny *any* direct or indirect support for military/paramilitary operations in Nicaragua." (*Presidential Letter to President Suazo of Honduras*, 2/20/85)

February 27, 1985: Lt. Col. Oliver North sends a memorandum to Robert McFarlane entitled "Cruz Control." Contra leader Arturo Cruz, Sr., North writes, has been a "CIA asset for several months." The chairman of the House intelligence committee, Lee Hamilton, has protested that it is illegal for Cruz to be on the CIA payroll and at the same time be the key lobbyist on Capitol Hill for the Contra cause. North's solution is to transfer Cruz from the CIA payroll to the accounts that he controls. (*[Cruz] Control*, 2/27/85)

March 4, 1985: Public relations specialist Edie Fraser sends a letter to Lt. Col. Oliver North on preparations for the Nicaraguan Refugee Fund dinner to be held in April. She adds a handwritten note: "Ollie, Very Imp. Two people want to give major contribs i.e. 300,000 and up if they might have one 'quiet' meeting with the President." Later, private meetings for donors with Ronald Reagan become the key device for fund-raising specialist, Carl "Spitz" Channell. (*[Handwritten Note Detailing Positive Responses…]*, 3/4/85)

March 5, 1985: Otto Reich, director of the State Department's Office of Public Diplomacy for Latin America and the Caribbean, writes a letter to the Pentagon requesting that military personnel from the 4th Psychological Operations Group at Fort Bragg, North Carolina, be detailed to Washington to enhance public diplomacy work. Among the tasks that required a "psyop" background, Reich explains, is preparing "a daily summary of exploitable information for S/LPD use." Five psyops officers join the staff of the Office of Public Diplomacy from June 4 to November 4, 1985. (*TDY Personnel for S/LPD*, 3/5/85)

March 6, 1985: In the early-morning hours, an explosion rocks the main Sandinista military depot in downtown Managua. The fire spreads to an adjacent military hospital causing its evacuation and extensive damage. Although the Sandinistas later claim the explosion was accidently set off by faulty wiring, Iran-Contra affair documents and testimony show it was a sabotage operation, undertaken by retired British Maj. David Walker at the behest of Lt. Col. Oliver North and with the help of Panamanian agents. In a May 1, 1985, memorandum to Robert McFarlane, North noted that $50,000 was expended "for the operation conducted in Managua against the ammunition depot at the EPS military headquarters." Later, during an executive session of the Iran-Contra Affair hearings, North is asked about the sabotage mission: "It is my understanding that Mr. Walker provided two technicians involved in that." Later the technicians are identified as Panamanians. (*FDN Military Operations, May 1, 1985; Oliver North, Testimony [Executive Session],* 7/9/87, p. 58; Document 23, *U.S. Government Stipulation on Quid Pro Quos with other Governments as Part of Contra Operations,* p. 39)

March 12, 1985: Lt. Col. Oliver North meets with Arturo Cruz, Sr., to discuss his salary as a future member of a unified Contra coalition. Cruz notes that his salary at the Inter-American Development Bank prior to becoming a Contra spokesman was $7,500 per month. North decides to transfer $6,250 into Cruz's bank account every month, drawing on monies being provided by Saudi Arabia. (*Meeting with Arturo Cruz,* 3/15/85)

March 13, 1985: Johnathan Miller, deputy director of the State Department's Office of Public Diplomacy for Latin America and the Caribbean, sends a memorandum to Patrick Buchanan, director of White House communications, entitled "White Propaganda Operation." The memo lays out five examples of S/LPD "white propaganda,"—planting or facilitating pro-Contra or anti-Sandinista stories in the press without acknowledging a government role. The key example, according to Miller, is the publication of an opinion piece in the *Wall Street Journal* by a paid consultant to S/LPD, Professor John Guilmartin (see entry for February 12, 1985). "I will not attempt in the future to keep you posted on all activities since we have too many balls in the air at any one time and since the work of our operation is ensured by our office's keeping a low profile," Miller concludes the memorandum. Later, when this memorandum is discovered by General Accounting Office investigators, it generates a major controversy over illegal propaganda activities conducted by S/LPD. (Document 11, *Memorandum for Patrick Buchanan, White Propaganda Operation,* 3/13/85)

March 16, 1985: Vice President George Bush meets with Honduran President Roberto Suazo Córdova in Tegucigalpa. They discuss the expedited delivery of U.S. military equipment, release of U.S. economic aid to Honduras, and enhanced security assistance programs. When the meeting becomes the source of public controversy four years later, Bush insists that no quid pro quo was discussed. (Document 23, *U.S. Government Stipulation on Quid Pro Quos with other Governments as Part of Contra Operations,* para. 58)

Terry A. Anderson, chief Middle East correspondent for the Associated Press, is kidnapped in Beirut. He is released on December 4, 1991. (NYT 12/4/86)

March 20, 1985: Describing U.S. policy toward the Iran-Iraq War, State Department spokesman Edward Djerejian says: "We continue to believe there can be no military resolution of the conflict and call upon Iran to join Iraq in accepting the many international calls for cease-fire and negotiated settlement. We do not provide arms to either side, either directly or indirectly, and we are making substantial efforts to diminish the flow of arms to Iran from free world sources as a means to induce Iran to end the fighting." (WP 11/11/86)

Lt. Col. Oliver North puts together a "Chronological Event Checklist" of over one hundred orchestrated events to be undertaken before the pending congressional vote on Contra aid. Tasks are to be undertaken by numerous officials and private-sector groups. Among other events, the State Department's Office of Public Diplomacy for Latin America and the Caribbean will release several prominent reports on Nicaragua; polls will be taken "to see what turns Americans against Sandinistas"; President Reagan will hold highly visible photo sessions with Contra leaders; the State Department will "release paper on Nicaraguan media manipulation." The purpose of this campaign is to influence media coverage of Nicaragua and the Contra issue, and, of course, the vote on Contra assistance. (*Chronological Event Checklist,* 3/20/85)

April 15, 1985: The Nicaraguan Refugee Fund dinner is held at a Washington, D.C., hotel. Ronald Reagan is the keynote speaker of the gala event, which boasts such celebrities as Bob Hope. The dinner is a significant public diplomacy event; Walter Raymond is involved in putting it together, as is Lt. Col. Oliver North. The National Endowment for the Preservation of Liberty and International Business Communications also participate in the preparations. Although over $300,000 is raised, in the end, only $3,000 is actually sent to the Contras. The rest goes to pay for expenses and consultants' fees. (AP 6/29/85)

April 21, 1985: Around this date, the Enterprise hires the *Erria,* a Danish freighter, to pick up a load of reconditioned Soviet AK-47 rifles and East European machine guns from Gdansk, Poland. The cargo ship then steams for Portugal where it takes on 461 tons of additional munitions. According to dock papers, the *Erria* is officially destined for Guatemala; three weeks later, however, the ship delivers its cargo to Contra representatives at Puerto Cortez in Honduras. This is only one of several shipments of Soviet-compatible weapons delivered to the Contras through the Enterprise in 1985–1986 and one of the many uses of the *Erria* in NSC-directed covert operations. A year later, the Enterprise purchases the *Erria* through a dummy corporation, Dolmy Business. (LAT 1/21/87; WSJ 1/23/87)

April 24, 1985: Five members of the Civilian Military Assistance team in Costa Rica are arrested: Steven Carr, Peter Glibbery, Robert Thompson, Claude Chaffard, and Joe Adams. Their arrests focus international attention once again on CMA and mercenary activity on behalf of the Contras. In La Reforma prison in San José, Carr and Glibbery begin to provide reporters with details of John Hull's support of Contra operations, including the charge that Hull is receiving $10,000 per month from the National Security Council, through a bank account in Miami. (Kerry Chronology, p. 152)

April 25, 1985: In Honduras, military officials react to the refusal of the U.S. Congress to renew aid to the Contras. Contra leaders are told that Honduras will no longer support them. A shipment of arms, arranged by the Enterprise, is intercepted by the Honduran military at the main FDN camp along the border. In response, Robert McFarlane recommends that President Reagan call the president of Honduras, Roberto Suazo Córdova, and pressure him to continue support for the Contras. "GOH [government of Honduras] cooperation with FDN logistics...must continue if the resistance is to survive," McFarlane writes. He recommends that Reagan signal U.S. commitment to "maintaining pressure" on the Sandinistas by telling Suazo that the United States is about to impose a trade embargo and/or downgrade diplomatic relations. President Reagan makes the call and takes notes on his conversation with the Honduran President. Suazo "expressed his support of me," Reagan writes, and will tell his military commander to deliver the seized ammunition to the Contras. Reagan also notes that Suazo raises the issue of an additional $15 million in U.S. aid to Honduras. (Document 24, *Recommended Telephone Call to Roberto Suazo Cordova*, 4/25/85)

Early May 1985: Lt. Col. Oliver North, Adolfo Calero, Richard Secord, and John Singlaub meet in North's NSC office to discuss weapons procurement. Singlaub, who is representing a private firm, GeoMiliTech Consultants Corporation, offers a lower price on surface-to-air missiles than Secord, but North and Calero decide the sale should go to Secord because he can provide training. Less than two weeks later, however, Calero places a $5 million order with Singlaub for weapons to be purchased through GeoMiliTech in Europe. Unlike Secord, whose

commission averaged 38 percent on weapons sold to the Contras, Singlaub adds almost no markup. The weapons are delivered to Central America on July 8, 1985. But Calero's authority to purchase weapons is soon removed by Lt. Col. Oliver North, and no other weapons are purchased from anyone other than Secord. (Iran-Contra Affair, p. 51)

May 1, 1985: In a memorandum classified "top-secret veil," Robert McFarlane transmits a CIA Memorandum of Notification (MON) to Ronald Reagan for presidential approval. The MON requests authorization for an "increase of $4.5 million in the authorized level for the Central American Covert Action Program," which includes revisions "relating to clarifying the nature of CIA support to Honduran Government [deleted]." (The *New York Times* later reports that part of the money is used for direct payments to Honduran officials.) "The Vice President, Department of State, Joint Chiefs of Staff, Department of Defense and OMB [Office of Management and Budget] concur with the MON as revised," McFarlane advises Reagan. The president approves the increase, which is part of the quid pro quo plan for Honduras recommended by the Crisis Pre-Planning Group in February. (*Memorandum of Notification for Increase in Authorized Funding Levels for Central America Covert Action*, 5/1/85)

Lt. Col. Oliver North reports to National Security Advisor Robert McFarlane on the status of Contra military operations. Of the money provided by Saudi Arabia, the "top-secret" memorandum states, $17,145,594 have been expended for arms, ammunition, combat operations, and support activities. Seven million additional dollars are to be allocated for increasing the Contra force, "a major special operations attack against Sandino airport," "a major ground operation," and "the opening of a southern front along the [Costa Rican] border which will distract EPS [Sandinista military] units currently committed to the northern front." (Document 34, *Memorandum for Robert McFarlane, FDN Military Operations*, 5/1/85)

May 4 or 5, 1985: NSC staff consultant Michael Ledeen travels to Israel, with the permission of National Security Advisor Robert McFarlane, to meet with Prime Minister Shimon Peres. The purpose of the meeting is to discuss the state of Israel's intelligence on Iran and to determine whether Peres would be willing to share that intelligence with the United States. According to Ledeen, Peres subsequently "constituted a group of people outside the government, not government officials, to work with us to study the Iran question and the Iranian terrorist issue." (Tower, p. B-5)

May 14, 1985: Lake Resources, Inc., is incorporated in Panama by Julio Quijano, an attorney working on behalf of the Enterprise. The front company is used as an account to deposit funds for Contra resupply operations. (NSA, p. 102)

May 17, 1985: Graham Fuller, the CIA's national intelligence officer for the Near East and South Asia, writes a five-page memorandum to CIA Director William Casey on current options for U.S. policy toward Iran. The memo begins, "The US faces a grim situation in developing a new policy toward Iran. Events are moving largely against our interests and we have few palatable alternatives…. The US has almost no cards to play; the USSR has many…. Our urgent need is to develop a broad spectrum of policy moves designed to give us some leverage in the race for influence in Tehran." Fuller goes on to present several suggested approaches, including encouraging U.S. allies to expand their ties to Teheran. A key element of this plan would be to "remove all restrictions in sales—including military—to Iran." Fuller's ideas are incorporated to a large extent in a Special National Security Estimate on Iran circulated by the intelligence community in June. (*Toward a Policy on Iran*, 5/17/85, pp. 1, 3; Document 60, *Draft National Security Decision Directive, U.S. Policy Toward Iran*, ca. 6/11/85; Tower, pp. B-6–7)

May 21, 1985: National Security Advisor Robert McFarlane transmits a briefing paper and talking points to President Reagan in preparation for the state visit of Honduran President Roberto Suazo Córdova. Among the purposes of the meeting is "to confirm our support for the Nicaraguan democratic resistance and the importance we attach to Honduran cooperation with the resistance forces." The briefing paper, drafted by NSC aide Raymond Burghardt, calls on Reagan to remind Suazo of the quid pro quo arrangements on the Contras: "Without making the linkage too explicit, it would be useful to remind Suazo that in return for our help…we do expect cooperation in pursuit of our mutual objectives. In this regard, you could underline the seriousness of our security commitment, which the Hondurans seem to regard as the main quid pro quo for cooperating with the FDN." (*Meeting with Honduran President Suazo*, 5/21/85)

May 28, 1985: David P. Jacobsen, director of the American University hospital in Beirut, is kidnapped. (NYT 12/25/86)

May 29, 1985: Texas businessman H. Ross Perot donates $200,000 to the Oliver North–directed program to ransom American hostages in Beirut. Although the money is apparently delivered to a DEA source in Lebanon, the plan falls through. (*DEA Support for Recovery of American Hostages Seized in Beirut*, ca. 5/85; Iran-Contra Affair, pp. 363–64)

June 3, 1985: CIA Station Chief William Buckley, a hostage in Lebanon since March 16, 1984, is believed by U.S. officials to have died on or about this date. (Tower, p. B-29 fn. 20)

June 10, 1985: Thomas Sutherland, dean of agriculture at the American University of Beirut, is kidnapped in Lebanon. (NSA, p. 112)

June 11, 1985: NSC staff aides Donald Fortier and Howard Teicher forward to Robert McFarlane a draft National Security Decision Directive aimed at countering perceived Soviet advantages in Iran. The document is based in part on a Special National Intelligence Estimate recently updated by the CIA at McFarlane's behest. McFarlane had requested the study following Michael Ledeen's return from discussions with Israeli Prime Minister Shimon Peres. Despite objections by Secretary of State Schultz and Secretary of Defense Weinberger, the ideas contained in the directive prevail, ultimately finding expression in the U.S.-sanctioned arms-for-hostages deals with Teheran of 1985 and 1986. (Document 60, *Draft National Security Decision Directive, U.S. Policy Toward Iran*, ca. 6/11/85; *U.S. Policy Toward Iran [Forwarding…a Copy of Draft NSDD….]*, 6/11/85; *U.S. Policy Toward Iran*, 6/17/85; *U.S. Policy Toward Iran: Comment on Draft NSDD*, 6/29/85; *U.S. Policy Toward Iran [Annotated Cover Sheet Attached]*, 7/16/85; *Draft NSDD re U.S. Policy Toward Iran*, 7/18/85)

On or about this date, Contra leaders meet in San José, Costa Rica, to announce formally the creation of a new coalition—the United Nicaraguan Opposition (UNO), The three leaders are Adolfo Calero, Alfonso Robelo, and Arturo Cruz, Jr. UNO is the brainchild of Oliver North, intended to create a more moderate civilian image for the Contras in order to enhance congressional support for restoring official U.S. aid for the Contra war. In a later memo to North, Robert Owen admits that "UNO is a creation of the USG[overnment] to garner support from Congress…. In fact, almost anything it has accomplished is because the hand of the USG has been there directing and manipulating." (Document 17, *Memorandum for BG, Overall Perspective*, 3/17/85)

June 12, 1985: The House of Representatives approves $27 million in "humanitarian assistance" for the Contras. The money is ostensibly only for food, medical assistance, and other nonmilitary goods, but the program becomes an elaborate cover for NSC's Contra resupply operations. Companies that are already involved in the clandestine NSC operations are hired to participate in the nonlethal assistance program. Robert Owen, Lt. Col. Oliver North's "eyes and ears" with the Contras, receives a $50,000 contract, which pays his salary and expenses. Owen proceeds to file one set of reports to State Department officials on nonlethal equipment needed by the Contras and a second set of reports to North on their need for lethal aid. (Iran-Contra Affair, p. 63)

June 14, 1985: Trans World Airlines Flight 847 is hijacked to Beirut. Iran's Speaker of the Parliament Ali Akbar Hashemi Rafsanjani plays a behind-the-scenes role in resolving the crisis, a fact that does not go unnoticed by U.S. officials (see entry for September 26, 1986). Washington views Rafsanjani's efforts both as evidence that Teheran holds sway over terrorists keeping Americans hostage in Lebanon and as the first concrete sign that the Khomeini government is ready to reestablish ties to the outside world. (WP 12/7/86; Wright, pp. 130–32)

June 17, 1985: Shortly after the successful resolution of the Trans World Airlines hijacking crisis, CIA Director William Casey learns of a proposition by Iranian arms dealer Cyrus Hashemi to arrange a meeting with high-level Iranian officials to discuss an arms-for-hostages exchange. Casey directs the chief of the Agency's Near East Division to follow up on the offer and inform the State Department, but without mentioning arms sales. Hashemi's contacts turn out to be Manucher Ghorbanifar and Mohsen Kangarlou, who later comprise the "first channel" of the U.S.-sponsored Iran initiative. Meanwhile, Hashemi's efforts produce no results. (*Release of Hostages,* 6/17/85; *Possible Iranian Contact via Cyrus Hashemi,* 6/22/85; Iran-Contra Affair, p. 171n48)

June 18, 1985: President Reagan declares, "Let me further make it plain to the assassins in Beirut and their accomplices, wherever they may be, that America will never make concessions to terrorists—to do so would only invite more terrorism—nor will we ask nor pressure any other government to do so. Once we head down that path there would be no end to it, no end to the suffering of innocent people, no end to the bloody ransom all civilized nations must pay." (*President's News Conference of June 18, 1985*)

June 28, 1985: Around this date, Lt. Col. Oliver North, Richard Secord, Adolfo Calero, and other Contras meet in Miami, Florida. According to Secord, North excoriates Calero for alleged corruption in providing equipment to Contra soldiers in the field. "[H]e had been receiving reports that the limited funds they had might be getting wasted, squandered, or even worse, some people might be lining their pockets." The decision is made at this meeting for Secord to oversee the creation of an "airlift project" to drop weapons to Contras in the field. North does not tell Calero that he has decided to transfer control of Contra finances to the Lake Resources bank account in Geneva—an account controlled by Secord, Albert Hakim, and North himself. (Richard Secord, Testimony, vol. 100-1, p. 58)

July 3, 1985: Around this date, Lt. Col. Oliver North asks Lewis Tambs, the U.S. ambassador-designate to Costa Rica, to help establish a southern front for the Contras along the Costa Rica–Nicaragua border. Tambs later testifies that his orders came from the "RIGlet"—a subgroup of the Restricted Inter-Agency Group established early in the Reagan administration to manage policy toward Central America. The RIGlet consists of North, Elliott Abrams, and Alan Fiers. His "pet project" is to facilitate the construction and use of a secret airstrip in northern Costa Rica for Contra resupply operations. (Iran-Contra Affair, p. 61)

Israeli Foreign Ministry official David Kimche meets with Robert McFarlane reportedly for the first time concerning contacts between Israeli and Iranian representatives. Kimche asks McFarlane how the United States would view the prospect of opening a political dialogue with Iran. He tells McFarlane that Iranians who have contacted Israel in this regard have proposed to demonstrate their legitimacy and good intentions by intervening with radical elements in Lebanon to help bring about the release of American hostages there. He adds that Teheran will require a show of good faith in return, "probably" in the form of weapons. McFarlane reports on the meeting to President Reagan and other top U.S. officials. (Tower, pp. III-5–6)

July 8, 1985: Israeli middlemen meet in Hamburg, West Germany, with Manucher Ghorbanifar and Hassan Karrubi, a politically powerful Iranian with ties to Ayatollah Khomeini. (Karrubi is referred to in the congressional committees' final report as the "First Iranian.") Following this meeting, Adolph Schwimmer, one of the Israelis, travels to Washington, D.C., to discuss with NSC consultant Michael Ledeen a proposal made at the meeting by Ghorbanifar to swap TOW missiles for hostages and to request a response to the idea from U.S. officials. Ledeen passes along the information to National Security Advisor Robert McFarlane. (Iran-Contra Affair, p. 167; *[Memorandum Forwarding Message from Michael Ledeen....],* 7/11/85)

Mid-July 1985: Lt. Col. Oliver North drafts a comprehensive three-phase plan to overthrow the Sandinista government. Entitled "U.S. Political/Military Strategy for Nicaragua," the plan explicitly calls for the overthrow of the Sandinista government. "The third and final phase would have the following objectives," according to North's scenario: "the defeat and demobilization of Sandinista and Sandinista armed forces [and] implementation of the UNO/FDN political program." Robert Owen carries a copy of the plan to Adolfo Calero during a trip to Central America. (Document 16, *U.S. Political/Military Strategy for Nicaragua,* 7/15/85; Transcript of Trial, *United States of America* v. *Oliver L. North,* Cr. No. 88-80 [D.D.C. April 7, 1989], p. 2236)

August 6, 1985: At a White House meeting, National Security Advisor Robert McFarlane informs President Reagan of an Israeli request on August 2 for authorization to sell one hundred TOW missiles from Israeli stocks to Iran. Vice President George Bush and top officials George Shultz, Caspar Weinberger, and Donald Regan are present. The president apparently makes no decision at this meeting but, according to McFarlane, telephones him several days later to grant approval for the plan. (Iran-Contra Affair, p. 167)

August 7, 1985: Saudi businessman Adnan Khashoggi, who plays an important financial role in the early stages of the U.S.-

sponsored arms sales to Iran, transfers $1 million to the bank account of an Israeli middleman in connection with first shipment of missiles from Israel. (Iran-Contra Affair, p. 168)

August 8, 1985: President Reagan signs the $27 million Nicaraguan humanitarian assistance bill into law. (WP 8/9/85)

August 8, 1985: The *New York Times* prints a front-page story on the NSC's role in supporting the Contras. The story causes a flurry of activity in Congress, where a number of representatives are concerned that the Boland Amendment prohibiting U.S. assistance to the Contras has been violated. (NYT 8/8/85)

August 11, 1985: Lt. Col. Oliver North travels to Costa Rica to confer with Ambassador Lewis Tambs and CIA Station Chief Joseph Fernandez about the creation of a secret airstrip at Santa Elena in northern Costa Rica for Contra resupply operations. The purpose of the trip, he writes in a PROFS note to Robert McFarlane, is "to discern what has gone wrong on Southern Front preparations which are now very late in getting underway." Later, North recruits an old Vietnam War colleague, William Haskell, to purchase the land from American businessman Joseph Hamilton. Haskell uses the alias Robert Olmstead, and subsequently the land is purchased through an Enterprise shell company, Udall Research Corporation, under the pretext that it is going to be used for Costa Rican tourism. (Iran-Contra Affair, pp. 61–62; *North Trip to San José,* 8/10/85)

August 16, 1985: Representative Michael Barnes writes a letter to National Security Advisor Robert McFarlane concerning press reports of Lt. Col. Oliver North's role in supporting the Contras. Barnes demands that the NSC turn over all information pertaining to North's contacts with the Contras since the enactment of the Boland Amendment in October 1984. When the letter arrives at the White House, McFarlane's deputy, John Poindexter writes a note on the transmission sheet: "Barnes is really a trouble maker. We have good answers to all of this" (see entry for August 28, 1985). (Document 54, *Letter for Robert McFarlane, August 16, 1985, with Cover Note,* 9/12/85)

August 19, 1985: Robert Owen travels to San José to meet with CIA Station Chief Joseph Fernandez and Costa Rican Minister of Public Security Benjamin Piza about the location of a secret airstrip for Contra resupply operations. "The area decided on is on the west coast, bordered by a National Park on the north, the ocean to the west, the Pan American Highway to the east, and mountains and hills to the south," Owen reports to Lt. Col. Oliver North. He also writes that the main concern "is how long the operation will remain covert." (Document 38, *Memorandum for BG, August 1985 Trip,* 9/25/85)

August 20, 1985: Brewery magnate Joseph Coors transfers $65,000 from his personal account to the Lake Resources' bank account in Geneva. As per Coors's agreement with Lt. Col. Oliver North, the money is to be used to purchase a Maule short-take-off-and-landing (STOL) plane for Contra resupply operations. (*[Bank Transfer of $65,000 to Switzerland to Purchase Maule],* 8/20/85)

Israel ships the first installment of ninety-six TOW missiles to Iran. There is no corresponding release of hostages. (Iran-Contra Affair, p. 168)

August 28, 1985: Over the next two weeks, National Security Advisor Robert McFarlane and his aide, Lt. Col. Oliver North, meet at least six times and confer by phone four times on the subject of altering documents relating to NSC aid to the Contras. Congressman Michael Barnes has requested any relevant materials as part of his inquiry into the matter. Six documents are identified that, according to McFarlane "raise[d] legitimate questions about compliance with the law." North alters one as a sample, which McFarlane later testifies, left the document "grossly at variance with the original text." McFarlane directs North to alter all the documents—a task, North later said, he did not complete until November 1986 when the scandal is about to break. (Iran-Contra Affair, pp. 124–26; Document 33, *Memorandum for Robert McFarlane, Assistance for the Nicaraguan Resistance,* 12/4/84; *Nicaraguan Arms Shipments,* 2/6/85; *[Guatemalan] Aid to the Nicaraguan Resistance,* 3/5/85; Document 56, *Memorandum for Robert McFarlane, Fallback Plan for the Nicaraguan Resistance,* 3/16/85; *FDN Military Operations,* 4/11/85; *The Nicaraguan Resistance's Near-Term Outlook,* 5/31/85)

Late August or early September 1985: Lt. Col. Oliver North is directed to prepare "contingency plans for extracting hostages…from Lebanon." This is apparently his first assignment in connection with the U.S.-sponsored Iran initiative. On August 30, he is given a passport in the name of William P. Goode for travel to Europe "on a sensitive operation" relating to the initiative. (Tower, p. B-25; Iran-Contra Affair, p. 168)

September 1, 1985: National Security Advisor Robert McFarlane reports to President Reagan, Vice President George Bush, and top administration officials George Shultz, Caspar Weinberger, and Donald Regan that Israel expects the imminent release of all the American hostages. (Events, p. 33)

September 4, 1985: NSC consultant Michael Ledeen meets in Paris with Manucher Ghorbanifar and Israeli middlemen David Kimche and Yaacov Nimrodi. It is a heated session punctuated by arguments over the failure of Iran to gain the release of any hostages following the first arms delivery from Israel. (Iran-Contra Affair, p. 168)

September 8, 1985: Lt. Col. Oliver North travels to Dallas, Texas, on a private jet with Carl "Spitz" Channell. The purpose of the trip is to solicit a donation for the Contras from billionaire Nelson Bunker Hunt. The three dine together and Channell presents Hunt with a list of munitions needed by the Contras which totals $5 million. As a result of the solicitation, Hunt writes two checks worth over $470,000 to Channell. (Iran-Contra Affair, p. 93)

September 10, 1985: Lt. Col. Oliver North's diary reflects a meeting with the Vice President's national security advisor, Donald Gregg, and Col. James Steele, the U.S. MilGroup commander stationed in El Salvador. His notes show that Contra resupply operations were discussed. The meeting becomes important later when Gregg claims he did not know of the Contra resupply operations until August 1986. (*[North Notebook Entries for September 10, 1985]*; "Donald P. Gregg on the Contras," 3/29/87)

September 12, 1985: Robert McFarlane sends a response to Representative Michael Barnes's request for information concerning Lt. Col. Oliver North's reported support for the Contras in violation of the Boland Amendment. The letter, drafted by North, contains numerous misstatements of fact. NSC officials, McFarlane claims, "have scrupulously abided by the spirit and the letter of the law. None of us has solicited funds, facilitated contacts for prospective potential donors, or otherwise organized or coordinated the military or paramilitary efforts of the resistance." Similarly worded letters are sent to Representative Lee Hamilton, chairman of the House intelligence committee, and Senator Patrick Leahy, ranking member of the Senate intelligence committee. These letters later become the basis of criminal charges against McFarlane and North for deliberately misleading Congress. (*[Response to Barnes Letter of August 16, 1985 regarding NSC Activities relating to the Contras]*, 9/12/85; see also Document 55, Robert McFarlane, *Draft of Letter to Congressman Michael Barnes*, 9/12/85)

September 15, 1985: The second shipment of TOW missiles (408 missiles in this installment) is delivered to Tabriz, Iran, by Israel. According to the congressional Iran-Contra committees' final report, President Reagan approved the delivery beforehand. The same day, Rev. Benjamin Weir, held captive since May 8, 1984, is released. President Reagan delays announcement of the release until September 18 in the hope that more hostages will gain freedom. (Iran-Contra Affair, pp. 168–69; WP 12/7/86)

September 20, 1985: Lt. Col. Oliver North writes a letter to Felix Rodriguez who is based at Ilopango air base outside San Salvador. The letter outlines plans to station aircraft at Ilopango

and requests that Rodriguez act as liaison with Salvadoran Gen. Juan Bustillo for Contra resupply airlifts to be run from Ilopango. "You must not advise the [CIA] Station Chief," North tells Rodriguez. (Document 36, *Letter to Felix Rodriguez*, 9/20/85)

October 1, 1985: International Business Communications begins work on a new $278,725 contract with the State Department's Office of Public Diplomacy for Latin America and the Caribbean. The contract is classified "secret," and is not actually signed until a year later on September 2, 1986. It calls for IBC to handle Nicaraguan defectors, conduct media work for Contra leaders, draft opinion pieces, and revamp the public diplomacy distribution system, among other tasks. The contract becomes the subject of considerable controversy in early 1987 when reporters learn that IBC is participating in an illicit lobbying campaign on Contra aid and has been a conduit for funds for the National Security Council's Contra resupply operations. (Document 12, *Office of Public Diplomacy Secret Contract with International Business Communications*, 10/1/85)

October 3, 1985: The three leaders of UNO, Arturo Cruz, Sr., Adolfo Calero, and Alfonso Robelo, send a letter to Robert Duemling requesting that the State Department's Nicaraguan Humanitarian Assistance Office employ Robert Owen, "an individual known and trusted by us," and Owen's company IDEA as a go-between in dispersing nonlethal aid to the Contras. The request is part of Lt. Col. Oliver North's plan surreptitiously to get NHAO to pay for Owen and his expenses to do the work he has already been doing for North. Duemling refuses initially but then, under pressure from North and Assistant Secretary of State Elliott Abrams agrees to hire Owen at approximately $50,000 per year (see entry for October 11, 1985). (*[UNO Request that NHAO Employ Robert Owen]*, 10/3/85)

October 4, 1985: Islamic Jihad claims it has "assassinated" CIA Station Chief William Buckley in retaliation for Israel's bombing of PLO installations in Tunis, Tunisia. However, U.S. officials believe that Buckley died of complications arising from torture and poor treatment in June 1985. (*U.S./Iranian Contacts and the American Hostages [Second of Two Versions of NSC's "Historical Chronology," Dated November 20, 1986, 2000 Hours]*, p. 6; Iran-Contra Affair, p. 169)

October 7, 1985: The cruise ship *Achille Lauro* is hijacked by a group under the direction of Palestine Liberation Front member Abu Abbas. Lt. Col. Oliver North takes part in monitoring the crisis. Drawing on assistance from Israel, the United States tracks down the hijackers and ultimately forces down the aircraft carrying them out of Egypt. The incident appears to be one of the earliest contacts between North and Amiram Nir, counterterrorism adviser to Israeli Prime Minister Shimon

Peres, who participated in monitoring the crisis on the Israeli side. Nir eventually supplants the other Israeli intermediaries in the arms-for-hostages deals in late 1985. He and North collaborate in planning several joint covert operations, the exact nature of which remains classified. (Oliver North, Testimony, vol. 100-7, pt. I, p. 223; Martin, pp. 240–41; [North Notebook Entries for January 27, 1986])

October 10, 1985: The first major supply flight of nonlethal Contra aid from the United States under the auspices of the State Department's Nicaraguan Humanitarian Assistance Office is seized in Honduras after officials there discover an NBC news team accompanying the plane. The Honduran government maintains the myth that Contras are not based in its country and therefore is extremely sensitive to news coverage of Contra assistance. (Iran-Contra Affair, pp. 61–63)

October 11, 1985: The Restricted Inter-Agency Group (RIG) on Central America, which manages administration policy toward the region, meets to discuss the humanitarian assistance program. Lt. Col. Oliver North argues that the fiasco in Honduras the previous day would never have happened if Robert Duemling, NHAO director, had hired Robert Owen. Assistant Secretary of State Elliott Abrams concurs, and Duemling agrees to hire Owen as a consultant. (Iran-Contra Affair, p. 63)

October 27, 1985: In one of a series of meetings, NSC consultant Michael Ledeen, Israeli intermediaries Yaacov Nimrodi and Adolph Schwimmer, Manucher Ghorbanifar, and several other Iranians discuss the developing arms-for-hostages deals. The Iranians insist they can gain the release of all the hostages without the Ayatollah Khomeini becoming aware of it. In return, they ask for HAWK missiles from the United States. (Events, p. 39)

November 14, 1985: National Security Advisor Robert McFarlane and his deputy, John Poindexter, meet with CIA Director William Casey and Deputy Director John McMahon. McMahon says McFarlane told McMahon and Casey of Israel's plans to ship arms to elements of the Iranian military who hope to overthrow the Khomeini government. (Iran-Contra Affair, p. 176)

November 15, 1985: Saudi financier Adnan Khashoggi borrows $8 million to finance Iran's arms purchases from Israel from Vertex Finances, a company directed by two Canadian businessmen. This is the first part of a $21 million loan. Later, when Khashoggi himself is not fully repaid, the Canadians reportedly threaten to expose the arms deals. (WSJ 12/12/86; NYT 12/13/86)

Israel's Defense Minister Yitzhak Rabin calls on National Security Advisor Robert McFarlane to inform him of plans to ship

more arms to Iran—this time, HAWK missiles. He asks for reassurance that the United States still supports the Iran initiative and that Washington still intends to replenish the weapons Israel has already sent to Iran from its own stocks. McFarlane informs President Reagan of Israel's plans. (Iran-Contra Affair, p. 176)

November 17, 1985: "[T]he night of November 17," Lt. Col. Oliver North says he is "thrown into" the HAWK missile shipment to Iran. He receives calls from Israeli Defense Minister Yitzhak Rabin and National Security Advisor Robert McFarlane. McFarlane tells him to take care of the problem of replenishing Israel's inventory of HAWKs, which Rabin has demanded before going forward with the shipment. (Iran-Contra Affair, pp. 177–78)

November 18, 1985: National Security Advisor Robert McFarlane informs President Reagan of the imminent shipment of HAWK missiles by Israel to Iran. (Iran-Contra Affair, p. 178)

The HAWK missile shipment runs into problems. The plan calls for the missiles to be shipped from Tel Aviv and loaded onto aircraft in Portugal for delivery to Iran. However, Portuguese officials refuse to grant landing clearances to the aircraft without written declarations from the United States as to the nature and purpose of the shipments. Lt. Col. Oliver North asks Richard Secord, who is already involved in North's Contra resupply operations, to help troubleshoot for the mission in Portugal. (Iran-Contra Affair, pp. 179–80; [Requesting Richard Secord's Assistance with the HAWK Missile Shipment…], 11/19/85)

November 21, 1985: Lt. Col. Oliver North calls in CIA official Duane Clarridge for help in clearing aircraft carrying HAWK missiles to Iran through Portugal. (Clarridge later maintains that he believed the cargo was oil-drilling equipment, not missiles.) The CIA's direct participation in the operation occurs without a Presidential Finding required to provide legal authorization for any CIA covert activity. The lack of a Finding in this case becomes a major focus of controversy when the Iran initiative comes to light in late 1986. (Iran-Contra Affair, pp. 180–83; NSC Mission, 12/7/85)

November 22, 1985: Logistical difficulties with aircraft and schedules add to complications that beset the HAWK missile shipment to Iran. On the morning of November 22, an El Al Airlines 747 leased by the Israeli Ministry of Defense departs Tel Aviv with eighty HAWKs on board, but problems obtaining landing clearances in Portugal force the plane to return. Because of the ensuing delay, Israeli middleman Adolph Schwimmer has to cancel a charter for two DC-8 aircraft he planned to use for the second leg of the trip, Portugal to Iran. A mad scramble to locate other aircraft ensues. (Iran-Contra Affair, pp. 181–85)

November 22–25, 1985: Despite extraordinary diplomatic pressure by U.S. officials, Portuguese authorities continue to deny clearances for aircraft transporting HAWK missiles to Iran. Entreaties by National Security Advisor Robert McFarlane and officials from the Department of State and CIA, in addition to gambits by Richard Secord, are to no avail. CIA official Duane Clarridge decides to shift his focus to Turkey and Cyprus as transit points for the shipment. Clearance problems arise again, but are eventually ironed out and an aircraft owned by the CIA proprietary, St. Lucia Airways, carrying only eighteen HAWKs (instead of the planned eighty missiles) finally arrives in Teheran. (Iran-Contra Affair, pp. 180–84; Document 76, *Cable for European CIA Station, NSC Request,* 11/25/85, #910344)

November 25, 1985: Deputy National Security Advisor John Poindexter informs President Reagan during a regular morning briefing that the shipment of HAWK missiles has arrived in Iran. The congressional committees investigating the Iran-Contra affair describe the shipment as "bad policy, badly planned and badly executed." The mission engenders a great deal of Iranian mistrust, because only a portion of the promised missiles are delivered—and those few fail to meet Iranian expectations. (The Iranians were mistakenly led to believe, possibly by Israeli middlemen, that HAWK missiles were capable of shooting down high-flying Soviet aircraft. Moreover, the missiles sent to Iran reportedly carried Israeli markings, which the Iranians found insulting). The mission also breeds ill will between American and Israeli participants who blame each other for the logistical snafus that arose. When the Iran initiative comes to light in late 1986, the HAWK mission is a focus for criticism on legal as well as policy grounds. (Iran-Contra Affair, pp. 187–88; *[Notes of Office Directors' Staff Meeting....],* 11/25/85)

November 27, 1985: Vice President Bush sends a Thanksgiving card to Lt. Col. Oliver North, which reads: "Dear Ollie, As I head off to Maine for Thanksgiving, I just want to wish you a happy one with the hope that you get some well deserved rest. One of the many things I have to be thankful for is the way in which you performed under fire in tough situations. Your dedication and tireless work with the hostage thing and with Central America really gives me cause for great pride in you, and thanks. Get some turkey." (*[Letter Thanking Lt. Col. Oliver North for Work on Hostage and Central America Issues],* 11/27/85)

Late November 1985: Around the end of the month, Lt. Col. Oliver North tells Richard Secord that $800,000 left over from an Israeli payment of $1 million for the November HAWK missile shipment is available for other uses. He says later it was spent on Contra operations. (Iran-Contra Affair, pp. 269–70)

December 1985: President Reagan holds a series of meetings with families of American hostages being held in Beirut. Lt. Col. Oliver North and other White House aides attend. After the emotional sessions, the president orders his advisers to redouble their efforts to gain the release of the hostages. (WSJ 12/22/86; NYT 1/12/87)

GeoMiliTech Consultants Corporation, an arms brokerage run by Barbara Studley with the assistance of John Singlaub, submits a plan to the CIA to arm rebel forces around the world outside of official U.S. government channels. The plan appears to embody what Lt. Col. Oliver North later describes as William Casey's desire to create an "off-the-shelf" independent covert capability. Its objective is "to create a conduit for maintaining a continuous flow of Soviet weapons and technology, to be utilized by the United States in its support of Freedom Fighters in Nicaragua, Afghanistan, Cambodia, Ethiopia, etc." The idea is to create a "three-way trade" involving the People's Republic of China, Israel, and the United States. The United States would provide credit to Israel for the purchase of high-technology equipment and information. Based on the value of that credit, Israel would deliver military hardware to China, which would allow the Chinese to upgrade their military forces and readiness. China would in turn ship Soviet-compatible weapons to a "neutral foreign trading company"—GeoMiliTech—which would then disburse those weapons "as per directions from the United States" to "freedom fighters worldwide, mandating neither the consent nor awareness of the Department of State or Congress." (*[Proposal to Use GeoMiliTech to Provide a Flow of Weapons to Insurgent Forces],* 12/86)

December 4, 1985: President Reagan announces Robert McFarlane's resignation as assistant to the president for national security affairs. Vice Admiral John Poindexter is named his successor, effective January 5, 1986. Lt. Col. Oliver North, at the time the principal member of the NSC staff dealing with terrorism, is designated to replace McFarlane on the Iran initiative. However, McFarlane continues to be informed of developments in the program through an NSC computer link-up that he retains at his home for ten months after resigning. (WP 12/7/86, 1/14/87; NYT 12/25/85, 2/14/87)

December 5, 1985: Lt. Col. Oliver North prepares a comprehensive review of the Iran arms sales initiative for incoming National Security Advisor John Poindexter. The NSC aide also takes the opportunity to propose a major new deal with Iran. In brief, the plan calls for Israel to deliver 3,300 TOW and fifty HAWK missiles to Iran in return for freedom for every American (and one French) hostage. The arms shipments would be divided into five installments, each to be followed by the release of one or more hostages, over a twenty-four-hour period. (*Private Blank Check,* 12/4/85, 02:02)

According to National Security Advisor John Poindexter, President Reagan signs a Presidential Finding, hurriedly composed at the insistence of CIA Deputy Director John McMahon, to cover retroactively the CIA involvement in the November HAWK missile shipment to Iran. A year later, to protect the president from political embarrassment, Poindexter destroys the only copy of the Finding. (Iran-Contra Affair, pp. 12–13, 18–19)

December 6, 1985: Lt. Col. Oliver North reportedly tells officials from Israel's Ministry of Defense that he plans to divert profits from the sale of arms to Iran to help the Contras in Central America. (Iran-Contra Affair, p. 270)

December 7, 1985: President Reagan meets with his principal national security advisors to review the Iran initiative. Secretary of State George Shultz and Secretary of Defense Caspar Weinberger express their strong opposition to continuing the operation on legal and policy grounds, while CIA Director William Casey is in favor. In later sworn testimony, several participants denied that the November HAWK missile shipment was discussed, but Weinberger's criminal indictment reveals evidence to the contrary. (Iran-Contra Affair, pp. 197–99; Weinberger Indictment, 6/16/92)

December 9, 1985: Lt. Col. Oliver North sends a memo to Robert McFarlane and John Poindexter discussing options for the Iran arms sales initiative. "There is a fifth option," North writes, "which has not yet been discussed. We could, with an appropriate covert action Finding, commence deliveries ourselves, using [Richard] Secord as our conduit to control Gorbanifahr [*sic*] and delivery operations." In January 1986 President Reagan signs such a Finding authorizing the United States to assume direct control over arms shipments using Secord as agent (see entry for January 17, 1986). (Document 77, *Memorandum for Robert McFarlane and John Poindexter, Next Steps*, 12/9/85, p. 3; Document 64, *Memorandum for the President, Covert Action Finding Regarding Iran*, 1/17/86)

January 2, 1986: Israeli counterterrorism official Amiram Nir travels to Washington, D.C., to meet with John Poindexter, Robert McFarlane, and Lt. Col. Oliver North. Nir proposes a way to get the Iran initiative back on track: according to Poindexter's notes, his plan calls for Israel to ship five hundred TOW missiles to Iran and, in turn, for Iran to release American hostages in Lebanon immediately thereafter. This would be followed by the release of certain Hezbollah prisoners held by the Southern Lebanon Army and the delivery of thirty-five hundred more missiles by Israel to Iran. Nir's plan presents almost no risk to the United States, limiting Washington's responsibility to replenishing Israel's stocks if the operation succeeds and guaranteeing to offer public support if it is exposed. Over the next three days, North, CIA Director William Casey and others review the plan and prepare draft Presidential Findings for consideration by the president. (*[John Poindexter's Handwritten Notes....]*, 1/2/86; Iran-Contra Affair, pp. 201–203)

January 6, 1986: President Reagan's morning national security briefing, attended by Vice President Bush, includes discussion of Amiram Nir's new proposal to resume the Iran initiative. President Reagan signs a draft Presidential Finding authorizing the U.S. to participate, apparently not realizing it is not a final version. According to a later press report, this is one of at least three dozen meetings Vice President Bush attends in 1985–1986 which deal with arms sales to Iran. (*[Presidential Finding on Iran—Signed by President Reagan]*, 1/6/86; Iran-Contra Affair, p. 203; WP 1/7/88)

January 7, 1986: President Reagan meets with the full National Security Council on the Iran initiative. The only objections to the new Israeli proposal come from Secretary of State George Shultz and Secretary of Defense Caspar Weinberger, who repeat their earlier concerns. All others present, including Vice President Bush, support the idea, according to Weinberger's notes of the meeting. Attorney General Edwin Meese cites a 1981 opinion by his predecessor, William French Smith, that the United States could legally transfer arms to Iran under the National Security Act rather than the Arms Export Control Act. (Iran-Contra Affair, p. 203; *CIA Exchange of U.S. Weaponry for [Excised]*, 10/5/81; Second Weinberger Indictment, 10/30/92)

January 9, 1986: The State Department's Nicaraguan Humanitarian Assistance Office begins payments to Frígorificos de Puntarenas, a Costa Rican seafood company, which the Senate Foreign Relations Subcommittee on Terrorism, Narcotics and International Operations later calls "a money-laundering and drug smuggling operation." Frígorificos is one of the main brokers in the purchase of nonlethal assistance for the Contras. Over the next four months, U.S. Treasury Department payments total $261,932. (Kerry Chronology, p. 153)

January 11, 1986: Manucher Ghorbanifar, deeply mistrusted by certain U.S. officials, submits to a polygraph examination in order to restore his credibility. According to the CIA official who administers the exam, Ghorbanifar shows deception on thirteen of fifteen questions. Nevertheless, CIA Director William Casey and Lt. Col. Oliver North manage to keep Ghorbanifar as part of the initiative. (*[Ghorbanifar Polygraph—Date (1985) Incorrect]*, 1/13/86; Iran-Contra Affair, p. 205)

January 12, 1986: Defense Department official Noel Koch meets with Avraham Ben Yousef of the Israeli Ministry of Defense at National Airport in Washington, D.C. They agree to set a price of $4,500 per TOW missile to be transferred to Iran. (Events, p. 55)

January 17, 1986: Culminating two weeks of feverish administration activity aimed at getting the next phase of the Iran initiative off the ground, the president signs a new Presidential Finding. In attendance are Vice President George Bush, Chief of Staff Donald Regan, National Security Advisor John Poindexter, and NSC aide Donald Fortier. The new Finding includes a reference to the participation of "third parties," which refers to Richard Secord, according to later testimony. The Finding represents a shift by the United States from an indirect role in support of Israel to a direct role in the transfer of weapons to Iran. Defense Secretary Caspar Weinberger and Secretary of State George Shultz both claim later they were unaware that the president had signed the Finding. (Iran-Contra Affair, pp. 208-209; Document 64, *Memorandum for the President, Covert Action Finding Regarding Iran,* 1/17/86)

January 18, 1986: Defense Secretary Caspar Weinberger directs his aide, Lt. Gen. Colin Powell, to start the process of transferring TOW missiles to the CIA under the provisions of the Economy Act. (Events, p. 57)

January 22, 1986: Lt. Col. Oliver North travels to London for his first meeting with Manucher Ghorbanifar since the new Presidential Finding was signed. During one session, according to North, Ghorbanifar "took me into the bathroom" and suggested that the United States could sweeten the notion of selling missiles to Iran by using "residuals" from the sales to help pay for Contra operations in Central America. North implies later that this is the first time the idea of diverting funds to the Contras occurred to him. However, the official Israeli account of the initiative notes that North told Israeli defense officials as early as December 6, 1985, that he planned to use money from the arms sales in Nicaragua. (Iran-Contra Affair, p. 216)

January 24, 1986: Lt. Col. Oliver North sends National Security Advisor John Poindexter a memo laying out a detailed "notional timeline" of events relating to the Iran initiative for the next month. The plan includes a recommendation to provide intelligence data to Iran and the following prediction for February 11: "Khomeini steps down." (NSA, p. 268)

February 1, 1986: National Security Advisor John Poindexter sends an update to Robert McFarlane on the views of top administration officials toward the Iran initiative. He notes that Secretary of State George Shultz and Defense Secretary Caspar Weinberger "still disagree on policy grounds, but are cooperating. Bill [CIA Director William Casey], [Attorney General]

Ed Meese, [Chief of Staff] Don Regan and I are fully onboard this risky operation, but most importantly, President and VP [Vice President] are solid in taking the position that we have to try." (*Secure Equipment,* 2/1/86, 16:33)

February 6, 1986: Saudi financier Adnan Khashoggi lends Manucher Ghorbanifar $10 million to help pay for the February shipment of TOW missiles from the United States to Iran. This is one of several loans by Khashoggi during the course of the Iran initiative. (Tower, p. B-74)

February 13, 1986: The U.S. Army turns over one thousand TOW missiles to the CIA. Two days later, the CIA delivers the weapons to Israel for final shipment to Iran. (*DD Form 1348 [Form for Shipping TOW Missiles],* 2/13/86)

February 17, 1986: The first installment of five hundred TOW missiles, having been transferred to Israel from Kelly Air Force Base by Southern Air Transport two days earlier, is shipped to Iran on Israeli aircraft. On its return flight, the Israeli aircraft transports seventeen rejected HAWK missiles back to Israel. (Iran-Contra Affair, p. 218)

February 25–26, 1986: Lt. Col. Oliver North meets with Mohsen Kangarlou, a deputy to Iran's prime minister, in Frankfurt, West Germany. Kangarlou is referred to as the "Second Iranian" in the congressional Iran-Contra committees' final report. Although it is immediately clear to members of the U.S. delegation that the two sides are on "different frequencies"— North pressing for hostage release, Kangarlou for Phoenix missiles—U.S. officials are optimistic afterward, believing they have finally established direct contact with the Iranian government. (Iran-Contra Affair, p. 219)

February 27, 1986: This month's second installment of five hundred TOW missiles is shipped from Israel to Bandar Abbas, Iran. Once again, as with the November HAWK operation, the transfer of U.S. arms to Iran results in no hostages being released. (*Exchanges,* 2/27/86, 20:11; *How Are Things?,* 2/27/86, 16:02; Iran-Contra Affair, p. 221)

The National Endowment for the Preservation of Liberty (NEPL) holds a press conference to introduce its multimillion dollar Central American Freedom Program (CAFP), a multifaceted lobbying campaign designed to influence the upcoming vote in Congress on $100 million in Contra assistance. The CAFP, according to internal NEPL records, is made up of three operations: "Freedom Fighter's Television," a media spot campaign designed to place pro-Contra advertisements in the home districts of swing Congress members; a Contra speakers program designed to bring Contra leaders into other congressional districts; and a lobbying campaign using Democratic lobbyists on Capitol Hill. Since NEPL is a nonprofit organization, prohibited by law from lobbying, the CAFP is described as an effort to "educate" the American public. (*Central American Freedom Program*, 2/16/86)

March 1986: Richard Secord retains former CIA operative Glenn Robinette to conduct surveillance on witnesses in the forthcoming Christic Institute lawsuit over the La Penca bombing (see entry for May 30, 1984). Jack Terrell, a former Civilian Military Assistance mercenary who is now telling journalists and congressional investigators about Contra corruption, is singled out. Both North and Robinette talk to the FBI about Terrell, advancing the idea that he is involved in a plot to assassinate President Reagan. Later, in July 1986, North goes so far as to write a memorandum for National Security Advisor John Poindexter to give to the president entitled "Terrorist Threat: Jack Terrell." The FBI places Terrell under surveillance and concludes he is no threat to the president. (Iran-Contra Affair, p. 113; *Terrorist Threat: Jack Terrell*, 7/17/86)

March 17, 1986: Robert Owen writes a comprehensive assessment of his experience with the Contras for Lt. Col. Oliver North. He warns North that the United Nicaraguan Opposition, is a fiction: "UNO is a creation of the USG[overnment] to garner support from Congress." Adolfo Calero and the FDN continue to dominate the Contra movement, Owen asserts. Their leadership is made up of men who are "liars and greed and power motivated. They are not the people to rebuild a new Nicaragua." Owen also reports on allegations of corruption by the Contra leadership. Humanitarian assistance funds are being sold on the black market and the profits are "divided up between the Honduran military, the suppliers and the FDN." (Document 17, *Memorandum to BG, Overall Perspective*, 3/17/86)

April 3, 1986: Manucher Ghorbanifar meets in Washington, D.C., with George Cave, the former CIA agent working on the Iran initiative, and the CIA's chief of the Near East (C/NE) Division. (Around this time, the C/NE job passed from Bert Dunn to his deputy, Thomas Twetten, according to subsequent reports.) The conversation centers on plans for a visit to Teheran by a U.S. delegation. Ghorbanifar promises that Iran will see to the release of all American hostages in Lebanon as soon as the U.S. delegation arrives in Iran. (Document 80, *Memorandum for the Chief of CIA Near East Division, Meeting with G[h]orbanifar 3 April*, 4/3/86; Iran-Contra Affair, p. 224; Martin, p. 339; C/NE deposition, vol. 5, p. 829)

April 4, 1986: On the last page of a five-page status report on the "Release of American Hostages in Beirut," Lt. Col. Oliver North notes that "residual funds" from the shipment of arms to Iran would be used in the following way: "$12 million will be used to purchase critically needed supplies for the Nicaraguan Democratic Resistance Forces. This material is essential to cover shortages in resistance inventories resulting from their current offensives and Sandinista counter-attacks and to 'bridge' the period between now and when Congressionally-approved lethal assistance... can be delivered." When the document, later known as the "diversion memo," is discovered in North's files in November 1986, this passage prompts the Reagan administration to expose publicly the Iran-Contra connection and places the diversion at the center of most subsequent investigations of the scandal. (Document 88, *Release of American Hostages in Beirut*, ca. 4/4/86)

April 11, 1986: The first mission of the Enterprise's Contra resupply airlift to the southern front is successfully carried out. North, Secord, and Owen engineer the use of an L-100 plane leased from Southern Air Transport to Airmach, Inc., for the humanitarian aid program. Once the plane is in Central America, it ferries a load of weapons to the drop zone. (Iran-Contra Affair, p. 66)

April 16, 1986: Lt. Col. Oliver North and National Security Advisor John Poindexter exchange messages on the upcoming April 18 meeting with Manucher Ghorbanifar to make arrangements for the May 25 Robert McFarlane–led mission to Teheran. Poindexter tells North, "I want several points made clear to [the Iranians]. There are not to be any parts delivered until all the hostages are free in accordance with the plan that you layed [*sic*] out for me before. None of this half shipment before any are released crap. It is either all or nothing." (Document 81, *PROFS Note to Oliver North, Private Blank Check*, 4/16/86, 19:02; Iran-Contra Affair, p. 227)

A schedule proposal for Vice President George Bush, initialed by Donald Gregg, lists a meeting with Felix Rodriguez, who has been working as a counterinsurgency specialist in El Salvador and as a liaison with the Salvadoran military on Contra resupply operations. The purpose of the meeting, according to the proposal, is "[t]o brief the Vice President on the status of the war in El Salvador and resupply of the Contras." Later, Rodriguez and Gregg deny that Contra resupply operations were discussed at the meeting or that Gregg even knew of such operations. (Gregg later claims to the Senate Foreign Relations Committee that the entry meant resupply of the "copters.") (*VP Meeting with Felix Rodriguez, a Counterinsurgency Expert Visiting from El Salvador*, 4/16/86)

May 1986: William Dwyer and Frank Tarallo, the two DEA agents assigned to Lt. Col. Oliver North since 1985 for hostage ransom efforts in Lebanon, come into play again. According to a new plan, $2 million would be paid to DEA contacts in Lebanon in return for one or more hostages. North again turns to Texas millionaire H. Ross Perot for the money, but the operation falls through when the contacts demand the cash up front. (Iran-Contra Affair, p. 365)

May 1, 1986: Vice President George Bush meets with Felix Rodriguez. At the end of the meeting, Lt. Col. Oliver North and U.S. Ambassador to El Salvador Edwin Corr join the meeting. Although briefing memoranda indicate that part of the agenda of the meeting is "resupply of the Contras," all participants later deny that the topic is discussed. (*VP Meeting with Felix Rodriguez, 4/16/86; Meeting with Felix Rodriguez, 4/30/86; Summary of Contacts with Felix Rodriguez, 12/15/86*)

May 3, 1986: Under Secretary of State Michael Armacost cables Secretary George Shultz a "very disturbing report" that Israeli middleman Amiram Nir has approached U.S. Ambassador to Great Britain Charles Price for help with an arms deal for Iran that reportedly has White House approval. (It is not entirely clear whether Nir is operating on his own or whether this is in some way sanctioned by Lt. Col. Oliver North.) Armacost guesses that the project "may be designed as a means of siphoning off additional materiel" for other unidentified operations. He adds, "Legal concerns seem not to impose any constraints whatsoever on our friends in the White House." Although Armacost is not told whether there is a CIA connection, he remarks, "I would be astonished if there was none." (*Arms Sales to Iran,* 5/3/86, State 139006)

May 6, 1986: Lt. Col. Oliver North, Amiram Nir, and George Cave meet with Manucher Ghorbanifar in London to "set the stage for the trip to Tehran." Cave also speaks with the Office of the Prime Minister in Iran to hammer out details. He reports that the U.S. delegation will meet in Teheran with Iran's president, prime minister and possibly Speaker of the Parliament Ali Akbar Hashemi Rafsanjani. In the end, none of these top officials meets with the Americans. (Tower, p. B-94)

May 12, 1986: President Reagan discusses Robert McFarlane's upcoming secret mission to Teheran at his morning national security briefing. (Tower, p. III-16)

May 20, 1986: Albert Hakim deposits $200,000 into the so-called Button account, which he has set up, reportedly without Lt. Col. Oliver North's knowledge, as an insurance policy for North's family in the event of his death. (Events, p. 80)

May 25, 1986: The Robert McFarlane delegation arrives in Teheran accompanied by a single pallet of HAWK spare parts. Members of the group include Lt. Col. Oliver North, CIA consultant George Cave, NSC aide Howard Teicher, Israeli official Amiram Nir, and a CIA radio communicator. The mission gets off to a poor start when no high-level officials are at the airport to greet the Americans. McFarlane has expected that Parliament Speaker Ali Akbar Hashemi Rafsanjani would be on hand. Over the next three days, the U.S. and Iranian delegations meet frequently but the negotiations founder over a variety of issues. The McFarlane group returns to Tel Aviv on May 28. (Iran-Contra Affair, p. 238)

May 29, 1986: Robert McFarlane briefs President Reagan on the recent mission to Teheran. Later interviews reveal that opinions differed among various players as to why the talks failed. Richard Secord and Albert Hakim blame McFarlane, saying they have no idea where he got the idea that all the hostages had to be released before more missile spare parts could be delivered to Iran. (The idea was in fact a condition set down by National Security Advisor John Poindexter before the mission.) Lt. Col. Oliver North and George Cave fault Manucher Ghorbanifar who, they say, misrepresented this point to Iranian officials. North has shown impatience with Ghorbanifar's trustworthiness since at least February. Whatever the reasons, despite McFarlane's pessimism about the future of the Iran initiative, the United States presses on and continues to rely on Ghorbanifar for several more weeks. (Iran-Contra Affair, pp. 242, 249; Events, p. 82)

May 31, 1986: One of the injured journalists in the La Penca bombing (see entry for May 30, 1984), Tony Avirgan, brings a suit through the Christic Institute against various members of the extraofficial group facilitating Contra operations on behalf of the Reagan administration. Those named in the suit include Richard Secord, Robert Owen, John Hull, Felipe Vidal, and René Corvo. The suit itself prompts a number of activities by the Enterprise and Lt. Col. Oliver North to discredit and silence witnesses; it is subsequently dismissed in June 1988 by a federal judge in Miami. (WP 7/3/86; NYT 2/6/89)

June 8, 1986: The *Miami Herald* runs a front-page story entitled "Despite Ban, U.S. Helping Contras," which names Lt. Col. Oliver North and outlines the White House program to evade the Boland Amendment. Two days later, the Associated Press runs a comprehensive article naming Lt. Col. Oliver North, Robert Owen, John Hull, and others as participants in illicit Contra operations. (MH 6/8/86; AP 6/10/86)

June 12, 1986: The CIA pays the Defense Department a total of $5.6 million for TOW missiles. The payment comes in the form of several checks, none of which exceeds $999,999.99, the maximum amount allowed before congressional notification is required. (Events, p. 84; *Support to Intelligence Operations,* 2/13/86)

June 16, 1986: Lt. Col. Oliver North, increasingly concerned that the resupply operations will be disclosed, sends a KL-43 message to CIA Station Chief Joseph Fernandez in Costa Rica. The cable states that North is sending Rafael Quintero, a former CIA agent, to Central America to facilitate a resupply drop. "I do not think we ought to contemplate these operations without him being on the scene. Too many things go wrong that then directly involve you and me in what should be deniable for both of us." (*[Report on Problems with Resupply Operation]*, 6/16/86, 21:30)

June 24, 1986: Texas Representative Ronald Coleman introduces a Resolution of Inquiry in Congress calling on the president to "provide to the House of Representatives certain information concerning activities of Lt. Col. Oliver North or any other member of the National Security Council in support of the Nicaraguan resistance." More specifically, the resolution calls for a complete list of North's communications with Robert Owen, John Singlaub, John Hull, as well as other private-sector intermediaries and foreign government officials. (*H.RES. 485*, 6/24/86; Iran-Contra Affair, p. 141)

June 25, 1986: The House of Representatives, in a major victory for the Reagan administration, narrowly passes the president's request for $100 million in renewed military and nonmilitary assistance for the Contras. "We can be proud that we as a people have embraced the struggle of the freedom fighters in Nicaragua," Reagan announces. "Today, their cause is our cause." The vote clears the way for full restoration of CIA involvement in the Contra war which begins again in October when President Reagan signs the bill into law. (Iran-Contra Affair, p. 72)

The CBS program *West 57th Street* airs a documentary on the Contra resupply operations. It identifies Robert Owen as "the bagman for Ollie North" and names John Hull as the key American working with the NSC in Costa Rica. In response to the program, North sends a PROFS note to Karna Small of the NSC calling the program "the single most distorted piece of 'reporting' I have ever seen." (*Question from CBS*, 6/27/86)

June 30, 1986: An Iranian intermediary informs George Cave, the retired CIA agent working with Lt. Col. Oliver North on the Iran initiative, that Iranian officials now believe they have been overcharged for HAWK missile spare parts by 600 percent. The Iranians made the discovery when they acquired a microfiche of actual factory prices for the parts. North, rather than refund any money, comes up with the idea of forging a price list to counter the authentic one in the Iranians' possession. The plan never gets off the ground. To make matters worse, the Iranians inspect the spare parts they have already received and find numerous defects and missing items. Iran's distrust of U.S. representatives rises markedly. (*[Discussion with Mohsen Kangarlou Regarding*

Price of HAWK Missile Spare Parts], 6/30/86; Iran-Contra Affair, pp. 247–48)

July 10, 1986: Albert Hakim and George Cave, who are attempting to develop a "second channel" to Iran on behalf of the U.S. government, meet with a contact of Hakim's in Washington, D.C. By late July, Lt. Col. Oliver North is informed that the contact, an Iranian who has agreed to help for a price, has come up with a colleague who has direct connections to the Iranian government. (Iran-Contra Affair, p. 249)

July 21, 1986: Lt. Col. Oliver North, George Cave and Amiram Nir meet in London with Manucher Ghorbanifar. They discuss an exchange of the remaining HAWK missile spare parts from the May mission to Teheran for the release of American hostages. (Tower, p. III-17)

July 26, 1986: Rev. Lawrence Martin Jenco, held hostage in Lebanon since January 8, 1985, is released. After the Tower Commission report finds that his freedom came in exchange for arms, Jenco says he would rather have remained a hostage than be a bargaining chip in a weapons deal. "I had to accept [President Reagan's] word that I was not exchanged for arms. Now…I have a deep question mark," Jenco said. (AP 3/1/87; WP 3/2/87)

July 29, 1986: Vice President George Bush meets with Israeli intermediary Amiram Nir in Jerusalem. According to notes taken by Bush aide Craig Fuller, Nir informs the Vice President of many details of the U.S.-sponsored Iran initiative. Among other things, Nir tells Bush that "we are dealing with the most radical elements" in the Iranian regime. This fact contradicts the purpose of the January 17 Presidential Finding authorizing the initiative, which directs that "third parties and third countries establish contact with moderate elements" in Iran. (Document 67, *Memorandum, The Vice President's Meeting with Mr. Nir*, 7/29/86; *Presidential Finding on Iran*, 1/17/86)

President Reagan approves a proposal by Lt. Col. Oliver North to transfer HAWK missile parts to Iran and afterward to arrange a meeting with Iranian intermediaries in Europe. The plan reverses National Security Advisor John Poindexter's earlier order not to deliver any additional military supplies to Iran before all American hostages have been released. (Document 66, *Memorandum for John Poindexter, Next Steps on the American Hostages*, 7/29/86, p. 3)

August 1986: By this month, Saudi businessman Adnan Khashoggi has been repaid a portion of his previous loans for use in the Iran arms deals by Lake Resources, a front company of the Enterprise. In October, Khashoggi's inability to square accounts with his own creditors leads them to threaten to expose the Iran initiative if they are not repaid. (Tower, p. 446)

August 3, 1986: Following President Reagan's authorization, twelve pallets of HAWK spare parts arrive in Iran from Israel. (SSCI, p. 29)

August 6, 1986: Acting on Representative Ronald Coleman's Resolution of Inquiry, the House intelligence committee invites Lt. Col. Oliver North to meet in closed session with its members. North lies or dissembles in response to almost every question. He states that his relationship with Robert Owen is "casual" and that he has not met with John Singlaub in 1985 or 1986. North states that he has "not in any way, nor at any time violate[d] the principles or legal requirements of the Boland Amendment." At the end of the hearing, according to notes taken at this time, Chairman Lee Hamilton "expresses his appreciation for the goodfaith effort" and "indicated his satisfaction in the responses received." When John Poindexter is informed of North's performance, he writes a PROFS note to him that says, "Well done." (Document 58, *PROFS Note to Oliver North with HPSCI Interview of North*, 8/6/86; Document 59, *Memo to the Files: August 6, 1986, 8:30 A.M.*, 9/3/86)

August 8, 1986: Lt. Col. Oliver North meets in London with Manucher Ghorbanifar for what turns out to be the last time. He agrees in principle to yet another proposal for the sequential release of American hostages to be followed in each case by further deliveries of U.S. weapons. (Iran-Contra Affair, p. 248)

Assistant Secretary of State Elliott Abrams flies to London to meet with a representative of the Sultan of Brunei. He travels under the alias "Mr. Kenilworth." Abrams and the official meet in a hotel and then take a walk through a nearby park, where Abrams solicits a donation of $10 million for the Contras. When asked what Brunei would receive in return, Abrams responds: "The President will know of this, and you will have the gratitude of the secretary [George Shultz] and of the president for helping us out in a jam." Abrams then gives the official a card with the number of a Swiss bank account for Lake Resources, an Enterprise front company. Later, it turns out that Fawn Hall, Lt. Col. North's assistant, has typed the number incorrectly, and the $10 million is deposited in the wrong account. (Iran-Contra Affair, p. 71)

August 12, 1986: Chairman of the House intelligence committee Lee Hamilton sends a letter to Representative Ronald Coleman which states that the committee will not support his Resolution of Inquiry. "Based on our discussions and review of the evidence provided, it is my belief that the published press allegations cannot be proven." The resolution is therefore tabled. (*[Letter from Hamilton to Coleman]*, 8/12/86)

August 25, 1986: Richard Secord meets with a new intermediary, Ali Hashemi Bahramani, a nephew of Iran's Parliament speaker. Bahramani, referred to as "the Relative" in various official reports, becomes the key figure in the "second channel" to Iran, which has been developed as an alternative to the discredited Ghorbanifar/Kangarlou avenue. His participation injects new life into the arms-for-hostages deals from the U.S. point of view. In a memo recommending the United States pursue this new contact, Lt. Col. Oliver North writes that he is "indeed a bonafide intermediary seeking to establish direct contact with the USG for Rafsanjani's faction within the Government of Iran." (U.S./Iranian Contacts and the American Hostages [Second of Two Versions...2000 Hours], 11/17/86; [Report on Meetings with Iranian Intermediaries in Brussels], 8/26/86, 1800; Next Steps with Iran, 9/2/86)

August 27, 1986: A new section of the Arms Export Control Act governing shipments of military equipment abroad goes into effect prohibiting arms exports to any country found by the secretary of state to support international terrorism. Iran was designated a sponsor of terrorism in January 1984. (Tower, p. III-3)

Late August 1986: Lt. Col. Oliver North meets with a representative of Panamanian Gen. Manuel Antonio Noriega two months after front-page headlines in the United States announce Noriega's ties to drug trafficking, money laundering, and the murder of Panamanian opposition leader Hugo Spadafora. In return for help in cleaning up Noriega's image and lifting a ban on U.S. military sales to Panama, the representative tells North, "Noriega would assassinate the Sandinista leadership for the U.S. government." North reports to Poindexter that Noriega has assets inside Nicaragua who could carry out significant sabotage operations. Poindexter responds that Noriega could be helpful to the United States, but that the U.S. government could not be involved in assassination. Poindexter urges North to meet directly with Noriega. (Document 23, *U.S. Government Stipulation on Quid Pro Quos with other Governments as Part of Contra Operations*, paras. 97–99)

September 1986: As the "second channel" in the Iran arms initiative begins to develop, some players in the arms-for-hostages deals sense that other problems are surfacing, namely the possible diversion of funds from the arms sales to the Contras. The CIA's Charles Allen and Manucher Ghorbanifar both suspect this possibility around this time. (SSCI, p. 31)

September 5–6, 1986: Lt. Col. Oliver North is alerted late at night that the Costa Rican government led by Oscar Arias is planning a press conference for the next day to expose the secret Contra resupply airstrip at Santa Elena. North's notebook entry for this day indicates a call from CIA Station Chief Joseph Fernandez: "Security Minister plans to make public Udall [Research Corporation] role w/Base West and alledge [*sic*] violation of C.R. [Costa Rican] law by Udall, Bacon, North, Secord, et al." North immediately calls Assistant Secretary of State Elliott Abrams and U.S. Ambassador to Costa Rica Lewis Tambs to discuss how to pressure President Arias to cancel the press conference. His notebooks reflect that he wanted Arias to be threatened with a cutoff of $80 million in AID funds appropriated for Costa Rica as well as with having a scheduled meeting with President Reagan canceled. Tambs does call Arias and succeeds in getting the press conference canceled, at least temporarily. (Document 47, ([*Notebook Entries for September 6, 1986]*))

September 9, 1986: Frank Herbert Reed, director of the Lebanese International School in West Beirut, is kidnapped. Ali Hashemi Bahramani, the principal figure in the second channel to Iran, tells U.S. negotiators later that Mohsen Kangarlou, the main contact in the first channel, was responsible for Reed's abduction. A later published report suggests that another group beyond Iran's control may have committed that act. (WP 11/26/86; NYT 12/25/86; Iran-Contra Affair, p. 261; Wright, p. 152)

At the president's morning national security briefing, the subject of the second channel to Iran's leaders is discussed, as is the possibility of mounting a hostage rescue operation. (Tower, p. B-152)

September 17, 1986: Lt. Col. Oliver North sends a PROFS note to National Security Advisor John Poindexter regarding the case of Honduran Gen. Jos_ Bueso Rosa, who has been charged with a plot to assassinate the president of Honduras and finance the operation by smuggling cocaine into the United States. Bueso Rosa had been a key liaison with NSC, CIA, and Defense Department personnel for covert Contra operations, and North is concerned that he will "break his longstanding silence about the Nic[araguan] Resistance and other sensitive operations." North refers to Bueso Rosa as "a friend" who deserves a "reward" and recommends an effort to get him off the hook. "Gorman, Clarridge, Revell, Trott and Abrams will cabal quietly in the morning to look at options: pardon, clemency, deportation, reduced sentence. Objective is to keep [Bueso Rosa] from... spilling the beans." The next day, Poindexter sends a computer message back to North stating, "You may advise all concerned that the President will want to be as helpful as possible to settle this matter." Bueso Rosa subsequently receives a five-year sentence in a minimum security prison. ([*Oliver North's Concerns....], 9/17/86*)

September 19–21, 1986: Ali Hashemi Bahramani, the key figure in the new second channel to Iran's leadership, meets with Lt. Col. Oliver North, George Cave, Richard Secord, and Albert Hakim in Washington, D.C. Bahramani and two associates

arrived in the United States under cover. Their stay includes a late-night guided tour of the White House by North. The substance of their discussions involves weapons sales, hostages, the fate of the Dawa prisoners in Kuwait and the future of Iraqi President Saddam Hussein, an enemy of Ayatollah Khomeini. Despite the history of previous disappointments in the Iran initiative, North once again feels able to report to John Poindexter that the talks have gone "extremely well." "You can brief RR that we seem to be headed in a v[er]y positive direction...." (Iran, 9/22/86, 09:22)

September 25, 1986: Costa Rican officials hold a press conference and disclose the existence of the secret airstrip at Santa Elena, which, they tell reporters, has been used for resupplying the Contras and for trafficking drugs. The Arias administration names Udall Research Corporation as the owner of the land and releases correspondence with Robert Olmstead, the alias of Lt. Col. Oliver North's covert intermediary, William Haskell. The field is permanently shut down. In a PROFS note to John Poindexter, North writes that "we have taken all appropriate damage control measures to keep any USG[overnment] fingerprints off this and with Elliott [Abrams] and [Joseph Fernandez] have worked up appropriate 'if asked' press guidance." (*Public Affairs Campaign on Central America*, 9/26/86)

September 26, 1986: Following a request by the new Iranian intermediary, Ali Hashemi Bahramani, for a public sign to support his position with the leadership in Teheran, North drafts an editorial for broadcast over the Voice of America thanking Iran for its help in resolving the Pan Am Flight 73 hijacking (see entry for June 14, 1985). (*Iran*, 9/26/86, 09:47)

October 5, 1986: A Fairchild C-123K belonging to the Enterprise is shot down by Sandinista soldiers over southern Nicaragua. Two American pilots, Wallace "Buzz" Sawyer and William Cooper, are killed. The cargo kicker, Eugene Hasenfus, parachutes out of the plane and is captured by the Sandinista army. Vice President Bush's office is the first within the administration to know about the crash when Felix Rodriguez, former CIA associate of Bush's national security advisor, Donald Gregg, calls Gregg's deputy, Sam Watson. The crash sets off a flurry of behind-the-scenes damage-control efforts by administration officials in an attempt to create a cover story and bolster denials of U.S. involvement. Almost immediately, the CIA station chief in Costa Rica, Joseph Fernandez, sends a KL-43 cable to Robert Dutton stating, "Situation requires that we do necessary damage control." Photographs of Eugene Hasenfus, the sole survivor, being led from the jungle by Sandinista soldiers are on the front page of almost every newspaper in the United States the next day. Under interrogation, Hasenfus identifies Felix Rodriguez by his code name, Max Gomez, as the man who managed resupply operations at Ilopango air base in El Salvador, and reveals a network of covert safehouses in San Salvador. He tells his Nicaraguan captors that he understood these Contra resupply flights to be part of a CIA-sanctioned operation. (*Iran-Contra Affair*, p. 144)

October 6–8, 1986: Lt. Col. Oliver North attends part of a series of meetings with the second channel in Frankfurt, West Germany. The U.S. delegation, including George Cave, Richard Secord, and Albert Hakim, brings a Bible signed by President Reagan a few days earlier. The Iranian side is again headed by Ali Hashemi Bahramani. North presents a list of seven points for consideration by the group but is forced to return to Washington to deal with the downing of Eugene Hasenfus's plane in Nicaragua before the Iranians can present their counterproposal. According to Albert Hakim, he is left to respond to Iran's list after the other Americans in the delegation also depart. At session's end on October 8, he and the Iranians have agreed to a nine-point plan that includes a number of concessions not on North's original list. Hakim hears soon afterward from North that the president approves of the final outcome, which the congressional Iran-Contra committees' final report later describes as a "retreat" for the United States. (*U.S. Proposal [Lt. Col. Oliver North's Seven-Point Proposal to Iran]*, 10/6/86; Document 84, *Memorandum of Understanding, Translation by Albert Hakim of the Farse Original of the "9 Points,"* 10/8/86; *Iran-Contra Affair*, pp. 254–58)

October 7, 1986: A week after the CIA's Charles Allen and Robert Gates meet to discuss the former's concerns about the Iran arms initiative, they raise the issue with CIA Director William Casey. Casey tells them that he has just received a telephone call on this very subject from Roy Furmark, a longtime business associate who also has ties to Saudi financier Adnan Khashoggi. Furmark's conversation confirms Allen's worst fears. According to Casey, Furmark has told him that two Canadian businessmen who loaned Khashoggi large sums of money for the arms-for-hostages deals have not been repaid and are prepared to expose the operation unless their investment-plus-interest is returned. Casey directs Allen to prepare a memo on the subject and informs National Security Advisor John Poindexter as well as the CIA's general counsel. A series of meetings between Allen and Furmark, and between CIA officials and Poindexter, follow in the next few weeks to work on ways to minimize the damage that might result from exposure of the initiative. (*[Charles Allen's Overview of the Iran Initiative]*, 10/14/86; *Ghorbanifar–[Excised] Channel*, 10/17/86; *Meeting with Roy Furmark*, 11/7/86; SSCI, pp. 45–49)

Shortly after CIA Director William Casey (on or about this date) tells him that the diversion of funds to the Contras from the Iran initiative may soon be exposed, Lt. Col. Oliver North

begins "shredding documents in earnest." (Oliver North, Testimony, vol. 100-7, pt. I, pp. 19–20)

The Restricted Inter-Agency Group on Central America draws up plans to orchestrate a cover story for the Hasenfus plane which will distance the U.S. government from the flight. According to a summary of the meeting sent to National Security Advisor John Poindexter, the decision is made to have the Contras claim credit: "UNO to be asked to assume responsibility for flight and to assist families of Americans involved." Press guidance is written admitting "no U.S.G. involvement or connection but that we are generally aware of such support contracted by the Contras." (Document 52, *PROFS Note to John Poindexter and Robert McFarlane, "Downed Plane,"* 10/8/86; *Iran-Contra Affair*, pp. 144–45)

October 8, 1986: Reagan administration officials, led by the president, begin a series of categorical denials of any U.S. role in the Hasenfus resupply flight. "There was no government connection with that at all," President Reagan tells reporters. "We've been aware that there are private groups and private citizens that have been trying to help the Contras—to that extent—but we did not know the exact particulars of what they're doing." The day before, Secretary of State George Shultz, after being briefed by Assistant Secretary of State Elliott Abrams, had been quoted on television as saying that Eugene Hasenfus was hired "by private people" and that "the people involved were not from our military, not from any U.S. Government agency, CIA included." (*Iran-Contra Affair*, p. 145)

October 9, 1986: Lt. Col. Oliver North's notebook entry on this day records telephone calls to CIA Central America Task Force Chief Alan Fiers and Contra leaders Arturo Cruz, Sr., and Adolfo Calero concerning the press guidance on the Hasenfus plane: "The A/C [aircraft] was providing humanitarian supplies to UNO fighters," state North's notes, referring to the cover story. In fact, the Sandinista inventory of the plane's cargo shows a significant number of weapons on board. (*[North Notebook Entries for October 9, 1986]*)

October 10, 1986: Assistant Secretary of State Elliott Abrams appears before the Senate Foreign Relations Committee and is asked about foreign donations to the Contras. "I think I can say that while I have been assistant secretary...we have not received a dime from a foreign government, not a dime, from any foreign government." (*[Abrams' Testimony]*, 10/10/86)

October 11, 1986: Assistant Secretary of State Elliott Abrams appears on the Cable News Network program, Evans and Novak, and is asked specifically whether Hasenfus was under "the control, the guidance, the direction, or what have you" of anyone connected with the U.S. government. He emphatically denies any U.S. government involvement: "That would be illegal. We are barred from doing that, and we are not doing it. This was not in any sense a U.S. government operation. None." (Iran-Contra Affair, p. 145)

October 14, 1986: The North-directed hostage ransom operation using agents of the DEA comes to an unsuccessful conclusion after more than eighteen months. North meets with DEA Deputy Administrator John Lawn to thank him for his cooperation. The previous June, President Reagan had sent a letter of appreciation to H. Ross Perot for his "discreet assistance" to the operation. (*[Appreciation for Ross Perot's Assistance in Attempting to Gain the Release of Hostages in Lebanon]*, 6/11/86; Iran-Contra Affair, p. 365)

CIA officials Clair George and Alan Fiers and Assistant Secretary of State Elliott Abrams appear at a closed hearing of the House Permanent Select Committee on Intelligence. According to a summary classified "top-secret Veil," committee Chairman Lee Hamilton asks for assurances "that the USG[overnment] was not involved in any way in supplying the Contras." George states "this was true for the Agency, and Mr. Abrams said it was true for the Government as a whole." Later Hamilton asks if there are any foreign governments providing support to the Contras. Abrams answers, "Not to our knowledge, and certainly not at our behest," even though he personally had solicited a donation from Brunei the previous August. (Document 53, *Memorandum for the Record: Testimony before the House Permanent Select Committee on Intelligence Regarding the Crash of a C-123 in Nicaragua*, 10/14/86)

October 21, 1986: American author Edward Austin Tracy is kidnapped in Beirut by the Revolutionary Justice Organization, a group with pro-Iranian connections. (WP 12/7/86)

October 28, 1986: Following the agreement in Frankfurt, West Germany, in early October between U.S. and Iranian negotiators, five hundred TOW missiles are delivered to Iran from Israel. By arrangement with the United States, Israel ships replacement missiles received from the United States in May because those missiles were judged not to meet the requirements of the Israeli Defense Forces. The United States agrees to replace them later with a more sophisticated version of the TOW missile. (Iran-Contra Affair, p. 259)

October 29, 1986: Lt. Col. Oliver North, George Cave, Richard Secord, and Albert Hakim meet once again with Iranian intermediaries, this time in Mainz, West Germany. The talks focus on the familiar issues of hostages, U.S. weapons, the Dawa prisoners, and the removal of Iraq's President Saddam Hussein. The Iranians also report that a student faction in Iran and a group within Hezbollah have independently published ac-

counts of various arms-for-hostages negotiations between Iran and the United States This has prompted the Iranians to consider closing down the initiative. Nevertheless, Bahramani announces that a joint commission representing different Iranian government factions that back the initiative has been established to oversee future negotiations. The Americans are stunned to learn that Mohsen Kangarlou, the key figure in the abandoned first channel, and the man Bahramani says is responsible for the recent kidnapping of American Frank Herbert Reed, is a member of the commission. Bahramani also assures the U.S. team that two or three hostages will be freed in the next few days. (*[Transmission of Message from Lt. Col. Oliver North on Talks with Iranians]*, 10/29/86, 22:23; Iran-Contra Affair, pp. 259–61)

November 2, 1986: Within days of the delivery of five hundred TOW missiles to Iran, American hostage David Jacobsen is released. Lt. Col. Oliver North expects other hostages to be released, but none are. In response to press inquiries, White House Chief of Staff Donald Regan acknowledges publicly for the first time the ongoing negotiations with Iran. (Tower, p. B-171; WP 12/20/86)

November 3, 1986: A Lebanese weekly, *Ash-Shiraa*, publishes an account of Robert McFarlane's secret May mission to Teheran. The story, immediately picked up by Western news services, marks the beginning of the end of the fifteen-month-long U.S. arms-for-hostages deal with Iran. The magazine's editor later reveals that his sources have ties to Mehdi Hashemi, a relative of Ayatollah Khomeini's designated political successor and a strong proponent of terrorist strikes against U.S. targets. (Hashemi has been arrested recently for treason (see entry for October 12, 1981). U.S. intelligence officials reportedly believe that Manucher Ghorbanifar may have tipped off Hashemi after being cut out of the secret deals. (*Al-Shiraa*, 11/3/86; Wright, pp. 151–52)

November 4, 1986: In the wake of the public exposure of the U.S. arms-for-hostages deals with Iran, Reagan administration officials begin to deliberate on official and unofficial responses. In a cable to National Security Advisor John Poindexter, Secretary of State George Shultz proposes divulging only "the key facts to the public," asserting that the president acted "within his Constitutional responsibility" and reaffirming "that our policies toward terrorism and toward the Iran/Iraq War stand." Poindexter responds the next day, advocating a delay before revealing details of the initiative. He argues that time is needed to work on gaining the release of other hostages and determining whether Washington may be able to influence an internal "power struggle" that he believes is underway in Iran. Poindexter adds: "Today I have talked with VP [Vice President George

Bush], Cap [Defense Secretary Caspar Weinberger] and [CIA Director] Bill Casey. They agree with my approach." (*U.S. Policy on Iran [Suggestion for Putting Best Light on Iran Operations]*, 11/4/86, #023003; Document 85, *U.S. Policy on Iran (TS)*, 11/5/86)

November 5–20, 1986: NSC officials begin to put together a chronology of the Iran initiative to help fashion a response to its public exposure. Among the principal contributors are Lt. Col. Oliver North, John Poindexter, Robert McFarlane, and North's aides, Robert Earl and Craig Coy. The chronology goes through several renditions, finally comprising seventeen pages of dates, names, events and rationales. Congressional investigators conclude later that Poindexter, McFarlane and North deliberately falsified key facts in the chronologies in order to protect the President and themselves (see the chronologies themselves, entitled *Chronology of Events: U.S.-Iran Dialogue* and *U.S./Iranian Contacts and the American Hostages*, dated from 11/7/86 through 11/20/86; Tower, pp. D-3–11; Iran-Contra Affair, pp. 298–300)

November 6, 1986: President Reagan declares that media reports of Robert McFarlane's trip to Iran have "no foundation." He denies that the United States reached a secret agreement with Teheran on the release of American hostages in return for arms. He goes on to say, "We will never pay off terrorists because that only encourages more of it." (Reuters 11/6/86; NYT 12/4/86; FBIS 11/10/86; Events, p. 107)

November 7, 1986: A CIA proprietary airline delivers five hundred TOW missiles from the United States to Israel. The missiles are replacements for TOWs Israel sent to Iran in February and October. (Tower, p. B-184)

November 8, 1986: Lt. Col. Oliver North, George Cave, Richard Secord, and Albert Hakim continue negotiations with Iranian intermediaries in Geneva, Switzerland, despite the revelation of the Iran initiative in the world press. Attention shifts to release of the Dawa prisoners in Kuwait as a precondition to release of American hostages in Lebanon. (Iran-Contra Affair, p. 262)

November 10, 1986: Top Reagan administration officials meet to discuss ways to deal with public revelations of the Iran arms initiative. The president decides on a basic response: "We have not dealt directly w[ith] terrorists, no bargaining, no ransom. Some things we can't discuss because of long-term consideration of people w[ith] whom we have been talking about the future of Iran." (*[Donald Regan's Notes of November 10, 1986, Meeting....]*, 11/10/86; Iran-Contra Affair, pp. 294–95)

November 12, 1986: White House officials brief congressional leaders for the first time on the Iran initiative. (*National Security Briefing of Congressional Leaders—12 Nov 86*)

November 13, 1986: President Reagan addresses the nation on the U.S. arms deals with Iran. He lays out the official rationale for the initiative, adding that he authorized a "small amount of defensive weapons and spare parts." He insists, "We did not—repeat—did not trade weapons or anything else for hostages nor will we." (*Iran-United States Relations [Address to the Nation]*, 11/13/86;)

November 19, 1986: President Reagan holds another news conference on the Iran initiative at which he denies three times that Israel played a role in the operation. Twenty minutes later, the White House issues a corrective statement acknowledging that "there was a third country involved in our secret project with Iran." (*Iran-U.S. Relations [President's News Conference]*, 11/19/86; WP 11/20/86, 12/7/86; NYT 12/4/86; MH 12/14/86)

November 20, 1986: Top administration officials, including Defense Secretary Caspar Weinberger, Secretary of State George Shultz, CIA Director William Casey, Chief of Staff Donald Regan, and Attorney General Edwin Meese review prepared statements of officials scheduled to appear before Congress the following day concerning the Iran initiative. State Department Legal Adviser Abraham Sofaer protests to Meese through an aide about gaps and inconsistencies in Casey's testimony. In the evening, Shultz holds "a long, tough discussion" with President Reagan about the accuracy of the information National Security Advisor John Poindexter is giving the president concerning the Iran program. Poindexter is coordinating the preparation of Casey's testimony. (Iran-Contra Affair, pp. 298–302)

November 21, 1986: CIA Director William Casey testifies before both congressional intelligence committees. Despite a review of his prepared remarks by top administration officials the night before, his testimony remains incomplete and misleading, particularly with reference to the November 1985 HAWK missile shipment. National Security Advisor John Poindexter also briefs Congress this day, telling members that one unpublicized object of the Iran initiative was to ship TOW missiles to the Afghan guerrillas. One legislator later characterizes Poindexter's presentation as "stonewalling." (Iran-Contra Affair, pp. 302–303; WP 1/20/87; WSJ 1/24/86)

Attorney General Edwin Meese, testifying later that he was concerned about the need for an accurate account of the arms sales to Iran, begins an "inquiry" into the affair. He is later criticized for the way he conducts the probe, using no senior investigators, turning down an FBI offer of assistance, and failing to take no notes of key interviews. (Iran-Contra Affair, pp. 305–16)

National Security Advisor John Poindexter destroys the December 5, 1985, Presidential Finding that authorizes retroactively the CIA's participation in the November 1985 HAWK missile shipment to Iran. He does so, according to later testimony, to save the president from political embarrassment. (Events, p. 117; Iran-Contra Affair, p. 13)

Lt. Col. Oliver North systematically shreds a stack of documents allegedly eighteen inches high to avoid their discovery by aides to Attorney General Edwin Meese. North has been told earlier in the day that Meese's aides plan to inspect NSC files as part of an inquiry into the Iran initiative. North's secretary, Fawn Hall, and aide, Robert Earl, are the other main participants in what North terms the "shredding party." Just prior to the shredding, North requests several original documents relating to the Contras from central NSC files and instructs Hall to retype them, altering or eliminating references to NSC military support and third-country aid to the rebels. Hall then returns the altered memos to the official in charge of the NSC's filing system. The destruction of documents apparently continues over the weekend of November 22–23. Some documents North apparently means to destroy are missed, however, and are discovered later by investigators. (Fawn Hall, Testimony, vol. 100-5, pp. 497–500; Oliver North, Testimony, vol. 100-7, pt. I, pp. 17–23; WP 6/14/87; PI 11/28/87; NYT 12/4/87)

November 22, 1986: Aides to Attorney General Edwin Meese looking into the Iran arms initiative, discover the so-called diversion memo, a document drafted by Lt. Col. Oliver North around April 4, 1986, which includes a description of a plan to divert $12 million to the Contras from the arms sales to Iran. Discovery of the memo, which links the Iran and Contra operations, subsequently leads the White House to fire North and accept the resignation of John Poindexter in order to avoid anticipated charges of a cover-up. A major focus of later official investigations into the Iran-Contra Affair is the question of whether President Reagan knew about the diversion. (Document 88, *Release of American Hostages in Beirut*, ca. 4/4/86, p. 5; SSCI, pp. 39–40; WP 11/26/86)

November 24, 1986: Attorney General Edwin Meese reports to President Reagan on the outcome of his inquiry into the program of arms sales to Iran. They meet once in the morning and again at a full National Security Planning Group meeting in the afternoon. At the afternoon meeting, Meese reportedly announces to the gathering that President Reagan did not know about the November 1985 HAWK shipment. Court documents indicate that "[n]o one contradicted Mr. Meese's incorrect statement...although several of those present... had contrary information. (Iran-Contra Affair, pp. 313–16; Weinberger Indictment, 6/16/92)

November 25, 1986: President Reagan and Attorney General Edwin Meese hold a noon press conference at which they publicly disclose the diversion of funds to the Contras from the arms sales to Iran. The president announces that National Security Advisor John Poindexter has resigned and that Lt. Col. Oliver North has been relieved of his duties. Meese gives more details of the Iran and Contra operations but declares that no one else at top levels of the Administration knew of the diversion. (Document 89, *Transcript of News Conference*, 11/25/86; *Transcript of Attorney General Meese's News Conference [November 25, 1986]*, 11/26/86)

At approximately 1:00 P.M., Fawn Hall forwards a call from President Reagan to Lt. Col. Oliver North at a hotel where he is meeting with Richard Secord. North later reports that the president called him "an American hero" and added, "I just didn't know." North interprets the latter comment to mean the president was unaware of the diversion of funds to the Contras. (Events, p. 129)

Assistant Secretary of State Elliott Abrams and CIA Central America Task Force Chief Alan Fiers appear before the Senate Select Committee on Intelligence shortly after Attorney General Edwin Meese's press conference on the diversion of funds. Questions from the senators focus on fund-raising for the Contras. Omitting any mention of his meeting in London in August with a representative of Brunei, Abrams tells the senators: "We're not—you know, we're not in the fundraising business," adding, "We don't engage—I mean the State Department's function in this has not been to raise money, other than to try and raise it from Congress." (*Transcript of Proceedings Before the Select Committee on Intelligence: Full Committee Briefing on Nicaragua*, 11/25/86)

Israeli Prime Minister Shimon Peres calls Attorney General Edwin Meese to inform him that Israel will deny certain statements made by Meese at the news conference today. Specifically, Israel asserts that it sold arms to Iran with U.S. permission and that it had no part in diverting funds to the Contras. (Iran-Contra Affair, p. 318)

November 26, 1986: President Reagan appoints former U.S. Senator John Tower, former National Security Advisor Brent Scowcroft, and former U.S. Senator and Secretary of State Edmund Muskie to the President's Special Review Board (known as the Tower Commission). Their charter includes an evaluation of the National Security Council system and an examination of the Iran-Contra Affair. (*President's Special Review Board, Executive Order 12575*, 12/1/86)

One day after Attorney General Edwin Meese's revelations about the diversion of funds to Contra resupply operations from the sale of arms to Iran, the CIA's chief of Latin American operations reports to his superiors that Costa Rican Station Chief Joseph Fernandez "might possibly have been involved in activities which at least technically could constitute an impropriety." The memo focuses on intelligence that the CIA provided to the Contras which was then given to the "PBs"—private benefactors—conducting the Contra resupply missions. The memo also reports on evidence that Fernandez received phone calls from the Contra resupply safehouses in El Salvador. (*Possible Impropriety in [Deleted]*, 11/26/86)

December 1986: As details continue to emerge in press accounts about the Iran-Contra Affair, Reagan administration officials are called upon repeatedly to explain and defend their policies. For their part, John Poindexter and Lt. Col. Oliver North plead the Fifth Amendment against self-incrimination during appearances before Congress. (NYT 12/4/86; WP 12/7/86)

December 6, 1986: The *Los Angeles Times* breaks the story of Assistant Secretary of State Elliott Abrams's trip to London to solicit Contra donations from the government of Brunei. (LAT 12/6/86)

December 8, 1986: Assistant Secretary Elliott Abrams testifies again before the Senate Select Committee on Intelligence (see entry for November 25, 1986) in the wake of press reports that he personally solicited $10 million from Brunei for the Contras. Some senators are furious at what they view as the misleading nature of his November 25 testimony. "Had you been under oath, that's perjury," states Senator Thomas Eagleton. "That's slammer time." Only after a break in the hearings, when several senators privately encourage Abrams to apologize, does he tell the committee, "I can only apologize that that testimony was misleading...." (*Transcript of Proceedings before the Select Committee on Intelligence: Full Committee, Testimony of Elliott Abrams*, 12/8/86)

December 13, 1986: Former CIA agent George Cave, who participated in several earlier meetings with Iranian intermediaries, teams up with State Department official Charles Dunbar to meet with an Iranian representative in Frankfurt, West Germany. The Iranian tells the Americans that Iran wants to continue with the initiative despite its public exposure. Dunbar tells him, however, that the United States will no longer ship arms to Iran. (Iran-Contra Affair, p. 263)

December 16–17, 1986: The Senate, followed the next day by the House of Representatives, names a special committee to investigate the Iran-Contra Affair. Senator Daniel K. Inouye will chair one panel, and Representative Lee H. Hamilton will chair the other. President Reagan calls for immunity for John Poindexter and Lt. Col. Oliver North. (CSM 1/2/87; *Statement by the Principal Deputy Press Secretary*, 12/1/86)

December 19, 1986: Following a request by Attorney General Edwin Meese, retired federal Judge Lawrence Walsh is appointed Independent Counsel in the Iran-Contra Affair by a three-judge panel of the U.S. Court of Appeals. His mandate includes investigating the arms sales to Iran, any diversions of funds from that operation, and support of any kind for groups involved in fighting the government of Nicaragua. (LAT 12/20/86)

Senator David Durenberger, chairman of the Senate Select Committee on Intelligence, briefs President Reagan for roughly twenty minutes on the contents of the committee's draft report on the Iran-Contra Affair. The next day, Durenberger briefs Vice President Bush for approximately ninety minutes. Bush later claims this is his first knowledge that the initiative amounted to dealing arms-for-hostages. The committee is not informed of either meeting until after the fact. (WP 1/21/87; WSJ 1/21/87)

January 20, 1987: Anglican Church envoy Terry Waite is taken hostage. A later published report speculates that his abduction may be a result of the recently exposed U.S.-Iran arms deals. Waite, the report says, has been viewed by many in the Middle East as a "front" for the United States. (Wright, p. 160)

January 27, 1987: Three more Americans, Allan Steen, Jesse Turner, and Robert Polhill, are kidnapped in Lebanon. (WP 2/18/88)

January 28, 1987: Iranian Speaker of the Parliament Ali Akbar Hashemi Rafsanjani holds a press conference at which he displays a Bible inscribed with a quotation from the Book of Galatians and signed by President Reagan, and a false Irish passport he says Robert McFarlane used to travel to Teheran in May of last year. (WP 1/29/87)

January 29, 1987: The Senate Select Committee on Intelligence releases a report of preliminary inquiry into the Iran-Contra affair. Although the report stops short of drawing explicit conclusions because of "limited fact finding," an earlier draft leaked to the press did not. The draft report concluded that the White House and CIA violated the Intelligence Oversight Act of 1980 by not fully informing the congressional intelligence committees "in a timely fashion" of foreign intelligence operations, and did not comply with Executive Order 12333 by not formally designating the NSC as the responsible agency for the Iran initiative. The draft report went on to fault the White House for failing to assess Israel's motivations in the arms sales fully and for monitoring the program inadequately. (NSA, pp. 629–30; SSCI, p. v)

February 2, 1987: CIA Director William Casey, suffering from a brain tumor, resigns. (NSA, p. 636; Events, p. 140)

February 9, 1987: Former National Security Advisor Robert McFarlane takes an overdose of Valium pills. He says later he tried to kill himself because he felt that he had "failed the country." (NYT 3/2/87, 2/10/87, 2/12/87; MH 2/10/87)

February 26, 1987: The Tower Commission releases its report. The commission concludes that the National Security Council system itself is sound but faults the president for failing to ensure that the system functioned properly; it lays particular blame on Chief of Staff Donald Regan and National Security Advisor John Poindexter for their performance. (Tower, pp. IV-10–11)

March 4, 1987: President Reagan addresses the nation on the Iran-Contra Affair. He says, "First let me say I take full responsibility for my own actions and for those of my own Administration." He continues, "A few months ago, I told the American people I did not trade arms for hostages. My heart and my best intentions still tell me that is true, but the facts and evidence tell me it is not. What began as a strategic opening to Iran deteriorated…into trading arms for hostages." (LAT 3/5/87)

April 29, 1987: Carl "Spitz" Channell becomes the first Iran-Contra figure to face criminal penalties. He pleads guilty to one count of defrauding the Internal Revenue Service by using the National Endowment for the Preservation of Liberty "for an improper purpose, namely, to solicit contributions to purchase military and other types of non-humanitarian aid for the Contras." At his plea-bargain hearing, Channell names Lt. Col. Oliver North and Richard Miller as coconspirators. (*United States of America* v. *Carl. R. Channell*, 4/29/87)

May 5, 1987: The joint congressional Iran-Contra hearings open with Richard Secord as the first public witness. His testimony reveals new information concerning Enterprise activities, the involvement of CIA Director William Casey, and the role of Lt. Col. Oliver North. In April 1987, the independent counsel charges Secord with several counts of perjury relating to parts of his testimony before the committees and other crimes. (WP 5/10/87)

May 6, 1987: Richard Miller pleads guilty to one count of conspiracy to defraud the United States. (Independent Counsel Fact Sheet, 6/92)

Former CIA Director William Casey dies of brain cancer. (Events, p. 140)

May 14, 1987: The Office of the Vice President issues a press statement on its review of all of George Bush's, Donald Gregg's and Samuel Watson's contacts with Felix Rodriguez. According to the press release, the review concludes that Bush's contacts with Felix Rodriguez "dealt entirely with the insurgency in El Salvador and there was no discussion, direct or indirect, on the Contra aid network." (*Statement by the Press Secretary*, 5/14/87)

September 30, 1987: After an investigation into the operations of the State Department's Office of Public Diplomacy for Latin America and the Caribbean (S/LPD), the GAO's Comptroller General concludes that the office had engaged in "prohibited, covert propaganda activities" that went "beyond the range of acceptable agency public information activities." The GAO reveals documents that show that S/LPD had conducted "white propaganda operations" in an ongoing effort to influence the media and public opinion in support of the Contras. (*[Regarding the Legality of S/LPD Activities]*, 9/30/87)

November 18, 1987: The joint congressional Iran-Contra committees issue their final report on the Iran-Contra affair. The 690-page volume includes a lengthy dissenting report by several Republican members, along with additional views by individual panelists. The majority report concludes that the Iran and Contra operations were characterized by "secrecy, deception, and disdain for the law." In addition to "policy contradictions and failures" and a "flawed policy process," the majority focuses on attempts by administration officials to avoid accountability to Congress for their actions. This, the report says, led to deception, abuses of the intelligence process, and the privatization of U.S. foreign policy. The majority report singles out Lt. Col. Oliver North, National Security Advisor John Poindexter, and his predecessor, Robert McFarlane, for blame on the operational level, former CIA Director William Casey for encouraging the affair, and former Attorney General Edwin Meese for inadequately investigating it, yet it concludes that "ultimate responsibility…must rest with the President." The minority report, on the other hand, rejects most of these conclusions and criticizes the majority for selective use of information and political bias. Dismissing the majority's depiction of the Iran-Contra Affair as "mostly hysterical," the minority sums up the scandal as "mistakes in judgment, and nothing more." (Iran-Contra Affair, 11/87)

March 11, 1988: Robert McFarlane pleads guilty in U.S. District Court in Washington, D.C., to four counts of withholding information from Congress relating to NSC support for the Contras in 1985 and 1986. (*United States of America* v. *Robert C. McFarlane*, 3/11/88)

March 16, 1988: John Poindexter, Oliver North, Richard Secord, and Albert Hakim are indicted on twenty-three criminal counts including conspiracy, wire fraud, obstruction of Congress, destroying government documents, false statements, and offering and accepting an illegal gratuity. The central charge is that all four men conspired to defraud the United States "by deceitfully and without legal authorization organizing, directing and concealing a program to continue funding of and logistical and other support for military and paramilitary operations in Nicaragua." According to the indictment, the four also conspired to defraud the U.S. government "by deceitfully exploiting for their own purposes" the Iranian initiative "rather than pursuing solely the specified governmental objectives of the initiative, including the release of Americans being held hostage in Lebanon." Poindexter, North, Secord, and Hakim are also charged with theft of government property because they "unlawfully, willfully and knowingly did embezzle, and convert to their own use and the use of others" some of the proceeds from the sale of arms to Iran. These central conspiracy charges relating to the diversion of funds are later dropped after a top-level administration panel refuses to release classified information on government covert operations in the Middle East, which are key to the legal proceedings. (*United States of America* v. *John M. Poindexter….*, 3/18/88; NYT 1/7/89)

February 21, 989: The long-anticipated trial of Oliver North gets underway. North is charged with twelve counts of illegal activity relating to the contra resupply operations and efforts to cover up the elements of the Iran arms-for-hostages operations. Over the course of eight weeks, the trial reveals substantially new information about the Reagan administration's efforts to sustain the Contras, including quid pro quo arrangements with numerous other nations. (North Trial Transcript)

March 3, 1989: McFarlane receives a sentence of two years' probation, a $20,000 fine, and two hundred hours of community service. (Independent Counsel Fact Sheet, 6/92)

May 4, 1989: North is convicted on three charges of obstructing Congress, destroying documents, and accepting an illegal gratuity; he is found not guilty on nine other counts. (WP 5/5/89)

July 5, 1989: North receives a sentence of twelve hundred hours of community service and a $150,000 fine. (WP 7/6/89)

November 8, 1989: As part of a plea bargain, Secord pleads guilty to a single false statement charge for denying that he knew money from the Enterprise went to benefit North. He is subsequently sentenced to two years' probation. (*Press Release*, 11/8/89)

November 21, 1989: Hakim pleads guilty to one count of supplementing North's salary. He is subsequently sentenced to two years' probation and fined $5,000. (Independent Counsel Fact Sheet, 6/92)

November 24, 1989: The case against Joseph Fernandez is dismissed because the Bush administration refuses to declassify CIA documents containing locations of three stations in Central America and descriptions of three CIA programs in the region, citing national security grounds. Independent counsel Laurence Walsh calls these "fictional secrets" and asserts that the CIA has a conflict of interest in seeking to protect this information. "We suggest that the injury to national security flows from support of illegal activities undertaken by former CIA officials, and not from their investigation and prosecution," he argues in a report Congress. (*Second Interim Report to Congress, 12/11/89*)

March 5, 1990: Jury selection begins in the trial of former National Security Advisor John Poindexter. Poindexter is charged with five felony counts: conspiracy, two counts of obstruction of Congress, and two counts of false statements. (WP 5/6/90)

April 7, 1990: After a month-long trial, Poindexter is convicted on all five charges against him. On June 11, he becomes the first Reagan administration official to receive a jail sentence—six months in prison. (Independent Counsel Fact Sheet, 6/92)

September 18, 1990: Thomas Clines is found guilty of four felonies: underreporting his tax earnings and falsely stating on his tax returns that he had no foreign financial accounts. He is sentenced to sixteen months in prison and $40,000 in fines, and becomes the only person involved with the scandal to serve a jail term. (Independent Counsel Fact Sheet, 6/92)

May 28, 1991: The Supreme Court declines to review North's case. (Independent Counsel Fact Sheet, 6/92)

July 9, 1991: Former CIA Central America task force chief Alan Fiers pleads guilty to two misdemeanor counts of withholding information from Congress about both the diversion of Iranian arms sales proceeds to the Nicaraguan Contras and about other military aid to the Contras. (Independent Counsel Fact Sheet, 6/92)

September 6, 1991: Former CIA deputy director Clair George is indicted on ten counts of perjury, false statements, and obstruction in connection with congressional and grand jury investigations of the Iran-Contra affair. George is accused covering up CIA knowledge of individuals working on the covert NSC contra resupply operations (George Indictment, 9/6/91)

September 16, 1991: U.S. District Judge Gerhard Gesell dismisses North's case because of problems caused by the "use immunity" granted to North by Congress in July 1987. (NYT 9/17/92)

October 7, 1991: Elliott Abrams pleads guilty to two misdemeanor charges of withholding information from Congress about secret government efforts to support the Contra rebels during a ban on military aid. A U.S. District judge later sentences Abrams to two years' probation and one hundred hours of community service. (Independent Counsel Fact Sheet, 6/92)

October 21, 1991: Oliver North begins a national book tour to promote his memoirs, *Under Fire: An American Story.* The book charges that "President Reagan knew everything"—although it provides little additional information regarding what Reagan was told and when. North also argues that the diversion issue was itself a diversion meant to protect the president from impeachment for other parts of the Iran-Contra operations. North and the book receive extraordinary publicity—including two appearances on ABC's *Nightline,* and two appearances on the *Phil Donahue* show. It remains on the best-seller list for more than two months.

November 15, 1991: A three-judge appeals panel reverses Poindexter's five convictions because of immunity issues relating to his testimony before Congress in 1987. (Independent Counsel Fact Sheet, 6/92)

November 26, 1991: Duane Clarridge is indicted on seven counts of perjury and false statements about a secret shipment of U.S. HAWK missiles to Iran. As of this writing, a trial date has not been set. (Clarridge Indictment, 11/26/91)

January 31, 1992: Fiers is sentenced to one year probation and one hundred hours of community service. (Independent Counsel Fact Sheet, 6/92)

June 16, 1992: Caspar Weinberger is indicted on five counts of obstruction, perjury, and false statements. The indictment charges that he willfully withheld seventeen hundred pages of contemporaneous notes on meetings and phone conversations relating to Iran-Contra operations. The indictment strongly implies that top Reagan administration officials participated in a cover-up of the November 1985 HAWK missile shipments to Iran. (Weinberger Indictment, 6/16/92)

July 13, 1992: The Clair George trial begins. Due to the inability of the jury to reach a verdict, the proceedings end in a mistrial. (Independent Counsel Fact Sheet, 10/92)

September 29, 1992: Judge Thomas Hogan dismisses the first obstruction count against Weinberger, leaving four others. A trial date is set for January 5, 1993. (Independent Counsel Fact Sheet, 10/92)

October 6, 1992: The Independent Counsel petitions the Supreme Court to review Poindexter's case. (Independent Counsel Fact Sheet, 10/92)

October 19, 1992: A retrial of Clair George on seven counts begins.

October 30, 1992: Independent counsel Laurence Walsh re-indicts Caspar Weinberger on a felony count of "making false statements to Congress" by denying he took notes relevant to Iran-Contra operations. The indictment replaces an earlier count of obstruction of Congress that has been dismissed by Judge Hogan. Unlike the previous indictment, this one quotes relevant parts of Weinberger's notes, including a passage relating to a meeting attended by former Vice President Bush on January 7, 1986, at which trading four thousand TOW missiles for five hostages is explicitly discussed. The new information immediately raises questions about Bush denial of "being in the loop"—questions he is forced to address during the final days of the 1992 presidential campaign. (Second Weinberger Indictment, 10/30/92)

November 3, 1992: Bill Clinton defeats George Bush in the presidential election. Bush is later reported to believe that the new Weinberger indictment broke his comeback momentum in the polls and contributed to his losing the presidency; Vice President Quayle charges that the independent counsel's release of the indictment on October 30—a date determined by the court schedule set by Judge Hogan—"smell[ed] of politics." High-ranking republicans, led by Senator Robert Dole, call for a both a congressional and executive branch investigation into the timing of the indictment's release. No such investigation is conducted. (WT 11/25/92)

December 7, 1992: The Supreme Court refuses a request by Independent Counsel Lawrence Walsh to review an appellate court decision overturning the convictions of John Poindexter. The decision forces the official dismissal of all charges against Poindexter. (WP 12/8/92)

December 9, 1992: The retrial of Clair George ends in a conviction on two felony counts of lying to Congress about his knowledge of Contra resupply operations. He is found not guilty on five other charges of perjury and obstruction. George becomes the first high ranking CIA official to stand trial and be found guilty of crimes committed while in office. (In 1976, former CIA director Richard Helms pleaded no contest to charges of lying to Congress about CIA efforts to overthrow the government of Chile.) In a press statement, Walsh called the convictions "an important deterrent to protect the Congress and the public from cover-ups by high-level national security officials." (WT 12/10/92)

December 10, 1992: Attorney General William Barr declines a request by Republicans on the Senate Judiciary Committee to appoint a special prosecutor to investigate the conduct of special prosecutor Lawrence Walsh. Barr says there is no basis for charges, made in the aftermath of the October 30 Weinberger indictment, that Walsh's office leaked the indictment to the Clinton/Gore campaign to undermine Bush's reelection bid. (NYT 12/12/92)

December 11, 1992: Judge Thomas Hogan dismisses the controversial re-indictment charge against Caspar Weinberger, issued by the independent counsel's office on October 30 before the presidential election. Hogan's ruling states that the charge of "false statements" before Congress violated the five-year statute of limitations and improperly broadened the original indictment against Weinberger. (NYT 12/12/92)

December 24, 1992: On Christmas Eve, President Bush issues a pretrial pardon for Caspar Weinberger, asserting that he is "a true American patriot" and that it is "time for the country to move on." He also pardons Duane Clarridge, Clair George, Robert McFarlane, Elliott Abrams, and Alan Fiers, on the grounds that "their motivation...was patriotism" and that they did not "seek to profit from their conduct." Bush attributes the Iran-Contra prosecutions to "the criminalization of policy differences." To offset anticipated allegations of a cover-up, Bush requests that a transcript of his deposition, taken by the OIC in January 1988, be released. Claiming that Iran-Contra has been "investigated exhaustively," the president also asserts that "no impartial person has seriously suggested that my own role in this matter is legally questionable" (see Document 100).

In response, Independent Counsel Walsh issues a statement condemning President Bush for using the pardons to sustain the cover-up of Iran-Contra. With the pardon of Weinberger before his trial "the Iran-Contra cover-up, which has continued for six years, has now been completed," Walsh states. The pardons demonstrate that "powerful people with powerful allies can commit serious crimes in high office—deliberately abusing the public trust—without consequence."

In a major revelation, the independent counsel discloses that President Bush himself concealed personal records relating to the scandal. Despite repeated requests for such documents, President Bush "failed to produce to investigators his own highly relevant contemporaneous notes," continuing a "pattern of deception and obstruction that permeated the highest levels of the Reagan and Bush administrations," according to the OIC. "In light of President Bush's own misconduct, we are gravely concerned about his decision to pardon others who lied to Congress and obstructed official investigations," reads Walsh's statement. "We will make a full report on our findings to Congress and the public describing the details and extent of this cover-up." (WP 12/25/92; see Document 101)

ABBREVIATIONS

AFP = Agence France Presse.

AP = Associated Press.

Clarridge Indictment = *United States of America* v. *Duane R. Clarridge,* November 26, 1991.

CSM = *Christian Science Monitor.*

Depositions = U.S. Congress. Senate Select Committee on Secret Military Assistance to Iran and the Nicaraguan Opposition; and House Select Committee to Investigate Covert Arms Transactions with Iran. *Report of the Congressional Committees Investigating the Iran-Contra Affair. Appendix B: Depositions, November 1987.* 100th Cong., 1st sess., 1988, vols. 1–27.

DOS Bulletin = *Department of State Bulletin.*

Events = U.S. Congress. Senate Select Committee on Secret Military Assistance to Iran and the Nicaraguan Opposition; and House Select Committee to Investigate Covert Arms Transactions with Iran. *Report of the Congressional Committees Investigating the Iran-Contra Affair. Appendix C: Chronology of Events, November 1987.* 100th Cong., 1st sess., 1988.

FBIS = *Daily Report, Near East and South East,* of the Foreign Broadcast Information Service.

George Indictment = *United States of America* v. *Clair E. George,* September 6, 1991.

Independent Counsel Fact Sheet = Office of Independent Counsel, Fact Sheet, June and October 1992.

Iran-Contra Affair = U.S. Congress. Senate Select Committee on Secret Military Assistance to Iran and the Nicaraguan Opposition; and House Select Committee to Investigate Covert Arms Transactions with Iran. *Report of the Congressional Committees Investigating the Iran-Contra Affair with Supplemental, Minority, and Additional Views, November, 1987.* 100th Cong., 1st sess., 1987.

Kerry Chronology = U.S. Congress. Senate Committee on Foreign Relations. Subcommittee on Terrorism, Narcotics and

International Communications. *Drugs, Law Enforcement and Foreign Policy. Hearings, May 27, 1987–July 14, 1988.* 100th Cong., 1st and 2nd sess., 1988 and 1989, pts. 1–4.

Kornbluh 1 = Kornbluh, Peter. *Nicaragua, the Price of Intervention.* Washington, D.C.: Institute for Policy Studies, 1987.

Kornbluh 2 = Kornbluh, Peter. "The Chilean Missile Caper." *The Nation,* May 14, 1988.

Kornbluh 3 = Kornbluh, Peter. "Another Fine Mess: Oliver North's Conviction Explodes the Official Story." *LA Weekly,* May 12, 1989.

LAT = *Los Angeles Times.*

Maas = Maas, Peter. *Manhunt.* New York: Random House, 1986.

Martin = Martin, David C. and John Walcott. *Best Laid Plans.* New York: Harper and Row, 1988.

Mayer = Mayer, Jane and Doyle McManus. *Landslide: The Unmaking of the President, 1984–1988.* Boston: Houghton Mifflin Company, 1988.

MH = *The Miami Herald.*

NSA = Armstrong, Scott, Malcolm Byrne, and Tom Blanton. *The Chronology: The Documented Day-by-Day Account of the Secret Military Assistance to Iran and the Contras.* New York: Warner Books, 1987.

NYT = *The New York Times.*

PI = *Philadelphia Inquirer.*

Reuters = Reuters News.

Second Weinberger Indictment = *United States of America v. Caspar W. Weinberger,* October 30, 1992.

SFE = *San Francisco Examiner.*

SSCI = U.S. Congress. Senate Select Committee on Intelligence. *Preliminary Inquiry into the Sale of Arms to Iran and Possible Diversion of Funds to the Nicaraguan Resistance.* 100th Cong., 1st sess., 1987.

Stipulation = Stipulation of Facts, *United States v. North,* Cr. No. 88-0080-02-GAG (D.D.C. 1989).

Testimony = U.S. Congress. Senate Select Committee on Secret Military Assistance to Iran and the Nicaraguan Resistance; and House

Select Committee to Investigate Covert Arms Transactions with Iran. *Joint Hearings on the Iran-Contra Investigation, May 5–August 6, 1987.* 100th Cong., 1st sess., 1988, vols. 100–1 thru 100–11.

Tower = Executive Office of the President. President's Special Review Board 1987. *Report of the President's Special Review Board [Tower Commission Report].* Washington, D.C.: Government Printing Office, February 26, 1987.

Weinberger Indictment = *United States of America v. Caspar W. Weinberger,* June 16, 1992.

Woodward = Woodward, Bob. *Veil: The Secret Wars of the CIA.* New York: Simon & Schuster, 1987.

WP = *The Washington Post.*

Wright = Wright, Robin. *In the Name of God: The Khomeini Decade.* New York: Simon & Schuster, 1989.

WSJ = *The Wall Street Journal.*

WT = *The Washington Times.*

ABOUT THE EDITORS

Peter Kornbluh is a senior analyst on U.S.-Latin America policy at the National Security Archive and Adjunct Assistant Professor of International and Public Affairs at Columbia University. He is the author of *Nicaragua: The Price of Intervention,* and coeditor of *Low Intensity Warfare: Counterinsurgency, Proinsurgency,* and *Antiterrorism in the Eighties.* He has also edited two Archive microfiche collections: *The Iran-Contra Affair: The Making of a Scandal, 1983–1988* (with Malcolm Byrne), and *Nicaragua: The Making of U.S. Policy, 1978–1990.* Most recently, he coedited the Archive's first reader, *The Cuban Missile Crisis, 1962.*

Malcolm Byrne is director of analysis at the National Security Archive. He has authored numerous articles on the Iran-Contra operations and edited the Archive's first book on the scandal, *The Chronology: The Documented Day-by-Day Account of the Secret Military Assistance to Iran and the Contras.* He also edited the Archive's microfiche collection, *The Iran-Contra Affair: The Making of a Scandal, 1983–1988* (with Peter Kornbluh). He currently is at work on another Iran-Contra book.

ABOUT THE NATIONAL SECURITY ARCHIVE

The National Security Archive is a nonprofit, nonpartisan organization that combines the functions of a foreign policy research institute, a library of declassified U.S. government documents, an indexer and publisher, and a legal advocate of the Freedom of Information Act and the public's right to know. The mission of the Archive is to serve scholars, students, journalists, Congress, public interest organizations, and concerned citizens by obtaining and disseminating internal U.S. government records that are indispensible for informed public inquiry and debate on important issues of foreign and national security policy. The Archive is supported by royalties from its publications and donations from foundations and individuals. The organization is located at 1755 Massachusetts Avenue, N.W., Washington D.C., 20036. The Archive's collections of indices and microfiched documents are available through Chadwyck-Healey, Inc., 1101 King St., Alexandria, VA, 22314.